Defending Muḥammad in Modernity

DEFENDING MUḤAMMAD IN MODERNITY

SHERALI TAREEN

University of Notre Dame Press

Notre Dame, Indiana

University of Notre Dame Press
Notre Dame, Indiana 46556
undpress.nd.edu

Published in the United States of America

Library of Congress Control Number: 2019952786
ISBN: 978-0-268-10669-0 (hardback)
ISBN: 978-0-268-10670-6 (paperback)
ISBN: 978-0-268-10671-3 (WebPDF)
ISBN: 978-0-268-10672-0 (Epub)

For Foi, Baba, and Dr. Moosa
The biological parents and the intellectual parent

Contents

Illustrations

Foreword

by Margrit Pernau

The division between different Muslim groups in nineteenth-century North India has caught the attention of historians for a long time. Not only were Indian Muslims highly divergent in their social and economic status as well as in their daily experiences, but Islam itself, or at least what the actors saw as the correct, legitimate and hence universally valid interpretation of Islam, was contested to a degree that could lead opponents to no longer recognize each other as Muslims. Scholars have struggled to name these parties, let alone understand what was at stake. It was not a division between *'ulamā'* and Sufis—both sides were learned scholars, they often even referred to the same curriculum, and both were deeply embedded in the Sufi tradition. It was not a division between different Sufi orders, as multiple initiations were the rule rather than the exception. It was also not a division between reformers and traditionalists, as both sides acknowledged the need to reform the life of the Muslims of their time and to preserve or return to the authentic traditions.

SherAli Tareen presents a book that looks at these developments in a new way. Drawing on a deep knowledge of the theological and philosophical discourses of the Islamic tradition and on linguistic skills that allow him to access an archive in Urdu, Persian, and Arabic, he provides a detailed reading of two debates. The first, between Fazl-i Ḥaqq Khayrābādī and Shāh Ismā'īl, took place in Delhi in the first decades of the nineteenth century. While Fazl-i Ḥaqq was known as one of the foremost *ma'qūlīs* of his time, an adherent of the tradition that was linked to both the recognition of the importance of reason (*'aql*) and Sufic practices, Shāh Ismā'īl was a scion of the Madrasa Rahimiyya, founded by Shāh Walī Ullah, which emphasized the unique role of the holy texts in accessing the truth (*manqūlāt*). The second debate took place in the last decades of the century and opposed Ashraf 'Alī Thānvī, a prominent scholar from the Deoband tradition, who spent most of his life as the guardian of the Sufi shrine in Thāna Bhavan, to Aḥmad Razā Khān, the leading figure of the Barelvī tradition, who is known as much for his defense of Sufi traditions as for his voluminous fatwa collection.

Through the intellectual history of these four well-chosen individuals (and those they interacted with), SherAli shows and explains the inner logic of their thinking, in detail and with a clarity that has rarely been achieved previously. Though debates like the one on the possibility of God creating a second Prophet Muhammad might appear to be no longer of interest to anyone except those wedded to theological intricacies of little relevance to other people, SherAli succeeds in showing what is at stake in this question for the authors, and how this debate can become a starting point through which to explore a whole cosmology and way of being in the world. These close-ups are consistently related to a more distant perspective, in which he shows what the Barelvī-Deobandī polemics mean for our current debates on political theology, but also on sovereignty—divine sovereignty as well as the establishment and legitimation of the colonial state.

This book is an invitation to an interdisciplinary dialogue, and in what follows I will take up this invitation from the perspective of a historian who has worked on the same time and the same region (and how I wish SherAli's book had come out ten years earlier to inform my own writing!). What SherAli convincingly shows is the importance theology had at this time and for these authors in order to make sense of their experiences, to create a language to communicate them, and thus to structure the myriad possibilities for acting in the world. The debate on God's sovereignty, which is at the core of many of the arguments, is also (without being reduced to it) a debate on how to live in the world and how to face colonial sovereignty. If we not only are interested in the facts related to political and ethical activities of subjects but also want to take into account the rationales given by the actors themselves for their choices, we have to take their theological foundation into account. This holds all the more true if we are interested in the moving border between the "theological" and the "nontheological," between the religious and the political. Giving the actors a voice in our debates is important, and SherAli has shown how this does not need to imply a renunciation of categories, concepts, and intellectual frames of our own. So for historians, dialogue with books like the present one is essential.

History, on the other hand, does more than provide a context for the reading of theological texts, showing where they are embedded in a life-world and how they lead to actions, and how they are also at times the result of processes that their authors are not necessarily aware of. Of course we need to know about the positionality from which Fazl-i Ḥaqq or Thānvī writes, we need to be aware of the experiences that stand at the basis of their interpretation, and we want to find out how their texts were communicated, how they reached their intended audience, and how they were read, as well as the way they moved people to act in a specific way (or not).

But as a historian, I would also be interested in the historical circumstances that muddy the clear divisions the texts establish and introduce more ambiguity. If we look only at the writings of Fazl-i Ḥaqq and Shāh Ismāʻīl, to take just the one example, the opposition between the two of them seems clear and is borne out by their actions. Not only did they condemn each other in no uncertain terms, they also positioned themselves in the public sphere in a very different way. While Fazl-i Ḥaqq spent a good part of his life in British service, Shāh Ismāʻīl distanced himself from the colonial power and went for *jihād* at the Northwestern Frontier. But here ambiguities come in already. If these choices were a result of their theologies, why did Fazl-i Ḥaqq leave his career in Delhi behind and seek employment at the surrounding courts, coming back only in summer 1857, when the city was under the rule of the rebels? How does the memoir he wrote as a prisoner on the Andaman Islands tally with his earlier texts? Things are more complicated than a biographical development might explain, for he is not renouncing his earlier writings; on the contrary. And Shāh Ismāʻīl, for all his emphatic justification of *jihād*, never fought against the British, but against the Sikhs. Moreover, those of his disciples who were still in the Northwest when the Revolt broke out did not turn against the British in large numbers. As Marc Gaborieau has suggested, the fact itself of fighting a *jihād* might have been more important than the details against whom it was fought and the results it generated.[1]

The blurring of the lines increases once we look beyond the writings of the key figures. It can be argued that many of the qasbahs in the Doab had a tradition of sending their young men for advanced training to the same place over generations, creating a network of affiliation either to Lucknow and the Firangi Mahal or to Delhi and the Madrasa Raḥīmīya. However, once we follow the students in their daily activities, we see that even those taking classes in *manqūlāt* at the Madrasa Raḥīmīya might go to Fazl-i Ḥaqq to read Arabic texts, spend their evenings at *samā'* sessions at the Naqshbandī shrine of Mīr Dard, and choose 'Abdul Qādir, the uncle of Shāh Ismā'īl, as their Sufi master. How were the theological differences and their worldly implications negotiated at this level—by the students, but also by their masters, who did not seem uncomfortable with these multiple allegiances? What do we make of the fact that even someone like Sayyid Aḥmad Khān, the founder of Alīgarh, who argued for a reconciliation of Islamic theology with European sciences, kept a deep veneration for Shāh Ismā'īl and his spiritual guide, Shāh Aḥmad, for all their *jihādi* rhetoric? Practices here add a second layer of meaning to the texts, which seems almost to stand in contradiction to the first, and which needs further exploration. What did the divide between the "Deobandīs" and the "Barelvīs" mean, and how stable was it?

None of this is to be read as a criticism of SherAli's fantastic book. Like the proverbial giant on whose shoulders the next generation will stand, he has provided the work from which such questions can now meaningfully be asked, and perhaps even answered. If his book shows one thing, then it is the importance of carefully researched work, which draws on the best disciplinary traditions, in order to establish a dialogue between disciplines. We need both the individual writing of masterpieces like the present one and academic structures that allow for a sustained dialogue, where scholars can come together across disciplines for more than a conference or two and work on common projects.

Acknowledgments

A number of wonderful people, institutions, and contingencies have made this book possible. My primary debt is to my guru and former graduate adviser Ebrahim Moosa. He quite literally taught me *'ulamā'* Urdu and Arabic and first introduced me to the treasure trove of South Asian *'ulamā'* traditions. Moreover, his insistence on and model of closely attending to the layers and complexities of Muslim intellectual thought, while constantly connecting that thought to broader theoretical questions and conversations in the humanities, have oriented and inspired the pages of this work. I was also fortunate that work on this monograph began in earnest during a sabbatical fellowship at the University of Notre Dame in 2015, where I again benefited from his guidance. This book, like all else I have published, is only a small footnote to the depth and promise of his scholarship. At Duke, I was also fortunate to study with two pioneers of the field of South Asian Islam in the academic study of religion: Bruce Lawrence and Carl Ernst. Bruce Lawrence is an intellectual dynamo whose abundant ideas inspire everyone around him. I have been a beneficiary of his unfailing support, encouragement, and wise counsel for many years, for which I feel most privileged and thankful. The idea of this book project initially germinated in an Urdu reading seminar with Carl Ernst when we read Ḥājī Imdādullah's *Fayṣala-yi Haft Mas'ala*. I have since accumulated many debts to Carl, not least through the meticulous training he provided in navigating Persian sources; his style of combining archival depth with conceptual precision and alertness has always been an excellent model to emulate. I am also indebted to miriam cooke for mentoring me and introducing me to various facets and intricacies of Arabic literature. Thanks also to Mona Hassan for reading and asking probing questions about an earlier draft of this book.

Working at the intersections of religious studies, Islamic studies, South Asian studies, and critical secularism studies has afforded me the pleasure and benefit of varied and outstanding interlocutors. In solidifying the conceptual frame of the project, I was most aided by David Gilmartin. To my good fortune, David was also working on questions of sovereignty and political theology when I was in the thick of writing this book; he went out of his way to read multiple versions of the manuscript and provided excellent and detailed feedback each time. Thank you, David! Muhammad Qasim Zaman has been a role model to me for many years; his work on Deoband and modern South Asian *'ulamā'* paved the way for more specialized studies such as this book. The various threads of his scholarship inform multiple moments in this project. He also generously read the entire manuscript and offered critical corrections and interventions. Margrit Pernau as well read the entire manuscript, asked terrific questions, and pushed me to clarify matters in ways that greatly improved the book. She also graciously offered to write a foreword to the book, for which I feel most honored.

The theoretical underpinnings of this project owe most directly to the thought and work of five scholars: Ananda Abeysekara, Saba Mahmood, Arvind Mandair, David Scott, and the *maṣdar al-maṣādir*, the *aṣl*, of critical secularism studies: Talal Asad. It was on a November evening in 2009 at the Davis Library at UNC-Chapel Hill, when, as a new ABD, I had been struggling to put the dissertation's first words on the computer screen, that I stumbled upon in the stacks, rather serendipitously, Ananda's *Colors of the Robe*. This was a turning moment in my intellectual journey. Since then, Ananda's friendship, his feisty yet always rigorous and dazzling critique of liberal secular promises and operations in academia and beyond, and his example of thinking carefully about the category of religion have sustained me as a scholar and writer. The writing of this book coincided with my falling in love with the work and intellectual depth, wonder, and courage of Saba Mahmood. I was blessed to have been in correspondence with her during her last couple years, and her support and encouragement meant the world to me. While this book is not a genealogical exploration of secular power, its aims and orientation are heavily indebted to Saba's scholarship. Arvind Mandair's *Religion and the Specter of the West* was one of those texts that shook and convulsed me, in all the right ways, while I was finishing my doctoral work. Arvind's work on political theology and Sikh reform, as even a casual reading of *Defending Muḥammad* will make abundantly clear, was pivotal to the composition of this book. My thinking about tradition, religion, and colonial power is deeply informed by the scholarship of David Scott; both *Refashioning Futures* and *Conscripts of Modernity*, and indeed his earlier work on Sri Lanka, were crucial to the formulation and navigation of the "problem space" of this book. And of course, Talal Asad's work on religion and the secular defines the theoretical stakes and stance of this project; I was also fortunate to have spent a week in his *ṣuḥba* as part of his master seminar on secularism at the New School in New York. That seminar presented critical ways to think through the question of secular power for a project primarily focused on the examination of Muslim scholarly texts and traditions.

Iqbal Sevea did a detailed reading of the manuscript and gave vital suggestions, especially with regard to the structure of the project. In addition to his intellectual generosity, Iqbal has been a great text message pal; our exchanges on all manner of things cricket, Hindī, and Panjābī cinema offered worthy study breaks. I am also most thankful to Radhika Govindrajan for her close reading of the manuscript and for her incredibly specific and brilliant observations. Rhiannon Graybill, Ali Mian, and Lena Salaymeh read and commented on different segments and versions of this project; their contributions were crucial in refining the book. Ali Mian has been a tremendous and tremendously generous friend who has always shared abundantly from his vast knowledge of the Deoband archive; his own work on Ashraf 'Alī Thānvī is sure to break new ground in the field. Venkat Dhulipala offered useful corrections for which I am grateful; I have also benefited greatly from our several generative and thought-provoking conversations. Other friends and mentors (not mutually exclusive categories) who informed this project include (in no order) Fuad Naeem, Muhammad Akram, Teena Purohit, Akbar Zaidi, Waris Mazhari, Gregory Lipton, Ketaki Pant, Meredith Minister, Zahra Sabri, Aysha Hidayatullah, Manzar ul-Islam, Brannon Ingram, Kecia Ali, John Modern, Barton Scott, Yasmin Saikia, Farina Mir, Hafsa Kanjwal, Jonathan Brown, Sonia Hazard, Ilyse Morgensten-Fuerst, Kathleen Foody, Rachana Rao-Umashankar, Sohaib Khan, Ermin Sinanovic, Shobhana Xavier, Kristian Petersen, Elliot Bazzano, Julianne Hammer, Anupama Rao, Cemil Aydin, Robert Rozehnal, Khurram Hussain, Anna Bigelow, Scott Kugle, Mashal Saif, Brett Wilson, Katherine Ewing, and Usha Sanyal. I should register my special thanks to Kecia Ali for her important recent work on and push for gender-sensitive/inclusive citation practices in Islamic studies that made this a better book.

Rizwan Zamir is my fiercest critic but also a vital friend who provided essential *desī* humor and support. Our conversations and provocations over the last decade have been critical to my academic and nonacademic life.

Few things in the academic profession can be more delightful than working in a cozy but brilliant religious studies department in a small liberal arts setting. Working at Franklin and Marshall College has felt like batting on a flat deck with no demons in the wicket, where the ball comes nicely onto the bat, where one can play through the line of the ball, and where one can pace one's innings according to one's desired plans and temperament. I thank all my friends in the department—Annette, David, John, Rachel, Sonia, and Stephen—for their solid support and intellectual nourishment. My thanks also to other faculty colleagues and friends at F&M, especially Secil Yilmaz, Sylvia al-Ajaji, Shari Goldberg, Hoda Yousef, Bridget Guarasci, Giovanna Lerner, and Michael Penn, for many fruitful conversations over the years. Kelseyleigh Reber, who was then an enterprising student at F&M, read and provided terrific comments on an earlier version of this manuscript as part of a summer research collaboration.

I remain deeply indebted to my professors and mentors at Macalester College: my many thanks to Joy Laine for first kindling my interest in the humanities through her class on Indian philosophies; to Jim Laine for demonstrating to me the brilliant idea that one can make a living through religion, for getting me into this business, and for continuing to shape my approach toward the category of religion through his own scholarship; to Adrienne Christiansen for rigorously coaching me in academic writing and for continuing to serve as a cherished mentor; and to Vasant Sukhatme for inspiring me to become a teacher.

In the nonacademic world, I am thankful to Jon Lentz, Shehryar Bokhari, Hassan Javaid, and Arsalan Ahmed for being, in very different ways, great friends. Many thanks also to the Menai family in Princeton for their avid and dependable friendship.

On the family front, I should begin by thanking my closest friend and wife Tehseen Thaver for providing just the right dose and mix of academic talk and otherwise chilled existence. Her enduring and steadfast support made every moment of this book possible. Thanks also to all the Thaver in-laws for being such wonderful and welcoming people; a special thanks to Mehreen and HS for being such generous hosts during our innumerable Manhattan visits. I am too close to my immediate biological family to formally "thank" them, as Imran Khan said in his defense when he was chastised for not thanking his team after winning the '92 World Cup, but let me register my gratitude nonetheless to Foi, Baba, SherAfgan, Mummy, and Shah Wali for everything. Thanks also to Aliya, Samia, Maya, John, and Mark for their hospitality over the years.

The staff at the University of Notre Dame Press have been a delight to work with. I am especially thankful to Stephen Little for steering this project and to Elisabeth Magnus for her expert and patient copyediting. Thanks also to Susan Berger, Matthew Dowd, Stephanie Hoffman, David Juarez, and Wendy McMillen for their support.

I presented different parts of this project at various conference panels and invited talks; I thank all the organizers, fellow panelists, respondents, and audience members at these venues. The research for this project was supported by the following institutions and grant programs, to all of which I am most grateful: a Luce Visiting Fellowship from the Kroc Institute for International Peace Studies at the University of Notre Dame; an International Institute of Islamic Thought Residential Fellowship; an American Institute of Pakistan Studies Long-Term Senior Fellowship; an American Academy of Religion Research Award; Franklin and Marshall College's Office of College Grants Resource Funds Award; and a Woodrow Wilson Charlotte Newcombe Dissertation Fellowship for Religious Ethics and Values. I profusely thank for all their assistance and patience the library staff at Punjab University Library, Lāhore; the Ganjbaksh Library, Islāmābād; the British Library, London; the Library of Congress, Washington, D.C.; the Van Pelt Library at the University of Pennsylvania; and the Shadeck-Fackenthal Library at Franklin and Marshall College. Thanks to Tsering Shawa at the Peter B. Lewis Library at Princeton University for his assistance with maps for this book. In Pakistan, I owe a special debt to Arif Naushahi for making my visits to the Ganjbaksh Library effortless, to Hamid Ali for going out of his way in making accessible manuscripts at the Punjab University Library, to Mujeeb Ahmad for all his time and efforts in connecting me to his vast network of Barelvī scholars and resources, and to Javaid Mujaddidi for providing critical clues about Persian manuscripts I should be hunting. In India, I owe many thanks to Waris Mazhari for being a trusted point person across the border and for his intellectual camaraderie. Manzar al-Islam, while based in the United States, is another *'ālim* brother and friend who was pivotal for my introduction to the vast treasure of the writings of Aḥmad Razā Khān.

Portions of this book have appeared in previous publications. Short segments of chapters 5 and 8, respectively, appeared in "Competing Political Theologies in Islam: Intra-Muslim Polemics on the Limits of Prophetic Intercession," *Political Theology* 12, no. 3 (June 2011): 418–33, and "Normativity, Heresy, and the Politics of Authenticity in South Asian Islam," *Muslim World* 99, no. 3 (July 2009): 521–52. I thank the original publishers for permission to use that material here.

I would be remiss not to mention and thank Yohanan Friedmann, a scholar I have never met in person, but whose scholarship on Islam and South Asia I consider closest to my own style and mode of operation. His work, especially *Prophecy Continuous*, is a favorite that continues to inspire. I would also be remiss to not thank all the authors I have interviewed as a host for the New Books Network for their time and intellectual hospitality.

Finally, thanks to Wayne Mutata and Wildon Layne, my fitness coaches, for making exercise a regular part of the writing process.

I dedicate this work to my parents, Foi and Baba, and to Dr. Moosa.

Note on Translation and Transliteration

While transliterating Arabic terms, I have followed the Library of Congress guidelines. For the sake of consistency and to prevent an explosion of diacritic marks, I have rendered Persian and Urdu terms according to the same format. So, for instance I use *khwāstan*, not *khvāstan*, and leave the *sa* in *sābit* (the Arabic *thābit*) without diacritics, though for proper names commonly spelled with a "v," like Thanvī and Nānautvī, I have kept the v in place. Similarly, in general, common spellings of names, places, and titles have been retained, so I use Bareillī, not Baraylī, and Hyderābād, not Haydarābād. Letters unique to Persian and Urdu are rendered phonetically as they sound: for example, *che* and *gāf* are rendered "ch" and "g" respectively. The Urdu aspirates تھ and ٹھ are both rendered as "th," whereas ڑ is rendered as a regular "r" and the aspirate ڑھ as "rh." All other aspirates are rendered as they sound: for example, "ph" for پھ. The diphthong "waw" is rendered as "aw,"—as in *awr* and *qawmī*, while the long vowel ے in both Persian and Urdu is rendered as "ay," as in *hay*, *kartay*, and the Persian *bar-way*. The nasal *nūn* in Urdu is left without diacritic mark as "n."

Generally, I have tried to transliterate terms in a manner that would keep them closest to the way they sound: hence Thānvī, not Thanavī (which sounds a bit too much like the Arabic "second"); Imdādullah, not Imdādullāh; Walī Ullah, not Walī Ullāh or Walī Allāh; Aḥmad Razā Khān, not Rizā Khān; et cetera. In rendering terms phonetically, I have also kept in mind the ethnolinguistic context of a name's articulation, so that at times I transliterate the same name differently on different occasions, as in the case of Shāh 'Abdul Qādir and Shāh 'Abdul Raḥim but 'Abd al-Qādir Jīlānī. Mostly I provide the Arabic, Persian, or Urdu term on first mention and then use the English translation afterwards. However, wherever useful for purposes of flow, I also use terms in the original language, especially recurrent terms such as *sharī'a*, *bid'a*, and *sunna*, and at times titles of texts such as *Manṣab-i Imāmat*. Names of South

Asian places have been transliterated with diacritics, except in the case of anglicized place-names like Delhi. Translations of particular terms are also at times repeated when I deem the reader might find a reminder useful. Transliterations from texts are usually given when a particular passage or thought is central or critical to an author's discourse, when the reader might find the original terminology or phrase useful and/or pleasurable to know, or when an author has said something sarcastic or humorous. Throughout this book, I have privileged the aesthetics and the ease, flow, and rhythm of the reading experience over fidelity to any transliteration system or conventions.

In the bibliography, bilingual or trilingual texts have been categorized under the most dominant language operative in the text. In an appendix, I have presented detailed suggestions for teaching this book in undergraduate and graduate courses on various themes and topics. Possible discussion questions connected with each chapter for in-class discussions or out-of-class assignments are also included. I hope this will be useful for colleagues wishing to use this book for their courses.

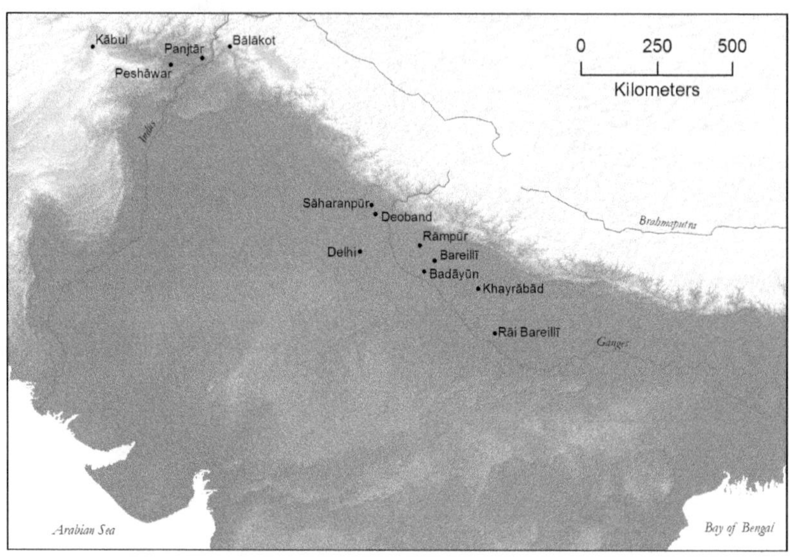

Figure I.1 Map identifying major places referred to in the book.

Introduction

In September 2006, ʿĀbid ʿAlī, an eighty-year-old man from the village of Aharaullah, around twelve miles from the town of Murādābad in North India, retook his marriage vows with his seventy-five-year-old wife of many decades, Asgerī ʿAlī. A few weeks earlier, their marriage had been annulled because they, along with two hundred other people, were declared non-Muslim by a local Muslim cleric, ʿAbdul Manān Karīmī. Karīmī made this radical pronouncement after he was informed about the circumstances in which these people had offered funeral prayers for a recently deceased elderly man in their village. There was nothing objectionable about participating in funeral prayers. However, in Karīmī's view, these villagers had committed a grave sin by offering funeral prayers that were led by a cleric from a rival doctrinal orientation.[1]

Karīmī and the two hundred villagers he had cast outside the fold of Islam belonged to what is known as the Barelvī orientation of Sunnī Islam. Abū Ḥāfiẓ Muḥammad, the cleric who had led the funeral prayers, was affiliated with the archrival Deobandī orientation. On the day of the funeral, because the local prayer leader was away, Muḥammad had stepped in as a substitute. For Karīmī, praying behind a Deobandī cleric had rendered the faith of the villagers invalid. And with that, the marriages of the couples among them had dissolved. Karīmī stipulated that the only way for them to get back together was to repent, profess their faith again, and then enter a new marriage contract. As he put it, "Repent, proclaim the testimony of faith, and get remarried" (*Tawba karo, kalima parho, awr nikāḥ parhwāo*). That is precisely what happened. In a public spectacle, over a hundred couples were remarried. A jubilant Karīmī trumpeted, "These weddings were free of any pomp or celebrations. Only the requirement of the presence of two witnesses was fulfilled."[2]

A few years after this rather bizarre episode in North India, another unconnected chain of events again brought the Barelvī-Deobandī rivalry into sharp focus, this time across the border in Pakistan. This next narrative further amplifies and clarifies the stakes and vectors of this ongoing rivalry.

On January 10, 2011, the antiterrorism court of Pakistan sentenced Muḥammad Shafī', a local prayer leader (*imām*) from the town of Muzaffargarh, and his son Muḥammad Aslam to life in prison on charges of blasphemy. They were originally arrested in April 2010 after being accused of removing a poster from their family-owned grocery store that advertised an event to commemorate Prophet Muḥammad's birthday.

According to the organizers of this event, who had also filed the case in court, Shafī' and Aslam had torn down the poster and trampled it under their feet.[3] The father and son were charged under Pakistan's controversial blasphemy law. In theory, the law prohibits blasphemy against any recognized religion. In practice, however, it is mostly applied against individuals found guilty of insulting the Prophet. The penalty can range from punitive fines to the death sentence.

The court verdict against Shafī' and Aslam was delivered six days after the much-publicized assassination of Salmān Tāseer, then the governor of the province of Panjāb. Tāseer was shot dead by his own bodyguard, a man named Mumtāz Qādrī who was driven to crime because he believed the governor had committed a sin in opposing the blasphemy law.[4] Following this high-profile assassination, several politicians, lawyers, and human rights activists in Pakistan decried the blasphemy law as unjust legislation that incited sectarian/interreligious violence and that was used primarily as a pretext to settle personal vendettas. Joining this chorus of protests against the law was 'Ārif Ghurmānī, the defense counsel for Shafī' and Aslam.

Ghurmānī claimed his clients had been unfairly prosecuted. In his view, his clients were victims of "intra-faith rivalries" among Sunnī Muslims. Ghurmānī said, "Both (the accusers and the accused) are Muslims. The case is the result of differences between Deobandī and Barelvī sects of Sunnī Muslims. . . . Shafī' is a practicing Muslim, he is the Imām of a mosque and he had recently returned from pilgrimage to Saudi Arabia. . . . I am defending them because I am convinced they are not guilty of blasphemy."[5] His clients belonged to the Deobandī orientation.

The "intra-faith rivalries between the Deobandī and Barelvī sects of Sunnī Islam" that Ghurmānī referred to represent a vexing yet important set of polemics between prominent Muslim scholars that date back to late nineteenth-century North India. Much like the controversy generated by Shafī''s alleged defilement of an advertisement for the Prophet's birthday celebration, this nineteenth-century debate animated opposing imaginaries of prophetic authority in South Asian Islam. It brought into view an ethical conundrum that has captured the imagination of Muslims for several centuries: How should a community honor the Prophet's memory and normative example?

This book is the first comprehensive study of the Barelvī-Deobandī controversy, a polemical battle that has shaped South Asian Islam and Muslim identity in singularly profound ways. Almost two hundred years separate the beginnings of this polemic from the present. However, its specter continues to haunt the religious sensibilities of postcolonial South Asian Muslims, both in the region and in diaspora communities around the world.[6] The logics, archives, and terrain of this controversy have indelibly informed the critical question of what counts as Islam and what counts as a normative Muslim identity in the modern world, in South Asia, and indeed globally.

As the two narratives with which I began show, the Barelvī-Deobandī polemic is not merely a matter of academic score settling. Rather, the terms and stakes of this debate pervade the everyday performance of Islam and shadow conversations ranging from defining blasphemy to organizing the choreography of a community's moral and devotional life. Too often, however, in both popular and academic discourses, the Barelvī-Deobandī controversy is approached through the framework of potent yet facile binaries like legal/mystical, puritan/populist, exclusivist/inclusivist, and reformist/traditional. Of these connected binaries, perhaps the one most commonly advanced as an explanation for the Barelvī-Deobandī controversy is the first. This debate is most often read, as I will demonstrate over the course of this Introduction, as the manifestation of a perennial divide between the mystical and legal traditions in Islam, or between Islamic law and Sufism. Through a close interrogation of the internal logics of the Barelvī-Deobandī polemic, this book illustrates the conceptual poverty and distortion of such binary constructions and explanations. These binaries are symptomatic of the liberal secular attempt to canonize the limits of life and religion, an attempt that is always destined to fail. They are conceptually simplistic and politically noisome and insidious.

As an alternative, I argue for a conceptual approach that views rival narratives on the boundaries of religion as competing rationalities of tradition and reform. The protagonists who articulate these rationalities seek to strategically control the limits of tradition. They strive to deflate the capacity of rival discourses to speak authoritatively about what should and should not count as religion. This operation involves mobilizing certain strategic practices of exclusion. For instance, such practices include demonstrating the logical incoherence of opposing arguments, showing their inconsistency with previous authoritative arguments, injuring the credibility of actors who articulate those rival arguments, and most importantly, offering alternative and contrasting programs of the normative.

The contested terrain in which such opposing discursive strategies battle for supremacy is never available for division into disciplinary binaries. Instead, it demands a practice of thinking (theory) that closely navigates the conflicting logics through which the parameters of a discursive tradition are fought out. It is precisely such an approach that this book attempts to employ. By examining competing nineteenth-century Indian Muslim rationalities of tradition and reform, it documents ways in which the limits of Islam in modern South Asia were articulated, brought into central view, and contested.[7]

Competing Political Theologies

More specifically, this book argues that the Barelvī-Deobandī polemic centered on competing political theologies. By *political theology* I mean the intimate interlocking of theological discourses and political and social imaginaries. At the heart of this polemic was the question of how one should imagine divine sovereignty and its relationship to Prophet Muḥammad's authority during the colonial moment when Indian Muslims had lost their political sovereignty.[8] Competing understandings of the relationship between God and his Prophet generated contrasting visions of what the ritual and everyday lives of the masses should look like. Put differently, the Barelvī-Deobandī polemic articulated opposing conceptions of the normative relationship between divine sovereignty, prophetic authority, and everyday ritual practice. At stake in it was the question of how one should understand the encounter between God, the Prophet, and the community during a moment of immense moral and political anxiety. This nexus between theology, law, and everyday practice is the conceptual thread binding this book, and I propose it as a way to interrogate traditions of intra-Muslim debate and argument.

A major theme of this book gravitates around the question of how the loss of political sovereignty generates conditions that intensify debates over divine sovereignty and its interaction with the everyday life of a community. With the onset of British colonialism, as centuries of Muslim rule over large parts of the Indian subcontinent came to an end, nothing seemed more urgent to the Muslim scholarly elite than securing the boundaries of faith from internal and external threats. This book tells how two rival groups comprising the most prominent and prolific nineteenth-century Indian Muslim scholars pursued this pressing task. This book deals more with the colonial context of the Barelvī-Deobandī controversy than with its postcolonial afterlives. This decision was not made to undermine the significance of recent developments, and it does not reflect a search for origins. Rather, it rests on the conviction that only through a sustained and careful consideration of the colonial context can the controversy's postcolonial ramifications be adequately understood and appreciated.[9] Through a close interrogation of the texts, actors, and narratives that populated the beginnings of this polemic, I provide a detailed example of how the boundaries of Islam as a discursive tradition are contested in conditions of colonial modernity.

The Big Picture

The emphasis of this book is on two contrasting movements and visions of Islam in South Asia, with beginnings in the early nineteenth century. The architects of these rival reformist traditions were distinguished scholars whose lives and intellectual strivings have deeply imprinted South Asia's Muslim heritage. Despite their vigorous disagreements, they held much in common. They were often connected through common scholarly genealogies, textual reference points and reading practices, and a shared geography (that of Delhi and northern India). Experts in the Muslim humanities, these scholars also occupied the common institutional space of the madrasas, Muslim seminaries where salvational knowledge, ethics, and piety are cultivated.

Most Muslim scholars (*'ulamā'*/sing. *'ālim*) in South Asia, including the nineteenth-century actors whose thought this book will engage, were and are trained in what is known as the Niẓāmī curriculum (*dars-i niẓāmī*). This rigorous (often six-year) curriculum brings together different aspects of the Muslim humanities (including Qur'ān exegesis, Ḥadīth studies, law, jurisprudence, and logic), with varying emphases depending on a madrasa's normative orientation. It is named after the famous seventeenth-century South Asian Muslim scholar Mulla Niẓāmudīn (d. 1677).

When viewed from the vantage point of the present, the competing Muslim intellectual traditions described in this book also hold in common the predictably stereotypical ways in which they are often viewed from the outside. In Western, Muslim-majority, and non-Western, Muslim-minority contexts alike, the madrasas, and their custodians, the *'ulamā'*, are often seen at best as experts of an arcane tradition irrelevant to the modern moment. At worst they are seen as agents of puritan obscurantism that stokes fundamentalism and militancy.[10] Madrasaphobia is a global phenomenon that brings together diverse and otherwise incompatible bedfellows from across ideological spectrums and time zones, from powerful Western neoimperial think tanks, to Zionist and Christian nationalists, to many liberals, modernists, and at times even Islamists within Muslim-majority countries. While such caricatured representations of madrasas and the *'ulamā'* boast a long history, they took on unprecedented prominence and intensity in the post-9/11 era, when madrasas became almost synonymous with the Taliban and terror. There is an entire cottage industry populated by self-professed experts who have made careers in the business of denigrating and dehumanizing madrasas and their scholars.

While this is a specialist scholarly book on a rather complicated intra-Muslim dispute, offering a corrective to this pathological narrative about South Asian Muslim scholars and their discursive universe is certainly among its major aspirations. To be clear, the point is not to glorify or romanticize madrasas either. As many scholars attached to them will be the first to admit, one could be critical of many aspects of madrasa traditions of knowledge, especially with regard to questions of gender justice and the treatment of religious minorities.[11] However, to develop a more complex and nuanced picture of South Asian Muslim scholarly traditions, it is imperative to bring into view the depth, details, and ambiguities of their internal disputes. That is exactly what this book seeks to do by sketching an intimate portrait of arguably the longest-running and most intellectually dense polemical encounter among *'ulamā'* in modern South Asian Islam: the Barelvī-Deobandī controversy. And through a close reading of this controversy, I aim to provide a detailed picture of an important and sizable fragment of the intellectual landscape of Islam in modern South Asia. So what precisely was this debate about, and who are the central characters that shaped it? I next turn to these questions as a way to further clarify and elaborate the purpose and argument of this project.

Competing Rationalities of Tradition and Reform

Throughout this book I present and explain two competing rationalities of tradition and reform advanced by two rival factions of the Indian Muslim scholarly elite. One was a group of scholars whose conception of tradition pivoted on securing the absolute exceptionality of divine sovereignty. To achieve this task, they articulated an imaginary of Prophet Muḥammad that emphasized his humanity and his subservience to the sovereign divine. They also assailed ritual practices and everyday habits that in their view undermined divine sovereignty or elevated the Prophet in a way that cast doubt on his humanity. One of the chief architects of this reform project was the early nineteenth-century Indian Muslim thinker Shāh Muḥammad Ismā'īl (d. 1831). His reformist agenda was carried forward in the latter half of the century by the pioneers of the Deoband school, an Islamic seminary and normative orientation established in the North Indian town of Deoband in 1866.

Another group of influential North Indian Muslim scholars sharply challenged this movement of reform. They counterargued that divine sovereignty was inseparable from the authority of the Prophet as the most charismatic and most beloved of God's creation. In their view, divine and prophetic exceptionality were not opposed but rather mutually constitutive and reinforcing. Moreover, they argued that undermining the distinguished status of the Prophet by portraying him as a mere human who also happened to be a recipient of divine revelation was anathema. As a corollary, these scholars vigorously defended rituals and everyday practices that served to venerate the Prophet's memory and charisma. The polymath thinker Aḥmad Razā Khān (d. 1921) spearheaded this counter-reformist movement. He was the founder of the Barelvī school, another ideological group that flourished in late nineteenth-century North India. The Barelvī ideology was named after the town of Bareillī in the North Indian state of Uttar Pradesh, where Khān was born. The Barelvī school was in many ways the intellectual heir of the nineteenth-century scholar Fazl-i Ḥaqq Khayrābādī (d. 1861), who had vigorously opposed Shāh Muḥammad Ismāʿīl.

At the core of this book is the task of describing the normative aspirations and conflicts that defined the intellectual lives of these scholars, who were fluent and wrote interchangeably in Arabic, Persian, and Urdu. I will have occasion to introduce these scholars in more detail as this book unfolds. For now, it will suffice to mention that they were among the most prolific, widely followed, and contentious figures in modern South Asian Islam who were at once prominent jurists and Sufi masters. Their rival programs of reform contributed to one of the most abrasive and intensely fought polemical battles in the narrative of modern Islam. Their dispute has produced several oral and written polemics, rebuttals and counter-rebuttals, juridical and theological pronouncements of unbelief (*takfīr*), and traditions of storytelling that valorize some scholars and caricature their rivals.

Before proceeding, I should clarify my use of the term *Barelvī-Deobandī polemic* throughout this book. This book engages both early and late nineteenth-century contexts with some important forays into the eighteenth century as well. So when I speak of the Barelvī-Deobandī polemic, I have in mind this longer context, even though the Barelvī and Deobandī orientations emerged in the late nineteenth century. I do not mean to endorse a teleological narrative that views the emergence of these groups as inevitable. Rather, I employ this term as a compact heuristic device to describe a debate on the relationship between divine sovereignty, prophetic authority, and ritual practice, beginning in the early nineteenth century and taking on a group-oriented character in the latter part of the century.

The discursive space of this debate is occupied by a myriad of interconnected questions. For instance, how was a community required to organize its life in a way that demonstrated its subservience to a sovereign divine? What was the nature of the Prophet's authority as a mediator between God and humans, in his capacity as an intercessor on the Day of Judgment? What kind of knowledge did the Prophet possess; did he have access to knowledge of the unknown (*'ilm al-ghayb*)? What was the normative status of rituals, devotional practices, and everyday habits that lacked a precedent from the practice of the Prophet and his Companions? Under what conditions did such practices become heretical? How was that decided? Another contentious question that drove this controversy had to do with God's capacity to lie or contravene a promise (*imkān-i kizb*; Ar. *kidhb*) or to produce another Prophet Muḥammad (*imkān-i naẓīr*). These questions were situated at the interstices of law, theology, and everyday practice in Islam. To repeat my argument: the Barelvī-Deobandī controversy was animated by competing political theologies, each of which generated competing imaginaries of law and boundaries of ritual practice.

This book is called *Defending Muḥammad in Modernity* because the intra-Muslim conflict it details centered on competing imaginaries of Prophet Muḥammad. What image of the Prophet should anchor a Muslim's normative orientation and everyday life? This question, at the kernel of the Barelvī-Deobandī controversy, assumed unprecedented urgency in the modern colonial moment. The condition of being colonized generated tremendous anxiety as well as anticipation about the aspiration of constructing an ideal Muslim public. And the contrasting images of Muḥammad made visible in the Barelvī-Deobandī controversy mapped onto divergent notions of an ideal Muslim subject and public. Muḥammad represented the hermeneutical key through which reform was imagined. Muḥammad was at stake in this polemic.

Almost all points of contention discussed in this book focus on Muḥammad: his capacity to intercede (on the Day of Judgment), transgressions against his normative model through heretical innovation, the status of his knowledge of the unknown, and the possibility of God producing another Muḥammad. In a certain sense then, this book is an account of how major Muslim scholars of modern South Asia wrestled with Muḥammad in modernity, proffering contrasting images of his character and persona in the arena of Muslim normativity. While harboring vigorous disagreement, all the Prophet's Indian men who drive the narrative of this book were in fierce agreement about the importance of mobilizing, managing, and defending their vision of "normative Muḥammad" as a vehicle for religious reform. The pioneers of the Deobandī and Barelvī movements were not alone in their zealous contestation of what Muḥammad represented in modernity. Rather, as Kecia Ali has importantly argued, in the nineteenth century the search for the authentic and historically verifiable Muḥammad also "came to dominate Western approaches to Muhammad's life." "Their preoccupations intersected with those of Muslim religious thinkers, traditional scholars, and Western educated reformers," Ali helpfully adds.[12]

The originators of the Barelvī-Deobandī polemic have passed on. But even today, almost two hundred years later, the questions and debates that captured the imagination of these nineteenth-century actors continue to generate passionate reactions. In both contemporary India and Pakistan, the stakes and arguments of this polemical encounter permeate not only Muslim institutions of learning, as the work of Arshad Alam shows, but also sites of everyday life such as neighborhoods, mosques, and public libraries, as Naveeda Khan has ably documented.[13] The onset of the digital age has further amplified the intensity and the geographic scope of the controversy. On various websites and in various polemical chat rooms—populated by both indigenous and diaspora South Asian Muslims from such places as the United States, the United Kingdom, and South Africa—rival ideologies and opinions are incessantly discussed, debated, dissected, and repudiated.[14] Far from having faded away over the years, this controversy has only gone viral.

This book is the first sustained study of the Barelvī-Deobandī polemic—its key moments, arguments, narratives, and ambiguities—that considers the entire swath of the nineteenth century as well as important precedents from the late eighteenth century. My sources include previously unexplored manuscript and print sources in Arabic, Persian, and Urdu, including polemical texts, reform literature, collections of sermons and letters, narrative histories, texts on law and theology, collections of legal opinions (*fatāwā*), and biographies. In addition to providing a close reading of legal and theological arguments, I have striven to draw vivid portraits of eminent South Asian Muslim scholars so as to bring to life the sensibilities, anxieties, and tensions that pervaded their intellectual lives and journeys. This project takes up a number of connected yet somewhat disparate conceptual themes and concerns. Thus I have drawn on a rather eclectic theoretical tool kit ranging from works in political theology, secularism studies, ritual studies, legal theory, and narrative theory. Throughout this book I have sought to contrapuntally engage the thought of South Asian Muslim scholars with Western philosophical and literary discourses. I have tried to do so in a manner that might clarify the depth, stakes, and particularities of the former while also connecting Muslim texts and contexts with questions and conversations in religious studies and the broader humanities. In a certain sense, then, this book represents a conversation between particular fragments of the Muslim and Western humanities, conducted in a fashion that will hopefully shed some productive light on both.

Conceptual Architecture

Conceptually, this work interrogates authoritative discourses invested in strategically controlling the boundaries of religion. Authoritative discourse, as described by Talal Asad, is "discourse which seeks continually to preempt the space of radically opposed utterances and so prevent them from being uttered."[15] This book exhibits the tactics and strategies through which rival custodians of tradition assembled their religious authority by seeking to preempt each other's space and capability to act as a rightful custodian. Their religious authority—their claim to represent authenticity—depended on the existence and conditions of their polemical encounter. Their entanglement in this contingent encounter, with unpredictable consequences, was what made possible their capacity to act and speak authoritatively as demarcators of tradition and its limits. As Asad famously put it, "An encounter, not a communication, lies at the heart of authority."[16]

Asad's conceptualization of authoritative discourse is closely tied to his famous prescription to approach Islam as a "discursive tradition,"[17] one of the most frequently mobilized concepts in Western academic studies on Islam. The idea of a discursive tradition offers productive avenues for conceptualizing the interaction of text, time, and practice in the life of a normative tradition like Islam. Approaching Islam as a discursive tradition means attending to the forms of reasoning, argument, and citational procedures through which the question of what the embodied life of a community should look like is authoritatively engaged and debated. What memories and models of the past should inform the disciplined life of a community in the present and the future? That question is at the heart of the idea of a discursive tradition. And since that question has varied and often oppositional responses, a discursive tradition is by its nature a conflictual enterprise.

Asad has more recently expounded on this crucial dimension of his presentation of a discursive tradition in a set of comments at once evocative and arresting: "Tradition," he writes, "is singular as well as plural. For subjects there are not only continuities but also exits and entries. Tradition accommodates mistakes as well as betrayal; it is not by accident that 'tradition' and 'treason' have a common etymology."[18] This book at its core is an exercise in applying Asad's call to approach Islam as a discursive tradition. It investigates ways in which a discursive tradition—Islam in modern South Asia—was invested with competing meanings and ideological projects in specific conjunctures of authoritative discourses and debates. It navigates the terrain in which opposing discourses sought to exclude one another from the boundaries of normative and authoritatively sanctioned forms of life and thought. In short, this book examines critical moments in the career of Islam in colonial South Asia when its limits were authoritatively contested in centrally visible ways.

Before proceeding, I should note that recently Asad's concept of a discursive tradition has been the subject of some unfortunately flagrant misreadings. One of many examples is found in Shahab Ahmed's monumental book *What Is Islam? The Importance of Being Islamic* (Princeton University Press, 2015). Ahmed completely misreads discursive tradition as a "prescriptive" and hierarchical concept invested in establishing an authoritative orthodoxy. As Ahmed puts it, "The subtle yet crucial problem with Asad's conceptualization of Islam as a 'discursive tradition' is his locating the definitive quality of the discursive tradition in the dynamic of authoritative prescription of the correct" (272). Such a prescriptive and authoritative notion of tradition, he further argues, cannot account for or include in the ambit of tradition "non-prescriptive," "non-authoritative," or what he calls "exploratory" discourses and practices. Thus, Ahmed concludes, remarkably I might add, that Asad's conception of discursive tradition generates "a binary of orthodoxy and un-orthodoxy/heterodoxy" that privileges "powerful statements of Islam as 'orthodox' and less powerful as 'heterodox'" (274). This is an untenable reading of Asad's thought. Its problems are many; let me touch on a few. First, more power or authority does not necessarily lead to orthodoxy, and less does not necessarily lead to heterodoxy. For Asad, orthodoxy is not a thing or condition empirically and readily available for institution. As Asad has argued, practitioners in a discursive tradition aspire to orthodoxy and coherence, but they do not always achieve it. And this aspiration for coherence through debate and contestation enables a shared form of life in a community. A discursive tradition presents a site of ceaseless contestation, never available for empirical or disciplinary canonization. An empirically calculable notion of orthodoxy whereby greater power produces more orthodoxy and vice versa is Ahmed's imposition on Asad's theoretical framework. Second, Asad's concept of a discursive tradition is not prescriptive or linear. Reducing the idea of a discursive tradition to a mechanism of establishing orthodoxy empties this concept of its most critical insights. A discursive tradition indexes the power relations through which the disciplined life of a community is lived and debated. It is an embodied moral argument "in which the use of distinct ideas, authorized by *power*, brings about not just shifts in the grammar of concepts and their meanings but also distinct sensibilities, passions, and aptitudes, with which one can act in particular ways and *not* in others."[19] In the arguments that constitute a discursive tradition, normative prescription is inseparable from exploratory practice. The idea of correctness in Asad's thought does not entail the normative prescription of a locatable orthodoxy. And a discursive tradition is not linear or hierarchical precisely because the temporality of such a tradition marked by contestation is never reducible to any objective continuity or stability. Finally, at the heart of the problem with Ahmed's misreading is a rather naive notion of discourse and power. As Michel Foucault so repeatedly pointed out, power is internal to and inseparable from discourse. Thus, no form of discourse—exploratory, contradictory, or otherwise—can escape power or encounters with authority. Ahmed wrongly assumes that exploratory discourse precedes power. But any form of exploration, the moment it is narrated, becomes embedded in power, and is always already authorized as a distinct capacity and sensibility. Indeed, the very idea of "nonauthoritative" discourse presupposes authoritative discourse.

In addition to Asad's idea of a discursive tradition, a conceptual key central to the concerns of this book is the category of "contingent conjunctures of debate." I have drawn this category from the work of the scholar of religion and Buddhism Ananda Abeysekara. Some years ago, in his brilliant study on contemporary Sri Lankan Buddhism, Abeysekara argued against imposing a priori conceptions of religion, tradition, and reform on subjects invested in controlling the boundaries of a religious tradition. Instead, he proposed that one interrogate the contingent and fleeting conjunctures of debate in which particular material, institutional, and epistemic conditions conjoin to determine what does and does not count as religion.[20]

Put differently, one cannot canonize the forms of religion manifested in intra- (or inter-) religious disputes by sorting them into readily available categorizations before the contingent conjunctures that make those disputes possible and in which they unfold. Ultimately, by highlighting the contingency of the process through which the boundaries of religion are contended, this approach constitutes an argument for the unavailability of religion for division into disciplinary binaries. I find Abeysekara's conjunctural approach to the examination of religion and religious life immensely attractive. It offers a way to navigate the logics and conflicts of a discursive tradition that does not succumb to the temptations of the liberal secular desire to define and canonize religion. Abeysekara, much like Asad (to whom he is heavily indebted), insists that religion, much like life, invariably escapes definition. In this book, I offer an examination of crucial conjunctures of debate in the narrative of Islam in colonial South Asia. I present and detail the competing rationalities of tradition and reform made visible during such conjunctures, as the question of what did and did not count as Islam was authoritatively contested. Through this exercise, I seek to disrupt the availability of these rationalities for canonization into disciplinary binaries like reformist/nonreformist, legal/mystical, and traditional/modern.

As an alternative, I propose and show that episodes of intra-Muslim contestation like the Barelvī-Deobandī controversy, animated by conjunctures of shifting visions of sovereignty, should be conceptualized as instantiations of competing political theologies. These competing political theologies reflect and articulate contrasting understandings of the interaction of law, theology, and everyday practice. They rest on opposing imaginaries of the relationship between God, Prophet, and the community. Again, that is the central argument of this book.

Before moving further, let me clarify the problem space of this project by reflecting on the broader conceptual and political intervention it seeks to make. In what follows I will be especially interested in elucidating ways in which internal Muslim contestations such as the Barelvī-Deobandī debate are inserted into and moderated by the new global politics of religion.

Beyond Good Muslim/Bad Muslim

Today, in both academic and nonacademic venues, the Barelvī-Deobandī controversy is most commonly approached as the manifestation of a perennial conflict between legal and mystical varieties of Islam or between Islamic law and Sufism. Scholars who oppose practices like the celebration of the Prophet's birthday or the *mawlid* are viewed as champions of law (*sharīʻa*), reform, and puritanism. This stereotype is commonly attached to the Deoband school. On the other hand, those who defend such practices, like the Barelvīs, are categorized as proponents of mysticism, populism, and a "soft" version of Islam.

One major problem with this framing is that both Barelvī and Deobandī scholars were major Sufi masters as well as prominent scholars of law. The Barelvī orientation never was or is mere saint worship; it has always represented a highly literate and textually anchored political theology. Similarly, Deobandī Islam has hardly ever lacked mystical dimensions.

Moreover, Barelvī and Deobandī pioneers, like their predecessors in South Asia and elsewhere, did not compartmentalize their lives and imprison themselves in neat binaries like legal/mystical. They did not wake up resolved to act mystically till the afternoon and then switch to a legal persona in the evening.

For example, when asked about the relationship between law and Sufism, the eminent Deoband scholar Ashraf 'Alī Thānvī (d. 1943) (about whom we will learn much in the course of this book) responded, "I trust the judgment of legal scholars more in matters of ethical practice, but this decision of mine is based purely on the intellect because on an instinctive level I am in love with the ways of the Sufis."[21]

Similarly, and contrary to his popular image, Aḥmad Razā Khān, the founder of the Barelvī school and one of the key protagonists of this book, was no antinomian Sufi. In fact, he was harshly critical of the tendency to bypass the authority of traditionally trained jurists by considering them secondary to or less important than charismatic Sufi masters. In a remarkable text entitled "Affirmations of the Mystics regarding the Nobility of the Law of the Jurists" (*Maqāl-i 'Urafā' fī I'zāz-i Shar'-i 'Ulamā'*), Khān marshaled a number of quotations from prominent premodern Sufi masters (most notably the medieval Sufi master 'Abd al-Qādir Jīlānī [d. 1166]) that denied the possibility of accessing mystical truth without a firm grounding in the ethical teachings of law.[22] Therefore, despite all their differences, for both Khān and Thānvī law and Sufism were part of a common ethical program that could not be divided into oppositional binaries.

In this book, I argue against the law/Sufism binary as both conceptually and historically wanting. It masks the complexities of intra-Muslim traditions of debate and argument by presenting an easy-to-digest but distorted narrative of such moments of contestation. Though *'ulamā'* actors, like the pioneers of Deoband, could at times be deeply critical of certain manifestations of the practice of Sufism in their midst, reducing moments of intra-Muslim contest like the Barelvī-Deobandī controversy to a battle between legal puritanism and mystical populism is untenable. The law/Sufism binary is intimately connected to a broader, more powerful, and ultimately a more insidious discourse of the good Muslim/bad Muslim,[23] in which "goodness" is invariably measured according to proximity to a secular liberal conception of good religion. This conception of good religion usually allies with US imperial designs and desires at a particular moment.

The good Muslim/bad Muslim binary, as Elizabeth Hurd's recent work shows, is woven into a broader global discourse about the "two faces of faith" that dominates much of the conversation on religion in international relations and public policy circles. In this framing, good religion is religion that is amenable and useful to neoliberal interests and mobilization, as in humanitarian and human rights campaigns. Bad religion, on the other hand, is religion requiring surveillance and discipline. It is religion that can slip easily into violence, intolerance, and fanaticism, hence requiring constant domestication. Hurd's argument is that this attempt to distinguish good from bad religion entails artificially constructing a distinct category of religion and of the religious subject as separate from politics. The discourse of a need to enact policies that scaffold good, tolerant religion evades and avoids historical complexities, local contexts, internal contestations, and the dynamics of embodied everyday life. But despite, or perhaps *because* of its intellectual mediocrity, the quest to construct good religion as a means of generating "religious freedom" has emerged as an immensely profitable industry. It has conferred power and wealth on a range of self-professed experts on religion, including academics, government officials, journalists, and diplomats populating a range of think tanks, foundations, and government bodies such as the US State Department Office of Religion and Global Affairs, launched in 2013.[24]

With respect to the case of Islam in South Asia, "the two faces of faith" narrative has often taken the form of trying to champion Sufism, which in turn is equated with the Barelvī orientation, to curb and marginalize the supposed threat of a *sharī'a*-centered Deobandī Islam. A particularly nauseating example of this logic is found in a widely circulated 2003 publication of the Washington, D.C., think tank the Rand Corporation titled *Civil Democratic Islam: Partners, Resources, and Strategies*. Authored by three self-proclaimed "Islam experts" including and led by novelist Cheryl Benard, this seventy-page text seeks to "promote democracy" by "assisting constructively in Islam's process of evolution."[25] Among other things, it tries to identify the merits and demerits of different kinds of Muslims as "potential partners" in the quest to "fix" the problem of "Islamic Radicalism" and to "foster the development of civil, democratic Islam."[26]

The document surveys the potential compatibility of different varieties of Muslims neatly categorized as "the secularists," "the fundamentalists," "the traditionalists," and "the modernists." As if evaluating the virility of different animals at a livestock fair, the authors found the modernists "the most congenial to the values and spirit of modern American democracy."[27] The secularists might seem like natural allies were it not for their "leftist ideologies and anti-Americanism."[28] Admittedly unsure about how to categorize Sufism in this mix, Benard and company proclaim: "Sufis are not a ready match for any of these categories, but we will here include them in modernism." While offering no explanation for this move, they proceed to describe Sufism as "an open, intellectual interpretation of Islam. . . . Through its poetry, music, and philosophy, Sufism has a strong bridge role outside of religious affiliations." Among other policy recommendations, this document states that "Sufi influence over school curricula, norms, and cultural life should be strongly encouraged in countries that have a Sufi tradition."[29]

A similar prescription is advanced in a 2010 report published by the Washington, D.C., think tank WORDE (World Organization for Resource Development and Education) called *Traditional Muslim Networks: Pakistan's Untapped Resource in the Fight against Terrorism*.[30] With delectable simplicity, this report calls for "the international donor community" to "help bolster the position of moderate religious leaders vis-à-vis extremist ideologues by providing financial assistance to a wide range of their activities."[31]

In this report as in the Rand document, the moderate allies and extremist villains are clearly marked and identifiable. While the Barelvīs are the mainstream Sufi moderates, the Deobandīs (called throughout this report "Deobandi-Wahhabi" or DW[32]) are the *sharīʿa*-driven extremists whose educational institutions are "centers of radicalization."[33] Through forging relationships and supporting (financially and otherwise) the former, the monstrous threat of the latter can be neutralized, the report concludes. A similar recommendation is advanced in another report published in 2009 by the influential think tank the Heritage Foundation.[34] Among the outcomes of such reports has been the drive to strengthen and support Barelvī institutions in Pakistan while also constructing new "Sufi universities" in different parts of the country.

Western state and nonstate powers have not been the only ones to promote Sufism as the moderate, apolitical, and softer brand of Islam. As Fait Muedini has pointed out, many governments in Muslim-majority states (such as Algeria, Morocco, and Pakistan) have also eagerly participated in this exercise.[35] They have done so because Sufism is often viewed as politically benign and thus of no threat to the state. Moreover, the support of a Sufi order can extend "religious legitimacy" to a political leader. Despite the power differentials involved, this is not a one-way process, as Sufi groups also benefit from state patronage through greater access to resources, and a boost in membership.[36] Such cooperation between the political elite and Sufi groups is by no means a modern invention.

Even in medieval and early modern Muslim societies, it was quite common for monarchs to bolster their political sovereignty by drawing on the charismatic authority of Sufi masters and for the latter to enjoy the ensuing fruits of royal patronage.[37] Indeed, this mutually beneficial arrangement was at the heart of the quintessential paradox of Sufism: the drive to renounce worldly pleasures and power while also depending on worldly networks of clients and institutions of patronage.[38] But for all the seeming resemblances with premodern contexts, state promotion of Sufism in the contemporary moment is radically different and unprecedented. This is so because today the valorization of Sufism invariably comes at the expense of what is presented as a competing variety of Islam: the puritan Islam of the *sharīʿa*. Sufism is portrayed as moderate or good Islam on the grounds of being inherently opposed to Islamic law or bad Islam, a category that always carries the threat of extremism.

Such a packaging of Sufism as the peaceful variety of Islam at odds with the Islamic legal tradition is a gross caricature of both Islamic law and Sufism. This stereotype ignores the fact that following the Sufi path requires adherence to the dictates of the law. Sufis do not reject the law and its imperatives. They instead consider it a first step toward higher spiritual refinement. Put simply, in Sufi thought the relationship between law and Sufism is presented not in the form of an oppositional binary but rather in terms of a hierarchy of progress on the path to divine reality, for which abiding by the law and its limits is a prerequisite. This hierarchical arrangement is reflected in the rhyming progressive (in a literal sense) formula "*Sharīʿa* (divine normative order)—*ṭarīqa* (the Sufi path)—*ḥaqīqa* (divine reality)."[39] A hierarchy is not the same as a binary.

The equation of Sufism with peace and "good Muslims" and of Islamic law with the threat of violence and "bad Muslims" is a Western Orientalist fantasy that remains potent in both Euro-American and many non-Western (including Muslim-majority) circles. As anthropologist Katherine Ewing sums up: "Regardless of the vicissitudes of how differences between Sufism and Islam or between Sufism and popular practice were characterized by various nineteenth-century writers—whether Sufism was 'good' in its sophisticated mystical inspiration and Islam was 'bad' because of its legalism, or the inverse, in which Sufism was 'bad' because of its ties to superstitious rituals and Islam was 'good' because of its rationality and strict monotheism—it was the split itself and its political and rhetorical force in the colonial environment that was to be crucially significant for the subsequent evolution of Sufism/*tasawwuf*."[40]

While the most coarse and pernicious expressions of the legalism-versus-Sufism stereotype are found in policy documents of neoimperial US think tanks, traces of this and other such moderating binaries can also be found in many instances of otherwise serious academic scholarship on Islam and South Asia. Take, for instance, anthropologist Pnina Werbner's article on South Asian Muslim immigrants in Britain, "The Making of Muslim Dissent: Hybridized Discourses, Lay Preachers, and Radical Rhetoric among British Pakistanis."[41] In this article, centered on the articulation of sectarian identities among diaspora South Asian Muslims in Britain, Werbner describes the contrast between the Deobandī and Barelvī schools as follows:

> For Deobandis . . . the stress on individual rationality as individual self-control is accompanied by an emphasis on legal reasoning (as against the mystical knowledge of the Sufis). . . . The [Deobandī] reform movement met with powerful organized opposition in defense of Sufi saints and *cultic practices* [emphasis mine] surrounding saints' tombs. This counter-reformation has come to be known as the Barelwi movement. . . . Thus, in South Asia at least two classes of "learned doctors" have emerged . . . reformer jurists and saintly jurists [who are] locked in continuous religious controversy.[42]

These statements are, to put it mildly, problematic. Werbner ignores the colonial legacy of descriptors such as "cultic practices surrounding saints' tombs" that she unhesitatingly employs. Her assessment is also factually incorrect, since, as I mentioned earlier, both Deobandī and Barelvī scholars were prominent jurists and Sufis. But most worthy of emphasis here is the way in which this description of the Barelvī-Deobandī rivalry rests on the assumption that law and mysticism are two readily identifiable and distinguishable discursive domains "locked in continuous religious controversy." While the trope of "reform" and hence the label of "reformer" is attached to scholars who "emphasize legal reasoning as against mysticism," their antagonists are conveniently encased in the category of "saintly jurists." The implication of the division between saintly jurists and reformer jurists is that the less jurists are invested in Sufism the more they will desire reform. This plays right into the unfortunate stereotype that the more seriously one takes the *sharī'a* the more one will be inclined to a harsh religious attitude and practice. More broadly, such a framing canonizes competing normative discourses into readily available binaries like reformist/saintly and legal/mystical, prior to the contingent conjunctures in which those discourses authoritatively contest the boundaries of such categories.

Another illustration of this tendency is found in the work of the prominent French historian of South Asian Islam, Marc Gaborieau. In his book *Un autre Islam: Inde, Pakistan, Bangladesh*, Gaborieau argues that the intellectual history of Islam in modern South Asia is characterized by two distinct and contrasting varieties of scholars. On the one hand, he proposes, are the "reformers." In Gaborieau's view, the reformist trend begins in the 1740s with the eminent eighteenth-century scholar Shāh Walī Ullah (d. 1762) and continues into the late nineteenth century and onwards in the form of modernist reformers like Chirāgh 'Alī (d. 1895), the pioneers of Deoband, and the Ahl-i Ḥadīth scholars. At the other end of the spectrum is an intellectual tradition populated by scholars whom Gaborieau labels as the "nonreformers" or the "unreformed." The nonreformist movement originates with Walī Ullah's son Shāh 'Abdul 'Azīz (d. 1823) and is carried forward in the nineteenth century by scholars attached to the Barelvī school.[43]

Aside from the unwieldy historicist gesture of lumping varied actors and discourses across two centuries into such generalized categories, this unabashedly dichotomous representation of South Asian Islam also imposes on indigenous normative traditions a prepackaged definition of reform. As I will show in chapter 9, contrary to Gaborieau's characterization, Barelvī scholars also imagined their role as that of reformers entrusted with the mission of preserving rituals and devotional practices of long standing. Their antagonism with the pioneers of Deoband was based, not on more or less reform, but on rival visions of what the work of reform entailed and demanded.

Such a bipolar representation of South Asian Islam is found in even starker terms in David Pinault's book on religion and popular culture in Pakistan, *Notes from a Fortune-Telling Parrot: Islam and the Struggle for Religious Pluralism in Pakistan*.[44] The manner in which he contrasts Deobandīs and Barelvīs captures quite well public and scholarly perceptions about the texture of the Barelvī-Deobandī conflict. Pinault defines Deobandīs as "adherents of the puritan ideology that spawned the Taliban."[45] He goes on to inform us: "The term Barelvi is used to characterize those Sunnis who admit the orthodoxy of Sufi practices."[46] According to Pinault's brief but telling descriptions, the Barelvī-Deobandī conflict represents a struggle between anti-Sufi puritans who eventually "spawned the Taliban" and defenders of "the orthodoxy of Sufi practices."

The conceptual assumption underpinning this narrative is that Islam represents a linear spectrum of views ranging from puritanism to Sufism. Concomitantly, following this logic, ordinary Muslims and Muslim scholars can also be readily compartmentalized as belonging to either one of these dualistically opposed categories. One should add here that precisely such a bifurcated understanding of Islam drives recent neocolonial attempts to frame Sufism as the "peaceful/apolitical" variety of Islam that stands in opposition to more "violent/political" articulations of the religion.[47]

To give one last example, a less flagrant but nonetheless problematic expression of the law/Sufism binary is found in Aamir Mufti's otherwise sophisticated book *Enlightenment in the Colony*. While discussing the thought and career of the twentieth-century Indian Muslim scholar and Urdu literary critic Muḥammad Ḥasan Askarī (d. 1978) (also a student of the Deoband pioneer Ashraf 'Alī Thānvī), Mufti writes:

> Askari's larger project here is nothing less than a transformation of the modern public sphere into the domain of traditional disputation. However, we must not confuse this project with those of what has come to be called Islamic fundamentalism, as his less careful critics are wont to do, for the shattered totality his work struggles to reconstruct is not *sharī'a* or Islamic law per se but the Sufi worldview (*taṣavvuf*) of the medieval Islamic world as interpreted in the work of such twentieth-century exegetes as Ashraf Ali Thanavi—a far cry, for instance, from the hyper-rationalist and hyper-literalist techno-Islamism of an increasingly global sort that now makes headlines worldwide.[48]

While Mufti's attempt to rescue Askarī's legacy from the jaws of fundamentalism is a laudable one (even though it rather dramatically generalizes fundamentalism), what I would like to point out is the opposition he sets forth between "*sharī'a* or Islamic law" and "the Sufi worldview (*taṣavvuf*) of the medieval Islamic world." There are two major problems with this formulation. The first is the contrast itself, signaled by the conjunction *but* between Islamic law and Sufism. The proposition that Sufism, medieval or modern, could operate to the exclusion of or be inversely related to the *sharī'a*/Islamic law would not have made much sense to a scholar like Thānvī. But more significantly, notice Mufti's attempt to exculpate Askarī from the sin of "hyper-rationalist and hyper-literalist techno-Islamism" by pointing to the latter's grounding in "medieval Sufism."[49] Medieval Sufism, according to this scheme, works as a moderating force to neutralize the violence of modern fundamentalism. And as exemplified by the phrase "not *sharī'a* or Islamic law but the Sufi worldview," the assumption that sustains this recourse to Sufism as the antidote to fundamentalism is that the more one adheres to the *sharī'a*, the more vulnerable one becomes to fundamentalism. This is precisely the assumption that nourishes contemporary neoliberal attempts to sell Sufism as the "good" Islam that promises relief from the horror of "bad" fundamentalist Islam. Mufti's "auratic" embrace of Sufism as the "other" of *sharī'a* and fundamentalism is untenable and riddled with serious problems.

To be clear, I do not mean to equate the work of these scholars with the nefarious politics associated with neoliberal abettors of empire. Rather, as Saba Mahmood has argued in a different context, what this unexpected convergence shows is the attraction and expanse of a normative attachment to a secular conception of good religion.[50]

My point is this: interpreting the contested terrain of South Asian Islam (or any other discursive tradition, for that matter) through binaries like reformer/non-reformer, revivalist/traditionalist, anti-Sufi/Sufi, and liberal/conservative obscures more than it reveals about the competing ideological claims that populate it. This book rejects the utility of such binary constructions.

As a way to move beyond the good Muslim/bad Muslim narrative, this book undertakes a detailed examination of the logics and strategies internal to a tradition through which its boundaries are debated and contested. A major assumption of this book is that the best strategy to delegitimate facile generalizations and binary representations is to give a voice to those about whom such generalizations are made. Through a close study of the texts, contexts, and normative aspirations that shaped the Barelvī-Deobandī controversy, I will show that this debate cannot be reduced to conflict between legal reformists and lax mystics. Let me further elaborate the stakes of that argument by commenting on the sort of intervention this book makes in the study of Islam, religion, and South Asia.

The Intervention

Despite the recent emergence of several excellent studies on Muslim reform movements in colonial India, the religious thought of pivotal Muslim scholars continues to cry out for more detailed and complex readings.[51] In the existing literature, one finds a much greater emphasis on the social, institutional, and political histories of South Asian Islam than on its intellectual/textual traditions.[52] Though there are some exceptions, most historians of South Asian Islam seem rather uninterested in navigating the hermeneutical logics and operations animating the religious thought of South Asian Muslim scholars. This is an unfortunate omission, as ultimately the religious discourses and debates of major scholars who constitute the discursive tradition of South Asian Islam were at the heart of their lives and careers. This is not simply a problem of coverage or of leaving a historiographic lacuna unaddressed. Inattention to the details and layered nuances of religious texts generates predictable or stereotypical impressions of South Asian Muslim reformist thought. Our understanding of the thick description—the narratives and internal contestations—of the meanings and limits of reform continues to be sketchy and driven by unhelpful generalizations. Take, for instance, the Barelvī-Deobandī polemic.

It is generally known that Deobandī scholars objected to rituals such as the Prophet's birthday celebration (*mawlid*) while the Barelvīs defended such practices. But the question of how they assembled their arguments on such contentious problems has not received any sustained attention. What was at stake for these rival scholars in whether the Prophet's birthday was celebrated or not? Through what discursive strategies did they authorize their own ideological program and unauthorize competing narratives of tradition? What conceptions of law, history, and temporality informed their social and religious imaginaries? What are some of the ambiguities and points of instability found in their discourses?

These are the kinds of questions that are pivotal to developing a richer narrative of Indian Muslim reform as a discursive tradition. I argue that what may seem as arcane and even petty intra-*'ulamā'* squabbles over inconsequential matters of theology, law, and ritual were in fact animated by and connected to profound questions of sovereignty, politics, and social order. The protagonists whose thought is explored in the pages of this book rarely engaged the machineries or institutions of electoral politics and democracy. However, as Saba Mahmood had famously argued, the political force of reform movements normatively invested in matters of piety and salvation lies in their capacity for individual and societal transformation.[53] Taking Mahmood's cue, this book documents in some detail the arguments, discourses, and conflicts that shaped rival *'ulamā'* imaginaries of moral individuals and publics. A close examination of the competing rationalities of tradition and reform that shaped their political horizons and expectations reveals the inadequacy of viewing reform projects like Deoband as "apolitical." As I will argue in due course, this view relies on and participates in a markedly limited and liberal notion of politics.

Again, such conceptual slippages in large measure result from insufficient attention to the religious thought and discourses of critical modern Indian Muslim reformers. Those of the early nineteenth-century scholars Shāh Muḥammad Ismāʿīl and Fazl-i Ḥaqq Khayrābādī, introduced above, are aptly illustrative. As I will show in Part I of this book, a heated debate between Ismāʿīl and Khayrābādī on the limits of prophetic intercession (*shafāʿat*) represented a crucial conjuncture in the narrative of intra-Muslim contestations in colonial India.

To this day, Ismāʿīl remains a deeply polarizing figure and the subject of countless refutations and apologetics. However, despite his importance to the Indian Muslim reform tradition, the primary Western source on his religious and political thought is a 1979 dissertation (much later published as a book) by former historian Harlan Pearson: "Islamic Reform and Revival in Nineteenth-Century India: The Tarīqah-i-Muhammadīyah."[54] Though an impressive work, Pearson's analysis is largely based on British official documents, at the expense of texts in Islamicate languages. Therefore, despite some intermittent discussions of indigenous religious discourses, he is unable to offer a detailed or complicated picture of their internal logics, aspirations, and ambiguities.

More generally, the study of Muslim scholarly traditions remains at a relatively nascent stage in the field of South Asian studies. Ebrahim Moosa aptly summed up this situation when he wrote:

> Historians of Islam in colonial India . . . will be the first to admit that they skate on the thinnest of ice if they claim to enjoy a complex knowledge of the 'Ulama' tradition in the region. Until recently, historians focused almost exclusively on cosmopolitan figures relevant to colonial and national politics, such as Sir Sayyid Ahmad Khan, the founder of Aligarh Muslim University, Muhammad Iqbal, the poet-philosopher interred in Lāhore, Abul Kalam Azad, the pre-eminent Muslim figure in the Indian National Congress or Muhammad 'Ali Jinnah, the first Governor-General of Pakistan. . . . Some five decades ago, it would have been rare to find in European sources any sustained discussion of the role of traditional religious scholars in the development of religious thought in South Asia. While some 'Ulama' were involved in the 1857 revolt, and the name of Fazl-i Haqq Khayrabadi is mentioned prominently, very little was said about his biography, scholarly work and the way he shadowed theological developments in twentieth century Muslim India. . . .

> The work of traditional scholars deserve[s] scrutiny to build a more comprehensive picture of Islam as a discursive tradition in South Asia.[55]

Though Moosa's comments are more than a decade old, they still hold largely true. This book addresses these gaps by offering a thickly textured presentation of Muslim intellectual traditions in colonial South Asia that brings the religious imaginaries of pivotal scholarly figures into central view. I give readers an extensive and multilayered tour of the logics, conflicts, and hermeneutical designs of modern Muslim intellectual traditions in South Asia. While examining intra-Muslim debates in colonial South Asia, I make frequent sojourns to premodern Muslim scholarly sources as a way to highlight the intellectual genealogy of those debates beyond South Asia. On this count, too, this book differs from most extant works on South Asian Muslim reformist thought, which rarely engage Arabic, Persian, and Urdu sources simultaneously. Thus this book seeks to integrate while operating at the interstices of the fields of South Asian studies, Islamic studies, and the study of religion more broadly. Also, by navigating a range of sources in Arabic, Persian, and Urdu emanating from the discursive landscape of *'ulamā'* knowledge traditions, I have tried to recover and highlight a critical and often sidelined corpus of the literary heritage of South Asia.

The Arc of the Book

The chapters in this book are thematically rather than chronologically organized, though they do follow a chronology of sorts as they traverse the late eighteenth and the nineteenth centuries. However, this book is not a chronological intellectual history. Rather, it examines specific conjunctures of authoritative and in many instances adversarial discourse invested in regulating the boundaries of Islam.

Parts I and II are bookended by shorter introductory chapters that discuss the intellectual and political context and conceptual terrain covered by the chapters that follow. Part I, "Competing Political Theologies," centers on the early nineteenth century, with frequent forays into the eighteenth century. It is occupied with polemical exchanges between

Shāh Muḥammad Ismā'īl and his rivals, primarily Fazl-i Ḥaqq Khayrābādī, over pressing theological problems such as the limits of prophetic intercession in Islam. While focusing on the opposing political theologies of these two (among some other) scholars, I try to describe two rival streams of South Asian Muslim reformist thought that took on a fiercely group-oriented identity by the late nineteenth-century. The theme of competing political theologies refers to the contrasting ways in which the relationship between divine sovereignty and prophetic authority is understood during junctures of political uncertainty such as India's transition from Mughal to British colonialism in the early nineteenth century. What languages and imaginaries of the political inform theological debates on the question of divine sovereignty? How do the political and the theological overlap and cross-pollinate each other? What are the competing rationalities of tradition engendered by competing political theologies? These are the central conceptual questions of the five chapters constituting Part I of the book.

Chapter 1, "Thinking the Question of Sovereignty in Early Colonial India," contextualizes the historical and theoretical terrain in which the following chapters are situated. This it does by meditating on the category of political theology as employed in this project and by highlighting some key shifts and continuities in the conceptual and sociological space of sovereignty from Mughal to British India. The next two chapters, "The Promise and Perils of Moral Reform" and "Reenergizing Sovereignty," explore the reformist career and thought of Shāh Muḥammad Ismā'īl, with a focus on his efforts to restore divine sovereignty, protecting it from what he saw as the threat of customs and habits widespread among North Indian Muslims. They combine a close reading of his most well-known and controversial Urdu text, *Fortifying Faith* (*Taqwīyat al-Īmān*), and his lesser-known but equally contested Persian text *One Day* (*Yak Roza*) with an account of his evangelical efforts to reform the public around him. Chapter 4, "Salvational Politics," outlines in some depth his theory and vision of ideal forms of politics and political rulers through a sustained discussion of his important but lesser-known Persian work *Station of Leadership* (*Manṣab-i Imāmat*). And chapter 5, "Intercessory Wars," sets its gaze on the question of prophetic intercession and on Fazl-i Ḥaqq Khayrābādī's rebuttal to Ismā'īl's thought. This chapter also introduces readers to Khayrābādī as a scholar and to the Khayrābādī school of thought.

Finally, in a brief conclusion to this section of the book, I wrestle with the problem of theorizing the interaction of colonial power and indigenous reformist thought as seen in the preceding chapters. More specifically, I address the question of whether the thought and career of a reformist thinker and activist like Ismāʿīl can be taken as an example of an emerging Islamic Protestant sensibility in South Asia. While concurring with some aspects of this possibility, I suggest and highlight important problems with such a conceptualization. I also suggest that perhaps the very problem space of the continuity/rupture debate regarding the nature of the encounter between colonial power and indigenous thought that has occupied so much of the study of South Asia and South Asian religions no longer yields the conceptual dividend it once may have, and I call for new theoretical framings such as the theme of "competing political theologies."

Part II, "Competing Normativities," shifts the focus to the later nineteenth-century context of the Barelvī-Deobandī controversy. An introductory chapter (chapter 6) called "Reforming Religion in the Shadow of Colonial Power" again sets the stage for subsequent analysis. It describes major features of the colonial reconfiguration of law, religion, and politics and the corresponding emergence of competing normative orientations (*masālik*, sing. *maslak*) among South Asian Sunnī Muslim scholars. The next few chapters examine the discourses of Deobandī and Barelvī pioneers on one of the thorniest legal and ethical problems that divided them: the definition and boundaries of heretical innovation (*bidʿa*) in Islam. *Heretical innovation* refers to practices and modes of being that oppose the normative model of the Prophet. But what those practices are and how should that be determined are questions that provoke intense controversy and disagreement, as they did in nineteenth-century Muslim India. Chapter 7, "Law, Sovereignty, and the Boundaries of Normative Practice," elucidates major elements of the Deobandī reform program by highlighting ways in which its pioneers imagined and contested the limits of heretical innovation.

Conceptually, I interrogate possible connections between a political theology invested in guarding the absoluteness of divine sovereignty and a legal imaginary anxious to control the boundaries of normative practice in everyday life. I show that according to Deobandī thought, the question of when innovation becomes heresy is one that operates at the interstices of law and theology. The crux of their reform project, much like that of Shāh Muḥammad Ismā'īl before them (which they avidly supported) was centered on reorganizing everyday life in a way that affirmed the radical exclusivity of divine sovereignty. If otherwise commendable ritual practices, such as the Prophet's birthday celebration, threatened or undermined divine sovereignty, they had to be deemed heretical and abandoned. For Ismā'īl and the Deoband pioneers, the work of reform entailed a revolution in prevailing habits, customs, and norms of sociability. They imagined their role as that of interventionists in history to change its course. Moreover, they authorized this interventionist model of reform by mobilizing a conception of time and history as marked by perpetual decline and disjuncture from an original moment of perfection. Chapter 8, "Forbidding Piety to Restore Sovereignty: The *Mawlid* and Its Discontents," presents a specific example of the application of Deobandī views on heretical innovation by considering the discourses by the acclaimed Deoband scholar Ashraf 'Alī Thānvī on the *mawlid* (the celebration of the Prophet's birthday), by far the most contentiously debated ritual in South Asia.

Chapter 9, "Retaining Goodness: Reform as the Preservation of Original Forms," provides a rival narrative of the boundaries of tradition and innovation in Islam. It discusses how the founder of the Barelvī School, Aḥmad Razā Khān, refuted Deobandī views on heretical innovation. Khān chastised his Deoband rivals for what he saw as their unwarranted assault on long-standing rituals and devotional practices in the guise of confronting heretical innovations. Reform for Khān was about retaining the normative goodness embodied in previously established practices in each successive present, rather than jettisoning such practices on the precautionary grounds of protecting divine sovereignty. He was especially scathing in his repudiation of any attempt to delegitimize rituals that served as a means of remembering and honoring the Prophet. For Khān and his Barelvī followers, questioning the cosmic centrality of the Prophet and downplaying the exceptionality of his spiritual status amounted to dismantling the entire edifice of tradition. Khān argued that the pioneers of Deoband, in their misguided and uninformed zeal to restore divine sovereignty, were committing precisely this kind of discursive sedition. This chapter elucidates the major features of that argument. But for all their bitter disagreements and disputes, there were also instructive areas of convergence and overlap in the reform agendas of Khān and his Deoband rivals. The next chapter (10), "Convergences," examines some of these points of overlap for the larger purpose of highlighting Barelvī understandings of reform and critiques of everyday religious life, so as to disabuse the popular stereotype that frames the Deobandīs as the objectors to and the Barevīs as the defenders of the ritual conduct of the masses in the public sphere. As I will show in this chapter, Aḥmad Razā Khān was often just as if not more condemnatory toward the habits and practices of the masses, especially women, as his Deoband rivals.

Chapter 11, "Knowing the Unknown: Contesting the Sovereign Gift of Knowledge," focuses on the question of the Prophet's access to knowledge of the unknown (*'ilm al-ghayb*). Despite all their other disagreements, it was in the context of this specific question that Khān had anathematized the Deoband pioneers (declaring them to be outside the fold of Islam) and had called them unbelievers. This chapter analyzes the opposing conceptions of the relationship between knowledge, sovereignty, and prophetic charisma that inspired Khān's dramatic judgment. I argue that at stake in this debate over the nature and capacity of the Prophet's knowledge was the very definition of knowledge and religion.

The question of whether the Prophet possessed knowledge of the unknown intimately depended on what counted as religious and salvationally beneficial knowledge. As a consequence, defining the limits of knowledge was inseparable from defining the limits of religion as an ideological category. The boundaries of what counted as knowledge and religion were mutually constituted, each reinforcing the other.

The final section of this book, Part III, "Intra-Deobandī Tensions," consists of a single chapter, "Internal Disagreements" (chapter 12). It addresses intra-Deobandī tensions and disagreements over disputed normative questions. More specifically, it discusses the disagreements between the pioneers of Deoband and their Sufi master Ḥājī Imdādullah Muhājir Makkī (d. 1899). Imdādullah was a distinguished Sufi master who was revered by his Deobandī disciples and by many other scholars and laymen in India and elsewhere. He had migrated to Mecca from India in the aftermath of the 1857 Mutiny when the British sought to arrest him for his organizing role in that mutiny. He stayed in Mecca until his death in 1899. While holding his Deoband disciples in great esteem, he disagreed with them on controversial normative questions in subtle yet noticeable ways. This chapter is devoted to an exploration of these subtle disagreements and their negotiation. Through the example of this disagreement between a prominent Sufi master and his disciples, I show how the internal logics of the differences it brought into view cannot be collapsed into a law/Sufism binary. I also highlight a remarkable narrative of how the Deoband pioneers negotiated love, loyalty, and disagreement.

In the Epilogue, I discuss some of the larger theoretical implications and contributions of this book in the fields of religious studies and South Asian studies. I especially reflect on ways in which a careful navigation of moral arguments in a religious tradition, as conducted in this book, can contribute to and build upon recent studies in religion that have questioned the religious/secular binary. I suggest that the uncovering of alternative logics of life, as showcased in the internal workings of a tradition, is crucial to the project of questioning the often-assumed universality of liberal secularism. Finally, in the brief postscript, "Listening to the Internal 'Other,'" I meditate on the political intervention of this project in contemporary South Asia, in conjunction with some thoughts on my own positionality with regard to it.

But first, a couple of clarifying comments. Since this book discusses an ongoing debate that elicits formidable investment and controversy, it would be apropos to clarify my own location in relation to it. I have conducted this project in the tradition of the academic study of religion. While marked as Muslim and South Asian (Pakistani), I am not a participant in this debate or affiliated with any of the individuals or groups invested in it. The objective of this study is not to decide in favor of or against a position or school. Nor is it to bring about a resolution to the controversy. Rather, I have striven to describe and interrogate its logics, stakes, and ambiguities as a way to add depth and nuance to our understanding of Muslim intellectual traditions, especially in the South Asian context.

I should not, however, be viewed as an "objective," "dispassionate" researcher uninvested in or detached from the figures he or she studies. While I am disinterested with regard to their normative positions, I have spent the last several years striving to understand and translate their thought, and I have obviously cultivated an intimate relationship with the scholars and texts that occupy this book. I have learnt much from them and owe them a tremendous intellectual debt. In what follows I try to honor their memory not through hagiography but through the procedures and protocols of the academic study of religion. This approach promises to reveal the layered complexities and tensions of tradition while also disrupting the moderating claims and assumptions of liberal secular conceptuality. That is the dual promise at the core of this book. I will have more to say on this problem in the Epilogue.

Another clarification: at various points in this book, I draw on indigenous collections of narratives and narrative-dominated histories and biographies. These sources range from the descriptive and analytical to the hagiographic and reverential. I should offer the disclaimer that I do not read these sources at face value or as repositories of empirical truth that reliably answer the question "What happened?" I am less interested in this question than in the political and normative work that narratives perform in the moral fashioning and strategic operation of a discursive tradition. Moreover, narrative represents a central rhetorical device and mode of argument in nineteenth-century South Asian Muslim reformist discourses, highlighted by the abundance of narrative-based texts in this tradition. Thus my mobilization of these narratives is also meant to recognize and record the discursive sensibilities that inform the texture of an archive.

Also, I have added brief notes on the chain of transmission/paper trail, or debates about authorship that accompany a text, where this was possible and where the information was available, though my focus throughout is more on the discursive content than on the material history of texts. The original manuscripts of most texts analyzed in this book are unavailable, and several biographical narratives, especially from the later twentieth century, rely on oral traditions or operate in the mode of reverential history. Thus it is useful to underscore that the intellectual lives and thought of the seminal figures who occupy this book often reach us through the mediation of a palimpsest of interpreters and are refracted by the particularity of their normative projects and attachments. Moreover, the texts through which we encounter these figures, especially those later translated from Arabic into Persian and Urdu, or from Persian into Urdu, are often products of the composite labor of figures stretching across a particular temporal bandwidth.[56] In the case of such texts, whenever possible, I have based my analysis on the text in the original language, while also considering its translation(s) to detect later insertions or deletions of a particular ideological cast.

I should add to these clarifications and disclaimers the plea that perhaps one ought to disturb the hierarchy implied by the subordination of always suspect native sources to Euro-American secondary sources that are charged with the mandate of inspecting, evaluating, and determining their historical reliability. I find this policing rather snobbish. All texts (including the one under way) are oriented if not determined by distinct normative registers and sensibilities and offer different kinds of strengths and benefits or weaknesses and pitfalls. For instance, for all their biases and explicit normative posturing, the detail, depth, and specificity of indigenous South Asian Muslim historiographies at many times far surpass Euro-American scholarship on South Asian Islam. While writing this book, therefore, I have tried to strike a balance between a hermeneutic of suspicion and a hermeneutic of submission. Striving for this balance might allow for a more thickly textured and sympathetically attuned encounter with the layered logics and projects that animate the stakeholders of a discursive tradition.

part one

Competing Political Theologies

chapter one

Thinking the Question of Sovereignty in Early Colonial India

Sometime during the first decade of the nineteenth century, the prominent North Indian Muslim reformer Shāh Muḥammad Ismāʿīl was teaching a lesson on the Ḥadīth while seated in the courtyard of the famous Jāmiʿ mosque in Delhi. A crowd of people carrying relics of the Prophet (*tabarrukāt*) swarmed the mosque, chanting reverential hymns and prayers in praise of the Prophet. Ismāʿīl was unmoved by the spectacle and continued his lesson. His lack of response, however, did not please the people associated with the procession. "Mawlānā, what kind of behavior is this?" one of them scolded Ismāʿīl. "Please stand up and show your reverence for the Prophet's relics."[1]

Ismāʿīl, however, remained unfazed. His continued indifference incensed the crowd. They repeated their demand, this time in an even harsher tone. Ismāʿīl finally responded by saying, "First of all, these relics are artificial; they are not real. Second, at this moment, I am serving as a delegate of the Prophet by performing the obligation of transmitting his message. Therefore, I cannot stand up." This scornful response further agitated an already angry crowd. An all-out brawl was prevented only because Ismāʿīl's loyalists at the mosque were as numerous as his detractors. Their skirmish was thus limited to a lively verbal duel and an exchange of verbal abuse.[2]

Severely offended by Ismāʿīl's behavior, the procession holders lodged an official complaint against him to Akbar Shāh (d. 1837), the Mughal emperor in Delhi at the time. They accused Ismāʿīl of insulting the Prophet and requested Akbar Shāh to punish him for his unruly attitude. The emperor summoned Ismā'īl to his court and demanded an explanation for his actions at the Jāmi' mosque on the day of this incident.[3] While at the court, Ismā'īl admitted that he had said the relics were artificial and that he was not inclined to venerate them. Akbar Shāh rebuked him, saying, "How impertinent that you call them [the relics] artificial." Ismā'īl smiled and responded mildly: "Sir, I only used words to say they were artificial, but you believe them to be so and also treat them as such." Akbar Shāh replied in bemusement, "How so?" "Sir, every year," Ismā'īl explained, "the procession of relics comes to visit you in your court, but you never leave your court to visit the relics." This response left the emperor speechless.

Ismā'īl then requested a minister at the court to bring a Qur'ān and the Ḥadīth collection of Bukhārī. When these two books were brought to him, he held them in his hands for a few moments and then returned them. He then proceeded to deliver a speech to those gathered at the court. In this speech, Ismā'īl again emphasized first, that it was debatable whether the relics were real or artificial. "But," he continued, "even if we were to accept their authenticity, the sacrality associated with objects such as a piece of garment or sandals worn by the Prophet is not deserving of personal or substantive honor [*sharaf-i zātī*]. On the other hand, there is no doubt about the Qur'ān being the word of God. Similarly, Bukhārī's book of Ḥadīth is undeniably the word of the Prophet; it is the most revered book in the tradition after the Qur'ān. There can be no doubt that the word of God and the word of the Prophet are more sacred than a garment once worn by the Prophet. But despite all this, when a copy of the Qur'ān and Bukhārī's Ḥadīth came before you, none of you stood up in reverence! From this it becomes apparent that all of you venerate the Prophet's relics not because of their sanctity but merely because of your addiction to established customs [*rasm parastī*]."[4]

As shown in this narrative, by the early nineteenth century, intra-Muslim contestations on the legitimacy of customs and traditions inspired by prophetic authority became centrally visible in the North Indian public sphere. Shāh Muḥammad Ismā'īl, the protagonist of this story, personified an emerging reform movement that vigorously critiqued long-established customs and conventions, calling them inessential if not outright harmful to religion. Venerating the Prophet's relics, for instance, was an unnecessary distraction that undermined the essentials of the religion. The material relics bore no imprints of the Prophet himself; they were mere objects devoid of any access to prophetic charisma. They lacked what religion scholar Robert Orsi would call the Prophet's "real presence."[5] In addition to zealously separating the real from the material, reformers like Ismā'īl also vigorously protested monarchical modes of life and politics that in their view encouraged a morally sluggish public. A politics of aristocracy, they argued, nourished a religious ethos that encouraged the entrenchment of superstitious customs in the public sphere and that undermined divine sovereignty. This antiaristocratic sentiment is clear in the above narrative's connection between the "addiction" of the masses to entrenched customs and the moral ineptitude of the Mughal emperor at the time.

But as the crowd's opposition to Ismā'īl for his refusal to venerate the Prophet's relics shows, the banner bearers of this reform movement met fierce resistance. A rival group of scholars vigorously challenged their authority and staunchly defended the traditions they had attacked. For this opposing group, practices like honoring the Prophet's relics were an ideal way to exalt and keep alive his memory. Therefore, anyone who challenged the normative validity of such rituals was guilty of detracting from the Prophet's exceptional status and charisma.

These contestations over the normative limits of tradition and prophetic authority were enabled by a conjuncture in Indian Muslim history marked by a crisis of sovereignty. In the decades following the death of the last recognized Mughal emperor, 'Ālamgīr Aurangzeb, in 1707, the political fortunes of the Indian Muslim elite plummeted. By 1757, after more than two hundred years of Mughal rule, a new imperial power had come to dominate the political landscape of the country, the British East India Company. Akbar Shāh, the Mughal emperor mentioned in the story above, was only a titular monarch whose effective authority was limited to the capital city of Delhi. He was among a series of Aurangzeb's descendants who "reigned" over an India in which sovereignty was gradually yet decisively shifting toward the British.[6]

This shift in political sovereignty also provided the conditions for intensified contestations on the question of sovereignty in the theological realm. Underlying these contestations was the question: What imaginaries of the political should inform the conceptualization of the relationship between God, the Prophet, and ordinary Muslims? Was this tripartite relationship organized in the form of a hierarchy whereby accessing the sovereign divine was possible only through the mediatory charisma of the Prophet? Or was the divine-human encounter founded on a politics of radical democracy that resisted any notions of hierarchy? What imaginaries of everyday life and practices did these contrasting political theologies demand?

Such questions generated a number of polemics and debates among the Indian Muslim intellectual elite during this transitional political moment. This section analyzes such a moment of polemical activity in the first three decades of the nineteenth century that brought into view competing understandings of the relationship between divine sovereignty and prophetic charisma in Islam. The actors who participated in this polemic were two prominent Sunnī scholars in Delhi, Shāh Muḥammad Ismā'īl (featured in the narrative above) and Fazl-i Ḥaqq Khayrābādī.

Their polemic centered on the normative limits of prophetic intercession (*shafā'at*) in Islam, and on the twin theological problems of God's capacity to lie (*imkān-i kizb*) and produce another Prophet Muḥammad (*imkān-i naẓīr*). *Shafā'at* or intercession refers to Prophet Muḥammad's role as an intercessor between God and human sinners on the Day of Judgment. By petitioning to God on behalf of sinners, the Prophet helps absolve their sins and hence secures them a place in heaven. The Prophet's capacity for intercession is well documented in traditional sources of normative authority in Islam, such as the Qur'ān and the Prophet's sayings. However, the scope of that capacity and its implications for divine sovereignty have remained subject to intense debate. For instance, in premodern Islam, scholars attached to the Mu'tazilī school of theology rejected the doctrine of intercession. The Mu'tazilītes found intercession an immediate threat to divine sovereignty.[7] Similarly, as Shaun Marmon has shown, the question of how one distinguished worldly or imperial intercession from eschatological intercession was keenly debated by Muslim scholars in medieval contexts like Mamlūk Egypt.[8]

In more recent times, proponents of the Wahhābī school of thought in Arabia have attacked the doctrine of prophetic intercession with much fervor. The most dramatic example of such an attack came in 1925 when the Saudi authorities destroyed the tombs of the Prophet's family and his closest companions, on the grounds that the masses had turned these tombs into sites of active worship, thus undermining divine sovereignty. The dispute between Ismā'īl and Khayrābādī described in this chapter occurred exactly a century before the Saudi destruction of the Prophet's family's tombs. In many ways, then, their polemic represents the beginnings of an ideological conflict that turned into a hurricane of debates and polemics in the following decades, often resulting in very material consequences, such as the destruction of tombs and shrines. While no bricks were broken, the outcome of Ismā'īl's and Khayrābādī's dispute was equally dramatic.

Khayrābādī charged Ismā'īl with anathema/unbelief (*kufr*) for insulting the Prophet and declared him an unbeliever who deserved to be killed. Ismā'īl, in turn, accused Khayrābādī of perpetuating a moral order that undermined the exceptionality of divine sovereignty and encouraged the proliferation of heresies and corruptions among the masses. Their hostility metastasized into a monstrous ideological battle among rival North Indian Muslim scholars in the latter half of the nineteenth century, as discussed in the following sections of this book. Before further discussing the intellectual careers of these actors, the texture of their debate, and the significance of their disagreement, in this introductory chapter to this section I want to highlight certain pivotal features of the politico-conceptual space in which this debate between Ismā'īl and Khayrābādī unfolded. I will do so through an exploration of the ways in which the idea of political theology might be productive in illumining the stakes and context of this conflict. I will follow that by sketching a brief genealogy of key shifts in the conceptual career of sovereignty in the transition from Mughal to British India as a way to set the contextual stage for the next chapters in the section.

Political Theology: Between the Global North and South Asia

Recently, the category of political theology has generated much debate and discussion in the Euro-American academy. Much of this discussion has centered on exposing the theological underpinnings of modern secular politics, especially of the modern state—an insight most often traced to the German theorist Carl Schmitt's influential 1922 publication *Political Theology*.

In this work Schmitt famously argued that "all significant concepts of the modern theory of the state are secularized theological concepts."[9] The modern state, while purporting to have overcome and eclipsed theology, is in fact deeply theological in the constitution of its sovereignty. In a probing recent study of Schmitt's thought, Paul Kahn sums up Schmitt's argument as "The state is not the secular arrangement that it purports to be."[10] Rather, the sovereignty of the supposedly secular state is homologous to that of the divine sovereign, hinging on the capacity to enact an exception to the normal rule. This suggestion has provoked the attention of a number of scholars who in different ways have extended, reworked, and critically engaged Schmitt to question the self-congratulatory narrative of a modern secular break from previously theological political orders. Such a line of inquiry, invested in fracturing the assumed exceptionalism of liberal secular politics, has been conducted in multiple domains of knowledge and life. For instance, notice the capaciousness of the way Graham Hammill and Julia Lupton approach the category of political theology as "the exchanges, pacts, and contests that obtain between religious and political life, especially the use of sacred narratives, motifs, and liturgical forms to establish, legitimate, and reflect upon the sovereignty of monarchs, corporations, and parliaments."[11]

On this account, political theology as a concept is not only relevant to religion. In fact, as Hammill and Lupton state emphatically at the outset of their book, "Political theology is not the same as religion."[12] Rather, political theology presents an important conceptual key to unlock the operations of secular power in such varied yet interconnected discursive avenues as religion, law, literature, politics, science, and economics. I am indebted to scholarship that has sought to mobilize the idea of political theology to highlight the tensions, contradictions, and theologies of secular power. In this work, though, I approach political theology with a slightly different emphasis.

I am interested less in the theological underpinnings of the political than in the political imaginaries, assumptions, and aspirations reflected in seemingly theological discourses and debates. My concern is the mutual imbrication of theology and politics, as reflected in discourses and debates on divine sovereignty. What are some of the ways in which theological debates and arguments about the nature of God's relationship with humanity are reflective of and informed by shifting understandings and manifestations of political sovereignty?[13] This in a nutshell is the question I pursue in the following chapters.

The problem space occupied by this question in many ways draws from another of Carl Schmitt's observations in *Political Theology*, namely that "the metaphysical image that a definite epoch forges of the world has the same structure as what the world immediately understands to be appropriate as a form of its political organization."[14] He further argued that the transition from conceptions of transcendence to those of immanence represents one of the key developments in European political theology from the early modern period. Through a radical "pushing aside" of the sovereign as the sole lawgiver of his kingdom, a democratic notion of legitimacy came to replace a previously monarchical one. The epoch of royalism came to an end because legitimacy no longer existed in the traditional sense. The seventeenth and eighteenth centuries, Schmitt argued, were dominated by the idea of the sole sovereign in the domains of both theology and politics. Schmitt, in effect, claimed that the metaphysical image that a particular epoch forges of the world parallels the structure of its political organization. Therefore, as conceptions of immanence increasingly influenced the political ideas and the state doctrines of the nineteenth century, they undercut monarchical authority, which was eventually supplanted by an order of radical democracy.[15]

The decisive quality that distinguished this new consciousness of democracy from its older monarchical counterpart was its complete intolerance for the state of exception, which in theological terms signifies miracles and dogmas that transcend human comprehension and critical doubt. As Schmitt put it, "Democracy is the expression of a political relativism that is liberated from miracles and dogma."[16]

Of course, as historian David Gilmartin has best elucidated, no conception of sovereignty, divine or state centered, can escape the irresolvable conundrum of representing a form of power that stands outside the realm of politics and everyday life and yet actively engages with them. Sovereign power exists simultaneously inside and outside its sphere of operation. Gilmartin captures this conundrum through the distinction between what he calls "legitimation," "a claim to authority transcending the everyday," and "governance," "the mundane process of actually managing and bringing order to society."[17] At the risk of getting a bit ahead of myself, one may note here that Gilmartin's observations on the conundrums of sovereign power can also be extended to highlight some of the inherent tensions in the idea of religious reform as a way of guarding divine sovereignty. The gesture of protecting divine sovereignty from the corruption of everyday customs and rituals remains arrested in the underlying contradiction that Gilmartin brings into focus: the divine sovereign stands apart from yet is threatened by the vagaries of everyday life, he is outside temporal existence and is nevertheless its most intimate architect.

That this conflict of sovereignty is not simply a matter of theoretical abstraction is fruitfully shown in historian Mithi Mukherjee's analysis of two contentious yet collaborative discourses of British colonial power in India: the "colonial" and the "imperial." The discourse of the colonial, as coined by Mukherjee, referred to matters of governance "driven by ideas of territorial conquest, power, violence, domination, and subjugation of the colonized."[18] The imperial, in contrast, "was based on a supranational deterritorialized discourse of justice under natural law" that sought to curb and censor the excesses of colonial power and governance.[19] These contrasting discourses of colonial power and imperial justice worked in tandem, the former operating invasively within society and the latter monitoring the former in a detached fashion from the outside. Their net effect was to elevate the institution of the Supreme Court and the figure of the lawyer as the most powerful mediators between the colonial state and native society. Colonial sovereignty was secured and advanced through the tensions and rifts between, on the one hand, governance through power and intrusion and, on the other, appeals to justice under the deterritorial umbrella of natural law.

In what follows, I want to extend these historical reflections on sovereign power to pursue the following question: How do changing imaginaries of political concepts and ideas fashion the ways in which such seemingly theological concepts as divine sovereignty and the human-divine relationship are thought about and conceived in particular historical conjunctures? My focus is not on Muslim intellectual meditations on the state, statecraft, and governance, things that are conventionally associated with politics (though I will have occasion to briefly take up that theme). I wish instead to look at the conceptions of politics and ideal polities that underlie intra-Muslim debates on the character of divine sovereignty, especially in relation to the figure of the Prophet and the everyday life of the community. How do competing notions of divine sovereignty and prophetic authority correspond to contrasting aspirations of an ideal polis? This question guides the interweaving of theology and politics in this section and in the broader project of this book. Interrogating the imbrication of the political and the theological can prove especially fruitful in the context of what one might call hinge moments when a long-standing political order is on the verge of dissipating and being replaced by another, such as periods of transition from monarchical to colonial power. This kind of problem space is particularly relevant to the case of South Asian Islam and its transition from Mughal rule to British colonialism, a gradual process of shifting power dynamics that took place between the seventeenth and the nineteenth centuries, roughly the same time period that occupied Schmitt's study.

Shifting Sociologies of Sovereignty

As historian Christopher Bayly has argued, the broader shifts and transformations in the informational and political networks of India that eventually enabled British colonial rule were well under way from the beginning of the eighteenth century onwards. In Bayly's account, India's transition from Mughal to British rule in the eighteenth and nineteenth centuries saw three major politico-economic developments: (1) the decentralization of political authority into smaller and more diffused networks of power, (2) the consolidation of a peasant class and a concomitant growth in the agricultural sector of the economy, and (3) an increased sophistication and mobility in both formal and informal networks of information sharing and intelligence gathering among various colonial and indigenous agents. Furthermore, this last trend decisively diminished the political authority and cultural capital of the older imperial and aristocratic elite.[20]

The conceptual significance of the transition to colonial power to the question of sovereignty is captured by political theorist Sudipta Kaviraj in his categorization of this shift as one from subsidiarity to sovereignty. Kaviraj claims that "all states before the coming of colonial modernity in India answered the description of a *state of subsumption/*

subsidiarity: they dominated society as a group of rulers distinct from the society below them, untied to their subjects by any strong emotive or institutional bond, like modern nationalism. Correspondingly, their ability to affect society's basic structure of the organization of everyday life was seriously restricted."[21] According to Kaviraj, gradually, and especially in the aftermath of the 1857 rebellion, such a politics of subsidiarity was overturned by the institution of the sovereign colonial state. The colonial state was conceptually distinct from its predecessors not only because it was much more powerful but more crucially because of the deliberate and direct fashion in which it bound its subjects to its sovereign authority. Indeed, for Kaviraj, speaking of the transition from a precolonial to a colonial state contains the misplaced "suggestion that we are talking about two historically different versions of the same object." In his account, when comparing modern colonial and earlier Islamic and Hindu notions of state authority, one confronts two fundamentally "different types of organization of political authority."[22] The idea of the sovereign state, with the capacity to actively regulate and make claims on the lives of its subjects, was thoroughly modern. More provocatively, Kaviraj further argues that in the Indian context the idea of the state "has been the primary source of modernity."[23]

Historian and anthropologist Bernard Cohn's seminal work on the colonial construction of sovereignty further amplifies Kaviraj's argument while connecting it more directly to my own concerns here. His work provides fascinating insights into the cultural effects of India's transition from Mughal to British colonialism. According to Cohn, during the early nineteenth century, the British continued the ritual idioms of their Mughal predecessors in establishing their political sovereignty over Indian society. However, the meaning they attached to those idioms was radically different than before. The British appropriation of Mughal symbols was an act of translation between two very different economies of imperial sovereignty. One of the most revealing theaters where such a process of translation took place was the *darbār* or royal court.

Throughout Mughal history, the royal court had served as a critical site of contact and exchange between the Mughal rulers and their subjects. More specifically, the ceremonial rituals conducted at the Mughal *darbār* served the function of incorporating indigenous subjects into the larger imperial project. For instance, one such ritual that took place in the *darbār* was the offering of gifts and valuables such as gold coins, elephants, horses, and jewels by indigenous elites to the Mughal emperor. This offering represented a gesture of their loyalty to the empire. The value of such an offering (*peshkash*; also called *naẓar*, or vow), was carefully calibrated according to the rank and status of the person who made it.

In return, the Mughal emperor would present that person with a *khelat* (Arabic *khil'a*): an item of clothing or a set of clothes that usually included a cloak, turban, and shawls. This process of exchange was suffused with symbolic significance; the *khelat* was a symbol "of the idea of continuity or succession . . . and that continuity rested on a physical basis, depending on contact of the body of recipient with the body of the donor through the medium of the clothing."[24]

In other words, far from a simply material exchange, the offering of *naẓar* and the receipt of *khelat* "were acts of obedience, pledges of loyalty, and the acceptance of the superiority of the giver of the *khelats*." Moreover, this ritualized demonstration of sovereignty and kingship enabled the incorporation of particular segments of indigenous society into the narrative structure of imperial rule. As Cohn elaborated, "The indigenous theory of rulership in India was based on ideas of incorporation, and a *theory of hierarchy* [emphasis mine] in which rulers not only outranked everyone but could also encompass those they ruled."[25]

However, in the late eighteenth and early nineteenth centuries, although the British as the new "Indian rulers" continued the practice of accepting *naẓar* and *peshkash* and of giving *khelats*, the meaning they ascribed to this moment of exchange had transformed. In contrast to the Mughals, the British tended to approach these acts primarily in material terms. The offerings of *naẓar* and *peshkash* were seen as paying for favors, which the British translated into rights related to their trading activities. They also "glossed the offering of *naẓar* as bribery and *peshkash* as tribute, following their own cultural codes, and assumed there was a direct *quid pro quo* involved."[26]

In the British inheritance of *darbār* rituals, a carefully choreographed performance of imperial sovereignty was translated as a materially driven instant of exchange. As Cohn explained, "Mughal ritual might seem to have been retained but the meanings had been changed. What had been, under Indian rulers, a ritual of incorporation now became a ritual marking subordination, with no mystical bonding between royal figure and the chosen friend and servant who was becoming part of the ruler."[27]

The most important point here is the subtle yet dramatic shift in the sociology of sovereignty precipitated by the emergence of British colonial rule in India. In the transition from Mughal to British rule, while the external forms of the imperial performance of sovereignty continued, the meanings contained in them changed. This combination of continuity and transformation reflected a larger contradiction in the political rationality of British colonial rule in India during the early nineteenth century. While seeking to maintain India as a feudal order, the British also looked to enact changes in indigenous society that would inevitably dissolve this feudal order and give rise to a new "modern" civic order.

This inherent tension in the logic of British colonial rule remained unresolved until the peasant uprising of 1857, which saw a brutal suppression of the rebellion and the eventual trial and imprisonment (in exile) of the last Mughal king, Bahādur Shāh Ẓafar (d. 1862). After this watershed event, through the Government of India Act of 1858, the British firmly vested in their monarch the political sovereignty of India.

More importantly, the symbolic capital attached to the figure of the Mughal emperor was now entirely desacralized. The previously complex navigation of indigenous mechanisms of legitimizing sovereign authority was now replaced by the brute demonstration of colonial power over its subjects. As Cohn summed up, "The trial of the emperor has to be seen in relation to the Government of India Act of 1858. The trial and the judicial exiling of the emperor and the end of Mughal rule were accomplished by completely desanctifying the previous political order of the society."[28]

Much as Kaviraj argued, Cohn's analysis makes clear that the conceptual economy of sovereignty also underwent a momentous transformation at the advent of colonialism in India. A previous notion of sovereignty tethered to considerations of privileges, hierarchies, and the importance of corporeal bonds with indigenous society made way for a markedly materialistic understanding of sovereign power. To be more specific, what Cohn's analysis highlights is the tension between idealized notions of how sovereign power ought to operate and how it actually works. For in critical respects, the political structure of British rule did not by any means completely overthrow the earlier structure of Mughal authority defined by genealogy, mediation, and intercession. Even under the British, processes of mediation continued to be extremely important in shaping how access to political power actually worked and how society was structured. However, despite these structural continuities, the sources, visions, and meanings that organized sovereign power were permanently altered. This is not to suggest that sovereignty was not debated and contested in the Mughal Empire but to point out key conceptual and political transformations in the sociology of sovereignty in the transition to another, very different form of imperial power.[29]

These transformations in the conceptual space and political performance of sovereignty also held major implications for indigenous imaginaries of social order and hierarchy. In her study *Ashraf into Middle Classes*, historian Margrit Pernau showed that the solidification of British colonial power in the latter half of the nineteenth century generated profound consequences for Muslim conceptions of nobility (*sharāfat*) in North India.[30] Following the 1830s, as the British more conclusively claimed political sovereignty and as the political, cultural, and racial boundaries separating the colonizers and the colonized crystallized, the focus and composition of nobility among Indian Muslims also shifted.[31] Until this point the domain of nobility had been restricted to the landowning elite (*jāgīrdār*) and the scholarly class, while merchants, traders, and artisans were counted squarely among the commoners. Moreover, lineage and descent from the Islamic "heartlands" was the primary marker of nobility distinguishing the noble (*ashrāf*) from indigenous converts (*ajlāf*), though claims to a noble lineage were often contrived as a mechanism for acquiring social recognition.

But these notions of nobility transformed in the late nineteenth century with developments such as the demise of the prospect of restoring Muslim political sovereignty in the aftermath of 1857, the rise of a public sphere dotted with colonial educational institutions, and the increasingly exclusive association of the *'ulamā'* with religious knowledge alone. While lineage continued to hold importance, nobility increasingly came to be associated with individual piety, a shift that Pernau described as one from "inherited values to lived values."[32] This shift coincided with and was facilitated by the emergence of a North Indian Muslim middle class that saw itself as distinct from both the upper and lower echelons of society. While by no means uniform, this middle class that took on the mantle of nobility was defined by its staunch opposition to aristocratic (*nawābī*) lifestyles and extravagance and by its affinity to the project of religious reform. The entanglement of piety and nobility in the late nineteenth century thus brought closer the scholarly elite, the *'ulamā'*, and merchants, traders, and other professional groups (the middle class) that had until then been excluded from the nobility. This crucial shift in the social order constitutes an important backdrop to the intra-Muslim debate described in this book, the career of which ran parallel to the historical arc of Pernau's project.

Finally, in elucidating the problem space of sovereignty in early modern and modern South Asia, the historian Azfar Moin's book *The Millennial Sovereign* is indispensably germane. In this work, Moin argued that Mughal understandings of political sovereignty were premised on the conjunction of kingship and sainthood. The sovereignty of the king was organized and performed according to the logic and grammar of the Sufi saint's charisma, suffused with millenarian authority and expectation. Kingship was interlocked with sainthood in "mimetic embrace."[33] According to Moin, such a millenarian conception of sovereignty, infused with and informed by saintly charisma, dominated the political and social landscape of early modern Muslim empires including Mughal India and Safavid Iran and was ruptured only with the onslaught of colonial modernity.[34] This book begins where Moin's ended. I am interested in the question of what happens to the career of sovereignty as a concept as the world that occupied Moin's study drew to a close of sorts.

More specifically, the question I address is this: How did the moment of transition from Mughal kingship to British colonialism in India's political history inform debates and contestation surrounding the conceptual economy of sovereignty among religious scholars and communities? I will focus on questions involving the normative relationship between the divine sovereign and the human subject that emerged as sites of tremendous intellectual fermentation and controversy among early nineteenth-century Indian Muslim scholars.

For instance, how was divine sovereignty to be imagined during a moment when political sovereignty was steadily disintegrating? How were Muslims supposed to perform their daily lives in a way that affirmed the absolute alterity of divine sovereignty? What did sovereignty depend on? Did divine sovereignty hinge on the capacity to enact exceptions, such as miracles? If yes, then how was one to understand Prophet Muḥammad's capacity as an intercessor (on the Day of Judgment) when through his charisma and blessings sinners were granted the exception of a pardon? Who decided on the exceptions—was there any tension between divine and prophetic claims to exceptionality? As I hope to show, these seemingly theological questions were intimately connected to how one imagined the normative horizons of the political. In what follows I will explore the interaction of the theological and the political through a close reading of a fierce polemical exchange between Shāh Muḥammad Ismā'īl and Fazl-i Ḥaqq Khayrābādī on the boundaries of prophetic intercession.[35] In addition, I will also analyze in some detail their competing positions on the controversial issues of God's capacity to lie (*imkān-i kizb*) or to create another entity like Muḥammad (*imkān-i naẓīr*).

I will argue that Ismā'īl's and Khayrābādī's opposing theological programs were informed by rival narratives of the political ethos that sustained the normative relationship between the human subject and the divine sovereign. I will show that at stake in these ostensibly theological debates was the larger political question of how should one understand the concept of sovereignty under conditions of political change and transition. My analysis thus is about the interplay, the overlapping, of theological and political imaginaries. The overarching theme I explore concerns ways in which Muslim theological discourses articulate and are informed by contrasting understandings of the political.

In preparation for that discussion, in the first chapter of this section I explore some key aspects of the life and intellectual career of an early nineteenth-century rabble-rouser whose writings and activities took Muslim India by storm: Shāh Muḥammad Ismā'īl. Ismā'īl's mark on the intellectual and social history of South Asian Islam is indelible, though the layers and tensions of his religious thought have been scarcely explored. I hope to make some progress in ameliorating this gap in what follows. But who was Ismā'īl, and why was he so controversial? It is by addressing these questions that I begin.

chapter two

The Promise and Perils of Moral Reform

The Fractured Memory of Shāh Muḥammad Ismā'īl

There are very few thinkers in the theater of South Asian Islam whose intellectual legacy is as controversial, contested, and polarizing as that of Shāh Muḥammad Ismā'īl (also known as Shāh Ismā'īl Shahīd). Born in 1779 in Delhi, Ismā'īl came from an illustrious family, boasting among the most distinguished and influential Muslim scholars in modern India. His grandfather was the famous and much heralded eighteenth-century scholar Shāh Walī Ullah. Ismā'īl's father was one of Walī Ullah's lesser-known sons, Shāh 'Abdul Ghanī. Ismā'īl received his religious education, including training in the Qur'ān, the Ḥadīth, jurisprudence, logic, and moral philosophy, primarily under the tutelage of his formidable uncles Shāh 'Abdul 'Azīz and Shāh Rafī' al-Dīn (d. 1821).

Ismā'īl was somewhat of an anomaly in this family of dazzling scholars. Among the things that most surprised and at times bewildered his family elders, especially his uncle Shāh 'Abdul 'Azīz, was Ismā'īl's passion for different martial arts and militaristic forms of physical exercise. In his biographical literature, Ismā'īl is presented as a masculine warrior-scholar who had been preparing for not only intellectual but also physical *jihād* from a very young age, as if he had always anticipated the course his life would take and the wars he would one day have to fight.[1] For instance, we are told that by the time he turned twenty-one Ismā'īl had mastered horse riding, archery, fencing, and swimming. In fact, at times he would spend three full days swimming in the river, only taking intermittent breaks at the river bank to teach students lessons and to eat dinner. Ismāʿīl also developed the skill of walking long distances (ten to eleven miles) on a single breath while not showing any signs of tiring. And so perfect was his control over sleep that not only could he last effortlessly without sleeping for eight to ten days, he could put his body to sleep or awake at any moment he so willed.[2]

In cultivating a battle-hardened masculinity, Ismāʿīl sought to distinguish himself not only from the generally less adventurous lifestyle of the Muslim religious scholarly elite but, more importantly, from the Mughal political elite of his time, whom he considered profligate, corrupt, and responsible for the political and moral decline of Indian Muslims. Rehearsing a theme that would occupy center stage in his reformist career, Ismāʿīl's biographers are keenly invested in showing his challenge to and repudiation of the Mughal political elite. Consider the following anecdote. Curiously, Ismāʿīl's fencing teacher, a certain Mirzā Raḥmatullah Bayg, was famous in Delhi as the instructor of most Mughal princes and sons of nobility. Once, on seeing Ismāʿīl practice fencing at the arena where Bayg coached his pupils, two young princes laughed at him mockingly, as if to lampoon a "religious scholar" exerting himself in a martial art commonly associated with the political aristocracy. After completing his lesson, Ismāʿīl turned to these two princes and lectured them:

> I am from the descendants of those [scholars] who disseminated Islam globally and established Muslim sultanates all over the world. And you are the offspring of those [aristocrats] who for the sake of their comforts and pleasures shattered the political sovereignty of Muslims to pieces. Hazrat ʿUmar [i.e., ʿUmar ibn al-Khaṭṭāb, the second caliph in Sunnī Islam, d. 644] was not a royal prince, the five hundred thousand Arabs who were working under him in the previously Roman and Sasanian empires were not denizens of the Red Fort [*lāl qilʿa*]. But what they achieved for Islam is not hidden to anyone, and [in contrast] the consequences of your ancestors' luxury-seeking habits are also all too well known.[3]

On hearing these damning charges, the two princes became remorseful and apologetic. Still, Ismāʿīl dared them to a fencing match, a challenge they reluctantly accepted. Within the first few rounds, Ismāʿīl's superior skills and training became apparent. The haughty princes realized that this "son of a mullah" (*mullah zāda*) whom they had scoffed at was much superior to them in a martial art usually associated with the aristocratic class. This narrative takes the mantle of masculinity away from the royal aristocracy and confers it on Ismā'īl. Moreover, it is the "luxury-seeking habits" of the Mughals that are held responsible for their downfall. Thus this anecdote narratively connects the masculine power and capacity of the male body with the capacity for political power and popular sovereignty.

Crucially, in seeking to cultivate a masculine body, Ismā'īl interrupted and departed from the noncombative mannerisms known among the religious scholarly elite. While they never objected or expressed any reservations, Ismā'īl's family members, such as his father and uncle, would often chuckle at his militaristic exercises. They would often register their perplexity at the sight of a member in their family with habits that were so distant from and at odds with a religious scholarly habitus (*mawlwīyāna mu'āsharat*).[4]

Ismā'īl's unusual predilection may also explain why, although he had strong intellectual bonds with his family, it was the charismatic figure Sayyid Aḥmad Barelvī (hereafter Sayyid Aḥmad, not to be confused with the Barelvī School;[5] d. 1831) who most profoundly shaped his reformist career. Sayyid Aḥmad is a curious figure on the intellectual and political map of South Asian Islam. Though he had studied the Qur'ān and the Ḥadīth from Shāh 'Abdul 'Azīz and Shāh 'Abdul Qādir, he was more a military warrior and mystic millenarian than a traditionally trained scholar. Nonetheless, Sayyid Aḥmad attracted a following that cut across elite and popular lines; besides Ismā'īl, Shāh 'Abdul 'Azīz's son-in-law and prominent Ḥanafī scholar 'Abdul Ḥaī (d. 1828) was among Sayyid Aḥmad's major disciples. Ismā'īl first met Sayyid Aḥmad in 1819 after the latter had returned to Delhi from the princely state of Tonk (today known as Rājasthān). He was sent there by 'Azīz to receive extensive military training from Amīr 'Alī Khān (d. 1834), who would later become the *nawāb* of Tonk. The encounter with Sayyid Aḥmad was a turning point in Ismā'īl's life.[6]

Before this moment, despite his intellectual promise, Ismā'īl had failed to develop any coherent agenda of reform. Generally lacking discipline, he had also refrained from taking up a stable profession. As the twentieth-century biographer and one of Ismā'īl's most ardent supporters Ghulām Rasūl Mehr (d. 1971) put it, "There was an element of carelessness [*be-parwā'ī*] in his temperament."[7] But after meeting Sayyid Aḥmad and pledging to him his allegiance, Ismā'īl experienced a dramatic conversion. His previous indifference and indiscipline gave way to a rigorous program of religious reform.

What distinguished Ismā'īl from most other scholars in his family was the way he combined scholarship with avid public activism. Ismā'īl took his reformist mission to arguably the most public of all venues in Delhi: the pulpit at the famous and centrally located Jāmi' mosque. There he delivered a number of rousing Friday sermons on themes like restoring divine sovereignty and abandoning heretical customs and traditions, themes that also occupied his intellectual career. He was a gifted orator, and his sermons attracted massive crowds every week. They generated equally passionate admiration and condemnation. Some lauded Ismā'īl for cuttingly diagnosing and laying bare the moral corruptions that afflicted Indian Muslims. Others chastised him for causing social havoc by insulting long-standing traditions and impugning the authority of pious saints and other revered figures. In fact, such was the fury precipitated by Ismā'īl's sermons that at one point his archnemesis Fazl-i Ḥaqq Khayrābādī petitioned to the British resident officer of Delhi to ban Ismā'īl from taking the pulpit at Jāmi' mosque. Khayrābādī was himself a part of the British bureaucracy. This petition was granted, and Ismā'īl was prohibited from delivering his sermons on grounds that they disturbed public order. Curiously, this ban was reversed only after Ismā'īl convinced the British resident that his sermons were not spreading any heresy and were in fact aimed at restoring divine sovereignty.

Reforming the Public

In the 1820s, the famous Presbyterian evangelist Charles Finney "rode on horseback from town to town" in upstate New York preaching his message of evangelical reform, as he spearheaded the "Second Great Awakening."[8] Thousands of miles away, at the same moment, Ismā'īl was also busy taking his reformist project to the public, in Delhi, and eventually across North India and beyond. In addition to delivering formal sermons at prominent venues like the Jāmi' mosque, he preached feverishly in public spaces such as markets and street corners. Much to the chagrin of his family members, he even ventured to famous brothels in Delhi, reminding dancing girls and their patrons of the "divine calamities" that awaited them. For instance, one night after offering his evening prayers at the Jāmi' mosque, Ismā'īl headed to the brothel of a famous prostitute in Delhi called Motī (Hindī for "pearl"). This brothel was frequented by some of the most affluent elite of the city. After pretending that he was a beggar seeking charity, Ismā'īl was let in to the brothel. Upon entering, he spread a piece of cloth in the courtyard, sat on it, and began to loudly recite *Sūrat al-Tawba* (the chapter of repentance) from the Qur'ān. He recited the chapter until the verse that reads "Thereafter we reduce him to the lowest of the low" (*Thumma radadnāhu asfal sāfilīn*). He then proceeded to deliver a fiery speech that painted a vivid image of torture on the Day of Judgment.

Gripped with remorse and panic, Motī and her elite patrons began smashing the drums and other musical instruments at the brothel. They also instantly repented. That same night when Ismā'īl returned to Jāmi' mosque, he was stopped at the staircase by his first cousin and the famous scholar of Ḥadīth, Muḥammad Ya'qūb Dihlavī. Dihlavī confronted Ismā'īl and reproached him for visiting a brothel. He said, "Your grandfather and your uncle were esteemed figures. You come from a family that kings have venerated for generations. But you are brashly ruining your reputation. What wisdom is there in bringing upon yourself such dishonor?" Ismā'īl responded confidently, "Mawlānā, I am bewildered at what you have just said. You consider what I did tonight a cause of dishonor. Well this was only the beginning. I will consider myself venerated the day the people of Delhi will mount me on a donkey, blacken my face, and take me around *Chandnī Chawk* while I will be roaring to them, 'God said such and such and God's Prophet said such and such' [*Qāla Allāh Kadhā wa Qāla Rasūl Allāh Kadhā*]."[9]

Widow Remarriage

One of the signature reformist campaigns in which Ismā'īl most earnestly participated was that of widow remarriage. In her important work on the topic of Hindu widow remarriage, feminist historian Tanika Sarkar has shown that in the mid-nineteenth century the question of widow remarriage was one of the most scandalous and incendiary disputes that consumed Hindu scholars and activists of varied and often opposing persuasions, as it did the colonial state. Moreover, according to Sarkar, opposition to widow remarriage "not only unified many Hindu castes—at least at the level of an ethical consensus—it also laid down the boundary line between Hindus and Muslims."[10] Eventually, after much dispute and debate spanning a few decades, the Hindu reformist position against the prohibition to widow remarriage triumphed in the arena of law. In 1856, the colonial state enacted a law (Act No. XV, July 1856) that abrogated "an earlier legal and prescriptive prohibition against the remarriage of Hindu widows."[11] This law had followed another law passed twenty-seven years earlier in 1829 that had prohibited the practice of widow immolation or *satī*. As Sarkar lucidly put it, "Between them, the two legal acts on sati and widow remarriage criminalized what was once a holy rite and legalized what had long been regarded as a form of religious immorality."[12]

Debates on the entangled problems of widow remarriage and widow immolation in the religious, political, and legal arenas of nineteenth-century South Asia have attracted some excellent scholarship.[13] However, in the field of South Asian studies, discussions on these questions tend to primarily center on the interaction of Hindu thought, actors, and the shifting priorities and attitudes of the colonial state over the nineteenth century. But these vexing controversies, especially around widow remarriage, did not just occupy Hindus and Hinduism; they also are a crucial node in the career of modern Muslim reform in South Asia, from the early nineteenth century onwards. Because of the social taboo associated with widow remarriage in certain Hindu traditions, this issue was of considerable interest for Muslim reformers, like Shāh Muḥammad Ismāʿīl, eager to cleanse Indian Islam of "Hindu" influences. And, as we will see in what follows, just as the opposition to widow remarriage represented a critical boundary marker between Hindus and Muslims for many Hindu castes, fighting the taboo against widow remarriage constituted an important reinforcement of that boundary for many Muslim reformers. Thus the early nineteenth-century Muslim reformist campaign against widow remarriage evinces a curious convergence of interests both with Hindu reformist voices opposed to the prohibition against Hindu widow remarriage and with Hindu scholars who vehemently defended the prohibition. While agreeing with the former on the ideological imperative of erasing the taboo against widow remarriage, Muslim reformers like Ismā'īl also shared with the latter an avid doctrinal and affective commitment to maintaining clear boundaries of separation between Hindu and Muslim bodies. The intimate yet volatile domains of conjugality and sexuality were particularly productive sites in which these boundaries were made visible, fought out, and demarcated. In what follows, I try to triangulate the discussion on widow remarriage by bringing into view important fragments of Muslim reformist contributions to this debate. I do so by presenting a narrative sketch of key moments of Ismā'īl's engagement with this issue.

The subject of widow remarriage was personal to Ismā'īl. His older sister was a widow who had not remarried for several years. By his own later admission, Ismā'īl said he too had absorbed and internalized the taboo attached to widow remarriage in North India at that time. As he recounted, "While teaching my sister the Ḥadīth collection of Mishkāt [by Muḥammad al-Tabrīzī (d. 1340)], I used to intentionally leave out prophetic reports about the virtues of widow remarriage. I was fearful that she might desire to remarry."[14] This apprehensive attitude changed after Ismā'īl took Sayyid Aḥmad as his spiritual guru. According to Ismā'īl, it was Sayyid Aḥmad who opened his eyes to the "fact" that the taboo against widow remarriage "was a Hindu custom that opposed the prophetic norm." Thereafter, Ismā'īl got his sister remarried to one of his close friends. The story of her remarriage is worth narrating.

One day, Ismā'īl was preaching on the subject of widow remarriage at the Jāmi' mosque. A man sitting in the audience raised his hand, gesturing that he had a question to ask. Ismā'īl immediately sensed that this man was going to ask him about his widowed sister, who was still unmarried.[15] He became very nervous and took the preemptive measure of calling the gathering off immediately, telling his audience, "I need to go take care of something very important, let's meet next week." Ismā'īl hurried out of the mosque and went running to his elder sister's house. As soon as she opened the door, he fell on his knees, and said, crying hysterically, "Oh sister, my career is in your hands, the efficacy of my sermons depends on you." Taken by complete surprise, she replied, "What are you talking about?" Ismā'īl explained, "If you get married, you will help me resuscitate an important prophetic norm and allow me to continue giving my sermons with authority." She tried to reason with him: "My dear brother, as much as I would like to revive a prophetic norm, I am just too old and sick to get remarried." But when Ismā'īl continued to insist, she finally succumbed and agreed to her brother's plea. She was married off to one of his close friends.[16]

Soon thereafter, buoyed by this personal victory, Ismā'īl launched a full-scale movement to get widowed Muslim women in North India remarried. He was joined by an army of associates who went village by village searching for widowed Muslim women eligible for remarriage. In fact, a certain Maulvī 'Abdul Raḥīm was so zealous to find widows in order to get them remarried that he became famous as "the widow remarriage mullah" (*Rāndon ke shādī wālay mullah*).[17]

Sayyid Aḥmad's influence on Ismā'īl's reformist awakening is unquestionable, even though the latter was a more accomplished and learned scholar. In a particularly poignant moment, Ismā'īl was once asked by someone: "Your uncles Shāh 'Abdul 'Azīz and Shāh 'Abdul Qādir love you passionately, and Sayyid Aḥmad Ṣāḥib is among their disciples. Why is it then that you are so much closer to Sayyid Aḥmad than you are to your own uncles?" Ismā'īl responded tersely, "All I will say is that when I used to teach my [widowed] sister the Ḥadīth collection of Mishkāt, I used to intentionally leave out prophetic reports about the virtues of widow remarriage, fearful that she might desire to remarry. But after my association with Sayyid Aḥmad blossomed, I myself took the lead in getting her remarried. From this you can discern why I am so close to him."[18]

The curious aspect of the narrative above is the way it readily admits the deep rootedness of a "Hindu taboo" among not only ordinary Muslims but also the Muslim scholarly elite. Ismā'īl's admission to have left out prophetic reports on widow remarriage while giving lessons on Ḥadīth to his sister is significant, for it shows that his reformist mission to regularize widow remarriage was as much a work of self-reform as it was aimed at reforming others. The desire to undo the taboo of widow remarriage among South Asian Muslims signals an implicit acceptance of their knotty entanglement with an Indic milieu in which the distinction between "Hindu" and "Muslim" geographies of normative attachments was not always so clear. Also, while Hindu and Muslim reformers differed markedly in terms of the context and purpose of their efforts, it is instructive to note their convergence not only in their endorsement of widow remarriage but also in their strategic presentation of the taboo against widow remarriage as a false custom that contravened scriptural authority—a task that hermeneutically at least was considerably more challenging for the former than it was for the latter. They also shared a view of the widowed woman's body as ever so vulnerable to the danger of sexual corruption and immorality if left outside the moral garrison of conjugal relations.[19] Indeed, one wonders whether the activism of Muslim scholars like Ismāʿīl and his compatriots played any role in generating conditions that paved the way for the eventual legal allowance accorded to Hindu widow remarriage by the colonial state a few decades later. Regardless of how one may evaluate this possibility, it is useful, as the preceding discussion has suggested, to at least consider South Asian Muslim reformist interventions in labors of reform conventionally understood as pertaining to "Hinduism" and Hindu actors. Identifying these often unacknowledged areas of convergence is also important precisely to unsettle the reformist fantasy of primordial and sharply delineated boundaries distinguishing religious identity and difference.

Domesticating Nondivine Charisma

Another curious incident that brings together the varied critiques undergirding Ismāʿīl's evangelical labor concerns his encounter with a reclusive yet spellbinding Sufi mystic called Jalāl Shāh.[20] Ismāʿīl took it upon himself to frequent prominent gatherings and events that showcased the mystical prowess of charismatic Sufi figures and that attracted large numbers of commoners and royalty. To camouflage his identity, he would go to such venues dressed in military garb. Jalāl Shāh was a thirty-eight-year-old Sufi with extraordinary powers and charisma. He was famous for his ability to overpower anyone at will in one moment simply by laying his eyes upon a person. In addition to his spiritual magnetism, Shāh was known for being astonishingly handsome. Every year during the month of *rabīʿ al-awwal*, for the first twelve days leading up to the Prophet's birthday, Shāh would hold elaborate spiritual assemblies at the shrine complex of Qadam Sharīf in Delhi.

These assemblies attracted close to two hundred people from varied backgrounds, including the poor, merchants, and the nobility, in addition to Shāh's large retinue of traveling disciples. While Shāh was a Sufi, his affective sensibilities were formed by a material culture of lavishness. Accouterments like fine Persian carpets and jewelry accompanied him in abundance. Despite this pomp, and his immersion in what the narrator of the incident calls a "corrupt moral economy," Shāh was generous in giving charity to the poor and showed traces of a pious subjectivity, as if anticipating the gift of reform and awakening. He was to soon encounter his awakener when one night, on the sixth of *rabī' al-awwal*, Ismā'īl attended one of Shāh's famed gatherings. He entered the Qadam Sharīf shrine at around ten p.m. when the spiritual festivities had just peaked. To Ismā'īl's surprise, when he entered the shrine, Shāh gestured toward him, inviting Ismā'īl to sit next to him. For a while Ismā'īl found nothing objectionable in the happenings of the gathering.[21]

That equanimity was disrupted as soon as relics of the Prophet were brought in; Jalāl Shāh and everyone else stood up in reverence. But Ismā'īl stealthily drew back, distancing himself from the performance of a ritual he so passionately despised. Though no one else noticed, Shāh did. However, he said nothing and showed no signs of anger or petulance. When the assembly resumed, Shāh again signaled Ismā'īl to take a seat next to him. For a while they exchanged no words, blending their breath in the majestic silence that pervaded Qadam Sharīf. Eventually, Jalāl Shāh broke the silence and made some small talk, asking Ismā'īl in a faint but audible voice, "Are you from Delhi?" When Ismā'īl responded in the positive, Shāh continued, "It is thanks to people like you that I come to Delhi so as to benefit from the pleasure and the illumination of your company."[22] As they began to converse more freely, Ismā'īl's eloquence and the wisdom of his speech so impressed Shāh's heart that he immediately called off the gathering, asking his disciples to pack up and leave. The usually spellbinding Jalāl Shāh was himself spellbound. Soon after, Ismā'īl and Shāh found themselves alone together. While the spiritual assembly that had attracted a massive crowd had ended prematurely, Ismā'īl's evangelical performance was just beginning.

But before Ismāʿīl could work his magic, Shāh had a question of his own: "Are you not Shāh Muḥammad Ismāʿīl?" he asked with the confidence of a student certain of having just aced his exam.[23] At first Ismāʿīl hesitated, but on Shāh's insistence he eventually confirmed his identity. He did wonder, though, how Shāh had come to find out who he was. Shāh explained that he would frequently receive descriptions of Ismāʿīl from the latter's opponents, accompanied by the exhortation to channel his mystical powers to overwhelm and kill him. But Shāh reassured Ismāʿīl that "he was not inclined to harm anyone without reason."[24]

Ismāʿīl then counseled Shāh by delivering an impromptu personalized sermon. He sought to lift the veil from the corrupt practices that saturated Shāh's life and that in turn corrupted the lives of his followers and disciples. Shāh shivered in agreement as he listened intently to Ismāʿīl's elaboration of what the Qur'ān and *sunna* demanded of him. In response, he wistfully reflected: "Yes, you are right. So many of the rituals I have steadfastly practiced, thinking they were central to Islam, like visiting graves of saints, blanketing those graves with flowers, and so on, are in reality touchstones of polytheism and heresy. God will hold me accountable for my own sins, but what answer will I furnish when he will ask me to account for all the people I led astray?" Here Shāh broke down in noisy tears.[25] Ismāʿīl consoled him and urged him to immediately repent by supplicating God for forgiveness. It was by now two a.m.; Delhi had retired into absolute quiet, and the only sound in the background was the intermittent clip-clop of the horses carrying local police officers (*kotwāl*).

Together Ismāʿīl and Shāh, eyes closed and hearts transfixed, beseeched God for the latter's forgiveness and repentance. The acceptance of their supplication was confirmed when a thundering yet comforting voice shook the heavens: "Jalāl, we pardon your sins, and from now on you are counted as among our friends." On hearing this, Shāh and Ismāʿīl both fell unconscious. On waking up an hour or so later, Shāh "found his heart beaming with divine splendor."[26] His conversion from heresy to normativity had been effected; he had joined the fold of the righteous ambassadors of Islam. After narrating this event, Ismāʿīl's biographer Mirzā Ḥayāt Dihlavī adds the curious comment, clearly taking a swipe at the philosophically oriented Khayrābādī school: "The emanation of a voice from the heavens might generate doubt and suspicion in the mind of the philosopher. But there is no doubt about the capacity of the heart to speak God's voice once it is cleansed of all worldly attachments."[27]

For Dihlavī, the purification of Jalāl Shāh's heart allowed it to serve as a receptacle of divine speech. Anyone who found such an occurrence rationally untenable could not comprehend or appreciate the intimate interlocking of the heart and divine being. In the body of a pious reformed subject, the heart's voice was God's voice. The narrative of Jalāl Shāh's transformation ties together the major threads binding Ismā'īl's reform project: the critique of nondivine sources of charismatic authority, the repudiation of ritual practices empowered by that authority, and the shunning of an aristocratic moral economy bound up with these two sources of dissatisfaction. The drama of Jalāl Shāh's conversion articulated the vision and desire of a reformed South Asian Muslim individual and public enraptured by nothing but the mission of upholding God's absolute and exceptional sovereignty.

Ismā'īl's Intellectual Oeuvre and Legacy

In addition to his evangelical activities, Ismā'īl wrote some of the most important religious texts in early nineteenth-century Muslim India. His writings encompass a remarkable range of themes and disciplines, including law, theology, logic, politics, and mysticism.[28] Moreover, Ismā'īl was remarkably adept at moving seamlessly between popular texts written for mass consumption and complex specialist texts. This book tries to present Ismā'īl with all his complexities by engaging his theological, legal, and political thought. While extensively discussing his most controversial text *Fortifying Faith* (*Taqwīyat al-Īmān*), I also bring into view some of his lesser-known texts, such as *Station of Leadership* (*Manṣab-i Imāmat*) on political theory, *One Day* (*Yak Roza*) on theology, and *Clarifying Truth* (*Īẓāḥ al-Ḥaqq*) on law and ritual practice. A more expansive consideration of his intellectual oeuvre reveals a far more complicated and nuanced thinker than what the label of a "puritan Salafī" often appended to him would suggest. Part of my objective in this book is to draw out the conflicts, paradoxes, and ambiguities that mark Ismā'īl's thought and career. But despite his voluminous and varied intellectual output, any thinking about Ismā'īl today cannot escape the thicket of polemics that blanket his memory. The dispute between Barelvī and Deobandī pioneers in the latter half of the nineteenth century has played a major role in intensifying the divisiveness of his persona. This is so because many of their polemical entanglements centered on some of Ismā'īl's most controversial statements.

Indeed, Ismā'īl's specter continues to haunt the polemical landscape of intra-Sunnī rivalries in Muslim South Asia (and in many places outside of South Asia) in profound ways even today. His supporters as well as his detractors are equally intense in their opinions about him. Both during his own life and later, Ismā'īl's supporters, most notably the pioneers of the Deoband, saw him as a champion awakener who had intervened in a situation of utter moral chaos in Muslim India.[29] For them, Ismā'īl was like a savior who reenergized the commitment of the masses and the scholarly elite alike to the primacy of divine sovereignty in Islam.

However, for his opponents, Ismā'īl was a person of questionable intellect who through his provocations against the Prophet and other revered figures of the tradition had been the first to plant the seeds of intra-Sunnī divisions in India. As the prominent present-day Barelvī scholar Yāsīn Akhtar Miṣbāḥī has put it, "Under Ismā'īl's standards of what constitutes normative Islam, the vast majority of Muslims from the last five hundred years of Indian history will have to be declared unbelievers. Before the publication of *Taqwīyat al-Īmān* there used to be only two groups of Muslims in India, Sunnīs and Shī'as. Now, because of his insidious agenda, the Sunnī community of India has been divided into countless groups and factions."[30] Ismā'īl's foes accused him of insulting the normative authority of the Prophet and of denigrating the sanctity of venerated traditions and devotional practices. In the deeply polemical environment of colonial India and also today, Ismā'īl is often labeled by his opponents as the first "Indian Wahhābī."[31] Moreover, his opponents sought to uncouple Ismā'īl from the legacy of his illustrious grandfather Shāh Walī Ullah by caricaturing him as the black sheep of the Walī Ullah family who did not even deserve to be called a scholar.

For example, notice the disdainful sarcasm with which one present-day Barelvī polemicist, Sayyid Muḥammad Na'īmuddīn, has described Ismā'īl's attitude as a student during the latter's youth:

> Shāh Ismā'īl was the bane of his teachers' existence. Always negligent about doing his homework, he would disrupt classes and cause havoc for other students with his obnoxious and unruly behavior. His only passions were kite flying [*patang bāzī*], physical exercise [*jismānī warzish*], and wasting time. Arrogant and boastful, Shāh Ismā'īl was a perpetual source of embarrassment to the elders of his family, such as his renowned uncle Shāh 'Abdul 'Azīz. How unfortunate that the Deobandī *'ulamā'* have taken this least competent member of the Walī Ullah clan as their religious guide while paying little heed to the thinking of its other exalted luminaries.[32]

The hyperbole of the above description aside, Ismā'īl's reformist activities later in life do seem to have generated a fair degree of consternation for the esteemed Ḥanafī scholars of his family. For instance, contrary to the Ḥanafī traditions of Muslim India, Ismā'īl preached and followed the practice of raising both hands (*raf' al-yadayn*) during prayers. This practice was a subject of intense contestation between Ḥanafī and nonconformist (*ghayr muqallidīn*) scholars of India. When Ismā'īl's uncle Shāh 'Abdul 'Azīz was informed about his nephew's endorsement of this practice and about the controversy it was generating, he shrugged in resignation and replied, "I am an old man now. He will not listen to what I say."[33] Shāh 'Abdul 'Azīz asked his younger brother Shāh 'Abdul Qādir to pacify Ismā'īl and to dissuade him from starting unnecessary scandals. Qādir responded, "Sir, I will do as you say. But he will not listen to me either. Instead, he will volley me with prophetic reports."[34] But Qādir did charge his own son and Ismā'īl's cousin Muḥammad Ya'qūb Dihlavī (also mentioned earlier) with this task.

Ya'qūb talked to Ismā'īl and advised him against engaging in provocative practices like *raf' al-yadayn*. Ismā'īl responded just as his younger uncle had predicted, by quoting a prophetic report. He said to Ya'qūb, "Considering the moral chaos [*fitna*] that has afflicted the masses these days, how are we to understand the prophetic report 'Whoever adheres to my practice in times of corruption will be rewarded with the reward of a hundred martyrs'?"[35] Ismā'īl continued, "Of course, when someone revives an abandoned prophetic practice [*sunnat-i matrūka*], there is bound to be controversy." When Shāh 'Abdul Qādir was told about Ismā'īl's response, he sighed. "We thought Ismā'īl had become a scholar. But he cannot even understand the meaning of a Ḥadīth. This principle applies only when an established prophetic practice is being opposed by a nonprophetic practice. But in this case both raising one's hands and keeping them down are among the Prophet's practices. So, in this context, the comparison is not between a prophetic norm and an opposing counternorm but between two different articulations of the same normative practice."[36]

Utopian Strivings

Apart from the controversy surrounding his intellectual life, Ismā'īl's legacy and memory have been much influenced by his central role in the North Indian *jihād* movement against the Sikhs during the years 1826–31 in what is today the Khyber-Pakhtūnkhwāh Province (formerly Northwest Frontier Province) in Pakistan. Under the charismatic leadership of Sayyid Aḥmad, Ismā'īl and some five hundred other scholars and laypeople waged war against the Sikhs to liberate the Pashtūn Muslims of that region from what they perceived as the tyranny of Sikh rule. The idea of this *jihād* movement is said to have originated through a tragic tale of abduction. In 1819, while in Rāmpūr, Sayyid Aḥmad was visited by a group of Afghan Pashtūn men. They told him a harrowing story that left him shaken as well as enraged. While traveling through Panjāb, these Pashtūn men had stopped at a well to quench their thirst. They saw some Sikh women operating the well. Unfamiliar with Indic languages, they signaled their desire for water through the silent gesture of placing hands under their lips. To their utter surprise, and later horror, these women, after looking around to make sure no one else could listen, began speaking in Pashto. They went on to reveal that they were not Sikh but Afghan women from different tribes and localities who had been abducted by the Sikhs to Panjāb, where they lived as their concubines. "Oh, Sayyid Aḥmad! Do something to save these women from unbelief," these visiting Afghan men pleaded. "God willing, I will soon launch *jihād* against the Sikhs," he responded in firm solemnity.[37]

Jihād, according to the hagiographic tradition surrounding Sayyid Aḥmad, was something he had been preparing for throughout his life,

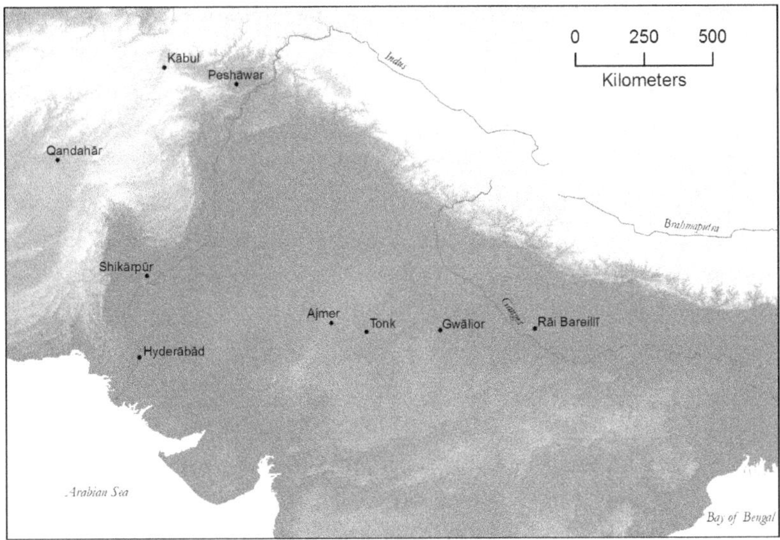

Figure 2.1 Map of the route of the *mujāhidīn.*

especially through his militia training while in Tonk. The Sikhs and their allegedly tyrannical rule over Pashtūn Muslims gave him a tangible target to put his lifelong training into practice. Sayyid Aḥmad's chief helpers and strategists for this task were two relatives of Shāh 'Abdul 'Aziz: his nephew Shāh Muḥammad Ismā'īl and his son-in-law 'Abdul Ḥaī. While Ismā'īl was a fiery orator and formidable military commander, Ḥaī in contrast was more of an introvert, whose calm and unflappable poise rendered him particularly well-suited for his role as Sayyid Aḥmad's chief political counsel and strategist.[38] Ḥaī, as I previously mentioned, was also a notable Ḥanafī scholar, adding to the doctrinal diversity of a mission that also included a fair number of nonconformists (those who did not subscribe to the canonical authority of the four schools of Sunnī law).

The route taken by these *mujāhidīn* (those who strive for *jihād*) was not constrained by the borders and boundaries of the modern nation-state. They made their way from Rāi Bareillī in North India to Gwālior, Ajmer, and Tonk in Rājasthan, to Hyderābād and Shikārpūr in Sindh, to Qandahār via the Bolān pass in Balochistān, leading to Kābul and eventually to Peshāwar via Khyber Pass.

While stationed in Peshāwar and its surroundings (especially Panjtār), Sayyid Aḥmad maintained active correspondence not only with scholars and notables in Delhi and North India, from which his campaign would receive an active supply of cash and fighters, but also with political leaders and tribal statesmen throughout Afghanistan and Central Asia. How did he and his top leadership imagine what they were doing as part of this campaign? And perhaps more importantly, how did they present their role, mission, and authority to others whose endorsement and support they often sought?

A letter in Persian that Sayyid Aḥmad wrote to the *sulṭān* of Herāt, Shāh Maḥmūd, during what seems from its contents to be the early stage of the *jihād* movement contains instructive clues to address these questions.[39] Sayyid Aḥmad explained the motivation and context of the *jihād* as follows: "Waging *jihād* and repealing rebellion and corruption are among the most important normative precepts of faith in all times and places. This is especially so in this moment, when the upheaval and unbelief unleashed by the unbelievers have reached their limit [*Khuṣūṣan dar-īn juzw-i zamān keh waqt-i shorish-i ahl-i kufr wa ṭughyān bi-ḥadī rasīdeh*]. The public markers of religion are devastated, and Muslim imperial political orders stand in ruin [*Takhrīb-i sha'ā'ir-i dīn wa ifsād-i ḥukūmat-i salāṭīn*]. This grand chaos has afflicted all parts of Hindustān, as well as Sindh and Khurāsān. In this situation, one cannot show indifference or laxity in confronting the unbelievers and the corrupt rebels;[40] that would be tantamount to the biggest and ugliest of sins [*Dar īn-ṣūrat taghāful dar muqaddimah-i istīṣāl-i kufrah mutamarridīn wa tasāhul dar bāb-i sarzanish-i bāghīyān-i mufsidīn az akbar ma'āṣī wa aqbaḥ āsām ast*]."[41]

A couple of things are worth noticing in this statement. First, as I will explore in much greater detail in chapter 4 while discussing Ismā'īl's political thought, Sayyid Aḥmad's diagnosis of catastrophe that authorized the imperative for *jihād* centered less on territorial loss than on the loss of public markers of Muslim distinction (*sha'ā'ir-i dīn*). The performance of Islam and Muslim identity in the public sphere was to him as crucial as and perhaps even more crucial than the acquisition of state sovereignty or territorial control. Second, Sayyid Aḥmad's inclusion of Sindh and Khurāsān, in addition to Hindustān in the ambit of geographies crying out for a rescue mission, a trio he repeatedly invoked in his letters, can mean two things. First, he imagined this *jihād* movement as an international campaign not limited to any specific locality, especially one contained by the borders of British India. And second, this was a strategic drive to gain sympathy, traction, and support from the political elite of these regions by convincing them that this campaign was as much theirs as it was his.

Indeed, in his letters, Sayyid Aḥmad frequently walked a fine line, impressing his authority as a religious leader (*imām*) who sought to establish a *sharī'a*-governed polity while also distinguishing himself from a political ruler (*sulṭān*) who might be seen as a threat to existing rulers and their power. This was not primarily an act of far-sighted anticipation but rather an attempt to fend off precisely such concerns about his political motives that were circulating among different regional groups and tribes. So, for instance, later in this same letter to Shāh Maḥmūd, as in several other such letters to Afghān and Pashtūn notables, Sayyid Aḥmad elaborated on the nature of his leadership as follows: "Since waging *jihād* against the people of unbelief and corruption is not possible without the anointment of an *imām*, the *mujāhidīn* and prominent [local] religious scholars have pledged to me their allegiance, and taken me as their *imām*; the Friday sermons are also delivered in my name." With this appetizer offered, Sayyid Aḥmad proceeded to the meat of the matter: "But there is a massive difference between the positions of religious and political leadership" (*Dar mayān-i manṣab-i imāmat wa manṣab-i salṭanat tafāwut-i 'aẓīm ast*).[42]

He continued, reassuring his addressee, "The appointment of a religious leader [an *imām*] is meant only for the purposes of waging *jihād* and repealing rebellion and corruption, not for colonizing countries and cities, or for seizing districts and regions." Sayyid Aḥmad closed this thought with a curious statement: "An *imām* and his followers have no personal objectives; they seek only to transfer the right of governance and rulership to its deserving custodians" (*Imām wa atbā'-i ān-rā maqṣudan li-zātihi namībāshad balkeh ḥaqq-i ḥukūmat wa salṭanat bimustaḥiqān-i ū mī-rasānand*).[43] Sayyid Aḥmad left open and ambiguous the time line for such a transfer of power. Nonetheless, his effort to clearly distinguish between his religio-political authority as an *imām* and the authority of political rulers illustrates his attempt to win the support of key regional players while also not threatening or offending them with his own claims to power.

This strategy seems to have initially worked. After some military success that saw the retreat of Sikhs from the region, Sayyid Aḥmad was

Figure 2.2 Sample page of Shāh Muḥammad Ismāʿīl's discourses during the *jihād*. Source: Shāh Muḥammad Ismāʿīl, *Maktūbat-i Shāh Ismāʿīl Dihlavī*, unpublished manuscript, MS 102, p. 26, Punjab University Library manuscript collections, Lāhore. Used with permission of the Punjab University Library.

anointed as the *imām* of the community in January 1827, with the support of the local political and religious elite. In Peshāwar, he was especially welcomed by the Yūsufzaī tribe. In fact, in their letters and speeches, both Sayyid Aḥmad and Ismāʿīl would often refer to their new surroundings as "the land of Yūsufzaīs" (*bilād-i/diyār-i/awṭān-i Yūsufzaī*).[44]

Over time, their support base expanded to include Pashtūn tribes such as the Afridīs, Khattaks, Momands, and Khalīls and places such as Swāt, Nangarhār, Buner, and Pakhlī. However, the frequency with which Sayyid Aḥmad defended his campaign and authority in his letters suggests that suspicions surrounding his role continued to persist. Note for instance his almost theatrical plea in a letter, written sometime between 1827 and 1830, to an influential tribal leader in Peshāwar, Yār Muḥammad Khān Durrānī, with whom Sayyid Aḥmad's relationship took many twists and turns, eventually turning fatally sour: "I swear to God," Sayyid Aḥmad proclaimed, "My call for *jihād* and my commitment to root out unbelief and corruption, truthfully and entirely, are not in any way at all

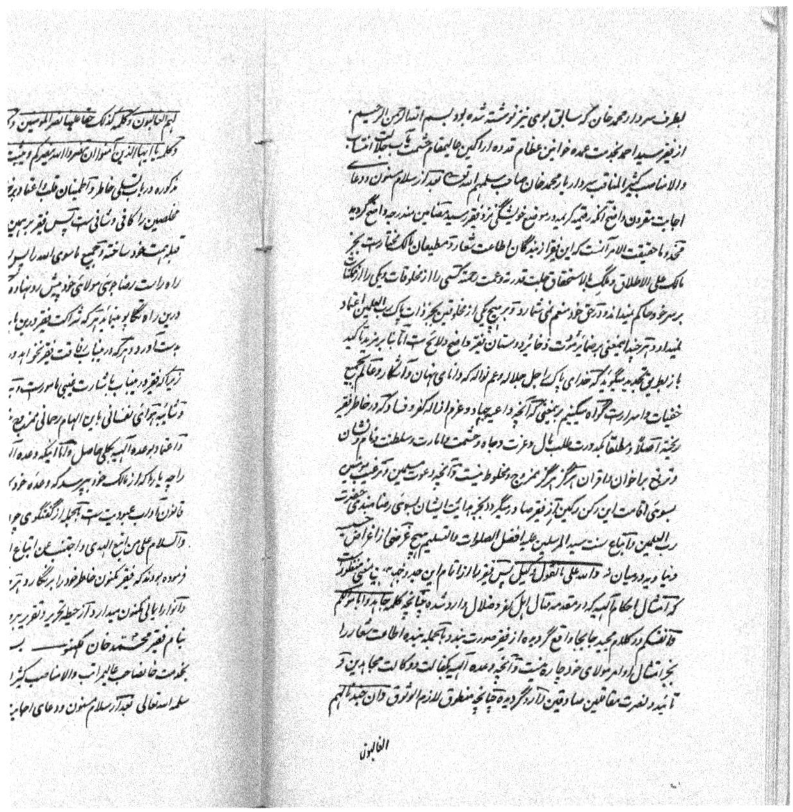

Figure 2.3 Sayyid Aḥmad's letter to Yār Muḥammad Khān Durrānī. Source: Sayyid Aḥmad Barelvī, *Makātīb-i Sayyid Aḥmad Shahīd* (Lāhore: Maktaba Rashīdīya, 1975), 13.

tainted by the stain of desiring wealth, status, rank, pomp, political power, sovereignty, name, recognition, or dominance over others" (*Dā'īyah-i jihād wa 'azm-i izālah-i kufr wa fasād keh dar khāṭir-i faqīr raykhteh aṣlan wa muṭlaqan bikudūrat-i ṭalab-i māl wa 'izzat wa jāh wa ḥashmat wa imārat wa salṭanat wa nām wa nishān wa taraffū' bar ikhwān wa iqrān har-giz har-giz mamzūj wa makhlūṭ nīst*).[45] In a fascinating discursive move, Sayyid Aḥmad further argued that he was "anointed" to his mission "by divine inspiration [*ilhām-i raḥmānī*] and by the decree of the unseen [*faqīr dar īn-bāb bi ishārat-i ghaybī ma'mūr ast*]." Thus there was "no possibility of any satanic whisper or a speck of selfish desire polluting this program."[46]

Despite Sayyid Aḥmad's assurances, the delicate task of acquiring power while not seeming to be doing so became too difficult to sustain. Over time, the local Pashtūn support for the *jihād* movement dwindled and eventually turned into outright opposition. The implementation of laws like the institution of the one-tenth land tax (*'ushr*) and a ban against high dowry rates played a critical part in this gradual but dramatic reversal of relations. Many Pashtūn tribal chieftains also resented and resisted Sayyid Aḥmad's use of the coveted title of "Commander of the Faithful" (*amīr al-mu'minīn*), a move they saw as a direct threat to their self-sovereignty.

For the North Indian reformers, these measures brought them closer to realizing the utopian mission of fashioning a society that replicated divine law. But for the local Pashtūns, such restrictions opposed established tribal norms and disrupted the order of life to which they were accustomed. This underlying philosophical rift regarding how law and society should interact resulted in irreparable animosity, to the extent that several powerful Pashtūn tribal leaders realigned with the Sikhs when they launched an all-out campaign to oust Sayyid Aḥmad and his followers from the region. The outcome was political and military catastrophe. Almost all the North Indian reformers save a few were killed at the hands of Sikhs and Pashtūns. Ismā'īl, along with Sayyid Aḥmad, was also killed during this campaign in December 1831, in the town of Bālākot, some 250 kilometers from Peshāwar. 'Abdul Ḥaī had died three years earlier in 1828—at that time a massive setback for the *jihād* campaign. Ironically, many of Sayyid Aḥmad's followers in India refused to accept his death and believed that he was living in hiding, armed with supernatural powers—precisely the sort of attitude that he and Ismā'īl had literally fought to death.[47]

The drama and shifting loyalties and alliances of this *jihād* campaign cry out for adoption as the screenplay of a blockbuster thriller, complete with a cast of Panjābīs, Pashtūns, and North Indians, scholars, warriors, and commoners, and a plot of espionage missions, conspiracy movements, political intrigue, utopian aspirations, looming suspicions, and action-filled military clashes. A detailed intellectual and political history of the *jihād* movement that carefully and extensively considers critical Arabic and Persian sources, especially the fascinating treasure

Figure 2.4 Sayyid Aḥmad's grave in Balakot, Khyber Pakhtūnkhwāh, Pakistan. Image courtesy Rizwan Zamir.

trove of Sayyid Aḥmad's and Ismā'īl's letters during these five years, is yet to be written. Such a task cannot be attempted within the parameters of this book, but I will briefly provide some sense of the internal tensions and rifts, as well as the competing ethical visions that inspired and often collided during the *jihād* movement. For this I want to turn briefly to a dramatic text composed by someone who, after having intimately and actively participated in the *jihād*, abandoned it midway, returned to Delhi, and wrote an eyewitness account.

The Case of a Curious Renegade

Sayyid Maḥbūb 'Alī Dihlavī (hereafter Maḥbūb 'Alī; d. 1864) was a prominent Sunnī Ḥanafī scholar from Delhi who was trained, like many notable scholars of his era, by Shāh 'Abdul 'Aziz and Shāh 'Abdul Qādir. Maḥbūb 'Alī pledged his allegiance to Sayyid Aḥmad in about 1815 while the latter was still in Delhi, and he joined the *jihād* campaign in June of

1827, accompanied by an army of some four hundred men.[48] While stationed close to Peshāwar, Maḥbūb ʻAlī traveled the expanse of the frontier region, diligently contributing to the *jihād* operation.

Around six months into his stay, however, he began to disagree sharply with Sayyid Aḥmad's tactics and strategies, finding them perilously harsh as well as uncalculated. More specifically, Maḥbūb ʻAlī was critical of Sayyid Aḥmad's resistance to privileging warfare over political negotiation with hostile Pashtūn leaders. He also found counterproductive what he saw as Sayyid Aḥmad's heavy-handed style of leadership that allowed little room for disagreement, critique, and consultation. Most interestingly, Maḥbūb ʻAlī found contrary to *sharīʻa* norms Sayyid Aḥmad's adoption of the title "Commander of the Faithful." This status doctrinally necessitated issuing the death warrant on anyone who refused acquiescence to Sayyid Aḥmad's leadership, a measure that he apparently had not hesitated from advocating. Qualifying for that title required that Sayyid Aḥmad first obtain the consensus of the South Asian *ʻulamāʼ* community on his position as the community's leader, Maḥbūb ʻAlī argued. Moreover, from a logistical standpoint, making such a grand claim to sovereignty was unnecessary to and distracting from the *jihād* campaign. Eventually, in 1828, a year after his arrival in Peshāwar, Maḥbūb ʻAlī reckoned that his differences with Sayyid Aḥmad had become irreconcilable, and he thus ventured back to Delhi.[49] Importantly, and this is a point I will soon repeat because it is so critical, despite his vigorous disagreement with Sayyid Aḥmad on the management of the *jihād* campaign, Maḥbūb ʻAlī remained desirous of its success. His internal critique did not change his overall attachment to the political and ethical mandate of the *jihād* movement, and he continued to wish Sayyid Aḥmad and Ismāʻīl well on their mission.

Nevertheless, on returning to Delhi, Maḥbūb ʻAlī faced massive backlash from some of Sayyid Aḥmad's most ardent supporters, who accused Maḥbūb ʻAlī of treason and disloyalty. Some also gave his return from an active battlefield a sectarian motive, pointing to his identity as a descendant of the Prophet's grandson Ḥusayn as among the factors explaining his lackluster commitment to Sayyid Aḥmad's *jihād* mission. It was in the context of this backlash and alleged defamation that Maḥbūb ʻAlī wrote a remarkable and massive text (numbering close to a thousand folios), primarily in Persian with parts also in Arabic, called "A History of Spiritual Masters in Remembrance of the Community's Leaders" (*Ta'rīkh al-Ā'ima fī Dhikr Khulafā' al-Umma*).[50]

In this rarely available text, to date found only in manuscript form, Maḥbūb 'Alī tried to write an intellectual history of the varieties of attack and resistance met by Muslim scholars throughout history, writing himself into that history. He introduced this text, which took him eight years to write, from 1828 to 1836, as follows: "In this book I will detail the events of God's vice-regents and elaborate what their rejectors and enemies tried doing with them; I want this book to serve for the public as a reminder of the afterworld and help orient their hearts towards [the attainment of] God's rewards."[51] This passage does not quite accurately describe the book, for a significant part of it is also devoted to the adjudication of controversial ritual practices in Islamic law, with a particular focus on the issue of the visitation of Sufi shrines (*ziyārat al-qubūr*).[52] At any rate, toward the end of the book, Maḥbūb 'Alī penned (in Arabic) a fairly lengthy eyewitness account of what he experienced and saw transpiring during the *jihād* campaign. Below I present in Maḥbūb 'Alī 's own words some key excerpts from this account. I have extracted them from different parts of his text, so as to give readers a selective but hopefully informative and representative sense of his firsthand experiences and observations. What follows is slightly lengthy for a quotation, but I would urge the reader to persevere till the end. As Maḥbūb 'Alī told the story:

> I set out from Delhi with the intention of waging *jihād* against unbelievers on the seventeenth of Sha'bān 1242 [roughly March 15, 1827], accompanied by four hundred men. After a few months, traveling via Bahāwalpūr, we reached Khunda, in the vicinity of Peshāwar. At this time, Sayyid Aḥmad, the leader of the Mujāhidīn, was in Panjtār [some 130 kilometers from Peshāwar], while "Abū 'Umar[53] Ismā'īl, the head of the military operations, was in Pakhlī [present-day Hazāra]; several scholars from North India, Sindh, and Khurāsān were also fighting alongside them. The local leaders of Peshāwar Yār Muḥammad Khān Durrānī and his brothers were vigorously opposed to Sayyid Aḥmad. To deal with their opposition, Sayyid Aḥmad wanted to subdue them through force rather than engage them in negotiations.

I feared the eruption of chaos between two warring groups of Muslims. I also saw that the decisions for the *jihād* were being based on spiritual intuition rather than consultative deliberation, as is the normative method for *jihād* [*Ra'aytu binā' al-umūr 'alā al-ilhām al-ghaybī lā 'alā al-mushāwara kamā huwa da'b al-muslimīn fi 'l-jihād shar'an*]. A person called Sayyid Shāh [had gained intimate proximity to Sayyid Aḥmad]; it was said about him that he was a spy of Durrānī's. It was on his advice that Sayyid Aḥmad had dispatched Mawlānā Ismā'īl to Phakhlī [instead of keeping him close to Peshāwar], a strategic blunder.

When I saw this state of affairs, I became certain that this man [Sayyid Aḥmad] was losing his grip over matters. So when I met him [in Panjtār] I said to him in private, "Oh Sayyid! *Jihād* is the most important normative obligation, and it can be conducted only through consultation. And warfare is based on hoodwinking [one's opponent]. But you are not hoodwinking anyone; rather, you yourself are the one being hoodwinked. Don't say things like "I am the Commander of the Faithful" or God's vice-regent on earth who demands every individual's obedience. Just stick around, don't antagonize the locals, and don't reveal your plans to them. Wait until twelve thousand more fighters from India have joined you, and only then assert your full authority." After hearing my opinion, Sayyid Aḥmad shot back: "You are ruining my project just when it has come together. You must stay quiet in my obedience like the silence of this mountain in front of me."

I pleaded with him: "Delegate to me the task of convincing the Peshāwar leaders to not prohibit people from pledging you their allegiance and to not block the path of the *mujāhidīn* travelers joining your ranks." He dismissed my suggestion, saying, "This is not possible. Yār Muḥammad does not have an ounce of faith in his heart; he will kill you instantly." I replied, "If he killed me, all the better then; that would unquestioningly legitimize your waging war [against him]." He did not say a word in response. So, I further pleaded, "Well then, send me as your delegate to that "dog of Lāhore" [Ranjīt Singh]. Send to him through me a note saying that "according to Muslim norms, we give our enemies the invitation to either submit to Islam or to accept paying a tax [*al-jizya*] [as a gesture of subservience]. So give your answer through this messenger and delegate of mine." To this suggestion, Sayyid Aḥmad replied,

> "I won't do this. He [Ranjīt Singh] will laugh at us, and for an unbeliever to laugh at Muslims is intolerable to me." When I saw this stubborn attitude, it became obvious to me that my staying longer would only increase discord and dissension, so I bid Sayyid Aḥmad [and the *jihād* campaign] farewell and made my way back to Delhi.[54]

If a faltering military campaign had frustrated Maḥbūb 'Alī in the Northwest, on returning to Delhi he had to contend with the vexation of being popularly considered as a traitor deserving of death. As he wrote in despair, "The [partisan] love of uninformed imbeciles for particular scholars and political rulers has destroyed the country" (*Fa'l-ḥaqq anna ḥubb al-jāhilīn bi'l-'ulamā' wa-l-umarā' kharraba al-diyār*).[55] Crucially, Maḥbūb 'Alī was critical not only of those who defamed him and sought his life but also of people who defamed and decried Sayyid Aḥmad, before and after the latter's death. As Maḥbūb 'Alī wrote, "Some of the ignorant people showed their malice toward the leader of the *mujāhidīn* [Sayyid Aḥmad] and labeled the *mujāhidīn* corrupt troublemakers. Such accusations are forbidden, as they fracture the community's political order" (*Ba'ḍ al-juhalā' abghaḍū sayyid al-mujāhidīn wa za'amū-hum mufsidīn wa kullu dhālika ḥarām wa takhrīb li-niẓām al-milla*).[56] He continued, rather poignantly, giving away a hint of regret and nostalgia for the promise of *jihād* that was never actualized: "In this matter, it is obligatory upon people to pray for the well-being of those who wage *jihād*, however, wherever, and whenever they were. And to pray [that God bestows his] mercy on Sayyid Aḥmad, who was the first to raise the flag of *jihād* for God and to win against the unbelievers" (*Fa'l-wājib 'alā al-nās fī hādha-l-bāb an yad'ū du'ā al-khayr li'l-mujāhidīn haythu kānū wa ayna kānū wa matā kānū wa turḥamū 'alā al-Sayyid Aḥmad raḥima-hu Allāh fa annahu awwal man rafa'a 'alam al-jihād fī sabīl Allāh wa fāza bi-muqābalat al-kuffār*).[57]

Despite Maḥbūb 'Alī 's break with Sayyid Aḥmad and all his reservations about the latter's military and political acumen, he continued to think highly of the broader aims and aspirations of the *jihād* movement. Notice especially his curious description "win against the unbelievers" for what was clearly a lost military campaign. Maḥbūb 'Alī did not imagine victory or loss in terms of the political outcome of warfare. Rather, it was the process of striving and aspiring for a just political order that mattered. Obviously, in Maḥbūb ʻAlī 's own narrative, he is the one who comes out looking the most impressive of all the characters: he is a prescient military strategist, intellectually well-versed, and politically wise. He becomes a victim of different shades and varieties of extremist ignorance. But one does not need to drop one's guard of hermeneutical suspicion to note the remarkable example of internal critique offered by his narrative. Maḥbūb ʻAlī illustrates that one could maintain an intensely critical attitude toward a person and movement while remaining deeply connected to and appreciative of their broader ethical and political aspirations.

Moreover, doctrinally, Maḥbūb ʻAlī was extremely critical of people who pinned the label of "Wahhābī" on scholars who wanted to prohibit doctrines and practices like prophetic intercession or visiting the shrines of saints. The rest of his text presents a stinging rebuttal to "anti-Wahhābī" polemics in North India. Maḥbūb ʻAlī was as perturbed by such polemicists as he was disturbed by those on the other side of the spectrum calling for his death because of his alleged "desertion" of Sayyid Aḥmad on the battlefield. As Maḥbūb ʻAlī put it, directing his anger at the first group (in Persian this time),

> These people are unhinged in their accusatory declarations of "So and so is a denier of the sainthood of saints, or has become a Wahhābī." Apparently, from their sanctimonious salvos, it seems as though they [have begun to] count themselves as among the friends of God! . . .They sit around their homes blabbering thoughtlessly. . . . They don't realize that bad-mouthing and defaming others is a horrible curse that ruins one's faith and livelihood. . . . They have become like the *Rawāfiz* [Ar. Rawāfiḍ; a derogatory term for the *Shīʻa*, meaning those who "reject"] who hasten to curse at and affix the label of "deniers of the *imāms*" on whomsoever they consider their opponents.[58]

Though Maḥbūb ʻAlī boasted of his descent from Fāṭima and Ḥusayn, his doctrinal hospitality did not support the Shīʻī other—an internal other who exhausted the limits of that hospitality. All this points to an obvious but often sidelined proposition: *ʻulamā'* actors, like all human actors, tend to be complex and complicated beings, not easily available for neat categorization and canonization.

Problematic Partisanship

It is precisely such a search for complexity that one finds sorely missing in historian Ayesha Jalal's pronouncement, in her informative but generally problematic book *Partisans of Allah*, that Sayyid Aḥmad and Shāh Muḥammad Ismā'il's *jihād* movement diluted the "high ethical values associated with jihad" by confusing "religion as faith and religion as a demarcator of difference . . . and pragmatic compromise."[59] These categories, the product of a liberal secular theology, are as vacuous as they are clumsy. According to this theology, good religion or "religion as faith" is a universal private inner experience. In contrast, bad religion is religion preoccupied with the external world of public ritual performance, the demarcation of difference, and the exercise of violence for the establishment and maintenance of that difference.

For Jalal, Sayyid Aḥmad and Ismā'īl were two in a series of ongoing Muslim actors who compromised the "high ethical values" of *jihād* as articulated in the Qur'ān by using *jihād* for material and pragmatic rather than "inner spiritual" purposes. That the material and the spiritual, the pragmatic and the utopian, can be intimately entangled is a possibility Jalal does not bother to consider. Good religion, "religion as faith," is religion peacefully contained in the vestibule of inner piety, sequestered from the turbulence of religion that is invested in external markers of ritual difference. Similarly, transposing her theory of religion to her theory of *jihād*, good *jihād* is the *jihād* of the heart or high ethical values. In contrast, bad *jihād* is the *jihād* of expansion, pragmatic calculation, demarcation of difference, and the exercise of violence. To be sure, the distinction between higher *jihād* (*jihād al-akbar*), the effort to discipline and protect the body from worldly desires and attachments, and lower *jihād* (*jihād al-aṣghar*) or warfare is found in Muslim intellectual thought.[60] But much like the relationship between Islamic law and Sufism, higher and lower *jihād* also interact as a hierarchical dyad and not in binary terms such as the binary of religion as faith versus religion as a demarcator of difference.

Jalal's diagnosis of the spiritual poverty and failure of Sayyid Aḥmad's *jihād* campaign is tethered to a broader rise-and-fall narrative of Muslim history. According to this narrative, an ethically flourishing view of *jihād* in the Qur'ān as grounded in justice became corrupted over time. This happened because Muslim scholars, the *'ulamā'*, married to the political calculations and power games of the political elite, uprooted *jihād* from its ethical moorings and turned it into a worldly instrument of political and material profit. In Jalal's own words: "The spokesmen of the Muslim community tended to sideline ethics as an intrinsic element of the Muslim faith. The implications of this became even more pronounced once Islamic law . . . detached itself from the ethical considerations spelled out in the Qur'an. The expansive Quranic conception of jihad was lost, and it assumed a reductive meaning in the Islamic legal tradition. . . . Classical juridical texts skirted around the spiritual and moral meanings of jihad to concentrate on the material facets of warfare."[61]

The bifurcation of the moral and the material, and the scripturalist valorization of the Qur'ān as the font of religious purity, only to be sullied by later generations of jurists—these moves are likely to make the most agnostic Protestant smile in delight. Jalal's reading of Muslim history is also animated by a thoroughly problematic embrace of an ethnoracial "cleavage" between what she calls "the Arabized and Persianized (ajami) forms of Islam." According to her, while "the Persian imprint was more widespread and remains to this day," "Arab influences . . . took the form of puritanical movements."[62] This is a ridiculous statement. A binary contrast between Arab puritanism and Persian inclusivism is historically and conceptually untenable.[63]

Jalal's broader conceptual framing also informs her assessment of Sayyid Aḥmad's and Ismā'īl's *jihād* movement. After a useful though somewhat laborious recapitulation of some aspects of Ghulām Rasūl Mehr's (one of Sayyid Aḥmad's hagiographers) account of the *jihād* campaign, Jalal dons the hat of a theologian and chastises Sayyid Aḥmad and Ismā'īl for having "scarred Muslim consciousness in South Asia" and for "inviting bitter controversy over religious belief (*aqida*) at the expense of faith (*iman*)."[64] She further claims that "they abandoned the spiritual element in their teaching, and strengthened their declining cause by appealing to the worst passions of the human heart,"[65] while quoting verbatim from that most sophisticated and nonpartisan of commentators, that epitome of colonial Orientalism W. W. Hunter! (d. 1900). I repeat: W. W. Hunter!

Announcing her formal entry into the polemical ring, Jalal challenges Sayyid Aḥmad's and Ismā'īl's "star studded gallery of admirers to offer a satisfactory answer to [Hunter's] stinging charges."[66] To be clear, I am not interested in defending Sayyid Aḥmad's *jihād* campaign or in passing a judgment on its ethical alignment with or departure from the "high values" of the Qur'ān. Attempting such a task would be wholly inappropriate for the academic study of religion; more crucially, I simply lack the theological credentials required for such an endeavor. My interest rather is in pointing out the conceptual and historiographic poverty of presenting particular actors as simplistic monological agents driven by political expediency, without considering in any detail or complexity their thought, texts, and intellectual careers. Such an approach does not promise a particularly nuanced account of either *jihād* or South Asian Islam. Indeed, the reader is left wondering who exactly the "Partisans of Allah" in this book refers to: the objects of the author's study or the author herself.

For a more sophisticated and helpful conceptualization of *jihād*, violence, and their intimate enmeshment with politics, one can gainfully turn to Talal Asad's insightful classic *On Suicide Bombing*. Throughout this text, Asad urges us to think critically about and bring into question the often-presumed opposition between violence and politics. This supposed opposition authorizes the fantasy of a contrast between the rationality of Western liberal politics and the irrationality of violent illiberal actors exemplified by the figure of the suicide bomber. When applied to the case of *jihād*, the liberal binary of violence/politics works to situate *jihād* as an eschatological pursuit of otherworldly bliss antipodal to politics' concern with worldly welfare and flourishing. *On Suicide Bombing* conducts a devastating indictment of such a self-congratulatory liberal narrative.[67] Most pertinent to my concerns is Asad's mobilization of an analysis by political theorist Roxanne Euben regarding the inseparability of *jihād* and politics. She writes, "Jihād is neither simply a blind and bloody minded scrabble for temporal power nor solely a door through which to pass into the hereafter. Rather, it is a form of political action in which, to use Hannah Arendt's language, the pursuit of immortality is inextricably linked to a profoundly this-worldly endeavor—the founding or recreating of a just community on earth."[68] Asad and Euben provide an immensely useful frame to think about the moral and political project at stake in Sayyid Aḥmad's and Ismā'īl's *jihād* movement. Approaching this movement solely through the prism of "puritan" Islam or through an evaluative judging of its normative underpinnings prohibits a more careful consideration of its discursive and political stakes and investments.

Postcolonial Appropriations

Returning to Ismā'īl, the *jihād* movement that ended his life, like most other aspects of his life, has become a subject of contested interpretations, fueled by ideological differences and postcolonial nationalist narratives. For some, the North Indian *jihād* movement against the Sikhs was a necessary moment of religious reform that had gone awry only because of the betrayal of the local Pashtūn tribes and their leaders who had turned against their own "liberators."[69] Further, according to this view, despite their military failure, the "martyrs of Bālākot" had paved the way for all future attempts to establish an Islamic state in South Asia. As Sayyid Abu'l A'lā al-Mawdūdī (d. 1979), the famous twentieth-century Indian-Pakistani Islamist political thinker and founder of the Jamā'at-i Islāmī, once wrote, "In the twelve-hundred-year history of Islam in South Asia, only the campaign led by Sayyid Aḥmad Barelvī and Shāh Ismā'īl Shahīd can be called *jihād* in the true sense of the word. While previous Muslim rulers in South Asia fought several wars, none of them was divinely inspired; these were mere wars, not *jihād* in God's cause. It was these two men who set aside all personal and political ambitions and waged war to enforce God's law on God's earth."[70]

When told by Ismā'īl's opponents such as the Barelvīs, however, this same event turns into a completely different narrative. According to this narrative, in their unbridled zeal for political power, Ismā'īl and his compatriots set the unfortunate precedent of causing bloodshed and chaos in a community populated by other Muslims. Further, had they genuinely desired the liberation of Muslims from non-Muslim rule, rather than traveling hundreds of miles to take on the Sikhs, they would have instead focused their energies on removing the more menacing threat of British colonialism within northern India.[71] In fact, so this story goes, the architects of this *jihād* movement were British agents charged with the task of dividing South Asian Muslims along ideological and sectarian lines. In response, Sayyid Aḥmad's and Ismāʿīl's supporters hastened to provide quotations from their discourses that cast the British in a negative light. Much of the introduction to the collection of Sayyid Aḥmad's letters and sermons is made up of moments where he either chided or expressed the desire to confront the British, whom he referred to interchangeably as "the European/Frank unbelievers" (*kuffār-i farang*) or the "Despicable Christians" (*naṣārā'ī nikohīdeh*). For instance, in a rather lengthy August 1827 letter to the *amīr* of Bukhārā, Naṣrullah Khān (d. 1860), Sayyid Aḥmad made frequent and rather unflattering mention of the British, at one point commenting, "These European unbelievers who have colonized India are extremely experienced, wily, masters of artifice, and tricksters" (*Kuffār-i farang keh bar hindustān tasalluṭ yāfteh and nihā'yat tajrabeh-kār wa hoshyār and wa ḥīla-bāz wa makār*).[72]

But both accusatory and defensive narratives of Ismāʿīl's and Sayyid Aḥmad's engagement with the British project nationalist desires and anxieties on actors who did not imagine politics through the confining prism of the modern state. So, for instance, even Sayyid Aḥmad's biting critique of the British in his letter to the *amīr* of Bukhārā was less an expression of anticolonial outrage than a warning to the *amīr* about the looming danger to the latter posed by British power. This in turn was a strategy to authorize a transregional *jihād* campaign, like the one Sayyid Aḥmad saw himself leading, the first stage of which involved battling the Sikhs. The binary politics of "pro-British" or "anticolonial" simply does not apply here. At any rate, Ismāʿīl's proponents and opponents continue to mobilize his memory for ideological projects, such as anticolonial nationalist politics, that he would not have recognized. His memory remains suspended between competing narrative paradigms.

"Shāh Muḥammad Ismāʿīl," as this name is inserted into different narrative constructs over time, becomes marked by such descriptors as "an inspiration for Deobandī thought," "the first genuine martyr in South Asian Islam" (as Mawdūdī would have it), "the first "Indian Wahhābī," and so forth. While some of these descriptors are laudatory and others condemnatory, what they have in common is the narrative desire to separate from the turbulence of history a fixed understanding of Ismāʿīl's legacy. In the discussion that follows, I am not interested in finding a historicist resolution to that legacy or in providing yet another narrative of how it should be understood. Indeed, given the density of polemical representations attached to the figure of Ismā'īl, it is impossible to historically resolve the controversy he continues to inspire. Instead, it will be more fruitful to examine his discourses in a way that clarifies his own social imaginary and also destabilizes all varieties of absolute claims on his memory. A critical discursive site that demands such an approach is his views on the theme of divine sovereignty, to which I next turn.

chapter three

Reenergizing Sovereignty

Arguably the most defining feature of Shāh Muḥammad Ismā'īl's intellectual career was his desire to reenergize the primacy of divine sovereignty in the religious imagination of Indian Muslims. His discourse on sovereignty was wrapped in a narrative of catastrophic moral chaos. To Ismā'īl, it was as if Indian Muslims had almost forgotten God's sovereign power. His diagnosis was premised on the observation that prophets, saints, and other nondivine entities had effectively colonized the religious lives of the masses: "These people think that no matter what we do in this world, some powerful saint or prophet will always intercede on our behalf and rescue us from God's wrath. This kind of an attitude is completely foolish and wrong. There is no source of mercy and redemption in the afterworld except the providential authority of God. These masses *forget God* [emphasis mine] in their unfettered reliance on saints, martyrs, and legends. They are thoroughly misguided."[1]

Although this sentiment is found in several of Ismā'īl's works, it was most forcefully articulated in one of his shortest yet most controversial books, *Fortifying Faith* (*Taqwīyat al-Īmān*) composed in Urdu and published in 1825, on the eve of the *jihād* campaign against the Sikhs.[2] This was the same year as the establishment of the American Tract Society, one of several print-centered organizations that launched the careers of prominent American evangelicals,[3] many of whom Ismā'īl might have enjoyed conversing with on common topics of interest. *Taqwīyat al-Īmān* continues to spark heated debates and polemics even today. In the almost two hundred years since its original publication, according to one count, more than 250 refutations of this book have been written![4] *Taqwīyat al-Īmān* was one of the first Urdu publications composed in the genre of a primer intended for a mass public audience rather than a specialist class of expert scholars. It was published during a moment in Indian Muslim history when Urdu was gradually yet decisively replacing Persian as the lingua franca of the religious and the literary elite.

The organizational structure of *Taqwīyat al-Īmān* comports with its intended popular audience. All sections of the book begin with a Qur'ānic verse or a prophetic report in Arabic, followed by a translation in Urdu and Ismā'īl's commentary on the selected verse/report. Among his signature practices in this text that reinforced its efforts at accessibility was his constant referral to God with the casual yet personalizing appellation of "Mr. Allah" (*Allāh ṣāḥib*). And a colloquial category he repeatedly invoked to express his desired ideal of Islam was "*ṭhait Islām*" or the purest most organic Islam, a term most often employed to express the purity of a person's ethnic or regional identity, as in *ṭhait Panjābī*. In his introduction to *Taqwīyat al-Īmān*, Ismā'īl announced that he deliberately wrote this book in vernacular Urdu so that common people would be able to comprehend its content with ease. Moreover, he urged his readers to reject the notion that they were in any need of specialist scholars for accessing religious sources of knowledge such as the Qur'ān and the Ḥadīth. As Ismā'īl put it, "There is a pervasive myth among the masses that understanding the Qur'ān and the Ḥadīth is difficult and that such a task requires a great deal of knowledge. They wonder how ignorant folk like them could understand these specialized sources of knowledge and act according to them. Such an attitude is completely unfounded because God declared in the Qur'ān, "We have bestowed upon you clear messages; no one denies their truth except the iniquitous."[5] In his push for vernacular popularity, Ismā'īl was riding the wave of a recent trend to make religious thought accessible to a broader public, seen most clearly in his uncle Shāh 'Abdul Qādir's idiomatic translation of the Qur'ān into Urdu called *The Accessible Qur'ān* (*Mūzīḥ al-Qur'ān*), written circa 1790 and first printed in 1829.[6] Through this translation, 'Abdul Qādir continued the vernacular translation movement of his own father, Shāh Walī Ullah, who had initially translated the Qur'ān into Persian in the face of much resistance. Similarly, *Taqwīyat al-Īmān* was not the only reformist text intended for a mass audience circulating during the early to mid-nineteenth century. Another prominent example of such a text, strikingly similar to *Taqwīyat al-Īmān* in its style, rhetoric, and indeed message, was a tract by a lesser-known contemporary of Ismā'īl, Khurram 'Alī (d. 1855), titled *Advice for Muslims* (*Naṣīḥat al-Muslimīn*) and published circa 1824.[7]

In *Taqwīyat al-Īmān*, Ismā'īl authorized his argument for restoring divine sovereignty by telling a particular story of moral fallen-ness in the present he inhabited, a present in which according to him several competitors to the sovereign authority of the divine were flourishing in the public sphere. According to this story, the vast majority of Indian Muslims, among both the masses and the elite, were drowning in the sea of polytheism and unbelief.

As he wrote, combining alarm with derision:

> These masses have turned saints, prophets, pious figures, angels, and fairies into their Gods. They supplicate before these entities for their needs, pray to them, offer food in their name, and name their own children after them. So today we find someone with the name 'Abdul Nabī (the Prophet's slave), someone else called 'Alī Bakhsh ('Alī's gift), or Ḥusayn Bakhsh (Ḥusayn's gift), Ghulām Muḥyīuddīn (the slave of the resuscitator of religion [referring to the famous thirteenth-century Andalusian Sufi Muḥyī al-Dīn Ibn al-'Arabī (d. 1240)]), and Ghulām Mu'īnuddīn (servant of the one who orders religion) [referring to the medieval South Asian Chishtī Sufi master Mu'īnuddīn Chishtī (d. 1236)].[8]

It was not as if people no longer believed in the absolute sovereignty of God or were declared atheists, Ismā'īl clarified. Rather, God's sovereignty was undermined by the entrenchment of certain attitudes, practices, and conventions in the everyday lives of the masses that were based solely on habit rather than any canonical authority. Ismā'īl's litany of such practices and conventions was overwhelming in number and variety. They ranged from matters of theology to everyday practice. While all or even most cannot be listed here, some examples included believing that any of the prophets or saints possessed knowledge of the unknown (*'ilm al-ghayb*), seeking the help of a saint to conceive a child, specifying certain animals as sacred or taboo without any normative justification, organizing and taking part in the birth anniversaries of the Prophet and saints while holding the conviction that they personally appeared at such gatherings [to bestow their blessings], seeking the intercession of saints in times of need and distress, engaging in leisurely activities like playing chess and attending poetry-reading assemblies with a discipline and regularity that simulated obligatory acts of religion such as praying and fasting, and holding the belief that a dead saint could harm or benefit living people.

If Grandfather Met Grandson: Walī Ullah, Ismā'īl, and Shifting Logics of Reform

The reformist mission Ismā'īl inaugurated was not entirely new, unprecedented, or unique to the nineteenth century. Even in the eighteenth century or before, Muslim scholarly protests against popular customs and conventions were plentiful. For instance, in his parting will, Ismā'īl's grandfather Shāh Walī Ullah sternly repudiated "putrid customs" like the taboo against widow marriage, which he attributed to Hindu influence and was eager for Muslims to stay clear of. He also warned Indian Muslims against their tendency to expend lavishly on occasions of festivity and sorrow. "Profligate spending," he had declared, "is among our horrible habits" (*Az 'ādāt-i shanī'a-yi mā mardum isrāf ast*).[9]

For another example, we can turn to Qāzī Sanā'ullah Pānīpatī (d. 1810), the late eighteenth-century Naqshbandī Sufi and Ḥanafī jurist/judge and chief disciple of Walī Ullah's famous contemporary Mirẓā Maẓhar Jān-i Jānān (d. 1781).[10] In his collection of juridical opinions (in Persian) titled *Inescapable Necessities* (*Mā Lā Budda Min-Hu*), Pānīpatī had expressly deemed forbidden widespread conventions and practices such as "chess, playing cards, especially when they involved placing bets, collecting pigeons, pigeon fighting, cock fighting, et cetera."[11] Further, in his will, written at the age of eighty when he was about to die, Pānīpatī gave elaborate instructions on the ritual choreography that must follow his death. Among these was the explicit instruction to his caretakers: "After I die, don't at all undertake worldly rituals like commemorating the dead and transmitting blessings to the deceased's soul by distributing food among community members on the tenth, twentieth, and fortieth day of death, or on the six-month and annual death anniversary [*ba'd-i murdan-i man rusūm-i dunyawī misl-i daham wa bīstam wa chehlam wa shishmāhī wa bar-sīnī hīch nah kunand*]. . . . The Prophet disallowed mourning for more than three days and categorically forbade the loud crying and wailing of women [on the occasion of death]."[12]

Now, these were the very sorts of issues that occupied the reformist energies of early and late nineteenth-century Indian Muslim scholars like Ismā'īl and later Ashraf 'Alī Thānvī, as we will see in the next chapters. Thus clearly there exist visible continuities between eighteenth- and nineteenth-century South Asian Islam. The vigorous critique of popular customs and conventions and an eager interest in the norms that should govern the nexus between divine sovereignty and everyday practice were not inventions of the modern colonial moment. However, these continuities notwithstanding, the intellectual career of a scholar like Ismā'īl also marks some major shifts. I will highlight three.

The first relates to the intensification of a tendency to make everyday life and practices the decisive arena and touchstone of religious authenticity. The breadth of everyday practices that came into the orbit of reform with a text like Ismā'īl's *Taqwīyat al-Īmān* was unprecedented. In earlier history, one would be hard pressed to find the kind of elaborate discussions of practices like wedding and engagement ceremonies, cockfighting contests, and kite flying, that one does in nineteenth-century reformist texts. Second, with the proliferation of technologies like print, the postal system, and railways, not only did reformist and counter-reformist voices reach much wider audiences, but the idea of a marked and defined public, available for assent and persuasion to competing visions of reform and normativity, also emerged.[13] Third, oral and written polemics, both live and recorded, reached an unprecedented volume, frequency, and intensity in the nineteenth century.

One also finds a subtle but crucial attitudinal shift in reformist approaches from the eighteenth to the nineteenth century. To capture this shift, one can gainfully turn to a comparison and contrast between the grandfather and grandson Shāh Walī Ullah and Shāh Muḥammad Ismā'īl regarding their respective methods of reform. Despite noticeable overlap in their thought (especially in their mystically oriented writings, such as Walī Ullah's *Lama'āt* and *Saṭa'āt* and Ismā'īl's *'Abaqāt*), Walī Ullah's temperament was markedly different from that of his more aggressive and maximalist grandson Ismā'īl. To give readers a sense of this contrast,

I want to rehearse a narrative from Walī Ullah's life that reaches us via 'Ubaydullah Sindhī (d. 1944), a twentieth-century Deoband-affiliated Muslim scholar/revolutionary activist who was one of the foremost commentators on Walī Ullah's thought. In his wide-ranging text on Walī Ullah's political theology and legacy *Shāh Walī Ullah and His Political Movement* (*Shāh Walī Ullah awr un kī Siyāsī Taḥrīk*), Sindhī narrates the following incident.

The renowned scholar Mawlānā Muḥammad Fākhir Allāhabādī (d. 1760) once came to Delhi to visit Walī Ullah.[14] While offering prayers at a local mosque, Allāhabādī (a nonconformist scholar) engaged in *raf' al-yadayn*, or raising both hands during prayers—a subject of immense controversy dividing South Asian Hanafīs from the nonconformists (*Ghayr Muqallidūn*).[15] On noticing Allāhabādī's aberrant ritual conduct, the congregation of Hanafīs present at the mosque turned against him, causing a major uproar. The mob almost resorted to violence and drew back only on discovering that Allāhabādī was Walī Ullah's guest from out of town. They took Allāhabādī to Walī Ullah's house so that the latter might adjudicate on the matter. When they asked Walī Ullah for his judgment, he tried to calm them, saying, "Relax! There exist Ḥadīth that legitimate the practice of *raf' al-yadayn*. I too at times perform it." On hearing this, the crowd dispersed. After they had left, Allāhabādī looked puzzled and said to Walī Ullah, "I did not know you performed *raf' al-yadayn*." Walī Ullah replied jokingly, "I actually don't, but had I not said so, you would have been killed today!" He added, "A wise one [*ḥakim*] is not he who without rhyme or reason turns the masses against himself."[16]

For Walī Ullah, then, much as for the Sufi master Ḥājī Imdādullah, whom we will learn more about in chapter 12, the maintenance of social order took precedence over judging the niceties of everyday ritual life. The chaos of an uprising was best avoided. For his grandson Ismā'īl, in contrast, it was through the meticulous ordering of everyday life that social order was realized. Until then, the world languished in a state of moral chaos, crying out for an aggressive treatment plan devised and implemented by the religious reformer. This attitudinal difference, I would submit, was not just a reflection of the contrast of temperament between a grandfather and his grandson. It was rather a product of broader shifts and transformations inaugurating the passage of South Asian Islam into the turbulently competitive nineteenth century. I will return to this theme of continuities and changes marking South Asian Islam's transition from the precolonial to the colonial era in the conclusion of Part I, and then again at the beginning of chapter 6. But first, let me return to Shāh Muḥammad Ismā'īl's political theology and reform project.

Protecting the Divine Sovereign: The Threat of Faux Religion

Ismā'īl's social imaginary was anchored in the assumption of a constant rivalry between human and divine norms. In his view, human habits and conventions had assumed the form of a counter-religion in the public sphere, what one might call a faux religion that simulated a divinely ordained normative order. As I will discuss in much greater detail in Part II of this book, this idea of simulating divinely sanctioned norms was at the heart of how Ismā'īl and then later the Deoband pioneers conceived the idea of heretical innovation (*bid'a*). Ismā'īl defined a heretical innovation as any habit or convention that despite not being divinely authorized as religion was adhered to with an intensity and passion that simulated religious practices.

This extension of the nonreligious into the domain of religion was heretical because it disturbed God's sovereignty as the exclusive decider of what did and did not count as religion. Therefore, law and theology, belief and practice, were inseparable in Ismā'īl's thought. As he put it, "Heresy in its essence hinges on attitudes of belief [*'aqīda*]: believing that a practice is beneficial when God has not called it beneficial and believing that a practice is harmful when God has not deemed it harmful. That is the definition of a pure heresy [*bid'a ḥaqīqīya*]."[17]

Therefore, for Ismā'īl, belief was not an internalized matter of rigid convictions but a dynamic object of knowledge. Belief and knowledge were inseparably intertwined; to know an act as harmful was to believe it to be so. "You believe what you know" was the maxim that guided Ismā'īl's thinking. Moreover, heresy represented the condition in which a divinely ordained program of correspondence between knowledge and belief was interrupted by the human act of choosing how that correspondence unfolded. Heresy, therefore, signified the act of choosing (*haeresis*):

choosing on the basis of one's own will an order of normativity that was not divinely sanctioned and, as a result, opposing the sovereignty of the divine as the sole author of law and its limits. To align this matrix of knowledge, belief, and practice to a divinely sanctioned template of normativity, it was vital, Ismā'īl argued, to cultivate a subject and in turn a public who were decisively intolerant toward any patterns of thought and activity that might cast any doubt on the absoluteness of God's sovereignty.[18]

The Locations of Sovereignty

But what were those signs of subordination that God had specified as exclusive to himself? What were those privileged sites of thought and practice through which humans affirmed and validated divine sovereignty and that were hence unavailable for any nondivine entity? In responding to this central question, Ismā'īl advanced four types of transgression, each corresponding to particular privileges reserved exclusively for the divine and therefore unavailable to any other entity. These types of transgression were transgression in knowledge (*ishrāk fi'l 'ilm*), transgression in the capacity to enact miraculous exceptions (*ishrāk fi'l taṣarruf*), transgression in devotional practices (*ishrāk fi'l 'ibādāt*), and transgression in everyday habits and practices (*ishrāk fi'l 'ādāt*). Let me briefly explain each of these categories as Ismā'īl understood them. Transgression in knowledge included all those practices and attitudes that undermined God's omniscience: for example, to constantly chant a saint's name, to call out his name with the belief that he was listening, or to think that all human conditions such as illness, destitution, life, and death were known to certain figures gifted with miraculous capacities. In short, transgressions in knowledge associated kinds of knowledge exclusive to the divine with nondivine entities.[19]

Similarly, transgression in the capacity to enact exceptions referred to such capacities as giving and taking life at will, fulfilling supplications, thwarting evil, curing illnesses, and afflicting with illness. These were all privileged capacities that established divine sovereignty and were therefore unavailable to any other entity. Transgression in devotional practices centered on the contexts in which one performed bodily gestures, movements, and activities that God had specified as signs of devotion to him: for example, prostrating, kneeling, standing with tied hands, giving charity in God's name, fasting, traveling long distances for the annual pilgrimage to Mecca, going on pilgrimage in a physical state that clearly distinguished the pilgrim from all other people, refraining from useless chatter and hunting around the site of pilgrimage, circumambulating the Ka'ba, covering it with a blanket, kissing the black stone, and refraining from cutting trees, plucking grass, and grazing animals around the Ka'ba. These were all practices that had been designated as indicators of God's sovereignty.

Performing such acts and gestures specific to the performance of obligatory devotional practices in other nonobligatory moments of devotion, such as when visiting shrines of venerated saints, represented heresy. In other words, transgression in devotional practices referred to the act of performing in other contexts actions that in Ismā'īl's view were specific to the affirmation of divine sovereignty. As he put it: "God has specified all these activities for his own devotion. Now if someone were to prostrate or kneel before the tomb of a saint or prophet, fast in his name, travel long distances to venerate him, hoist a flag in his name, light candles at that venue, venerate the forest and plantations in the neighboring areas, or cover the walls of the tomb with blankets, all of these activities would be transgressions in devotion, meaning that they would be venerating a nondivine entity as if it were divine [*ghayr Allāh kī ta'ẓīm Allāh kī sī karnā*]."[20]

Transgression in everyday habits and practices was the most expansive of the four categories. It was also the category that most clearly connected Ismā'īl's theology to his larger critique of aristocratic modes of organizing life. Some of the practices in this category included the excessive veneration of other people in everyday discourse, referring to other people with such reverential epithets as "the highest excellency" (*janāb-i a'lā*) or "his majesty" (*qibla*), taking pride in one's ancestral lineage (*iftikhār bi'l ansāb*) by boasting one's affiliation with noble lineages such as Pathān, Rājpūt, and Mughal, and kissing the hands of pious figures or elders as a show of reverence. Transgression in everyday habits and practices, in short, involved allowing a nondivine entity the same intensity of veneration in everyday life that was exclusively reserved for God. Each of these forms of transgression, Ismā'īl claimed, was thriving among Indian Muslims.

Tradition as the Repetition of Origin

According to Ismāʿīl's reformist narrative, the drama of early Islam pitting Prophet Muḥammad and his fledgling community against hostile pagans, Jews, and Christians in seventh-century Arabia was being repeated in his own nineteenth-century Indian present. While the actors had changed, the narrative plot was the same. The path of normativity, defined by submission to an absolutely sovereign divine, was opposed by heretics of various stripes who thoughtlessly followed the practices of their ancestors. Was this not the condition of ignorance that had given rise to Islam and the Prophet's mission? Moreover, Ismāʿīl argued, much like Islam's antagonists during the Prophet's career, Muslims in nineteenth-century India were also completely unaware of the rut of heresy in which they found themselves. While most people claimed to be believers, they were in fact stuck in the quagmire of unbelief. On the pretext of venerating saints and prophets, such people disseminated heresy, without even being cognizant of their own sins. Again, Ismāʿīl's vivid description of this condition of ignorance gives a view into the way he imagined the sort of dissatisfaction he saw himself overcoming. While rehearsing the kinds of objection most often thrown at him, he lashed out:

> When someone confronts these people, and warns them against mixing the opposite paths of belief and unbelief, they confidently reply, "You cannot charge us with unbelief because all we are doing is showing our love for prophets and saints. Moreover, you could accuse us of polytheism only if we considered these entities as equal to God. But we regard them as God's creations that are divinely bestowed with certain miraculous capacities. They are God's beloveds. To call them for help is to call God. To find them is to find God. The closer we get to them, the greater our proximity to God."[21]

Ismāʿīl's rebuttal to this potential line of argument against his project provides us with instructive clues about the way he imagined tradition and its relationship to time. He claimed that such justifications were identical to those advanced by polytheists and unbelievers during the early years of Islam. Even during Muḥammad's prophetic career, he reminded his readers, unbelievers regarded their idols not as equal to God but only as his creation. Their sin had never been outright unbelief, for they often recognized that these entities did not possess divine capacities. But by engaging in practices like making vows in the name of idols and petitioning them for forgiveness they challenged divine sovereignty. Why? Because these were practices that God had designated as markers of his own sovereignty, and engaging in them for anyone else questioned that sovereignty. For this reason, Ismā'īl claimed, God had chastised Jews and Christians for venerating their saints and prophets, even though they did not worship idols. This was best reflected in the following Qur'ānic verse: "They take their priests and their anchorites to be their lords in derogation of Allāh, and [they take as their Lord] Christ the son of Mary; yet they were commanded to worship but One Allāh. There is no god but him. Praise and glory to him: [far is he] from having the partners they associate [with him]."[22]

Thus, Ismā'īl extended his analogy, there was little to separate Indian Muslim masses of his own era who undermined divine sovereignty by venerating saints and prophets from the unbelievers during Islam's formative years. Both were guilty of a common sin: associating privileged sites of divine sovereignty with nondivine entities. Similarly, Ismā'il further argued, the tendency among Indian Muslims to undermine the Prophet's humanity by excessively venerating him was identical to the way Christians had divinized Jesus. According to Ismā'īl, the Prophet had himself warned his community against imitating Christians in this regard when he said: "Don't excessively exalt me the way the Christians exalted Jesus son of Mary. I am but God's slave. So call me God's slave and God's messenger."[23]

On another occasion, the Prophet cautioned his followers, "Don't elevate me above the status [of a human] that God has assigned to me. I am Muḥammad, son of 'Abdullah, and God's slave and his messenger."[24] For Ismā'īl, these prophetic admonitions were meant to establish a non-negotiable boundary between divine reality (*ḥaqīqat-i ulūhīya*) and Muhammadan reality (*ḥaqīqat-i muḥammadīya*), a boundary that Indian Muslims routinely transgressed in the guise of showing their love for the Prophet. This excess replicated the way Christians ascribed divine qualities to Jesus or Meccan pagans turned their idols into divine figures. In other words, in Ismāʿīl's view, despite the temporal distance between these two moments, Islam in early nineteenth-century India and the Prophet's career in seventh-century Arabia shared a common moral and aesthetic space. This space was defined by a preponderant and imminent threat to the exceptionality of divine sovereignty. Moreover, after the Prophet, it was the task of prophetic reformers like Ismāʿīl to battle this threat by expending their evangelical energies to quash real or potential competitors to the divine sovereign. While the battlefield had changed, the battle to be fought was essentially the same.

Ismāʿīl's move of narratively connecting prophetic time to his own moment of reform is quite revealing of how he approached the interplay of tradition and time. For Ismāʿīl, as shown in his comparison between Indian Muslim masses with Jews and Christians in early Islam, the narrative drama of prophetic time was being reenacted in colonial India. Notice that crucial to such a conception of tradition—as the repetition of an origin—is the role of translation.[25] For Ismāʿīl, prophetic time and his present were perfectly translatable. More, by arguing for the perfect translatability of these two temporal moments, he attempted to cast the story of the antagonism between tradition and heresy as the ongoing repetition of an origin. In Ismāʿīl's imaginary, reforming the present rested on the promise of inheriting a tradition that seamlessly traveled through time. The past was always perfectly translatable as an object of inheritance. Moreover, the figure of an immutable divine sovereign effectively erased the distinction between past and present. The absolute stability of divine transcendence defeated the dynamicity of time. Rather than an evolving project of contested meanings, tradition was the repetition of an eternal origin. That origin was indistinguishable from the totalizing figure of a sovereign divine.

Ismāʿīl dismissed the idea of modifying the limits of tradition according to temporal changes and accompanying shifts in the lived experiences and aesthetic sensibilities of subjects. Such modifications were not required, since prophetic time and the present were perfectly translatable. Ismāʿīl most strikingly affirmed this sentiment of perfect translatability in a telling moment when he sought to establish the equivalence between the Prophet's era and his own time. He wrote, "Babies were born then too, women used to menstruate, children were circumcised, people used to get married, suffer from illnesses and die, graves used to be constructed—so one must always ask, what did the Prophet do in these situations, and how were these practices of everyday life undertaken by his succeeding Companions?"[26] As this statement amply shows, for Ismā'īl, tradition represented an oracle from the past that was always readily available for replication in the present. But this desire for replication was entangled in the aporetic logic of seeking the repetition of an originary prophetic moment when that moment was no longer available for repetition. Ismā'īl's project of reform (like many other such projects?) could not resolve this irresolvable contradiction.

Can God Create a Million New Muḥammads?

The most controversial aspect of Ismā'īl's theology was the absolute terms in which he argued for the radical alterity of divine sovereignty. In relation to the sovereign divine, he claimed, all other entities, whether prophets, jinns, Satan, spirits, fairies, or saints, were equally radically inferior. It was not only his argument but the way he presented his argument that generated much fury and controversy. As he grandly proclaimed: "Even if all human beings and jinns from the time of Adam to the end of time became like archangel Gabriel and Muḥammad, the splendor of his kingdom would not increase, and if they all became like Satan and the anti-Christ, that splendor would not diminish. In all conditions, he is the most sovereign of all sovereigns and the king of all kings; no one can harm or benefit him."[27] And in an even more dramatic affirmation of the divine capacity to enact the exception, in what has since proven to be the most controversial moment in this text, Ismā'īl also declared, "God is so powerful that in one moment, just by uttering the command 'Be,' he can create millions of new prophets, saints, jinns, angels, Gabriels, and Muḥammads."[28]

In his stinging rebuttal of *Taqwīyat Īmān*, Fazl-i Ḥaqq Khayrābādī, Ismā'īl's archnemesis, took grave exception to this claim by pointing out that accepting the possibility of a second Muḥammad equates to accepting that God can lie and renege his promise of Muḥammad's finality. Thus, Khayrābādī continued, one would have to consider it possible for

God to be defective, as lying is a defect. In replying to this charge in a work called *Yak Roza* (in Persian), Ismāʿīl set the stage for yet another controversy that consumed South Asian Muslim scholars and nonscholars for decades to follow: what came to be known as *imkān-i kizb* or God's capacity to lie. Ismāʿīl is said to have written *Yak Roza* (meaning "one day") after he was interrupted on his way to the Jāmiʿ mosque to say his prayers, as someone shared with him a copy of Khayrābādī's refutation.

After offering his prayers, Ismāʿīl sat in the mosque courtyard and finished this text on that same day, hence its name "One Day." In this text, rather than shying away from Khayrābādī's suggestion, Ismāʿīl confidently contended that yes indeed, God possessed the capacity to lie or contravene his own promises. So, for instance, while God had promised to send Pharaoh, Abū Lahab, and Hāmān to hell, he might well undo that promise by sending them to heaven. Ismāʿīl argued that disallowing God the capacity to lie would mean that God could not do something that humans easily could, lie, thus necessitating human capacity to exceed divine capacity (*lāzim āyad keh qudrat-i insānī azyad az qudrat-i rabbānī bāshad*). More specifically, Ismāʿīl framed his argument by drawing on the distinction between potentiality (*imkān*) and actuality (*wuqūʿ*). He argued that although God had the capacity to create a million new Muḥammads or to lie/contravene his own promise, he would never actually do so.[29] Let me elaborate. His precise argument was that the actual occurrence of something contravening a statement was what necessitated the falsity of that statement, not the possibility or potentiality of such an occurrence (*Wuqūʿ-i chīz-i keh mukhālif-i chīz-i bāshad mustalzim-i kizb-i ān chīz ast, na imkān-i wuqūʿ-i ān*).[30]

We can usefully amplify and flesh out Ismāʿīl's argument here by noting its resemblance with what the theorist Giorgio Agamben has described as the distinction between potentiality and actuality in Aristotle's thought. In Aristotle's conceptualization, Agamben argued, "potentiality precedes actuality and conditions it, but also seems to remain essentially subordinate to it. . . . Aristotle always takes great care to affirm the autonomous existence of potentiality—the fact that the kithara player keeps his potential (*potenza*) to play even when he does not play and the architect keeps his potential to build even when he does not build."[31] Agamben drew from Aristotle the critical insight that for potentiality to have its own autonomous existence it must be able not to pass over into actuality. As Agamben put it, "If potentiality is to have its own consistency and not always disappear immediately into actuality, it is necessary that potentiality be able not to pass over into actuality, that potentiality constitutively be the potentiality not to (do or be), or, as Aristotle says, that potentiality be also im-potentiality (*adynamia*)."[32]

The crux of Agamben's argument is that the sovereign is precisely that zone of indistinction where pure potentiality and actuality are indistinguishable. Now similarly, Ismā'īl's propositions that "God may well create a million new Muḥammads" or "contravene his own promise" are situated precisely in this zone of indistinction where the divine potentiality to enact the exception to the rule never passes over into actuality. It instead maintains itself in suspension, in the relation of a "sovereign ban" on itself such that the potentiality to do something is also the potentiality not to do something.

Ismā'īl's argument that God can contravene his promise or create a million new Muḥammads is arguably the thorniest and most controversial aspect of his thought and legacy. Thus let me briefly touch on some key forms of evidence for this argument that he advanced in *Yak Roza*, as a way to capture the highlights of this hugely important but rarely studied text. This will also better prepare readers for Fazl-i Ḥaqq Khayrābādī's rebuttal of his argument, which I will get to in subsequent chapters. From the Qur'ān, Ismā'īl primarily (though not exclusively) proffered eschatologically oriented verses that establish God's capacity to bring to life human and nonhuman entities on Judgment Day. What purpose would such verses serve him? Let us find out by briefly considering his reading of a couple such verses. For instance, Ismā'īl cited verses 81 and 82 of chapter 36, or Sūrah Yā Sīn: "Does not the One [God] who created the heavens and earth possess the capacity to create the likes of them? Of course he does! He is the all-knowing Creator. His command is such that when he wants something, he just says, 'Be!' and it becomes."[33]

Since this verse described the Day of Judgment, Ismā'īl argued, the phrase "the likes of them" applied to all those entities, including all humans, who would then be brought back to life (*Pas zamīr-i muzakkar rāji' ast bi-sū'ay jamī' banī Ādam zīra keh āya-yi karīma-i mazkūra dar maqām-i bayān-i mu'ād wāqi' gardīda, pas har-keh dar mu'ād zinda khwāhad shud ān dākhil ast dar āyat-i karīma*).[34] God possessed the capacity to create the likes of everyone who would be resurrected on Judgment Day; this verse demanded the necessity of this correlation (*Har farday az afrād-i insānī dar mu'ād zinda shudanī ast pas misl-i ū bi-muqtazā'ay karīma-i mazkūra dākhil-i taḥt-i qudrat-i ilāhīya bāshad*).[35] Now, it was among the necessities of religion to have faith in the tenet that the Prophet was a human being who would come alive on Judgment Day (*Nabī dar ma'ād zinda khwāhad shud*).[36] Therefore, Ismā'īl continued, connecting the dots, God must according to this verse possess the capacity of creating another Muḥammad (*Pas wujūd-i misl-i nabī dākhil bāshad taḥt-i qudrat-i ilāhīya bi-muqtazā'ay karīma-i mazkūra*).[37] Why? Because God possessed the capacity to create the likes of whoever would come to life on Judgment Day. "And that was my point [in *Taqvīyat al-Īmān*]," Ismā'īl concluded in triumph.

Similarly, he put forward another curious Qur'ānic verse where again the iconic phrase "Be! And he became" appeared: verse 59 of chapter 3 in the Qur'ān, Sūrah Āl-i 'Imrān: "To God, Jesus is like Adam. He created Jesus from dust, then said to him: 'Be!' And he became."[38] The import of this verse is that Jesus, like Adam, was born without a father through God's sovereign command, "Be!" For Ismā'īl, the similitude between Jesus's and Adam's creation from God's perspective showed that God's capacity to bring an entity into existence in itself indicated his capacity to produce a second such entity. This was a point at the heart of Ismā'īl's argument in *Yak Roza*: "Prophet Muḥammad's very existence represents a proof for the possibility of the existence of Muḥammad's like" (*Wujūd-i nabī khud dalīl bāshad bar imkān-i wujūd-i misl-i īshān naẓar bi qudrat-i ilāhīya*).[39] "The sequence of this argument goes like this," Ismā'īl clarified: "In every instance that the Prophet's existence is under God's capacity, the existence of another Muḥammad must also be inclusive in that capacity."[40] Shifting from Persian to Arabic, he emphasized that this was so because "according to [the meaning of] the Qur'an's uttered speech, on the matter of being subservient to a form of power or of not being so, two like entities carry the same rule or principle" (*Li-anna ḥukm al-mathalayn wāḥid fi'l-dukhūl taḥt al-qudra wa 'admihi bi-manṭūq al-Qur'ān*).[41]

Other than his presentation of specific Qur'ānic verses, the central argument that sustained Ismā'īl's line of defense in *Yak Roza* was that

God's contravening his promise or creating a second Muḥammad was not essentially impossible (*mumtanaʿ bi'l dhāt*) but only indirectly impossible (*mumtanaʿ bi'l ghayr*). These two categories, *mumtanaʿ bi'l dhāt* and *mumtanaʿ bi'l ghayr*, were at the heart of the debate about God's capacity to contravene a promise or create another Muḥammad. *Mumtanaʿ bi'l dhāt* referred to a logical impossibility, something that was impossible in essence or substance. On the other hand, *mumtanaʿ bi'l ghayr* referred to an impossibility that was impossible not in essence but by virtue of something else—in other words, indirectly impossible. Now remember, Ismāʿīl was in complete agreement with his opponents like Khayrābādī that there had never been, was never, and never would be another Muḥammad. The creation of another Muḥammad was impossible. There was no debate about that.

The crux of the disagreement, then, was the nature of this impossibility. For Ismāʿīl, to repeat, God's lying or producing Muḥammad's like was not essentially impossible but only indirectly impossible. God could do these things if he wanted; however, he did not and would not, for the nonessential (in the literal sense of that term) reason that these acts did not fit his theological program. In contrast, for someone like Fazl-i Ḥaqq Khayrābādī, as we will soon see, these were essentially impossible acts. To conclude the discussion on Ismāʿīl's position with a bit more specificity, the central dictum driving his argument was that "every indirect impossibility is essentially possible and every essential possibility is under God's sovereign power" (*Har mumtanaʿ bi'l ghayr mumkin bi'l dhāt wa har mumkin bi'l dhāt dākhil-i taḥt-i qudrat-i ilāhīya*).[42]

On the basis of this principle, he launched the case that since the absence and impossibility of Muḥammad's replica were not essential but indirect, the presence of such a replica was essentially possible. And since God could obviously enact what was essentially possible, it was proved that God possessed the capacity to produce another Muḥammad, or, for that matter, to renege his own promise. That was all he had tried to say in *Taqwīyat al-Īmān*, Ismāʿīl pleaded, like an author battling to control the reception history of his own text. But these explanations, as we will soon see, hardly satisfied his antagonists and only made them more scornful of what they saw as the intellectually degenerate provocations of a lightweight vanity scholar. Soon after writing *Yak Roza*, Ismāʿīl set out for that fateful *jihād* against the Sikhs. However, he left behind him plenty of theological ammunition and land mines for future generations of South Asian Muslim scholars and commoners to employ, contend, and negotiate. If we are to believe that *Yak Roza* was indeed written in only one day, then few texts can boast such a staggering disproportionality between the time taken to compose them and the durability of their many futures and afterlives. Before I turn to some other critical aspects of Ismāʿīl's thought and political theology, allow me a momentary and hopefully enjoyable detour from India.

Kindred Spirits

In his zeal for restoring the primacy of divine sovereignty, Shāh Muḥammad Ismāʿīl would have found much in common with the thought of the eleventh-century Italian Christian reformer Peter Damiani (d. 1072). Much like Ismāʿīl, Damiani was a vigorous polemicist who was deeply invested in the question of divine sovereignty, as the title of his most influential work *De divina omnipotentia* (The divine omnipotence) clearly suggests.[43] In this text, Damiani attacked a range of Christian thinkers before him, most notably the prominent Thomistic scholar St. Jerome (d. 420), who had argued for the boundedness (*protestas ordinata*) of divine power in a way that precluded God from undoing what he had already done. For instance, taking the example of virginity, he had claimed that "although God can do all things, he cannot raise up a virgin after she has fallen."[44]

St. Jerome was very uncomfortable with the idea of a capricious God who might do as he wished. In his attempt to introduce some degree of order to divine sovereignty, he drew a distinction between "absolute power," which established God's radical alterity from any other being, and "ordained power," which referred to what he actually did. While absolute power was unrestricted, ordained power was regulated by a certain notion of divine reason that was reliable, orderly, and therefore accessible to humanity.

But Damiani, who followed St. Jerome seven centuries later, found such philosophical maneuvering an attempt to limit something that was inherently unlimited. Responding directly to St. Jerome, he wrote, "How . . .

dare we doubt that God can restore the virginity of a fallen woman? For God can undo the past—that is, so act that an actual historical event should not have occurred."[45] Notice the uncanny resemblance to Ismā'īl's declaration that "God may well create a million new Muḥammads" in the following pronouncement by Damiani: "God has no need of any creature and is judged by no necessity to create, out of that nothing into existence draw this natural world of ours . . . imposing upon it its customary laws. Incapable in his omnipotence and in his eternal present of suffering any diminution or alteration of his creature power, *that natural order he could well replace, those laws at any moment change* [emphasis mine]."[46] In other words, according to Damiani, God's claim to absolute sovereignty rested on his capacity to enact the exception of undoing what had already been done, of replacing the past within a moment's notice. Ismā'īl's theology, much like Damiani's, was informed by precisely such an understanding of sovereignty that hinged on the absolute capacity of the sovereign to enact the exception.

So far I have been discussing Ismā'īl's conception of theological sovereignty and its implications for the sort of moral and societal order he sought to shape. But to develop a more thorough understanding of his political theology, a question that is apropos to address here is: What conception of politics did he imagine and advance? What to him constituted ideal political forms, structures, and leaders? I address these questions in the next chapter by examining another of Ismā'īl's seminal Persian texts that to my knowledge has not yet received any detailed analytical treatment, *The Station of Leadership* (*Manṣab-i Imāmat*). In this text he most explicitly articulated a political theory of sorts. In what follows, I will highlight key aspects of his political thought as presented in this text. I will also point to ways in which this text connects to his broader reform project, as articulated in other texts such as *Taqwīyat al-Īmān*. Despite major differences in language and styles of composition, thematic points of emphasis, levels of difficulty, and intended audiences, these two texts nonetheless combined as part of a rather coherent reform agenda: so I plan on demonstrating in the following chapter.

chapter four

Salvational Politics

Politics for the Preservation of Public Markers of Distinction

Ismāʿīl composed *Manṣab-i Imāmat* (in Persian) on the eve of the *jihād* campaign against the Sikhs that eventually cost him his life. His death halted the completion of the book, though he had written a substantial chunk; the print version of the book is around 150 pages long. Despite the timing of *Manṣab-i Imāmat*'s composition, it is not directly occupied with his and his master Sayyid Aḥmad's experiment of establishing an Islamic State in the frontier region, even though that context is central to its background. In tone and tenor, *Manṣab-i Imāmat* is drastically different from *Taqwīyat al-Īmān*.

This is not a popular text written primarily for the masses. Rather, *Manṣab-i Imāmat* is a rather dense philosophical meditation on the purposes of politics and on different categories of political structures and rulers. The language of this text is also markedly less polemical and at several times rather dense. That Ismāʿīl composed this text in Persian rather than in Urdu (though it was later translated into Urdu) also shows that he imagined for it a more scholarly audience. On several occasions in this text, Ismāʿīl wrote in rhyming prose, a feature readers can observe in some of my transliterations in this chapter. In what follows I will try to extract some of the key themes and arguments of *Manṣab-i Imāmat* as a way to trace the major lineaments of Ismāʿīl's political thought.[1]

To anticipate and summarize, Ismāʿīl's focus was less on presenting an exact template of an ideal political state and more on detailing the types of political orders and leaders best suited for the objective of moral reform and salvation. As I will show in a bit, Ismāʿīl's chief concern was with the effects of political leaders on the moral life of a community, not with their piety. Of foremost interest to him was the imperative of keeping current public markers of Muslim distinction (*sha'ā'ir-i Islām*), an imperative for which he was willing to tolerate a morally sluggish leader.

Curiously, and crucially, Ismā'īl equated the loss of Muslim sovereignty more with the extinction of such public markers of identity (primarily concerning distinctly Muslim practices) than with the loss of a Muslim state or territory per se. The erasure of the public performance of distinctly Muslim rituals was for him analogous to the intolerable condition of being dominated by unbelievers (*ghalbah-yi kuffār*). This condition necessitated from all Muslims of a community (*farz-i 'ayn*) a response of active rebellion and aggressive warfare against the current political order and ruler, even if that ruler was marked as Muslim. And if that was not possible, then they must migrate to a different polity, Ismā'īl argued.

But the question of whether a non-Muslim ruler who preserved Muslim practices and markers of distinction was tolerable to Ismā'īl remained ambiguous in his discourse. His political thought pivoted not so much on detailing a coherent theory of the state as on impressing politics on the fabric of everyday practice. And it was this underlying emphasis on moral reform as a means to salvation that united Ismā'īl's projects in *Taqwīyat al-Īmān* and *Manṣab-i Imāmat*, despite their discursive dissimilarities. Ultimately, the effectiveness of political as well as theological sovereignty hinged for him on the cultivation of a moral individual and public. With this brief summation of some of the highlights of Ismā'īl's argument in *Manṣab-i Imāmat*, let me now turn to a fuller elaboration of the reasoning that went into the making of that argument. While his discourse drew to some extent on major strands of medieval Sunnī political thought, especially in its aversion to rebellion and instability, much of his thought was novel and particular to him.[2] Moreover, what I am about to present in some detail is an expression of salvational politics not so easily amenable to being mapped onto or through the conceptual grid and space of either the modern nation-state or the premodern caliphal state. Ismā'īl's political calculus was firmly tethered to an imperial Muslim political theology, but at its heart was less the desire for the territory of a defined state and more the promise of securing and keeping alive public markers of Muslim distinction in the realm of ritual and everyday life: the maintenance of Muslim distinction in the public performance of religion, rather than the territorial construct of an Islamic state that indexed and signaled sovereign power. In a certain sense then, what I am about to detail and delineate is an illiberal model of Muslim political theology that challenges the liberal fantasy involved in privileging the modern state as the centerpiece of politics.

A final note before I dive into Ismā'īl's *Station of Leadership*: by analyzing a major Indo-Persian text on political theology composed at the cusp of colonial modernity and explicitly invested in the interaction of salvation and everyday piety, this essay also diversifies and complicates our understanding of a genre of thought that is typically associated with the heyday of Mughal rule and occupied primarily by Persianate notions of ethics and kingship.[3]

Politics as an Expression of Prophetic Love and Talent

For Ismā'īl, the primary purpose of politics was the reform of human beings: reform aimed at benefiting their lives in this world and elevating their salvational prospects in the afterworld. Politics, he argued, was among the prophetic talents (*kamālāt-i nabawī*).[4] More specifically, his political thought rested on a crucial distinction between what he called salvational politics (*siyāsat-i īmānī*) and imperial politics (*siyāsat-i sulṭānī*).[5] Salvational politics was the kind of politics associated with prophetic talents. It combined the goal of ordering worldly affairs with that of ensuring salvation in the afterworld.

The animating source and force of salvational politics was the abundant love (*wufūr-i shafqat*) that prophets held for their communities. This love made them strive for the moral correction of their followers. On the other hand, and in contrast, imperial politics revolved primarily around the accumulation of the ruler's personal benefits. Fulfilling the desires of oneself, rather than shepherding the moral lives of one's subjects, drove imperial politics (30). As Ismā'īl described, "The underlying political objective of such rulers is not the moral refinement of their subjects. Rather, the obedience and approval of subjects is sought only as an instrument of support for the realization of their own selfish desires" (*Pas maqṣūd-i īshān az siyāsat-i afrād-i insān mujarrad iṣlāḥ-i ḥāl-ī īshān nīst bal-keh aṣl-i maqṣūd hamīn ast keh īshān iṭā'at wa rafāqat ikhtiyār kunand tā beh i'ānat-i īshān aghrāz-i nafsānīya-i khud bi-dast āyad*) (30).

The driving force of imperial politics was the commanding ego-self (*nafs-i ammāra*) that steered and controlled a leader's actions and decisions. The more that this ego reigned supreme, the more the imperial political order was corrupt and distant from salvational politics. Politics was defined by this incessant competition between captivity to the sovereign self and salvation through prophetic talents. Thus, while *Manṣab-i Imāmat* and *Taqwīyat al-Īmān* were very different in tone and focus, they shared a broader conceptual structure: a political theology defined by the struggle between the sovereignty of the self and God's sovereignty. The goal of guarding divine sovereignty against the threat of human transgressions and desires was central to both: *Taqwīyat al-Īmān* pursued it by focusing on everyday practices and rituals, while *Manṣab-i Imāmat* set its sights on political order and leadership. But as the following discussion will show, in *Manṣab-i Imāmat* Ismā'īl expressed rather minimal requirements for an acceptable political order. Though he saw imperial politics as the opposite of salvational politics, he was quite tolerant of an imperial political order, so long as it did not extinguish the signature markers of Islam in a polity.

Prophetic Talents

At the heart of Ismā'īl's political philosophy was the idea that there existed a spectrum of political orders and leaders of varying legitimacy and acceptability. A political structure approached the ideal to the extent that it was infused with prophetic talents. These talents were (1) esteem (*wajāhat*), the prestige and high rank of prophets in the eyes of God, angels, and pious servants (humans); (2) sainthood (*wilāyat*), or prophets' capacities of knowledge such as wisdom, intuition, and discernment; (3) resurrection (*ba'that*), the training and education that prophets imparted to their communities—in its deeper meaning a talent expressing the absolute capaciousness of prophetic love; (4) guidance (*hidāyat*), which concerned charismatic qualities such as miracles and eloquence through which prophets attracted followers; and (5) politics (*siyāsa*), which brought together these talents for the formation of a moral community (3–36).

The more that a leader and his political order embodied these prophetic talents, the more prophetically endowed they were. Indeed, the perfect leader (*imām-i akmal*) was someone who fully embodied all these prophetic talents. Such a person had all the qualities of a prophet. He was not a prophet only because he was not allowed to be one, Ismā'īl provocatively claimed (54). "Otherwise, if there had been a prophet after Muḥammad, it would have been such a person" (*Dar ḥaqq-i misl-i īn shakhṣ tawān guft keh agar ba'd-i khātim al-anbīyā' kasay bi martabah-'i nubūwwat fā'iz mī shud har ā'īna hamīn akmal al-kāmilīn fā'iz mī-gardīd*) (54). The only distinction between such a leader who embodied all prophetic talents and Muḥammad was that the former was not a recipient of revelation (*Dar mayān-i īn imām-i akmal wa dar mayān-i anbīyā' Allāh imtiyāzay ẓāhir nakhwāhad shud illā beh nafs-i martabah-'i nubūwwat*) (54). This, he went on to explain, was the import of the Prophet's statement describing his relationship to his cousin/son-in-law 'Alī (d. 661), "You are to me what Aaron was to Moses, [with the difference] that there will be no prophet after me" (*Anta minī bi manzalat Harūn min Mūsa illā anna-hu lā nabīya ba'dī*).[6]

The crucial point to keep in mind here is that prophetic talents were not limited to prophets alone; they could also be found among nonprophets, and even among common people of faith. Nonprophets could never achieve the same level or magnitude of prophetic talents as prophets had, Ismā'īl was careful to clarify. However, there could be a conceptual similitude (*ma'nā-yi mumāsalat*) between the prophetic talents of nonprophets and those of prophets (52). The different gradations and stations of political leadership depended on the degree of similitude with prophetic talents. In a political leader, the stronger and more extensive that similitude, the more prophetically imbued he was. And ideal leadership (*imāmat-i ḥaqīqīya*) was characterized by absolute similitude (*mushābahat-i tāma*) with any of the prophetic qualities.

The best example of such ideal leadership was found in the period of the four "Rightly Guided" Caliphs immediately following the Prophet. This was a moment when, according to Ismā'īl, "The lamp of leadership glowed in the glass of the caliphate" (*Chirāgh-i imāmat dar shīsha-'i khilāfat jalwa gar gardīd*) (74). Such a state signified the perfection of God's investment in the moral fashioning and upbringing of humanity (*Ni'mat-i rabbānī dar bāb-i parwarish-i nū'-i insānī bā tamām rasīd*) (74). A rightly guided caliph was the ideal leader. This was so regardless of how acceptable or popular the caliph was to his community. At times a rightly guided caliph might not receive the complete support of his community, as was the case during 'Alī's tenure. However, even a chaotic reign, though less preferable than an orderly one, did not detract from the caliph's authority or stature (75). Ismā'īl explained that some caliphs did better than others in attracting their communities' loyalty, much as some prophets were more successful in disseminating their message to people than others. But this difference did not translate into any elevation or diminution in their station of leadership.

Yet a rightly guided caliphate was stable in addition to having all the qualities necessary to fulfill the aspirations of salvational politics. The Caliphate of 'Umar (the second successor to Muḥammad in Sunnī Islam) was a prime example of such an ideal order. Here Ismā'īl introduced a critical and potentially far-reaching caveat: the rightly guided caliphate was not restricted to any particular period of time, such as the three decades following Muhammad's death.

In making this case, Ismā'īl defined "a rightly guided caliph" as "someone who ascended to the station of leadership and actualized the conditions of salvational politics" (*Khalīfa-i rāshid 'ibārat ast az shakhsay keh ṣāḥib-i manṣab-i imāmat bāshad wa abwāb-i siyāsat-i īmānī az ū ẓāhir shawad*) (77). According to Ismā'īl, these defining characteristics were not limited to any specific temporal time frame or to the four successors to Muḥammad (*Khwāh dar zamān-i sābiq ẓahir shawad khwāh dar zaman-i lāḥiq khwāh dar awā'il-i ummat bāshad khwāh dar awākhir-i ān*) (77). Moreover, there was no stipulation that the title "Rightly Guided Caliph" could be affixed only to people of any particular lineage or ancestral background, such as say the Quraysh, the tribe to which the Prophet belonged. As for the prophetic reports circumscribing the period of the rightly guided caliphate to thirty years, Ismā'īl contended that they referred only to a continuous and unbroken period of thirty years. While such a caliphate was interrupted thirty years after the

Prophet's death, the possibility of further caliphates was not terminated. In an evocative analogy, Ismāʿil likened the reemergence of salvational politics, instituted by a rightly guided caliph, to the invariable appearance of daylight after a sustained period of darkness at night. Political orders, he argued, shifted and changed as in the cyclical alternation of night and day. The anticipated daylight inevitably overcame the darkness of night (*Tabaddul-i qismayn-i khilāfat rā tabaddul-i layl wa nahār qiyās bāyad kard keh baʿd az zamāna-'i layl nahār āshkārā mī-gardad*) (80). Similarly, people of faith must always pray and keep alive their hope and striving for the dispensation of the divine gift of a rightly guided caliphate. "One should never lose hope," Ismāʿīl almost wistfully urged (*Har-giz māyūs na-bāyad shud*) (80).

Imperial Politics: The Body Politic and Its Affective Horizons

But although the establishment of a rightly guided caliphate that would usher in salvational politics was the ideal, it was far from the only acceptable option. Ismāʿīl combined his idealistic vision with the realist proposition that even an imperial political order that did not fulfill the requirements of a rightly guided caliphate was worthy of support and submission. The only exception to this rule was the case of a political ruler and order that explicitly championed unbelief and brazenly opposed the prophetic norm; only in that case was rebelling against the ruler permitted. Ismāʿīl explained by drawing an analogy between religious normativity and the human body and senses.

A human, he said, was composed of a physical exterior body consisting of muscle, bones, and so on, and then the deeper sensoria like sight, taste, hearing, and the imagination. Similarly, laws and normative injunctions had an exterior form and then a deeper reality connected to their underlying purpose. In this way the *sharīʿa* was like a human being, Ismāʿīl claimed (*Sharīʿa rā bi-mushābah-i yak shakhṣ-i mujassam bāyad fahmīd*) (56). Politics was structured in the same manner. The ideal political order of salvational politics, driven by a rightly guided caliph, signified and brought to life the innermost realities of politics and political leadership (*imāmat-i ḥaqīqīya*). Such a leader was the Prophet's shadow on earth that brought to life the foundational aspirations of divine law (56).

In contrast, imperial politics was like the exterior body of law and politics, uncoupled from their inner spirit and deeper purposes. Ismāʿīl explained the interaction between salvational politics and imperial politics with the graphic image of the adulteration of pure sweet water with foul and noxious water. The more the polluted water seeped into pure water, the more repugnant and unamenable to use that water became. Similarly, as salvational politics was corrupted by imperial politics, over time, the latter overpowered the former, emerging as the dominant political order (89). But what precisely was the difference between salvational and imperial politics? On what did their distinction rest?

Ismāʿīl argued that whereas salvational politics had as its foundational purpose the moral reform of the community, imperial politics was animated by the fulfillment of the ruler's personal wishes and desires. Rightly guided caliphs who steered the ship of salvational politics had no interest in satisfying any aspect of their ego. Serving the prophetic mission of nurturing the salvational prospects of their community was their only aim. They considered indulging the desires of the self a form of polytheism, in competition with obedience to God. In stark contrast, the imperial ruler could not help but satisfy the desires and ambitions of the self (*hawā-yi nafsānī*).

This imprisonment to the urges of the self (*muqtaziyāt-i nafs*) could take varied forms. While the thirst to conquer other lands consumed some rulers, others were gripped by the goal of assembling a loyal fan club among friends and associates. While some were driven to amass wealth, others could not escape the temptation of attending to bodily pleasures. Though the symptoms differed, the disease that generated them was the same: an unceasing occupation with satisfying the self. While boosting political power and dominance, the net effect of such imperial politics was to harm the foundations of the *sharīʿa*. As Ismāʿīl put it, "The seed of this thorn is destructive for [the goal of] establishing servitude [to God]" (*Tukhm-i īn khār nuqṣān ast dar maqām-i ʿubūdīyat*) (91).

But for all the tragedy surrounding the overpowering of salvational politics by imperial politics, the latter was not necessarily deserving of outright rejection or rebellion. Indeed, such a hostile attitude toward a political ruler was permissible only in the most extreme circumstances. Crucial to Ismāʿīl's argument was a consideration of the degree to which rulers were consumed by their ego. Gauging the scale of the problem was essential, he argued. He presented four distinct categories of rulers and corresponding political orders, each calling for a different reception and response. Let me elaborate the key features of these categories, as sketched by Ismāʿīl. His understanding and characterization of each category provide an illumining window into his political imaginary and into the extent of transgression in the political sphere that he was willing to tolerate.

The Just Empire

The first category of imperial politics/leadership was what Ismāʿīl called a "just empire/just ruler" (*salṭanat-i ʿādila/sulṭān-i ʿādil*). This was the least corrupt and problematic kind of politics. However, even so, just imperial rulers suffered from all the problems of imperial politics. They were power hungry, indulgent, and enamored with pomp and bodily comforts. They considered things like building tall monuments, collecting fine horses and weaponry, and creating sumptuous gardens examples of major achievements. Moreover, while dispensing justice, they often allowed personal likes and dislikes to color their judgment, treating some criminals more favorably than others, even when the same crime was committed (94).

However, crucially, despite all their follies, they maintained the public persona of people of faith and piety and strove to remain within the bounds of the religion. While entertaining the desires of the ego, they were careful not to overstep the boundaries of *sharīʿa*. They reined themselves in just at the threshold of transgression. Their ego enticed them toward misdeeds, but their fear of God helped them resist that enticement. Ismāʿīl explained this behavior through a curious example: "Say this ruler falls in love with someone, and the yearning for sexual intercourse leaves him in a state of unrest. Yet he contains his sexual urges until entering into a marriage contract. Now, he may well run amok in his eagerness to get married, and spend excessive time and money in realizing that wish. But still, by waiting till marriage, he manages to avoid committing an explicitly forbidden act and thus remains within the bounds of permissibility" (99). "The flame of faith," Ismāʿīl continued, "flickers in the heart of such a ruler. But it is camouflaged under the smoke of his desire and ego. And while the lightning of certainty illumines his heart, the darkness of a fickle intention keeps it hidden" (*Aṣl-i shu'la-'i īmān dar dil-i ū afrokhta ast fa-ammā dūd-i hawā wa hawas bā ū āmaykhteh wa barq-i yaqīn bar dil-i ū darakhshandeh fa-ammā ẓulmat-i taghayyur-i nīyat ū rā poshīdeh*) (100).

Though not advancing the salvation of the masses, just imperial rulers do excel at other affairs of statecraft such as waging war, quashing rebellions, and establishing peace and security. Therefore, although such rulers do little for the moral pedagogy of their community or for the elevation of their spiritual condition, they do protect the outer manifestations of the *sharī'a* (by maintaining Muslim political supremacy). Thus, Ismā'īl advised, the subjects of such rulers should offer them full support. In fact, he further recommended, they should adopt the practice of exaggerating their achievements, magnifying their efforts, and turning a blind eye if rulers ever act contrary to the prophetic norm (*Ba'zay 'umūr khilāf-i sunnat az ū ẓāhir mī-gardad wa az ān chishm bāyad poshīd wa dar khayr khwāhī-yi ū bi-jān wa dil bāyad koshīd. Sa'ī-yi qalīl-i ū rā bi-jāy-yi kasīr bāyad shumard wa 'amal-i ṣaghīr-i ū bi-jāy-yi 'amal-i kabīr*) (104). "They should think like this," Ismā'īl proposed, summing up his position: "Yes, he [the just imperial ruler] is occupied with satisfying the pleasures of the self, but concurrently he is also [publicly] seen as serving God's religion" (*Ḥisāb bāyad kard keh har chand bi-istīfā-'yi lazzāt-i nafsānīya mashghūf ast ammā bi khitmatguzārī-yi dīn-i rabb al-'ālimīn mawṣūf*) (104).

Despotic and Misguided Empires

The next two categories of imperial political orders, as Ismā'īl described them, were the "despotic empire" (*salṭanat-i jābira*) and the "misguided empire" (*salṭanat-i zāla*). Despotic rulers were completely captive to the commands of their ego-self (*nafs-i ammāra*). They did as their ego directed them to do, indifferent to whether their actions kept within or transgressed the limits of religious normativity. They were equally indifferent to their responsibility of serving as moral exemplars for the masses. As was the case with the first category, the moral depravities of despotic rulers could take many forms, depending on the temperament and inclinations of a particular ruler. In what seemed like a clear swipe at the Mughal aristocracy, Ismāʿīl listed among such depravities the ingestion of intoxicants, an attachment to exquisite clothes and food, and the patronizing of music and dance concerts and chess games. The only talent connected to these habits was wastefulness (*isrāf*). In turn, wastefulness was the only talent that these habits advanced (104–7).

The tendency to privilege luxury and self-pleasure on the part of the ruler shattered the moral economy of the polity, while also intensifying injustice and exploitation. This was so, Ismāʿīl lectured, because wastefulness required the constant accumulation of wealth. And this insatiable need to compound wealth opened numerous avenues for injustice such as the economic exploitation of the poor and complete disregard for the interests of merchants and agriculturalists. Moreover, as the political elite occupied itself with play and luxury, the polity's state of security and systems of justice were compromised. Distant from the care and concern of the ruler, subjects also began to treat each other unjustly and oppressively. Thus the debauchery and wastefulness of the sovereign undermined the moral architecture of the entire community. Such an empire was "a massive catastrophe" (*balā'-i aẓīm*) (107), Ismāʿīl declared.

But despite all the catastrophes unleashed by such rulers, their subjects had to give them their loyalty and support. Returning to his minimalist view, Ismāʿīl explained that despite all his destructive inclinations, the despotic ruler at least "counted himself as among Muslims" (*jān-i khud rā az muslimīn shumārad*) (116). "Therefore," Ismāʿīl continued, "every now and then the fervor of religion and pride in its normative structures might [just] enflame his heart and push him to strive for the elevation of Islam" (*Gāh gāh ḥamīyat-i dīn-i matīn wa ghayrat-i shar'-i mubīn az dil-i ū mījoshad wa binā bar ān dar i'lā'ay kalima'-yi rabb al-'ālimīn mīkoshad*) (116). Central to Ismāʿīl's argument was the contention that even if the despotic ruler was inattentive to the prescribed boundaries of religion and oblivious to the counsel of religious scholars, he might still bring some benefit to Islam and some harm to the unbelievers. This he could do in a few ways. Most importantly, though the despotic ruler was distant from God, one would expect him, simply by virtue of identifying as a Muslim, to privilege people of faith over unbelievers. For example, while appointing ministers, viziers, and other important members of his bureaucracy, he would always prefer appointing Muslims over unbelievers. In effect, though not the most beloved to God, he still contributed to strengthening the societal standing of Muslims while simultaneously harming the position of unbelievers (115). One could think of this ruler as being like "a blind man carrying a torch" (*kor mash'al dār*) (116).

Second, even the transgressions of such rulers could at times be well intentioned or at least open to such a charitable interpretation, Ismā'īl suggested. For instance, say the ruler was spendthrift and fond of channeling his treasury funds into erecting big and tall monuments. But every now and then he might also fund the building of a magnificent, opulent, and lustrous mosque as an expression of his devotion to God. This act of extravagance, Ismā'īl admitted, would constitute wastefulness, something that was certainly undesirable according to the *sharī'a* and displeasing to God. But it could also be interpreted in a different light. The ruler could be spending extravagantly on devotional acts like building mosques to maximize his spiritual rewards. He may have reasoned, "The more I spend [on such pious projects] the greater the dividends in the afterlife" (115). Thus, even though such extravagance was undesirable, his subjects should be focusing on the sincerity of his attempt at piety. His subjects, especially the religious elite, should consider the despotic ruler an excellent candidate for receiving their moral guidance and instruction, Ismā'īl suggested. In fact, they should consider the explication of truth in the presence of such a ruler the highest form of worship because he was without doubt in need of moral pedagogy (*Sulṭān-i jābir bilā rayb muḥtāj-i 'amr bi'l ma'rūf ast wa iẓhār-i ḥaqq bihuzūr-i ū afzal-i 'ibādāt*) (116).[7] However, Ismā'īl was quick to add a cautionary note: "This guidance and instruction should never turn into conflict or opposition that reaches the point of rebellion. Rebelling against or desertion of the despotic ruler is not normatively permissible [*khurūj bar imām-i jābir shar'an jā'iz nīst*]" (117).

The next category of ruler discussed by Ismā'īl, the "misguided ruler," had all the bad qualities of the despotic ruler, but in more pronounced and stark terms. The misguided empire was one in which all the corruptions and depravities that afflicted the despotic empire became institutionalized and deeply sedimented in political and everyday life. In all aspects of life, a competing normative order opposing the divine and prophetic order took hold. That which God declared forbidden was celebrated in public, and that which he deemed obligatory was sidelined. This stark inversion of normative injunctions and boundaries was manifested in the proliferation of such practices as attaching titles like "Emperor of Emperors" to political rulers, using dishware made of gold and silver, and celebrating non-Muslim festivals like the Persian new year (*nawroz*), Dīwālī, and Holī. And while these corrupt practices became popular, practices specifically associated with Islam, such as responding to the greeting "Peace be on you" (*As-salāmu 'alaykum*), performing the pilgrimage to Mecca, and attending and benefiting from assemblies of meditation and intellectual exchange, were erased to the point of seeming forbidden (116–20).

But again, despite all this moral misery, the saving grace of such rulers was that at least they proclaimed themselves to be Muslims. Ismā'īl pointed out that "although in reality this ruler is among the unbelievers destined for hellfire, the fact that he presents himself as a Muslim in public means that his unbelief remains undisclosed and his faith in Islam visible to the public eye. . . . This apparent claim to a Muslim identity shields him from outright unbelief" (*Har chand amsāl-i īn salāṭīn fi'l ḥaqīqat az qabīl-i kuffār-i ashrār and wa az jins-i ahl-i nār fa-ammā az bas-keh bi-zabān-i khud da'wā-yi Islām mī-kunand pas kufr-i īshān mastūr ast wa īmān-i īshān ẓāhir wa shāhid*) (120). Concomitantly, despite the moral havoc enveloping the polity, at least the minimum markers of Muslim religious performance, such as "getting girls married according to Islamic norms, celebrating Eid/'Īd, and following Muslim burial rites," continued unabated in the public sphere (120). The currency of these basic Muslim practices indicated that a community had not completely bid farewell to the *sharī'a*. So in this condition, should a community rebel against the political sovereign? This question was open to debate, Ismā'īl claimed. There existed cogent scholarly arguments both for and against that option.

His own opinion on this question was contingent on the consequences of such a move. Consistent with the pragmatic stance of this text, he argued that if rebellion led to chaos and a political vacuum, it was undesirable. But were it certain that such rebellion would result in the emergence of a rightly guided caliphate or a just imperial order, then it was commendable. Rather than a strictly legal calculus, Ismā'īl's argument was primarily based on consideration of what was most beneficial for the community. In contrast to his firm prohibition of rebellion against the first three types of imperial political orders, his view in the case of the misguided empire was more ambiguous. As he put it, rather dramatically, and again in rhyming prose (see transliteration): "The misguided ruler is the king of the corrupt, the leader of heretics. The state he governs is for religion fatal poison, his leadership according to God and the Prophet absolute falsehood. But so long as he associates with Islam, the question of his unbelief remains ambiguous, and the connected question of announcing rebellion and disobedience against his rule is subject to debate." (*Sulṭān-i muzall har chand ra'īs al-mufsidīn ast wa imām al-mubtadi'īn wa riyāsat-i ū beh nisbat-i dīn simatay qātil wa imāmat-i ū biḥukm-i kitāb wa sunnat wa hamay ast bāṭil ammā az ānjā keh rāh-i mu'āmala-'i Islām bā ū maslūk ast takfīr-i ū mashkūk binā'an 'alayhi iẓhār-i bughā bar-way wa khurūj az iṭā'at-i ū nīz az masā'il-i ikhtilāfīya ast*) (122). But Ismā'īl did add that one should exercise caution in this matter hastening neither to instigate a rebellion nor to censure or rebuke someone else who did.

Empire of Unbelief

But there was no ambiguity, debate, or consideration of restraint or caution regarding the course of action to be taken in the context of the fourth and worst form of imperial political order, what Ismā'īl called "the empire of unbelief" (*salṭanat-i kufr*). The empire of unbelief did not mean a political order governed by unbelievers, Ismā'īl was careful to clarify. Rather, the ruler was marked as Muslim but otherwise opposed the normative injunctions of the *sharī'a* with unabashed virulence. Drowned in worldly pleasures and concerns, such a ruler and his supporters had lost all faith in doctrinal covenants like divine oneness, prophethood, and the afterworld. Moreover, and this is the point on which Ismā'īl fumed most aggressively, they constantly ridiculed and called idiotic those who did not subscribe to their agenda of complete attachment to worldly pleasures and acquisitions. In his own words: "They regard heeding the normative practice of the Prophet as foolishness, abiding by the limits of religion in everyday affairs and habits as lowliness, and putting one's trust in God as a sign of weakness and torpor" (124).

Most devastatingly, Ismāʿīl lamented, this mocking attitude cheapened the stature and authority of divinely mandated norms (*sharʿ-i rabbānī*) in the eyes of the ruler's followers and subjects. In effect, imperial law (*qānūn-i sulṭānī*) trumped divine law in all affairs of life. Even more disconcertingly, while following the injunctions of the imperial normative order was associated with intelligence and discernment, attending to the practices required by the *sharīʿa* was stigmatized as useless and foolish (124).

Inevitably, such rulers took their arrogance and self-love to the limit by claiming prophecy and eventually the status of divinity. Thus their brazen contempt for divine sovereignty reached its apex, and an alternative moral and political order, reeking of unbelief and entirely bereft of any salvational aspiration, came to be erected. Ismāʿīl was unequivocal in his prescription for Muslims in such a polity. It was incumbent on every one of them (*farz-i ʿayn*) to wage war in rebellion, or, if unable to do so, to migrate to another Muslim domain. Ismāʿīl's reasoning as to why rebellious warfare or migration represented the only two options before a Muslim community in this situation presents a critical window into his political theology. He argued that a Muslim polity that exhibited all signs of unbelief simulated the dominance of unbelievers over Muslims (*bi mushābah-i ghalbah-i kuffār ast*) (125). The ruler of such a polity normalized the markers of unbelief in the public sphere. That is why, for Ismāʿīl, "resisting and killing this ruler was the essence of Islam" (125). And if that was not possible, one was then required to migrate to another place where the public markers of Islam were current, Ismāʿīl concluded (125). This reasoning reveals a crucial aspect of Ismāʿīl's political thought and imaginary.

In evaluating the legitimacy of political leadership, Ismāʿīl seems concerned less about the intentions or individual piety of political leaders than about the effects of their leadership on the power and performance of Islam in the public sphere. Even a leader steeped in moral corruption was acceptable to him so long as that leader was able to secure the political dominance of Islam and keep alive in public the distinctive ritual markers of the religion. A Muslim leader was unambiguously unacceptable only when the polity began to resemble a political order dominated by unbelievers. In Ismāʿīl's evaluative calculus, the moral depravity of a leader was problematic primarily on account of its deleterious effect on political power and as a consequence on the normative gravitas of practices enjoined by the *sharīʿa* in the public's eyes. The foundations of Ismāʿīl's political thought were informed and prioritized by an imperial political theology invested above all in maintaining Islam's political dominance. So long as that objective was achieved, he was willing to tolerate even significant departures from the ideal of a rightly guided caliphate. That tolerance was exhausted only by the case of a political ruler and order substantively equivalent to the sovereignty of unbelief.

Imperial Political Theology

So to return to the question with which I began this chapter: What was Ismāʿīl's conception of ideal forms of politics? What the preceding analysis shows is that his political thought considered a wide range of possibilities ranging from the ideal to the minimally acceptable. But throughout he demonstrated an overarching concern with the moral economy of the community. The purpose of politics was moral reform, animated by the prophetic mandate to elevate the salvational prospects of a community. A political leader, Ismāʿīl contended, was someone who invited (*ṣāḥib al-daʿwa*) his community to salvation. The quality of that invitation, however, varied radically. It ranged from promising the realization of prophetic talents to only ensuring the performance of basic acts of piety. But as long as political leaders offered some form of that invitation, they remained legitimate and worthy of obedience. Only when the expectation of the invitation to moral reform and salvation was completely lost did a political order and leader cease to attract any legitimacy.

In conclusion, some instructive ambiguities in Ismāʿīl's views on political leadership deserve mention. Most notably, it is difficult to correlate the theoretical aspects of his discussion with the political conditions and actors that occupied his life. Clearly, Ismāʿīl's assault on aristocratic habits and practices, replete with examples such as grandiose architecture and fixation with chess, was directed at the Mughal elite. But otherwise, it is difficult to tell exactly how he categorized early nineteenth-century India in terms of its political acceptability. That he did not explicitly call for Indian Muslims to migrate elsewhere shows that he did not consider India an "empire of unbelief." But then what was it? Complicating the matter further is Ismāʿīl's silence on the question of the status of a polity led by a non-Muslim in which the basic requirements of the *sharīʿa* were fulfilled. Was any non-Muslim ruler unacceptable or only one who was an avowed unbeliever or one who explicitly opposed the *sharīʿa*? Another curious ambiguity surrounds the status of his mentor and the leader of the *jihād* campaign against the Sikhs, Sayyid Aḥmad, purportedly the key player dominating the context of this text. Did Ismāʿīl see him as a rightly guided caliph or as a just imperial ruler (the first category of imperial politics)? Clearly, lending legitimacy to Sayyid Aḥmad's leadership of the community that was to emerge from the *jihād* campaign against the Sikhs serves as an important backdrop to this text. But how exactly did Sayyid Aḥmad fit its conceptual grid—or, to phrase it differently, what exactly was his "station of leadership"? It is difficult to tell; perhaps that was to be the part of the text Ismāʿīl never got around to writing. The almost complete erasure in Ismāʿīl's discourse of British colonialism is also rather telling.

In any case, a central point emerging from *Manṣab-i Imāmat* is that the conceptual architecture of Ismāʿīl's thought there was shaped most by an imperial Muslim political theology that enlaced political power and dominance with the promise of piety and salvation. The condition of Indian Muslims as an increasingly colonized community seemed less immediate to his concerns and operative logics. And it was on this issue that the underlying aspirations of *Manṣab-i Imāmat* and *Taqwīyat al-Īmān* coincided, despite palpable differences in the tone and points of emphases of the two texts. While *Taqwīyat al-Īmān*'s focus was on the relationship between divine sovereignty and the everyday performance of religion, *Manṣab-i Imāmat* approached that question from the perspective of political power and leadership. But ultimately, at the heart of both texts was the problem of regulating everyday religious life in a manner that preserved the sovereignty of divine law.

Finally, juxtaposing these two texts shows the elasticity of Ismā'īl's discursive temperament and orientation. In *Taqwīyat al-Īmān*, he adopted a noticeably maximalist outlook radiating with apocalyptic urgency and slashing discontent with the world around him. The Ismā'īl of *Manṣab-i Imāmat*, in contrast, was not only stylistically more measured and less hostile but also remarkably minimalist in many of his positions. Rather than view this difference as a contradiction, perhaps one could see it as an illustration of Ismā'īl's ability to couch his projects according to their varied intended objectives and audiences. While a shock and awe strategy might have been appropriate for a popular text like *Taqwīyat al-Īmān*, Ismā'īl nimbly changed gears to present a more cautiously calibrated account of politics in *Manṣab-i Imāmat*. However, as I just pointed out, the overarching intellectual framework and project that inspired these seemingly varied texts were similar. In the next chapter, I continue my interrogation of Ismā'īl's political theology by considering one of the most controversial arenas of this thought: his discourse on the limits of prophetic intercession. I do so by returning to *Taqwīyat al-Īmān*.

chapter five

Intercessory Wars

The subject of intercession is inextricable from the question of sovereignty. The capacity to pardon a sinner signifies the ability to enact an exception, a departure from the normal rule. The sovereign, remember, at least according to the Schmittian notion, is he who enacts the exception. The role of an intercessor in this process can cause some tension. To be sure, an intercessor serves only as a petitioner who mediates between a sinner and the sovereign decision maker. But what is one to make of an intercessor whose petitions are never refused, whose status allows him to have all his requests for an exception approved? Does that in any way compromise the sovereignty of the sovereign?

These questions were central to Ismā'īl's discussion on intercession. He was most troubled by the tendency of the masses to associate sovereign powers with human intercessors such as pious saints and prophets. The way they understood the idea of intercession, he contended, confused the exceptionality of divine sovereignty with the intercessory authority of nondivine entities. He saw intercession as one of the principal arenas that threatened the radical alterity of divine sovereignty. In the discussion that follows, I am interested less in the coherence of Ismā'īl's argument according to traditional Islamic theology than in the language in which he delivered his argument. What kinds of symbols, metaphors, and images populated his discourse? What political postures and desires might we discern from this seemingly theological discussion? What does his mode of argumentation reveal about his social imaginary?

Ismā'īl's discourse on intercession, consistent with his larger argument in *Taqwīyat al-Īmān*, sought to radically undercut the authority of intermediaries and nondivine entities, including the Prophet, in the realm of salvation and redemption. To use Schmittian terms, Ismā'īl argued that it was only God who possessed the sovereign power to grant the exception of forgiveness and salvation to a sinner who would otherwise, according to the normal rule, be destined for hell. In formulating his argument, Ismā'īl presented a number of prophetic reports in which the Prophet himself emphasized his fallibility and vulnerability as a human being. For instance, in one such report, the Prophet said, "By God! Even though I am God's messenger, I have no idea what will be done to me or to you [in the afterworld]."[1] On another occasion, the Prophet assembled his family members and declared to them: "Save yourselves from hellfire. I will be of no help to you in God's [court of accountability]."[2] The Prophet, Ismā'īl argued, was acutely concerned that his followers not divinize him or confer superhuman qualities on him and thus undercut God's absolute sovereignty. Moreover, Ismā'īl argued that the aura and majesty of the Prophet depended not on any extraordinary salvific capacities but on the perfection of his humanity. In other words, the paradigmatic example of his unwavering submission to divine sovereignty was what made the Prophet extraordinary.

To support this argument, Ismā'īl adduced an array of verses from the Qur'ān in which God instructs the Prophet to declare his incapacity to harm or benefit his community in the afterworld. For example, "Say: It is not in my power to cause you harm or to bring you to right conduct. Say: No one can deliver me from God (If I were to disobey him), nor should I find refuge except in him."[3] In his commentary on this verse, Ismā'īl exhorted his readers to take note of the Prophet's keenness to establish his subordination to the divine. This he emphasized to prevent his community from transgressing the limits of his own authority. Here Ismā'īl spoke for the Prophet as follows: "Do not transgress the limits by thinking that our intermediary is extremely exalted and our intercessor very beloved [*hamārā wakīl zabardast aur hamārā shafī' barā maḥbūb*] so that we can do whatever we wish and he will save us from God's punishment. Even I [the Prophet] tremble before God and do not seek anyone else as my refuge."[4] Ismā'īl continued, "From this verse it becomes apparent what misguided transgressors these Indian Muslim masses are who forget the sovereignty of the divine in their reliance on saints and holy figures. The master of prophethood [*sarkār-i risālat*] himself used to fear God day and night and find solace in nothing other than his mercy. Then who are these commoners to be following a different path?"[5]

Ismā'īl also cited a number of other verses that underscore the absoluteness of divine sovereignty while criticizing the role of intermediaries in the salvific realm. For example, these included "They serve, besides God, things that neither hurt them nor profit them, and they say: 'These are our intercessors with God.' Say: 'Do you indeed inform God of something he knows not, in the heavens or on earth? Glory to him! And far is he above the partners they ascribe [to him]!' "[6] and the verse "Who is it in whose hands is the governance of all things, who protects [all], but is not protected [by any]? [Answer] if you can."[7]

At the same time that Ismā'īl vigorously advanced his argument for limiting the scope of prophetic intercession, he faced a formidable conundrum: contrary to his theological project, traditional sources of Muslim normativity, including the Qur'ān, contain several references that do in fact affirm a normative role for human intercessors in the domain of salvation. Some such moments in the Qur'ān are verses like "On that day shall no intercession avail except of him whom the Beneficent God allows and whose word he is pleased with"[8] and "Intercession will not avail aught with him save of him whom he permits."[9] Confronted with this obstacle, Ismā'īl was presented with the challenge of devising a hermeneutical strategy that might advance his argument for the exclusivity of absolute divine sovereignty while also honoring the normative permission offered to nondivine intercessors in traditional Islamic sources.

How did he go about this task? What kind of a strategy did he employ in attempting to shift the parameters of normativity in relation to the question of intercession? In what follows, I will briefly recount how Ismā'īl performed this hermeneutical operation as a way of examining the larger political program that inspired his theology. Notice in what follows the way Ismā'īl mobilized political characters and symbols to assemble his theological argument. As I hope to show, his argument for the absoluteness of divine sovereignty was intimately bound to a scathing repudiation of monarchical politics and forms of life. Moreover, it was precisely by drawing a radical contrast between divine and worldly sovereignty that he sought to establish the supremacy and exclusivity of the former. Observing in some detail the steps of his argument should clarify this point.

Varieties of Intercession

In *Taqwīyat al-Īmān*, Ismā'īl advanced a tripartite typology of intercession. The three types of intercession, according to him, are intercession based on high esteem (*shafā'at-i wajāhat*), intercession based on love (*shafā'at-i muḥabbat*), and intercession through permission (*shafā'at bi'l idhn*). Intercession based on high esteem refers to a situation in which an official from a king's entourage is greatly esteemed at court. This official is thus granted the capacity to intercede on behalf of a criminal. When the official petitions for a criminal's exoneration, the king invariably grants it. The king fears that if he upsets or insults such an important member of his kingdom his authority will be weakened. Thus, keeping in mind the best interests of his government, he pardons the criminal.[10]

Intercession based on love is very similar. This type of intercession involves a situation where someone whom the king loves a great deal petitions on behalf of a criminal. For example, such a person could be a close relative or a friend for whom the king holds deep affection. The king accepts the petition because he feels that in hurting his relative or friend he would hurt himself. Ismā'īl argued that these two types of intercession are not found in God's court; they can operate only in worldly monarchies. Only the third variety of intercession, intercession by permission, is even conceivable in God's kingdom.[11]

According to Ismā'īl, intercession by permission involves a situation in which a criminal has already repented for his crime and has vowed to never commit it again. Moreover, he is not a habitual criminal but has just once succumbed to his desires and transgressed. He is extremely ashamed and regretful about his actions. Fearing punishment day and night, he keeps his head bowed in guilt and sorrow. Such a criminal does not go around looking for a courtier or a minister to intercede on his behalf. Rather, agreeing that he deserves to be punished, he anxiously awaits the king's verdict. The king feels pity for the miseries of the criminal and wants to pardon him. But he hesitates from following through on his inclination, reasoning that were he to forgive a criminal in this manner, other subjects in his kingdom might begin to take lightly the severity and authority of his justice system.

In this moment, a courtier or minister from the king's court comes forward and petitions on behalf of the criminal. Importantly, the motivation behind this petition is not to help the criminal but to add weight to the king's original inclination to pardon the criminal. The king accepts the minister's petition, and in the guise of honoring an esteemed member of his court he goes on to exonerate the criminal. Ismā'īl insisted that when the Qur'ān talks about the capacity of certain prophets to act as intercessors, it is this third type of intercession that is intended.[12]

Most important to note here is that even in this third scenario, although the king exonerates the criminal only after receiving a petition from an exalted minister in his court, the decisive factor is that the criminal has already repented and has resolved to never commit a crime again. The petition of an intercessor only facilitates the process; it is not in itself the main cause of the criminal's exoneration. The sole cause is the sovereign authority of the divine, not the authority of any other entity. Ismā'īl's insistence on emphasizing the "already repentant" character of the criminal is significant here.

Even while allowing for the legitimacy of some form of intercession, Ismā'īl did not emphasize the capacity of an intercessor to mediate on behalf of criminals. To the contrary, he argued that a minister (and by analogy Prophet Muḥammad) intercedes on someone's behalf only when the sovereign king (and by analogy God) has already arrived at the decision to exonerate him. As Ismā'īl wrote: "The only reason ministers intercede for such a criminal is that he has already repented his crimes and the king has decided to forgive him. Ministers do not act as intercessors for the benefit of the criminal. Rather, their intercessory labor is solely invested in serving the king. They [ministers] are not supporters [*ḥimāyatī*] of criminals; they are obedient subjects [*farmānbardār*] of the king."[13]

In a sense, Ismā'īl's argument is somewhat counterintuitive: intercession is legitimate only when it is not sought and when it plays a marginal role in the eventual exoneration of the criminal. One might wonder, then, as Ismā'īl's opponents later did, what one is to make of the authority of an intercessor whose intercession is unwanted and peripheral to the redemption of a sinner. Ismā'īl did not address these ambiguities in any detail. However, what must be underscored here is the larger political program encoded into his theological discourse on intercession.

The Cross-Pollination of Political and Theological Imaginaries

The promise of egalitarianism found in Ismā'īl's theological imagination was intimately connected to a larger critique of worldly monarchies and royal kingdoms that in his view privileged a hierarchical order of political authority. Ismā'īl's theological project was inseparable from his political goal of exposing the aristocratic hubris that in his view poisoned the Mughal moral economy in the waning years of that empire. A political theology of radical sovereignty required a moral economy of simplicity that jettisoned monarchical modes of being.

The rhythms of everyday life had to be orchestrated in such a manner that all habits, customs, and norms of socialization that threatened to undermine the sovereignty of the divine were abolished. For Ismā'īl, the exclusivity of divine power was constantly undermined in a community that flocked to saints for assistance in moments of distress, and in which a culture of aristocracy and privileged nobility thrived in the public sphere. Correcting this condition of moral and political malaise required establishing God as radically and absolutely different from and sovereign over all his creation.

In trying to achieve this task, Ismā'īl sought to establish a decisive difference between worldly and divine exercise of sovereign power. Particularly telling in this regard is the way he contrasted the accessibility of the divine with the arrogant aloofness that characterizes worldly monarchs. As he explained, "God is not an arrogant elitist like worldly kings who dispense their mercy and generosity in a bureaucratic and selective fashion. Access to God's court does not require any petitions or endorsements from viziers, princes, or people of nobility. Even though God is the king of all kings [*sab bādshāhon kā bādshāh*], he is not arrogant like worldly kings who pay no heed to the supplications of their subjects."[14]

Ismā'īl argued that in the realm of divine justice one does not need to go through a chain of bureaucrats and intermediaries to have one's supplications heard and answered. Moreover, it is not as if God makes himself available only for the major and most critical supplications of his subjects while delegating all minor affairs to his ministers. Unlike worldly monarchs, while dealing with his subjects, God does not delegate at all. Citing a well-known prophetic report, Ismā'īl claimed that one should not hesitate to ask God for even a shoelace when it breaks (*ḥatā yas'alahu shish' na'lihi idhā inqaṭa'a*).[15] In short, Ismā'īl argued that since God's generosity and mercy are endless and immediately available to the human subject, seeking the intercession of saints and prophets is unnecessary, illogical, and illegitimate.

To make this point, Ismā'īl mobilized a powerful analogy: "Imagine a person was sitting in the king's company all by himself, and he enjoyed that king's complete and undivided attention. If, despite this intimate private hearing, this person were to cry out for the help of some governor, minister, or vizier who was far away, the only conclusion one could draw would be that this person was blind or had lost his mind."[16] This analogy is illustrative of the way Ismā'īl approached the relationship between divine sovereignty and human agency. In his view, human agency was secured through submission to the absolute sovereignty of the divine. By affirming God's absolute otherness, one attained God's absolute proximity.

As noteworthy as Ismā'īl's argument is the rationally driven discourse in which he framed it. Calling an intercessor for help is not only illegitimate and heretical, it signifies that a person has "lost his mind" and become irrational and blind because of his dependence on nondivine sources of authority. If someone has received the providential gift of intimate proximity with the divine, seeking the intercessory services of a distant, nondivine entity is foolishness.

Ismā'īl further argued that to seek the immediate intercession of someone other than God is to take God's prerogative as the sole dispenser of mercy and hand it to another entity who does not deserve it. Here again, the language in which Ismā'īl articulated this idea is very revealing. In a style that combined polemical abrasiveness with pedagogical rebuke, Ismā'īl wrote, "Handing the creator's prerogative of divine sovereignty to someone among his creation is like stealing the prerogative of the most exalted and giving it to the most base, it is like taking off a king's crown and placing it on the head of a 'low-caste' leather worker [Chamār]. What could be more unjust?"[17]

He continued, even more emphatically, "You can be sure that the most exalted person, and the most powerful angel, when compared to the majesty of God, has a status lower than that of a 'low-caste' leather worker."[18] This statement is pregnant with irony. After all, the construction of a moral order that transcended hierarchies of caste and lineage was at the heart of Ismā'īl's reform project; he was scathingly critical of the practice of boasting about one's lineage, which he found repugnantly common in late Mughal India. But his mobilization of the racially charged symbol of the Chamār shows the selective nature of that outrage. As readers will see in the next few chapters, for all their disagreements and polemics, rival groups of nineteenth-century Muslim scholars were remarkably united in their disdain for the Chamār, for many of them a degraded being at the very bottom of the social ladder.[19] Even for Ismā'īl, who believed that submission to divine sovereignty flattened all worldly distinctions and privileges, there were some taboos that even God's sovereign power could not undo.

Sovereignty and the Imperative of Ontotheology

In theorizing the overlapping of theological and political imaginaries in Ismā'īl's thought, it is helpful to return to Carl Schmitt's proposition that the sovereign is he who has the ability to enact the state of exception, the capacity to suspend the application of the normal rule in the domain of law. As I have argued, central to Ismā'īl's theory of intercession was a complete repudiation of all nondivine forms of authority in the realm of salvation; protecting the absoluteness of God's sovereignty necessitated that the authority of all saints and prophets must be severely restricted. In other words, only God can break all the rules he made himself, or, in Schmittian terms, has the power to enforce the state of exception, to suspend the rule by granting the miraculous exception of a pardon to a habitual criminal.

But an important question that emerges here is: What kind of a subject was articulated and imagined in Ismā'īl's discourse? More specifically, in what ways was Ismā'īl's theology of divine transcendence connected to a desire for the constitution of a sovereign subject in the public sphere? How did his argument for the absolute alterity of divine sovereignty also construct a particular conception of popular sovereignty? Critical to addressing these questions is the larger question of what we mean by the category of transcendence. Here I want to return to the work of Arvind Mandair, and specifically to his brilliant reading of Martin Heidegger's meditation on transcendence. Mandair observed that for

Heidegger, as reflected in his *Metaphysical Foundations of Logic*, "transcendence," with its signification of passing beyond limits, could be understood in two different ways: (1) in contradistinction to immanence and (2) in contradistinction to contingency.[20] In the first modality, which Heidegger called "epistemological transcendence," the transcendent is "that which does not remain within but is without, what lies outside the soul and consciousness . . . what is outside the borders and encompassing wall of consciousness."[21]

In this conception of transcendence, the key relation is that between the interior and the exterior, with the immanent being the interior, what remains within the soul/subject, and the transcendent being what lies outside the soul and consciousness. On the other hand, when set in opposition to contingency, transcendence is a theological concept. It refers to that which is beyond all that pertains to us, all that touches us; it is "stepping-over" in the sense of "lying beyond all conditioned beings . . . as the entirely unattainable."[22] "Being beyond in this case expresses the infinite difference between the creator and the created."[23] Heidegger further argued that in almost all forms of theological metaphysics these two conceptions of epistemological and theological transcendence are conjoined so that "the problem of the existence of the external world is implicated in the problem of the knowledge of God and the possibility of proving God's existence."[24] This kind of a framework, in which a subject's possibility of knowing the external world is bound up with his or her knowledge of a transcendent divine, is what Heidegger called "ontotheology." To break it down, ontotheology brings together being (*onto*), God (*theos*), and knowledge/reason (*logos*).

The critical point to remember is that an ontotheological argument for transcendence constructs a figure of a divine sovereign that reproduces itself in the figure of a sovereign subject. Divine sovereignty and popular sovereignty are mutually constructed, each reinforcing the other. A similar ontotheological apparatus sustained Ismā'īl's discourse on intercession. His argument for the exceptionality of divine sovereignty was as much about the constitution of a sovereign subject in the public sphere as it was about God. The divine and Indian Muslim identity were not independent but mutually co-figured in the discursive space of Ismā'īl's statements on divine sovereignty.

In *Taqwīyat al-Īmān*, Ismā'īl propounded a political theology that cognitively bound the performance of an Indian Muslim identity in the public sphere with the demand for that identity to affirm the transcendence of an immutable sovereign God. From within this ontotheological framework, the relationship of a subject to him- or herself and to others pivoted on fidelity to the sovereignty of the divine. Each individual in a community shared a collective responsibility to affirm divine sovereignty.[25] The affirmation of divine sovereignty was the basis of solidarity in a community. All members of a community were allied in their shared allegiance to the divine sovereign. However, that solidarity was maintained at the price of constant anxiety over transgressing the limits of divine sovereignty. Every thought, practice, and rhythm of everyday life required constant regulation so that all potential rivals to the sovereign divine would be denied any access to the domain of sovereignty.

In such an environment of heightened vigilance and anxiety, ontology (being) was always bound to theology. The limits of life and the limits of identity were inextricably tied to the figure of a divine sovereign. According to this logic of identity, all forms of thought and practice that might threaten or undermine the cultivation of such a subject had to be eliminated. Ismā'īl's litany of transgressions that in his view opposed divine sovereignty was animated precisely by this ontotheological logic. In his view, these transgressions undermined a divine-human relationship in which all moments of human life were dedicated to the duty of affirming the absoluteness of divine sovereignty.

Moreover, in Ismā'īl's theological imaginary, the sovereignty of the self was secured through the promise of immediate access to the sovereign divine. A subject was empowered with freedom through the act of handing over all power to God. There was no need for any intermediaries such as prophets and saints to mediate between God and his human subjects. God was immanently available to his subjects to hear and answer their requests and supplications. In effect, God's absolute sovereignty relieved the individual subject, and in turn, the collective public, of any dependence on nondivine sources of authority. Individual and collective salvation depended solely on allegiance to the sovereign divine. But, and this is the critical point, that salvation was conditional.

It was available only to someone who consciously and actively shunned all potential competitors to divine sovereignty. Anyone who through his actions or convictions bolstered the authority of rivals to the sovereign divine was denied the gift of salvation. Such a person who undermined the absolute alterity of divine sovereignty was guilty of committing theological treason. Maintaining the integrity of divine sovereignty required absolute allegiance to the sovereign divine during all moments of a community's life. For divine sovereignty to have any coherence, it had to be absolute. This way of imagining divine sovereignty bears a striking resemblance to how the modern state authorizes its sovereignty over its citizens.

Much as the modern state demands from its citizen absolute allegiance to its sovereignty, in Ismāʿīl's political theology, God's sovereignty could be secured only if it were absolute and unassailable by any threat of competition. And just as challenging the state's sovereignty results in the loss of citizenship and makes one vulnerable to the charge of treason, for Ismāʿīl, challenging divine sovereignty made one an outsider to the faith. In other words, the limits of Indian Muslim identity, individually and collectively, were ontologically engraved in a theology of divine transcendence. But this ontotheological arrangement was marked by a profound contradiction.

On the one hand, Ismāʿīl articulated a theology of radical democracy. According to this theology, a community, in handing all power to God, kept that power away from all human and nondivine entities. In return for its fidelity to the exclusive sovereignty of God, the community was gifted with God's absolute proximity. But to achieve God's absolute proximity, a subject had to affirm God's absolute otherness. God was at once both within and outside the community. He was within the community as its most accessible member. However, he was also outside it as the sole sovereign who at any moment could enact the exception and alter all existing rules. The moment of enacting the exception required God to step outside the bounds of the community to suspend the rules and laws that he had put in place. In effect, in relation to his subjects, God was at once absolutely proximate and absolutely distant. He was radically immanent, yet radically transcendent. God was everywhere, and yet he was nowhere. No notion of sovereignty, whether associated with the religious divine (God) or with the secular divine (the state), can escape this irresolvable contradiction. Ismāʿīl's political theology was also entangled in the contradictory logic of securing divine sovereignty by conjuring up a public that was obligated to unceasingly affirm and guard that sovereignty.[26] This was an impossible task.

Ismāʿīl's controversial views on prophetic intercession and his stinging critique of monarchical authority in late Mughal India did not go unchallenged. Indeed, perhaps no other nineteenth-century Indian Muslim thinker has been more attacked for his ideas. As mentioned earlier, his religious career and discourses have continued to influence intra-Sunnī polemics in South Asia and in immigrant South Asian Muslim communities in such places as Britain, South Africa, and the United States for several decades. However, in his own lifetime Ismāʿīl's most formidable and unsparing intellectual opponent was the famous Delhi philosopher, poet, and logician Fazl-i Ḥaqq Khayrābādī. It is to the latter's devastating refutation of Ismāʿīl's discourses on divine sovereignty, composed in a Persian text entitled *The Definitive Opinion on the Falsity of Unbelief* (*Taḥqīq al-Fatwā fī Ibṭāl al-Tughwā*), that I now turn.

Fazl-i Ḥaqq Khayrābādī and the Politics of Prophetic Love

The publication of *Taqwīyat al-Īmān*, coupled with Ismāʿīl's ongoing reformist activities in Delhi, precipitated a flurry of debates and arguments among the scholarly elite of the city. The book, especially its more controversial passages, was intensely debated and dissected. In fact, so divisive was the climate at this time that even Ismāʿīl's own first cousin, Muḥammad Mūsā Dihlavī (d. 1864), squared off against him in a famous public debate in 1826.[27] As Ismāʿīl's sermons at the Jāmiʿ mosque began to draw more and more people, a countermovement to silence his ideas also gathered steam. This movement was spearheaded by the influential Delhi scholar and aristocrat Fazl-i Ḥaqq Khayrābādī.

Khayrābādī, twenty years younger than Ismāʿīl, is an extremely important figure in the history of South Asian Islam whose thought has received far too little attention from Western scholars. A native of the town of Khayrābād in northern India, Khayrābādī is most vividly remembered today for his political activities against the British, for which he was charged with treason and exiled from India to the Andaman Islands, in what is today the country of Myanmar. He died there in 1861 after spending close to two years in prison. During his imprisonment, Khayrābādī wrote his memoir in exquisite Arabic, much of it in rhyming prose, later titled *The Indian Rebellion* (*Al-Thawra al-Hindīya*). This book contains fascinating insights into not only Khayrābādī's career but also the broader Indian political milieu of this decisive era.[28] The first words with which Khayrābādī launched this text poignantly reveal his melancholic resignation, in the final days of a life of imprisonment and defeat under the unforgiving yoke of colonial power. "This book of mine," he wrote, "is a book written by a lost heartbroken prisoner, wistful for what has left him, suffering from every harrowing pain, incapacitated to bear one bit more tribulation, longingly expectant of some relief from his Lord" (*Fa-inna kitābī hādhā kitāb asīr kasīr khasīr, 'alā mā fāta min-hu ḥasīr, mubtalā bi-kull 'asīr lā yuṭāq wa law fī an yasīr, muntaẓir li-faraj 'alā rabbihi yasīr*).[29]

Intellectually, Khayrābādī is most well known for his writings on Islamic philosophy and on logic, and for his massive output of Arabic poetry. He is said to have penned close to four thousand Arabic poems. Khayrābādī also boasted a diverse and widespread network of students not only from all over India but also from Central Asia, Iran, and the Arab Middle East. The scholarly hub of the Khayrābādī school of thought was centered in North India, especially the towns of Khayrābād, Badāyūn, Rāmpūr, and Sāharanpūr. A distinctive feature of the Khayrābādī intellectual temperament, shaped most decisively by Fazl-i Ḥaqq and his luminary father and teacher Fazl-i Imām Khayrābādī (d. 1829), was its focus on nonrevealed rationalist disciplines such as logic and philosophy. The elder Khayrābādī, who had also established a leading seminary in Delhi, was the author (among other important texts) of the popular textbook in logic *The Ladder* (*Mirqāt*). Similarly, Fazl-i Ḥaqq composed the widely read text of logic *The Gift of Contentment* (*Al-Hadīya al-Sa'dīya*), among other prominent texts and commentaries on the works of his father and other major exponents of the rationalist disciplines.[30]

The Khayrābādian intellectual legacy was carried forward by Fazl-i Ḥaqq's students, most notably his prolific son 'Abdul Ḥaqq Khayrābādī

(d. 1899) and the son of his bosom friend and intellectual companion Fazl-i Rasūl Badāyūnī (d. 1872), 'Abdul Qādir Badāyūnī (d. 1901). The Khayrābādīs were well aware of their indubitable scholarly stature in South Asia and beyond, and hardly shy of embracing it. For instance, once a certain Maulvī Ikrāmullah Shahābī asked 'Abdul Ḥaqq Khayrābādī: "Brother, how many scholars in human history can be counted as among the sages [*ḥakīm*]?" 'Abdul Ḥaqq confidently replied, "There are three and a half sages in the world: first the original teacher Aristotle, next the second master [the famous tenth-century Muslim philosopher] al-Farābī (d. 951), third my father Fazl-i Ḥaqq Khayrābādī, and the remaining half yours truly."[31] 'Abdul Ḥaqq's triumphant claim is certainly debatable. But it is difficult to not appreciate the impact of the Khayrābādī clan's scholarly output, especially Fazl-i Ḥaqq Khayrābādī's (henceforth the intended referent to Khayrābādī). Indeed, a measure of his prominence in the intellectual history of South Asian Islam can be discerned from the fact that even in biographical dictionaries less partisan to his thought, such as 'Abd al-Ḥayy al-Ḥasanī's (d. 1922) well-known *Nuzhat al-Khawāṭir*, he is described as "the foremost scholar of Arabic, philosophy, and logic of his era."[32]

The Triad of Āzūrda, Khayrābādī, and Badāyūnī

Other than his students and family members, two other scholars intimately connected to Khayrābādī and to the Khayrābādī school of thought were Muftī Ṣadruddīn Āzurda (d. 1868) and Fazl-i Rasūl Badāyūnī. Khayrābādī and Badāyūnī were only a year apart and were about a decade younger than Āzurda. The three men held much in common. They shared a passion for poetry and the rationalist disciplines, were at some point employed by the British, eagerly participated in the 1857 rebellion, and had a common teacher in Fazl-i Imām Khayrābādī.[33] In addition, Badāyūnī shared with Fazl-i Ḥaqq Khayrābādī an intense antipathy toward Ismā'īl. While the industry of anti-Ismā'īl polemics and rebuttals boasted many names, Badāyūnī and Khayrābādī were perhaps its foremost producers. A practicing physician as well as a scholar, Badāyūnī showed such polemical prowess that it earned him the title "God's Slithering

Sword" (*sayf Allāh al-maslūl*), a title also often attached to the Prophet's cousin and son-in-law 'Alī ibn Abī Ṭālib.[34] Badāyūnī authored some of the most devastating rebuttals against Ismā'īl, including *Muḥammadan Thunders for Decimating the Satans of Najd* (*Al-Bawāriq al-Muḥammadīya li-Rajm al-Shayāṭin al-Najdīya*), *A Conclusive Victory for the Intercession of the Intercessors* (*Al-Fawz al-Mubīn bi Shafā'at al-Shāfi'īn*), *The Colossal Slithering Sword against the Enemies of the Pious Authorities* (*Sayf al-Jabbār al-Maslūl 'alā a'dā' al-Abrār*), *Confirming Truth and Falsifying Falsehood* (*Iḥqāq al-Ḥaqq wa Ibṭāl al-Bāṭil*), and *The Decisive Refutation* (*Al-Mu'taqad al-Muntaqad*);[35] all were composed in Persian except the last, which was in Arabic.[36]

These texts, like the work of Khayrābādī that is analyzed in this chapter, took up themes such as prophetic intercession, the finality of the Prophet, and the Prophet's knowledge of the unknown. Indeed, their lines of attack frequently intersected, and Badāyūnī often drew on and cited Khayrābādī's texts. I will not have the opportunity to conduct a detailed examination of Badāyūnī's scholarly corpus. But given his importance to the early nineteenth-century intellectual landscape, I here summarize five major discursive goals and strategies that run through his polemical work. These are (1) framing Ismā'īl and Muḥammad ibn 'Abd al-Wahhāb as part of a common transnational conspiracy against traditionalist Sunnī Ḥanafī normativity, (2) establishing anti-Ismā'īl South Asian scholars like Badāyūnī himself and Khayrābādī as intimate colleagues and collaborators with the Ottoman Ḥanafī scholars in Arabia, (3) dissociating Ismā'īl from the intellectual lineage of the Walī Ullah family by presenting his reform agenda as contrary to the thought of Walī Ullah and his sons, (4) liberally mobilizing proof texts from the Qur'ān and the Ḥadīth as a way to dispel the notion that the Badāyūnī/Khayrābādī school of thought was too reliant on arcane rationalist sources and arguments, and (5) casting Ismā'īl as a modern Mu'tazilī opposed to avenues of prophetic exaltation such as intercession.[37] These moves and strategies, especially the first three, were repeated abundantly by Aḥmad Razā Khān in the late nineteenth-century context, as I will discuss in some detail in chapters 9, 10, and 11. Thus, in the arena of polemical warfare, Khān was in many ways an intellectual heir to Badāyūnī. It is consequently of no surprise that Khān also composed an important commentary on what was arguably Badāyūnī's most significant polemical text, *The Decisive Refutation* (*Al-Mu'taqad al-Muntaqad*),[38] entitled *An Authoritative and Corroborated Foundation for Eternal Salvation* (*Al-Mu'tamad al-Mustanad Binā' Nijāt al-Abad*).

In slight contrast to Badāyūnī's incontrovertible polemical credentials and massive output, the record on Āzurda's attitude toward Ismā'īl is much more ambiguous. For instance, while Āzurda was among the signatories to Khayrābādī's legal opinion declaring Ismā'īl an unbeliever, he nonetheless wrote in Ismā'īl's favor on the sensitive issue of God's capacity to create a second Muḥammad.[39] And apparently, Khayrābādī's animosity toward Ismā'īl is said to have greatly perturbed Āzurda, prompting him to often criticize and disagree with his close friend's handling of the issue. But Āzurda could also be quite critical of Ismā'īl's harsh rhetoric, even while agreeing with him on certain contentious questions, suggesting that Āzūrda was ultimately interested in reducing the polemical heat emanating from Delhi.

Patrolling the Boundaries of Thinkability: The Khayrābādian Response

Returning to Khayrābādī, in the context of this chapter, an important element of his biography relates to his economic background as an affluent aristocrat in nineteenth-century Delhi. Khayrābādī hailed from a family with deep ties and affinities to the Mughal nobility in India. In fact, just like his father, Fazl-i Imām Khayrābādī, he actively served as a high-ranking official in the Mughal court. Moreover, even after the fall of the Mughal Empire, Khayrābādī continued to work as an influential bureaucrat in the British Empire, until he was eventually charged with treason and deported from India by the British. In fact, Khayrābādī was so highly regarded among colonial administrators that on his request the British resident officer in Delhi banned Shāh Muḥammad Ismā'īl from delivering sermons at the Jāmi' mosque. Khayrābādī's request was granted after he argued that Ismā'īl's sermons posed an imminent threat to communal peace and harmony in Delhi. This ban lasted forty days. The historiography is murky on the question of how Khayrābādī's previously close relations with the British so rapidly deteriorated that he was declared an enemy of the state and imprisoned in exile until death. His allegedly central role in orchestrating the Indian Mutiny of 1857 seems to have been a major catalyst in this reversal of relations.[40]

Khayrābādī's aristocratic background is well documented in the biographical literature connected to his life. For example, as a young boy, when Khayrābādī used to go for his Ḥadīth classes at the house of Shāh 'Abdul 'Azīz, his later nemesis Ismā'īl's uncle, he would always travel on an elephant, escorted by a servant especially designated for this task. This servant was responsible for protecting young Khayrābādī from the sun by holding an umbrella over his head. His opponents would later invoke Khayrābādī's elite background to delegitimize his pietistic credentials. For example, in *Nuzhat al-Khawāṭir*, he is said to have "displayed the comportment of monarchs, not of religious scholars" (*Kāna zayyuhu zayy al-umarā' dūn al-'ulamā'*).[41] Shāh Muḥammad Ismā'īl and Fazl-i Ḥaqq Khayrābādī lived in the same urban intellectual milieu of early nineteenth-century Delhi. In fact, as just mentioned, Ismā'īl's illustrious uncle Shāh 'Abdul 'Azīz and his younger uncle Shāh 'Abdul Qādir (whom we met in chapter 2) were Khayrābādī's primary Ḥadīth teachers.

However, despite the overlap in the networks of scholarship that these thinkers belonged to, their social imaginaries were sharply opposed. Khayrābādī found Ismā'īl's theological program at once coarse and subversive. In his view, under the pretense of defending divine sovereignty, Ismā'īl was inventing a new tradition that demeaned the Prophet. What Khayrābādī found most threatening about Ismā'īl's agenda of reform was the way it opened the possibility of imagining a moral order that disregarded previously unassailable ranks, distinctions, and privileges. For Khayrābādī, if the masses were lured into imagining a world that disrespected hierarchies or that refused to situate the Prophet at its cosmic center, the very foundations of tradition would crumble.

At the heart of the controversy generated by Ismā'īl was the way he challenged the horizons of thinkability. Once it became thinkable that God might well create a million new Muḥammads or that he might contravene his own promise, the logic of tradition was bound to unravel. For instance, consider the fascinating diagnosis of Khayrābādī's contemporary hagiographer Asīd al-Ḥaqq Badāyūnī (not to be confused with Khayrābādī's contemporary Fazl-i Rasūl Badāyūnī) that Ismā'īl's slanderously nonchalant attitude toward prophets, saints, and other pious figures paved the way for the later "[Aḥmadī] rejection of the Prophet's finality" (*inkār-i khatm-i nubūwwat kī rāh hamwār hu'ī*).[42] Thus, to Badāyūnī and many of Khayrābādī's other followers, Ismā'īl was a proto-Aḥmadī, someone who generated the conditions that made a claimant to prophecy like Mirzā Ghulām Aḥmad (d. 1908) possible.[43] For Khayrābādī himself, Ismā'īl's cardinal sin was his assumption that prophetic charisma and divine sovereignty were separable. In Khayrābādī's view, the figure of the Prophet and that of God were part of a common cosmological program. Therefore, any attempt to uncouple the Prophet from the political economy of salvation could only invite chaos.

The textual time line and sequence of Khayrābādī's discursive skirmish with Ismā'īl went as follows. After the publication of *Taqwīyat al-Īmān* in 1825, Khayrābādī published a very brief rebuttal in Persian titled "Treatise of Objections against *Taqwīyat al-Īmān*" (*Taqrīr-i i'tirāzāt bar Taqwīyat al-Īmān*). This text of only a few pages focused on the issue of God's capacity to produce a second Muḥammad, refuting Ismā'īl's claim that "God may well create a million new Muḥammads." In response, Ismā'īl composed *Yak Roza* (One day), which I discussed a bit earlier in chapter three. Following that, Khayrābādī authored a detailed refutation of both *Taqwīyat al-Īmān* and *Yak Roza*, again in Persian, titled *The Definitive Opinion on the Falsity of Unbelief* (*Taḥqīq al-Fatwā fī Ibṭāl al-Tughwā*), a close reading of which informs the bulk of my analysis in what follows.[44] All this happened in the turbulent year of 1825, only a few months before Ismā'īl's military campaign against the Sikhs that ended his life, thus effecting an involuntarily compelled cease-fire to this short but intense dispute. Khayrābādī registered the intensity of his contempt and displeasure toward Ismā'īl and his theology from the very beginning of *The Definitive Opinion*:

> His [Ismā'īl's] extravagant and superfluous words are all pervaded by the most insidious lies and the most warped idiosyncrasies. His entire discourse bears no hint of having encountered truth and honesty [*Īn kalām-i lā ṭā'il az akāzīb-i aqāwīl wa a'ājīb-i abāṭīl hargiz az rāstī masāsay wa bi ṣidq iltibāsay na dārad*]. While describing the types of intercession, he has committed numerous abominations. In direct contradiction to the

consensus of both modern and premodern luminaries of the tradition, he has undermined the exalted status of the most noble of all nobility, the Prophet Muḥammad. In doing so, he has sold the sanctity of his faith and planted the seed of discord and misguidance in the hearts of the ignorant masses.[45]

Khayrābādī accused Ismāʿīl of insulting the Prophet, saints, and angels, and judged him as "an unbeliever who deserved to be put to death" (235). In what follows, I examine how Khayrābādī arrives at this dramatic judgment. By analyzing his refutation of Ismāʿīl's views on prophetic intercession and on God's capacity to lie or create another Muḥammad, I aim to describe a competing political theology in early nineteenth-century Indian Muslim thought.

Love as the Marker of Exception

Fazl-i Ḥaqq Khayrābādī's discourse on intercession was marked by four key elements: (1) establishing God's relationship with the Prophet as one characterized by exceptional love and proximity; (2) presenting an extremely loving, generous, and authorial Prophet who continually sought to intercede on behalf of sinful subjects to redeem them of their sins; (3) arguing for a decisively hierarchical intercession model with clear and non-negotiable boundaries between Prophets, saints, and the common folk with respect to their stature in God's court; and (4) refuting Ismāʿīl's claim in *Taqwīyat al-Īmān* that the only type of intercession operative in God's court was that of intercession by permission (*shafāʿat bi'l idhn*).

Khayrābādī's central charge against Ismāʿīl was that the latter had undermined the exceptionality of prophetic charisma. The status and privilege that God had conferred on the Prophet, Khayrābādī contended, was radically exceptional. No other entity was as privileged as the Prophet (*Ṣubḥānahu ān janāb rā beh fazl wa karāmat ikhtiṣāṣ bakhshīd kasay dīgar rā az khalq*) (283). More crucially, the exceptionality of the Prophet's status was affirmed by his unrivaled capacity for intercession. The Prophet's capacity to intercede on behalf of sinners distinguished him from all other beings and authorized his status as the most exceptional of all beings. Intercession was the mechanism of establishing the Prophet's exceptionality. It was the exception that made the Prophet exceptional.

Khayrābādī further argued that intercession was the primary discursive site that ensured the continuity of prophetic charisma in the afterworld. In other words, the esteem attached to the office of prophecy in the temporal world was carried forward in the afterworld through the gift of intercession. In assembling this argument, Khayrābādī cited the prominent thirteenth-century Qur'ān exegete 'Abdallāh Ibn 'Umar al-Bayḍāwī (d. 1286), who said that "esteem in this world is prophecy, and esteem in the afterworld is intercession" (*Al-wajāha fi-l-dunyā al-nubūwwa wa fi-l-ākhira al-shafā'a*).[46]

In fact, Khayrābādī continued, the Prophet's status in the afterworld would be even higher than it was in the temporal world. On the Day of Judgment, he would be rewarded for his exemplary conduct and obedience to God with the capacity to intercede for his community. Intercession was the reward and gift for prophetic experience; it both rewarded and confirmed the sanctity of prophecy. In other words, for Khayrābādī, the gift of intercession was intrinsically bound up with the institution of prophecy. Intercession enabled the perpetuity of prophetic charisma in the afterworld. As a corollary, any attempt to compromise the Prophet's capacity to intercede was a direct assault on the very logic of prophecy. That is why Ismā'īl's discourse on intercession was anathematic to Khayrābādī.

In addition, Khayrābādī found Ismā'īl's hyperbolic rhetoric particularly problematic. He argued that Ismā'īl's provocative statements were hardly relevant to the latter's supposed argument about the primacy of divine sovereignty. For instance, the statement about God's capacity "to create a million new Muḥammads" was an unnecessary provocation with no substantive relationship to the restoration of divine sovereignty.

"Suppose," Khayrābādī explained, "that a king is completely subservient to a minister or vizier in the workings of his kingdom. The king does whatever that minister tells him to do. Now in order to restore this king's sovereignty, it makes no sense to say that he may well make a million new ministers, or that he may turn the masses into ministers. How does that at all resolve the problem of the minister's interference in the king's governance over his kingdom?" (332). All that Ismā'īl needed to say, Khayrābādī advised, was that "there is no possibility of any interference in God's domain of sovereignty" (*Bāyastay guft keh kasay rā dar kārkhānijāt-i ilāhī mudākhalat hīchgūneh nīst*) (333). Yet instead of putting forward this simple proposition, Ismā'īl had resorted to playing rhetorical games that did nothing to advance his argument and that insulted the Prophet in the process. This was at once a show of poor judgment and poor etiquette.

Apart from what he saw as Ismā'īl's penchant for unhelpful rhetorical flourishes, Khayrābādī repudiated him for ignoring the significance of love to the conceptual architecture of God's relationship with the Prophet. The centerpiece of Khayrābādī's theology was an intense lover-beloved relationship between God and the Prophet. Satisfying the demands of one's beloved, he argued, was an essential requirement for a relationship based on love to succeed and thrive. Therefore, just as a true lover would never do or say anything that would hurt, disappoint, or disrespect his beloved, God also took great care in ensuring the satisfaction of his most beloved subject, the Prophet.

Moreover, for a relationship of love to survive, it was necessary for the lover to accept his beloved's petitions advanced on someone else's behalf. Therefore, in sharp contrast to Ismā'īl, Khayrābādī unreservedly permitted the operation of intercession based on high esteem (*wajāhat*) and love (*muḥabbat*) in God's court. Since God had declared the Prophet as his most beloved subject, he would always follow through on the latter's petitions on behalf of sinful people. In emphasizing the intense proximity that marked God's relationship to those he loved, Khayrābādī quoted the famous Ḥadīth Qudsī "When I make a beloved of someone, I become the ears through which he hears, the eyes through which he sees, the feet with which he walks, and the tongue with which he speaks."[47] What is remarkable about this text is the way it emphasizes the embodied force of love. God's love for his beloved is not simply a cognitive state; rather, that love colonizes the senses, infusing every faculty of the beloved's being. Thus, for Khayrābādī, the Ḥadīth Qudsī not only established beyond doubt the extremely elevated status of God's beloveds but also amplified his broader argument about the embodied intimacy and inseparability of divine and prophetic ontologies. Moreover, Khayrābādī emphasized that the politics of love in God's court was neither democratic nor egalitarian (*Ṣubḥānahu āfrīdagān-i khud rā bimarātib-i mutafāwata wa madārij-i mutabā'ada āfrīda*) (268). Instead, the framework of his dispensation of love and standing to all entities was unabashedly and meticulously hierarchical; each of God's beloveds had a distinct and clearly marked position and status (*Har yakay az muqarrabān-i bārgāh-i khud 'alā qadar-i tafāwut-i darajātihim wa 'alā ḥasb-i marātibihim manzilatay wa makānatay bakhshīda*) (268). The efficacy of someone's intercession depended on the rank and position he held in God's court. To be more accurate, the capacity to intercede demonstrated God's love for the intercessor.

Love, Power, Distinction

In Khayrābādī's imaginary, love was inseparable from power. Love authorized distinction. Love determined the hierarchy of salvific authority. Intercession in turn was the gift of love, a gift that signaled the rank of an entity in relation to others. Therefore, the supplications and petitions of prophets and pious saints were more likely to be answered than those of common folk and sinful people. Khayrābādī authorized this hierarchical arrangement of salvific power by citing the Qur'ānic verse "Those apostles we endowed with gifts, some above others: to one of them God spoke; others he raised to degrees [of honor]."[48]

Khayrābādī agreed with Ismā'īl that the sovereignty of the divine was absolute, exclusive, and unalterable. Furthermore, all beings, whether humans, angels, prophets, illiterates, kings, or slaves, were equally obligated to demonstrate their complete subordination (*bandagī*) to God. There was no disagreement on that foundational covenant. However, Khayrābādī was equally emphatic in pointing out that there was no contradiction between the absoluteness of divine sovereignty and the carefully calibrated hierarchy according to which God had ordered his creation. Each entity in God's court had been assigned a specified status (*manṣab*) and degree of exaltedness.

He explained that while some entities were given proximity and honor, others were shunned as rejected, lost, or misguided. The degree of esteem and authority accorded entities in God's court corresponded with their stature. A beloved of the divine could never occupy the same stature as a rejected one, and so on. Concomitantly, the effectiveness of the petition of intercessors on behalf of sinners also corresponded with their stature and with the intensity of God's love for them. Put differently, an intercessor's capacity to intercede depended on his or her position in the bureaucracy of divine love. Moreover, and this was the most important point, God's acceptance of intercession affirmed that position (263–65).

Forgiving a sinner for crimes was only an apparent function of intercession. More crucially, the practice of intercession reinforced the distinguished status occupied by God's beloveds. As Khayrābādī put it, "The acceptance of an intercession is among the effects of love [*āsār-i muḥabbat*]" (334). And in support of his point he quoted the couplet: "Someone asked a lover: Which is better? Union with the beloved or separation? / The lover replied: whatever pleases the beloved" (*Bi gufta waṣal bah ya hajar az dūst / Bi gufta har cheh mayl-i khāṭir-i ūst*) (288).

In the divine politics of love, no entity, Khayrābādī claimed, occupied a more noble, exalted, and authorial status than the Prophet Muḥammad. As he wrote, "On the Day of Judgment, no one will be allowed to speak [intercede] in God's court except prophets" (275). In contrast to Ismā'īl, who found the attachment of extraordinary intercessory capacities to the Prophet a threat to divine sovereignty, for Khayrābādī divine sovereignty and prophetic exceptionality were mutually constitutive.[49]

In fact, Khayrābādī declared that demonstrating one's love for the Prophet was a necessary condition for having faith. "A faithful Muslim," as he put it, citing a well-known Ḥadīth, "must consider the Prophet more beloved than his own self, father, son, and the rest of humanity" (400). Moreover, for Khayrābādī, there was no tension between divine and prophetic authority. It was precisely by affirming the cosmic qualities of the Prophet that a subject enacted subordination to the divine. This view, Khayrābādī argued, was clearly stated in the Qur'ān when God said to the Prophet, "Verily, those who pledge their allegiance to you pledge their allegiance to me. The hand of God is over their hands."[50] Khayrābādī also cited a number of Ḥadīth that for him incontrovertibly demonstrated the Prophet's exalted status: for example, "When angels roam around the world, they most frequently visit houses where people called Muḥammad live. This gesture is meant as a show of reverence for Muḥammad's majestic authority" (295) and "On the Day of Judgment, the Prophet will be occupied with nothing other than interceding on behalf of his people. While all the other prophets will worry for their own fate and cry 'Myself, myself' [*Nafsī, nafsī*], the Prophet will cry only, 'My community, my community' [*Ummatī, ummatī*]" (322).

Perhaps most illustrative of how Khayrābādī imagined the interaction of divine and prophetic authority was his narration of the following prophetic report:

> On the Day of Judgment, while all the other prophets will be seated at their respective pulpits [*manābir*], I will be standing at the most elevated part of God's court. God will ask me, "Oh my beloved, what do you want me to do with your community [*Mā turīd an aṣna' bi-ummatik*]?" I will reply, "Oh God, account for them quickly." Then they [the Muslim community] will be brought in and accounted for. Some of them will go to heaven because of God's mercy and some of them because of my intercession. (327–28)

Also notice the comprehensiveness of the Prophet's care for his community's salvation as communicated in this report: "On the Day of Judgment I will tirelessly intercede on behalf of my community, even for those who were otherwise destined to go to hell, to the degree that the doorman of hell will say to me, you did not allow anyone in your community to taste the wrath of God's anger" (328).

To sum up, the two main arguments that undergirded Khayrābādī's discussion on intercession were: (1) God always accepts Muḥammad's petitions on behalf of sinners because of the latter's status as the most beloved and exalted member of his court, and (2) the Prophet will work incessantly on the Day of Judgment to ensure that whoever seeks his intercession is granted forgiveness and a place in heaven.

Distinguishing a Petition from a Command

Khayrābādī's model of intercession raises an obvious question: If God always heeds the petitions of his beloved (the Prophet), then what are we to make of God's own sovereignty in managing the affairs of his court?

In other words, if God never rejects the petitions advanced by the Prophet, then what is the nature of God's own legislative authority? Khayrābādī addressed these potential doubts by drawing on and emphasizing the distinction between a petition (*sifārish*) and a command (*taḥakkum*). "Every thinking person and imbecile knows that a petition and a command are two different things: there is no compulsion in [the acceptance of] a petition" (*Har āqil wa nādān mī dānad keh sifārish dīgar ast wa taḥakkum dīgar. Dar sifārish taḥakkum na mī bāshad*) (264), Khayrābādī explained, with a tinge of disdain for the fact that he had been pulled into making such an obvious point. God's acceptance of a petition does not imply that an agent other than him possesses any authority over his kingdom. God responds favorably to the petitions of those close and beloved to him to reinforce their esteemed status in his court. However, the decision to accept or reject a petition remains strictly his personal prerogative. In short, God accepts his beloveds' petitions not under compulsion or duress but out of love (263–70).

Here Khayrābādī trod a slippery slope while negotiating the interplay of divine and prophetic authority. On the one hand, God is the ultimate sovereign over his kingdom who does not take orders from anyone. On the other hand, the Prophet enjoys such an elevated and authorial status in God's court that his petitions are never rejected. Does this risk the confusion of divine and prophetic authority? In Khayrābādī's view, no, it does not. The key variable that allowed him to separate these two modalities of authority was that of causation. God accepts a petition not out of any fear or duress but out of his love for the petitioner.

Khayrābādī further reasoned that if it were duress that caused God to accept petitions, then he could not be said to have any sovereignty over his kingdom to begin with. In that situation, God would be akin to a powerless monarch who was only a ruler in appearance. In reality, it would be his ministers who effectively controlled all the workings of his kingdom. Such a politically castrated monarch would acquiesce to whatever his associates told him to do. He would be fearful that not obliging their demands would result in his losing his already tenuous grip on power. Since such a king would effectively be subservient to his ministers, his acceptance of a petition would represent a form of obedience and reverence, not intercession (*Farmānbardārī wa iṭā'at ast na qubūl-i shafāʿat*) (264). This kind of a situation, Khayrābādī argued, could never exist in God's court.

Khayrābādī chastised Ismāʿīl precisely for not taking into account this crucial distinction between a request and a command. A request for intercession and outright coercion are two completely separate things, he explained. It is not fear but the desire to honor and affirm the exalted status of a beloved that drives a sovereign's decision to accept an intercessor's request. What Ismāʿīl failed to understand, Khayrābādī argued, is that love can serve as the exclusive cause for the acceptance of intercession, independent of any coercion or duress. Khayrābādī was particularly critical of Ismāʿīl for undermining the liberating capacity of prophetic munificence and for spreading among the masses the poison of hopelessness. As he wrote, rather poignantly, "This man [Ismāʿīl] has equated hope in prophetic mercy with sinfulness. He has turned those who hope for the Prophet's intercession into disobedient sinners. But in fact, it is he who is wrong and who has wronged himself. . . . Whoever has no hope in intercession, may he stay hopeless!" (*Īn qāʾil umīdwārī rā beh farāmoshkārī nāmīda, bā gunāhgārān-i bay-ṭāʿat umīdwārān-i shafāʿat rā bi ghalaṭkārī nisbat kardeh, khud dar ghalaṭ wa taghliṭ uftādeh. . . . Har keh az shafāʿat nawmīd [nā-umīd] bāshad nawmīd mānad*) (330).

Khayrābādī also took Ismāʿīl to task for completely misrepresenting the concept of intercession by permission. Remember, Ismāʿīl had described intercession by permission as the situation in which the king, prior to receiving a request for intercession, had already decided to pardon the criminal. Intercession only served to reinforce this original inclination; it did not cause the king's decision. Khayrābādī took serious exception to this logic. He argued that for intercession to not be useless and superfluous, it had to be the immediate cause for a criminal's exoneration (335). According to Khayrābādī, Ismāʿīl's contention that intercession by permission worked only if the king had already decided to pardon a criminal rendered the very idea of intercession meaningless (*Dar īn ṣūrat shafāʿat laghw wa baykār ast*). Of what good was intercession, he protested, if the king had already shown his mercy on a sinner prior to receiving a petition for intercession? As he summarized his point, "Intercession is valid only when it is effective" (335). Khayrābādī summed up his assessment of Ismāʿīl's scholarly credentials with a less than flattering review: "Either the author is an ignorant fool who is posing as a scholar and does not understand the meaning of intercession, or he is a scholar exhibiting vast ignorance by inverting the very meaning of an intercessory petition" (*Qā'il yā jāhil muta'ālim ast keh ma'nā-yi sifārish dar fahm-i ū na mī āyad yā 'ālim-i mutajāhil ast keh ma'nā-yi sifārish wāzh gūneh mī namāyad*) (330).

In Schmittian terms, Khayrābādī was a custodian of a monarchical social imaginary par excellence. Not only was he a believer in the state of exception—the miracle of intercession—but he stipulated it as a necessary condition for a commoner to have any chance of absolving his sins in God's court. Khayrābādī explicitly declared that no one would be able to attain repentance on the Day of Judgment without seeking Muḥammad's intercession. Particularly instructive in this context is how Khayrābādī's subjectivity and position in society were revealed in the way he articulated his argument for the extent of prophetic authority. Again, the language of his argument is as critical to my concerns as the argument itself.

The symbolism of Mughal bureaucracy permeated Khayrābādī's discourse on intercession. For example, while describing the scene on the Day of Judgment, Khayrābādī sketched a vivid image of the Prophet sifting through the files (*dafātir*) of sinners who had requested his intercession. The Prophet went through all the files himself and granted each of his plaintiffs an executive pardon, and in effect a place in heaven. Indeed, Khayrābādī's conception of the Prophet as the most exalted officer in God's court was intimately connected to a larger project of safeguarding a political ethos founded on hierarchies and distinctions.

Scandalous Provocations: Let the Impossible Remain Impossible

To complete my analysis of Khayrābādī's refutation, let me turn to and briefly highlight key aspects of his rebuttal of Ismā'īl's twin claims regarding God's capacity to lie (*imkān-i kizb*) and to produce a second Muḥammad (*imkān-i naẓīr*). Remember, Ismā'īl's position in this context, as I detailed in chapter three, was that while these occurrences would never happen, and were hence indirectly impossible (*mumtana' bi'l ghayr*), they were not essentially impossible (*mumtana' bi'l dhāt*). God did not lie and would never create another Muḥammad, but he might well do so if he so wished; potentiality would never pass into actuality. Khayrābādī, in contrast, found this position at once logically and normatively untenable while also morally repugnant and incendiary. For Khayrābādī, God's lying or creating another Muḥammad was essentially impossible. The possibility of another Muḥammad would mean the possibility of another Prophet, thus necessitating the falsification of the conclusive text of the Qur'ān (152–53).

This was so because the Qur'ān had explicitly and famously stated: "Muḥammad is not the father of any of your men; he is [rather] God's messenger and the seal of all Prophets."[51] Khayrābādī urged his readers and the masses to not take Ismā'īl's claims casually. He was not only claiming that another entity could share the humanity of Muḥammad; that claim would not have posed any doctrinal problems and would hardly represent a subject of debate. Rather, Khayrābādī reminded sternly, Ismā'īl was arguing for the possibility of another entity that shared with Muḥammad all of the latter's perfect attributes (*awṣāf-i kāmila*), most significantly that of the highest of all perfections: prophethood.

Khayrābādī also warned his readers to beware of Ismā'īl's cunning sleight of hand in making it seem as if he was only arguing for the potentiality and not the actuality of another Muḥammad. That Ismā'īl's intent and emphasis were on the actuality of another Muḥammad's creation, as much as he insisted otherwise, was obvious from the very language he had used to make his claims. More specifically, Khayrābādī invited readers to evaluate for themselves the semantic outcome and focus of the Urdu construction "*kar dālay*" (he may well do so) that Ismā'īl had employed while declaring in *Taqwīyat al-Īmān* that "God may well create a million new Muḥammads." This was a fascinating discursive moment in which Khayrābādī, while writing himself in Persian, interrogated the semantic features of Urdu.

Had Ismā'īl simply intended to mean the potentiality for a second Muḥammad, Khayrābādī noted, he could have used a phrase to the effect of "If so and so wanted, he could do X [*kar sakay*]" (348). The difference between "may well do so" (*kar dālay*) and "could do so" (*kar sakay*) was that while the latter referred to the capacity or potentiality of undertaking an act, the former emphasized the actual execution of an act. The phrase "may well do so" emphasizes the agency of the actor to actualize an act, not his or her capacity or potentiality to do so (*Ma'nā "kar dālnā" īlqā'-i fi'l wa bi wujūd āwardan ast nah qurdrat wa tawān bar ān*) (348). So, Khayrābādī concluded, if Ismā'īl had wanted to indicate God's capacity or potentiality to create a million Muḥammads, he would have used the verb form *kar saknā* (could do) and not *kar dālnā* (may well do) (*Tarjumah-i qudrat wa tawān dar zabān-i Urdū 'kar saknā' ast nah 'kar dālnā'* ") (348). But in Khayrābādī's view, semantic problems were only part of what was wrong with Ismā'īl's grandly misguided and dangerous propositions.

More seriously, Khayrābādī argued, Ismā'īl's strategy of mobilizing Qur'ānic verses to show God's capacity to bring into existence any animate or inanimate entities by just proclaiming "Be!" (Qur'ān 3:59; 36:81–82) was fatally flawed. The central problem with this hermeneutical move was that it was inapplicable to the figure of Muḥammad. Moreover, Ismā'īl's argument was tenable only through an egregiously decontextualized reading of such verses, Khayrābādī insisted. Take, for instance, Ismā'īl's use of the verse "Does not the One [God] who created the heavens and earth possess the capacity to create the likes of them? Of course, he does! He is the all-knowing Creator. His command is such that when he wants something, he just says: 'Be!' And it becomes."[52]

Ismā'īl's intellectual failure in citing this verse was that he did not consider its audience. The verse, Khayrābādī schooled Ismā'īl, was intended as a response to the recalcitrant unbelievers who had denied the afterworld and had rejected God's capacity to bring human bodies and bones to life on Judgment Day. They had mockingly asked, as recorded a few verses earlier, "Who could possibly give life to these decrepit bones?" (*Man yuḥyā al-'iẓām wa hīya ramīm*).[53] The verse in question responded to this provocation. If God could bring to life gigantic and supreme entities like heaven and earth, how could he not possess the capacity to bring back to life tiny and lowly human bodies, bones, and organs? That was the intended meaning and emphasis of this verse (*Pas madlūl-i īn āyat taṣḥīḥ-i qudrat bar i'ādī-yi abdān wa raf'-i istib'ād-i munkirān ast*) (364). The phrase "the likes of them," Khayrābādī stressed, referred to the fragile materiality of the human body (*Murād az misal dar īnjā misal ast dar ajzā'ay badanī . . . misal dar kotāhī wa ḥaqārat ast*) (364). Therefore, this phrase could not, by any stretch of the imagination, be made to refer to the equal of the possessor of all perfections, the Prophet. There was no relationality or vector of comparison between bringing the human body back to life and creating the like of the possessor of all human perfections (*Zikr-i misal dar jamī'-i kamālāt az bayān-i ḥashar-i jismānī wa i'āda-i abdān bi-wajhay ta'alluq wa munāsabat na dārad*) (364–65). Citing a Qur'ānic verse that referred to the former and extending its meaning to encompass the latter was a work of exegesis unbefitting a competent scholar. Such misguided hermeneutical theatrics could only be the outcome of Ismā'īl's peculiar brand of whimsicality, Khayrābādī concluded.

According to Khayrābādī's analysis, a similar absence of interpretive imagination was shown in Ismā'īl's proffering of the following Qur'ān verse to make his case for God's capacity to create another Muḥammad: "To God, Jesus is like Adam. He created Jesus from dust, then said to him: 'Be!' And he became."[54] Just as in his first example, in Khayrābādī's view, Ismā'īl was making an inappropriate comparison. The similitude between Jesus's and Adam's parentless creation was simply inapplicable to the potential case of Muḥammad's second becoming. The underlying flaw in Ismā'īl's argument, Khayrābādī explained, was its failure to take into account the different modalities of attributes (*awṣāf*). Attributes, he reminded his readers, were of two kinds (*Awṣāf bar dū gūneh ast*): those that were mutually sharable (*mumkin al-ishtirāk*) and those that could not be shared (366). The similitude between the conditions of Adam's and Jesus's birth resulted from the first variety of attributes. Adam's parentless birth did not prohibit Jesus from sharing that same attribute. However, in contrast, the finality of Muḥammad's Prophethood represented an attribute the embodiment of which prohibited any other entity from sharing that attribute. This was where Ismā'īl's analogy and thus his argument disastrously failed.

To make his case worthy of a hearing, Khayrābādī elaborated, Ismā'īl had to first demonstrate that all of Prophet Muḥammad's attributes were of the first kind, available for sharing and replication (*Dar ṣūrat-i qābil-i samā'at tawānad būd keh īn qā'il awwal bi-isbāt rasānad keh jamī'-i awṣāf keh dar zāt-i satūda ṣifāt-i ānhazrat . . . mawjūd būdeh and az qism-i awwal ya'nī mumkin al-ishtirāk and*) (367). There was an irresolvable contradiction at work here. If the finality of Muḥammad's prophethood was available for sharing, it would not be finality. And if that finality was indeed exclusive to Muḥammad, then there was no possibility of another Muḥammad. No matter which direction it swerved, Ismāʿīl's argumentative machine was unyieldingly stalled.

No, God Cannot Lie!

Precisely such a careless inability to think through conceptual categories impaired Ismāʿīl's argument in favor of God's capacity to lie (*imkān-i kizb*), Khayrābādī continued in his indictment. He was particularly incensed by Ismāʿīl's reasoning that if God did not possess the capacity to lie, human capacities would exceed divine capacities. What this warped logic did not consider, Khayrābādī admonished Ismāʿīl, was that capacities were of two kinds: absolute capacity (*qudrat-i kāmila*), which was specific to God, and defective or limited capacities (*qudrat-i nāqiṣa*), which were associated with God's creation. The second kind, which included the capacity to perform defective or taboo acts (*nuqṣ wa ʿayb*) like lying, was infinitely inferior to the first kind (*Bi marātib-i ghayr mutanāhīya nāqiṣ ast*) (354). These two typologies of capacities were infinitely distant and distinctive.

Therefore, if humans were capable of a defect like lying and God was not, that did not in any way undermine the latter's sovereign power. Neither did it imply that human capacity exceeded divine capacity. For that to be so, Khayrābādī again lectured Ismāʿīl, one would first have to prove that human capacities consisted of divine capacities. "Perhaps the meaning of 'excess' did not cross his [Ismāʿīl's] mind," Khayrābādī commented sarcastically (*Shāyad maʿnā-yi lafẓ-i "ziyādat" bi khayāl-i sharīf naguzasht*) (354). All matters of interpretation aside, raising the very question of the possibility that God could possess a shamefully defective quality like lying, Khayrābādī pointed out, demonstrated the insidious workings of Ismāʿīl's mind. "He [Ismāʿīl] admits that lying is a shameful defect, yet he harbors no qualm about attributing the possibility of lying to God. This clearly shows that he is at peace with the possibility of God being defective and tainted" (352). In Khayrābādī's assessment, Ismāʿīl's deliberately derogatory discursive bravado proved beyond doubt that his demeaning statements about Prophet Muḥammad, other prophets, angels, and saints were not generated by the passions raised in a heated dispute. Rather, such statements clearly reflected what he actually believed in. For someone who did not spare even God from the sledgehammer of offensive speech, there was nothing extraordinary about his offending God's creation, including the Prophet, Khayrābādī concluded.

Mind the Language

Indeed, Khayrābādī was perturbed perhaps less by the content of Ismā'īl's scandalous provocations than by the language in which he argued for those positions and by the potential effect of that language on the masses. The question of language was also central to the way Khayrābādī's protest tied back to his political theology. While trying to prove that Ismā'īl's hypothetical propositions concerning the Prophet in *Taqwīyat al-Īmān* constituted an affront to the Prophet, Khayrābādī made an arresting set of comments. He argued that the determination of whether a speech act constituted offense or injury depended not on its veracity or lack thereof but on the agent and context of its utterance. In illustrating his point, Khayrābādī again turned to the spatial and conceptual space of the imperial court. Imagine, he suggested, that a king, in a show of his sovereign power, told an extremely powerful and exalted prime minister in his court: "If I so wanted, I could fire you, appoint to your ministry the lowliest of my subjects, throw you in jail, and execute you." These words, harsh as they were, would not constitute an affront to the prime minister because they were uttered by the sovereign king. But if an ordinary infantry officer said that if the king so wanted, he can do those very things, then that same speech act would constitute a form of offense (370).

Similarly, in the theological realm, verses of the Qur'ān that instructed the Prophet to declare his humanity such as "Say: I am human like you" (Qur'ān 18:110) did not diminish the Prophet's elevated stature (371). Why? Because that instruction came from God. But a mortal member of the Prophet's community would have no business saying these words; doing so would equate to insulting the Prophet. Shooting down a possible objection before it arose, Khayrābādī clarified that reciting these words from the Qur'ān would not count as a form of insult. His reasoning here was interesting. This was so, he argued, because at the moment of reciting the Qur'ān, a human being was simply repeating and rehearsing God's words; the speaker had no ownership over those words and hence no responsibility for their content (372).

But the deliberate composition of sentences like "God may well create a million new Muḥammads" blatantly disfigured the protocols of hierarchy that needed to accompany any discourse about the Prophet. Thus, Khayrābādī summed up, Ismā'īl had unabashedly insulted and cast aspersions on the Prophet. Moreover, he had confused the masses by raising obscure theological puzzles that only an expert familiar with concepts like "essentially impossible" (*mumtana' bi'l dhāt*) or "indirectly impossible" (*mumtana' bi'l ghayr*) could adequately tackle. For Khayrābādī, even if Ismā'īl's arguments had been perfectly sound and valid, airing them so publicly, beyond the circles of the intellectual elite, could only sow chaos and confusion. Curiously, Khayrābādī was profoundly perturbed by the accessibility of *Taqwīyat al-Īmān's* language and examples and by the book's composition in the vernacular Urdu. As he ruefully wondered, "Why did he [Ismā'īl] have to write his text in the accessible vernacular? And in order to prove God's all-encompassing sovereignty, was there no other illustrative example left but the possibility of a million other Muḥammads?" (445).[55]

So how would Ismā'īl have responded to the charge that he was an offensive provocateur destroying the religion of the innocent masses? From the clues he left us, it is obvious that he took strong exception to such a menacing characterization of his reformist discourse and labor. What to Khayrābādī was chaos and confusion, to Ismā'īl represented some much-needed clarity and precision during a historical moment otherwise characterized by moral decay and fragmentation. Rather than hiding sensitive theological problems from the gaze of the masses in the name of maintaining etiquette and hierarchical stability, laying such matters bare was a much wiser strategy, Ismā'īl argued. In fact, he claimed, not doing so was precisely what germinated confusion, puzzlement, and anxiety among the masses. On the specific charge that he had insulted the Prophet, Ismā'īl responded in *Yak Roza* that "reinforcing the Prophet's subservience to God does not constitute any form of insult or breach of etiquette, nor can it be described as an instance of misguiding the masses. Rather, it is an expression of the Prophet's servitude and humanity that is among the most conclusive objectives of the religion" (*Tanqīṣ-i ānjināb beh nisbat-i hazrat-i*

Ḥaqq aṣlan isā'at-i adab bi-ānjināb wa izlāl-i 'awwām nīst balkeh iẓhār-i 'ubūdīyat-i ānjināb ast keh az atam maqāṣid-i dīn ast).[56] To sum up, on the question of what counted as offensive speech, Ismā'īl's and Khayrābādī's positions were bound up with competing imaginaries of divine sovereignty, the Prophet's body and charisma, and the everyday religious lives of the masses. In other words, their disagreement over the etiquette of speech, much like their broader polemical encounter, was animated by competing political theologies.

Competing Political Theologies

To be clear, I do not wish to suggest a neat causal relationship between Khayrābādī's or for that matter Ismā'īl's theological and political imaginaries. To the contrary, I am dubious about conceptualizing theology and politics as two distinct discursive economies that are readily available for the exercise of determining what causes what. Instead, throughout this section, I have tried to explore the often-latent imaginaries of the political, broadly conceived, that inform arguments focused on such seemingly theological concepts as divine sovereignty and prophetic authority. It is the synchronicity, not the causality, of the theological and the political that I have tried to capture. The polemical moment described in this section brought into central view two radically opposed narratives of political theology.

Ismā'īl emphasized the Prophet's humanity as part of a larger political program that bound the promise of individual freedom to the unyielding affirmation of the radical alterity of divine sovereignty. Moreover, for him, any crack in the exclusivity of God's capacity to enact the exception would inevitably undermine the exclusivity of his sovereignty. In contrast, Khayrābādī considered anathema even the possibility of a cosmological hierarchy that did not position the Prophet at its apogee. Further, in his view, the exception was a gift that announced the relative privilege enjoyed by an entity in God's court. The divine gift of intercession secured the Prophet's status as the most exalted and venerated being. Moreover, that gift ensured the continuity of the Prophet's charisma in the afterworld.

Therefore, for Khayrābādī, any attempt to steal the Prophet's gift of intercession constituted an intolerable doctrinal breach and irreparably fractured a logic and rationality of tradition held together by prophetic exceptionalism. This was the underlying source of alarm that made him escalate to anathematizing Ismāʿīl. For both Ismāʿīl and Khayrābādī, political and theological imaginaries were inextricably intertwined. However, the specific trajectories of their political theologies were radically opposed.

Theorizing the Interaction of Colonial Power and Indigenous Reform beyond the Rupture/Continuity Binary

Fazl-i Ḥaqq Khayrābādī and Shāh Muḥammad Ismāʿīl's dispute over prophetic intercession gives us an important snapshot of the sociology of sovereignty during early nineteenth-century India. This controversy sprang up during a specific conjuncture in the political history of South Asia, one marked by the ascendancy of the British and the waning of the Mughal Empire. As Carl Schmitt had argued, political and theological imaginaries are always intertwined. The narrative of Western modernity, he further claimed, was marked by the emergence of a political theology that shifted the locus of sovereignty to the figure of the modern citizen. Moreover, encoded in this new political theology was a discourse of rationalism that sought to transcend theological states of exception, as the authority to enact the exception was increasingly claimed by the modern state.

But how might the polemical moment described in this section point to the limits of Schmitt's theory of political theology? More precisely, can this dispute indeed be conceptualized as a competition between a newly emerging modern secular consciousness and a traditional social imaginary? Should we think of a figure like Ismāʿīl as an indigenous reformer who through his political theology furthered a modern rationalist episteme critical of hierarchies, distinctions, and privileges? Put differently, was his drive to outlaw traditions that seemingly threatened divine sovereignty an expression of a newly emerging, colonially inspired, Protestant Islamic modernity in South Asia? There are reasons to answer these questions in the affirmative.

As I previously argued, the ontotheological framework of Ismāʿīl's discourse inextricably connected the enunciation of an Indian Muslim identity with the affirmation of divine sovereignty in the public sphere. Therefore, his theology of transcendence was as much about the construction of a reformed Indian Muslim subject as it was about God. Ismā'īl's argument against prophetic intercession did not explicitly call for the cultivation of popular sovereignty in a nationalist sense. However, central to his political theology was the promise of a subject who, by affirming the radical alterity of divine sovereignty, secured radical proximity to the divine. This kind of ontotheological political theology seems quite consistent with Schmitt's description of a modern notion of sovereignty whereby "the will of the people becomes identical to God's will; it is in the voice of the people that God's voice is heard."[57] As scholars of the American evangelical tradition in the eighteenth and nineteenth centuries such as John Modern and Michael Warner have argued, the stories of American secularism and evangelical reform are intimately tied together.[58]

These authors have shown that the evangelical critique of earlier patterns of religiosity was critical to the production of a normative understanding of religion privileging inner piety and the immediacy of the transcendent. This new conception of religion, in turn, was central to facilitating and emphasizing the operation of secularism as a moral and political project. This model of interaction between secular power and evangelical reform both does and does not work in the case of a reformer like Ismā'īl.

On the one hand, the propagation of reformist programs like Ismā'īl's was indeed indebted to the technological and institutional conditions inaugurated by the British in nineteenth-century India. The vernacularization of languages through which Urdu emerged as the lingua franca of the Indian Muslim scholarly elite, the expansion of print, the efflorescence of commerce and information networks were all developments that played an important role in the flourishing of Muslim currents of reform such as Ismā'īl's. For instance, the kind of popularity and circulation achieved by a text like *Taqwīyat al-Īmān* would have been unimaginable before the technologies of print inaugurated by the British.[59] However, with all that said, reading such moments of Muslim reform as a product of British colonial modernity also has limits that are useful to point out.

It is difficult not to discern an apparent affinity between Muslim reformist discourses eager to restore divine sovereignty and modern colonial narratives of religion. Both these discursive regimes sought to empower the individual subject (or believer) through the promise of accessing a transcendent truth (divine or otherwise) without recourse to hierarchies. They were both invested in securing the immediacy of the transcendent. However, this apparent affinity does not always translate into a relationship of imposition and reaction.

While indebted to the emerging conditions of colonial power, the specific trajectory and modality of Ismāʿīl's reform project do not fit the paradigm of Protestant Islam very well. This point can be usefully fleshed out in conversation with the case of other religious reform movements in South Asia that are often theorized as products of a modern colonial episteme. Perhaps the most sophisticated example of such an argument is found in the work of Arvind Mandair on Sikh reformist thought in colonial India.[60] My objective in what follows is not to disagree with Mandair's argument; to the contrary, I find his analysis profoundly convincing. Rather, by engaging his conceptualization of Sikh reformist thought, I hope to highlight subtle, yet critical differences in the texture of the encounter with colonial power of varied instantiations of religious reform in South Asia.

To paraphrase a complex analysis, Mandair argued that Sikh reform movements like the Singh Sabhā (established in 1873) strove to present Sikhism as a monotheistic world religion with a clearly articulated theology. They did so in response to and in imitation of a colonial knowledge regime that deemed the absence of a divine sovereign in a tradition as a lack. Overcoming this lack was a prerequisite to gaining entry into the world religions club. In their quest to overcome this lack, the Singh Sabhā reformers translated and reconfigured the Sikh path (the Sikhī) into the modern religion of Sikhism centered on the figure of a sovereign God. Mandair called this process "religion-making," meaning the appropriation of a dominant and prior colonial idiom to refashion one's tradition in a manner that conforms to that dominant idiom's expectation of what counts as religion. While offering entry into the global world religions matrix, shaped in the image of the West and Christianity, "religion-making" also forecloses the ambiguities and possibilities offered by a tradition's precolonial heritage.[61] The most crucial aspect of Mandair's argument to my meditation here is the way he presents the hierarchy of power through which thought travels from the colonizer to the colonized: "It is possible to reconstruct the colonizer/colonized relation in terms of a hierarchical differentiation between the colonizer's idiom (or the 'first idiom') and the idioms that come to be articulated by the colonized through interaction with the colonizer. The first idiom is provided by the British. It comprises the institutions, concepts, language, and intellectual heritage of the colonizer—not to mention the terms of their critique of native traditions, given through Indological, ethnographic, and missionary literature."[62]

According to this hierarchical schema, it was through the imposition of the colonial idiom that the intellectual horizons and reformist programs of the indigenous scholarly elite came to be imagined and articulated. One finds similar processes of the colonial rationalization of indigenous religion in the programs of other late nineteenth-century South Asian reform movements. Though these are disparate in their goals and orientation, one may mention here the Brahmo Samāj, the Aryā Samāj, the Alīgarh School, and Sinhalese Buddhist reformers, for whom Gananath Obeyesekere coined the famous term "Protestant Buddhism."[63]

Despite their apparent convergence, the case of Ismā'īl is rather different from these reformist currents. Ismā'īl lived a few decades before the late nineteenth century when many of these reformist streams flourished. But also, his formative training contrasted significantly from that of the pioneers of these movements, who were either well immersed in the colonial milieu or educated at Anglo-vernacular institutions. There is no evidence to suggest that Ismā'īl was versed in colonial knowledges on religion or that he was familiar with British institutions of learning. In this situation, it is difficult to assimilate his focus on the restoration of divine sovereignty or his critique of hierarchies to the imposition of a modern colonial episteme.

Rather, it would be more accurate to say that Ismā'īl's reformist program occupied a parallel discursive domain similar but not reducible to a modern Protestant understanding of religion. His discourse on divine sovereignty may have simulated colonial narratives of religious authenticity, but it was not immersed in the colonial discursive economy. The conceptual assumptions and apparatus that informed his reformist agenda were not imposed on him by colonial power, even though that power generated the conditions conducive for the propagation of that agenda. The conditions of an emerging colonial order, marked by a crisis of political sovereignty, certainly facilitated reformist projects like Ismāʿīl's. Moreover, it is not as if Ismāʿīl did not have to contend with or negotiate colonial power. He certainly did, as best exemplified by the banning and then restoration of his sermons by the British resident in Delhi. That incident clearly showed that a new authority was in town. However, in thinking about the encounter between colonialism and indigenous reformist thought, it might be useful to distinguish between the institutional and technological conditions of colonial power on the one hand and its epistemic interventions on the other. The two are obviously related. But making this distinction promises a more nuanced understanding of reformist discourses, like Ismāʿīl's, that even while contending with the encroaching presence of colonial power were not inspired by its knowledge regimes.

Clearly, Ismāʿīl's provocations and Khayrābādī's response to them occurred in an arena marked by a slowly but surely expanding colonial state. But the set of moral virtues, questions, and anxieties that animated their arguments were part of a long-standing Islamic discursive tradition, hardly derivative of or reducible to modern Protestant rumblings. Thus one must be cautious to not conflate the emergence of new political and institutional conditions with a narrative of intellectual influence and imposition. An apparent similarity between Muslim reformist and modern Protestant critiques of hierarchies and emphasis on the figure of a divine sovereign does not mean these critiques can be assimilated into each other.

Let me avert a potential misreading here. My point here should not be confused with an attempt to excavate "native agency" by pointing to the limits of colonial power. This now fashionable line of argument suffers from major conceptual problems, as scholars like Arvind Mandair, David Scott, and Ananda Abeysekara have shown in different ways.[64] For instance, approaching the agency of the colonized in terms of resisting or subverting colonial power depends on a less-than-nuanced understanding of power as necessarily negative, without an appreciation of the productive ways in which power operates. Hunting for agency thus makes a mockery of much of what Michel Foucault taught us about power. Also, as Abeysekara has usefully pointed out, positing the limits of colonial power perpetuates the unsound assumption that such power is empirically measurable so that one may decide on its limits.[65] Moreover, the desire to extricate native agency from colonial influence rests on the erroneous assumption that "'influence' is something that lies *outside* one's own 'agency,' that agency is given and prior to 'influence'–a notion that has a complex modern genealogy within colonialism and liberalism."[66] Mandair has also highlighted the problematic nature of the interactionist or dialogical model of the encounter between colonial power and the colonized elite that is integral to the project of uncovering native agency. As he usefully points out, such a model "depends on an implicit model of communication in which both parties are assumed to be capable of speaking and thinking freely with each other."[67] In other words, the quest for native agency fails to consider the power dynamics and differentials of the terms and terrain on which the native allegedly enters into dialogue with the colonizer.

I am not interested in recovering native agency. My point here is very different. I have tried to draw attention to some specific aspects of the polemical moment described in this section to caution against the temptation of reading it as yet another example of a familiar colonial contamination of indigenous religious thought. The diffusion of colonial power in this case displayed a trajectory that cannot be seamlessly accommodated into a hierarchical grid of colonial imposition and indigenous absorption. At the risk of stating the obvious: South Asian reform movements followed varied trajectories in terms of their entanglement with colonial discourses on religion. And it is useful to highlight such intrareformist differences and variations lest one include them all in a uniform scheme of the colonial reconfiguration of the epistemic foundations of indigenous religious thought. It is the particularity of Ismāʿīl's case that I have found important to emphasize. While haunted by colonial power, the grammar of that hauntology was distinctive and particular.

Again, this is not to stake a claim for the authenticity or purity of Ismāʿīl's thought by absolving him from the stain of colonial intellectual influence. I am not after salvaging native thought unaffected by colonial power. Rather, Ismāʿīl's example offers the possibility of conceptualizing discursive projects of reform in a manner that neither seeks from them remainders of native agency nor collapses them with colonial modernity. Ultimately, agency hunting and the assimilation of indigenous religious discourses to colonial power are both unsatisfactory pursuits. Attachment to either side of the agency/assimilation binary precludes a closer look at the styles, strategies, and conflicts that inform the articulation and contestation of the distinctive forms of life and excellence constituting a tradition. It is precisely such a close look at the terms and stakes of a discursive tradition that has occupied the last few chapters of this book.

Let me gesture in passing that perhaps it is time to look beyond the very continuity/rupture problem space and debate that have occupied so much of South Asian studies, especially the study of South Asian religions, in the last few decades. I take my cue here from David Scott's astute provocation when he asks "whether the moment of normalization of a paradigm is not also the moment when it is necessary to reconstruct and reinterrogate the ground of questions themselves through which it was brought into being in the first place; to ask whether the critical *yield* of the normal problem-space continues to be what it was when it first emerged."[68] Thinking with Scott, one wonders whether the continuity/rupture problem space still offers the sort of critical purchase it once may have. Has not the very question "Does colonialism constitute a rupture from or continuity with the precolonial past" assumed a certain staleness and air of predictability in the sorts of answers it invariably elicits?

The most obvious answer to this question, of course, is that there are continuities as well as ruptures. So rather than offering sweeping narratives and judgments of continuity or rupture, we might find it more profitable to excavate and identify new problem spaces generated from the specificity of particular discursive archives. The theme of competing political theologies that has anchored the preceding chapters represents such a novel problem space. It is derived from the normative concerns, investments, and religious thought of Muslim actors rather than from the vestibules of nationalist politics. I am not advocating a reversion to some sort of nativism. I am simply pointing to the limits of persisting with a question-and-answer space that has lost its former conceptual urgency and payoff. Such persistence only forecloses the possibility of asking new questions more attuned to the specific normative vectors orienting a discursive archive. I am advocating the formulation of new sorts of questions and problem spaces in the study of South Asian Islam and religion conceptualized through the close and energetic reading of critical texts and contexts. This mandate especially promises the possibility of widening and deepening the analytical horizons informing South Asian Muslim studies, especially in relation to the South Asian *'ulamā'* tradition.

To wrap up, in this section I have explored the logics and rationalities through which the limits of a discursive tradition were authoritatively contested in a particular debate. I have pursued such a line of inquiry by focusing on a specific polemical moment in early nineteenth-century Muslim India when the boundaries of religion and reform were struggled over. Moreover, I have sought to show that the rival logics of tradition made visible during this polemical moment cannot be canonized into such binaries as traditional/modern, mystical/rational, religious/secular, or liberal/conservative. One could not have entered the discursive site of Ismāʿīl's and Khayrābādī's debate armed with a priori assumptions about the knowledges, logics, and stakes that animated it. The rival narratives of tradition and its limits that these scholars articulated were authorized within the contingent conjuncture of their polemical encounter. It was precisely the antagonistic space of their debate that obliged them to confront each other's argument and destabilize its normative coherence and that allowed them to authoritatively debate what could and could not count as Islam. The identity of Khayrābādī's argument depended on establishing the otherness of Ismāʿīl's and vice versa. Each was the other's condition of possibility.

The personal rivalry between Ismāʿīl and Khayrābādī ended after Ismāʿīl's death in 1831. However, the debate over prophetic authority that they had begun only metastasized in the following decades, as colonial power became further entrenched. In the next few chapters, I shift my focus to that later context of intra-Muslim rivalries in North India during the latter half of the nineteenth century. Thematically, I will now consider the competing understandings of law and normative practice in everyday life corresponding to the competing political theologies discussed in this section. Remember, the interaction of theology, law, and ritual practice is the conceptual thread that binds this book together.

How does a political theology invested in the radical sovereignty of the divine translate into a legal imaginary invested in the promise of regulating embodied practices in a way that affirms that sovereignty? That is the major question connecting the following section to the one just concluded. I will address this question by focusing on one of the most contentious categories in Islam that is located precisely at the nexus of law, theology, and everyday ritual practice; the category of heretical innovation (*bidʿa*).

part two

Competing Normativities

chapter six

Reforming Religion in the Shadow of Colonial Power

On a Friday afternoon in 1890, a foreign black Muslim scholar (*siyāh wilāyatī*) (we are not told his country of origin) visited the town of Deoband in Uttar Pradesh, India. Interested in becoming involved with the local community and their devotional practices, he asked Ḥājī Muḥammad ʻĀbid Ḥusayn, one of the less well-known founders of the Dār al-ʻUlūm Deoband, the prestigious seminary of the town, if he could deliver the Friday sermon as part of the weekly congregational prayers. ʻĀbid Ḥusayn willingly obliged the foreigner's request, took him to Deoband's congregational mosque, and extended him the coveted pulpit. It so happened that Rashīd Aḥmad Gangohī, another one of the madrasa's founders and a leading scholar in the Deoband hierarchy, was also visiting the town and thus attended the weekly congregational prayer. Since it was the month of *rabīʻ al-awwal*, during which the Prophet was born, the guest prayer leader devoted his Friday sermon to the virtues of the *mawlid* ceremony (the celebration of the Prophet's birthday).

Gangohī was bitterly opposed to the *mawlid* as practiced in India. He considered it a serious heretical innovation, one that lacked a precedent in the normative tradition of the pious ancestors. Moreover, in Gangohī's view, the *mawlid* had become terminally corrupted because the ignorant masses had turned the ritual into an orgy of transgressions. Given his disposition toward the *mawlid*, Gangohī grew increasingly agitated as he listened to a sermon expounding on its sanctity. At some point during the sermon Gangohī lost his patience and interrupted the preacher. "Mawlānā, please wrap up your sermon."[1]

The preacher, who clearly did not recognize Gangohī, reproached him in terms of the etiquette of prayer: "Be quiet, it is forbidden [*ḥarām*] to interrupt a Friday sermon." "Don't you lecture me on what is *ḥalāl* and *ḥarām*," an infuriated Gangohī retorted. "You deserve to be taken by your hand and dragged down from the pulpit. According to the rules of jurisprudence [*fiqh*], one ought to shorten the sermon and lengthen the prayers. You are doing the exact opposite." "Be quiet," the preacher reprimanded again.

Some of the congregants, now offended by the preacher's unruly attitude toward Gangohī, refused to pray behind him. They asked Gangohī to lead the prayers, but he declined, fearing that some people might think he had orchestrated the altercation in order to gain control of the pulpit. Eventually, Muḥammad Ya'qūb Nānautvī, another prominent Deoband scholar and a close associate of Gangohī, led the prayers. Gangohī hastily left the mosque after the prayers. Thereafter, the black foreigner said to Ya'qūb Nānautvī: "Call that Wahhābī[2] over here who rudely interrupted the sermon and was rambling like a buffoon for the longest time ever."[3]

Nānautvī wanted to confront the foreigner but feared that if he did so members of the already agitated congregation might join in the fray with unpredictable consequences. So he restrained himself, acted as if he had not heard the offensive comments, and busied himself in rituals. In doing so, he averted what could potentially have escalated into mob violence.[4]

This narrative provides a vivid glimpse of the climate of bitter polemics that enveloped the Muslim learned elite of North India during the late nineteenth century. As this story shows, debates over the limits of the Prophet's normative model, especially with regard to the legitimacy of controversial popular conventions such as the Prophet's birthday celebration, resulted in heated divisions. At stake in Gangohī's altercation was not only the texture of the community's ritual life but, equally important, the question of who controlled and managed the public yet intensely communal space of the mosque in which the rhythms of ritual life unfolded.[5] This narrative also underscores the intimate relation between elite scholarly contestations and the buildup of communal tensions in the practices of everyday life. Over time these tensions broke out in rampant mutual anathematizing and name-calling among different Muslim groups across North India. It was not new for prominent Indian Muslim scholars to be engaged in vitriolic debates over contentious questions of normative practice.

Even during the heyday of Muslim power in North India in the fifteenth and sixteenth centuries, it was common to find individual Muslim scholars embroiled in bitter and often very personal intellectual disputes. This trend continued until the early half of the nineteenth century, as we saw in the previous section on the exchanges between Shāh Muḥammad Ismā'īl and Fazl-i Ḥaqq Khayrābādī. However, the polemical fervor of the late nineteenth century was quite different from previous eras in important ways.

Most notably, in the period following the 1857 Mutiny (in which Indian Muslims were brutally defeated by the British), the learned elite of Muslim India were divided into competing "normative orientations" (*masālik*, sing. *maslak*) with contrasting programs of religious reform. Paradoxically, the loss of Muslim political sovereignty generated the conditions for unprecedented intellectual fermentation, as competing groups of scholars wrestled with the question of how must one reform Islam and Muslims under the new conditions of British colonialism.[6]

In the British proclamation of sovereignty over Indian subjects as recorded in the Government of India Act of August 2, 1858, all Indian subjects "were to enjoy the equal and impartial protection of the law . . . and they were to be secure in the practice of their religions."[7] The colonial state's seeming munificence of according indigenous religious communities protection under the law was inextricable from the liberal secular operation of evacuating the domain of religious beliefs, practices, and debates as separable from and yet subservient to the protection of the state and its laws. As David Gilmartin has argued, this arrangement followed the colonial bifurcation between the allegedly universal, rational, and scientific realm of the colonial state and the realm of indigenous cultures and communities defined by their particular norms and characteristics (religious, tribal, etc.).[8]

This distinction between the universal and the particular did more than establish the universality and hence exceptionality of the colonial state. It also put in place the artificial yet powerful separation between the public domain, which oversaw the operation of law and politics, and the particular domain housing religious sensibilities and practices. Thus Gilmartin famously argued that in the late nineteenth-century context it is more helpful to talk about the public and the particular than about the more familiar distinction of public/private. It was precisely by recognizing and claiming to protect the particularities of indigenous religious communities that the universality and superiority of the colonial state and its control over affairs of law and politics were instituted.[9] But as Julia Stephens has shown, the promise of protecting religions through the law only added to the ambiguities surrounding the relationship between religious liberty and legal protection, often generating intensely volatile debates and situations.[10] Indeed, the colonial evacuation of religion as a distinct and particular domain of life so that it could be managed and protected by the state had the paradoxical effect of rendering that domain ever more conflictual, polemical, and competitive. Conceptually, this is not surprising.

The more one seeks to define and limit a category (in this case religion), the more avidly its definition and limits will be contested.[11] It is not a coincidence that the nineteenth century was a moment of unprecedented intrareligious and interreligious adversarial activity in South Asia. Further, the polemical warfare of the nineteenth century was facilitated not only by the political and epistemological reordering of religion as an increasingly reified and competitive category but also by technologies such as print, railways, and the postal system. As Arvind Mandair has usefully pointed out, in colonial India two separate yet interconnected fields of moral contestation simultaneously operated. One was the field of interreligious polemics that pitted against each other Hindus, Muslims, Sikhs, and Christian missionaries. At stake in this contest with external "others" was the legitimacy of individual religious identities. The other field was the site of dialogue with internal "others." These internal antagonisms stemmed from competing views on the limits of authenticity and tradition. While the first domain concerned the negotiation of the self's relationship with the other, the second revolved around the character of the authentic self.[12] Thinking with Mandair, one may further observe the remarkable symmetry between episodes of intrareligious debate that occupied the late nineteenth century. Take the cases of the major Hindu, Muslim, and Sikh reformers and counter-reformers. While these are obviously different and particular, one finds a striking resemblance in the objects, composition, and frameworks of their debates and contentions.[13]

While a range of Indian Muslim scholars expressed a desire for reform, what reform meant to them varied considerably, generating numerous arguments, debates, and polemics.[14] Among the most prominent of these reform movements was the Deoband school, simultaneously an Islamic seminary and an ideological orientation. The Deoband madrasa was established in the North Indian town of Deoband, Uttar Pradesh, in 1866 by a group of prominent Indian Muslim scholars (*'ulamā'*). More specifically, it was the charismatic scholars Rashīd Aḥmad Gangohī and Qāsim Nānautvī (d. 1877) who laid the foundations of this educational institution of religious learning that has affected the intellectual, social, and political history of South Asian Islam in profound ways. Today, some 150 years later, with its parent institution in India, the Deoband madrasa boasts the largest network of satellite madrasas all over Pakistan and Bangladesh as well as neighboring countries in Asia and beyond, as far afield as the Caribbean, South Africa, Britain, and the United States. Deobandī madrasas number circa fifty thousand to sixty thousand institutions on the Indian subcontinent alone, with the largest concentration in India.

However, it is important to stress here that although numerous Islamic seminaries in various countries call themselves "Deobandī," their ties to the founding school in the town of Deoband, which continues to this day, may well be only tenuous or even nonexistent. This is an important point because it illustrates that besides the physical institution of the seminary, the term *Deobandī* also connotes a certain ideology, or a particular thought-style within Sunnī Islam in the modern world. Further, in colonial as well as postcolonial South Asia, the Deobandī orientation was never monolithic or uniform. As the last chapter of this book shows, even on crucial questions of law and practice, Deoband scholars, including the pioneers of the school, have often disagreed.

Moreover, from the late nineteenth century to the present, Deoband scholars have differed, at times radically so, on questions of politics, political alliances, and participation in electoral democracy. Thus, while some leading Deoband luminaries (such as Shabbīr Aḥmad Usmānī, d. 1949) supported or even played a formative role in the Pakistan movement, others (most notably Ḥusayn Aḥmad Madanī) vigorously opposed it.[15] Further, some Deoband scholars like Thānvī were intensely attached to the ideal of reforming the masses through the purification and reordering of their ritual lives. Others, like his contemporary 'Ubaydullah Sindhī (d. 1944), were much less if at all invested in the orchestration of devotional rituals. For instance, Sindhī understood reform primarily through the lens of revolutionary politics and socioeconomic justice, a view that was informed by his travels in Afghanistan, Soviet Russia, and Turkey during the mid-twentieth century.[16] Thus, the Deobandī orientation included various and at times conflicting ideological trajectories.

In late nineteenth-century India and in the following decades, among traditionally educated scholars, the authority of the Deoband madrasa was most eagerly challenged by its chief competitors, the Barelvī and Ahl-i Ḥadīth schools. These rival ideological formations—the Deobandīs, Barelvīs, and Ahl-i Ḥadīth—articulated overlapping yet contrasting narratives of ideal norms of life and ways of interpreting those norms.

The Ahl-i Ḥadīth school, in contrast to the Barelvī and Deobandī schools, rejected the canonical authority of the four established academies of Sunnī law. They argued for restricting the sources of religious norms to the Qur'ān and the normative model of the Prophet. Curiously, though, while the Ahl-i Ḥadīth championed the populist promise of accessing the Qur'ān and *sunna* in the absence of the mediating authority of legal schools and scholars, certain key features of the movement were incongruent with that promise. Consider, for instance, the intellectual and social profile of the most prolific and well-known thinker associated with the Ahl-i Ḥadīth, Ṣiddīq Ḥasan Khān (d. 1890). Unabashedly aristocratic, he was married to the princess of the princely state of Bhopal. Moreover, he wrote almost exclusively in Arabic in a bid to raise the intellectual profile of the school among scholarly circles in the Arab Middle East, a decision that could hardly have made his thought more accessible to the Indian masses. For Ṣiddīq Ḥasan Khān, hermeneutical minimalism, aristocratic sociality, and Arabicist elitism went together. Apart from their hermeneutical disagreement, Ahl-i Ḥadīth scholars also quarreled with their Indian Ḥanafī counterparts on the normative legitimacy of three specific practices related to the performance of the fivefold daily prayers: raising both hands (*raf' al-yadayn*) during prayers, saying "*Āmīn*" (Oh Allāh, respond) aloud after reciting the *fātiḥa* (*āmīn bil-jahr*), and reciting the *fātiḥa* behind a prayer leader (*fātiḥa khalf al-imām*).

The rivalry between Deobandī and Barelvī scholars, on the other hand, centered on competing views of the Prophet's charisma and the limits of his normative model. Their conflicts, as this and the next three chapters will show, focused on the critical questions of how the prophetic norm (*sunna*) must manifest in the everyday lives of the masses and how to guard religious practice from the threat of heretical innovations (*bida'*, sing. *bid'a*). The nature and scope of the Prophet's knowledge were also pivotal points of disagreement (discussed in chapter 11).

What Is a *Maslak*?

The growth of the Deoband school into a movement in 1866 and the formation of the Ahl-i Ḥadīth and Barelvī ideologies decisively altered the intellectual landscape of Sunnī South Asian Islam. From this moment, the production and dissemination of knowledge took on an unprecedented group-centered orientation. This group solidarity and concentration is best captured in the term *maslak*, which became the most visible referent to a distinct Muslim reformist program in colonial South Asia. Indeed, the concept of *maslak*, which in its Urdu modality can best be rendered as a "normative orientation," flowered as never before in the latter half of the nineteenth century in Muslim India. What, then, is a *maslak*? *Maslak* is a malleable and often ambiguous and multivalent category. Derived from the Arabic term *sulūk*, or "proper conduct," at its core *maslak* relates to the cultivation of a subject's virtues and ethical formation.

In the modern South Asian context, however, the ethical aspect of *maslak* is intimately entwined with, and perhaps even overshadowed by, its implicit signaling of competition over normativity. From the late nineteenth century onwards, *maslak* has become a resoundingly competitive concept. It denotes not only a salvational program but one empowered by an exclusive claim to normativity over other competing claimants. There is thus an irresolvable tension and ambiguity at the heart of the concept. Belonging to or associating with a *maslak* marks an exclusive claim to normativity, yet the very existence of multiple conflicting *maslaks*, and the dependence of *maslak* identity on the presence and existence of competing others, suggest the fragmentation and instability of normativity. In other words, *maslak* is a claim to normativity that also announces the absence and impossibility of any absolute claim to normativity.

This underlying tension in the concept of *maslak* is most palpable in the oscillation between embracing and eschewing a *maslak* identity often found among Deobandī, Barelvī, and Ahl-i Ḥadīth actors. Embracing and embodying a *maslak* identity honors the genealogy of scholarly authority and the signature indices of tradition that distinguish a particular *maslak* from its rivals. But eschewing such designations as "Barelvī" and "Deobandī" clears the way for claiming the mantle of Sunnī normativity in a manner that transcends *maslak* differences and distinctions. While not exactly opposite, the particularity of a *maslak* and the universality of Sunnī normativity are nonetheless interlocked in productive tension, thus provoking the seemingly contradictory gestures of embrace and repudiation.

But let me return briefly to the question of what a *maslak* is. How might one conceptualize the crux of the difference between the competing normative orientations of Deobandī, Barelvī, and Ahl-i Ḥadīth? In a nutshell, the *maslak* is situated at the interstices of knowledge, practice, and hermeneutics. Belonging to a particular *maslak* signals a practitioner's fidelity to a distinct normative orientation governing three major questions connected to three variables: (1) knowledge: What sources of the tradition must inform one's engagement with key legal, ethical, and theological problems? (2) hermeneutics: How and through what interpretive protocols should one translate the premodern legacy of the canonical tradition in the modern world? and (3) practice: What patterns of ritual and everyday life emerge from the way one imagines authoritative knowledge and hermeneutics (1 and 2)? This knowledge-hermeneutics-practice combination is at the heart of *maslak* differences and polemics in South Asia.

The Barelvī-Deobandī disagreement centered on hermeneutics and practice. While disagreeing vigorously on their interpretation of the canon, the two schools nonetheless agreed on the sanctity and indispensability of a converging if not common canon. The Ahl-i Ḥadīth, however, rejected the very canonicity of that presumed canon. Yes, they also disagreed with their Ḥanafī rivals on matters of practice. But that disagreement was based on the question of what counted as authoritative and normative knowledge. To sum up, attending to the interaction of knowledge, hermeneutics, and practice offers a compact and potentially effective analytical strategy to capture the category of *maslak*.

The late nineteenth-century ideological reification of Sunnī Islam in North India, as exemplified in the emergence of competing normative orientations, gave rise to an unprecedented intensity of polemics. All reformist groups, including Deobandīs, Barelvīs, and Ahl-i Ḥadīth, vigorously participated in the ensuing polemical warfare. The most well-known of these polemics, on which this book focuses, were those between the

Barelvīs and Deobandīs. The dispute involved major Barelvī scholars such as the founder of the school, Aḥmad Razā Khān, and their Deobandī counterparts, including the pioneers of Deoband Qāsim Nānautvī and Rashīd Aḥmad Gangohī, and their successors such as Khalīl Aḥmad Sāharanpūrī (d. 1927) and Ashraf ʻAlī Thānvī.[17] Despite being affiliated with the same Ḥanafī school of Sunnī law, these two groups were bitterly opposed regarding the limits of the Prophet's normative model and its institution in the public sphere.

Louis Dumont noted in the context of Hindu communalism in modern India that with "the replacement of the king as sovereign . . . Dharma is replaced by the People as a collective individual mirroring itself in a territory."[18] Similarly, in the context of Islam in colonial India, the normative model of the Prophet emerged as a synecdoche representing the entirety of law, *sharīʻa*. The central locus of normativity was now firmly established in the figure of the Prophet. In the absence of any tangible and legitimate political authority, the Prophet's normative example emerged as the primary discursive arena where opposing factions of North Indian *ʻulamā'* articulated and contested their religious authority. But each rival group defined prophetic normativity very differently, even antithetically. In this regard, the case of the Barelvī-Deobandī polemics is particularly illustrative.

At the heart of Deoband's reformist platform was an egalitarian imaginary of Prophet Muḥammad's authority. For example, in the view of Deobandī scholars, calling the Prophet one's brother would not amount to offensive or disrespectful speech or conduct. On the contrary, such an affirmation of the Prophet's human qualities was to be encouraged. The well-known prophetic saying "I am unlike any of you" (*lastū ka aḥadin minkum*) referred only to Muḥammad's unique status as a recipient of divine revelation, the Deobandīs argued. In all other matters of human existence, he was much like anyone else. Therefore, for the Deobandī scholars, it was intolerable to believe that the Prophet possessed knowledge of the unknown (*ʻilm al-ghayb*). As I will show in chapter 8, this theological position was central to their opposition to rituals such as the celebration of the Prophet's birthday, during which he personally appeared at multiple gatherings simultaneously. In a manner very similar to Shāh Muḥammad Ismāʻīl, for the pioneers of Deoband the perfection of Muḥammad's prophecy was enabled by the perfection of his humanity.

As Ashraf ʿAlī Thānvī once said while contrasting the Deoband school against its opponents, "They turn the Prophet into a God but a defective one. We understand him to be a servant [of God] but a perfect one. So they detract from the Prophet's authority and we affirm his perfection" (*Bidʿatī huzūr ko ilāh māntay hayn magar nāqiṣ. Ham unhayn ʿabd māntay hayn magar kāmil. Tuh tum huzūr kī tanqīṣ kartay ho awr ham kamāl ke qāʾil hayn*).[19] Thānvī tried to defend the Deobandī emphasis on the humanity of the Prophet by pointing to the proclamation uttered by all Muslims during the five-daily prayers: "I bear witness that there is no God except God and that Muḥammad is his servant and his messenger." What must be noticed in this proclamation, Thānvī instructed, was that the affirmation of Muḥammad's servitude to God preceded the mention of his role as a messenger. Therefore, the Prophet's position as God's servant (*ʿabduhu*) took priority over his status as God's messenger (*rasūluhu*). The Prophet's humanity was the most defining aspect of his persona.[20]

In contrast, the centerpiece of the Barelvī ideology valorized above all the element of love characterizing the Prophet's relationship with God. For the Berelvīs, much as for Fazl-i Ḥaqq Khayrābādī, whom they held in great reverence, any normative argument that might undermine the Prophet's charisma as God's most beloved subject, such as questioning his ability to intercede on behalf of sinners or calling his birthday celebration a heretical innovation, was unacceptable. Moreover, it was not only distasteful but also heretical for anyone to even think of, let alone speak of, the Prophet as one's brother. Any speech or conduct that even theoretically diminished Muḥammad's prophetic aura was unpalatable to Barelvī sensibilities. For Aḥmad Razā Khān, for instance, God's intimacy with the Prophet was interwoven with the very logic and temporality of revelation. The reason why the Qurʾān was revealed not in one installment but gradually over more than two decades was precisely the cultivation of love and intimacy between God and the Prophet. The Prophet's knowledge of the Qurʾān at the completion of this process, and through it his knowledge of all that there was and all that would follow (*mā kāna wa mā yakūn*), was a manifestation of God's love for the Prophet.[21] It was this entwinement of love, knowledge, and revelation that made the controversy over the Prophet's knowledge of the unknown (*ʿilm al-ghayb*), examined in chapter 11, so pivotal and sensitive for

Khān and his followers. But as I mentioned in the introduction to this book, it would be singularly problematic to frame the Deobandī-Barelvī rivalry as one between proponents of populist Sufism (Barelvīs) and custodians of legal conservatism (Deobandīs).

Deobandīs and Barelvīs were deeply invested in both Ḥanafī law and Sufism. Where they differed from one another was on the question of what it meant to be a Sunnī Ḥanafī Muslim under conditions of colonialism. Their opposition was based on competing ideologies of prophetic normativity, not on claims to disparate canons of law. It is crucial to make this distinction between *madhdhāhib* (canonical schools of law) and *masālik* (normative orientations) to recognize the epistemic neighborliness underlying the Deobandī-Barelvī dispute. It was precisely because these two groups were so similar in their broad outlines, and in the potential followers they sought to attract, that their polemics were often so personal and caustic.

The Deobandī-Barelvī polemics began in the late nineteenth century, a few decades after Shāh Muḥammad Ismāʿīl's death in 1831. However, the figure of Ismāʿīl was at the center of these polemics. The pioneers of Deoband vigorously defended his views and heralded him as an exemplary religious reformer. For instance, once, while commenting on some of Ismāʿīl's controversial statements in *Taqwīyat al-Īmān*, Rashīd Aḥmad Gangohī declared: "*Taqwīyat al-Īmān* is a majestic book that contains the very essence of the Qur'ān and the Ḥadīth. Its author was a person of great repute. Anyone who calls him [Ismāʿīl] an unbeliever or a person of bad character is himself satanic and cursed by God."[22] Hermeneutically, Ismāʿīl's reform project was more marked by a nonconformist streak than that of the Deoband pioneers.

Remember, in *Taqwīyat al-Īmān*, Ismāʿīl had urged the masses to not rely on specialist scholars for accessing and interpreting normative sources of the religion such as the Qur'ān and the Ḥadīth. Moreover, although Ismāʿīl was well versed in Ḥanafī jurisprudence, he did not identify himself as a Ḥanafī jurist per se. In fact, as I discussed in chapter 2, on certain contentious issues such as raising both hands during prayers (*rafʿ al-yadayn*), Ismāʿīl had departed from the practice of Ḥanafī scholars in his own family, causing them much consternation. Therefore, for the Deoband pioneers, who were staunch Ḥanafīs and who vigorously opposed the nonconformist Ahl-i Ḥadīth school, to so passionately embrace and defend Ismāʿīl seems somewhat odd. But a couple of factors may explain this apparent inconsistency. First, unlike the late nineteenth-century Ahl-i Ḥadīth scholars, Ismāʿīl did not reject the principle of conforming to a canonical school of law (*taqlīd*) or demean the authority of esteemed Ḥanafī scholars of the past. So in Ismāʿīl's discourse one does not find any discernible doctrinal views on the question of conforming to a canonical school of law that might have offended the Ḥanafī sensibilities of Deoband scholars.

Second, in Ismāʿīl the Deoband pioneers found an excellent spokesperson for their own reform agenda. Ismāʿīl's focus on the theme of restoring divine sovereignty and, as I will show in the next chapter, his views on the limits of innovation in everyday practice, deeply resonated with the Deoband ideology. Thus, despite differences of hermeneutical temperament, the doctrinal affinity between Ismāʿīl and the Deoband pioneers made possible a robust strategic alliance between them.

In contrast, Aḥmad Razā Khān and his Barelvī followers were as dramatic in their condemnation of Ismāʿīl's intellectual and political contributions as the Deobandīs were celebratory. For Khān, Ismāʿīl and his Deobandī admirers were part of a common intellectual genealogy that thrived on cheapening the Prophet's charisma in a misguided quest to restore divine sovereignty. Like Fazl-i Ḥaqq Khayrābādī, Khān launched a scathing attack against the thinking of Ismāʿīl and the Deoband pioneers and sought to frame them as a dire threat to South Asian Islam and Muslims. In many ways, then, the Deobandī-Barelvī polemics in late nineteenth-century India represented a more ideologically defined and group-centered episode of a doctrinal rivalry that Ismāʿīl and Khayrābādī had ignited a few decades earlier.

These controversies were in large measure driven by a fundamental ethical question that had captured the imagination of Sunnī Muslim thinkers for several centuries: What are the limits of innovation to the normative model of the Prophet and his Companions? In other words, when does innovation in the realms of devotional and customary practices turn into heresy, or, to phrase it differently, what is the etiquette governing the application of the doctrine of heretical innovation (*bidʿa*) in Islam? These are among the questions that occupy the next chapter.

chapter seven

Law, Sovereignty, and the Boundaries of Normative Practice

Mutual Dependence of the Limit and Its Transgression: Toward an Archaeology of *Bid'a*

Bid'a (literally "innovation") is at once one of the most controversial and most elusive and supple categories in Muslim thought. *Bid'a* announces simultaneously the limits of tradition and the always imminent threat and possibility of transgressing those limits. Limits and transgression, as Michel Foucault asserted, are mutually entangled and constitutive; each is the other's condition of possibility and, one might add, impossibility. As he instructively put it, "The limit and transgression depend on each other for whatever density of being they possess: a limit could not exist if it were absolutely uncrossable and, reciprocally, transgression would be pointless if it merely crossed a limit composed of illusions and shadows. But can the limit have a life of its own outside of the act that gloriously passes through it and negates it?"[1] Foucault's words here capture the conceptual complications shadowing *bid'a* as an index of transgression in Islam. Committing *bid'a* means transgressing the limits of the Prophet's normative model, the *sunna*, but precisely the threat and the actuality of transgression give life to those limits. *Sunna* and *bid'a*, the normative and the heretical, the limits of tradition and the transgression of those limits, are intimately interwoven and mutually dependent. Normativity and heresy are co-constitutive, harkening Mary Douglas's important argument in her classic *Purity and Danger* that the ideas of contagion and purification are intimately bound together. As she eloquently put it, in words that remarkably resemble the conceptual architecture undergirding the relationship of *sunna* and *bid'a*: "if uncleanness is matter out of place, we must approach it through order. Uncleanness or dirt is that which must not be included if a pattern is to be maintained."[2]

The intellectual genealogy of *bid'a* is traceable to two well-known prophetic sayings: "Every innovation is a misguidance, and every misguidance leads to hell" and "Whoever innovates in this matter of ours that which is not a part of it is rejected."[3] However, the modality of transgression associated with the word *bid'a* hardly corresponds to the sense of violation in contemporary positive law. To charge someone with committing *bid'a* is to accuse that person of insulting the normative authority of the Prophet, opposing the tradition of the pious ancestors, and most fundamentally, breaking the foundational covenant of lordship and servitude that binds a human subject to God. *Bid'a* is a potent category of intra-Muslim "othering" in large measure because it is as expansive as it is malleable; it can be attached to a panoply of perceived transgressions of devotional rituals, theology, and everyday customs and practices.

As Maribel Fierro, in her encyclopedic examination of the numerous premodern Muslim scholarly books on *bid'a* (*kutub al-bida'*) shows, things accused of being *bid'a* can range from objectionable styles of Qur'ānic recitation to the placement of fans at the entrance of mosques![4] The doctrines, practices, and habits that might fit in the *bid'a* category are indeed multitudinous and span a variety of reformist projects and temperaments. The South Asian *'ulamā'* whose thought on *bid'a* takes up much of this section participated in a long-standing genre of scholarship, while adding their own individual touches to the accumulated intellectual and social history of a fraught concept.

The ominous symbolism attached to the term *bid'a* persists to this day. For example, in an essay on the application of *bid'a* in Islam, contemporary American Muslim scholar Umar Faruq Abd-Allah remarks that "the allegation that something is *bid'a* is often made rashly, marginalizing new ideas and making creativity difficult. For some Muslims, the term has become a rhetorical sledgehammer to vindicate their own ideas by obliterating others."[5] As Abd-Allah's commentary suggests, the dilemma over the negotiation of innovation and creativity in Islam with the imperative of upholding the sanctity of the normative order established by the example of the Prophet and his Companions is as vexatious today as it was many centuries ago. At stake in how one imagines the parameters of *bid'a* are the very boundaries, and by extension the very content, of Islam as a discursive tradition. Indeed, the question of "when innovation turns into heresy" equates to asking what defines Islam and its limits.[6]

In this chapter, I examine some of the ways this crucial question was addressed by the pioneers of the Deoband school and by Shāh Muḥammad Ismā'īl before them. Since there is significant overlap in the thought of these scholars on this issue, for purposes of illustration the bulk of this chapter focuses, though not exclusively, on the discourses of the most prolific early Deoband thinker, Ashraf 'Alī Thānvī.

Popularly known as the "physician of the community" (*ḥakīm al-ummat*) by his followers, Thānvī is arguably the most influential and certainly one of the most widely read modern South Asian Muslim scholars. His writings are said to number over a thousand. He wrote extensively on almost all facets of Islam, including Qur'ānic exegesis, Ḥadīth studies, law and jurisprudence, Sufism, and philosophy. Thānvī was both an accomplished jurist and a leading Sufi in the Chishtī order. Originally from the town of Thāna Bhawan in Uttar Pradesh, Thānvī graduated from Deoband in 1883, at the age of twenty.[7] His intellectual career was influenced not only by one of Deoband's founders, Rashīd Aḥmad Gangohī, but also by the eminent nineteenth-century Indian Chishtī Sufi Ḥājī Imdādullah Muhājir Makkī.

Ḥājī Imdādullah served as the Sufi guru for all of the Deoband pioneers, including Gangohī, Nānautvī, and Thānvī. Though not trained as a jurist, he was arguably the most charismatic and widely followed Sufi master in colonial India. Like Thānvī, Imdādullah was a native of Thāna Bhawan. He was accorded the title "the Meccan Migrant" (Muhājir Makkī) because he fled to Mecca in the aftermath of the 1857 Mutiny after the British accused him of involvement in that rebellion. Imdādullah stayed in exile in Mecca for the rest of his life, where he continued to attract Indian and non-Indian disciples of varied ideological orientations (see chapter 12). Thānvī became Imdādullah's disciple in 1884 while he was in Mecca for his first pilgrimage. Imdādullah played a formative role in

Thānvī's development as a Sufi master. In turn, Thānvī played a pivotal part in preserving and shaping Imdādullah's legacy, as we will see more fully in the final chapter.

After graduating from Deoband in 1883, Thānvī taught for fourteen years in a seminary called Jāmi' al-'Ulūm in the city of Kānpūr in Uttar Pradesh. He then returned to his hometown of Thāna Bhawan in 1897 and took up the leadership of the Sufi lodge that his own guru Imdādullah had managed before leaving India. While at Thāna Bhawan, Thānvī trained a number of disciples and established himself as a prolific and influential author. He remained closely connected with the Deoband school and served as its patron-in-chief (*sarparast*) for many years. Thānvī's disciples came from all over India. Among the most prominent of them were his nephews Ẓafar Aḥmad 'Uthmānī (d. 1974) and Muftī Muḥammad Shafī' (d. 1976), both of whom went on to become major religious figures in Pakistan after the partition of 1947.[8]

Thānvī devoted a large part of his intellectual oeuvre to the theme of heretical innovation.[9] His writings on this concept are found across varied textual genres, including popular reformist texts (*iṣlāḥī taṣnīfāt*), juridical opinions (*fatāwā*), and reverential aphorisms (*malfūẓāt*) meticulously compiled by his disciples. These discursive archives provide important insights into Thānvī's social imaginary as a religious reformer and also into the Debandī orientation more generally.

In the discussion that follows, I analyze critical fragments of his thought in the hope of documenting and highlighting ways in which Deoband scholars imagined the limits of innovation both theologically and in relation to religious practice. While it is well known that Deoband scholars opposed several popular conventions and devotional rituals, the question of how they went about that task has not received much attention in the Western academy. By what hermeneutical means did they try to construct the limits of normativity and heresy? How did they imagine the very idea of innovation? What are some of the ambiguities found in their conception of moral reform? These are some of the questions I address in this chapter. Initially, however, I want to briefly explain the way I approach the categories of normativity and heresy, as a way of outlining my theorization of the concept of heretical innovation or *bid'a* in Islam.

Theorizing Normativity and Heresy in Islam

By the term *normativity*, I mean the clusters of theological commitments and patterns of embodied practices that a community deems to be normatively demanded for the cultivation of moral excellence and virtue. As philosopher Christine Korsgaard, in her book *Sources of Normativity*, frames this concept, "Ethical standards are [always] *normative*. They do not merely *describe* a way in which we in fact regulate our conduct. They make *claims* on us; they command, oblige, recommend, or guide [emphases in original]." Similarly, she states that "concepts like knowledge, beauty, and meaning, as well as virtue and justice, all have a normative dimension, for they tell us what to think, what to like, what to say, what to do, and what to be."[10] In a religious tradition like Islam, the sources of normativity are always varied, multiple, and interrelated, ranging from the pastoral authority of expert scholars to the accumulated weight of repetitive disciplined practice. I prefer the category of normativity over orthodoxy because it affords a greater degree of fluidity and ambiguity in the location of religious authority among a set of competing claimants.[11] The category of orthodoxy, even if assumed to be subject to constant contestation, creates the wrong impression that one can in fact generate a set of names and addresses where the custodians of orthodoxy may be identified and marked as such. In the absence of a dominant ecclesiastical authority in Islam, the heuristic value of the term *orthodoxy* seems questionable. Moreover, and more crucially, "orthodoxy," like "sect," is one of those categories that at the very moment of its invocation becomes caught up in the "machine of [Christian] political theology."[12]

In his brilliant study *Two: The Machine of Political Theology and the Place of Thought*, philosopher Roberto Esposito demonstrates the conceptual entwinement of Christian political theology and modern secularism.[13] Moreover, he shows the machine-like process through which this political theology forces itself into conceptual categories employed while examining non-Western traditions and cultures. As Esposito points out, the "entire linguistic tissue that enervates our conceptual categories is imbued with political theological undertones."[14] Building and commenting on Esposito's contribution, Arvind Mandair sums up the problem at stake: "Central to the operations of (especially modern) Western language and thought," he writes, "is a metaphysical apparatus whose key task is to organize difference (among persons, cultures, concepts) by reducing it to structures of identity (for example, noncontradictory unity, analogy, individuality, personhood)."[15] One can fruitfully add "orthodoxy" to Mandair's latter list of structures of identity assembled by the machine of secular Christian political theology and transposed into other contexts through an act of "generalized translation."[16] It is this insidious yet powerful theology of translation that various attempts to defend or resuscitate the category of orthodoxy in Islamic studies have failed to consider.[17] To draw on Gil Anidjar, this category is too soaked in the "blood" of Christian political theology that is the foundation of secular conceptuality to be allowed to so freely and cheerfully circulate through the study of Islam and South Asian religions.[18] This category is also unhelpful with regard to the specific context of investigating modern South Asian *'ulamā'* discourses and contestations.

The major Muslim reformist schools in British India, the Deobandīs, Barelvīs, and the Ahl-i Ḥadīth, were all part of the same so-called orthodoxy of the learned religious elite; where they differed from one another was in their interpretation of the prophetic norm, and consequently the normative expectations they held for the masses. The binary construct of orthodoxy/heterodoxy is quite unhelpful in capturing the range of contesting opinions on the borders separating the normative from the heretical. The category of normativity affords greater flexibility and theoretical breathing space for the analysis of scholarly debates on the boundaries of normative practice in Islam.

In approaching the category of normativity, I find particularly compelling anthropologist/sociologist Pierre Bourdieu's idea of *habitus*, as developed in his two books *The Logic of Practice* and *An Outline of a Theory of Practice*. Bourdieu described *habitus* as "a product of history [that] produces individual and collective practices—more history—in accordance with the schemes generated by history. *Habitus* ensures the active presence of past experiences, which, deposited in each organism in the form of schemes of perception, thought, and action, tend to guarantee the '*correctness*' (emphasis mine) of practices and their constancy over time, more reliably than all formal rules and explicit norms."[19]

For Bourdieu, *Habitus* is a form of embodied history that at every moment structures new experiences in accordance with the structures produced by past experiences. The relationship of *habitus* to normativity is best captured when Bourdieu writes, "The *habitus* tends to generate all the 'reasonable,' 'common sense' behaviors (and only these) which are possible within the limits of these regularities, and which are likely to be *positively sanctioned* [emphasis mine] because they are objectively adjusted to the logic characteristic of a particular field, whose objective future they anticipate."[20]

Closely aligned to Bourdieu's category of *habitus* is his concept of *doxa*: a collection of bodily rhythms and dispositions that come to be taken for granted by members of a community as an established cosmological order, perceived not as arbitrary (i.e., as one among others) but as a self-evident natural order recurrently reproduced without any questioning or second-guessing.[21] Central to theorizing the category of normativity in Islam is the question of how a set of authoritative religious discourses become embodied in a community's practice of everyday life. In this context, particularly insightful is Bourdieu's astute observation that "the stabler the objective structures and the more fully they reproduce themselves in the agents' dispositions, the greater the extent of the field of *doxa*, of that which is taken for granted."[22]

I find Bourdieu's twin concepts of *habitus* and *doxa* helpful in deepening the conversation on the normative expectations and conflicts underlying intra-Muslim contestations over the boundaries of heresy in Islam. In a certain sense, the discourse on *bid'a* in Muslim thought is driven by competing imaginaries of an ideal "*Islamic habitus*," or, to be more precise, a *habitus* informed, formed, or shaped by the *sunna*. What must be emphasized here is that the *sunna* is not simply a juridical category applied to derive legal rulings. Rather, it signifies practices and rhythms of life intended to assume the status of a naturalized, spontaneous *habitus*—a normative model with the weight of embodied history behind it. As Bourdieu reminded us, "*Habitus* tends to ensure its own constancy and its defense against *change* through the selection it makes within new information by *rejecting information* capable of calling into question its accumulated information, if exposed to it accidentally or by force, and especially by *avoiding exposure* to such information" (emphasis mine).[23]

The insight that *habitus* defends against change is particularly relevant to the interplay of constancy and change that hovers over the *sunna-bid'a* debate in Islam. *Sunna* signifies the sanctioned normative *habitus* embodying a community that shares a history and tradition. Therefore, the community and its history and tradition all have to be protected against the threat of external exposure and new information that might devour its purity, destabilize its constancy, and, in effect, compromise its normative authority as a set of discourses demanding embodied assent from its followers. *Bid'a*, on the other hand, is the inverse of *sunna*, denoting those unsanctioned habits and rhythms of disciplined activity that are introduced in the face of an already agreed-upon structure of normativity. Before I dig deeper into the hermeneutical aspects of *bid'a*, I want to briefly reflect on its narratological dimension so as to further clarify its epistemic and normative stakes. For this, I turn to the thought of arguably the most formidable scholar in medieval and early modern Islam to have written on the concept of *bid'a*: the renowned fourteenth-century Andalusian/Granadian Mālikī jurist Abū Isḥāq Ibrāhīm al-Shāṭibī (d. 1388).

The Narratology of *Bid'a*: Normativity, Heresy, and Estrangement

Bid'a is as much a narrative category as it is a doctrinal, legal, and theological one. In fact, attending to its narrative function promises to broaden and deepen the analytical view and approach to this category. More specifically, Muslim intellectual discourses on *bid'a* are often enfolded in what one may call a "narrative of estrangement," in which the archetypal narrative of the Prophet's and his community's estrangement and exile at the hands of unbelievers in early Islam is mobilized as a blueprint for each successive episode of antagonism pitting the upholders of normativity against the purveyors of heresy. Committing to the normative path invariably brings estrangement. But this estrangement also indexes an individual's and a community's commitment to the Qur'ān, the *sunna*, and the teachings of the pious ancestors. In what follows, I elucidate the sorts of moral claims and desires invested in the mobilization of such a narrative of estrangement in Muslim intellectual and reformist discourses on *bid'a*. As literary theorist Hayden White best put it, "Where, in any account of reality, narrativity is present, we can be sure that morality or a moralizing impulse is present too. . . . Could we ever narrativize *without* moralizing?"[24]

For a particularly effective and instructive illustration of the articulation of such a narrative, I briefly turn to the most systematic and one of the most detailed premodern works on the concept and application of *bid'a*: *Adherence* (*Al-I'tiṣām*), a text by the fourteenth-century Mālikī jurist Ibrāhīm al-Shāṭibī. Al-Shāṭibī died almost exactly a century before the death of the Muslim emirate of Granada. His works on Islamic law and jurisprudence (such as his other classic, *The Reconciliation* (*Al-Muwāfaqāt*) are widely considered as among the most sophisticated and influential in early modern Muslim thought.[25] While I will have occasion to engage select aspects of his discussion on interpretive aspects of *bid'a* in a moment, I focus here on his remarkable introductory chapter in *Adherence*.

In this introduction, al-Shāṭibī framed his investment in composing a book on *bid'a* through a sustained meditation on the Prophet's evocative saying: "Islam began as a stranger and will return as a stranger the way it began, so blessed are the estranged" (*Budi'a al-Islām gharīban wa sa ya'ūdu gharīban kamā budi'a fa ṭūbā li-l-ghurabā'*). Ebrahim Moosa's commentary on this prophetic saying brings its multiple facets into relief. "Here," Moosa wrote, "the idea of being a stranger or exile is idealized in manifold ways. It evokes a certain tyranny of the world and of time. Under such anticipated conditions, those who seek the truth become exiled and marginalized by the tyranny of the majority. The marginalized are exiles in their suffering and give solidarity to each other. Exile here has many permutations ranging from the physical and spiritual to the political and to other conceivable forms of suffering and marginalization."[26] Being estranged, often considered a horrifying prospect, is in fact laced with the beauty of divine and prophetic blessings, this prophetic report suggests. Moreover, this prophetic saying connects a narrative of estranged beginnings to a teleology that returns to those beginnings. This quality of repetition is crucial to the way the saying brings together narrativity and temporality. "Narrative repetition," as Paul Ricoeur puts it, enables "reading the end into the beginning and the beginning into the end," so one can "learn to read time backward, as the recapitulation of the initial conditions of a course of action in its terminal consequences. In this way, the plot does not merely establish human action 'in' time, it also establishes it in memory."[27]

Al-Shāṭibī saw this saying of the Prophet as the encapsulation of a constantly repetitive battle at the heart of Islam: the battle between submitting to divine sovereignty and following the customs, habits, and traditions of one's ancestors. This battle had rendered the Prophet a stranger in his own community, the object of rebuke and slander from those who not long before had been among his dearest friends and kin. This was how al-Shāṭibī recounted the psychic pain of the Prophet's misery: "All the people of peace declared war on him, his dearest friends turned against him as [agents of] torturous pain. Those closest to him in kin became farthest from his friendship. And those affixed to him in a relation of the womb cultivated the bitterest sentiments against him in their hearts. What kind of estrangement can equal this estrangement?" (*Wa ṣāra 'ahl al-silm kuluhum ḥarban 'alayhi wa-l 'āda al-walī al-ḥamīm 'alayhi ka-l-'adhāb al-'alīm fa 'aqrabuhum 'alayhi nasaban kāna ab'ad al-nās 'an muwālātihi wa 'alṣaquhum bi-hi raḥman kānū 'aqṣā qulūban 'alayhi. Fa 'ay ghurba tuwāziy hādhihi-l-ghurba?*).[28] Why did the Prophet encounter such resistance to his mission? Because he challenged "what people were used to" (*kharaja 'an mu'tādihim*) (13). Central to the narrative plot of the battle between *sunna* and *bid'a*, normativity and heresy, is the temptation and power of sedimented habits that oppose divine norms.

The Prophet sought to shake and interrupt long-standing habits among pagans and other non-Muslims in Arabia; he and his small band of followers were thus shunned. But despite this inevitable hostility, they held on to the rope of divine normativity that kept them together, empowering and unifying them through dire tribulations. It is this image of holding on to God's rope that inspired the title of al-Shāṭibī's book, "Adherence" or "Holding On" (*Al-I'tiṣām*) derived from the iconic Qur'ānic verse "And hold on, together, to God's rope, and do not be divided."[29] Al-Shāṭibī's adoption of his book's title from this verse indicates that for him departing from the prophetic norm and succumbing to heretical innovations constituted more than a doctrinal or eschatological breach. *Bid'a* was a threat to the political order, unity, and power of the community. For al-Shāṭibī, it was thus a dual assault on individual salvation and on social order and cohesion.

Al-Shāṭibī's argument for the destructive power of *bid'a* was framed in a distinct narrative. He told the story of Islam's unfolding in the centuries after the Prophet's passing and his own place in that story through the emotive images of estrangement and exile. As Islam grew, so did the heresies within it multiply, fulfilling the alarming prophetic prognostication that "my community will be divided into seventy-three factions," much as had happened with Judaism and Christianity before it. Slowly but surely, Islam's power and unity dwindled, as practitioners of heresies and whimsical self-indulgence overpowered the upholders of prophetic normativity (*Fa takālabat 'alā sawād al-sunna al-bida' wa-l-ahwā'*) (15).

In enticingly simple yet telling words, al-Shāṭibī summed up the close relation between upholding normativity and experiencing estrangement. "When put next to the people of falsehood, the people of truth will always be small in number" (*Inna 'ahl al-ḥaq fī janb 'ahl al-bāṭil qalīl*) (15). He continued: "An estranged community is marked by erasure or paucity. This is when the normative becomes the taboo,[30] what should be taboo becomes normative, heretical innovations take the place of prophetic norms, and prophetic norms begin to seem like heretical innovations" (*Al-ghurba lā takūn 'ilā ma' faqd al-'ahl aw qilatihim wa dhālika ḥīna yaṣīru al-ma'rūf munkaran wa-l-munkar ma'rūfan wa taṣīru al-sunna bid'atan wa-l-bid'a sunnatan*) (15).

In al-Shāṭibī's view, the relationship between *sunna* and *bid'a* was absolutely inverse. "Every innovated heresy kills a parallel normative practice" (*Mā min bid'a tuḥdath ilā wa yamūt min al-sunan mā huwa fī muqābalatihā*) (19), he wrote with the precision of a mathemetician, and reinforced his point by quoting the Prophet's famous Companion 'Abdullāh Ibn 'Abbās (d. 687): "There is not a year that passes when people don't innovate heresies and kill the *sunna*, thus [constantly] resucitating heretical innovations and strangling to death prophetic norms" (*Mā yā'tī 'alā al-nās min 'ām ilā aḥdathū fī-hi bid'atan aw 'amātū fī-hi sunnatan*) (19). Thus for al-Shāṭibī the estrangement of the upholders of normativity followed a predictable regressive temporal pattern. Each successive generation of scholars found the world around them imprinted with fewer vestiges of the prophetic norm than the generation before. In impressing this point, al-Shāṭibī recounted an exchange between the Prophet's close Companions 'Abū al-Dardā (d. 652) and his wife 'Umm al-Dardā (an erudite scholar and jurist in Umayyad Damascus). Despite having died only a few decades after the Prophet, they were already bemoaning the state of the world around them. One day 'Abū al-Dardā entered their home looking visibly angry. "What made you angry?" his wife inquired. He responded, "By God, I don't recognize anything from the Prophet's practice except that people still pray together" (*Wallāh mā 'ārifu shay'an min 'amr Muḥammad 'illā annahum yuṣallūna jamī'an*) (16).

Similarly, al-Shāṭibī continued, inserting himself into his narrative, when he had plunged into his scholarly journey and begun addressing the masses, he found himself besieged by all varieties of heretical innovations. As he put it: "I found myself a stranger among my contemporaries" (*Wajadtu nafsī gharīban fī jumhūr ahl al-waqt*) (16). Al-Shāṭibī's dramatic account of the alienation he experienced deserves to be presented in his own words, as they capture to good effect the interaction of narrativity, normativity, and estrangement that I have been delineating in the last few pages.

> My intellectual options were clear. First, I could have adhered to the *sunna* on the understanding that I would be opposing what people were accustomed to. In this scenario, it was inevitable that what had happened to the opponents of heresies before me would also happen to me. This would be especially so if I called on them to follow only the *sunna* and nothing else. This option presented a mighty burden but also a generous reward. Second, I could have followed the path of the heretics at the expense of opposing the normative model of the Prophet and his pious Companions, in which case I would have come under the banner of misguidance, God forbid. In this situation, I would have condoned the habit [lit. "the habitual"] [of heresy]. And I would have been considered [by people] an agreeable person rather than a disagreeable antagonist. (17)

"But," al-Shāṭibī continued, more emphatically, "it became clear to me that destruction on the path of normativity is the very essence of salvation [*ra'ytu anna al-halāk fī 'itbā' al-sunna huwa al-nijāt*]. And that other people cannot detract anything from my commitment to God. So I began by choosing the method of gradualism in some matters. [Yet] all hell broke loose! Humiliation and rebuke were heaped upon me. Censure shot its arrows at me. I was associated with heresy and misguidance and was placed in the category of buffoons and fools [*fa qāmat 'alaīya al-qiyāma wa tawātarat ʿalaīya al-malāma wa fawwaqa ʿillaīya al-ʿitāb sihāmahu wa nusibtu ʿilā al-bidʿa wa-l-ḍalāla wa ʿunziltu manzilat ʿahl al-baghāwa wa-l-jahāla*]" (17).

Despite all these hardships, al-Shāṭibī asserted, in a flourish that congratulated himself for his own heroism: "I continued to investigate the heresies that the Prophet had highlighted and warned about . . . and to search for prophetic norms whose light was about to be extinguished by heretical innovations so I could help restore their glow with my actions and be counted on Judgment Day as among those who resuscitated the *sunna* [*ʿabḥath ʿan al-sunan allatī kādat tuṭfīʾ nūrahā tilka al-muḥdathāt laʿllī ʿajlū bil-ʿamal sanā-ha*]" (19).

Note how al-Shāṭibī crafted the narrative of his scholarly strivings as if he were telling the Prophet's biography. The narrativity of *bidʿa* was intimately tied to the construction of his own religious authority as the inheritor of the Prophet and of the prophetic mandate. Embodying the Prophet's experience of physical, emotional, and psychological estrangement during the early years of his prophetic career confirmed one's place on the path of normativity. The trope of estrangement, in other words, signified occupying the right side of history in the temporal realm and achieving salvation in the eschatological domain. Most importantly, prophetic reformers in every epoch were fated to estrangement. The Prophet's Companion ʿUways al-Qaranī (d. 657), to whom the Sufi practice of establishing spiritual intimacy or discipleship in the physical absence of one's master/beloved (*ʿuwaysī* initiation) is also attributed, best summed up this sentiment: "Commanding the normative and forbidding wrong does not leave the faithful with any friends" (*Inna al-ʿamr bi-l maʿrūf wa-l-nahī ʿan al-munkar lam yudʿā li-l muʾmin ṣadīqan*) (19).

I now turn to some key hermeneutical aspects of defining *bidʿa* and its limits. I will do so by staying with al-Shāṭibī for a few moments before venturing again to South Asia.

The Hermeneutics of *Bidʿa*: Heresy as Faux Religion

Central to the definition of *bidʿa* is the capacity of the human subject to cultivate a parallel order of normativity that might rival God's authority as a sovereign legislator. Indeed, it is this fundamental sin of choosing that constitutes *hairesis* (heresy): the exercise of the human will in selecting a faux architecture of normativity is what invests *bid'a* with its symbolic currency as one of the most incendiary discourses of exclusion and taboo in Islam. To be more precise, the category of *bid'a* operates at the interstices of law and theology; the prohibition against innovating in the presence of a prophetic norm is anchored in a larger theological imaginary eager to guard the absoluteness of God's sovereignty. For example, in *Adherence*, al-Shāṭibī defined *bid'a* "as an innovated practice in religion that simulates the *sharī'a* [in the intensity and discipline with which it is undertaken]" (*ṭarīqa fī-l-dīn mukhtara'ah tuḍāhī al-sharī'a*) (23). "Simulating the *sharī'a*," he explained, meant "resembling the path of the *sharī'a* without in reality being that [path]" (*Tushābih al-sharī'a min ghayr 'an takūn fī-l-ḥaqīqa kadhālik*) (25).

In excavating the deeper dynamics at work in the desire to simulate a normative order, al-Shāṭibī offered a curious reading on the psychology of the heretical innovator. The heretical innovator, he claimed, strove to make his heresies resemble established normative practices so that he might disguise the former as the latter (*taltabis 'alayhi bi'l-sunna*). That was his best bet to confuse people into thinking that his new heresies are indeed normative—a necessary task because "a human being is not inclined to imitate a practice unless that practice exudes the air of normative legitimacy" (25). In other words, to paraphrase al-Shāṭibī, if you want to ensnare people into becoming your followers, you must give what you are selling the appearance of normativity. It is precisely this power of duplicity, this capacity for subterfuge, that made the heretical innovator (*mubtadi'*) and heretical innovations so very dangerous.

Thus for al-Shāṭibī, as for several other scholars, the quality of simulation was crucial to how *bid'a* functioned as a borderline discourse in Islam separating normative and heretical modes of practice. The boundaries of normativity were transgressed when someone chose to establish what one might call a "faux normativity" by adhering to an unsanctioned practice with the rigor and passion required for adherence to the *sharī'a*. Such religious adherence to a non-normative order of innovated norms sanctified what had not been divinely sanctioned. For this reason I render *bid'a* as "heretical innovation" instead of just "innovation," as it is often translated. Rendering *bid'a* as simply "innovation" is problematic because it nourishes the stereotype that casts Islam as a religion inherently opposed to all forms of innovation and creativity in the realms of law and jurisprudence. Both the legal discourse on and the social baggage carried by the category of *bid'a* are inseparably bound up with a psychology of unceasing rivalry between humanly invented and divinely mandated orders of normativity.

This is also a good opportunity for further elaboration and explanation of my translation of *bid'a* as "heretical innovation." The "heretical" in "heretical innovation" does not equate to expulsion from religion or the community of the faithful. *Bid'a* is not the same as unbelief (*kufr*) or apostasy (*irtidād*). The idea of ingratitude for God's sovereignty or *kufr* is closely tied to the theme of challenging divine sovereignty that undergirds the concept of *bid'a*. But the latter does not carry the same magnitude of eschatological consequence. However, I have persisted with translating *bid'a* as heretical innovation rather than as, say, "blameworthy innovation" or "reprehensible innovation" because the idea of *hairesis* or choosing is inseparable to its conceptual architecture. The reprehensibility of *bid'a* lies precisely in the human attempt to choose an order of life that is not divinely sanctioned and that hence challenges God's sovereign power. Indulgence in *bid'a* does not signal outright unbelief. Perhaps even more dangerous, it presages a lurking threat that operates at the threshold of unbelief, always threatening to cross over but never explicitly doing so. It holds the potential for unbelief. And it is that potentiality that renders *bid'a* subversive, theologically and sociologically. The specter of transgression shadowing *bid'a* lives off the mimetic sedition involved in the human decision to simulate God's sovereign decisions. It is this sin of hairesis or choosing a faux normative order that lends *bid'a* its ominous character doctrinally and communally. That is why I render it as "heretical innovation."

The discourse on *bid'a* in nineteenth-century North Indian Muslim reformist thought was very similar in its mind-set of constant competition between human and divine norms. For example, in their major texts on *bid'a*, Shāh Muḥammad Ismā'īl and Ashraf 'Ali Thānvī argued that any pattern of ritualized activity (*rasm*) begins to threaten the legislative authority of the divine and its expression as a normative example of the

Prophet when it is performed with the degree of passion, commitment, and discipline reserved exclusively for acts of religion such as praying and fasting that are normatively demanded of believers and that serve as means to attain greater proximity (*taqarrub*) to God.[31]

This category of *rasm* (pl. *rusūm*), derived from the Arabic roots *r-s-m*, literally meaning "to imprint, draw, or sketch a pattern," is a critical component of Indian Muslim discourses on *bid'a*. In its Urdu modality, *rasm* can best be rendered as customs and habits that through a process of repetitive performance and reiteration become an entrenched part of a community's underlying *habitus*. In other words, a *rasm* can be likened to a *doxic* condition that over time comes to be taken as a self-evident, unspoken reality rather than as one of several alternative and equally arbitrary possibilities.

Rusūm: Conceptual Continuities and Transformations

The intellectual trajectory of the category of *rasm* in South Asian Muslim scholarly discourses underwent a subtle yet significant shift from the eighteenth to the early and late nineteenth century. The modality of this shift is usefully captured if one attends to the discussion of this category by the iconic eighteenth-century scholar Shāh Walī Ullah in his magisterial magnum opus in Arabic, *God's Conclusive Argument* (*Ḥujjat Allāh al-Bāligha*). *God's Conclusive Argument* is a dizzyingly layered and multivalent text. In a nutshell, though, one may describe it as a commentary on the cosmological foundations of a pious and morally sound political economy. A central category that binds this text together is what Walī Ullah called "tools or instruments of moral cultivation" (*irtifāqāt*),[32] also commonly translated as conveniences or supports for civilization. In its conceptual outlines, *God's Conclusive Argument* seems closest to the hugely influential twentieth-century book by the German sociologist Norbert Elias, *The Civilizing Process*.[33] Though occupied with remarkably similar concerns about the cultivation of civility, Walī Ullah's text in fact offers a useful corrective to Elias's Eurocentric narrative by presenting a competing imaginary of disciplined life.

In a section of *God's Conclusive Argument* entitled "Dominant Customs/Conventions among the People" (*Al-rusūm al-sā'ira fī'l-nās*),

Walī Ullah argued that habits and customs, or *rusūm*, were "among the instruments of moral cultivation that are as critical [to the moral fashioning and advancement of a community] as the heart is to the body." Further, "They are the foremost and most essential object of revealed normativities" (*Al-rusūm min al-irtifāqāt hīya bi manzilat al-qalb min jasad al-insān wa 'iyāhā qaṣadat al-sharā'i' awwalan wa bi'l-dhāt*).[34] While offering an archaeology of the concept of *rusūm*, Walī Ullah identified multiple sources that could serve as the cause for their becoming entrenched in the everyday life of a community. In addition to the influence of prophets and sages, and the pressure exerted by kings, customs and habits could manifest intuitively in people's hearts. Walī Ullah contended that when dominant norms (*al-sunan al-sā'ira*) emanated from the truth, they protected the moral fabric of the community and guided its people toward intellectual and practical talents. In the absence of such norms, he continued, those people would be like animals (*Lo lā-hā li'l-taḥaqa akthar al-nās bi'l- bahā'im*). Walī Ullah made the arresting claim that most often people found it impossible to enunciate or explain their motivations for participating in such disciplined practices of moral cultivation. As he put it:

> Consider the number of men who, say, enter marriage and take part in other such commonly expected moralizing norms. If you ask him [one such man], Why do you restrain yourself with these constraining practices? he will not have a good answer other than to say, "I am doing what people do" [*Lam yajid jawāban 'ilā muwāfaqat al-qawm*]. The most one can say about such a person is that he has an intuitive synoptic knowledge [*'ilm ijmālī*] of the motivations underlying his actions—though even that much he will not be able to articulate, let alone be able to explain his actions as a prelude to moral advancement. (100)

In other words, for Walī Ullah, the motivation to lead a disciplined life, was not always readily articulated. Life was, as Talal Asad would have it, "essentially itself."[35] Moreover, what interests me most about Walī Ullah's discussion is his recognition of the subjectivity of the masses as a source of normativity. In subtle contrast to his nineteenth-century successors, Walī Ullah seemed much more confident about acknowledging the intuitive capacities of the masses to chart a pious life.

That said, it would be misleading to suggest that he was not critical of several customs and practices in his midst. He was far from a practitioner of hermeneutical charity. The dominant norms of a community, he argued, were ever vulnerable to corruption. And the foremost cause of such corruption was the rise to power of a morally sluggish political elite unable to see or understand the broader interests (*al-maṣāliḥ al-kulīya*) of a community (100).

Like Ismāʿīl and the Deoband pioneers, Walī Ullah was deeply critical of aristocratic habits and customs, especially in the realm of everyday life. These included profligate habits of dress and eating, or the expenditure of excessive time on idle forms of entertainment like chess, hunting, collecting pigeons, and playing musical instruments. Such habits not only required that one earn a lot of money (*taḥtāju ʿilā taʿammuq balīgh fī'l-ʿaksāb*) but also made a person indifferent to matters of worldly livelihood and the afterlife (*ʿihmāl ʿamr al-muʿāsh wa'l-muʿād*) (101–2). As people with such corrupt habits assumed power and political authority, the masses, unable to oppose or resist the might of the powerful, fell in line with abject imitation, he continued this narrative. This happened because the masses lost the capacity in their hearts to strongly incline toward pious or for that matter impious acts; they simply adhered to the practices they saw among those in power (101). And those who refused to surrender their moral compass and remained steadfast in piety tended to keep away from others around them, relegating themselves in silence to the sidelines (*Wa yubqā qawm fiṭratuhum sawīya fī ʿukhrīyāt al-qawm lā yukhāliṭūnahum wa yaskutūna ʿalā al-ghayẓ*) (101). By this silence they expressed anger and disavowal toward the dominant population around them. This was how a morally harmful norm was established and reinforced (*Fa-tanʿaqidu sunnatan sai'yatan wa tataʾakkadu*) (101). Walī Ullah urged the scholarly elite with expansive knowledge to not adopt such a disengaged, pacifist attitude. "They must expend their efforts to spread the truth and make it circulate in society, and they must actively resist and circumvent falsehood. This may well take some fierce quarreling and opposition [*mukhāṣamāt wa muqātalāt*]" (101).

From this discussion, it is apparent that Walī Ullah, much like his grandson Ismāʿīl a few decades later, clearly espoused a reform agenda that was intensely critical of habits and customs or *rusūm* attached to the Mughal aristocracy. However, the conceptual space of *rusūm* in Walī

Ullah's discourse also differed from Ismā'īl's reform agenda in some crucial ways. For Walī Ullah, while *rusūm* were vulnerable to corruption, the corruption emanated from moral cracks in the political economy and leadership driving a community. The focus of Walī Ullah's thought was on the interaction of cosmology, politics, and the moral fashioning of everyday life. He seemed relatively unconcerned about the incapacity of the masses to distinguish between obligatory and nonobligatory practices, or about their tendency to confuse the two, in the performance of their ritual lives.

Yet as I will show in this section, such concern and anxiety were at the heart of Ismā'īl's and Deobandī discourses on heretical innovation. Indeed, over the nineteenth century, the category of *rusūm* or customs became increasingly synonymous with that of *bid'a*, heretical innovation. This was one of the central conceptual transformations in the mobilization of *rusūm* in South Asian Muslim reformist discourses from the eighteenth to the nineteenth century and beyond. For Walī Ullah, *rusūm* impressed a cosmological template of normativity upon the affairs of the temporal world. Good norms and customs attracted the prayers and blessings of the Highest Council (*al-malā' al-a'lā*) and the satisfaction of the Supernum Plenum (*ḥaẓīrat al-quds*) in the cosmological realm. Corrupting norms and customs, on the other hand, invited their opposition and anger (101).[36]

Now, even nineteenth-century reformers like Ismā'īl and his Deobandī interlocutors could think about the broader cosmologies underlying their reformist visions. However, one finds in their discourse a much firmer equation of *rusūm* with heretical innovation or *bid'a*, coupled with a more sharply delineated distinction between customs (*rusūm*) and devotional practices (*'ibādāt*). Let me make this point more simply and colloquially. In contrast to Walī Ullah, whose reading of *rusūm* was cosmologically oriented, in the discursive universe of nineteenth-century South Asian Muslim reformist thought *rasm/rusūm* increasingly acquired negative connotations, signifying heretical innovations opposing the Prophet's normative model. In other words, the constriction of what counted as normative religion necessarily entailed the expansion of what counted as heretical innovations. The normative legitimacy of an unprecedented plethora of everyday customs and conventions became suspect and subject to debate and contestation. This, I would argue, was a subtle yet profound transformation not only in the category of *rasm/rusūm* but in the intellectual and social careers of South Asian Muslim thinkers more broadly from the eighteenth to the nineteenth century.

An excellent illustration of this transformation is found in the contemporary Deoband scholar Sa'īd Aḥmad Pālanpūrī's Urdu translation of and commentary on Walī Ullah's *God's Conclusive Argument* (*Ḥujjat Allāh al-Bāligha*), entitled *God's Capacious Mercy* (*Raḥmat Allāh al-Wāsi'a*).[37] While commenting on the section of this text I have just now addressed, Pālanpūrī employed the phrase "customs [*rusūm*] and heretical innovations [*bid'āt*]" as a tautological compound, as if they were synonymous. Take, for instance, the following statement of Walī Ullah's, excerpts of which I also discussed earlier: "The learned elite with expansive knowledge must expend their efforts to spread the truth and make it circulate in society, and they must actively resist and circumvent falsehood. This may well take some fierce quarreling and opposition. All this is counted as among the best acts of piety" (101). Now compare with this statement Pālanpūrī's translation and commentary: "Correcting/reforming heretical innovations and customs is a most excellent practice [*Bid'āt wa rusūm kī iṣlāḥ karnā beḥtarīn 'amal hay*]. . . . When customs and heretical innovations take root in a community, they become incredibly difficult to dislodge."[38] Pālanpūrī's confident repetition of the "heretical innovations and customs" (*bid'āt wa rusūm*) compound throughout his commentary betrays the fact that in this section Walī Ullah never even used the word *bid'a*, either independently of or with reference to the category of *rusūm* or customs. Yet in the late twentieth century, a scholar like Pālanpūrī took the equation of these terms as almost a given. This presumed synonymity of *rusūm* and *bid'ā* had a lot to do with the thought and intellectual impact of prominent nineteenth-century South Asian Muslim reformers like Shāh Muḥammad Ismā'īl and Ashraf 'Alī Thānvī. I now turn to a detailed examination of their discourses on and contributions to shaping the conceptual architecture of *bid'a* as a concept and construct.

Defining "Heretical Innovation"

At the heart of the controversy surrounding the limits of *bid'a* in South Asian Islam was the question: Under what conditions do such customary conventions (*rusūm*) begin to oppose or threaten the monopoly of the *sharī'a* and especially that of the Prophet's normative model as the sole body of norms operative in the realm of religious practices? In other words, at what point, if ever, do humanly innovated norms come to challenge the supremacy of divinely sanctioned norms?

Different scholars, depending on their normative temperament, responded to this central question in disparate ways. Moreover, their response to this question holds the key to the much larger question of how they imagined their own authority as members of the religious elite vested with the task of safeguarding the religion's normative boundaries. Ismā'īl and Deobandī scholars such as Rashīd Aḥmad Gangohī and Ashraf 'Alī Thānvī who followed him were deeply suspicious and cautious about the capacity of customary practices to develop into what one might call a faux-*sharī'a*: a counternormativity reflective of human desire rather than divine decree. The masses, these scholars argued, could not be trusted in matters of religion. If a tight leash on their activities was not maintained, they would be certain to compromise the primacy of the *sharī'a* with their religious adherence to non-normative conventions.

The Deobandī reform project was primarily aimed at protecting the primacy of religious obligations against the threat of seemingly pious and spiritually rewarding rituals that, despite being permissible (*mubāḥ*), were not obligatory. The Deoband pioneers feared that the masses might easily mistake voluntary acts of piety for obligatory acts. For instance, Thānvī likened such voluntary rituals to tempting sweets (*mithā'ī*) that made young gullible children salivate. While mesmerizingly pleasurable when ingested, these sweets could only harm the health of the young and earnest in the long run.

Thānvī continued his analogy by drawing a comparison between parents and religious scholars. It was the responsibility of parents to train their children and prevent them from being seduced by such delicious yet harmful sweets. Similarly, Muslim scholars had to nurture the lived religion of the masses so that they might achieve immunity from seductive rituals that provided immense satisfaction in this world but caused only pain and anguish in the afterworld. *Bid'a*, according to this interpretation, functioned much like a tabooed act whose performance could tempt others. As Freud memorably remarked, in his problematic but productive classic *Totem and Taboo*, eerily echoing Thānvī, "An individual who has violated a taboo becomes himself taboo because he has the dangerous property of tempting others to follow his example. . . . He is therefore really *contagious*, in so far as every example incites to imitation, and therefore he himself must be avoided."[39] The originator of *bid'a*, the heretical innovator or *mubtadi'*, was similarly dangerous because he carried the contagion of temptation and the threat of normalizing the taboo through inciting imitation. Defeating such a pathological agent of contagion required not only intellectual overpowering but also social shunning.

In Thānvī's view, *bid'a* was much more dangerous than other sins. Why? Because *bid'a* could wear the mask of religion. Thānvī claimed that people who engaged in heretical innovations did so driven by the assumption that they were taking part in pious devotional practices. This made *bid'a* different from other sins. In the case of most other sins, at least the sinner knew that he was engaging in a wrongdoing for which he had to repent at some point. By contrast, the biggest tragedy about *bid'a*, Thānvī lamented, was that its perpetrators were never given the opportunity to repent because they understood their heresies as acts of religion.[40] Moreover, because such practices assumed the status of religion, a person who participated in them was lauded for pietistic excellence, and someone who refrained from them was collectively censured, reproached, and singled out as a heretic.

Indeed, this was the defining quality of a heretical innovation or a faux religious convention. The communal insistence, the peer pressure, if you will, to participate in such a practice had reached a level that anyone who voluntarily abstained from it was attacked. Such conventions were perpetuated by the invisible pressure of communal expectations and norms, not adherence to the dictates of divine law. Shāh Muḥammad Ismā'īl's definition of *rasm* or convention/custom illustrates this point very well. He defined *rasm* as "a nonobligatory practice that becomes so deeply ritualized in a community that anyone who abandons it becomes the target of his community's rebuke and censure. Moreover, conformity to the habits of ancestors or the peer pressure of contemporary friends, relatives, and community members represents the foundational source of the popularity that such rituals achieve."[41] Therefore, a nonobligatory or simply permissible practice was performed with as much dedication and regularity as if it were obligatory. But how did this happen? What was the process through which rituals became ritualized? How did individual practices become so entrenched in the life of a community that their abandonment was no longer thinkable?

Law, History, and the Normative

In one of his lesser-known but fascinating and rich texts *Clarifying Truth* (*Īzāḥ al-Ḥaqq*), devoted almost entirely on the subject of *bid'a*, Shāh Muḥammad Ismā'īl addressed some of these questions in enticing detail.[42] Critical to his narrative of how nonobligatory rituals assumed the aura of obligatory practices was the relationship between normativity, community, and history. All rituals, he explained, originally entered into a community's life to serve particular benefits. Moreover, the intellectual elite of a community endowed those rituals with specific forms so that the attached benefits were maximized and attained as easily as possible. Gradually, those specific forms became current and dominant among the masses. However, as those forms became an unquestioned part of a community's everyday life, the foundational purpose or benefits for which those forms had been originally instituted were forgotten.

People lost sight of the original reason underlying particular rituals as their attachment to the current form (*ṣūrat-i murawwaja*) of those rituals intensified.[43] Over time, form and purpose became completely divorced. At this point, the passion of the masses remained solely invested in preserving the outer forms of rituals, even if those forms no longer yielded the benefits for which they had originally been put in place. Therefore, even if the purpose of the ritual could be fulfilled through other means, its current form would not be discarded. And anyone who chose not to abide by the specificities of that current form became subjected to the community's wrath.

Ismā'īl presented the example of the ritual of transmitting blessings to the deceased (*īṣāl-i sawāb*) by distributing food among family and community members. Almost ubiquitous among South Asian Muslims even today, this ritual is also known as the *fātiḥa*, since participants recite the opening chapter of the Qur'ān over food for the transmission of blessings to the souls of relatives, friends, or prominent saints and scholars. The *fātiḥa* is usually undertaken on the third and fortieth day of a person's death, events that are hence called *sīwam* (the third) and *chālīsvān* (the fortieth) respectively. In case of famous saints and scholars, the *fātiḥa* is most frequently held on the occasion of their birth anniversaries. The size and scope of these events can vary from a gathering of only a few households in a neighborhood to the assembly of massive crowds encompassing whole villages and towns. Despite the widespread popularity of the *fātiḥa*, Ismā'īl considered this practice a heretical innovation that had been terminally corrupted by the manner and intention with which it was performed. He explained that originally the logic of this ritual had centered on feeding the destitute relatives of the deceased as an act of charity. The blessings attained from this moment of charity were then transmitted to the soul of the deceased. Since destitute relatives were the most deserving recipients of all kinds of charity in Islam, on this occasion also they were prioritized as the foremost recipients of food.

However, Ismā'īl protested, in his day Indian Muslims were so compulsively attached to this specific mode of performing the ritual that its original purpose and rationale were lost on them. Thus he observed that when the relatives and close friends of the deceased were provided food, no one explicitly said things like "This food is charity on behalf of the deceased" or that "It is a source of support for the destitute." If such statements announcing the original purpose of this practice were uttered, Ismā'īl predicted, most relatives and family members would not even accept the food.[44] In fact, they would consider it an insult.

Moreover, their complete intolerance for any other means of fulfilling the supposed purpose of the ritual, namely transmitting blessings to the deceased, confirmed that they understood this specific form as obligatory. Ismā'īl argued that even if someone expended all kinds of charity on behalf of the deceased it would not be socially accepted. Why? Because people were fixated on the requirement that food be distributed exactly according to the ritual. If the food was not distributed in this manner, the person performing the ritual would be the target of abuse and censure. However, if that same person spent nothing on charity on behalf of the deceased and simply distributed food in accordance with established norms, he would be spared any verbal or emotional injury. Therefore, Ismāʿīl concluded, the practice of distributing food for the transmission of blessings to the deceased was no longer a devotional activity. It had become a mere convention divested of its original purpose and objective.[45]

It is important to note here the pivotal role of history in Ismāʿīl's narration of the formation of normativity. History, he argued, authorized rituals in ways that made it impossible to unauthorize them. The original purpose of offering food as a means of transmitting blessings to the deceased, for instance, had become buried in time and history. Indeed, history had made this ritual normative, a taken-for-granted part of a community's life that was no longer thought about before it was done.

According to Ismāʿīl, the original purpose of this ritual was invisible, hidden by history/time because, as one might say, it had been there for some time. But how did Ismāʿīl go about demonstrating the illegitimacy of this ritual as it was currently practiced in India? By turning to history itself. Ismāʿīl's argument rested on showing that this ritual had been "brought into history" for a specific purpose that it no longer served. His historicist posture sought to make visible the contingent authorization of this ritual as a way to disrupt its unquestioned necessity. The irresolvable contradiction in this operation was this: it was through history that Ismāʿīl attempted to reveal what had been hidden by history. In trying to combat the power of normalization enabled by history, Ismāʿīl mobilized more history. Even while protesting the intimacy of normativity and history, he could not think beyond history.

For Ismāʿīl, the labor of reform required one to remind the inhabitants of the present of their responsibility to the past. What he did not consider was the unavailability of the past to make demands on the present and the precariousness of temporality that rendered impossible the promise of historicizing life into a seamless thread connecting the past, present, and the future. In launching his evangelical program to transform embodied life by making appeals to history, what Ismāʿīl missed was that, as the theorist Jean-Luc Nancy has observed, history is not metaphysics but community or the commons. Nancy memorably wrote that "history—if we can remove this word from its metaphysical, and therefore historical, determination—does not belong primarily to time, nor to succession, nor to causality, but to community, or to being-in-common."[46]

Nancy's provocation aims to dehistoricize history. His goal is to show that the moral present of a community is not bound to how the history of its past is told. In other words, the pasts of a community are no longer transparently available for translation in the present. However, in Ismā'īl's historical imaginary, the past was an all-important and transparent category. In his conception of the relation between normativity and history, the determination of a community's moral life ought to be derived from an empirical history of its pasts. Ismā'īl's was a quest to construct and then narrate an objective history of the community. On the basis of that model he sought to reform the community.

But in the process he also objectified community into a group of ideologically self-aware agents who might readily shun embodied practices to demonstrate their fidelity toward that community's ideal history. The continued prevalence of such rituals in the everyday lives of South Asian Muslims today suggests that this way of imagining the relationship between community and history is untenable. It is untenable because the promise of transforming embodied life by reminding that life of its responsibility to history is never fulfilled. This promise cannot be fulfilled and remains deferred to an unspecifiable future.[47]

An almost identical promise to transform embodied life inspired Ashraf 'Alī Thānvī's discourses on *bid'a*. Thānvī was in complete agreement with Ismā'īl's analysis of the moral maladies afflicting Indian Muslims and with the latter's strategies to cure those maladies. Much like Ismā'īl, he believed that most popular rituals that seemingly fulfilled devotional objectives were in fact only means to show off wealth and conform to the pressures of the community. As an illustration of this argument, he took the example of commemorating the fortieth day of someone's death, the *chalīsvān* or the fortieth, as it is popularly called. While ostensibly serving the purpose of collecting rewards and blessings for the soul of the deceased, he claimed, the money spent on this ceremony, primarily on the preparation and distribution of food, was intended solely for the public display of wealth and social status.[48] To test the true motivation of the organizers for hosting this event, Thānvī proposed an interesting experiment.

He suggested that the organizers of this event should be advised that rather than publicly feeding members of their community (*birādarī*), they should privately give charity to someone destitute or donate funds to a mosque or a seminary. After all, the more needy and desperate the recipients of charity, the more rewards and blessings it would bring to the deceased. If presented with this suggestion, Thānvī predicted, the organizers would inevitably reply with something to the effect of "Good Lord! [*Subḥān Allāh*]! Do you really expect us to spend our money without anyone even hearing about it? How can we let that happen?"[49] According to Thānvī, ostentation (*riyā'*) and the fear of being shamed by the community were the driving motives for all these sorts of gatherings. The resistance to adopting any means of transmitting blessings that would not involve a public show of wealth confirmed this conclusion.

For Thānvī, this condition defeated the entire logic of transmitting rewards to the deceased. After all, he explained, the way this process worked was that living people accumulated rewards by doing good deeds with the right intention, and they then transmitted those accumulated rewards to the souls of the deceased. But in this situation, since the very intentionality underlying such rituals was corrupt and founded on affectation, the living were not even earning any rewards that could then be passed on. As he sarcastically put it, "When the balance [in this world] is zero [*ṣifar*]. what is left to be gifted [to the deceased]?" (*Jab yahān hī ṣifar hay tuh wahān kyā bakhsho gey?*)[50]

Here an important clarification must be registered: Ismā'īl and Thānvī were not opposed to rituals such as transmitting blessings to the deceased in absolute terms. To the contrary, they considered such rituals pious acts that were laudable in essence. But they found problematic the intentions with which the masses performed these rituals. The attachment of corrupt attitudes had rendered impermissible these otherwise permissible practices. And critical to Ismā'īl's and Thānvī's argument was the role of history in the formation of a community's normative boundaries.

In the view of these scholars, the moral corruption encrusted on otherwise pious rituals was invisible to the masses. This was so because the masses were so unconsciously attached to the historically generated forms of these rituals that they were blind to the original purpose of those forms. As a result, in the guise of performing pious acts, they were in fact perpetuating a public sphere plagued by moral corruptions. For Ismā'īl and Thānvī, the work of reform involved awakening the masses to this dissonance between the normative boundaries mandated by religion and established norms that dictated the practice of everyday life. Put differently,

Ismā'īl and Thānvī saw their role as one of intervening in history in order to interrupt its course. They sought to transform prevailing habits by showing how those habits transgressed the limits of tradition. But what kind of a legal imaginary and hermeneutical model sustained and channeled such a program of socioreligious reform?

When Innovation Becomes Heresy: The Hermeneutics of *Bid'a*

For Shāh Muḥammad Ismā'īl and the Deoband pioneers, it was not only the practice and era of the Prophet (the early seventh century) that was sacrosanct. In addition, the authority of the pious ancestors, meaning all the Companions of the Prophet, their successors, and other recognized religious figures in the Sunnī tradition, was equally binding and immune to criticism.[51] Indeed, while it is convenient to translate *sunna* as the "normative model of the Prophet," the meaning usually intended when the trope of *sunna* is placed in contradistinction to its inverse other, *bid'a*, is really the body of norms generated and sanctioned from the first three generations of Islam (*qurūn-i salāsa, Ar. Al-qurūn al-thalātha*). The pioneers of Deoband argued that the era of the Prophet and the eras of his Companions and their successors belonged to the same temporal complex.

It was impossible, they claimed, for any practice or convention current and widespread during the era of the Companions and their successors to lack either an explicit or an indicative precedent or proof text from the Prophet's normative example.[52] So the development of Arabic grammar and lexicography, the establishment of the doctrine of Qur'ān's inimitability, the creation of legal maxims and principles—all these were examples of seeming innovations that had been added to the tradition after the Prophet's physical departure from the world. But far from opposing the *sunna*, these later inventions in fact enhanced its normative stature or further aided in its explication. Therefore, they could not be called heretical innovations.

The Deoband pioneers argued that the often-made distinction between the categories of commendable innovations (*bid'a ḥasana*) and reprehensible innovations (*bid'a sai'yya*) was superfluous. For them, the term *bid'a* always signified unsanctioned practices that opposed the normative model of the Prophet. The so-called commendable or good innovations, they advised, should instead be labeled as "attachments to the *sunna*" (*mulḥaq bi 'l-sunna*). This was so because these later additions did not establish a new normative precedent but simply revealed an already established precedent.[53] Let me explain.

According to Deoband scholars, the normative model of the Prophet constituted those beliefs, practices, and habits that were dominant during the first three centuries of Islam without objection (*shuyyū' bi-lā nakīr*). It was not as if bad things did not happen during this exemplary stretch of time. Even then, people lied, cheated, and committed all varieties of crimes. However, these wrongdoings were both limited and objected to. Therefore, in the Deobandī legal imaginary, the concept of heretical innovation did not signify every new thing that did not materially exist during the first three generations. Rather, it meant alteration or opposition to the logic of norms dominant during that chosen era. In a very useful discussion Ashraf 'Alī Thānvī elaborated this principle in some detail.

According to Thānvī, two kinds of innovations sprang up after the first three generations of Islam's beginnings.[54] The first category comprised innovations that were new in both their form and the motivational cause (*sabab-i dā'ī*) for their existence. Moreover, these innovations were necessary for the fulfillment of obligatory religious practices. For example, the writing and cataloguing of religious books, the construction of religious seminaries and Sufi lodges, and the development of Arabic grammar were all new developments that were nonexistent during the Prophet's life and, more importantly, had no reason to exist then either.

Over time, however, these innovations became necessary for the completion of the religion's obligations. Why? In addressing this pivotal question, Thānvī presented a story of how a general decline in the human capacity to preserve and protect religion, as that religion became more and more removed from its moment of origin, necessitated the emergence of new tools and inventions that might assist in that task. Thānvī argued that during the first three centuries of Islam, the capacity of that early community to protect religion from harm was so advanced and finely adapted that there was no need for any external tools or mechanisms of assistance. For instance, the memory of the people during that era was impeccable. They remembered everything they heard. Their understanding of religion and its subtleties was so acute that they required no one to lecture or instruct them on such points. Similarly, a culture of recording and documenting prophetic discourses and events was also thriving.[55]

After this initial era of impeccability that lasted three generations, Thānvī continued, a second phase set in that witnessed a steady and steep decline on a number of fronts. People were no longer as enthusiastic about preserving religion as they once had been. A general indifference became the order of the day. Heretics and people who privileged rationalism over revealed truth assumed a position of dominance.[56] At this moment, Muslim scholars realized that their tradition was under threat and that if they failed to take immediate remedial action, religion would gradually die out. Therefore, they invented specific tools and mechanisms for preserving the tradition in a moment of potential crisis.

These innovations included the writing and publication of religious books, the systematization of such disciplines as jurisprudence, principles of jurisprudence, and the discourses of the Prophet that were authenticated and canonized long after the Prophet's death. The intellectual elite also constructed religious schools where these newly emerging disciplines could be taught and transmitted. Similarly, the prominent Sufis of that era invested in lodges and centers of learning to consolidate their genealogies of religious knowledge and authority.

The motivating cause that gave rise to all these new intellectual developments and activities, Thānvī emphasized, was absent in the lifetime of the Prophet and his immediate followers. All these developments might appear to be innovations. However, in reality, they served as necessary preludes and preconditions to the fulfillment of obligatory religious practices. Therefore, Thānvī further explained, according to the juridical rule that a prelude to an obligation was also obligatory (*muqaddimat al-wājib wājib*), these innovations should in fact be called obligatory.

These new practices and forms of knowledge did not threaten the coherence of tradition. Rather, they were requirements for the continued subsistence of tradition. In other words, these seeming innovations constituted what one might call the deferred prophetic norm. Although their outer form was new, in substance they seamlessly connected with the logic of the Prophet's normative model. These innovations served as necessary means to materialize the deferred promise of the prophetic norm in a world where the memory of that norm was constantly fading away.[57]

The second category of innovations consisted of practices that were new in their form but not new in the "motivating cause" underlying their origination. For example, the "motivating cause" for celebrating the Prophet's birthday was to express happiness and joy at the event of his birth. This foundational cause was also present during the Prophet's life and the era of the Companions. Had they so wished, they could also have celebrated the Prophet's birthday. It was not as if the inauguration of this ritual was unthinkable for the Prophet and his Companions, Thānvī emphasized. Yet they never organized or participated in such a gathering.

For Thānvī, the absence of an act during the first three generations of Islam even when the rationale and motive for performing it were present in that era clearly showed that such an act was not authorized by the Prophet's normative model. Put more simply, if the Prophet and his Companions did not invent a practice when the logic for its invention was available to them, it was obvious that their normative model did not endorse this practice. Therefore, Thānvī continued, the later innovation of such practices was heretical because it injected into religion a kind of newness that the Prophet and his Companions did not inject even when they could have. Such innovations, Thānvī concluded, were new not only in their outward appearance but, more critically, also in their substance. This substantive departure from the prophetic norm was heretical because it cast a doubt on the completeness and the finality of that norm. It contradicted the prophetic norm by questioning its completion and perfection.[58]

For Thānvī, at stake in this entire debate over the limits of innovation in Islam was the sovereign authority of the prophetic norm and by extension, that of divine law. As he argued, "Someone who innovates in religion is a claimant to Muhammad's prophecy in veiled terms [*Dar pardah mudda'ī-yi nubūwwat hay*]. By attempting to add something new to the *sharī'a*, such a person implicitly accuses the *sharī'a* of deficiency and incompletion. Moreover, he implicitly boasts that he has the sovereign authority to rectify the deficiencies of the *sharī'a* by introducing new items to it."[59] The next analogy presented by Thānvī illustrates this point even more vividly. "Say someone printed a copy of the government's [the English word used by Thānvī] constitution and at the end of the document randomly added a clause of his own. Even if this additional clause were extremely beneficial for the country and its government, such unauthorized tampering with the constitution would still be called a crime, and its perpetrator would be severely punished." "Therefore," he continued, "if adding one unauthorized clause to the law of this world is a crime, how can such an addition to divine law be condoned?"[60]

The central difference between these two kinds of innovation, Thānvī further explained, could be most clearly understood by focusing on the prophetic saying, "Whoever innovates in this matter of ours that which is not a part of it is rejected" (*Man aḥdatha fī amrinā hādhā mā laysa min-hu fa huwa radd*).[61] The first variety of innovations, those that were necessary for the completion of religious obligations, corresponded to the part of this saying that read "included in it" (*min hu*). To the contrary, the second category of innovations that opposed the normative tradition of the Prophet and his Companions corresponded to the segment that read "that which is not" (*mā laysa*).

Another way to remember this distinction, Thānvī suggested, was to think about the difference between the expressions "innovations for religion" (*iḥdāth li'l-dīn*) and "innovations in religion" (*iḥdāth fi'l-dīn*).[62] *Innovations for religion* appeared new in their outward form but substantively (*ma'nan*) conformed to the normative model of the Prophet. On the other hand, *innovations in religion* not only were new in their outer appearance but also altered the substantive logic of the Prophet's normative model. In effect, while *innovations for religion* further solidified the Prophet's status as the ultimate exemplar and the foundational source of normativity in Islam, *innovations in religion* undermined his normative authority by challenging the perfection and finality of his salvational program.

"Everything Should Stay within Its Limits": Heresy as Excess and Disorder

For Ashraf 'Alī Thānvī, *bid'a* was another name for disorder. He described disorder as opposition to a prescribed order of things (*khilāf-i zābiṭa*). For example, he explained, imagine that someone while praying offered five cycles of prayer instead of the prescribed four. In this scenario, because of adding onto and hence disturbing the logic of an already designated order of devotional activity, this person would have corrupted his entire prayer; he would not receive any rewards for even the first four cycles. Now this person might not find such excess heretical in any way; after all, he might argue, how could there be anything wrong with the display of some excess in the most pious act of praying? However, the central sin committed in this case, Thānvī argued, was that of opposing an already established order of normativity. Thānvī further elucidated this innate antagonism between order and excess with an insightful analogy, again revealing his embeddedness in a modern colonial technological landscape: "If someone attached a one-rupee stamp on an envelope that required only eighty *paisas* [100 *paisas* = 1 rupee], then that envelope would become ineligible for delivery. That is so because by exceeding the designated postage rate, the sender used his stamp improperly and opposed the prescribed order of norms."[63]

For Thānvī, the importance of maintaining order in the performance of everyday life was paramount even in regard to imitating the Prophet. He argued that the desire to replicate every detail of the Prophet's personal life was commendable so long as that desire did not interrupt or undermine the fulfillment of religious obligations. The Prophet's normative model, he further explained, consisted of two dimensions: practical (*fi'lī*) and discursive (*qawlī*). The practical dimension was composed of the specific aspects of his daily life: for instance, the things he ate, the way he wore his turban, held his stick, kept his house, and so on. This practical dimension, in other words, consisted of his personal habits. Thānvī argued that later Muslims were not obligated to replicate the specificities of the Prophet's personal habits in their own lives. The discursive dimension of his model, on the other hand, included practices that were explicitly devotional in their import. In contrast to the practical dimension, it was obligatory to embody the limits stipulated by the discursive dimension of his model, though humans were granted a fair degree of autonomy to choose within those limits according to their own temperament.

Thānvī described people who went the extra mile by replicating every moment of the Prophet's life, even when they were not obligated to do so, as "passional lovers" (*'ushshāq*) of the Prophet. According to Thānvī, ordinary people could not emulate such passional lovers. As he put it, "Love is the foundational source for the passion to replicate every moment of prophetic life [*iss kā manshā' muḥabbat hay*]. . . . These lovers have the capacity to choreograph their entire lives on the model of the Prophet; they eat, drink, and wear exactly what he did. But for ordinary people like us, these restrictions are not obligatory so long as we remain within the general discursive limits of the Prophet's normative example."[64] "In all matters," he continued, "one must vigilantly guard the limits of normativity; everything should stay within its limits [*Har shai' ko apnī ḥadd par rehnā chāhīyay*]."[65]

Most importantly, Thānvī warned that one must never so exaggerate in imitating the Prophet's personal life that the obligations of religion were compromised. In fact, an act of imitation that obstructed the fulfillment of an obligatory practice should be discarded. For instance, Thānvī explained, the Prophet used to offer eight cycles of supererogatory prayers every night. The imitation of this nonobligatory practice, if someone possessed the requisite capacity and desire, was commendable. But imagine a scenario where a person offered supererogatory prayers all night and, as a result, was unable to wake up for the obligatory prayers at dawn. In this situation, it was incumbent upon that person to cast aside the voluntary prayers, go to bed early, and plan to wake up in the morning to offer the obligatory prayers at dawn. The passion to imitate every moment of the Prophet's life was commendable so long as it did not threaten the primacy of obligatory devotional practices. When religious passion threatened obligations, then that passion had to be tempered or altogether extinguished. Thānvī recognized and appreciated the passionate love that overwhelmed some followers of the Prophet. However, even in demonstrations of one's love for the Prophet, erotic excess that undermined order was intolerable.

Preserving the Aura of Obligations

The foundation of Thānvī's interpretive architecture was the legal principle that turning nonobligatory practices into obligations was prohibited. According to Thānvī, permissible practices (*mubāḥāt*) became forbidden when the masses mistook those practices for religious obligations. In fact, even if an encouraged (*mustaḥabb*) practice was elevated to the status of an obligation, it needed to be abandoned. Thānvī argued that this principle was a hallmark of the Ḥanafī legal tradition.

For example, Thānvī frequently cited the influential early nineteenth-century Ḥanafī scholar Muḥammad Amīn Ibn ʿĀbidīn (d. 1836), who in his widely read text *Radd al-Muhtār* categorically warned against elevating nonobligatory practices to the status of religious obligations. For instance, Ibn ʿĀbidīn noted that reciting the three Qur'ānic chapters, *Al-A ʿlā* (The Loftiest; chapter 87), *Al-Kāfirūn* (The Unbelievers; chapter 109), and *Al-Ikhlāṣ* (Fidelity; chapter 112) while performing the voluntary night prayers (*witr*) was among the prophetic practices. However, if one insisted on reciting only these three chapters and not any other chapter from the Qur'ān, then that insistence would turn an otherwise encouraged practice into a prohibition. Why? Because such a specification imparted to a nonobligatory practice the aura of obligation. Therefore, according to Ibn ʿĀbidīn, one should refrain from following any fixed pattern while choosing parts of the Qur'ān for recitation during prayers.[66]

Similarly, according to Thānvī, the Prophet's Companions also explicitly warned against undertaking permissible and encouraged practices with a discipline that made it appear as if those practices were obligatory. In this regard, Thānvī was particularly fond of quoting a statement by the Prophet's Companion ʿAbdallāh Ibn Masʿūd: "You should not give away a part of your prayer to Satan by thinking that it is necessary to turn [after finishing prayers] toward one's right side. Indeed, I have seen the Prophet often turn toward his left side also."[67] According to the Prophet's normative model, turning rightward after prayers was an encouraged (*mustaḥabb*) act. However, when people began to understand this act as obligatory, Masʿūd intervened and reminded them that there was no harm in turning leftward either. In fact, he equated the insistence on only turning rightward to "giving away a part of prayer to Satan." Commenting on this report, the prominent scholar of Ḥadīth and Shāfiʿī law Ibn Ḥajar al-Asqalānī (d. 1448) declared that "encouraged acts [*mustaḥabbāt*] become abominable [*makrūh*] if those acts are elevated above their designated status."[68]

The larger logic underlying these examples was that nonobligatory practices, even those that were prophetically sanctioned, had to never simulate obligatory practices. This was the foundational principle, Thānvī insisted, that people did not consider when they accused Deobandī scholars of forbidding permissible practices. This charge against Deoband scholars, he emphatically insisted, was unfair. They never forbade permissible practices. They forbade only practices that served as a prelude to forbidden practices. Just as the means to an obligatory practice were also obligatory, the means to a forbidden practice were also forbidden (*Muqaddimat al-ḥarām ḥarām*). The critical point to remember, Thānvī emphasized, was that at the moment when a so-called permissible practice became a means to a prohibition, it lost its membership in the category of permissible practices (*mubāḥāt*) and itself became a forbidden practice.[69]

According to Thānvī, the moral value attached to a given act depended on the conditions in which that act took place. The morality of a practice was always contingent on the circumstances of its occurrence. Even a meritorious act might become undesirable if it was not performed under appropriate conditions. For example, Thānvī reasoned, praying was universally acknowledged as a good act. However, even praying became abominable if performed when nature called (*Pāh khānā kā taqāzā ho tuh iss waqt namāz makrūh ho jātī hay*).[70] This was the "secret," as Thānvī put it, to why otherwise permissible practices were sometimes forbidden. "But," he lamented, "this subtle point was beyond the understanding of the masses."

Thānvī explained, mixing pedagogy with humor:

> When I forbid them [the masses] to perform practices like celebrating the Prophet's birthday, they complain that I am disallowing them from participating in pious activities. I agree that these are indeed pious practices. They are not problematic in their essence. However, what renders these practices heretical is the stipulation of particular specifications as necessary for the attainment of divine rewards. To make such specifications necessary has no place in the *sharī'a*. But what of this subtle reasoning will these masses understand? Therefore, while talking to them I do not go into the details of my argument and simply forbid them sternly to do what they should not be doing. For example, once a villager protested, "Why does the Friday congregational prayer [*jum'a*] not take place in rural areas?" I silenced him by responding, "First tell me this: why is there no *ḥajj* [annual pilgrimage to Mecca] in Bombay?"[71]

Blocking Goodness to Prevent Harm: Who Decides and How?

Thānvī emphasized that the decision on whether a permissible practice should be forbidden on grounds that it might lead to corruption was not available for everyone. Only the most accomplished jurists possessed the authority to judge whether the kind of corruption likely to be caused by a permissible practice was grave enough as to necessitate its being forbidden.[72] But how was that decision to be taken? What were the criteria determining whether a permissible practice should be forbidden on cautionary grounds? To address these critical questions, Thānvī offered his readers a fascinating scenario to ponder.

He proposed the following thought experiment. Suppose a practice was meritorious and good in its essence. But the public considered it taboo and blameworthy. Therefore, there was a high probability that whoever engaged in that practice would be subject to the censure of the community. In this situation, what should the law governing such a practice be? Should the jurist deem this practice permissible and ignore the controversy that participating in it would generate? Or should he call for the abandonment of this practice to avoid its potentially harmful social consequences?[73]

Thānvī argued that this kind of a practice could be categorized neither as absolutely forbidden nor as absolutely permitted. It required, not a straightforward answer but a very complex engagement with the traditional sources of normativity, one that only the most accomplished jurists were qualified to undertake. Thānvī elaborated his argument by discussing two incidents in the Prophet's life that in his opinion best demonstrated the multiple possibilities available to a jurist confronted with such a scenario. At stake in each of these two incidents was the ruling on a commendable act that was likely to cause a massive backlash from the community. In one of those situations, the Prophet abandoned the act so as not to cause any social unrest. In the other situation, however, he decided to complete the act despite the attached risks. The same theoretical situation yielded two very different outcomes.[74]

The first incident was the famous case of the wall called Ḥaṭīm, to the southwest of the Ka'ba in Mecca. After the Muslim conquest of Mecca in 628, the Prophet was presented with an excellent opportunity to bring this wall within the vicinity of the Ka'ba. Until that moment, this wall had been external to its territory. But the project would have required destroying the Ka'ba before reconstructing it. Despite the apparent goodness of this act, the Prophet decided to postpone the reconstruction plan. He reasoned that by destroying the Ka'ba, he might well offend both Muslim and non-Muslim Meccans who held the Ka'ba in great reverence. In other words, the Prophet realized that given the very nascent and fragile stage in the career of Islam at that point, undertaking such a potentially provocative project would not be wise. Therefore, even though reconstructing the Ka'ba and including the Ḥaṭīm within its vicinity was the correct and sound thing to do, the Prophet chose to drop the plan because of the hostility and uproar it was likely to cause.

Prophetic Decisions and Desires: Prophecy, Sexuality, Intimacy

The second incident was the Prophet's marriage to Zaynab bint Jaḥsh (d. 633), who had been divorced by Zayd Ibn Ḥāritha (d. 629), the Prophet's adopted son and one of the earliest Muslims.[75] This is among the most remarkable episodes in early Muslim history, entangled in a curious web of prophecy, sexuality, and the intimacy of human relations. It is the narrative of the Prophet's desire for the wife of his former slave turned adopted son, who in the course of its unfolding was unadopted and changed from being a son to being an (albeit still close) Companion. As David Powers has argued, this narrative has profound implications for the conception of prophecy in Islam, since if Muḥammad had not unadopted Zayd and if the latter had outlived the Prophet, the prophetic lineage and thus prophecy might well have continued.[76] Let me first turn to Thānvī's exploration of the Zayd-Zaynab-Muḥammad saga and then add some narrative dimensions he left out, as a way to highlight possible ambiguities marking his hermeneutic.

Thānvī centered his discussion on the calculus of the Prophet's decision to marry Zaynab after she was divorced by Zayd (Thānvī kept silent on the reasons for or the circumstances leading up to the divorce). This act was pregnant with the possibility of a scandal, since it could have been perceived by the "ignorant masses" of that time as a case of the

Prophet marrying his own daughter-in-law. Again, the Prophet was confronted with a moment in which a commendable act was likely to become an object of repudiation and unrest. In this situation, however, contrary to the episode of the Ḥaṭīm, God instructed the Prophet to undertake this act, despite its likely volatile consequences.[77] Therefore, the Prophet followed through on the commendable yet potentially controversial act of marrying Zaynab.

The dynamics of these two situations were almost identical, Thānvī explained. In both cases, the fulfillment of a commendable act would have led to the censure of the community. However, the decisions in the two cases were opposite. In one situation, the likelihood of controversy attached to an action was considered strong enough for abandoning that act altogether. In the other scenario, the action was carried out. The critical point to remember here, Thānvī instructed, was that the decision on whether a commendable act should be abandoned because of the likelihood that it would generate communal unrest could be made only by a distinguished scholar. In other words, the question of whether the apparent benefits associated with such an act should be foregone in consideration of the dissension it might produce in a community was one that only the most accomplished of jurists could answer.[78] This was so because there was no fixed or predictable pattern of adjudication governing such situations, as the Prophet's differing decisions in these structurally identical situations showed. But Thānvī did not stop there.

In his signature probing style, he went one step further to speculate on why might God have allowed the Prophet to marry Zaynab while disallowing the inclusion of the Ḥaṭīm within the Ka'ba. After all, these were both commendable acts that were likely to be met with the community's displeasure and hostility. Why, then, the contrasting decisions? In addressing this question, Thānvī first congratulated himself for having found the solution to it. "Thank God, the contrast between these two scenarios has become obvious to me," he wrote.[79] He then argued that the vital question to be asked while deciding whether an otherwise commendable act should be disallowed on grounds that it would become infamous (*bad nāmī*), censured, or scandalous was whether that act fulfilled any obligatory or essential objectives of religion. If it did, then that act, regardless of the negative consequences attached to it, must not be abandoned. On the other hand, if an act were neither obligatory nor a means to fulfilling any essential objectives of religion, preventing scandal and censure should take precedence and the act should be abandoned.

Thānvī explained that the Prophet's marriage to Zaynab was a vital act of religious reform while the inclusion of the Ḥaṭīm in the Ka'ba was not. In that era, he historicized, the practice of marrying the divorced wife of one's adopted son was considered illegitimate and forbidden. Furthermore, this taboo was so pervasive and entrenched that it could not have been uprooted only by verbal admonishment; practical demonstration would be necessary. To conduct the work of reform, it was not enough for the Prophet to just verbally preach his message; he had to live what he preached. His marriage to Zaynab represented such a moment of demonstration.

This marriage fulfilled an essential objective of religion by catalyzing the reform of a corrupt taboo. Therefore, according to Thānvī, the Prophet did not worry about the potential scandal his marriage to Zaynab might cause. The promise of reform attached to this act outweighed the danger of censure that it carried. In contrast, Thānvī continued, no essential objective of religion pivoted on the inclusion of the Ḥaṭīm in the Ka'ba. While a commendable act, it was by no means critical for either protecting or reforming religion. Therefore, in this situation, the high probability of the provocation that such a move was likely to cause outweighed its potential benefits, hence legitimizing its abandonment or deferral.[80]

Thānvī presented a number of other cases from the Prophet's career when he had not abandoned a practice despite its repercussions in the community. The quintessential example was the Prophet's call to monotheism. His community responded to his message of radical monotheism with intense and unyielding rejection. But that did not lead him to abandon his message. Similarly, after the Prophet returned from his ascension to heaven (*mi'rāj*), his first cousin Umm Hānī, from whose house he had embarked on that journey, urged him to not announce this event to the community, lest he be charged with lying. But the Prophet refused to accept her advice because at that moment publishing the story of his ascension was critical to advancing his prophecy. Therefore, regardless of the uproar and accusations of lying that his public narration of this event was likely to engender, this act of narration fulfilled an essential objective of religion and consequently could not be abandoned.[81]

Framing the Prophet as a Reformer-in-Chief

Thānvī's hermeneutical framework here is revealing of his larger conception of reform. Most significantly, note that the very question of whether an act fulfills an objective of religion involves an a priori demarcation of what does and does not count as religion. The juridical program that Thānvī outlined here also served the task of distinguishing activities and spheres of life that properly belonged to the category of "religion." Thānvī's declaration that the inclusion of the Ḥaṭīm in the Ka'ba was something unrelated to religion, whereas the Prophet's marriage to Zaynab and for that matter his ascension to heaven were deeply religious acts, was authorized through a discursive regime of separating the religious from the nonreligious. This moment of separation was also a moment of translation—of translating the limits and boundaries of religion, of making the sovereign decision as to what could and could not be called religion.

Second, in his discourse on the Prophet, Thānvī articulated a particular conception of prophetic persona and authority. According to this conception, all of the Prophet's life was readily available for interpretation and translation. Moreover, the singular objective of that life was either to establish law or to reform religion. The Prophet's subjectivity as a desiring sexual human subject was not given much weight or reflection in Thānvī's juridical estimations. For example, Thānvī never entertained the possibility that perhaps the Prophet married Zaynab because he desired to do so, with little or secondary interest in reforming religion or in ridding society from corruption. It was as if Thānvī saw himself in the Prophet and/or the Prophet in himself: primarily as a reformer of the masses. Other aspects of his subjectivity, such as his sexuality, were subservient to and overshadowed by his reformist mandate. Thānvī deftly avoided the remarkable narrative and background of the Prophet's marriage to Zaynab, which highlights the Prophet's humanity in striking terms. For that we can fruitfully turn to literature.

Indeed, one of the most engaging discussions of this narrative is found in the 2016 novel *The Televangelist*, by Egyptian novelist Ibrahim Essa.[82] The novel tells the story of an enterprising but conflicted young religious scholar in Egypt, Sheikh Hatem, who surges to household celebrity status through his widely watched television program on Islam. One day a person by the name of Raouf calls in to the show from Alexandria to seek Hatem's counsel on a vexatious problem: a Christian colleague at work has been taunting Raouf about his faith. Specifically, when Raouf has tried to evangelize this Christian colleague, the latter has responded with the claim that the Prophet "looked at" (with the implication of lusting after) Zaynab, the wife of his neighbor and adopted son Zayd.[83]

In his response, Hatem urges the caller to confidently engage rather than feel embarrassed by his colleague's provocation. The circumstances that led to the Prophet's marriage with Zaynab are well documented in the normative sources of the tradition, Hatem lectures. The clearest reference in this regard is available in the Qur'ān where God says to the Prophet, "You hid in your heart that which God was about to make manifest: you were afraid of the people, but it is more fitting that you should fear God."[84] Regarding this verse, the Prophet's wife Ayesha said, "If the Prophet of God had suppressed anything that God revealed to him, he would have suppressed this verse because it is so hard on him."[85] What God was about to make manifest was the Prophet's attraction for Zaynab, whose own marriage to Zayd was faltering, in large part because of their sexual incompatibility. When Zayd shared his marital travails with the Prophet and expressed his desire to divorce Zaynab, the Prophet counseled him to instead work on mending his marriage.[86]

But the Prophet had also fallen in love with Zaynab, who was said to have been among the "finest" and most "fair-skinned" women in the Quraysh. As Hatem narrates, citing the early Qur'ān commentator Muqātil ibn Sulaymān (d. 767): "The Prophet came looking for Zayd one day, and he saw Zaynab standing there. She was fair-skinned, beautiful, and buxom. . . . He fell for her and said, "Praise be to God who turns men's hearts."[87] Zaynab, overhearing this, realized that she had made an impression on the Prophet and mentioned it to Zayd when he came home. Zayd then again asked the Prophet for permission to divorce her.[88] In his book on Zayd, David Powers presents a slightly more elegant and accurate rendition of Muqātil ibn Sulaymān's commentary: "The Prophet caught a glimpse of Zaynab as she was in the act of rising to her feet [*fa-abṣara Zaynab qāʾimatan*]. She was beautiful and white of skin, one of the most perfect women of Quraysh. The Prophet—may God bless him and grant him peace—immediately experienced sexual desire for her [*hawiyahā*], and he exclaimed, 'Praise be to God who has the power to transform a man's heart [in an instant].'"[89] Powers also adds the curious detail that when Zayd returned home, Zaynab, who is said to have been a boastful woman, did not just tell him about her "extraordinary encounter" with her father-in-law but asked Zayd "if he wanted to hear the story again, and again, and again." As a consequence, "Relations between the couple went from bad to worse." Ironically, Zayd, who had once implored the Prophet to ask Zaynab's family for her hand in marriage, "now pleaded with him for permission to divorce his haughty, condescending, and sharp-tongued wife."[90] The Prophet at first advised Zayd to not divorce her. He also resisted and kept secret his own urge to marry Zaynab, deterred by the taboo of marrying his adopted son's former wife. Eventually, though, with God's help and intervention, he followed through on his desire and married Zaynab. Moreover, in the interim between Zaynab's divorce with Zayd and the Prophet's marriage to her (during Zaynab's waiting period of three monthly periods), the Prophet disinherited Zayd as his adopted son.[91] By so doing, the Prophet had, according to dominant traditional readings, anticipated and fulfilled the mandate of abolishing adoption, as laid out in verse 4 again of chapter 33, the relevant parts of which read: "God has not put two hearts inside any man, . . . nor has He made your adopted sons your [real] sons."[92] Perhaps more significantly, this act of disinheritance also sealed the institution of prophecy from the threat of any potential claimants after the temporal departure of the Prophet.[93] Zayd remained close to the Prophet, though, as one of his most intimate Companions and allies (*mawālī* sing. *mawlā*); a formidable military commander, he died in 629 while leading an expedition against the Byzantines in the village of Mu'tah in southern Jordan.[94]

Most remarkable about this narrative is the way it brings together varied threads of the Prophet's life: family, sexuality, prophecy, and his relationship to God. This episode intertwines sexual, familial, and theological intimacy. As Sheikh Hatem, the protagonist of *The Televangelist*, urges his viewers: "There is nothing to embarrass us in this story. On the contrary, we can be proud that the Qur'ān has taught us to be completely transparent about the Prophet's important private and intimate affairs."[95]

Particularly noteworthy is the intervention of the Qur'ān in the most intimate of the Prophet's desires and anxieties. The divine intervention and dialogue with the Prophet regarding what hid in the latter's heart collapse the separation of the private and the public, the concealed and the revealed.

The Qur'ān served as the divine disclosure of the Prophet's seemingly private feelings. "You were afraid of the people but it is more fitting that you should fear God."[96] This verse may well be taken as an exhortation to enact religious reform and dissolve existing taboos. But such a reading underplays the riveting drama of the divine-prophetic encounter fueling this verse. Perhaps more than a mandate to reform the people around him, what we find in this verse is God assisting and empowering the Prophet, his most beloved subject, during a moment of enormous unease and uncertainty. Indeed, perhaps the most poignant aspect of this narrative is the self-doubt that may well have enveloped the Prophet on the verge of a potentially terrible misdeed.

God rescues the Prophet from the torment of his desire by legitimizing that desire. Certainly, this divine solace may well have held the potential for religious reform. However, it is difficult not to observe the profound celebration of the Prophet's humanity and of his vulnerability as a human enacted in the text and context of this verse. Returning to Thānvī, such considerations of the Prophet's humanity were a less prominent part of his hermeneutical apparatus, trumped by the imperative of viewing the Prophet's body primarily as a vehicle for the reform of the masses. The desires, doubts, and vulnerabilities of that body were of scant use and relevance to the labor of religious reform. Similarly, one may observe in passing that Thānvī's question, whether the Prophet's decision to abandon the plan to include the Ḥaṭīm in the Ka'ba fulfilled a religious objective, assumed that religion was the main determinant of the Prophet's actions. As Thānvī had himself pointed out, this decision by the Prophet could well have been an astute political calculation designed to prevent any fragmentation in a fledgling community, with no conscious, self-aware deliberation over whether the act fulfilled a religious objective or not.

But in Thānvī's juridical imagination, the Prophet's life was always translatable in religious terms. More accurately, for Thānvī, the limits of the religious and the nonreligious within the Prophet's life were always available for discursive representation, interpretation, and translation. In this framework, the Prophet's life story emerges as an elaborately schematized set of discourses, actions, and gestures readily mobilizable for the task of demarcating the boundaries of religion. This way of imagining the Prophet's memory was fully attuned to the ideological demand of neatly defining what did and did not count as religion. Put simply, in Thānvī's hands, the Prophet was thoroughly religionized. In the next chapter I continue my examination of Thānvī's religious imaginary by attending to his discourses on what was arguably the most controversial and intensely contested ritual among the Muslim scholars of colonial India: the celebration of the Prophet's birthday, or what is known as the *mawlid*.

chapter eight

Forbidding Piety to Restore Sovereignty

The *Mawlid* and Its Discontents

No other ritual was as vigorously contested among nineteenth-century Indian Muslim scholars as the *mawlid* or the celebration of the Prophet's birthday. The debate over *mawlid* in colonial India has indelibly informed the continuing controversy surrounding this practice in the present. Popularized first in Fatimid Egypt during the eleventh century, today the *mawlid* is widely performed in almost all Muslim communities. It takes place annually on the twelfth day of *rabīʿ al-awwal* (the third month in the Islamic calendar), the day on which the Prophet was born. Usually undertaken in the form of a festival, the specific elements of the *mawlid* vary from region to region. However, the most characteristic feature of the *mawlid* is the recitation of poems about the Prophet that begin with an account of his birth and then praise his life and virtues.[1]

The debate over the *mawlid* generates passionate responses from its supporters and detractors alike. In the South Asian context, the most contested element of the *mawlid* is what is called the *qiyām*. The *qiyām* refers to the practice of standing up in honor of the Prophet to offer him salutations and to receive his blessings in return. It usually coincides with the recitation of the praise poetry. Its effectiveness hinges on the conviction that the Prophet himself appears at this gathering to bestow his blessings upon the participants. The opponents of the *qiyām* argue that showing faith in the Prophet's simultaneous appearance at multiple *mawlid* gatherings threatens to divinize the Prophet. Why? Because it risks the attachment of omniscience and omnipresence, both strictly divine attributes, to the being of the Prophet. Moreover, the act of reverentially standing up elevates the Prophet in a way that undermines his humanity.

On the other hand, as I will detail in the next two chapters, the supporters of the *qiyām* consider it a most virtuous practice that honors God's most exalted creation, the Prophet. Rather than a threat to divine sovereignty, they argue, the *qiyām* is a physical affirmation of the Prophet's unrivaled spiritual status. Apart from the debate about the *qiyām*, the question of the *mawlid* brings together certain pivotal theological and legal issues at the heart of the ideological rivalries between competing Muslim scholars in colonial India. For instance, these include the specification of a date (*tawqīt al-waqt*) for nonobligatory rituals, the danger of imitating non-Muslim religious practices (*tashabbuh*) such as Christmas, the legitimacy of potentially carnivalesque practices like singing and playing music, and the use of lights, incense, and perfume in embellishing the venue where the *mawlid* is held. In addition to these communal and phenomenological aspects, the *mawlid* raises a critical hermeneutical problem: the status of new practices and rituals that are neither expressly forbidden nor explicitly sanctioned in the *sharī'a*. The *mawlid* is a quintessential case of a ritual that is not found in the practice of the Prophet or his Companions but that is undertaken for the commendable purpose of venerating the Prophet's memory. It is empirically an innovation. But is it heretical?

This question has remained a subject of much contestation in the medieval and early modern Islamic legal tradition. While some scholars have extolled the *mawlid* as among the most meritorious ritual practices, others have expressed greater skepticism regarding its doctrinal validity. The views of the prominent scholars Jalāl al-Dīn al-Suyūṭī (d. 1505) and Taqī al-Dīn Ibn Taymīya (d. 1328) on the *mawlid* capture well these opposing tendencies. A leading figure in the Shāfi'ī school of law, Suyūṭī was a staunch advocate of the *mawlid*. According to Suyūṭī, although the *mawlid* was invented long after the Prophet and the Companions, it was a positive innovation that exalted the Prophet and honored his memory. The purpose of this ritual was the demonstration of one's love for the Prophet and the expression of gratitude to God for sending the Prophet to this world. Since these objectives were undeniably pious, Suyūṭī concluded, there was no doubt about the normative validity of the *mawlid*.[2]

Ibn Taymīya, a prolific medieval scholar who preceded Suyūṭī by a couple of centuries, agreed with the latter that the commemoration of the Prophet's birthday fulfilled certain pious objectives. As Ibn Taymīya wrote, "Someone who performs the *mawlid* may deserve a great reward [*ajr ʿaẓīm*] because of his good intentions [*li-ḥusn qaṣdihi*] and his exaltation of the Prophet."[3] But although Ibn Taymīya acknowledged the potential goodness attached to the *mawlid*, he still considered this ritual a heretical innovation because the *mawlid* lacked a precedent in the normative model of the Prophet and the Companions. Ibn Taymīya argued that since the Prophet's Companions—who loved and venerated him best, and were the most diligent in performing good works—did not institute a celebration for the Prophet's birthday, clearly the *mawlid* ought not to be celebrated.[4] Suyūṭī's and Ibn Taymīya's divergent opinions on the *mawlid* provide a snapshot of the ambiguity surrounding its normative status in Islam.[5] The *mawlid* is an ideal case of a ritual that might carry spiritual benefits but that lacks a precedent in the Prophet's and his Companions' normative example. How then should its legitimacy be determined?

Like their premodern predecessors, Muslim scholars in colonial India contested this question with much passion. Both supporters and critics of the *mawlid* expended copious ink in defending their respective positions. The pioneers of Deoband, as reflected in the story with which this section began, vigorously opposed the *mawlid* as practiced in India. Again, it was Ashraf ʿAlī Thānvī who explained the Deobandī opposition to the *mawlid* most thoroughly, in a treatise entitled *Ṭarīqa-yi Mawlid Sharīf* (The normative method of the *mawlid*).[6] In this treatise, Thānvī presented a systematic legal argument aimed at establishing the *mawlid* as a heretical innovation.

In this chapter I conduct a close analysis of Thānvī's legal framework on the question of the *mawlid*. Through this analysis, I want to provide a concrete illustration of the theoretical arguments about Deobandī views on *bidʿa* discussed in the previous chapter. What are the specific ways in which Thānvī rationalized and called for the illegitimacy of the *mawlid* gathering? What does his argument reveal about the way he imagined the interplay of knowledge, time, and subjectivity? Through what discursive strategies did he construct his own authority as the gatekeeper of tradition and its limits? These are among the questions I will address.

In the *Ṭarīqa-yi Mawlid Sharīf*, Thānvī articulated five principles governing the legitimacy of a ritual such as the *mawlid* that is neither completely permitted nor entirely abominable according to the *sharī'a* but that lacks a precedent from the normative model of the Prophet and his Companions. Crucial to Thānvī's hermeneutical paradigm was the legal dictum that whenever permissible and prohibitive causes join in a given act, the prohibition always receives the preference. A close consideration of each of these principles will allow for a deeper understanding of his legal imaginary and hermeneutical sensibility.

Principle 1: "*If a nonobligatory practice is made into an obligation, it should be abandoned.*" (46)

As I have argued throughout this section, the centerpiece of Thānvī's reform project was to protect the primacy of religious obligations against the threat of nonobligatory rituals that the masses might easily confuse for obligatory acts. Despite being permissible in essence, these conventions turned into heretical innovations because they simulated the specifications exclusively reserved for obligatory religious practices. Such an epistemic transgression was confirmed, moreover, when a community began to reproach someone who voluntarily abstained from such rituals and to consider him worthy of punishment.

The *mawlid*, according to Thānvī, was the ideal example of such a ritual. In essence, Thānvī never tired of reminding his readers, the *mawlid* was not only permissible (*mubāḥ*) but even encouraged (*mustaḥabb*). Organizing and participating in the *mawlid*, in Thānvī's view, were without doubt spiritually beneficial acts. But this was so only if the gathering was free from any restraints imposed by the weight of customs and conventions (*quyyūd-i murawwaja*). For example, if certain people were to gather coincidentally without a special invitation from anyone, or if they came together for another unrelated purpose and in this gathering either verbally or through reading the Qur'ān expressed their reverence for the Prophet by remembering his character, personal traits, miracles, and virtues in a manner consistent with the established prophetic reports, then such an assembly was permissible without any reservations.

However, where things got problematic, Thānvī emphasized, was when the *mawlid* was elevated from its status as merely permissible to one that the masses began to understand as obligatory. At this point it turned into a heretical innovation. Moreover, if the insistence on participating in the *mawlid* reached a level that equaled or surpassed the enthusiasm with which people were summoned to perform obligatory acts, then such insistence compromised the normative authority of the *sharī'a*. And as in the case of all simply permissible practices, the censuring of a person who willingly abstained from the *mawlid* was the main symptom revealing such a transgression of limits. For Thānvī, when voluntarily opting out of the *mawlid* became a target of communal censure, there remained no doubt that the masses had come to understand it as an obligation.

A trope Thānvī repeatedly invoked in this discussion was "conditionality of obligation on that which is not normatively demanded" (*iltizām mā lā yalzim*). If the insistence on engaging in a nonobligatory practice reached a point that whoever abstained from it was subjected to shame (*'ayb*) and reproach (*ṭa'n*), then those responsible for cultivating such a culture of insistence were guilty of innovating a counternorm rivaling the normative order sanctioned by the prophetic example. For Thānvī, such innovators were heretical (*mubtadi'ūn*). They deserved to be punished, shunned, and rendered pariahs so that they were incapacitated from infecting the religion of others in their communities.

Another symptom that revealed the simulative property of the *mawlid*, according to Thānvī, was the attachment of specifications that had no source (*'aṣl*) in law. For instance, the specification of a date on which the *mawlid* had to be performed every year (typically the twelfth day in the month of *rabī' al-awwal*) was an example of an additional humanly invented specification. Thānvī adduced a prophetic report to cement his argument: "Don't specify Friday night as a night of staying up for prayers and other devotional exercises, and don't designate Friday as a day of fasting" (47).

> Principle 2: "*Every permissible and even encouraged (mustaḥabb) act becomes impermissible and forbidden if it is polluted and mixed with an illegitimate act or condition.*" (47)

Thānvī claimed, for example, that "accepting an invitation to a gathering is encouraged and in fact sanctioned by prophetic reports. However, if an illegitimate activity takes place at this gathering, then going to it will also be deemed impermissible" (48). This criterion reflects Thānvī's concern with maintaining the purity of religious practices. Moreover, it is also revealing of the pathology-centered social imaginary that drove his method of adjudicating the legitimacy of contested devotional practices such as the *mawlid*. For Thānvī, normative religion was like the human body in that it had to be protected from all corrupting and polluting influences. Therefore, even if an otherwise pious activity such as commemorating the Prophet's birthday became infected by external corruptions, it had to be abandoned lest it harm the community as a whole. Some of the corruptions that Thānvī listed are illuminating with regard to his conception of a moral public. Notice also the intensity of their focus on fashioning the affective choreography of the senses:

—Boys who are good-looking or have good voices (*khush alḥān*) sing panegyric tunes during the ceremony.
—Participants wear inappropriate and impermissible clothes.
—Music and singing at the gathering produce the possibility of sexual attraction, as when a good-looking man or woman sings.
—The expenditure on decorating the venue, putting up lights, and other embellishments is too exorbitant.
—The venue is permeated with excessive amounts of perfume and incense.
—It is considered obligatory to distribute sweets to the participants.
—The enthusiasm displayed in bringing people together is highly exaggerated, to the extent that such efforts exceed the care taken to gather people for obligatory prayers and preaching ceremonies.
—The Prophet is understood to be omnipresent (*ḥāzir*) and omniscient (*nāẓir*) at the gathering.
—The organizer's intention is that of indulging in vanity and pride. (39–48)

The two main moral principles that guided Thānvī's litany of corruptive influences were simplicity and sobriety. Indeed, simplicity and sobriety were among the most decisive normative values undergirding the Deobandī orientation. The pioneers of Deoband, including Rashīd

Aḥmad Gangohī, Khalīl Aḥmad Sāharanpūrī, and Thānvī, were united in their condemnation of all forms of devotional practices that might ignite unwarranted passion and desire among practitioners. In their view, a moral economy tolerant of affective excess invariably injured the capacity of the masses to distinguish between sanctioned normativity and innovated heresies.

Consistent with the larger Deobandī narrative of reform, Thānvī argued for a political economy of piety in which subjects committed to simplicity and sobriety enabled a community where wastefulness, public displays of grandeur, and erotic modes of being generated taboo and shame.[7] Therefore, it is a mistake to understand projects of moral reform, such as Thānvī's, as a push for a retreat to a "private sphere" concerned exclusively with the cultivation of pious subjects. To the contrary, the hallmark of Thānvī's discourse on *bid'a* was its connection of the moral architecture of the self to the political economy of the community. His discourse defied any distinction between private and public spheres. I return to this point in the conclusion of this chapter.

> Principle 3: "*It is the responsibility of the religious elite to shepherd and protect the religion and conscience of the masses.*" (48)

Thānvī argued that religious scholars, because of their capacity to attract the imitation of the masses, must exhibit extreme caution and care while publicly performing their religion. In Thānvī's view, it was the responsibility of the religious elite to nurture and protect the moral health of their communities. Therefore, if there was ever any danger that the masses had begun to understand a simply permissible practice as obligatory, it was incumbent upon the religious elite to abandon that practice. As moral exemplars, religious scholars were required to remain mindful of how their actions influenced the actions of people in their communities. Thānvī admitted that religious scholars, thanks to their extensive knowledge and experience, had a superior capacity to distinguish between obligatory and nonobligatory practices. However, in view of their power to attract emulation, the religious elite, in order to protect the religion of the masses, should jettison otherwise beneficial practices that the masses might mistake for obligations. The foremost duty of religious scholars, Thānvī emphasized, was to save the masses from being harmed by doctrinal and moral corruption.

Thānvī explained his argument by drawing on and elaborating two categories of his own construction: what he called individual harm (*zarar-i lāzmī*) and extensive harm (*zarar-i muta'addī*). Individual harm, he explained, involved a situation in which only an actor himself was negatively affected by engaging in a harmful act. Extensive harm, on the other hand, took place when others were also affected by his actions. Thānvī argued that just as a permissible act had to be forbidden when it implied individual harm, in the same way, an act had to be prohibited when it might cause extensive harm. For example, "Say someone was ill and the doctor allowed him to break his fast. In this situation, his eating and drinking would be permissible in essence. However, if there were a probability that another person would look at this situation and break his fast too, then this seemingly permissible action [the breaking of one's fast in times of sickness] would also become impermissible" (57).

The elite, then, had to constantly monitor nonobligatory practices that held the potential for confusing the normative boundaries separating simply permissible from divinely mandated acts, and thus for causing either individual or extensive harm. Moreover, the elite needed to enforce the abandonment of a practice that at any point threatened to become elevated above and beyond its normatively designated status. For example, Thānvī noted that the act of seeing the family of the bereaved on the day of death used to be among the prophetic practices. However, when people began understanding this ritual as an obligatory act, the elite declared it prohibited and worthy of abandonment. Similarly, the practice of prostrating before God as a gesture of exhibiting gratitude was customary and permissible at the time of the Prophet, but because people started understanding it as a form of emphasized prophetic practice (*sunnat-i maqṣūda*), it was outlawed.

There was, however, one major addendum that Thānvī stipulated to this rule: if a legally obligated practice became corrupted by certain abominable features, then that practice, instead of being abandoned altogether, should simply be corrected and purified of the attached corruptions. For example, if a funeral cortege (*janāza*) was accompanied by a woman who was crying excessively (*noḥa*), then the ceremony of burial didn't need to be abandoned altogether; such women should just be silenced. But with regard to an unnecessary or a nonobligatory act such as accepting an invitation to a gathering, the invitation itself had to be turned down if the gathering contained any abominable or corrupt qualities (49). This according to Thānvī was the crucial difference in the rules pertaining to simply permissible and obligatory acts. And as I will have occasion to emphasize in the next chapter, it is precisely on this point that the Deoband pioneers most clearly disagreed with their Barelvī rivals.

But apart from its hermeneutical aspects, this discussion is also quite revealing of Thānvī's imagination of his own role as a member of the learned elite vis-à-vis the masses. In his social imaginary, the religious elite were perpetually burdened with the responsibility of serving as exemplary models to be emulated. It was through the demonstration of the elite that the masses cultivated and performed their religion. If the elite acted irresponsibly in their demonstration, they would influence the religion of the masses in a detrimental fashion. And if they took seriously their capacity to attract the emulation of the masses, they would contribute to the cultivation of a morally sound and healthy community.

In this context, a rhetorical device employed frequently by Thānvī and several other Indian Muslim reformers (both Deobandīs and Barelvīs) was that of equating the masses to a herd of cattle. This sentiment was exemplified in the Arabic aphorism, cited frequently by South Asian Muslim scholars of varied stripes, "The masses are like cattle" (*Al-'awāmm ka-l-an'ām*). In this view, the masses were unsophisticated and gullible, in constant need of a class of herders to provide them religious guidance and moral direction. There is a certain irony to this attitude because the mode of discourse that jurists like Thānvī usually engaged in tended to be highly specialized and linguistically challenging. One wonders, then, just how accessible such discourses and the hermeneutical complexities contained in them really were to the "cattle-like" masses they sought to reform and morally purify. Indeed, perhaps more than anything else, the equation of the masses to cattle served to scaffold the religious authority of the scholars who invoked it. By casting the relationship between the religious elite and the masses in the image of the interaction of a herder with his herd, this aphorism intertwined the normative authority of the former with the assumed mimetic predispositions and dependency of the latter.

> Principle 4: "*Spatial, temporal, and empirical observations can produce different outcomes in matters that are designated as temporarily abominable [makrūh-yi 'ārzī].*" (49)

As mentioned earlier, several prominent medieval and early modern Muslim jurists such as al-Suyūṭī had commended the *mawlid* as an undeniably legitimate and exemplary ritual. This fact created for Thānvī a normative challenge, as his opposition to the *mawlid* could well have been taken as an affront to the intellectual integrity of these earlier luminaries. Thānvī's articulation of this principle was meant to confront this challenge. In a moment of interpretive determinism, Thānvī argued that these earlier scholars had called the *mawlid* a commendable act because during their lifetime it had not been polluted by the moral corruptions later added to it. As Thānvī wrote, "Had these jurists been adjudicating on the *mawlid* today, they would also deem it forbidden" (49). Therefore, according to Thānvī, the value attached to a practice did not have to be constant or permanent across time and space. It was possible that an action currently categorized as abominable might well have been regarded as permissible in a previous era.

Thānvī applied the same line of reasoning to geographic differences in customs: an act considered permissible in one country (on the basis of its prevalent internal conditions) might well be deemed impermissible in another. Similarly, two equally accomplished jurists might arrive at opposite legal opinions on the same matter because of different experiential and observational knowledge sets. Thānvī reasoned that if a jurist were unaware of the moral corruptions attached to an otherwise permissible practice, he would obviously not find it problematic. Yet the experience and observation of another scholar might persuade him that a practice led to abominable behavior. Therefore, he would declare that same practice to be impermissible.

Thānvī insisted, anticipating and warding off his opponents' objections, that this seeming opposition "was only on the level of appearance and not that of reality. It was merely superficial [*ṣuwarī*], not meaningful [*ma'nawī*]" (49). Therefore, Thānvī succeeded in holding on to his prohibitory stance on the *mawlid* while also affirming his loyalty to prominent pre-modern jurists such as al-Suyūṭī, who might have held a different legal opinion on this point.

According to Thānvī's hermeneutical framework, the moral value of an act was contingent on the conditions under which that act took place. Ultimately, this relativistic framework worked to magnify Thānvī's own authority as a reformer jurist. This was so because the underlying decision on the morality of a practice in a given moment and place rested with him. In performing the work of reform, Thānvī sought to supervise a moral order that replicated the normative expectations and boundaries of divine law. But the decision on what those expectations and boundaries were rested with Thānvī and with his evaluation of the present. He exercised his own will to approximate divine will.

Moreover, Thānvī's interpretive posture was intimately connected to an ambiguous understanding of temporality and its relationship to the formation of a community's norms. On the one hand, Thānvī's legal apparatus was anchored in a dynamic imagination of temporality. According to this dynamic imagination, normative rulings on contested ritual practices did and in fact needed to change according to shifting temporalities and social conditions. Hence, even though previous scholars like al-Suyūṭī might have declared the *mawlid* commendable, when the conditions in which the *mawlid* was performed changed, so too did its normative status. The normativity of a practice was dynamic and variable according to the conditions under which that practice was undertaken.

Law in this case was imagined as a flexible discursive space that adapted to the changing temporal conditions under which it operates. Yet the very desire to replicate the normative model of the Prophet in all temporalities and geographies, a desire at the heart of Thānvī's reform project, presumed time to be unchanging and constant. Another moment from Thānvī's discourse further reveals the ambiguity over the question of time found in his thought. While clarifying his argument about the necessity of adopting legal opinions according to the external contingencies found in particular temporal moments, Thānvī stated that "in the Prophet's time, women were allowed to pray in mosques because the possibility of attraction between the two sexes was not there. Later on, however, on observing the changed conditions, the Companions declared this practice censurable" (50).

In this example, the original context of the Prophet's lifetime served as the master temporal framework to which the present had to always harken and respond. The model of temporality underpinning such a sentiment was animated by what one might call an oracular mode of history whereby life in the present unfolded in the image of an oracle (the prophetic time) from the seventh century. Such an oracular imaginary of history is resistant to change and dynamism; it presumes and is nourished by a conception of time that is constant and unchanging. However, even as Thānvī embraced an oracular understanding of history and time, he was also at ease with adopting a dynamic notion of time. This was most clearly evident in his endorsement of the Companions' prohibition of the presence of women inside mosques, a clear departure and change from the Prophet's time. In this instance, Thānvī championed the flexibility of law and endorsed the capacity of law to change according to changing social conditions. In contrast to an oracular model, this flexible and dynamic attitude toward law valorized the present as the temporal context most relevant to the fashioning of a community's normative ethical program. Concomitantly, in contrast to the oracular mode of imagining law and history that obligated time to be constant, this latter attitude was anchored in the dynamicity of time. Clearly then, Thānvī sought to strategically control the constancy or dynamicity of time in his discourses on *bid'a* according to the kind of argument he wished to make. Constant time and dynamic time coexisted and cooperated in his discourse, presenting an unresolved yet productive ambiguity.

There is another ambiguity in Thānvī's explanation of the prohibition against the presence of women inside mosques during the era of the Companions: On what historical grounds must one accept such radical shifts in human nature over time? For instance, on what basis could Thānvī argue that the possibility of attraction between the two sexes inside mosques was absent during the time of the Prophet, only to emerge after his death? Thānvī did not address these ambiguities. However, more interesting than the coherence of Thānvī's argument was the conception of history and time it presumed and articulated. One may respond to this question by observing that the rise-and-fall narrative of Muslim morality that underpinned Thānvī 's argument was tethered to the conviction that the further one went back in history, the more pristine form of Islam one would find, with the Prophet's era serving as the ultimate model of an uncorrupted moral economy. Most importantly, to Thānvī, his negative evaluation of time in his present authorized his own position as a custodian of the tradition's moral purity. A pessimistic view of the present accentuated the need for and the authority of prophetic reformers who could reorient the masses from the path of heresy to that of normativity. In fact, Thānvī's entire project of the strict epistemological policing of religious obligations would have ceased to be urgent if it had not been ensconced in a narrative of pandemic moral failure.

To be more precise, Thānvī wove his religious authority by placing in contradistinction a utopian imagining of the past and a dystopian sketch of the present and the future. In Thānvī's discourse, the utopia (the era of the Prophet and his Companions) was behind us; it was a figment of history that could be retrieved only through a comprehensive and ongoing program of transforming a community's *habitus* so that it might reenact the absent memory of the past in the present. But that promise of retrieval remained unfulfilled. It remained an impossibility deferred to the future.

Here I should add that precisely this always deferred promise of reenacting the prophetic past in the present fuels the apocalyptic urgency of moral crisis found in the popular Muslim reformist trope of *fasād al-zamān* (corruption of time), a trope Thānvī recurrently invoked in his discourses on *bid'a*. The symbol of *zamān* (time) in this construction is a metonymical substitution for people, the masses, who cultivate habits and practices that cause an exponential rise in the index of corruption during each successive epoch. Moreover, it was in the irresolvable aporia enabled by the simultaneity of utopian and dystopian temporalities in Thānvī's discourse that his religious authority as a watchdog and reviver of the prophetic norm was enshrined.

> Principle 5: "*An unlawful act cannot be permitted on the basis that it produces certain benefits and welfare for the community. If those attached benefits are not necessary according to the sharī'a, then that act will remain unlawful.*" (50)

In articulating this principle, Thānvī was responding to the argument propounded by the defenders of the *mawlid* that the beneficial outcomes of this ritual, such as the physical nourishment of the poor, the propagation of Islam among non-Muslims, and the flowering of a religious community, justified its legitimacy. Thānvī counterargued that the communal benefits generated by the *mawlid* could not offset the harmful effects of the corruptions attached to it. Moreover, according to Thānvī, if the supposed benefits associated with the *mawlid* were not legally obligatory or if there were other means to achieve them, then those benefits could not legitimate the *mawlid*. For instance, one might have argued that the *mawlid* provided for a community a shared ritual space that facilitated intracommunal harmony. For Thānvī, though, this benefit was not good enough to sanction the *mawlid*. In his social imaginary, guarding the normative boundaries of the *sharī'a* was a much more pressing, urgent, and worthwhile imperative than the cultivation of a vibrant community.

Maintaining the integrity of divine law took precedence over all other objectives. As Thānvī commented, "From good intentions a permissible act might assume the status of a devotional practice [*'ibāda*], but an abominable act [*makrūh*] can never become permissible, even if the latter contains a thousand benefits and profitable consequences" (50). He further elaborated (using a Robin Hood–like hypothetical): "Say someone engaged in injustice and coercion to collect money with the intention of distributing it to the poor. In this situation, injustice and coercion would not become permissible even if millions of people were expected to benefit from this apparent act of generosity" (50).

Giving Meaning to a Profane Reality: Thānvī as the Mediator of Divine Goodness

After outlining his five principles, Thānvī tested the legitimacy of the *mawlid* according to those principles. Thānvī argued that first one had to determine whether the masses understood taking part in the *mawlid* as obligatory. Second, one had to ascertain if the *mawlid*, as performed by Indian Muslims, had been corrupted by any polluting influences. With respect to the *mawlid*, on both of these counts, Thānvī decisively answered in the affirmative. As he wrote:

> What must be ascertained is whether such permissible actions are producing harm in our time: if one finds harm being generated, then these acts must be forbidden. Otherwise, they will remain permitted. And this ascertainment can be easily derived through observation and experience.

> So in the case of the *mawlid*, through my years of experience with this matter, I can unhesitatingly declare that nearly everyone among the masses considers this ceremony as legally obligated and partakes in its festivities as if it were equal to or even higher in stature than the obligations of the *sharīʿa*. (51)

Thānvī did not outlaw the *mawlid* in absolute terms; in essence and in and of itself, he continued to maintain, the *mawlid* was permissible. However, the litmus test that he set for the demonstration of its permissibility was severely restrictive. According to him, if participants at this gathering could demonstrate, through both their words and their actions, that they considered the *mawlid* a nonobligatory ritual, it would remain permitted. How might they do so? The way they could do so, Thānvī suggested, was by adding some variety to the specifications attached to the ceremony—specifications that would otherwise simulate the *sharīʿa* in the intensity with which they were adhered to.

I will let Thānvī's own words elaborate the mechanism of presenting and establishing a ritual like the *mawlid* as nonobligatory:

> If distributing sweets is a regular part of the ceremony, then on certain occasions the participants should introduce variations and, say, give out cash or clothes or wheat to the poor in private. At still other times they should completely abstain from any form of philanthropy. Similarly, when the virtues and personal traits of the Prophet are being announced during the ceremony, if one is gripped by passion and ecstasy and as a result stands up, there is no reason to fix a specific time for that standing up to take place. One should stand up whenever one feels dominated by ecstasy, whether that happens in the beginning, middle, or the end of the ceremony. Yet at other times, one should also control one's passion and keep sitting. Moreover, one must not specify the *mawlid* ceremony as the only venue where one stands up when overcome by ecstasy. One should also experience this ecstasy and stand up in venues other than the *mawlid* when the virtues and traits of the Prophet are recited. (52)

Thānvī's discussion here presents an important modification to a point I made earlier. Note that for all the emphasis on sobriety, the ecstatic still had a place in his normative imaginary. It was not the excision of the passions but their proper management and harnessing that defined a morally upright and stable subject. I will return to this point in the conclusion of this chapter. Thānvī was quick to point out that it was almost impossible to find a person who met all these requirements, that is, someone who did not confuse the *mawlid* for an obligatory practice in the way he performed this ritual. As he sarcastically commented, "This kind of a person is as rare as a phoenix" (51).

Thānvī's interpretive methodology rested on what one might describe as a relativistic mode of ethics. For Thānvī, it was the external contingencies (*'awāriz-i khārijīya*) under which an act took place that determined its legitimacy. Again, this hermeneutical posture accentuated his own religious authority. By shifting the debate from the inherent and essential merit of an act to the conditions under which it took place, Thānvī bolstered his legislative authority as a jurist. This was so because ultimately it was he who decided whether a given set of external contingencies were negative or positive, corruptive or salutary. In their book *Justice Miscarried: Ethics, Aesthetics and the Law*, legal theorists Costas Douzinas and Ronnie Warrington argue that the gradual expansion in the legislative power of the human will is the most characteristic feature of the development of law in modernity. Under conditions of modernity, they write, "Modern conscience and free will become legislative: the subject can now examine the rules themselves and can reject and replace them if they do not fulfill criteria that may vary according to circumstance and belief."[8] Similarly, in the *Ṭarīqa-yi Mawlid Sharīf*, Thānvī articulated specific juridical criteria that grounded moral obligation in a highly systematic process of ratiocination mediated through the prism of human reason. By considering the normative value of practices that were neither expressly sanctioned nor definitively prohibited by divine law as dependent upon external contingencies, Thānvī elevated his own authority as a master jurist (*mujtahid*). While acting as the mediator of divine will and intent, Thānvī positioned himself as the bestower of meaning upon a profane reality.

Thinking beyond the "Inward Turn"

To conclude, in the last two chapters I have shown that central to the programmatic of normativity undergirding Shāh Muḥammad Ismā'īl's and

Ashraf 'Alī Thānvī's discourses on *bid'a* was a desired synchronicity between the epistemic boundaries established by the *sharī'a* and the ontological patterns governing everyday habits and practices. In the view of these scholars, an act turned into heresy when it transgressed its normatively assigned value of "allowed" (*ḥalāl*), "permissible" (*mubāḥ*), "mandatory" (*wājib*), "abominable" (*makrūh*), or "forbidden" (*ḥarām*) as delineated according to a given interpretation of the *sharī'a*. In other words, the normative values of the *sharī'a* functioned as a panoptic apparatus of knowledge to which the rhythms of individual habits and practices had to correspond and harmonize. When this harmony between knowledge of the law and acquired dispositions was broken, heresy ensued. Epistemic chaos led to ontological and social disorder. It is useful to observe here that this knowledge-practice complex was also at the centerpiece of Bourdieu's theory of *habitus*, as Michel De Certeau has observed.

De Certeau argued that the key variable connecting the objective structures of a community to its *habitus*, in Bourdieu's model, was that of acquired learning. According to De Certeau, Bourdieu's theory "seeks to explain the adequation of practices to structures through their genesis. This 'genesis' implies an interiorization of structures (through learning) and an exteriorization of achievements (what Bourdieu calls the *habitus*) in practices. A temporal dimension is thus introduced: practices (expressing the experience) correspond adequately to situations (manifesting the structure) if, and only if, *the structure remains stable* [emphasis mine] for the duration of the process of interiorization/exteriorization."[9]

A very similar configuration of correspondence between structures and dispositions can be found in Muslim reformist discourses invested in protecting the primacy of the *sharī'a* as a sovereign structure of normative commands. The stability of the epistemic checkpoints and boundaries stipulated by the *sharī'a* can be ensured only through the exteriorization of acquired dispositions that publicly enact and affirm those checkpoints and boundaries. However, these boundaries and limits are never a settled matter. The power struggle over whose version of "normative dispositions" comes to dominate the *habitus* of a community is always an ongoing process that is susceptible to ceaseless contestation. In other words, the very contestability of an idealized *doxa* indicates its absence; for in the presence of a *doxa,* even the possibility of any alternative choices becomes unthinkable and is excised from the realm of consciousness. This struggle over competing *doxas*, I would argue, serves as the master narrative-plot underlying the saga of intra-Muslim contestations over the meaning and scope of *bid'a*.

The analysis conducted in the last two chapters also calls into question historian Barbara Metcalf's assertion that the Deoband founders articulated a project of religious reform focused on the private sphere of personal piety. In her pioneering book on the early years of the Deoband madrasa, Metcalf argued that the Deobandī ideology was characterized by what she called an "inward turn," a renewed emphasis on reforming the individual as a believer. In her own words, the Deoband scholars "fostered a kind of turning away from issues of the organization of state and society, toward a concern with the moral qualities of individual Muslims."[10]

In his landmark study on Deoband, Muhammad Qasim Zaman critiqued Metcalf's argument by noting that it cannot explain "the public and political dimension of the activities of Deobandi 'Ulama' in the twentieth century" and does not "prepare one for the radical sectarianism in Pakistan in the last quarter of the twentieth century."[11] Zaman's point is well taken. But here I should like to add that Metcalf's argument suffers from a more elemental problem, namely its assumption that the public and the private spheres can be readily distinguished as separate domains of life. Metcalf's conceptual frame imposes liberal secular binaries such as inner/outer and public/private on actors who did not live their lives or organize their ideas of reform under the limits of such binaries.

As I have shown repeatedly in this section, Deobandī discourses on *bid'a* operated at the nexus of law, theology, and everyday practice. A subject's salvational prospects intimately depended on the superintendence of a public sphere that affirmed a political theology of radical and absolute divine sovereignty. The purification of the individual believer required the cultivation of a society committed to embodying the limits of divine law in the performance of everyday life. The defining feature of the Deoband reform project was not the interiorization of Islam or a "turning away from issues of the organization of society," as Metcalf argued. To the contrary, the Deoband pioneers strove to transform society in a way that would restore the primacy of divine sovereignty in the religious imagination of Indian Muslims. The task of reforming the self was inseparable from the imperative of reorganizing society.

The intimacy of self, society, and political theology comes across with glistening clarity in a remarkable and memorable moment in Thānvī's intellectual oeuvre: his assault on the rituals of wedding and engagement ceremonies as practiced in North India. As part of his comprehensive critique of popular everyday practices in his widely read text *Mending Conventions* (*Iṣlāḥ al-Rusūm*), Thānvī conducted an exhaustive ethnography of these rituals.[12] He described the precise ritual sequence and sociological dynamics enfolding a couple's betrothal and nuptials in encyclopedic and graphic detail, recounting hundreds of stages that went into a wedding alone. Indeed, from the breadth and depth of Thānvī's knowledge of these rituals, one is almost driven to think that surveilling weddings and engagements was his favorite hobby, if not an abiding obsession. But while Thānvī the ethnographer was meticulous, he was hardly sympathetic to his subjects. In fact, he gave wedding and engagement ceremonies the apocalyptic names "the greater doomsday" and "the lesser doomsday" (*qiyāmat i-kubrā wa qiyāmat-i ṣughrā*) respectively. While rehearsing "the horrifying events" attached to weddings, Thānvī lodged a telling if curious protest that gets to the heart of my point. He complained sarcastically: "At the beginning, the male members of a clan get together and send off the local barber to deliver a letter to the bride's family as a way to fix the wedding date. People are so attached to this custom that even if it were pouring, the roads were blocked and flooded, and the barber was vulnerable to a permanent send-off, they must do it this very way. Tell me: What is this if not necessitating that which God did not deem necessary; what is this if not establishing a counternorm that challenges the *sharī'a*?"[13]

It is Thānvī's next set of comments that most interest me: "What fools these people are. They pay a rupee and a quarter to someone to deliver a message when they could buy an envelope and stamp costing only fifty *paisās*. Why can't they simply put the letter in the mail? And if they must deliver the letter via an intermediary, can they not find for this task a more honorable member of the community than the local barber!"[14] These sentiments nicely capture the interlacing of theology, law, and the promise of a moral public. The force of customs like weddings did more than threaten the sovereignty of the *sharī'a*. It also disturbed the order of ranks and hierarchies that went into the making and preservation of a moral public. Moreover, Thānvī's utilitarian championing of the cost- and time-effective postal system shows the striking synergy between his reform project and the trappings of the colonial discursive and institutional economy. However, one should also be careful to not overvalorize Thānvī's utilitarian impulse as a constitutive element of his intellectual makeup. His utilitarian impulse was inseparably bound to his passional pastoral concern for the everyday life and salvational prospects of the masses. Passional love for the religion of the public and a utilitarian rationality governing the religious performance of that public went hand in hand.[15] The passional and the rational were mutually entangled and inseparably intimate.

To sum up this minidiscussion: in conceptualizing the religious thought of Deoband scholars, it is impossible to make such distinctions as inward/outward, personal piety/public religion, subject/society, or rational/passional. These divisions seek to canonize imaginaries of tradition and its limits that are not available for disciplinary canonization. In the next chapter, I describe a competing understanding of tradition and reform by examining a scathing critique of Deobandī normativity, especially on the question of heretical innovation, advanced by Deoband's archrival Aḥmad Razā Khān. Khān sought to unauthorize the credibility of the Deoband pioneers as reliable custodians of the Prophet's memory. Moreover, he tried to puncture the coherence of their reform project by casting it as a heretical innovation that opposed the opinion of prior and existing authorities of the tradition. The next chapter elucidates how Khān framed his Deoband rivals as heretics who posed a looming threat to Islam in India.

chapter nine

Retaining Goodness

Reform as the Preservation of Original Forms

In January 1906, while in Arabia for his second pilgrimage, Aḥmad Razā Khān presented a juridical opinion (*fatwā*; pl. *fatāwā*) to thirty-three leading jurists in Mecca and Medina. In it he had anathematized, or declared outside the fold of Islam, some prominent Indian Muslim scholars. Khān urged his Arabian interlocutors to endorse his judgment of anathema (*takfīr*).[1] He played the role of a troubled informant educating his foreign colleagues on the different brands of "heretics" and "unbelievers" that in his opinion were thriving in India at that time. As Khān wrote, addressing his Arabian interlocutors: "Tell me clearly if you agree with my assessment of these leaders of misguidance. Do you agree with my judgment of anathema? Or should we refrain from calling them unbelievers just because they are so-called scholars (*'ulamā'*) and *Maulvīs*, even though they are Wahhābīs who curse at God and the Prophet? Should we not save the masses from these people who deny the necessities of religion, and who proudly publish and spread their contemptuous ideas?"[2]

Apart from the founder of the Aḥmadī movement, Mirzā Ghulām Aḥmad, these "leaders of misguidance," as Khān called them, included the pioneers of Deoband: Rashīd Aḥmad Gangohī, Qāsim Nānautvī, and their immediate successors, Khalīl Aḥmad Sāharanpūrī and Ashraf 'Alī Thānvī. This juridical opinion, composed in Arabic, was later published under the title *The Sword of the Holy Sanctuaries at the Throat of Unbelief and Falsehood* (*Ḥusām al-Ḥaramayn 'alā Manḥar al-Kufr wa-l-Mayn*).[3] Khān succeeded in acquiring endorsements from his counterparts in Mecca and Medina. In his opinion, these endorsements, issued by scholars from the bastion of Sunnī Islam, had made official the defeat of his Deoband rivals.

More seriously, they had also authorized the Deobandīs' exit from the fold of Islam. This was an unprecedented event in Muslim South Asia.

There was nothing new about the eruption of fierce polemics and debates among the Indian Muslim scholarly elite. However, by anathematizing prominent fellow Ḥanafī scholars, Khān had set a novel precedent. His judgment of anathema on Deoband scholars represented a culmination of two decades of polemical activity between the pioneers of these two schools. This fury of contestation was facilitated by the technological possibilities of a new colonial public sphere in which the publication and dissemination of printed materials had become easier than ever.

Deobandī and Barelvī scholars pummeled each other with stinging refutations and counter-refutations. Two texts in particular—*Glistening Lights in Defense of the Mawlid and the Fātiḥa* (*Anwār-i Sāṭi'a dar Bayān-i Mawlūd wa-l-Fātiḥa*), henceforth *Glistening Lights*, and *Conclusive Proofs on the Darkness of Glistening Lights* (*al-Barāhīn al-Qāṭi'a 'alā Ẓalām al-Anwār al-Sāṭi'a*, also known as *Barāhīn-i Qāṭi'a*), henceforth *Conclusive Proofs*—are canonical examples of such contestation.[4] The formidable yet rarely studied scholar 'Abdul Samī' composed *Glistening Lights* in 1885 (with a second edition in 1890). He wrote it in response to two brief legal opinions (of four and twenty-four pages) that had chastised the *mawlid* and the *fātiḥa* as practiced in North India. Published by the Hashmi Press (Maṭba' Ḥāshmī) earlier that same year in 1885, these opinions featured Rashīd Aḥmad Gangohī among their major signatories. In *Glistening Lights*, Samī' undertook a devastating critique of Deobandī positions on various questions of theology and ritual practice, mostly focusing on the issues of prophetic knowledge, the celebration of the Prophet's birthday, and the transmission of blessings to the deceased. Samī' was not a disciple of Aḥmad Razā Khān. Therefore, technically, it would be inaccurate to call him a "Barelvī scholar." However, his views on the major contentious questions of theology and ritual practice that divided Deobandī and Barelvī scholars almost entirely overlapped with those of Aḥmad Razā Khān.

Samī' was a prominent Sunnī Ḥanafī scholar from the North Indian town of Rāmpūr (hence he is also known as Abdul Samī' Rāmpūrī). He received his initial education from Raḥmatullah Kayrānwī (d. 1891), a distinguished nineteenth-century scholar and noted polemicist in his own right, in a seminary Kayrānwī had established in his native Kayrāna.[5] In 1854, Samī' ventured to Delhi, where he studied with prominent religious scholars and poets including Muftī Sadruddīn Azūrda and the famous Asadullah Khān (popularly known as Mirzā Ghālib; d. 1869). Samī''s poetic pen-name was "The Heartless" (*be-dil*); hence he is also popularly known as Abdul Samī' Bedil. After dabbling for a while in the composition of *ghazal* and other forms of Urdu poetry, Samī' turned his attention more exclusively to religious scholarship. Samī' spent the last forty-two years of his life in the Lāl Kurtī Bazār (lit. Red Blouse Market) area of Meerut, living next to a large mosque abutting the bungalow of a well-known aristocrat Shaykh Ilāhī Bakhsh (d. 1883). With no children of his own, Ilāhī Bakhsh had appointed Samī' as the teacher for his nephews; when Samī' died in 1900 he was buried in the family graveyard of the most well-known of these nephews, Khān Bahādur (d.n/a). Curiously, major Deoband scholars, including one of the founders of the school Qāsim Nānautvī, the Sufi master of the Deoband pioneers Ḥājī Imdādullah, and the notable Ḥadīth scholar Aḥmad 'Alī Sāharanpūrī (d. 1880), were among Samī''s formative teachers. In fact, he was among those rare disciples of Imdādullah's whom the latter had personally granted the investiture of discipleship.[6] But despite the influence of important Deobandī scholars in his intellectual genealogy, by composing *Glistening Lights*, Samī' emerged as among the fiercest and most unsparing critics of the Deoband school.[7]

Samī''s *Glistening Lights* met with a trenchant rejoinder from the Deoband scholar Khalīl Aḥmad Sāharanpūrī, Rashīd Aḥmad Gangohī's chief disciple. Sāharanpūrī served as the president of the Deoband-affiliated Maẓāhir al-'Ulūm madrasa in the North Indian town of Sāharanpūr for several years. He mentored and inspired some of the most influential twentieth-century Indian Muslim scholars, including the founding luminaries of the transnational evangelical movement Tablīghī Jamā'at, Muḥammad Ilyās Kāndlavī (d. 1944), and his nephew Muḥammad Zakarīya Kāndlavī (d. 1982). Therefore, Sāharanpūrī represents a pivotal connection between the Deoband school and the Tablīghī Jamā'at. Sāharanpūrī was primarily a scholar of Ḥadīth. Among his most well-known texts is an extensive commentary on Abū Dawūd's (d. 889) Ḥadīth collection entitled *A Painstaking Endeavor of [Explicating] Abū Dāwūd's Prophetic Reports* (*al-Badhl al-Majhūd fī Sunan Abī Dāwūd*).

In addition to his role as a notable scholar of Ḥadīth, Sāharanpūrī was a major player in the Barelvī-Deobandī controversy. In 1887, at the behest of his master Gangohī, Sāharanpūrī composed a point-by-point refutation of 'Abdul Samī''s *Glistening Lights* that he appropriately titled *Conclusive Proofs on the Darkness of Glistening Lights*. This text was originally published as a 276-page book by Bilali Steam Press in Sadhaura (present-day Haryāna).[8] Today in most printed editions, these two texts appear together, *Glistening Lights* on the top of the page and *Conclusive Proofs* on the bottom, with a running refutation of the former by the latter. These two texts, extracts of which I will analyze in detail at different points in this chapter and chapter 11, exemplify the intensity, density, and sarcastic tone of Barelvī-Deobandī polemics. Samī' and Sāharanpūrī wrestled for the mantle of normativity by proffering competing and often laboriously complex readings of the Perso-Arabic canonical tradition (especially the Ḥanafī legal tradition) as they jostled to discredit each other. I will return to them and to these texts in due course.

Aḥmad Razā Khān also contributed prolifically to this burgeoning industry of polemics. Moreover, he was not to be outshone in the department of menacing titles. Indeed, the titles that Khān chose for his polemical texts against Deoband scholars and Shāh Muḥammad Ismā'īl show his passionate disdain toward them: *Decimating Wahhābīs for Their Desecration of Muslim Graves* (*Ihlāk al-Wahhābīyīn 'alā Tawhīn Qubūr al-Muslimīn*), *A Shining Star about the Unbelief of the Father of Wahhābīs* (*al-Kawkaba al-Shahābīya fī Kufrīyāt 'abī Wahhābīya*), *Drawing the Indian Swords on the Unbelief of the Masters of Najd* (*Sall al-Suyūf al-Hindīya 'alā kufrīyāt Bābā 'an al-Najdīya*), and *Destructive Spears against the Unbelief of Unbelievers* (*Rimāḥ al-Qahhār 'alā Kufr al-Kuffār*).[9]

As some of these titles and the passage quoted at the beginning of this chapter suggest, Khān strategically attempted to brand his Deoband opponents as "Indian Wahhābīs." Despite their purported loyalty to the Ḥanafī tradition, Khān claimed, Deoband scholars were actively assaulting the normative practices and beliefs sanctioned by that tradition, in the same vein as the eighteenth-century Arab reformer Muḥammad ibn 'Abd al-Wahhāb. Khān's accusation is, however, undercut by the fact that neither the pioneers of Deoband nor Shāh Muḥammad Ismā'īl before them harbored any strong connections with the Wahhābī movement or ideology in Arabia.

Moreover, Deoband scholars were adamantly opposed to the nonconformist Ahl-i Ḥadīth school in India, who could in theory bear the closest resemblance to the Wahhābīs. In fact, Deobandī hostility toward nonconformists (*ghayr muqallidīn*) was often much more intense than their opposition to the Barelvīs. According to the Deobandī imaginary, the Barelvīs, despite their penchant for heretical rituals and conventions and their tendency to divinize the Prophet, were nonetheless part of the same tradition of Ḥanafī scholarship and learning. The Barelvīs at least honored the authority of the same texts and personalities as the Deobandīs. While their interpretations differed, the interpretive framework was still the same. That was not the case with the Ahl-i Ḥadīth, who rejected the very legitimacy of that framework by denying the canonical authority of the four Sunnī schools of law.

Ashraf ʻAlī Thānvī summed up the distinction between Barelvīs and Ahl-i Ḥadīth, as seen from the Deobandī perspective, with an illuminating pair of comparisons. He wrote, "The Barelvīs are like members of one's own household who have gone astray. The Ahl-i Ḥadīth and nonconformists, in contrast, were never part of the household to begin with. . . . The Barelvīs have moral etiquette but no faith [*be-dīn bā-adab*]. The Ahl-i Ḥadīth, on the other hand, have faith but no moral etiquette [*bā-dīn be-adab*]."[10] Continuing the analogy to describe the broader landscape of modern South Asian religious movements, Thānvī likened the clash between Indian Ḥanafīs and the nonconformists to the disagreement between the Āryā Samāj and the Sanātan Dharmīs in Hinduism. On the surface, the Āryā seemed like the (normatively sound) monotheists while the Sanātans seemed like the (normatively questionable) nonmonotheists. But on probing further, Thānvī claimed, one found that the Sanātan Dharmīs showed much better etiquette in their reverence for the authorities of the Hindu tradition than the Āryās did. Further, he added, "Even the Āryā claim to monotheism is questionable. They consider three things—matter, soul, and *parmeshwar* [highest lord/God]—to be eternal in essence [*qadīm bi'l dhāt*]. Where is the monotheism here?"[11]

In any case, Khān's insistence on attaching the label of "Wahhābī" to his Deoband opponents reflects the fearsome associations of this term by the late nineteenth and early twentieth centuries, in both India and Arabia. Ideological battles between Ḥanafī scholars and their nonconformist antagonists had been raging in the Ḥijāz since the late eighteenth century.[12] These battles provided Khān with an ideal moment to authorize his own normative agenda in highly visible ways. Indeed, it was a time when specific institutional, political, and material conditions conjoined to allow Aḥmad Razā Khān to come into central view and authoritatively argue for the exclusion of Deoband scholars from Islam in *Ḥusām al-Ḥarāmayn*. For following the establishment of the Saudi Kingdom in 1932, no juridical pronouncements endorsing Khān's understanding of tradition and difference came forth.

Why precisely did Khān anathematize the pioneers of Deoband? What was at stake for him in this antagonism? How did Deoband scholars defend themselves from Khān's accusation of anathema? And most fundamentally, what were the pivotal intellectual disagreements that separated Barelvī and Deobandī imaginaries of tradition and its limits? These are among the questions addressed in this and the following chapters. I will address them by focusing on two central objectives: (1) highlighting the major ways in which Khān's conception of heretical innovation contrasted with that of his Deobandī rivals, and (2) presenting their opposing views on the relationship between knowledge, sovereignty, and prophetic authority. I will pursue this second task in chapter 11 through a close examination of a debate over the Prophet's capacity for knowledge of the unknown (*'ilm al-ghayb*) that was the immediate context for Khān's judgment of anathema against the Deoband pioneers. Let us begin with a brief introduction to Aḥmad Razā Khān and his intellectual persona.

Aḥmad Razā Khān: An Arch-Defender of Tradition in Modernity

Born in the North Indian town of Bareillī in 1856, one year before the Indian Mutiny against the British, Aḥmad Razā Khān was one of the most prolific, charismatic, and controversial scholars of his era. A staunch Ḥanafī jurist with impeccable credentials as a Sufi master in the Qādirī order, Khān was the founder of the Barelvī orientation in South Asia. His followers remember him as the foremost reviver (*mujaddid*) of Islam in modern South Asia. Khān came from a family of Afghan migrants to North India (more precisely to the region of Rohilkand) in the seventeenth and eighteenth centuries. His immediate ancestors had joined the Mughal imperial bureaucracy as soldiers and soldier-administrators.[13]

In fact, Khān's great-grandfather, Ḥāfiẓ Kaẓim 'Alī Khān, even served as the Nawāb of Awadh in Lucknow, though for the most part his family was part of the local landed elite who were awarded land by the imperial authorities in return for their military service.[14] It was only in the middle of the nineteenth century that his grandfather, Razā 'Alī Khān (d. 1866), ended the family tradition of serving in the military by becoming trained as a jurist and a Sufi in the Qādirī order. The gradual erosion in the fortunes of the Muslim landed elite and the rising unemployment of Muslim soldiers during the nineteenth century precipitated this transition.

In addition to being an accomplished jurist and prolific scholar of Ḥadīth, Aḥmad Razā Khān was immersed in such disciplines as logic, philosophy, philology, and rhetoric. He also composed a commentary on and a translation of the Qur'ān in Urdu. Khān received his juridical training in the traditional Dars-i Niẓāmī curriculum from his father, Naqī 'Alī Khān (d. 1880), who was known as a prominent scholar and as a member of the aristocratic elite. Naqī 'Alī Khān was also an arch-opponent of Shāh Muḥammad Ismā'īl. He was one of several scholars in the generation following Ismā'īl's death who wrote refutations of *Taqwīyat al-Īmān*.[15] Indeed, much of Aḥmad Razā Khān's antipathy toward Ismā'īl and toward Wahhābī ideology was inspired and nurtured by his father.

Khān completed his education in the Dars-i Niẓāmī curriculum at the precocious age of thirteen. Henceforth, he took on the responsibility of writing juridical opinions on behalf of the Miṣbāḥ al-'Ulūm (Lamp of knowledges) Islamic seminary that his father had established in Bareillī in 1872.[16] Khān soon achieved recognition and fame for his thoughtful juridical opinions. By 1880, he had positioned himself as one of the foremost jurists and jurisconsults in India. On any given day, more than five hundred requests for juridical opinions would arrive at Khān's desk, not only from all over India but also from such places as the Ḥijāz, China, Central Asia, Africa, and even the United States.[17] Khān continued the practice of writing juridical opinions at his own seminary, Manẓar-i Islām (The sight of Islam), which he established in Bareillī in 1904.

Apart from his father, another major influence on Khān's intellectual career was his Sufi master Shāh Āl-i Rasūl (d. 1879), a charismatic figure from the North Indian township of Mārhara. Āl-i Rasūl belonged to a highly venerated family of Sufi masters, the Barkatīya, who were also descendants of the Prophet (*sayyid*, pl. *sādāt*). Khān had become Rasūl's disciple before embarking on his first pilgrimage to Mecca in 1878, only a year before Rasūl's death. But despite the relatively short time Khān served as Rasūl's disciple, the latter played a critical role in shaping his outlook on Sufism and prophecy.

Khān's two pilgrimages to the Ḥijāz in 1878 and 1905 were formative moments in his intellectual career. During these visits, he established close relations with prominent scholars of that region; some of them also served as his teachers. For instance, the acclaimed Meccan Shāfi'ī scholar Aḥmad Zaynī Daḥlān (d. 1886) was an important influence on Khān's intellectual formation. Khān had studied with Daḥlān during his first pilgrimage to Mecca in 1878. Like Khān's father in India, Daḥlān was a zealous antagonist of Wahhābī ideology and wrote important tracts refuting the thought of Muḥammad ibn 'Abd al-Wahhāb.[18] As I will show in this chapter, Khān frequently mobilized Daḥlān's ideas for his own assault against Shāh Muḥammad Ismā'īl and the Deoband pioneers.

Another important Arabian mentor for Khān was 'Abd al-Raḥmān Sirāj Makkī (d. 1883), a well-known Ḥanafī jurist and the chief jurisconsult of Mecca and Medina during the late nineteenth century. Like Daḥlān, with whom he was closely associated, Sirāj Makkī actively participated in the anti-Wahhābī campaign that occupied a number of Ḥanafī scholars in the Ḥijāz during this era. In addition to benefiting from his Arabian interlocutors, Khān seems to have made a deep impression on them through his scholarly acumen.

For instance, it was on the request of the prominent Meccan Ḥanafī scholar Ṣāliḥ Kamāl that Khān composed his celebrated Arabic work on the question of the Prophet's knowledge of the unknown, *The Meccan Gift on the Matter of the Unknown* (*Al-Dawlat al-Makkīya bi-l-Mādat al-Ghaybīya*), discussed in chapter 11.[19] Kamāl had sought Khān's assistance in February 1906 after Wahhābī scholars issued a provocative pamphlet with five questions on the subject of the Prophet's knowledge of the unknown, challenging Ḥanafī scholars to answer them. Khān obliged Kamāl's request and wrote *Al-Dawlat al-Makkīya* within a few days. This book was touted by scholars of the Ḥijāz in glowing terms as the most definitive refutation of Wahhābī views on the Prophet's knowledge. It was also presented to the *sharīf* of Mecca at that time, 'Alī Pāsha ibn

'Abdallāh (d. 1932), and was read aloud in his court. After listening to the contents of the book, the *sharīf* exclaimed, "God gifts [the Prophet knowledge of the unknown] and they [the Wahhābīs] forbid it" (*Allāh Yu'ṭī wa hum yamna'ūn*).[20]

Khān's writings encompass a remarkable range of themes and subjects, including Qur'ān exegeses, Ḥadīth criticism, law, theology, philosophy, and logic. Almost all of his works were published in 2006 in thirty-two volumes as *Al-Fatāwā al-Rizvīya* by the Barelvī press Markaz-i Ahl-i Sunnat in Gujarāt, India. Each volume ranges from five hundred to seven hundred pages and contains, on average, ten to fifteen articles. Although Khān wrote primarily in Urdu, he also composed several works in Arabic and Persian.

An excellent visual illustration of how Khān's religious authority is remembered and constructed by his followers today can be found on the front cover of each of his *fatwā* volumes, presented in figure 9.1. This illustration provides a snapshot of the Barelvī self-imagination of their tradition, centered on the charismatic authority of Aḥmad Razā Khān.

On the category of tradition, Ebrahim Moosa has evocatively commented:

> Tradition is both construct and covenant. Meticulous rules and protocols as to how one engages with those who belong to an intellectual and spiritual kinship of tradition is what I call "construct." One's imagined family—often more intimate than blood-ties—create a chain of links between the past and present. Unlike anthropologists and tourists, persons who self-identify with tradition do not do fieldwork, nor do they take trips into the past. Folks of tradition claim to do ontology: an investigation into the nature of being. But more than that, it is more about how they belong to that chain of being. The how is facilitated by covenant and contract: specific modes of practices and beliefs are signatures of participation in particular forms of life.[21]

Figure 9.1 mirrors Moosa's description of tradition. It shows us the sources and hierarchies of normativity that enabled Aḥmad Razā Khān's religious authority as a Sunnī Ḥanafī scholar. At the top of the hierarchy is of course the Qur'ān (represented by the book at the very top of the

Figure 9.1 Barelvī foundations of normativity. The thirty-two volumes of Aḥmad Razā Khān's *fatāwā* are shown to spring from an interpretive framework of canonical texts, which in turn rest on the Ḥadīth, which in turn rest on the Qur'ān. Source: Aḥmad Razā Khān, *Al-Fatāwā al-Rizvīya* (Gujarāt: *Markaz-i Ahl-i Sunnat*, 2006), cover page. Insertions are my own.

image), followed by the six canonical traditions of Ḥadīth in Sunnī Islam. Next, we find the weight of tradition, the interpretive framework that authoritatively connects prophetic time to the present: several canonical texts from various epochs, disciplines, and regions, including al-Ghazālī's *al-Mustaṣfā*, al-Taftazānī's *Sharḥ al-Maqāṣid*, al-Marghinnānī's *al-Hidāya*, Jāmī's *Nafaḥāt al-Uns*, and Fazl-i Imām Khayrābādī 's *al-Mirqāt*. All of these cumulatively constitute the "normative orientation of Aḥmad Razā Khān," *maslak-i A'lā Hazrat* (inscribed inside the bricks), from which the thirty-two volumes of his *fatāwā* spring forth as knowledge that connects the past to the present and establishes a normatively sanctioned "chain of ontological belonging." Indeed, reading any of Khān's writings feels much like taking a trip through the arcade of tradition. Khān was a master of citation. Almost all his works follow a common discursive pattern: fortifying an argument by overwhelming the reader with a deluge of successive quotations from varied authorities and sources across time, space, and disciplines of knowledge.

The defining feature of Khān's understanding of tradition was the active veneration of the Prophet as the most exalted of all beings. For Khān and his followers, honoring the Prophet's status as God's most beloved subject was a non-negotiable doctrinal imperative. Anyone who even hinted at lessening Muḥammad's exalted status had to be confronted, repudiated, and discredited. Khān's passion for guarding the sacrality of Muḥammad's prophetic status was intimately connected to a larger political imaginary driven by an uncompromisingly hierarchical worldview. Indeed, a hierarchical vision of both the social order and the religious order was one of the hallmarks of Khān's conception of tradition.[22] The human-divine relationship could be sustained only by the mediating authority of saints and the Prophet. Moreover, each entity occupied a successively advanced station (*martaba*) in the hierarchy of salvific activity. Khān's theological imaginary also informed his social imaginary.

In the social arena, Khān maintained the superiority of the Prophet's descendants and people belonging to particular noble lineages (*sharīf aqwām*) such as Mughal Pathāns, Anṣārīs, Ṣiddīqīs, and Farūqīs, over the rest of Indian Muslims.[23] To be more precise, people of nobility were not exempt from the requirements of religion and did not receive any special concessions in the realm of law and justice.[24] However, for Khān, nobility and noble lineages were important factors in how a community organized its norms of sociability and calibrated everyday rhythms and habits. For example, with regard to such matters as norms of greeting each other, sitting in public gatherings, and conducting oneself in the marketplace and other spheres of public interaction, it was important to cultivate an aesthetic taste or ethical predisposition (*zawq*) amenable to a vision of society that affirmed certain boundaries, privileges, and hierarchies.

Moreover, Khān argued that it was imperative for people of noble descent, especially women, to take lineal compatibility into consideration when deciding on the marital compatibility or suitability (*kafā'a*) of a spouse. For example, in one of his books devoted entirely to the subject of noble genealogies and their normative status in society, *Demonstrating Moral Etiquette for the Noble in Lineage* (*Irā'at al-Adab li Fāḍil al-Nasab*), Khān declared, "It is impermissible for a Mughal or Pathān girl [*mughlānī wa pathānī*] who has not yet reached the age of marriage to marry a Muslim weaver [*julāhā*]."[25] One must again stress that Khān was not tolerant of impiety or moral sluggishness in people who boasted a noble lineage. On the contrary, he explicitly declared that virtuous practices could never be replaced by lineal nobility. Furthermore, he was extremely critical of people who took excessive pride in their lineage or tribal affiliations; Khān argued that such an attitude could only reflect someone's utter ignorance about the normative model of the Prophet and the pious ancestors.

In a telling moment, Khān was once asked for his opinion on the practice of ridiculing people by the name of their family occupation, a practice that seems to have been quite pervasive in Muslim North India at that time. As his questioner put it, "What is the opinion of the *'ulamā'* on calling someone by the name of his ancestral occupation such as 'weaver' [*julāhā*], 'farmer' [*kāshtkār*], 'fisherman' [*māhī-furosh*], 'hunter' [*shikārī*], or 'crooked-nosed weaver' [*nūrbāf*] as an insult when that hurts his feelings or breaks his heart [*dil shiknī*]?"[26] Khān responded decisively, "To break someone's heart by calling such names is impermissible in the case of not only a Muslim but also an unbeliever under Muslim protection [*kāfir zimmī*], even if the content of the insult is actually true. For every truth is verifiable but not everything verifiable is true [*fa inna kulla ḥaqqin ṣidq wa laysa kulla ṣidqin ḥaqq*]."[27]

On another occasion, a questioner asked Khān, "The prayer leader in our mosque has memorized the Qur'ān and steadfastly performs his five daily prayers. However, he is a butcher by profession. Is it permissible to pray behind him?" Khān responded, "Yes, as long as he is not a Wahhābī, Deobandī, or someone who holds such corrupt beliefs, it is fine to pray behind him. Being a butcher does not disqualify someone from serving as a prayer leader. Several pious ancestors also engaged in this profession."[28]

As these examples show, Khān was not an elitist supremacist by any means. However, he was unwavering in his claim that genealogical distinctions (*tafāzul-i ansāb*) were indispensible to a community's norms. He firmly repudiated the modern notion that genealogies and the social distinctions based on them were insignificant or useless. "Such an opinion," Khān argued, was "rejected and false" (*Nasab ko muṭlaqan maḥaz be qadar barbād jān-nā mardūd wa bāṭil hay*).[29] Most important to note here is the affinity between how Khān understood the capaciousness of prophetic authority and his conception of the ideal norms of human relations in society at large. In both the salvific and social domains, a hierarchical arrangement of power was imperative. Moreover, exaltation of the Prophet as the highest cosmic and ontological reality was the ultimate template for such a hierarchical political theology. And it was precisely this horizon of the political that was at the center of Khān's rivalry with the early Deoband scholars. Khān's refutation of Deobandī views on heretical innovation, to which I now turn, illumines this underlying disagreement very well.

Don't Tamper with the Law: Khān's Refutation of Deobandī Views on Heretical Innovation

Aḥmad Razā Khān vigorously attacked Deoband scholars and Shāh Muḥammad Ismā'īl for their views on the limits of innovation in the arena of ritual practices. His most elaborate discussion on the theme of heretical innovation in Islam is found in a text entitled "Unleashing Hell against the Attacker of Standing to Exalt the Venerable Prophet" (*Iqāmat al-Qiyāma 'alā Ṭā'in al-Qiyām li Nabī Tihāma*).[30] In this text, while focusing on demonstrating the legitimacy of standing when one is reciting the salutation in honor of the Prophet, Khān offered a much broader critique of what he regarded as his opponents' erroneous understanding of the concept of heretical innovation. In the discussion that follows, I highlight the most salient elements of that critique.

Khān was most troubled by the readiness of his opponents to outlaw rituals that served as a means to honor the Prophet's memory and example, such as his birthday celebration. He chastised them for cultivating a public sphere in which the exaltation of the Prophet and the pious ancestors was almost criminalized. Hermeneutically, he argued that an act could be deemed impermissible or forbidden only if a conclusive proof text (*naṣṣ-i qaṭʿī*) establishing such a judgment was available. The default value of all other practices that had not been forbidden by the *sharīʿa* was that of permissibility (*ibāḥat*). In explaining this principle, Khān cited the sixteenth-century jurist Muḥammad al-Qasṭalānī (d. 1517), who in his well-known text *Al-Mawāhib al-Ladunīya* had proclaimed, "The existence of an act [in the Prophet's practice] indicates its permissibility, but the nonexistence of an act does not indicate its impermissibility" (*Al-fiʿl yadull ʿalā al-jawāz wa ʿadm al-fiʿl lā yadull ʿalā al-manʿa*).[31]

The principle that all nonforbidden practices were essentially permissible was also established by the Prophet's saying "Those practices that God has declared as lawful in the Qur'ān are normatively lawful. Those practices that God has declared as forbidden in the Qur'ān are normatively forbidden. And those practices about which God has said nothing [in the Qur'ān] are neither normatively sanctioned nor forbidden" (*Al-ḥalāl mā aḥalla Allāh fī kitābihi wa-l-ḥaram ma ḥarrama Allāh fī kitābihi wa mā sakata ʿan-hu fa huwa mimā ʿafā ʿan hu*).[32] In legal terms, the implication of this prophetic saying was that unless a practice was explicitly forbidden in the *sharīʿa* it was permissible.

Khān accused his Deobandī rivals of falsifying divine law by prohibiting practices that were permissible in essence. Divine law, he emphasized, was eternal (*abadī*). Therefore, when the original normative value (*aṣl*) attached to an act was that of permissibility, calling it prohibited was equivalent to manufacturing an unsanctioned novel law. For Khān, such tampering with the normatively designated values of law undermined the sovereignty of that law.

The cardinal sin of Deoband scholars and Shāh Ismā'īl, in his view, was their hubris in altering the logic of normativity by outlawing permissible practices.[33] Khān would have agreed with his Deoband rivals (such as Thānvī) that the attachment of corruptions makes otherwise permissible practices heretical. However, where he sharply diverged from them was in their evaluation of the present and its moral condition. In Khān's view, there was no immediate emergency or moral chaos that necessitated dissuading people from undertaking rituals centered on venerating the Prophet. In fact, he argued, so long as there was no threat to divine sovereignty, prohibiting any means to exalt the Prophet by calling it heretical was itself heretical. For Khān, the celebration of the Prophet's birthday and especially the act of standing up in reverence to him (*qiyām*) were no ordinary acts that could be discarded at will. Since this ritual was a means to remember and honor the Prophet, it was indispensible to the tradition.[34]

Competing Logics of Time and Tradition

Conceptually, Khān's major complaint against his opponents was the way they understood the interaction of tradition and temporality. According to Khān, the Deoband scholars held a very restricted and mistaken view of sacred time. As he put it, "All of them suffer from the disease of making time the ultimate sovereign on the boundaries of normativity [*zamān ko ḥākim-i shar'ī banāyā hay*]. Their only concern is whether a practice existed during a certain period in history [the era of the Prophet and Companions] or not. If a practice existed during that era, they will endorse it, and if it did not, they will outlaw it."[35]

As a counterview to such a temporally driven hermeneutic, Khān argued that the normative validity of an act depended on its inherent goodness or lack thereof, not on the period in history in which it occurred. A good act was good whenever it might be undertaken. Similarly, a bad act, regardless of when it happened, was bad. Instead of evaluating the inherent quality of a practice, Khān lamented, his opponents were solely interested in determining whether it had occurred during the first three generations of Islam (*qurūn-i salāsa*).

A hermeneutic so fixated on an original sacred time was bound to produce a very myopic understanding of tradition, Khān argued. No doubt, the era of the Prophet, his Companions, and their successors was most exemplary and sanctified. However, and this was the most crucial point, the sanctity of prophetic time did not mean that the rest of time—the nonprophetic past, the present, and the future—was doomed to the abyss of moral failure. Goodness was not restricted to any specific time period, even to the first three centuries. Here Khān cited the evocative prophetic saying, "My community is like rain; one cannot tell which is better, the beginning of a rain shower or its end" (*Mathal ummatī mathal al-maṭar lā yudrā awwalahu khayr am ākhiruhu*).[36]

For Khān, this prophetic report clearly showed that the horizon of goodness was not limited to any single moment. The memory of an exemplary prophetic time was supposed to inspire the moral capacities of those who inhabited the present, not cripple them with the anxiety of living in the shadow of an irrecoverable past. For Khān, reform was animated by the mission of ensuring the continuity of the normative goodness embodied in ritualized practices in each successive generation. Those who called such practices heretical were themselves committing the heresy of forbidding practices that had been sanctioned by esteemed scholars and luminaries of the tradition for several centuries.

In this regard, Khān's conception of reform differed dramatically from that of his Deoband rivals. As I showed in the previous chapters, the reform project of Deoband scholars such as Ashraf 'Alī Thānvī was anchored in a narrative of constant moral decline that necessitated an act of radical intervention by the learned elite. Given the urgency of the situation, even otherwise pious practices, such as the celebration of the Prophet's birthday, were to be abandoned. The moral crisis confronting the present necessitated the conscious decision of discarding certain ritualized practices that had thrived in the past but that were now terminally corrupted.

Time, Goodness, Disciplined Life

Because this point is so important—the contrast in Barelvī and Deobandī imaginings of the interaction of temporality and normativity—I want to clarify and deepen my analysis. To do so, I will briefly turn from Khān's discourse to further elaboration of the Deobandī position on temporality as a way to sharpen its contrast with the Barelvī position. For this purpose, I turn to the lively discourse of Deoband scholar Khalīl Aḥmad Sāharanpūrī in his polemical text *Conclusive Proofs* before returning to Khān. (Remember, this text was written as a refutation of Maulvī ʻAbdul Samīʻs anti-Deobandī text *Glistening Lights*.)

Samīʻ, in an argument mirroring Khān's, had accused the Deoband pioneers of wrongly restricting the era of goodness (*khayrīyat*) to the time of the Prophet and the first three generations of Islam. Such a view erroneously snatched from all successive generations of Muslims the possibility of embodying and accessing goodness, Samīʻ had complained. In his response, Sāharanpūrī took Samīʻ to task for generalizing the category of goodness. How? By not distinguishing between the absolute virtue (*fazl-i kullī*) of the first three generations and the partial or subsidiary virtue (*fazl-i juz'ī*) embodied by what followed. The faithful of the first three generations, because of their promixity to God and prophetic knowledge (*ʻilm-i nubūwwat*), possessed absolute virtue. On the other hand, the pious folk who came after that era, on account of their faith in Islam despite the Prophet's absence (*īmān bi'l ghayb*), carried subsidiary virtue. Critically, these two varieties of goodness or virtue, though hierarchically ordered, were not contradictory or opposed.[37]

In hammering his point home, Sāharanpūrī treated his readers to an unseemly but entertaining analogy. The superiority of absolute to subsidiary virtue, he explained, was much like the superiority of a mouthwatering *palāo qorma* (a rice- and meat-based North Indian delicacy) to the agricultural manure (*khād*) available in human excrement (*pākhāna*).[38] Clearly, the *qorma* does not have the benefit of the manure and cannot perform the manure's task. Nevertheless, the manure cannot match the absolute goodness of the *qorma*. Equating the goodness of the first three generations with that of all successive generations, as Samīʻ had done,was like equating the delicacy of the *palāo qorma* to excrement [*palāo awr pākhāna ko musāwī batānay lagay*]. "This author [Samīʻ] is not even familiar with the concepts of universal and subsidiary virtue, hence his superficial hermeneutical moves. . . . Had he expended even an ounce of thought, he would not have authored such senseless drivel" (*Mu'allif fazl-i kullī fazl-i juz'ī ko jāntā hī nahīn jo yeh tawjīhāt-i rakīka kartā hay. . . . Kuch bhī samajhtā tuh aysī charbūz taqrīr taḥrīr na kartā*), Sāharanpūrī concluded in a burst of indignation.[39]

Let us set aside for a moment the scatological imagery evoked by Sāharanpūrī's discourse. There is a crucial dimension of his argument that must be emphasized here. What separated the first three generations from the rest of time was not only the difference in their magnitude of goodness but the difference in the types of goodness they embodied. The goodness inherent in the virtuous practices of the first three generations had the normative function of sanctioning law and ritual practice for all future generations. In other words, it was attached to a grammar of assent (*ḥukm-i ittibā'*); it provided successive generations a normative template to follow and assent to. In contrast, the goodness of acts beyond the first three generations did not have this normative function or authority. So, for instance, such acts as a husband treating his wife well or a community benefiting another community, if performed after the first three generations, could not have served as the basis for law and normativity. The goodness of these acts, in contrast to the virtuous deeds of the first three generations, was detached from a grammar of assent: they were not normative.[40] As I explained in chapter 7, the Deobandī position was not that everything happening in the first three generations was good and everything happening later was bad, though opponents like Aḥmad Razā Khān and 'Abdul Samī' sometimes caricatured it that way. Nonetheless, Khān was on to something in pointing out that the Deobandī outlook was characterized by a view of human degeneration following the first three generations of Islam, as the preceding discussion of Sāharanpūrī's thought clearly testifies.

Let me return to Khān. His view of temporality was starkly opposite. Philosophically, he objected to viewing history as entailing continuing degeneration. Such pessimism produced a markedly stagnant notion of time as divided into an original sacred time followed by a progressively profane time. This duality was at odds with the example of none other than the Prophet's Companions themselves, Khān argued. The Prophet's Companions, he stressed, celebrated the dynamic nature of tradition.[41] When evaluating the legitimacy of a new practice, they invested their energies in determining the inherent merit of that practice rather than the time period in which it occurred. For example, Khān narrated the story of a debate between the first two caliphs in Sunnī Islam, Abū Bakr and 'Umar, over systematizing the text of the Qur'ān. In the aftermath of the battle of Yamāma in 632, several Companions who had memorized the Qur'ān died. Following this development, 'Umar became concerned that given the rapidity with which memorizers of the Qur'ān were dying (in battles), a significant portion of the text might soon be lost.

He urged 'Abū Bakr, the caliph at that time, to begin the work of compiling and systematizing the Qur'ān in earnest. At first, Abū Bakr hesitated. He protested, "How can we do something that the Prophet did not do?" 'Umar responded to his senior colleague's hesitation by saying, "By God, it is a good thing to do" (*Huwa wallāhī khayr*). As they engaged in this debate, Abū Bakr's heart gradually opened up to 'Umar's suggestion. Eventually, he was convinced that this was indeed a meritorious act that demanded urgent attention. The project of systematizing the Qur'ān soon commenced.[42]

For Khān, the most noteworthy aspect of this story was this: when Abū Bakr initially hesitated to start a new practice that was not found in the Prophet's life, 'Umar did not respond by valorizing the sacred temporality that shielded the Companions from any wrongdoing. He did not say, for instance, that the prohibition against innovation might have existed in a previous era but that Companions of the Prophet who occupied the temporal space of the first three generations were exempt from such considerations. Rather, he tried to convince Abū Bakr on the basis of the essential goodness of the act that he had advocated. It was the inherent quality of an act, not its presence or absence in a particular time period, that drove 'Umar's argument.

In other words, Khān emphasized, 'Umar's imagination of normativity and its limits was not shackled to any singular hegemonic temporality that colonized the moral choices of all subsequent generations. To the contrary, he, like all other Companions, viewed tradition as continually blossoming, as a continuously evolving moral project that was firmly rooted in its sacred origins. Khān vividly sketched such a relationship between temporality and tradition through the metaphor of a garden (*bāgh*).

Islam, he analogized, was Muḥammad's garden, a garden that continued to grow in splendor and magnificence over time. The original caretakers of the garden laid the foundational soil that ensured its capacity to survive during its early years. However, they did not have the time or the opportunity to develop it any further. But gradually, the garden blossomed. It became luscious green, elaborated with breathtaking flowers, leaves, and fountains, as each generation of scholars and saints added new layers of beauty to what they had inherited from their predecessors.

Khān argued that tradition, like a blooming garden, was a palimpsest of temporalities and thought-styles bound by a shared narrative of the moral good. Moreover, just as new varieties of flowers in a garden sprang from their originals, new practices that were essentially good seamlessly connected with the logic of the Prophet's normative example. Someone who objected to a praiseworthy act because it had not existed during the first three generations of Islam was as foolish as someone who denied the beauty of new flowers in a garden, Khān claimed; "Ultimately, such an ignorant fool will remain deprived of the garden's fruits and flowers."[43]

For Khān, devotional rituals that were new in their form but meritorious in essence were comparable to the new flowers of a garden. Disputing their legitimacy was foolish. Moreover, the most esteemed of such rituals were those that venerated the Prophet's status, such as the celebration of his birthday. He further argued that any innovated act that exalted the Prophet was inherently praiseworthy and immune to critique unless that act undermined God's sovereignty. Khān authorized this position by quoting the sixteenth-century Shāfiʿī scholar Ibn Ḥajar al-Haytamī (d. 1567): "All means of venerating the Prophet that do not undermine the exclusivity of divine sovereignty are praiseworthy" (*Taʿẓīm al-nabī bi-jamīʿ anwāʿ al-taʿẓīm allatī laysa fī-hā mushārakat Allāh taʿālā fi'l-ulūhīya `amr mustaḥsan*).[44]

Haytamī's cautionary precondition, Khān explained, referred to brazenly problematic gestures such as prostrating before the Prophet or saying his name instead of proclaiming "God is great" before sacrificing an animal. But all other expressions of honoring the Prophet, such as standing up in his honor, were the loftiest of pious acts. Khān challenged his opponents to present a conclusive proof text from the Qur'ān or prophetic reports if they wished to deny the legitimacy of practices that exalted the Prophet. In the absence of such a proof text, to outlaw an essentially good practice that was deemed permissible by the *sharīʿa* was a challenge to the sovereignty of the *sharīʿa*. Therefore, Khān concluded, scholars who opposed rituals such as the celebration of the Prophet's birthday, including his Deobandī rivals, were playing God.[45] They were outlawing rituals that God had not outlawed. Far from protecting divine sovereignty, such an inversion of divine law undermined that sovereignty. Furthermore, by calling heretical rituals that were a source of remembering the Prophet and other pious figures in the tradition, these scholars were inventing a new law that contradicted all previous norms of moral etiquette. Indeed, for Khān, this debate was as much about proper moral etiquette as it was about law.

The enthusiasm of the Deoband scholars to prohibit avenues of exalting the Prophet was symptomatic of their lack of respect for the Prophet. That was why, Khān argued, Shāh Muḥammad Ismā'īl and his Deobandī followers instructed the masses to address the Prophet in the same manner as they addressed each other, to not hesitate to call him their brother, and why they discouraged people from naming their children "the Prophet's gift" (*nabī bakhsh*). These dramatic measures confirmed their disregard for the uniqueness of the Prophet's charisma. They were turning the Prophet into merely an ordinary person. This view of prophetic authority radically opposed the tradition of the pious ancestors. The Companions had not diminished the Prophet's stature. To the contrary, they had choreographed their entire lives around the imperative of demonstrating their love for him. Khān cited the example of the preeminent eighth-century jurist and eponymous founder of the Mālikī school of law Mālik Ibn Anas (d. 795):

> When prospective students visited Mālik, a slave girl would receive them and say, "The Shaykh asks what you wish to study: problems of jurisprudence or Ḥadīth?" If they replied "Jurisprudence," Mālik would immediately come out and begin the lesson. However, if they answered "Ḥadīth," he would take his time in preparation. He would perform ablutions, put on new clothes, apply perfume, and put on his turban. Then a special seat would be placed in front of him on which he would sit at an elevation. Only then would he begin the lesson. If someone inquired about the reason for such ceremonious preparations, he would respond: "I love exalting the Prophet's words. Therefore, I don't utter those words until I am in a state of utmost purity and physical excellence."[46]

This was the kind of passion for elevating the Prophet's being that was sorely lacking among scholars who wished to outlaw the Prophet's birthday celebration, Khān claimed. To sum up, in Khān's view, the Deobandī reformist platform was not only legally invalid. More importantly, it also contravened long-established norms of moral etiquette.

Distinguishing Law and Habit

Barelvī and Deobandī attitudes toward the limits of innovation also differed on another subtle yet significant point, the role of habit in the construction of a community's normative boundaries. As we saw in the previous chapters, the Deobandī reform project was animated by the promise of disrupting habits and conventions that simulated obligatory religious practices. In the view of Deoband scholars, even praiseworthy rituals had to be abandoned when they became so entrenched to a community's life that whoever voluntarily abstained from them was collectively rebuked and censured. The emphasis of the Deoband school, therefore, was on transforming the practice of a community's everyday life so that it replicated the normative boundaries of divine law.

Philosophically, this position was authorized by the assumption that normative law and embodied habits were separable, with the latter always conforming to the boundaries stipulated by the former. Aḥmad Razā Khān, on the other hand, articulated a very different conception of the relationship between law and habit. Khān argued that the law governing a community could not be divorced from its habits. Therefore, he found nothing problematic with the regularization of customs and conventions that were essentially good and that served pious ends, even if they lacked a precedent in the Prophet's normative model.

As I explained earlier, for Khān the decisive factor in determining the normative legitimacy of an act was its inherent goodness, regardless of when it had been invented and introduced into the life of a community. Moreover, if a community agreed on regularizing certain pious practices in a way that conformed to its temperament and practical needs, that was to be encouraged and not repudiated. So, for instance, Khān, in stark contrast to the pioneers of Deoband, was untroubled by the specification of a date or time (*tawqīt al-waqt*) for undertaking rituals such as celebrating the Prophet's birthday or commemorating the birth anniversary of prominent saints. His argument here is worth considering in some detail, for it shows specifically how his legal imaginary differed from that of his Deoband rivals.

Khān explained that in relation to the performance of devotional practices, there were two kinds of temporal specifications: those that were normatively demanded (*tawqīt-i sharʻī*) and those that were non-normative (*tawqīt-i ʻādī*). The first category included practices that according to the *sharīʻa* could be performed only during specified blocks of time: for instance, performing the five daily obligatory prayers at specified times, undertaking the sacrifice of an animal in the three days following the annual *ʻĪd* celebration (*ayyām al-nahr*), and completing the rites of pilgrimage during the months of *Shawwāl*, *Dhul Qaʻda*, and *Dhul Ḥijja* in the Islamic calendar. On the other hand, non-normative specifications of time were not necessary and merely served as a means to actualize and regularize ritual practices. As Khān put it in very simple terms, "For something to happen, there must be a specified time for it to happen."[47] Therefore, the birth/death anniversary of pious figures was commemorated every year or every six months. Similarly, gatherings for the transmission of blessings to the deceased were organized on the third and the fortieth days of a person's death. The specification of a time served as a means to remind participants about the occurrence of such rituals. "When there is a specified time for an act, it is more likely to happen," Khān explained.[48]

Importantly, he explicitly warned that the temporal specifications attached to such practices must not be confused with normatively demanded specifications (such as those for daily prayers). Here he was in complete agreement with his Deoband rivals. However, for Khān, as long as people did not understand non-normative specifications as obligatory, there was no harm in them. To the contrary, specifying a date, he reasoned, represented a necessary means to ensure the continuity (*mudāwamat*) of spiritually beneficial practices over time.[49] Khān further argued that the normative practice of the Prophet and the Companions provided ample examples of temporal specifications for pious practices.

For instance, the Prophet visited the graves of martyrs at the beginning of every year, a practice continued by Abū Bakr and ʻUmar. Similarly the Prophet's close Companion ʻAbdallāh ibn Masʻūd (d. 650) had specified Thursday as a day for delivering his sermons. The most important thing to remember here, Khān urged his readers, was that none of these specifications were elevated to become normative; they remained at the level of habit and custom. It was not as if Ibn Masʻūd considered all days other than Thursday as inadmissible, inappropriate, or any less propitious for delivering sermons. His intention in specifying Thursday for delivering sermons was the regularization of a laudable practice. There was nothing illegitimate or harmful in regularizing a spiritually beneficial practice through the specification of a date.

Moreover, Khān continued, even if the specification of a date for a pious practice did not serve any obvious purpose or benefit, that specification could still not be called forbidden. Individual subjects had the choice to specify a date if they so wished or to not specify a date if they so wished. In the case of all non-normative specifications (*ta'ayyunāt-i 'ādīya*), the decision on instituting them or not rested solely with the individual practitioner, with no rewards or punishments attached to it. For Khān, this was the import of the Prophet's saying, "Specifying Saturdays as a day for fasting will bring you neither rewards nor any punishment" (*Ṣiyām al-sabt lā laka wa lā 'alayka*).[50] This prophetic saying meant that the specification of Saturday as a day for fasting was a neutral choice that carried no normative consequences, positive or negative. Further, the choice to institute and regularize Saturday as a day on which to fast was the prerogative of each individual subject.

Therefore, according to Khān, the objection of his Deoband rivals to specifying a date for permissible ritual practices opposed the normative model of the Prophet and the Companions. The heightened concern of the Deoband scholars that the specification of a date would cause permissible practices to simulate obligatory practices was a concern not shared by the Prophet. To the contrary, the Prophet showed remarkable confidence in the capacity of ordinary Muslims to choreograph the performance of their religious lives. Moreover, Khān advised, in case someone among the masses understood such specifications as normative or obligatory, then that attitude should be corrected on a case-by-case basis. A permissible ritual should not be altogether abandoned because of the potential threat that someone might understand it as obligatory.

In Khān's view, the Deobandīs, rather than taking the measured approach of preventing corruptions in pious rituals or educating the masses on correct practice, had imposed an absolute ban on those rituals. As a result, even people who did not hold corrupt beliefs, among both scholars and the masses, were denied participation in rituals that were deemed beneficial or permissible according to divine law. Here we find a subtle yet critical point of difference between Khān and the Deoband scholars.

For the latter, such as Ashraf 'Alī Thānvī, the specification of a date for nonobligatory rituals simulated obligatory practices and hence undermined the primacy of religious obligations. Hence, such a specification rendered otherwise permissible practices heretical. In stark contrast, for Khān, specifying a date made possible the ritualization of pious acts. As a result, it facilitated the secure transmission of the goodness embodied in those acts from one generation to the next. In Khān's imaginary, there was no reason to interrupt goodness unless there was an urgent need to do so.

Since divine law was eternal, the manifestation of that law in the life of a community did not require constant epistemological policing on the part of jurists and scholars. The job of a jurist was to ensure that the promised goodness of divine law became ritualized as part of a community's everyday life. For Khān, the function of law was the perpetuation, not the prohibition, of morally beneficial rituals crafted in accordance with a community's aesthetic sensibility. He argued that the prophetic saying "Associate with people in accordance with their [good] character and oppose them in their [sinful] deeds" (*Khāliqū al-nās bi akhlāqihim wa khālifūhum bi a'mālihim*) clearly substantiated his position.[51]

Khān summed up his argument by citing the polymath eleventh/twelfth-century scholar Abu Ḥāmid al-Ghazālī (d. 1111), who in his magnum opus *The Resuscitation of Salvational Knowledges* (*Iḥyā' 'Ulūm al-Dīn*) wrote: "Every community has its own conventions. It is imperative to deal with people in accordance with the goodness of their character (as stated by the Prophet), especially in relation to practices that enable good conduct or the purification of hearts. And whoever calls such practices heretical innovations because the Companions did not take part in them is mistaken. The Companions did not transmit the totality of all permissible practices. Only a practice that opposes the normative model of the Prophet and the Companions can be called a heretical innovation."[52]

To Eat or Not to Eat? Food, Text, and Competing Hermeneutical Strategies

I want to conclude this discussion on law and habit by delving deeper into the precise hermeneutical mechanisms and citational practices through which Deobandī and Barelvī pioneers contested the boundaries of tradition. Thus far, I have had occasion to elaborate individual Barelvī and Deobandī positions on particular contentious matters. Here I want to walk readers through a specific example of how competing logics and readings of tradition unfold within the specific conjuncture of a polemical back-and-forth. Think of what follows as the highlights package of a live textual polemical showdown. For this task, I turn again to 'Abdul Samī''s *Glistening Lights* (*Anwār-i Sāṭi'a*) and Khalīl Aḥmad Sāharanpūrī's polemical rejoinder *Conclusive Proofs* (*al-Barāhīn al-Qāṭi'a*).

I will juxtapose their opposing views on the controversy surrounding the *fātiḥa* or the distribution of food on the occasion of death to transmit blessings (received from this act of charity) to the deceased's soul. I have chosen to highlight their discursive skirmish on this particular issue because it brings together in particularly effective ways varied conceptual nodes and analytical threads. These include the interaction of materiality and affect; the relationship between law, ritual, and habit; and, as we will see, the status and charisma of the Prophet's body. In what follows I will be interested not only in the texture and layers of Samī''s and Sāharanpūrī's arguments but also, and especially, in the contrasting interpretive strategies through which they accessed and mobilized authoritative sources of tradition, particularly sources from the Ḥanafī legal tradition. After this analysis, I will return to Aḥmad Razā Khān's quest to dismantle the Deobandī claim to the mantle of normativity. I begin, however, by exploring the major lineaments of Samī''s spirited defense of the ritual benefit and normative validity of the *fātiḥa*, as practiced in colonial South Asia.

In *Glistening Lights*, while defending the *fātiḥa* from the onslaught of Deobandī critique, Samī' argued that offering food or sweets as a means of transmitting spiritual blessings and rewards to the dead is a practice that joins bodily and monetary devotions (*badanī wa mālī 'ibādāt*).[53] The bodily devotion relates to the recitation of the opening chapter of the Qur'ān (*al-fātiḥa*) or that of any other liturgical prayer over the food, with the intention that those prayers be transmitted to a specified deceased person. It is because of this particular moment in the ritual, Samī' explained, that it is called the *fātiḥa*. So when the masses say that today is the *fātiḥa* of such and such a saint (*buzurg*) or of such and such a deceased person, they are referring to this gesture of reciting the *fātiḥa*. In addition to this bodily devotion, Samī' continued, in the tone of a lecturer warming up an audience, there is a monetary devotion attached to this ritual, namely the expenditure of financial resources to acquire food and sweets. Each of these components, Samī' argued, the bodily and the devotional, is normatively sanctioned by the tradition. In assembling his case, Samī' cited the famed fourteenth-century Muslim Persian polymath Sa'd al-Dīn al-Taftazānī. In his Arabic commentary on the text of another twelfth-century Persian polymath, Najm al-Dīn al-Nasafī's (d. 1142),[54] *Tenets of Faith* (*Al-'aqā'id*), al-Taftazānī had categorically declared: "Except the Mu'tazila, all [Muslims] agree that the prayers and charity of the living for the dead benefit the latter" (*Wa fī duā' al-aḥyā' li-l-amwāt wa ṣadaqatihim 'an hum nafa'a la-hum khilāfan li-l-mu'tazila*).[55] Similarly, Samī' further validated his position by drawing on the prominent seventeenth-century Ḥanafī jurist Muḥammad al-Hirawī (d. 1605; popularly known as Mullāh 'Alī al-Qārī), who in his commentary, also in Arabic, on Abū Ḥanīfa's seminal text *The Loftiest Jurisprudence* (*Al-Fiqh al-Akbar*), had said, "Abū Ḥanīfa and all other members of the patristic community agreed on the [permissibility of] transmission of rewards to the dead" (*Dhahaba Abū Ḥanīfa wa jumhūr al-salaf 'ilā wuṣūlihā*).[56] Closer to his home and the present, Samī' also presented as a way of building his case the thought of the noted eighteenth-century South Asian jurist and Sufi master Qāzī Sanā'ullah Pānīpatī, who in his Persian text *Remembering the Dead* (*Tazkirat al-Mawtā*) had proclaimed: "All jurists have ruled that the rewards of every [such] devotional practice reach the deceased" (*Jamī'-yi fuqahā ḥukm karde and ke sawāb-i har 'ibādat bi-mayyat mī rasad*).[57]

The import of the view of these leading intellectual giants in the Ḥanafī canon was the same, Samī' argued. Since bodily and monetary devotions were individually permissible, a practice that aggregated these two components was, by necessity, also permissible. In other words, if the two parts (*ajzā'*) making up a ritual were normatively legitimate, it made little sense to question the normativity of the eventual product (*murakkab*), that is, the ritual itself. In elucidating his argument, Samī' constructed a culinary analogy, much as his archnemesis Sāharanpūrī had done in the example I earlier discussed. If *palāo qorma* had kindled Sāharanpūrī's gastronomic imagination, Samī''s illustrative dish of choice was *biryānī*. Samī' argued that prohibiting the ritual of the *fātiḥa* was as ludicrous as banning the consumption of *biryānī*. What, one might wonder, was the correlation? Well, just as the *fātiḥa* represented a composite of bodily and monetary devotions, *biryānī* was also a composite of varied ingredients including rice, meat (the possibility of a vegetarian *biryānī* did not cross his imagination), and, in some cases, saffron. "Only a fool would lodge the protest: 'Yes, these individual ingredients are permissible, but show me a proof text ('*aṣl*) from the Qur'an and Ḥadīth authorizing the consumption of the actual *biryānī*.'"[58] This was the level and sort of ridiculousness exhibited by Deoband scholars who forbade the *fātiḥa*, Samī' claimed. To summarize, Samī''s argument rested on establishing the normative validity of combining two different types of devotional activities (*jam' bayn al-'ibādatayn*).

Samī' expanded his argument by juxtaposing the mobilization of Ḥanafī sources with an example from the Prophet's life and practice. During the Battle of Tabūk (in 630), Samī' narrated, the Prophet had prayed over food on 'Umar's request. As a million people witnessed, this embodied devotional act on the Prophet's part multiplied the food in abundance, feeding all those present. This act not only showcased the miraculous charisma of the Prophet's body but also established the normative soundness of praying over food as a devotional act, Samī' confidently argued. If the Prophet did not hesitate to pray over food, who were the Deoband scholars to voice their doubts and hesitation about doing so? Samī' concluded his attack on the Deoband pioneers, in relation to this particular issue, with a devastating Persian aphorism: "I have no hope in your doing any good, [but at least] keep the bad to yourself" (*Marā bi khayr-i tū umīd nīst bad ma risān*).[59]

Sāharanpūrī's response to this attack began with the reminder that Deoband scholars had no objection to transmitting blessings and rewards to the deceased through acts of charity such as the distribution of food. Their objection concerned the specific manner (*hayyat-i ḥāṣila*) in which this practice unfolded among Indian Muslim communities, with the food placed in front of the supplicant, who then recited the *fātiḥa* over it. Even more specifically, what Deoband scholars rejected was the insistence on reciting the *fātiḥa* in this particular manner only, with the belief that otherwise the rewards of the act would not reach the deceased.

This particular ritual form, and the insistence on adhering to it, were heretical innovations not only because they had no precedent in Islam's first three generations. They carried the added contagion of imitating the "Hindu" practice and custom (*tashabbuh-i hunūd*) of praying over food placed in front of the supplicant. In fact, the widespread currency of this particular ritual mode among Hindus was precisely the cause for its spread into and preponderance among the Indian Muslim community, Sāharanpūrī asserted.[60]

But what about the appetizing metaphor of the *biryānī* that Samī' had so earnestly advanced to argue that the ritual product of two permissible components must also be permissible? What fault could Sāharanpūrī possibly find with an analogy about the perfectly permissible, if not deliciously aromatic ingredients of the *biryānī*? Sāharanpūrī responded that while the essential goodness of the ingredients was never in question, it behooved the chef to inspect their condition before putting them to use. If, for example, an intoxicant were found in the saffron (*za'frān*) that went into preparing the *biryānī*, then that otherwise permissible *biryānī* would become prohibited. Similarly, if an otherwise permissible ritual became corrupted by abominable or prohibited ingredients, it would no longer be permissible. In the case of the *fātiḥa*, imitating a Hindu practice and making necessary a specific new action that was unprecedented in the era of the Prophet and his community was such an abomination (*karāhat*) and prohibition (*ḥurmat*). The broader hermeneutical principle at work in Sāharanpūrī's thought was this: the original permissibility (*ibāḥat-i aṣlīya*) of a practice could be sustained only in the absence of a prohibitory authoritative proof text (*naṣṣ-i māni'*). With regard to the *fātiḥa*, the prophetic sayings "Every innovation is a misguidance and every misguidance leads to hellfire" and "Whoever imitates a people becomes one of them" were two such prohibitive proof texts. For Sāharanpūrī, these prophetic sayings clearly established the prohibition of the specific form of this ritual as current among the masses of India.[61]

But perhaps the most fascinating part of Sāharanpūrī's tug-of-war with Samī' had to do with his meditation on the narrative of the Prophet's praying over food during the Battle of Tabūk. Here his view of the Prophet, the materiality of food, and the relationship between the canonical tradition and the present was strikingly divergent from Samī''s.

Sāharanpūrī did not disagree with Samī' that the Prophet had indeed prayed over food at Tabūk, with the food placed right in front of him. But like a humanities scholar scolding an empiricist social scientist, Sāharanpūrī urged that the empirical accuracy of an event was hardly its most important aspect: what mattered was the interpretive frame through which one interpreted a said event. It would be absurd to deny that the Prophet had recited the Qur'ān or some other prayer over food because he used to recite prayers every moment of his life; there was nothing noteworthy about that.[62] The Deobandī argument, Sāharanpūrī reminded his readers, was not that the Prophet never prayed over food but that the specific form of this practice, as dominant among Indian Muslims, was not found during Islam's first three generations.

But the obvious question that emerged here was: If praying over food by placing it in front of oneself was one of the central problems with the ritual performance of Indian Muslims, and if that was precisely what the Prophet also did, what then was the difference? How could these two seemingly identical acts be so opposed? Sāharanpūrī's answer to this foundational question was at once curious and revealing. He argued that the prophetic reports cited by Samī' such as the one about the Battle of Tabūk showed only that the Prophet had prayed over food to increase its quantity. Moreover, the Prophet's supplication to increase the quantity of the food was necessitated by a situation of urgency. Had the Prophet not prayed over food, its quantity would not have increased, and the Muslim army would have starved. And since the intention of the Prophet in this context was to increase the quantity of food, it was obvious only that he prayed with the food placed right in front of him.[63]

However, Sāharanpūrī continued, this moment from the Prophet's life could not be employed as an authoritative precedent legitimizing the Indian ritual of the *fātiḥa*. The key to Sāharanpūrī's argument was his judgment that in Samī''s example the Prophet's act of praying to increase the quantity of the food and the practice of the *fātiḥa* were not analogous (*qiyās ma'l-fāriq*). Why? Because, Sāharanpūrī argued, the Prophet's supplication was an act of repair and restoration; it was intended to increase the food and to prevent its depletion (*izāla-i nuqṣān-i qadar-i ṭa'ām*). Casting the Prophet as first and foremost a "reformer," Sāharanpūrī argued that the Prophet's supplication was much like any other act of worldly reform intended to remove corruption and ameliorate harm. Through his prayer, the Prophet tried to reform and correct the situation of a lack of food.[64]

But the *fātiḥa*, in stark contrast, was a practice that had a corrupting influence on food (*ifsād-i ṭa'ām*) because it caused the food to go cold in the time that elapsed between its preparation and the recitation of prayers over it. Moreover, the desire (*shahwat*) of both the diners (*ākilīn*) and the reciter (*qārī*) would be transfixed on consuming the food. Hence, this practice also had a corrupting influence on the enthusiasm and intentionality of the diners. Therefore, Sāharanpūrī concluded, one could not make a beneficial and restorative act, the Prophet's supplication to increase the quantity of food and remove its inherent capacity to deplete, an analogy for an act that was inherently corrupting: the *fātiḥa*. Such a ridiculous analogy, he asserted, only showed Samī''s intellectual inferiority; no serious scholar would utter such nonsense (*Fi'l-i muṣliḥ ko muqīs 'alayhi fi'l mufsid kā banānā fahm-i mu'allif kā hī hay awr koī ahl-i 'ilm aysī laghawīyāt nah kahay gā*).[65]

Sāharanpūrī's interpretive approach, in noticeable contrast to Samī''s, stripped the Prophet's body of its miraculous charisma by turning him into a reformer-in-chief. Moreover, it made the materiality of food subservient to the Prophet's reformist mission. The food had no agency other than to serve as an instrument of prophetic reform. Again, this stood in some contrast to the role and place of food in Samī''s social imaginary. For Samī', the materiality of food was integral to the very possibility of the *fātiḥa* as a communal ritual. Food was what made the ritual and the human choreography around it possible. But in Sāharanpūrī's account of the Prophet's bodily gesture of praying over food at Tabūk, food was primarily a synechdoche for community. The Prophet, ever animated and always occupied by the mandate of reform, reformed and restored food much as he sought to reform and restore the moral lives and salvational prospects of his community.

But what about Ḥanafī luminaries like Mullāh 'Alī Qārī, Sa'd al-Dīn al-Taftazānī, and Sanā'ullah Panīpatī, whose opinions, as mobilized by Samī', seemed to clearly diverge from those of Sāharanpūrī and the Deobandī pioneers? Sāharanpūrī's strategy in dealing with this seeming dissonance was quite similar to Thānvī's, as I detailed in the previous chapters.

It pivoted on emphasizing the specificity of the late nineteenth-century North Indian Muslim context that was the object of Deobandī critique and reform. As Thānvī had argued in the case of the *mawlid*, so Sāharanpūrī claimed with respect to the *fātiḥa*: had these past authorities known the specific conditions of the Indian Muslim context, they would have taken the exact same prohibitive position as the Deoband scholars did.

This brings us to the critical question of how two groups of scholars, who revered and followed an almost common genealogy of texts and authorities, harbored such opposing reform agendas. How could that be possible? The key to answering this question is to withhold evaluation or judgment about which group, the Barelvīs or the Deobandīs, established themselves as the more sound or loyal Ḥanafīs. It is far more instructive to attend to the varied and often opposed hermeneutical strategies through which they read and approached a common intellectual lineage. For scholars like Samī‘ and Aḥmad Razā Khān, the form of the text, much like the form of the Prophet's body and status, demanded integrity and was not available for tampering. If scholars like Taftazānī had stamped their approval on a particular doctrine or practice through a clear textual precedent, searching for ambiguities in or alternate readings of that precedent was intolerably transgressive. The coherence of tradition depended on a hermeneutical strategy and temperament eager to preserve the stability of the text. It was the stability of the text that ensured the durability of the Prophet's body and charisma.

The Deoband scholars, on the other hand, were far more inclined and open to the procedures of a certain version of process theology. The canonical tradition was sacrosanct, but its application had to contend and accord with the shifting temporalities and conditions marking the moral (or in the Deobandī imagination amoral) landscape of the present. Crucially, Deoband pioneers like Sāharanpūrī and Thānvī saw such a hermeneutical approach, not as some innovation or departure from the Ḥanafī or the Muslim jurisprudential tradition more broadly, but rather as firmly grounded in its intent, spirit, and application. Nonetheless, their self-perceptions and projections not withstanding, the seeming incongruence between their positions on contentious ritual and doctrinal matters and the apparent precedents from major and long-established sources of normative authority did leave them vulnerable to precisely this charge of departing from established tradition. This was a vulnerability too delectable for Aḥmad Razā Khān to not relish and pounce on. How he did so is an important and instructive aspect of his discursive strategy to injure the Deobandī normative project. Returning to Khān and his discourse, I next survey some key illustrations of this strategy.

Opposing the Authority of Tradition

Aḥmad Razā Khān sought to frame his Deoband rivals as an aberrant group of Indian heretics whose ideology opposed all traditional sources of authority in Islam, past and present. In Khān's view, the Deoband pioneers contravened the established consensus (*ijmā'*) of Sunnī Muslim scholars. Why? Because Deoband scholars outlawed rituals that leading luminaries of the tradition not only had extolled as meritorious but had personally participated in with no reservations. For instance, contrary to the Deobandī position, an overwhelming majority of Muslim scholars had sanctioned the Prophet's birthday celebration and the practice of standing up to offer salutations to the Prophet. Khān mobilized a variety of authorities to construct his case.

For example, according to the prominent eighteenth-century Medinese scholar Sayyid Ja'far al-Barzanjī (d. 1766), "All learned scholars are in agreement that standing up to offer salutations to the Prophet is a laudable practice. Anyone who engages in this act with the intention of elevating the Prophet receives divine blessings."[66] The eminent nineteenth-century Shafi'ī scholar in Mecca, Aḥmad Zaynī Daḥlān, who was also among Khān's teachers, echoed this sentiment when he wrote, "Expressing joy on the night of the Prophet's birthday, reciting panegyrics in his honor, feeding those gathered at this ceremony, and all such similar customs are meant to venerate the Prophet. These practices represent different articulations of piety [*min anwā' al-birr*]. Numerous scholars have established the goodness of these practices in several books that contain a plethora of proofs and evidence. There is no need to say more."[67]

Khān cited a range of other scholars from varied intellectual persuasions, geographical backgrounds, and moments in history who had categorically pronounced the *mawlid* and offering salutations to the Prophet as commendable acts. Some of these scholars included Jalāl al-Dīn Suyūṭī, Aḥmad Qasṭalānī, 'Alī Ibn Burhānudīn al-Ḥalabī (d. 1634), Tāj al-Dīn al-Subkī (d. 1370), Muḥammad Ibn Yaḥyā al-Tādifī (d. 1556), Yūsuf Ibn Yaḥyā al-Ṣarṣarī (d. 1258), and 'Abdul Wahhāb Sha'rānī (d. 1565). According to Khān, the Deobandī opposition to pious practices such as the *mawlid* contravened the consensus established by all these scholars. Khān argued that the ideology of the Deoband pioneers challenged the validity of the Prophet's saying, "My community does not coalesce around a misguidance" (*La tajtami' ummatī 'alā al-ḍalāla*).[68] If one held the Deobandī view that the *mawlid* and the practices attached to it were heretical innovations, then one would have to concede that all these leading scholars were also heretics. The choice, in Khān's view, was clear and stark.

As he put it, addressing his readers, "You decide. Is the consensus of so many scholars from Mecca, Medina, Syria, Egypt, Yemen, Daghistan, Andalusia, and India unreliable? Or should we assume that these pillars [*'amā'id*] of the tradition are in fact heretics and people of bad faith who for hundreds of years have been misguiding their communities by calling repugnant heresies pious and praiseworthy?"[69] Khān next suggested to his readers a vivid exercise:

> For a few moments, cleanse your heart from the thought of all the rival ideologies in Muslim India. Forget about their competing positions on contentious questions. Just close your eyes, bow your head, and imagine. Imagine that several preeminent scholars, past and present, are all alive and have gathered in a magnificent place. The question of the legitimacy of the *mawlid* and that of standing up to venerate the Prophet comes before them. All of them say in one voice, creating a mesmerizing crescendo, "No doubt it is a commendable practice. Who calls it bad? He should dare come before us." Now consider the splendor and glory of these scholars. And then reflect on the status of these few Indian detractors [Deobandīs] of the Prophet. In this moment will any one of them have the courage to step into this gathering and confront the assembled crowd of leading scholars?[70]

Khān curiously argued that the Deoband pioneers were able to freely express and disseminate their heretical views because of the absence of an Islamic state and ruler in late nineteenth-century India. The Deobandīs, he argued, were taking full advantage of a political environment in which there was no sovereign authority to reprimand them for their derogatory views on the Prophet. In a functional Muslim polity, it would have been incumbent on the ruler to formally punish (*ta'zīr*) the Deoband scholars for their brazen opposition to the consensus of the community.

The absence of an institutional framework to regulate religious discourse had provided the Deobandīs the opportunity to say whatever they wanted. Khān argued that the Deobandī ideology would never have survived in a Muslim state. In other words, in Khān's view, British colonialism represented the condition of possibility for the emergence and flourishing of the Deoband school. However, Khān emphasized, although his Deoband rivals were spared punishment by a worldly colonial government, they were certainly destined to hell in the afterworld according to the Prophet's saying, "Follow the greatest majority of believers, for he who deviates from that majority deviates into hell" (*Ittabi'ū al-sawād al-a'ẓam fa inna-hu man shadhdha shadhdha fi'l-nār*).[71] In short, for Khān, the Deoband pioneers were cheapening the doctrinal authority of consensus by articulating a reformist agenda that overwhelmingly opposed the practice and opinion of leading scholars.

Contradicting the Walī Ullah Family

In Khān's view, the Deobandī assault on certain ritual practices was even contrary to the life and practice of seminal authorities that the Deoband scholars themselves counted as among their intellectual forebears. More specifically, Khān argued that the Deoband reform project entirely contradicted the thought of the celebrated eighteenth-century scholar Shāh Walī Ullah and his prominent sons Shāh 'Abdul 'Azīz and Shah Rafī' al-Dīn. Since this was arguably the most revered scholarly family whose legacy was eagerly claimed by Muslim scholars and movements of all kinds in colonial South Asia, Khān was well aware of the significant damage that dissociating them from Deoband pioneers would inflict on the credibility of the latter's reform agenda. According to their official narrative, Khān contended, the Deoband pioneers were the true inheritors of the Walī Ullah legacy. However, on closer inspection, one found a stark disparity between the position of Walī Ullah and his sons and that of Deoband scholars on the legitimacy of contested rituals. For example, Khān highlighted Walī Ullah's unequivocally charitable attitude toward the ritual of transmitting blessings to the deceased (*īṣāl-i sawāb*) through the offering (*naẓar*) of food (also known as the *fātiḥa*).

According to Khān, in contrast to Deobandīs and Shāh Muḥammad Ismā'īl, who called this ritual a corrupt heretical innovation, the Walī Ullah family unreservedly participated in this practice and encouraged others to do so. For instance, Shāh Walī Ullah once recalled that his father, the famous Ḥadīth scholar Shāh 'Abdul Raḥīm, had prepared and distributed food every year to transmit blessings to Prophet Muḥammad's soul. One year, because of financial hardship, Shāh 'Abdul Raḥīm was unable to procure any food except fried chickpeas (*ḥimsan maqlīyan*), which he distributed among people. Later that night, the Prophet appeared in Raḥīm's dream. The Prophet was smiling and gleaming, with the chickpeas nestled in his hands.[72]

Shāh Walī Ullah himself had categorically stated that there was no harm in cooking and feeding pasted sweets (*malīda*) and rice pudding (*shīr-i birinj*) with the intention of transmitting blessings (acquired through this act of charity) to the soul of a saint (*Agar malīda wa shīr-i birinj binā bar fātiḥa-i buzurg-i bi-qaṣd-i īṣāl-i sawāb beh rū-yi īshān pazand wa bukhurānand muzā'iqa nīst*).[73] On another occasion, Walī Ullah had instructed his followers to "recite the opening chapter of the Qur'an [*al-fātiḥa*] every day over some sweets [*shīrīnī*] to transmit blessings to the celebrated Sufis of the Chishtī order" (*Bar qadr-i shīrīnī-yi fātiḥa be nām-i khwājagān-i chisht bi khwānand wa hamīn ṭawr har rūz mi khwāndi bāshand*).[74]

Similarly, in his well-known text on Shī'ī thought and history *The Gift of the Shī'īs* (*Tuḥfat Ithnā 'Asharīya*), Walī Ullah's son Shāh 'Abdul 'Azīz stated that "all Muslims regard 'Alī and his blessed family as their spiritual leaders and guides who are connected to divine orders of existence [*umūr-i takvīnīya*]. Reciting prayers and panegyrics, expending charity, making vows, and giving offerings of food in their name is common and widespread among people, just as these practices are common in relation to all revered friends of God." (*Hazrat-i amīr wa zurīyat-i ṭāhira-i ū rā tamām ummat bar misāl-i pīrān wa murshidān mī purastand wa umūr-i takvīnīya rā wābasta bi īshān mī dānand wa fātiḥa wa durūd wa ṣadaqāt wa naẓar wa mannat bi nām-i īshān rā'ij wa ma'mūl gardīde chunānche bā jamī'-yi awlīya' Allāh hamīn mu'āmala ast.*)[75]

Further, in his commentary on the *Qur'ān Tafsīr-i 'Azīzī*, Shāh 'Abdul 'Azīz likened the soul of a recently deceased person to someone who was about to drown: "Just as a drowning person desperately screams for assistance, a recently deceased person cries out for the prayers and blessings of those he has left behind in the world. In these moments all forms of prayers, charity, and offerings of food provide much benefit and solace to the deceased." "This is why," he explained, "in the year following someone's death and especially during the first forty days, people do their utmost to assist the deceased by performing such acts of piety."[76]

Shāh Walī Ullah and his sons endorsed the practice of transmitting blessings to the deceased by distributing food or by reciting the *fātiḥa* over food in general terms, Khān insisted. Moreover, in contrast to the Deobandīs, they were unconcerned about the attachment of specifications to this ritual that were not found in the *sharī'a* but that conformed to local customs and habits. For instance, Shāh Rafī' al-Dīn (Shāh 'Abdul 'Azīz's younger brother) explicitly declared that the specific manner in which a ritual was organized and conducted should depend on the convenience and temperament of its participants.

For example, Rafī' al-Dīn argued that there was no harm associated with the specifications usually attached to the ritual of transmitting blessings to the deceased by distributing food among people.[77] In his view, there was nothing problematic about the popular Indian custom of specifying food items for distribution according to the deceased person to whom blessings were transmitted. So the practice of specifying rice lentils (*khichdī*) for transmitting blessings to the Prophet's grandson Ḥusayn or flour balls (*tosha*) to transmit blessings to the famous sixteenth-century Indian Ḥadīth scholar 'Abdul Ḥaqq Dihlavī was completely valid. Rafī' al-Dīn argued that the decision to institute such specifications rested entirely with the organizers of an event of this kind. Moreover, he explained that these kinds of humanly invented specifications initially entered into a community's life because they fulfilled certain practical benefits. Gradually, they become ritualized as part of that community's everyday habits and customs (*Īn takhṣīṣāt az qism-i 'urf wa 'ādat and keh bi-maṣāliḥ-i khāṣa wa munāsabat-i khufīya be ẓuhūr āmadeh wa rafta rafta shuyyū' yāft*).[78] There was nothing objectionable about this process of ritualization, Shāh Rafī' al-Dīn argued. Therefore, the attachment of such specifications to devotional rituals, specifications that enabled the regularization of those rituals, was not illegitimate or normatively unsound.

In Aḥmad Razā Khān's view, Rafī' al-Dīn's generous opinion about the ritualization of customary habits and conventions entirely contradicted the reform project of the Deobandīs and that of Shah Muhammad Isma'il. In contrast to the pioneers of Deoband, Shāh Walī Ullah and his sons did not suffer from hyperanxiety about the elevation of nonobligatory practices into religious obligations. Rather, consistent with the view of authoritative past and present Sunnī scholars, they were willing to accommodate a community's aesthetic choices and practical welfare in the determination of its normative boundaries. Further, unlike their so-called Deobandī heirs, they did not rush to outlaw pious practices and rob the masses of avenues to honor revered figures in the tradition.

Khān further argued that Walī Ullah and his sons were not driven by an attitude of vigilantism that led them to constantly police embodied life in search of signs of corruption and moral decay. Rather, they empowered the community to attain the normative goodness found in pious rituals in accordance with its temperament, character, and practical needs. In contrast, the Deoband pioneers and Shāh Muḥammad Ismā'īl cultivated a public sphere that was perpetually pervaded by the fear of transgression. Because of their excessively pessimistic outlook on the capacity of the masses to organize their religious lives, the Deobandīs criminalized praiseworthy rituals that their own intellectual forebears had explicitly sanctioned. This contradiction, Khān claimed, showed the unabashed hypocrisy of the Deoband pioneers. The Deobandīs were unsparing in chastising anyone who participated in rituals such as the *mawlid* or the *fātiḥa*. Yet they raised no objection against their own intellectual masters when the latter engaged in and praised those very practices.

As Khān put it, "According to the Deobandī ideology, Walī Ullah and his sons are without doubt guilty of 'innovating in religion' and of committing blatant heresies. They clearly invented rituals that were never found in previous centuries. But the Deobandīs would never call them lost or heretical. Instead, they call them esteemed scholars, leaders of faith, and renowned mystics. . . . But in comparison, other people who participate in those same rituals are damned as misguided heretics."[79] "Perhaps the sin of everyone else," Khān continued sarcastically, "is that they take part in certain praiseworthy practices in a manner that is sanctioned by the *sharīʿa*. What can one say to such warped jurisprudence [*īn taḥakkum-i be-jā rā che gufta āyad*]?"[80]

To sum up, according to Khān, the Deoband scholars were inventing a new *sharīʿa* that opposed all authorities of the tradition (including their own predecessors) and that punished people for engaging in pious and normatively sanctioned practices. Ironically, while pretending to combat heresy and innovation, the Deobandīs were in fact engineering a heretical moral order that inverted the logic of all previously established conceptions of normativity.

Most importantly, in Khān's view, the Deoband pioneers were playing God by haphazardly vetoing the established consensus of the community and imposing over it their own sovereign will. By tampering with divine law, the Deobandīs were questioning the eternality of that law. In effect, they were brazenly challenging God's sovereignty as the sole author of law and its limits. Therefore, Khān argued, the supposed Deobandī passion for restoring divine sovereignty was nothing but a farce. For in the guise of protecting divine sovereignty, the Deobandīs in fact arrogated that sovereignty to themselves. In the process, they cheapened the sovereign force of divine law and demeaned its sanctity. As Khān sarcastically demanded of his Deoband rivals, "Is the *sharīʿa* your household business that you may twist and play whenever you so wish?" (*Sharīʿat kār-i khānagī-yi shumāst keh har chūn khwāhīd pahlū gardānīd?*)[81]

chapter ten

Convergences

So far, I have tried to highlight major differences between Khān and his Deoband rivals on how they approached and defined the idea and threat of heretical innovation. Here I will show some important points of convergence between these opposing camps of scholars. The central question I will take up is: What was Aḥmad Razā Khān's conception of *bid'a*? How did he imagine transgression? What was his notion of reform? What did he find objectionable in the religious and everyday lives of the masses and why? Let me briefly clarify my intent in pursuing this line of inquiry. In what has preceded I have largely presented the objection of the Deoband pioneers regarding certain rituals and customs and Khān's defense of their normative legitimacy. But the picture will remain incomplete and skewed if we simply regard the Deobandīs as the objectors to and the Barelvīs as the defenders of Muslim ritual life in colonial South Asia.

A close examination of Khān's thought reveals that, critical as he was of Deoband scholars, he was also deeply and at times even more trenchantly critical of the manner in which the masses engaged in particular rituals and customs. His disagreement with the Deobandīs was premised on hermeneutical differences regarding forbidding permissible practices, especially those that honored the Prophet. He and the Deobandīs also differed sharply on the interaction of tradition and temporality, as I detailed in the preceding chapter. However, these conceptual disagreements did not mean that Khān was any less dissatisfied with the everyday conduct of the masses. Khān was no lax libertine. He was no inclusivist Sufi who could be readily contrasted to the allegedly rigid legalism of the Deobandīs. To the contrary, Khān was urgently invested in securing and guarding the purity of an imagined Indian Muslim identity against what he perceived as the threat of both internal and external others. He was intimately concerned with the shape and rhythm of everyday life among Indian Muslims. Moreover, much as with his Deoband rivals, his efforts to regulate the religious lives of the masses were at once highly gendered and predicated on a less-than-charitable opinion about the ability of the common folk to abstain from transgression. Let me offer some examples.

Death, Food, and Hospitality

Consider the following query once posed to Khān regarding the practice of women gathering at the house of the deceased immediately after that person's death:

> In most parts of India, it is common for women among the friends and relatives of the deceased's family to descend on the latter's house on the day of death. Usually they stay there for three, ten, sometimes even forty days. They turn the home of the deceased into a site of festivity, as if they came to attend a wedding. For the duration of this extended stay, the deceased's family invariably takes up the responsibility for the entertainment of these guests, defraying the cost of food, drink, and the consumption of betel leaves [*pān*] and betel nuts [*chālīya*]. To meet these expenses, they are often stretched financially and at times even compelled to take out loans on which they must pay interest. And if they refuse to play good hosts, they risk being subjected to the community's ridicule and shaming. Is this normatively permissible?[1]

In answering this question, Khān registered his exasperation with it by firing a sarcastic salvo at the questioner himself: "Good Lord, O Muslim! You ask 'Is this normatively permissible?' You should instead ask: 'How many repugnant and loathsome qualities does this filthy custom coalesce?' "[2]

Leaving all else aside, turning the home of the deceased into a place for a large social gathering was in itself impermissible, Khān contended. The family of the deceased must not be burdened with the responsibility of hospitality. In assembling his case, Khān cited *Sharḥ Fatḥ al-Qadīr* (a commentary on the canonical Ḥanafī text *al-Hidāya*), by the fifteenth-century Egyptian Ḥanafī jurist Ibn al-Humām (d. 1457): "It is abominable for the family of the deceased to assume [the responsibility of] hospitality by offering food [to guests]. Hospitality has been normatively designated for occasions of happiness, not for moments of tragedy. This is a reprehensible innovation" (*Yukrahu ittikhādh al-ḍiyāfa min al-ṭa'ām min ahl al-mayyit liannahu shuri'a fi-l-surūr lā fi-l-shurūr wa hīya bid'a mustaqbaḥa*).[3] The more appropriate and normatively sound course of action, Khān advised, was for mourning family members of the deceased to be fed by their neighbors and relatives on the day of death, so that they would be relieved of all other worries while grappling with their loss. But, Khān lamented, the situation was often reversed.

Rather than being aided and comforted in their mourning, a bereaved family was compelled to bear the costs and burden of hosting and entertaining a large number of people. That they were often pushed to accumulate debt for this purpose added to the horror of this ritual. But what most bothered Khān was the conduct of women at such gatherings. As he dismissively described: "These women gather at the home of the deceased and partake in all sorts of objectionable acts. They theatrically wail, cry hysterically, beat their breasts, and cover their faces in feigned attempts at looking sorrowful. All such gestures fall under the category of 'wailing' [*niyāḥat*], which is forbidden. The friends and relatives of the deceased should not even send food to a house where such women gather, for that would equate to sponsoring sinfulness."[4]

Ashraf 'Alī Thānvī and Khān's other Deoband rivals would have endorsed these sentiments with little hesitation. Both the Barelvī and Deobandī critiques of custom were wrapped in a heightened concern to suppress what they saw as the contagious threat of women to moral order and stability. As Faisal Devji, commenting on the intensified focus on female bodies in Muslim reformist imaginaries in colonial South Asia, so memorably put it, "Every one of the reformers viewed the woman, for example, as the agent of a sinister, debilitating corruption. . . . This feeling of masculine vulnerability vis-à-vis the marginal feminine could occur only when these men had themselves been marginalized by colonialism."[5] Back to Khān: his underlying point was that while offering food for the transmission of blessings was permissible, serving food [on the occasion of someone's death] as means of extending hospitality was forbidden. This was so because if the solemn occasion of death was turned into a quasi-party, then the gravity and tragedy of such a moment would evaporate. When someone died, rather than reflecting on death and loss, people seemed more eager to reflect on the dining menu. In stressing this point Khān presented a rather cynical reading of the Arabic saying "The food served on the occasion of death kills the heart" (*Ṭa'ām al-mayyit yumīt al-qalb*). This saying, Khān argued, described the condition of people who sat around waiting for someone in their community to die so they might enjoy the food served afterwards. The hearts of such people died because their attachment to the pleasures of food made them detached from the thought and the seriousness of death (*Khānā khātay waqt mawt se ghāfil awr iss kī lazzat mayn shāghil*). This was the unfortunate outcome, Khān warned, of turning someone's death into an occasion for large gatherings and feasts.[6]

According to Khān, besides feeding the family of the deceased (on the day of death), the only normatively approved option was to distribute food to the poor. There was no point in either inviting other members of the community or distributing food to them. And the rich should especially refrain from consuming such food; should they receive it, they should pass it on to the poor. Again, the Deoband pioneers would have found little to disagree with here. But despite these convergences, Khān clearly departed from his Deoband rivals on one key question: specifying a day for the distribution of food (to the destitute). In contrast to Deoband scholars, Khān found nothing problematic about specifying, say, the third, tenth, or fortieth day after a person's death for that purpose, as was common practice. The specification of a day served the convenience and interest of the community (*maṣāliḥ-i 'urfīya*). Hence it was permissible, Khān argued.[7]

Conditional Salvation

But while showing flexibility on some issues like specifying a day for distributing food, Khān was anything but flexible when it came to the religious identity of people who could receive such food or of the souls who could benefit from its distribution. Only the soul of a Muslim who had not contravened the necessities of the religion could attain the blessings reaped from an act of charity like distribution of food among the poor, Khān argued. And only a person with the same unblemished profile was allowed to receive and consume such food. Non-Muslims of all variety, polytheist and nonpolytheist, did not qualify. Similarly, even Muslims who undermined the necessary doctrines of Islam, such as Shī'ītes who rejected or insulted the authority of the first two Sunnī caliphs Abū Bakr and 'Umar (Rāfiḍī/Tabarā'ī), were excluded from the category of legitimate recipients or beneficiaries.[8]

In this regard, most telling was Khān's attitude toward "low-caste" leather workers, Chamārs. Let me elaborate with a brief interruption of the discussion on food and blessings after death. Khān was once asked about the status of Hindus who converted to Islam. More specifically, he was asked if after their conversion it was permissible for them to continue being associated with the caste or social standing they had held before becoming Muslim. In his reply Khān pointed out that since one's religious identity was not bound to any specific group or tribe, there was no harm in being associated with one's tribe or community even after conversion. This was common practice during the Prophet's time. Khān explained that there was no honor or exaltation higher than that of joining the fold of Islam, thus rendering all previous social or caste standings infinitesimally insignificant in comparison.[9]

However, even so, social privilege before conversion was not entirely irrelevant. The Islamic legal tradition had in fact stipulated that if an exalted member of [another] community comes to you, then exalt him (*Idhā atākum karīmu qawmin fa-kramūhu*). So, for instance, Khān translated in the Indian context, if a Hindu Thākur or Rājpūt came to a Muslim, the latter had to honor him. This was so because Thākurs/Rājpūts were known to have a privileged social standing in India. Conversion to Islam, or, as Khān phrased it, "breaking [all ties with the previous religion] and becoming one of us" (*bilkul tūt kar ham mayn ā milā*), would multiply that elevated status a thousandfold more. "*Even when a Chamār becomes Muslim* [emphasis added]," Khān tellingly proceeded, "viewing him with disdain is expressly forbidden because after converting he became our brother in religion."[10] In other words, for

Khān, conversion to Islam gave those of lower caste the opportunity to lose all social stigmas and begin afresh. And for those with an already privileged status, becoming Muslim made them even more privileged—a thousandfold more.

However, this opportunity was available only for someone who had crossed the bridge of conversion. On another occasion Khān was asked about his opinion on the practice of distributing food to non-Muslim destitute Chamārs for the transmission of blessings to the deceased. As the questioner put it, "Often on the third day of a person's death, people recite the first chapter of the Qur'ān over chickpeas, some of which is distributed among Muslims and the rest of which is given to polytheist Chamārs. Should the chickpeas over which the Qur'ān has been recited be fed to [Hindu] Chamārs?"[11] Khān's response was sharply negative: "Giving this food to a polytheist or [non-Muslim] Chamār is sinful, sinful, and sinful! [*gunāh, gunāh, gunāh*]."[12] For Khān, the Chamār's body was capable of extending any salvific benefit only if it was marked as Muslim. The social dignity as well as the moral stature of the Chamār was contingent on his officially becoming a Muslim. Once converted, he or she could legitimately enter or participate in the Muslim ritual economy. But this possibility was closed off before the moment of becoming "one of us." Only on entering the right home could the Chamār's body expect any form of hospitality, before or after death.

Public Distinction: Preserving the "Self" by Differing from the "Other"

Khān was acutely invested in preserving Muslim markers of distinction in the public sphere. In the acerbity of his opposition to participation in or imitation of non-Muslim (especially Hindu) rituals, he equaled and perhaps even surpassed his Deoband rivals and Shāh Muḥammad Ismā'īl. For instance, once Khān was asked for his opinion on Muslims visiting Hindu festivals like Rāmlīlā (the dramatic reenactment of Rāmā's life) and Dusehra (the commemoration of Rāmā's victory over Rāvana). More specifically, he was asked about the normative consequences of spending time in such spaces, where statements and chants that signaled polytheism or unbelief were openly aired. Would that harm one's doctrinal status as a Muslim?[13] Khān's response was calibrated according to the nature of the festival, why someone went there, what that person did there, and most critically, what happened to him or her while there.

In Khān's view, if the festival was religious in nature, then visiting it was forbidden in almost all situations because such a gathering would invariably involve discourses and activities that conflicted with the doctrinal necessities of Islam. But while forbidden, merely visiting such a festival would still not constitute unbelief. However, a positive reaction to what went on there could portend dire salvational consequences. Khān argued that if, for example, a Muslim began to think favorably of Hindu chants and rituals that promoted polytheism and the rejection of divine sovereignty, then he or she risked being charged with unbelief. This risk was also great for someone who took such chants and rituals lightly and did not pay much heed to the offense they caused. Such people would not only be expelled from the fold of Islam; additionally, as a consequence, their marriage contract would be annulled.[14] An expensive visit to a festival indeed!

Even if it were not a religious festival but one primarily involving nonreligious entertainment, it was best to avoid spaces dominated by Hindus, Khān advised. "It is not possible for such events to be free of objectionable and repulsive activities."[15] But what about Muslim vendors and traders who went to such places only for their business and livelihood? They were allowed to do so, Khān admitted, provided there was no sign of polytheism or unbelief, and they neither saw nor involved themselves in anything repugnant. Again, though, it was best if they avoided such venues altogether.

For Khān, there was only one situation in which attending Hindu festivals, religious or nonreligious, was not only absolutely permissible but in fact good and praiseworthy: if a Muslim scholar went there to educate people about and invite them to Islam. The Prophet himself used to frequently make such visits to invite non-Muslims to Islam, he pointed out, in his attempt to authorize this exception to the rule.[16] So for Khān, only a Muslim scholar with the appropriate skills of pedagogy and persuasion could frequent Hindu festivals. Only a scholar with the capacity to attract, guide, and save the otherwise salvationally doomed was insulated from the threat posed by the deviant heretical spaces, discourses, and festivals. Such a scholar entered the dangerous terrain of heresy and unbelief equipped with the required intellectual gear and armor. As for the rest, the common folk, it was best if they kept away from such dangers lest their salvational prospects prematurely implode.

As I have argued in more detail elsewhere, Khān's efforts to shield the purity of Indian Muslim identity was enfolded in an imperial political theology that assumed and sought to maintain Muslim superiority and dominance over other religious communities.[17] In the absence of Muslim political power, the focus of such a quest fell squarely on the realm of everyday rituals and practices. So, for instance, Khān had chastised the leaders of the early twentieth-century Khilāfat movement (an early twentieth-century anticolonial movement to preserve the Ottoman Caliphate) for their alliance with and proximity to Gāndhī (d. 1948). Khān was perturbed less by the politics of such an alliance than by its implicit promotion of Hindu-Muslim intimacy in the public sphere. For him, as for his Deoband counterparts, at stake was the preservation of public markers of Muslim distinction (*Sha'āi'r-i Islām*). If friendship with Hindus was endorsed, which is what he saw the Khilāfat leaders doing, the public distinction and with it the moral superiority of Muslims would inevitably be erased. This anxiety about erasure loomed large in his pastoral concerns.[18]

But Khān was far from an absolute radical exclusivist; he displayed a great interest in pragmatic politics. For instance, during the Khilāfat movement years, he vehemently opposed the call of scholars attached to that movement, like Abu'l Kalām Āzād (d. 1958), to wage *jihād* against the British. Such a call to take on a mighty imperial force was outright foolishness, Khān contended. Moreover, he rejected the call to abandon all relations with the British, as the Khilāfat movement (in accordance with Gāndhī's noncooperation movement) had urged. Such anticolonial agitation, Khān had argued, would only damage Muslims socioeconomically while doing no harm to British power. In fact, he was convinced that the so-called boycott of the British was only Gāndhī's ruse to lower the socioeconomic standing of Indian Muslims. In his view, this was a conspiracy to which the Khilāfat leaders/scholars had either knowingly or unwittingly signed on.

Jettisoning the radical anticolonial posture of launching *jihād* against the British, Khān adopted the more pragmatic position of engaging them in civic transactions and relations, despite their non-Muslim status. His argument was based on a distinction he drew between substantive friendship (which was not permitted with non-Muslims) and mere transactional relations (which were permitted). In fact, he had even permitted Muslims to dissimulate friendship with the British if need be, given the latter's hegemony and power.[19]

All this is to point out that Khān's views on the external "other" exhibited enough shades of complexity so as not to be captured by binaries like inclusive/exclusive, peaceful/violent, and reformist/nonreformist. He certainly espoused an agenda for reform, one that joined the desire for embodied purity with a more realistic acknowledgment of the impossibility of Muslim political power in conditions of British colonialism. One might say that his political realism was matched by his idealism in the realm of everyday life, as he strove to establish the purity and superiority of Muslim markers of distinction in the public sphere. Let me probe a bit further into this crucial aspect of Khān's understanding of reform: the regulation of everyday norms of sociability.

Regulating Everyday Life

For Khān as for his Deoband opponents, the limits of law were not a matter of theoretical abstraction. Stipulating and enforcing legal boundaries was meaningful only if it shaped a moral public with carefully patterned social norms and priorities. Take, for instance, his discussion of such widespread leisure activities in colonial North India (which continue to this day in South Asia) as flying kites, playing chess and cards, staging quail- and chicken-fighting contests, and hunting animals. In addition to prohibiting these practices, Khān went a step further. He outlined, often in great specificity, the conduct one should adopt while engaging with people who did take part in such practices. So, for instance, Khān instructed that if one encountered a person who organized chicken-fighting contests or spent hours flying pigeons, it was best to not initiate the customary greeting of "Salām." And it was not obligatory to return the greeting of such a person either. In Khān's normative imaginary, it was not enough to legally prohibit an act by declaring it forbidden. Legal prohibition had to be accompanied by a public display of affective displeasure. The perpetrators of transgression not only called for discursive rebuke; they also deserved social ridicule and, if necessary, explicit shunning.[20]

Khān's reasoning on forbidding animal hunting for leisure illustrates his investment in fashioning a moral public in particularly revealing ways. He argued that animal hunting (*shikār*) was completely permissible if it fulfilled a substantive purpose. So, for example, there was nothing problematic about hunting animals as a source of food or medicine, or any other purposeful benefit. What was forbidden was hunting or fishing for sport or leisure. But how could one distinguish or ascertain whether someone had hunted for leisure or for a legitimate purpose like procuring food? What was the determinant of the distinction between leisure and necessity/purpose? Khān's answer is of great interest as it clearly brings into view the utilitarian foundations of his critique.

What confirmed the profligate and purposeless attitude of socially elite hunters in his time, he argued, was their reluctance to subject their bodies to even a hint of discomfort in other everyday situations. As he put it: "These elite hunters are so self-possessed that they consider stepping out of their homes to buy their essential groceries and clothes an insult to their majesty. And so pampered are they that they refrain from walking even ten steps under the sun to go to a mosque to pray."[21]

"It was preposterous to think that such people," he continued derisively, "would abandon their homes for days, walk and camp for hours in unforgiving deserts burning in scorching heat, and get slapped by blasts of hot air for the purpose of procuring something to eat!"[22] As if reminding readers of the obvious, Khān pointed out that there were much easier ways to get food, such as buying fish from a local market. But the insistence on going hunting/fishing for long hours, despite the availability of easier ways of obtaining food, was the surest indicator that pleasure and entertainment, rather than food or any other utility, were what drove such expeditions. Moreover, most often, the animals killed during hunting were distributed among other people and were rarely cooked and eaten by the hunters themselves, Khān asserted. All this confirmed that these were mere hunting games and that the people who played them had little interest in satisfying their hunger or in fulfilling any other concrete purpose.

Pivotal to Khān's prohibitive logic was a normative investment in fashioning a moral economy that resisted frivolity, extravagance, and the instrumentalization of life and nature for seemingly inessential purposes like sports and entertainment. Though this was not how he framed it, Khān's utilitarian emphasis on "purposeful" hunting honored the integrity and sanctity of the animal by forbidding its violation for unnecessary human gratification. While this was not an animal rights activist position by any means, it is nonetheless intriguing to note the possibility of some space for such a position in a rather strict traditionalist framework like the one espoused by Khān.

Wedding Hell

Khān resembled his archrival Ashraf 'Alī Thānvī most strikingly in the fact that the custom drawing his most visceral condemnation was that of wedding ceremonies. To Khān, as for Thānvī (see end of chapter 8), Muslim weddings in North India were a cesspool of abominations. More than any other customary event, they brought together all the prominent varieties of moral failures that afflicted the masses: wasteful spending, the collapse of proper gender norms, extravagant splendor, inexplicable attachment to financially burdensome and at times morally reprehensible customs, and the imitation of non-Muslim (especially Hindu) rituals of festivity. Taken together, these corruptions were at once damaging the piety and salvational prospects of the public and crumbling their financial status and power.[23]

The part of the wedding ceremony that most angered Khān was the carnivalesque singing and musical performances that primarily women engaged in. The songs sung during such ceremonies were often full of obscenities and vulgar expressions, with frequent references to illicit sexual behavior. Rather than harboring any shame or remorse, the gathered women could hardly contain their uproarious guffaws. And while young unmarried girls witnessed and absorbed such scandalous spectacles, the "shameless, reckless, spineless, and rotten men" would not say a word in opposition and allowed all this to go on unhindered.[24] In Khān's assessment, Indian Muslims had learnt such questionable habits from the Hindus. As he summarized, "These insolent asses and ignorant knuckleheads have learnt this filthy and cursed ritual from the Satanic Hindus, the accursed decadents" (*Woh nā-pāk awr mal'ūn rasm keh buhat kharān-i be tamyīz aḥmaq jāhilon ne shayāṭīn-i hunūd malā'īn-i be bahbūd se sīkhī*).[25] The rhyming prose in which Khān delivered his onslaught is difficult to reproduce in translation. But I hope the pungency of his disgust wafts through.

Again, anxiety over the threat of imitating the undesirable "other" was central to his protest. And much as in the earlier examples I presented, here again Khān was intimately concerned with shaping everyday norms of sociability. The clearest indication of this concern was the way he went beyond just highlighting or describing the "corrupt practices" that in his view pervaded wedding ceremonies. He also issued express instructions on what one must do in the event that one encountered such practices while in attendance at a wedding. As soon as guests began to sense that immoral exhibitions like the singing of profane songs were about to take over a wedding, they were supposed to immediately get up and head for the exits, Khān commanded. He urged emphatically: "Don't subject your wives, daughters, mothers, and sisters to vulgar profanities!"[26] But ideally, people must avoid attending such weddings altogether.

Lest one think that Khān was an unsparing killjoy, he made it clear that he was not opposed to all modes of wedding celebrations. Celebrating the occasion of someone's marriage was fine as long as it did not transgress the boundaries of law. So, what did a normatively sound wedding look like? In offering a template of such an acceptable wedding, Khān looked toward practices during the Prophet's time. There was nothing wrong, for instance, in beating drums (*daf*) as a way to announce the solemnization of a marriage, as was customary during the Prophet's time. Or, for example, in Medina it had been common to recite simple poetic verses on the occasion of arriving at the groom's house, such as "We have come to you, we have come to you. May God keep us alive, and keep you alive too" (*Ataynākum ataynākum, faḥayyānā wa ḥayyākum*).[27] For Khān, there was no harm in such proper talk. But, he hastened to add, even this much was not permissible in India. Why? Because, he explained, if Indian women were allowed any opportunity, there was no hope that they would be able to abide by the limits that were set for them. Therefore, it was best to institute a complete embargo on any kind of celebration during a wedding, so that "the doors to moral chaos were entirely shut off" (*Siray se fitna kā darwāza hī band kīyā jā'ey*).[28]

Khān was especially adamant about excluding from weddings "vulgar and morally questionable women of bad repute [*bāzārī fāḥisha fājira*] such as dancers [*randīyon*] and low-caste singing girls [*domnīyon*]."[29] His reasoning exhibits his acute class consciousness. Such women needed to be kept away not only because it was impossible for them to honor the boundaries of normative law but, more significantly, because they could harm women belonging to "families of good repute" (*sharīf zādīyon*). As Khān put it, "Even the sight of such morally loose and corrupt women should be kept away from girls of reputable pedigree. For the company of bad [people] is a fatal poison [*suḥbat-i bad zehr-i qātil hay*]."[30] He rounded off his argument with an assertion that brought his gender imaginary into sharp relief: "Women are delicate glass; if they break they are destroyed."[31] Khān's pastoral anxiety brought together class and gender in striking ways. While the capacity of all women to observe the limits of law was suspect, those from the lower classes and castes were the most likely to corrupt the rest. They were the primary threat to the integrity of the moral and social order, an order that was reflected in and held in place by the purity of the female body—a body delicate as glass, ever susceptible to death and destruction. One might say that in regulating the norms governing wedding ceremonies, Khān strove to play the part of the brown man saving brown women from other brown women.

One final note on Khān and weddings: the moral and legal aspects of his critique of Indian Muslim weddings were intimately tied to a narrative of socioeconomic decay. Among the most unfortunate effects of people's uncompromising insistence on fulfilling the prevailing mores and customs of weddings was the financial burden of such insistence, he argued. Khān's juxtaposition of moral and socioeconomic decay is best reflected in the following sentiment: "Some people are so unwavering in their attachment to marriage customs that even if they are forced to sin they will do so; but they will not let go of a custom. They will take out loans on exorbitant rates of interest, often losing their lands and homes in the process. *It is these frivolous expenses that have destroyed the properties and assets of [Indian] Muslims* [emphasis mine]."[32] As this statement shows, for Khān, much as for his Deoband rivals, moral and financial economies were inseparable. Moreover, the decay of one's salvational prospects from the transgression of God's law also meant the decay and destruction of one's temporal power and welfare.

My central objective in what has preceded has been to mobilize enough evidence (there is much more available) to dispel the notion that Aḥmad Razā Khān did not have a cogent program of religious and moral reform. As should be clear by now, approaching the Barelvī-Deobandī polemic as a contest between reform and antireform is at once conceptually and empirically untenable. Despite their intense disagreement, Khān and his Deoband rivals shared the view that reforming the masses was an urgent imperative. Moreover, not only was their object of critique often similar (as in the case of weddings), but they also shared many of the same assumptions regarding gender, class, and their imagination of their own role as caretakers of normativity. While Khān vehemently objected to the Deobandī insistence on forbidding certain ritual practices like the *mawlid*, he was at times even more strident in his criticism of popular customs and everyday habits. He was no libertine populist.

To the contrary, a less-than-charitable opinion about the capacity of the masses (especially women) to organize their lives in a normatively sound fashion was central to his religious imaginary. When compared to his Deoband opponents, he was as dissatisfied as they were, if not more so, with the performance of everyday life among the Indian Muslim masses. And as I have shown, he expressed that dissatisfaction and articulated strategies of reform to overcome it with much purpose and passion.

Competing Political Theologies Revisited

But these convergences of Khān with Deoband scholars in some of their programs and assumptions of reform should not lead us to underplay the stakes and magnitude of their disagreements. While these two parties may have been equally critical of popular social customs like weddings, their understandings of the interaction of law, theology, and ritual practice were diametrically opposed. At the heart of this disagreement was the question of how divine law must interact with a community's conception of the moral good. For Khān, a community's imagination of moral goodness largely reflected divine will. This, he argued, was the import of the prophetic saying that "what Muslims consider good is good in God's view" (*Ma ra'ā-hu-l-muslimūn ḥasan fa huwa 'inda Allāh ḥasan*).[33] Divine will and the embodied life of a community were mostly in harmony, even if there were moments of dissonance that required urgent attention and intervention. Therefore, the habits and conventions of a community, as long as they did not explicitly oppose the *sharī'a* (this condition was critical), did not require a complete overhaul by the scholarly elite. The task of scholars was to preserve the eternality of the normative values prescribed by divine law instead of tampering with those values, a sin of which he found the Deobandīs guilty. Khān emphasized this hermeneutical position especially in the context of rituals involving the exaltation of the Prophet, such as the *mawlid*.

But as I labored to show in the previous section of this chapter, this emphasis on the continuity of established norms did not equate to giving the masses a free pass on doing as they wished. Khān was deeply critical of many popular customs and practices and of the manner in which people indulged in them. The critical point here is: his was a hermeneutical argument for the continuity of divinely stipulated norms in a community's devotional and ritual life. And this argument was grounded in a hierarchical cosmology zealously committed to defending the Prophet's status as the most exalted of all created beings. This was not an argument for populist leniency or flexibility.

To sum up, the last four chapters have presented outlines of two contrasting imaginaries of tradition and reform. In contrast to Khān and the Barelvī orientation, the emphasis of the Deobandī pioneers' agenda of reform was on transformation, not continuity. Reform, in their view, meant the transformation of a community's *habitus* and the interruption of its continuity. Shāh Muḥammad Ismā'īl and the Deoband scholars called for a break with the habits and customs of the past that in their view threatened the radical absoluteness of divine sovereignty.

Aḥmad Razā Khān articulated a competing logic of tradition and reform. For Khān, reform entailed the preservation of authorized traditions, not their reinvention. He argued that the Deobandī zeal for transforming embodied life was misplaced and excessive. Moreover, he accused his Deoband rivals of sabotaging established customs and traditions that provided moral guidance to the community and that exalted the Prophet and other exemplary figures in the tradition. In the guise of purifying conventions from accumulated corruptions, Khān argued, Shāh Muḥammad Ismā'īl and the Deoband scholars denied the masses the normative goodness of the past. In the process, they also tampered with divine law by prohibiting practices that God had not prohibited and that had been sanctioned by esteemed Muslim scholars for many centuries. Therefore, in Khān's view, Deoband scholars not only outlawed rituals that venerated the Prophet, they also challenged the authority of revered scholars from the tradition by questioning the soundness of their judgment. In short, Khān accused his Deoband rivals of tampering with tradition in a way that compromised its integrity and detracted from the Prophet's charisma.

In fact, from the analysis I have presented, the major difference of opinion between Aḥmad Razā Khān and his Deobandī opponents was a very subtle disagreement over what should one do when simply permissible practices that served as means to honor the Prophet became corrupted by the manner in which or the intention with which the masses engaged in them. In Aḥmad Razā Khān's view, in this kind of a situation, rather than condemning that practice altogether, religious scholars should try to correct and reform the corruptions attached to it. In other words, for Khān one could not outlaw practices that honored and exalted the Prophet or served other pious purposes. On the other hand, in the view of Deoband scholars, removing a palpable threat to divine sovereignty took precedence over venerating the Prophet or any other nonobligatory expression of piety. For them, the corruption in the attitude of the masses was too terminal for any possibility of recovery or reform; outlawing such practices was the only viable option. This subtle hermeneutical disagreement cannot be collapsed into an inherent opposition between Islamic law and Sufism and cannot be approached through easily apprehended but ultimately misleading binaries like rigid/flexible, reform/antireform, or moderate/conservative.

To amplify and further layer this point, let me return to the theme of political theology that has undergirded much of this book. The competing normative programs advanced by Barelvī and Deobandī pioneers mapped onto competing political logics and assumptions, even though those logics and assumptions were not explicitly articulated as such. By *political*, I mean less their conceptions of the state or electoral politics than the way they understood the interaction of the individual, the social order, and their own religious authority as shepherds of the individual and society. In a nutshell, the Barelvī-Deobandī controversy brought into view an underlying difference in conceptions of the relationship of the individual to the social. In Deobandī imaginings of reform, the individual was encouraged to harness the capacity to resist societal pressures and the contingencies of everyday life. The individual stood apart from society while also seeking to transform it.

The fulfillment and preservation of divine sovereign power and the replication of prophetic time in the present required that one develop an immunity from a social order drenched in the unceasing putridity of everyday corruption. That in turn required the cultivation of moral individuals who could realize the boundaries of the divine normative order, as reflected in the *sharī'a*, by actively—indeed, proactively—undoing that corrupt social order. The individual was an agent who acted upon a world from which he or she stood apart, who injected into a world of chaos and corruption the sanitizing potion of divine normativity. In terms of the boundaries of religion, religion in such a worldview existed outside the unstable contingencies of the social. The dictates of religion came from a sovereign source beyond the messiness of history. Religion represented an abstracted ideal of divine power and prophetic time that impinged on the world through the agency of moral people.

And *bid'a* was precisely the confusion of this vision of religion with normative pressures and orders that came from the world—the taboos, habits, and pressures that emanated from the realm of the social, what the Deoband scholars called faux *sharī'a*. But this vision was steeped in irony. While endowing the individual with the agency to resist and stand apart from the social, Deoband pioneers continued to frame the masses as cattle dependent on the leadership and guidance of the scholarly elite. The promise of a moral individual empowered to enact the divine mandate in the world was interlocked with that individual's subservience to the religious authority of the scholar. The promise was impossible without the mediating authority and pedagogical interventions of the *'ulamā.'*

Aḥmad Razā Khān and his Barelvī followers shared many aspects of this worldview. As I showed earlier, he too was deeply suspicious of the masses and of their capacity to lead moral lives. However, in his thought one finds much greater allowance for not divorcing the individual from the social context in which he or she operated. Most crucially, despite all the corruptions in society, it was precisely the ritual life of a community—made up of practices such as the celebration of the Prophet's birthday—that kept alive the Prophet's memory. And even more crucially, the Prophet was intimately tied to the social, as best reflected in his presence during his birthday celebration. The Prophet was there when he was invoked and honored during the *mawlid*. The moral individual, with the help of the scholar, had to regulate and keep a check on the vicissitudes of everyday life. But that regulation had to refrain from dismantling the salvific potential of the social, blocking in the process embodied avenues of exalting the Prophet. It was through human engagement with the social that the Prophet's nobility and exceptional status were publicly marked, enacted, affirmed, performed, and routinized. The religious authority of Muslim scholars, the *'ulamā,'* in turn, was tied to the preservation of a social structure affectively and narratively committed to upholding the ontological exceptionality of the Prophet. And this was possible only through an individual's orientation toward the social: the individual, while suspicious of its workings, was nonetheless entangled in its fabric. Thus, the competing conceptions of law, temporality, and history that fashioned the Deobandī-Barelvī antagonism were also anchored in contrasting visions of a moral polity. Embedded in their contestation over the meaning and boundaries of *bid'a* were implicit political theories on the relationship of the individual with the social and on the place of the religious elite in mediating that relationship.[34]

Despite Khān's serious differences with Deoband scholars on the limits of heretical innovation, this was not the reason for his judgment of anathema (declaring someone outside the fold of Islam) against them. That judgment was delivered for a much more specific reason, namely certain controversial statements aired by the early Deoband scholars regarding the Prophet's capacity for knowledge of the unknown (*'ilm al-ghayb*). This debate was animated by competing views on the normative relationship between knowledge, sovereignty, and prophetic authority. A close analysis of this debate will further sharpen our understanding of the normative fault lines that divided Deobandī and Barelvī imaginings of tradition. It is this task that the next chapter addresses.

chapter eleven

Knowing the Unknown

Contesting the Sovereign Gift of Knowledge

Aḥmad Razā Khān and his Deoband rivals agreed that knowledge and prophetic authority were intimately intertwined. They also agreed on the doctrinal tenet that of all God's creations the Prophet was the most knowledgeable, authoritative, and beloved. However, they sharply departed on the critical questions of how should one define knowledge and what precisely its relationship was to prophetic authority.

These were also the underlying questions that precipitated a controversy that eventually led Aḥmad Razā Khān to anathematize the pioneers of Deoband: Rashīd Aḥmad Gangohī, Khalīl Aḥmad Sāharanpūrī, and Ashraf 'Alī Thānvī.[1] At the center of this polemic were two statements by Sāharanpūrī and Thānvī on the Prophet's capacity for knowledge of the unknown (*'ilm al-ghayb*). Since their original utterance, these statements have achieved the status of what one might call canonical discursive moments that have been incessantly dissected and debated for more than a century. Khān had declared the Deoband pioneers unbelievers on the specific charge that these two statements contravened the necessities of religion (*zarūrīyāt-i dīn*).

In this chapter, I examine the content and context of these statements, Khān's refutation of them, and finally, the Deobandī response to Khān's refutation by the twentieth-century Indian Deoband scholar Manẓūr Nu'mānī (d. 1997). Through a close investigation of this polemical moment, I will highlight the opposing ways in which Khān and his Deoband rivals imagined the relationship between knowledge, sovereignty, and prophetic authority, an issue that remains the most explosive point of disagreement between the Barelvī and Deobandī schools.

I will show that at stake in this polemic seemingly centered on the limits of prophetic knowledge was the very definition of religion in modernity. The question of whether the Prophet possessed knowledge of the unknown pivoted on an a priori specification of what counted as knowledge. In turn, the decision on the boundaries of knowledge depended on defining the kinds of knowledge that counted as religious. As a corollary, defining religious knowledge was inextricable from defining religion. Indeed, this polemic was as much about the limits of religion as a category of life as it was about competing understandings of prophetic knowledge and authority.

The Beginnings

This debate had originally erupted on the question of the Prophet's appearance during his birthday celebration to bestow blessings on the participants at the gathering. Deobandī scholars including Gangohī, Sāharanpūrī, and Thānvī opposed such a possibility. They argued that a belief in the Prophet's capacity to visit multiple venues simultaneously would lead the masses to think that he was omniscient. Therefore, they contended, the masses would begin attributing divine qualities to the Prophet.[2] The prominent North Indian scholar 'Abdul Samī' tried to rebut this argument in his scathing refutation of Deobandī thought *Glistening Lights*, which has been introduced in previous chapters.

In *Glistening Lights*, Samī' chastised Deoband scholars for their position that a belief in the Prophet's capacity to visit multiple venues during his birthday celebration constituted polytheism. He counterargued that this belief posed no threat to divine sovereignty, as the Deoband scholars claimed.[3] Samī' explained that polytheism meant associating with a non-divine entity the kind of knowledge that God possessed. However, he emphasized, knowledge of all the venues where the Prophet's birthday was held could not be compared with God's infinite knowledge.

God was omniscient of and omnipresent in every moment of time and in every corner of all universes. In comparison to this infinite knowledge, knowledge about the places where the Prophet's birthday was celebrated was infinitesimally miniscule, Samī' argued. Therefore, a belief in the Prophet's capacity to appear at multiple places simultaneously could not possibly imply the equation (*barābarī*) of prophetic and divine knowledges. Nor could it be taken to mean that the Prophet had assumed partnership in the divine attribute (*mushārakat-i ṣifāt-i ilāhī*) of absolute knowledge. That interpretation would be valid, Samī' insisted, only if God's knowledge and presence were also limited to *mawlid* gatherings. Since that was not the case, a belief in the Prophet's appearance during his birthday celebration did not oppose or threaten divine sovereignty, nor did it create any possibility of polytheism.[4]

Samī' explained that a divine attribute (*ṣifat*) was something that was found only in God and not in anyone other than him (*Yūjad fī-hi wa lā yūjad fī ghayrihi*). The capacity to be present at all places in the world, he claimed, was not among those attributes. This capacity was not specific to God. For instance, Samī' elaborated, the ability of the angel of death (*malik al-mawt*) to traverse the entire universe was well known. He had access to all humans, beasts, insects, and birds. Wherever any of God's creation died, he was present. Moreover, Samī' argued, even Satan followed all of humanity day and night (except those who are protected by God's mercy). God had granted Satan the capacity to be present at all places at all times, just as he had gifted that capacity to the angel of death. Therefore, according to Samī', by negating that same capacity for the Prophet, Deoband scholars were effectively calling the Prophet lesser in status (*fazl*) than Satan and the angel of death.[5]

In Samī''s view, by denying the comprehensiveness of the Prophet's knowledge, the Deobandīs were demonstrating their own incapacity to perceive prophetic grace. Samī' clarified that his argument should not be taken to mean that the Prophet necessarily visited every gathering of his birthday celebration. Rather, his point was that a person who held this belief could not be called a polytheist. Why? Because even entities that were lesser in status than the Prophet, such as Satan and the angel of death, possessed the capacity to be present at innumerable sites simultaneously.

It was thus inconceivable for the Prophet to not possess that same capacity. Anyone who even hinted that the Prophet's knowledge was inferior to the knowledge of Satan and the angel of death was guilty of insulting and demeaning the Prophet.[6] This in a nutshell was Samī''s charge against the Deoband school on the question of prophetic knowledge.

Khalīl Aḥmad Sāharanpūrī led the Deobandī response to Samī‘'s allegation in *Conclusive Proofs*, his rebuttal of *Glistening Lights*, which I have already discussed on a few occasions. In the section of this text that I am about to dive into, Sāharanpūrī tried to discredit Samī‘'s claim that Deoband scholars considered Satan more knowledgeable and hence of a higher status than the Prophet. His response is at the center of this dispute. I thus analyze it in some detail next.

Uncoupling Knowledge and Status: Sāharanpūrī's Response to Samī‘

In his rejoinder, Sāharanpūrī scoffed at Samī‘'s suggestion that Deobandīs regarded Satan as higher in status than the Prophet. While clarifying their position on knowledge and prophetic authority, he explained that God had gifted each entity among his creation with a specific amount of knowledge. Further, to associate with any entity even one bit more knowledge than what it had been divinely ordained constitutes polytheism.[7]

For Sāharanpūrī, God's privilege to gift knowledge and to limit the degree of knowledge possessed by all entities other than him was incontrovertibly established in the Qur'ānic verse "God has the keys to knowledge of the unknown; no one knows it except Him."[8] Sāharanpūrī underscored that the sin of polytheism was not limited to equating divine and prophetic knowledge. Even the mere association of a divine privilege such as his absolute knowledge with a nondivine entity was polytheism. This rule applied to all nondivine entities, including the Prophet.[9] As evidence for this principle, Sāharanpūrī cited the Ḥanafī ruling (contained in texts such as *Baḥr ar-Rā'iq* and *Durr al-Mukhtār*) that whoever undertook a marriage contract (*nikāḥ*) taking God and the Prophet as active witnesses at the ceremony became an unbeliever.[10]

This was so because of the implicit assumption that the Prophet possessed knowledge of the unknown. The crucial point to keep in mind, Sāharanpūrī reminded, was the categorical prohibition against associating knowledge of the unknown with the Prophet. There was no qualification that polytheism would occur only if one quantitatively and qualitatively (*kamman wa kayfan*) equated divine and prophetic knowledges. Had that been the case, Sāharanpūrī continued, one would have to concede that the Arab polytheists during the Prophet's time were not really unbelievers. After all, they did not associate absolute sovereignty and knowledge with any one divinity. They used to believe in multiple false divinities (*ma'būdān-i bāṭila*), each with its separate domain of authority. According to Sāharanpūrī, all nondivine entities, including all prophets, Satan, and the angel of death, were divinely ordained with a specific capacity (*wus'at*) for knowledge that they could neither exceed nor fall short of.[11] Most importantly, Sāharanpūrī argued, that gifted capacity for knowledge was unrelated to spiritual status. Indeed, Sāharanpūrī's entire argumentative apparatus rested on the claim that status did not depend on knowledge of the physical world. An entity with lesser knowledge might well have a higher status. For example, he explained, Moses was much more exalted and privileged than the revered figure in the Qur'ān, Khidhr, though Moses's capacity for the unveiling of knowledge (*'ilm kā mukāshafa*) was much less advanced than Khidhr's. The capacity for knowledge of both men was limited to what they had been gifted by God, despite the marked disparity in their status.

Sāharanpūrī concurred with Samī' that the expansive knowledge provided by God to Satan and the angel of death was incontrovertibly established by conclusive proof texts (*nuṣūṣ-i qaṭī 'a*). However, on that basis, one could not advance the analogy that a more privileged and exalted entity, such as the Prophet, must have at least as much if not more knowledge than Satan and the angel of death. To the contrary, Sāharanpūrī advised, several conclusive proof texts established the Prophet's inability to access knowledge of the unknown. For example, the prophetic saying, "I do not know what will be done to me or to you [on the Day of Judgment]" (*Lā adrī mā yuf'il bī wa lā bikum*) clearly showed the Prophet's own repudiation of associating knowledge of the unknown with him. The critical flaw in Samī''s hermeneutic, Sāharanpūrī maintained, was his inability to differentiate between status and knowledge. The Prophet was more privileged than Satan, but that did not mean he must also be more knowledgeable.[12] Knowledge and status were not proportional, as Samī' had erroneously assumed.

Sāharanpūrī also chastised Samī' for mobilizing an analogy in opposition to a conclusive proof text. Questions on tenets of faith (*'aqā'id ke masā'il*), Sāharanpūrī sternly warned, could not be resolved through analogies. They required conclusive proof texts. In the absence of a conclusive proof text demonstrating the Prophet's extensive knowledge of the physical world, Samī''s argument was invalid.

At this point Sāharanpūrī said something that would haunt his legacy and ignite polemical battles for several decades: "Satan's and the angel of death's immense capacity for knowledge of the physical world [*'ilm-i muḥīṭ-i zamīn*] are established from conclusive proof texts. Show me a conclusive proof text that proves such a capacity for the Prophet! What is it if not polytheism to contravene conclusive proof texts with the corrupt analogy [*qiyās-i fāsida*] that since the Prophet holds a higher status than Satan and the angel of death he must also possess more knowledge than them?"[13]

According to Sāharanpūrī, knowledge was the primary constituting force of sovereignty. In his view, the divine privilege over knowledge of the unknown was critical to maintaining the absolute alterity of divine sovereignty. Moreover, divine sovereignty was at once generated and mediated by knowledge. In Sāharanpūrī's discourse, God had gifted all entities other than him a fixed proportion of knowledge. The capacity of all nondivine entities to possess knowledge was predetermined according to a divinely authorized epistemological program. Most importantly, God's sovereignty depended on the integrity of that program. Any disturbance to that program threatened the sovereignty of its architect, God.

This is why the suggestion that the Prophet could visit multiple sites simultaneously during the *mawlid* ceremony was noxious to Sāharanpūrī. What Sāharanpūrī found heretical was the implication that the Prophet had exceeded the limits of knowledge that God had gifted him. In Sāharanpūrī's theological imaginary, knowledge was God's gift to others. The gift of knowledge also established God's sovereignty over the recipients of that gift. One might put it this way: by gifting knowledge to others, God gifted to himself his sovereignty. The gift of knowledge secured the gift of sovereignty. And most importantly, no nondivine entity, even the Prophet, was allowed to trespass the limits of that divinely sanctioned gift.

But Sāharanpūrī's attempt to dissociate knowledge (*'ilm*) from status (*fazl*) was not free of ambiguities. Perhaps the most ambivalent aspect of this attempted separation of knowledge and status was the status he accorded to knowledge itself. On the one hand, Sāharanpūrī's entire argument rested on the claim that knowledge and status were not necessarily proportional or even related. It was this move that allowed him to simultaneously venerate the Prophet as the most exalted being and humanize him as someone whose knowledge was less than that of Satan and the angel of death.

But his argument for the absolute exclusivity of divine sovereignty hinged precisely on the exceptionality of divine knowledge. A central question that emerges here is this: If status and knowledge are indeed disproportional or unrelated, why must an absolutely sovereign God also be an absolutely knowledgeable God? In other words, if someone's position in the hierarchy of spiritual perfection is unconnected to knowledge, how can God's sovereignty depend on that very knowledge? These were the kinds of questions that (as we will see a little later in this chapter) emerged as objects of intense contestation over the import of Sāharanpūrī's statement cited above. Moreover, for his opponents, as troubling as Sāharanpūrī's argument was the language in which he delivered that argument. Sāharanpūrī's rhetorical choice to draw comparisons between the Prophet and Satan made him particularly vulnerable to the accusation that he was being irreverent toward the Prophet. Another Deoband luminary whose comments on the issue of the Prophet's knowledge of the unknown made him a target of this accusation was Ashraf 'Alī Thānvī.

Can the Prophet Be Called "Knower of the Unknown"? Ashraf 'Alī Thānvī's Contribution to the Debate

Much like his senior colleague Sāharanpūrī, Thānvī was troubled by the possibility that the masses might confuse the distinction between prophetic and divine knowledge. In one of his shorter epistles entitled *Guarding the Faith* (*Ḥifẓ al-Īmān*), Thānvī addressed the question of whether it was permissible to call the Prophet "Knower of the Unknown" (*'ālim al-ghayb*). Thānvī was asked this question by a disciple seeking clarity on whether an entity that received knowledge of the unknown through God's mediation (*bi'l wāsiṭa*) qualified for this title. As this questioner put it, "Zayd [a hypothetical interlocutor] says that knowledge of the unknown is of two kinds: essential (*bi-zāt/Ar.bi'l-dhāt*) and mediated (*bi-wāsṭa/Ar.bi'l-wāsiṭa*). He argues that while the first type is reserved for

God, the second is available to the Prophet. Therefore, the Prophet can also be called 'Knower of the Unknown.' Is this interpretation correct?"[14]

In his response, Thānvī decisively rejected the possibility that the Prophet could be called "Knower of the Unknown." Thānvī argued that since God was the sole possessor of absolute hidden knowledge, no nondivine entity, even the Prophet, deserved this title.[15] The attachment of this title to any of God's creation, he claimed, opened the doors to polytheism. It was for the same reason, he explained, that referring to the Prophet with epithets like "Our Shepherd" (*rā'inā*) and "My Lord" (*rabbī*) was prohibited.

Thānvī further argued that apart from revelatory proofs showing the partiality of the Prophet's knowledge, the Prophet's own career attested to that. For instance, the Prophet's use of spies and informants to gather intelligence and his lack of knowledge about the date of Doomsday both demonstrated his lack of access to absolute hidden knowledge. Therefore, the title "Knower of the Unknown" was exclusive to God and inapplicable to the prophet. To further stress his point, Thānvī offered a hypothetical analogy that generates controversy even today. He wrote:

> If one accepts that it is correct to attach the title "Knower of the Unknown" to the blessed being of the Prophet, then the question that must be asked is: What kind of hidden knowledge is intended here, absolute or partial? If what is intended is partial hidden knowledge, then that is nothing specific to the Prophet. Every boy, lunatic, in fact, even every animal and beast knows something that no one else knows. Therefore, if one followed this logic, all these entities should also be called "Knower of the Unknown." . . . And if what is intended [by this title] is absolute hidden knowledge, then that claim can be refuted through both rational and revelatory proofs.[16]

In presenting this provocative analogy, Thānvī sought to underscore the distinction between divine and prophetic authority. According to Thānvī, only God was the absolute sovereign who possessed the privilege of absolute hidden knowledge. The Prophet did not enjoy that privilege. But in presenting his point, Thānvī, much like Sāharanpūrī, adopted a rhetorical style that would haunt him and the legacy of the Deoband school for many decades. Thānvī's comparison of the Prophet's knowledge with that of animals, beasts, and lunatics supplied his opponents with ammunition to launch the argument that the Deobandī ideology demeaned the Prophet.

This was precisely the argument that drove Aḥmad Razā Khān's refutation of Deobandī views on prophetic knowledge, to which I next turn. As I mentioned before, the above two statements by Sāharanpūrī and Thānvī were the immediate catalyst for Aḥmad Razā Khān's judgment of anathema against the Deoband pioneers. Despite all his other disagreements with Deoband scholars, he declared them unbelievers specifically on the charge that these two statements contravened the necessities of religion.

The Perils of Satanic Theology

In *Ḥusām al-Ḥaramayn*—the tract composed as a legal opinion for the endorsement of Ḥanafī scholars in Arabia—Aḥmad Razā Khān categorized Gangohī, Sāharanpūrī, and Thānvī as a group of "satanic Wahhābīs" (*Wahhābīya Shayṭānīya*).[17] He accused them of insulting the Prophet and glorifying Satan. He began his assault with Sāharanpūrī. For Khān, the suggestion that the Prophet, God's most beloved subject, might possess lesser knowledge than Satan and the angel of death was unthinkable. Khān found offensive not only Sāharanpūrī's argument but also the way he presented that argument.

Posing provocative questions like "Where is there a conclusive proof text that establishes the Prophet's knowledge of the unknown?" was an insult to the Prophet. Moreover, the act of drawing comparisons between the Prophet's and Satan's knowledge confirmed an attitude of complete irreverence toward the sanctity of the prophetic example. Note the combination of alarm and revulsion in Khān's tone regarding Gangohī's and his followers' attitude toward the Prophet:

> Beware, O Muslims, beware those who believe in the Prophet. Reflect a little on what this man [Gangohī] is claiming. He claims that he is among the loftiest of scholars and that he is a master of faith and mystical knowledge. He is known as the "pivot and savior of this age" among his henchmen. But look how he curses at the Prophet [*kayfa yassub Muḥammadan*] without any inhibition. He proudly announces his belief in the

> capacity of his master Satan's knowledge. But he demands a proof text for the knowledge of that most exalted being whom God taught what he did not know, on whom God has showered his infinite grace, whose light illuminates whatever comes before him, and to whom God gifted the knowledge of the past, future, and everything that exists from East to West. What is this if not faith in Satan's knowledge, and unbelief in the knowledge of the Prophet [*hal laysa hādhā īmānan bi 'ilm iblīs wa kufr bi 'ilm Muḥammad*]? He goes on at length to prove Satan's comprehensive knowledge of what happens in the world, but when someone affirms that same capacity for the Prophet, he calls it polytheism.[18]

Khān accused Sāharanpūrī of calling Satan more knowledgeable than the Prophet. Moreover, he argued that there was no substantive difference between calling the Prophet less knowledgeable than a nondivine entity and brazenly cursing him. Therefore, in Khān's view, Sāharanpūrī was guilty of cursing the Prophet (*sabb al-rusūl*), and he deserved the punishment of anathema or departure from the fold of Islam.[19]

Further, according to Khān, Sāharanpūrī was as enthusiastic about establishing Satan's capacity for knowledge as he was militant about denying that same capacity for the Prophet. While calling the Prophet's access to knowledge of the unknown "polytheism," Sāharanpūrī found nothing problematic in attributing that same access to Satan. Therefore, Khān argued, despite Sāharanpūrī's supposed anxiety about the association of divine qualities with the Prophet, he was all too keen to establish Satan as God's partner. Satan was the only beneficiary of such an absurd theology, Khān bemoaned. According to Khān, in one flash of rhetorical hyperbole, Sāharanpūrī had at once insulted the Prophet and exalted Satan by positioning the latter as the most worthy recipient of divine grace. In other words, Sāharanpūrī had completely inverted the logic of tradition by replacing the Prophet with Satan. Such a satanic theology could only uproot the foundations of the religion, Khān declared.[20]

Robbing the Prophet's Privilege

Khān next turned his attention to Ashraf 'Alī Thānvī. He introduced Thānvī to his Arabian interlocutors as follows:

> Among the most esteemed of these satanic Wahābbīs is another of Gangohī's associates [*min adhnāb Gangohī*], a person called Ashraf 'Alī Thānvī. In a treatise of not more than a few pages, he says that the Prophet's knowledge is just like that of a boy, lunatic, animal, and beast. He further argues that if someone claims that the Prophet possesses knowledge of the unknown, the question one must ask of that person is this: Does the Prophet possess partial knowledge of the unknown or absolute? If it is partial knowledge, then that is nothing specific to the Prophet. Every boy, lunatic, in fact all animals and beasts also possess that kind of knowledge. And if one claims that the Prophet possesses absolute knowledge of the unknown, then this claim can be shown to be false through both rational and revelatory proofs.[21]

Khān accused Thānvī of equating (*yusāwī*) the Prophet with animals and lunatics. As if urging his interlocutors to participate in his fury, Khān thundered, "Look how he has abandoned the Qur'ān, bid farewell to faith, and stooped to question the difference between the Prophet and an animal" (*Unẓur kayfa taraka-l-Qur'ān wa wadda'a-l-īmān wa 'akhadha yas'al al-farq bayna-l-nabī wa-l-ḥaywān*).[22] The simple thing that Thānvī did not consider, Khān lectured, was that the kind of hidden knowledge that all nonprophetic entities possessed is merely speculative (*ẓannī*). Only prophets were the true and original recipients of conclusive knowledge over hidden matters. God enabled no other entity to command hidden knowledge except his favorite prophets, he emphasized. Those exalted prophets then transmitted part of this knowledge to nonprophetic entities.[23]

Khān's major philosophical objection against Thānvī was that he had rejected the idea that knowledge served as a marker of privilege. In Khān's view, knowledge and privilege were hierarchically organized, each reinforcing the other. An entity's capacity for knowledge signified its rank and stature in God's hierarchy of privilege. But Thānvī, Khān argued, had erased this correspondence between the hierarchies of knowledge and privilege. Instead, in Thānvī's discourse, one found a bipolar division between an absolutely knowledgeable God and all nondivine entities, which were equally radically inferior to God in terms of their capacity for knowledge.

What Thānvī did not consider, Khān continued, was that the knowledge possessed by all nondivine entities was not uniform or homogeneous. Rather, there was a hierarchy of knowledge that clearly distinguished more privileged entities such as prophets and saints from less privileged ones such as ordinary humans and animals. But because Thānvī chose to ignore these distinctions and hierarchies, he found nothing repugnant in comparing the Prophet's knowledge with that of children, lunatics, and beasts.

In the *Meccan Gift* (*Dawlat al-Makkīya*), Khān's most extensive text on the question of the Prophet's knowledge of the unknown, also composed in Arabic and also intended for an Ottoman scholarly audience, Khān proposed to his readers an experiment for Thānvī's consideration. "If you want to know his reality," he advised them, "go to him and greet him with the salutation "Oh you who are equal to dogs and pigs in knowledge and stature." This unexpected salutation, Khān predicted, "will cause him [Thānvī] to burn with outrage and die of anger." "Then ask him," he continued, " 'Does your knowledge encompass everything like God's knowledge?' If he replies yes, he will have committed unbelief. And if he replies no, then say, 'What is so special about your knowledge? Even dogs and pigs have knowledge of some things. So why do you call yourself a scholar and not your counterpart dogs and pigs [by the same name]?' " (*Fa-in shi'ta an tarā ḥaqīqat dhālika fa-a'thu wa khāṭibhu bi-qawlika "Yā musāwī al-kalb wa-l-khanzīr fi'l 'ilm wa-l-tawqīr." Sa-tarā yaḥtariq ghayẓan wa yakād yamūt ghanzan. Fas'al-hu: hal ahaṭta bi-kul sha'yyin 'ilman ka-mithl Allāh ṣubḥānahu wa ta'ālā fa-in qāla na'm fa-qad kafara wa-in qāla lā fa-qul la-hu: "Ay khuṣūṣīya la-ka fi'l 'ilm fa-inn al-'ilm bi-ba'ḍ ḥāṣil la-ka wa-li kul kalb khanzīr. Fa mā la-ka tusammā 'āliman dūn naẓarā'ika al-kilāb wa-l-khanāzīr?"*)[24]

According to Khān, the underlying flaw in Thānvī's argument was its failure to distinguish between different kinds of knowledge. More specifically, Khān argued that Thānvī had collapsed the distinction between the categories of pure knowledge of something as it existed (*muṭlaq al-'ilm*) and unconditionally unrestricted knowledge (*al-'ilm al-muṭlaq*).[25] The first category of pure knowledge referred to the essence of something in and of itself, without any added meaning or intent. This kind of knowledge was reserved for nondivine entities, including the Prophet. God gifted pure knowledge to entities among his creation in accordance with their spiritual status and privilege. On the other hand, the second category of unconditionally unrestricted knowledge was knowledge that was beyond human fathoming. Humans could not comprehend its size or content. It was unrestricted by any conditions. This kind of knowledge was available only to God.[26]

Khān argued that according to Thānvī's model, a privileged status was available only to someone who possessed knowledge of the unconditionally unrestricted variety. In other words, a privileged status was available only to an absolutely sovereign God. But Thānvī showed no regard for the hierarchy of privilege corresponding with differential capacities for pure knowledge among God's creation. Instead, Thānvī placed all recipients of pure knowledge on the same level. Such a radically uniform understanding of pure knowledge made it impossible to distinguish the Prophet from the rest of the world.

In Khān's view, because of his monological conception of pure knowledge, Thānvī had erased the distinction of the Prophet. He had dispossessed the Prophet of his privilege. Thānvī's equation of the Prophet with lunatics, animals, and beasts was an acute symptom of this deeper hermeneutical malady that afflicted his thought, Khān argued. As he explained: "He [Thānvī] makes no distinction between different kinds of pure knowledge; knowledge of a word or two and that which is infinite are all the same to him. He limits privilege to the possessor of unconditionally unrestricted knowledge [*al-'ilm al-muṭlaq*]. For him, a privileged status is available only for someone who possesses the totality of unconditionally unrestricted knowledge. [Therefore] he has to rob from prophets the privilege accorded to them through pure knowledge."[27]

As this quote shows, in Khān's view, Thānvī had robbed the Prophet of his exceptional status by constructing an excessively stark binary between prophetic authority and divine sovereignty. In Khān's theological imaginary, much like that of Fazl-i Ḥaqq Khayrābādī before him, divine sovereignty and prophetic privilege were mutually constituted. As a corollary, divine knowledge and prophetic knowledge, although distinct in their quantity and scope, were nonetheless part of a shared discursive venture. Khān framed the Prophet's capacity to know the unknown as an expected gift from God.

Much like the capacity for intercession, the knowledge gifted to the Prophet by God functioned as the signifier of the Prophet's elevated and unrivaled spiritual status. The gift of knowledge distinguished the Prophet from the rest of creation. It was a sign of God's love for his most beloved subject, the Prophet. For Khān, in clear contrast to his Deoband rivals, the Prophet was not merely a recipient of divine knowledge. He was also an active participant in that knowledge. Moreover, Khān further argued, "robbing" the Prophet of his gift of knowledge of the unknown equated to denigrating the sanctity of divine knowledge itself.

In Khān's view, those who undermined the Prophet's aura also cast aspersions on God. God's sovereignty and the Prophet's exalted status were not mutually exclusive, as the Deobandīs had erroneously assumed. Rather, they were inseparably intertwined. As Khān wrote, "You will never see someone who detracts from Prophet Muḥammad's glory and also exalts his Lord. By God! People who diminish the Prophet are those whom God has diminished" (*Lā tarā abadan man yanquṣ sha`n Muḥammad wa huwa mu'aẓẓimun li rabbihi. . . . Wallāhī innama yanquṣuhu man yanquṣuhu rabbuhu*).[28]

Khān considered Thānvī an exemplar of someone "who diminishes the Prophet's glory." For Khān, Thānvī's hypothetical scenarios that compared the Prophet to lunatics, animals, and beasts were not just an affront to the Prophet's persona and authority. Much more than that, such provocative comparisons threatened the very integrity of Islam. Khān explained that if one followed Thānvī's reasoning, an unbeliever or someone hostile to Islam might apply the same logic to question the concept of divine sovereignty. Following Thānvī's reasoning, Khān argued, it might be plausible for that unbeliever to say:

> If Muslims claim that God is sovereign, then one must ask: Is that sovereignty over all things or just some things? If it is only over some things, then there is nothing special about God, since several other entities, including humans, animals, lunatics, children, and beasts, also enjoy sovereignty over some matters. And if it is said that God is sovereign over everything, this proposition can be refuted with both revelatory and rational proofs. For instance, one may then argue that since God's being is also included in the category "everything," he must be subject to his own sovereignty. In that case, his sovereignty will no longer be necessary. In effect, he will no longer remain God.[29]

For Khān, this was the kind of doctrinal chaos that Thānvī's discourse set in motion. Again, what Khān found most troubling about Thānvī's language was the way it extended the boundaries of thinkability. As soon as a comparison between the Prophet, lunatics, and beasts became thinkable, it was only a matter of time before the very doctrinal foundations of Islam, such as the covenant of divine sovereignty, could be exposed to such scandalous comparisons. It was this deeper anxiety over defending the underlying foundations of religion that propelled Khān's judgment of anathema on the Deoband pioneers.

Can God Lie or Produce Another Muḥammad?

This anxiety comes across with even greater clarity if one considers Khān's devastating indictment of the position of Shāh Muḥammad Ismā'īl and the Deoband pioneers on the twin issues of God's capacity to lie or contravene a promise (*imkān-i kizb*) and to create another Prophet Muḥammad (*imkān-i naẓīr*). To give some necessary background, recall from chapter 3 that Ismā'īl's argument had pivoted on the distinction between potentiality and actuality. Though God might enact the exception and thus exercise his absolute sovereignty by actualizing these exceptional occurrences, he would not actually do so. This potentiality that never became actuality for Ismā'īl served as the touchstone for divine sovereignty. As Ismā'īl was attacked for this position in his lifetime and later, Deoband scholars, especially Gangohī and Sāharanpūrī, rushed to his defense. For instance, Gangohī tried to clarify that no one, including Ismā'īl and himself, disagreed that holding the conviction that God actually lied made a person an unbeliever. There was no doubt or disagreement about that. However, the point that Ismā'īl's detractors refused to understand, Gangohī complained, was that the former's focus was on establishing God's capacity to enact the exception, not on attributing to God qualities like lying. For example, Gangohī explained, rehearsing Ismā'īl's earlier argument, although God had already pronounced that he would send Pharaoh, Abū Lahab, and Hāmān to hell, he was not incapacitated (*'ājiz*) from sending them to heaven.[30]

Sāharanpūrī amplified the Deobandī position on this matter and its contrast from the position of the Barelvīs by pointing to the theological debate between the Ash'arīs and the Mu'tazilīs in early Islam. In an effort to discredit his Barelvī opponents, Sāharanpūrī argued that the Barelvīs were modern Mu'tazilīs. The Mu'tazilīs, he reminded his readers, considered it impossible for God to even hold the capacity to reward rather than punish a disobedient person or to punish rather than reward an obedient subject. Thus the Mu'tazilīs had insisted that God in essence was necessarily just and must by necessity act justly at all times. In this they were much like the Barelvīs, who insisted that God in essence did not even possess the capacity to contravene his promise or to produce another Muḥammad. In contrast, the Ash'arīs, who eventually came to represent the dominant theological school in Sunnī Islam, had called out the farcicality of this position by showing that God's capacity for an undesirable quality like injustice or lying did not constitute a defect undermining God's sovereignty. The Deobandīs, like Ismā'īl before them, were only acting like faithful Ash'arīs, Sāharanpūrī had declared.

But for Aḥmad Razā Khān, these explanations could not conceal a deadly discursive agenda headed for moral and doctrinal catastrophe. Again, his argument revolved around the threat of extending the boundaries of thinkability to alarming territories of imagination. If one began to think that God could potentially lie, Khān argued, the veracity of anything that he said or promised no longer remained necessary. As he put it: "When God's lying becomes possible, his truthfulness becomes unnecessary" (*Jab iss kā kizb mumkin hūa tuh iss kā ṣidq zarūrī nā rahā*). Religion itself, therefore, became vulnerable to upheaval. Rewards and punishments in the hereafter, resurrection, heaven and hell: none of these transcendental promises and truth claims remained incontrovertible or worthy of unwavering faith. In effect, faith collapsed.

Combining sarcasm with contempt, Khān pointed out that if imagining God to lie became fair game, there was nothing stopping people from attributing to God any number of repulsive, degrading, or vulgar acts. God could also then "engage in adultery [*zinā karay*], drink alcohol [*sharāb pīyay*], steal [*chorī karay*], worship idols [*buton ko pūjay*], urinate [*pishāb karay*], defecate [*pākhāna bharay*], burn himself in fire [*apnay āp ko āg mayn jalā'y*], drown himself in the sea [*daryā mayn dubā'y*], and have shoes thrown at him [*jūtīyān khā'y*]."[31]

Lying, Khān argued, was such an abominable sin that anyone with even a trace of self-respect would do the utmost to try and avoid it. The language in which Khān expressed this sentiment is quite revealing of the way he imagined the society around him. The benighted figure of the "low-caste" leather worker (Chamār) again appeared in his discourse. As he put it, "Even a 'low-caste' leather worker [*bhangī Chamār*] would consider association with the sin of lying a source of shame and embarrassment" (*Har bhangī Chamār bhī apnī taraf iss ki nisbat se 'ār rakhtā hay*).[32] How, then, could a Muslim even imagine that a source of such impurity, a sign of such immorality, could be attached to God? Khān sought to delegitimize his rivals by again citing the fourteenth-century Muslim Persian polymath Sa'd al-Dīn al-Taftazānī's *Sharḥ al-Maqāṣid*: "Muslim scholars are in consensus that lying is a sinful defect that cannot be associated with God" (*Al-kidhb muḥāl bi-ijmā' al-'ulamā' li'anna al-kidhb naqṣ bi-ittifāq al-'uqalā' wa huwa 'alā Allāh ta'ālā muḥāl*).[33] For Khān, the most disturbing aspect of Ismā'īl's and Deobandī positions was what he perceived as their utter irreverence toward a foundational covenant of Islam for the sake of scoring some philosophical points. Again, much as in the case of the Prophet's knowledge of the unknown, Khān felt that the speculative discursive and doctrinal maneuvers of his Deoband rivals verged on blasphemy. But for the Deoband pioneers, the discursive risks they ran paled in comparison with the stakes of securing divine sovereignty in a moment of moral crisis and chaos.

Knowledge, Information, and the Limits of "Religion": Manẓūr Nu'mānī's Rebuttal

As one might expect, Khān's attempt to anathematize the founding scholars of Deoband did not pass unchallenged. The publication of *Ḥusām al-Ḥaramayn* ignited a series of rebuttals and counter-rebuttals that consumed Deobandī and Barelvī scholars alike. As Usha Sanyal memorably put it, "There was a fatwa war."[34] As with any other moment in this polemical encounter, these events were also entangled in irresolvable competing narratives. According to the Barelvī narrative, leading Arabian scholars' endorsement of *Ḥusām al-Ḥaramayn* brought such embarrassment to the Deoband school that Khalīl Aḥmad Sāharanpūrī, who was in Mecca at that time, was forced to flee back to India. On the other hand, according to the Deobandī narrative, Khān's self-declared triumph, one that was achieved only through blatant fabrications, was short-lived. The scholars of Ḥijāz had initially endorsed his epistle in the tradition of trusting a fellow scholar's intentions and intellectual honesty. However, most of them retracted their endorsements after acquiring a more accurate understanding of Deoband scholars and their ideology. They also repudiated Khān for having misled them. In bringing about this reversal, it was Sāharanpūrī who played a pivotal role by composing a text (in Arabic) in November 1907 called *The Sword against the Fabricator* (*Al-Muhannad 'alā al-Mufannad*).[35] In this text, Sāharanpūrī answered in detail twenty-six questions/doubts that the *'ulamā'* of Ḥijāz had raised about the Deoband school and its normative precepts. The focus of these questions was on the Prophet's knowledge and status in Deobandī thought, and on theological problems like the twin issues of God's capacity to lie or produce another Muḥammad, with frequent references to the controversial passages of Deoband scholars that Aḥmad Razā Khān had cited in *Ḥusām al-Ḥaramayn*.[36] Allow me to leave aside here the historicist question of "what really happened" during this episode and which side actually won over the scholars of Arabia. Instead, during the remainder of this chapter, I continue my analysis of the competing normativities characterizing the Deobandī and Barelvī orientations by considering another important discursive fragment attached to this polemic, the thought of the twentieth-century Deoband scholar Manẓūr Nu'mānī.

In the decades following the publication of *Ḥusām al-Ḥaramayn*, Nu'mānī emerged as arguably the most ardent and astute defender of the Deoband pioneers from the charge of anathema that had been leveled against them by Aḥmad Razā Khān. Primarily a scholar of the Ḥadīth, Nu'mānī was one of the most influential and authoritative Deoband scholars in postcolonial India. Originally from Bareillī, Nu'mānī spent most of his life in the city of Lucknow, where he also served as a distinguished instructor of the Ḥadīth in the Nadwat al-'Ulamā' seminary, an institution with which he maintained close relations throughout his career. His most well-known publications are a four-volume work on the Ḥadīth called *Knowledges of the Ḥadīth* (*Ma'ārif al-Ḥadīth*) and a more introductory primer, *What Is Islam?* (*Islām Kiyā Hay*). Both of these books have been translated into English and have circulated worldwide.

Nu'mānī also excelled as a debater. In 1934, twenty-eight years after the publication of *Ḥusām al-Ḥaramayn*, he composed a rebuttal entitled "The Decisive Polemic" (*Fayṣala kun Munāẓara*).[37] According to Nu'mānī, he had prepared this text for an oral debate that same year in Lāhore against representatives of the Barelvī school, a debate for which the renowned Indian Muslim poet Muḥammad Iqbāl was to serve as a disinterested adjudicator. In the weeks leading up to it, this debate was much touted as a decisive event that promised to resolve the dispute once and for all. "But alas, the Barelvī scholars failed to show up!" Nu'mānī sighed (94). He then decided to publish the remarks he had prepared for the debate in the form of a book also entitled *The Decisive Polemic*. My interest in Nu'mānī's rebuttal, however, does not come from the eventful circumstances of its publication.

Rather, his contribution to the Barelvī-Deobandī polemic is instructive for how it connects the question of knowledge and its relationship to sovereignty with larger questions about the boundaries of the "religious" and the "nonreligious" in modernity. As I will show in the following discussion, with considerable help from Nu'mānī, at stake in the debate surrounding the Prophet's capacity for knowledge of the unknown was the very definition of knowledge. Defining knowledge in turn was inseparable from the task of demarcating the boundaries of religion. Encoded in this debate was thus the critical question of what did and did not count as religion. In what follows, I will develop this argument through a close reading of Nu'mānī's rebuttal of *Ḥusām al-Ḥaramayn*.

Manẓūr Nu'mānī accused Aḥmad Razā Khān of deliberately misrepresenting Sāharanpūrī's and Thānvī's statements to Arab scholars not familiar with Urdu: "It seems that while writing *Ḥusām al-Ḥaramayn*, Aḥmad Razā Khān vowed to refrain from telling the truth or from showing any honesty" (184). Nu'mānī argued that Khān either willfully or unknowingly failed to consider the context of Sāharanpūrī's and Thānvī's remarks before passing his devastating judgment of anathema. For instance, Nu'mānī clarified that Thānvī's statement (see earlier in this chapter) was a response to the following question: Is it permissible to call the Prophet "Knower of the Unknown" (*'ālim al-ghayb*)? Thānvī was not even addressing the question of whether the Prophet possessed hidden knowledge, he stressed.

All that Thānvī was trying to show was that the Prophet could not be accorded the title "Knower of the Unknown," Nu'mānī claimed (184). There was a massive difference, he continued, between the questions "Does the Prophet possess knowledge of the unknown?" and "Can he be called Knower of the Unknown?" In elaborating his point, Nu'mānī advanced the philosophical principle that the actualization of an attribute in a given entity does not make it permissible for that entity to be named after the actualized attribute. For example, he explained, God had declared himself the creator of all existence in the Qur'ān. Moreover, all Muslims had to believe that everything in this world, minor or major, magnificent or trivial, was God's creation. However, in spite of that, calling God "creator of monkeys and pigs" was impermissible. Similarly, it was well known that the Prophet was so self-sufficient that he used to repair his own shoes and also milk his own sheep. However, despite this fact, it would be highly inappropriate to call the Prophet "Shoe-Mender" (*khāṣif al-na'l*) or "Sheep Milker" (*ḥālib al-shāt*).

As Nu'mānī urged his audience, "What I want readers to understand is that the debate on whether the Prophet possesses hidden knowledge and the question of whether the title 'Knower of the Unknown' can be attached to his blessed being are two entirely separate issues. They are not connected" (185). According to Nu'mānī, all that Thānvī was trying to argue in *Guarding Faith* was that the title "Knower of the Unknown" could not be affixed to the Prophet. The Prophet could not be called "Knower of the Unknown" in the same manner as he was called "Seal of All Prophets" (*khātim al-anbīyā'*), "Master of All Messengers" (*sayyid al-mursalīn*), "Mercy for All the Worlds" (*raḥma li'l 'ālamīn*), and so on. This was because the title "Knower of the Unknown" could be attached only to someone who acquired hidden knowledge without the help of an intermediary. There was no such entity other than God. Therefore, the title "Knower of the Unknown" was also unavailable for all nondivine entities, including the Prophet, Nu'mānī explained (185).

The upshot of Thānvī's discourse, Nu'mānī elaborated, could be understood as follows: if one agreed to call the Prophet "Knower of the Unknown," this could be true either because he had access to all unknown knowledge or because he had access only to some. The first scenario could not be true because only God had access to absolute hidden knowledge. And the second scenario could not be true because even the most debased entities in the world, such as animals, beasts, and lunatics, were privileged with some forms of knowledge that were unknown to anyone else. Therefore, if one abided by the principle that access to some knowledge of the unknown qualified an entity for the title "Knower of the Unknown," then the entire world would have to be accorded that title. Moreover, Nu'mānī probingly inquired, inverting the logic of Aḥmad Razā Khān's protest: How could a title that applied to everything in the world possibly exalt the stature of the Prophet? To the contrary, such a universally applicable title would only diminish the Prophet's aura (185–88). Nu'mānī further defended Thānvī's position with an instructive analogy:

> Imagine a country is ruled by a king renowned for his philanthropic generosity. He feeds thousands of destitute people day and night. Now suppose some fool, say Zayd, announces that he will call this king "the Sustainer" [*al-rāziq*]. At this moment, another person, say 'Umar, asks Zayd the following question: When you call this king "the Sustainer," is it because he provides sustenance to all of humanity, or because he feeds some of humanity? The first proposition is obviously false because the king clearly does not feed all human beings. And if the king is called "the Sustainer" because he feeds some people, then that is nothing specific to that king. Even the laborers of a country at least feed their own children. Setting aside humans, even birds feed their offspring. So, if one were to extend your logic, one would have to call every laborer and bird "the Sustainer." (196)

The most important thing to notice in the above analogy, Nu'mānī emphasized, was that 'Umar's statement could not be interpreted to mean that he considered the magnanimous king and every laborer or bird as equal in status or in terms of philanthropic capacity. This was exactly how Thānvī's rejection of attaching the title "Knower of the Unknown" to the Prophet should be understood. He (Thānvī) never intended to compare, let alone equate, the Prophet's knowledge with that of beasts, lunatics, and animals.

Nu'mānī summed up the central principles undergirding Thānvī's argument as follows: (1) only God possessed absolute knowledge of the unknown, and (2) there was nothing exclusive about the Prophet's possession of partial knowledge of the unknown. The suggestion that Thānvī declared beasts and lunatics more knowledgeable than the Prophet was solely a construction of Khān's imagination. As Nu'mānī chuckled, "On hearing Khān's sensationalist interpretation of Thānvī's otherwise clear and unambiguous statement, even Satan would hasten to seek refuge from unbelief" (188).

Like a prosecutor brandishing incriminating evidence to the jury, Nu'mānī marshaled a number of instances in Aḥmad Razā Khān's own writings when he had demonstrated the accessibility of some hidden knowledge to entities other than the Prophet. For example, in a collection of his edificatory discourses (*malfūẓāt*), Khān had touted his father's ability to foretell (*peshgo'ī*) the future as an affirmation of the latter's spiritual achievements (193). Moreover, Khān had argued that even nonhumans assented to such unperceivable matters of dogma as belief in God and the finality of the Prophet. "Every tree, plant, leaf, and sand dune is obligated to assent to the unity of God and the prophecy of Prophet Muḥammad. They all bear witness to Muḥammad's prophethood and praise the divine," Khān had declared.[38]

In light of such statements by Khān, Nu'mānī argued, there was no substantive difference between Thānvī's and Khān's positions on hidden knowledge. Both were in agreement that while absolute hidden knowledge was available only to God, partial hidden knowledge was accessible to almost all human and nonhuman entities. Therefore, Nu'mānī concluded, Khān was creating the impression of a radical disagreement with Thānvī when there was none.

Defining Knowledge and Religion: Nu'mānī's Defense of Sāharanpūrī

Nu'mānī also accused Khān of deliberately taking Khalīl Aḥmad Sāharanpūrī's statement out of context in a bid to make it appear scandalous. He argued that Khān was dead wrong in his assessment that Sāharanpūrī had called Satan more knowledgeable than the Prophet. Nu'mānī explained that Sāharanpūrī was simply refuting 'Abdul Samī''s original analogy that since even Satan possessed extensive knowledge about the physical world (*'ilm-i rū-yi zamīn*), it was inconceivable for the Prophet to not possess that knowledge.[39] Sāharanpūrī, Nu'mānī stressed, was trying to debunk the soundness of this analogy by demonstrating that just because the Prophet's status was higher than Satan's, it did not mean that the Prophet's empirical knowledge of the physical world must also be greater. The critical point to remember, Nu'mānī lectured, was that the kind of knowledge under discussion in Sāharanpūrī's discourse was not absolute knowledge or knowledge connected to salvation and the advancement of human perfections (*kamālāt-i insānī.*) Rather, Sāharanpūrī was talking only about knowledge of the physical world that had nothing to do with religion or salvation (151).

Nu'mānī further elaborated this point by positing a crucial contrast between the categories of knowledge (*'ilm*) and information (*ma'lūmāt*). He defined knowledge as something that actively enabled a subject to attain salvation and greater proximity to God. Knowledge directly related to matters of religion. On the other hand, information either was irrelevant to salvation or might even detract from it. Most importantly, Nu'mānī emphasized that when a person was called "more knowledgeable" (*a'lam*) than someone else, it was only because of the superiority of his or her religious or salvationally beneficial knowledge.

The acquisition of all other forms of knowledge that were unrelated to religion did not make someone more knowledgeable. For this reason, Nu'mānī argued, even if an illiterate person possessed more information about trivial and secondary events than, say, a Prophet, that person could not be called more knowledgeable on that account. For instance, knowledge of such things as "Sanskrit, English, geography, magic, and poetry" was mere information that had nothing to do with human perfections or religion. Nu'mānī illustrated the distinction between knowledge and information with a set of comparisons that are quite indicative of how he imagined the boundaries of religion and knowledge.

He wrote:

> These days a European heretic possesses a great deal of information about material and industrial inventions [*mādī awr ṣan'atī ikhtarā'āt*] that the great jurists Imām Abū Ḥanīfa and Imām Mālik never even heard of. Similarly, even the loftiest and most pious religious scholars do not have the extensive information [*ma'lūmāt*] about theaters and

> cinemas that these morally depraved and corrupt spectators [*tamāshā bīn*] who frequently visit such venues do. But only a fool [*aḥmaq*] would argue that the heretics of Europe [*Europe ke mulḥidīn*] or the habitual spectators of movies at cinemas are somehow more "knowledgeable" [*a'lam*] than Imām Abū Ḥanīfa, Imām Mālik, Shaykh 'Abd al-Qādir Jīlānī, or any other esteemed religious scholar. (185)

The quote above provides important clues about Nu'mānī's social imaginary. Nu'mānī's example of "corrupt cinema spectators" captures his dissatisfaction with the moral economy he found around him. In his view, Indian Muslims had become so enamored by trivial and harmful "nonsalvational" activities that they had lost any connection with Islam and its intellectual heritage. Nu'mānī's discourse also shows a divide between a salvational and a profane world.

The salvational world was populated by people of religion such as leading scholars of the tradition. The profane world was contaminated by modern developments like European industrial inventions, knowledge of "un-Islamic" languages such as English and Sanskrit, and the proliferation of public theaters and cinemas. In Nu'mānī's social imaginary, the division between knowledge and information corresponded with a larger division between salvational and profane spheres of thought, practice, and public life.

Most importantly, the construction of this binary between salvational and profane worlds was intimately connected to Nu'mānī's argument that the Prophet's lack of knowledge about the temporal world did not in any way undermine his status. The Prophet's status as a perfect human being depended on the capaciousness of his salvational religious knowledge. The Prophet's status had no relation to the kind of profane nonreligious information that interested people of questionable moral character.

In Nu'mānī's view, the exclusivity of the Prophet's status depended solely on knowledge connected to human perfections and religion. Therefore, the Prophet's ignorance about particular events in the world did not undermine his perfection and status. There was no example, Nu'mānī argued, that better demonstrated this point than the Prophet's own life. The Prophet had himself declared to his followers, "You know better [than I do] the affairs of your worldly lives" (*Antum a'lam bi 'amr dunyā-kum*).

Moreover, during the Prophet's life, he had no knowledge about several secondary events that took place around him. For example, during his tenure in Medina, he mistook many hypocrites for good believers. Only through revelation did he eventually become aware of these hypocrites' true intentions (182).[40] Similarly, Nu'mānī reasoned, the Qur'ān declares, "We did not teach [the Prophet] poetry, nor is it necessary for him."[41] It is obvious from this verse, Nu'mānī claimed, that the Prophet was not taught poetry, even though several unbelievers and "morally depraved people" had mastered the art of poetry. But knowledge of poetry did not make them more knowledgeable. It simply added to their acquisition of trivial information. As Nu'mānī put it: "Imru' al-Qays [the pre-Islamic Arabic poet, d. 575] was the worst kind of unbeliever, but he was also a renowned poet. Firdawsī [d. 1020] was a morally corrupt Shī'a. However, he was among the most accomplished of Persian poets. But one cannot conclude that because even unbelieving and immoral people like 'Imru' al-Qays and Firdawsī excelled in poetry, the Prophet must have as well. . . . In fact, if knowledge of poetry were in any way related to status and moral superiority, then every pious Muslim would be a better poet than 'Imru' al-Qays and Firdawsī" (153).

This distinction between religious knowledge and nonreligious information was also central to how Nu'mānī defended Khalīl Aḥmad Sāharanpūrī from the accusation that the latter had called Satan more knowledgeable than the Prophet. Sāharanpūrī's argument was exactly to the contrary of this accusation, Nu'mānī claimed. According to Nu'mānī, Sāharanpūrī had in fact argued for a radical difference between the Prophet's unrivaled knowledge of religion and Satan's mastery over profane worldly information.

As Nu'mānī explained:

> Indeed, God has granted Satan all the resources of information that he might need to misguide humans and to test their faith. For instance, Satan should be familiar with human desires and temperaments so he may exploit them. He should know that in such and such a place a vulgar dance gathering is taking place so he may tempt vulnerable youth to go there and engage in debauchery. Satan requires extensive information about the lowly affairs of the world to fulfill his satanic goals. But prophets and

> other beings dear to God have nothing to do with such trivial and vulgar information. Their job is not misguidance but guidance and moral instruction. Therefore, God has gifted them an unlimited abundance of knowledge suited for that task. (159)

Here one can see how Nu'mānī defended Sāharanpūrī by constructing a binary between "religious knowledge" and "profane information." According to Nu'mānī, when Sāharanpūrī had said that Satan's knowledge of the physical world was greater than the Prophet's, he was referring only to the kind of nonsalvational profane information that religious people had nothing to do with. In fact, people of religion, most prominently the Prophet, would strive to keep away from those kinds of information and from the spheres of mental and physical activity they encompassed. Therefore, contrary to Khān's accusation that Sāharanpūrī had demeaned the Prophet by calling him less knowledgeable than Satan, Sāharanpūrī had in fact established the absolute superiority of the Prophet's religious knowledge over Satan's capacity for nonreligious profane information.

To sum up, Nu'mānī's argument pivoted on the claim that the Prophet's knowledge of matters unrelated to salvation and the advancement of human perfections might well be less than that of a non-Prophet, an unbeliever, or even Satan. However, a deficit in knowledge of worldly affairs and events in no way undercut the Prophet's status as the most knowledgeable being. Khān had failed to consider this basic principle before accusing Sāharanpūrī of calling Satan more knowledgeable than the Prophet, Nu'mānī concluded.

What interests me most about Nu'mānī's argument is the conception of knowledge and religion it articulated and on which it rested. In Nu'mānī's imaginary, the definition of *knowledge* was restricted to "religious knowledge." More precisely, religious knowledge represented those forms of knowledge that God had deemed necessary for salvation. For instance, these included the Qur'ān, the Ḥadīth, and the *sharī'a* more broadly, though he did not provide an explicit list of disciplines that counted as "religious." However, Nu'mānī's exercise of consciously defining knowledge also involved defining the boundaries of religion.

His decision on what counted as knowledge was also a sovereign decision on what did and did not count as religion. Moreover, this exercise of defining the proper limits of knowledge and religion produced a noticeably constricted conception of both. For instance, consider the way Nu'mānī compared the knowledge of prominent premodern Muslim jurists with that of scholars from other disciplines in the tradition. He wrote:

> Imām Abū Ḥanīfa had mastered millions of disciplines connected to the *sharī'a*. In comparison, although Ibn Rushd (d. 1198) was also a fairly accomplished scholar of the *sharī'a*, his knowledge was not even one-tenth that of Abū Ḥanīfa. On the other hand, Ibn Rushd's *information* [emphasis mine] about Greek philosophy was certainly far superior because Greek philosophy had not been translated into Arabic during Abū Ḥanīfa's life. However, on that basis, one cannot call Ibn Rushd more knowledgeable than Abū Ḥanīfa. Similarly, despite their wealth of knowledge about the Qur'ān and Ḥadīth, Imām Bukhārī (d. 870) and Imām Muslim (d. 875) did not have as much *information* [emphasis mine] about history as did Ibn Khaldūn (d. 1406) and Ibn Khālikān (d. 1282). But Ibn Khaldūn and Ibn Khālikān, or for that matter any contemporary historian, cannot be called more knowledgeable than these [Bukhārī and Muslim] luminaries of the religion. (150)

Nu'mānī's privileging of knowledge over information was authorized by a discursive program of controlling the limits of knowledge that counted as "religious." In defining "religious knowledge," he excluded history, philosophy, poetry, and a range of other disciplines from the domain of religion. For Nu'mānī, these knowledge traditions were mere information. They were inconsequential, if not detrimental, to a subject's salvational goals. In Nu'mānī's discourse, the boundaries of knowledge and religion were mutually, indeed simultaneously, constructed. Each enabled the other in the instant of the decision on what counted as knowledge and religion. Most importantly, for Nu'mānī, both knowledge and religion were readily available for division, definition, representation, and translation.

Life was readily available for the sovereign operation of separating religion from the nonreligious and knowledge from information. Ultimately, it was Nu'mānī who as the sovereign jurist decided the definition of knowledge and, by extension, that of religion. As shown in the quote just cited, his sovereign decision produced a remarkably reified understanding of religion, one that was confined to law. Law and religion were rendered synonymous. There was nothing more to religion than law. There was nothing more to knowledge than knowledge of the law. All else was nonreligious, nonsalvational, and potentially profane information. As a useful contextual backdrop to Nu'mānī's discourse, Margrit Pernau has keenly observed that from the mid-nineteenth century "The concept of the ulama began to assume the connotation of scholars concerned exclusively with religious knowledge."[42] During the early nineteenth and eighteenth centuries, in contrast, at the level of the scholarly elite, "No distinction was made . . . between those who specialized in religious and in secular knowledge. The erudition of scholars like Fazl-e Haqq and Sadr ud Din Azurda qualified them equally for a career in the colonial administration, a position at the court of a prince, or a teaching post at a madrasa."[43] Nu'mānī's reifying views on knowledge and religion seem to confirm Pernau's analysis. As the authority and expertise of the *'ulamā'* came to be associated with religious knowledge exclusively, their conception of both religion and knowledge also turned increasingly exclusionary.

Nu'mānī's discursive paradigm was paradoxical in many ways. Even as he strove to secure the primacy of knowledge that was "truly religious," his project was driven by the modern promise of dividing life into readily available compartments like religion/nonreligion and knowledge/information. The subject, according to this modern imaginary, did not only live life within its limits. Empowered by the sovereign power of decision, he or she decided on the limits of life. The question of the boundaries separating the religious from the nonreligious or knowledge from information was no longer subject to uncertainty and doubt. Instead, these boundaries were always available for translation, representation, and decision.

Nu'mānī's discourse seems to be restricted to a debate over the character and limits of Prophet Muḥammad's knowledge of the unknown. However, as I have shown, at the heart of his argument was something much more radical: a sovereign decision on what did and did not count as religion. The site on which he issued that decision was knowledge. The limits of knowledge symmetrically corresponded with the limits of religion. The moment of distinguishing knowledge from information was also the moment of defining the location of religion.

In short, Nu'mānī's discourse on the relationship between knowledge and prophetic status was inextricable from a politics of "religion making" invested in demarcating the ideological boundaries of what counted as religion. Moreover, as Nu'mānī objectified the limits of religion, he also objectified the Prophet's knowledge and, in effect, the imaginary of the Prophet as a font of normative guidance. By religionizing religion, Nu'mānī also religionized the Prophet.[44]

Competing Imaginaries of Tradition and Reform

The controversy generated by Thānvī's and Sāharanpūrī's remarks about prophetic knowledge clearly shows the opposing points of emphasis characterizing Deobandī and Barelvī understandings of tradition. For each, the other was heretical. In Aḥmad Razā Khān's view, the pioneers of Deoband were diminishing the Prophet's aura to make obscure and untenable arguments. More seriously, he anathematized them for violating the religious necessity to honor the Prophet. In turn, both early and later Deoband scholars such as Manẓūr Nu'mānī accused Khān of manufacturing baseless allegations by deliberately falsifying their arguments. More substantively, they also accused Khān of undermining God's sovereignty under the pretense of venerating the Prophet. As Rashīd Aḥmad Gangohī once commented, "They diminish God's majesty and give it the name 'love for God's Prophet'" (*Ḥaqq-i ta'ālā kā shān ghatātay hayn aur iss kā nām ḥubb-i rasūl Allāh rakhtay hayn*).[45] For both Aḥmad Razā Khān and his Deoband rivals, knowledge and sovereignty were intimately intertwined. However, the ways in which they understood that relationship and mobilized it for their programs of religious reform were radically opposed.

But from the preceding analysis of this polemic, one can also conclude that Aḥmad Razā Khān and his Deoband rivals were in many ways talking past each other. Substantively, notwithstanding their disagreements, their theological ideas overlapped in significant ways. Both agreed that absolute hidden knowledge was available only to God. They also agreed that God gifted part of that knowledge to nondivine entities, including the Prophet. Moreover, theoretically, Khān would have agreed with Thānvī that the title "Knower of the Unknown" was inapplicable to the Prophet if it meant the possessor of absolute knowledge of the unknown.

In light of these obvious points of agreement, one should note, as I have throughout this book, that this controversy had as much to do with the etiquette of talking about the Prophet as with competing visions of his authority. For Khān, the way in which Deoband scholars talked about the Prophet was unnecessarily provocative and outright offensive. Even if their arguments had been logically consistent, the manner in which they articulated those arguments was reprehensible. In Khān's view, through their unabashed comparison of the Prophet with Satan, lunatics, and beasts, his Deoband rivals were making a complete parody of religion. Khān found such comparisons and hypothetical scenarios an imminent threat to tradition because they stretched the limits of thinkability in alarming ways. That the etiquette of language was among Khān's gravest concerns with Deobandī discourse is captured in this statement of his in the *Meccan Gift*: "We also affirm that God gifts only some knowledge to the Prophet. But there is a difference of night and day between their 'some' and our 'some.' The 'some' of the Wahhābīs is a 'some' of hate and insult. And our 'some' is one of reverence and exaltation [*Fa-ba'ḍ al-wahābīya ba'ḍ bughḍ wa tawhīn wa ba'ḍuna ba'ḍ 'izz wa tamkīn*]."[46] As this statement shows, even when Khān recognized substantive agreement between Deobandī and Barelvī positions, what he perceived as the irreverence of Deobandī discourse left him aghast. On the other hand, in addition to disagreeing with Khān's characterization, the pioneers of Deoband would also have argued that taking some discursive risks to secure the primacy of divine sovereignty was appropriate. The urgency of the situation required some degree of discursive daring.

Ultimately, the polemical moment described in the last few chapters brought into central view two competing imaginaries of the moral goods most integral to the coherence of a tradition. Moreover, it was within a contingent conjuncture of antagonistic activity that Aḥmad Razā Khān and the pioneers of Deoband fought out and made centrally visible their opposing views on the limits of tradition. It was precisely by working through and against opposing arguments that the identities of these two schools took discursive shape. Identity and difference were mutually constituted in the moment of their encounter. Therefore, one could not have entered this polemical moment armed with a priori conceptions of what counted as Islam. Rather, the specific questions about the limits of

Islam and the answers provided to them were produced within the antagonistic space of the debate. The pioneers of the Barelvī and Deobandī schools articulated competing visions of what they considered normatively coherent programs of tradition and reform. Their rival narratives of tradition cannot be conceptualized through such binaries as law/Sufism, reformist/nonreformist, or traditionalist/modernist. These binaries set the ideological horizons of normative discourses on the limits of tradition and reform before the contingent conjunctures of debates in which those limits became centrally visible. Instead, the Barelvī-Deobandī debate demands an analytical approach centered not on the empiricist question of who won and who lost but on the political question of how and through what kinds of discursive and nondiscursive relations claims about the scope and boundaries of tradition were made, put on display, and contested.[47]

part three

Intra-Deobandī Tensions

chapter twelve

Internal Disagreements

Once Rashīd Aḥmad Gangohī visited his Sufi master Ḥājī Imdādullah in Mecca. Incidentally, during his visit, a *mawlid* gathering had been organized in the neighborhood where Imdādullah resided. Imdādullah asked Gangohī if he would like to attend the *mawlid* with him. On hearing this request, Gangohī emphatically refused and said, "Ḥājī Ṣāḥib: How can I attend a gathering of the *mawlid* when I am the one who forbids others in India from attending this evil gathering?" Upon hearing this reply, Ḥājī Imdādullah smiled and said to Gangohī, "May Allāh reward you. I would not have been any happier with you had you decided to attend the *mawlid* with me than I am in your refusal to do so, because you are steadfast in what you believe in." Later that day, when Ḥājī Imdādullah did finally attend the *mawlid* gathering, a student of Gangohī's, who was accompanying the latter on this trip, tagged along with Ḥājī Imdādullah, without informing his master. At the end of the ceremony, this student of Gangohī declared, "Had my Shaykh, Mawlānā Rashīd Aḥmad Gangohī, attended the *mawlid* gathering, he would not have condemned it, for it was free from all evil and impermissible affairs."[1]

This narrative captures some of the subtle variations and attitudinal differences found among the Deoband pioneers on contested ritual and normative practices. The difference showcased in this narrative cannot be collapsed into a law/Sufism binary or described as a case of absolute or even explicit disagreement. Rather, what we find here is an example of disagreement that conforms to the etiquette of a relationship of love and fidelity. Imdādullah and Gangohī clearly differed from one another in their attitude toward the *mawlid*. But they negotiated that difference in a manner that did not strain or break the bond or sanctity of the master-disciple relationship. The dynamics and process of such negotiations are the focus of this chapter.

More broadly, this chapter examines internal disagreements and tensions among the pioneers of the Deoband school on contested questions of normative practice. A consideration of these tensions reveals important examples of the subtle but critical variations in the attitudes of Deoband pioneers toward such questions. Moreover, they point to ways in which difference and disagreement were negotiated within a shared normative franchise. While maintaining relations of love and loyalty, the Deoband pioneers also disagreed with each other in nuanced yet visible ways. This negotiation of love and disagreement forms a key theme of this chapter. More specifically, the chapter addresses the role and contribution of Ḥājī Imdādullah in the Deobandī-Barelvī controversy. It does so by discussing an instructive text that Imdādullah wrote in an attempt to cool down the polemical fervor that had gripped late nineteenth-century Indian *'ulamā'*. This text, composed in Urdu, is called *Faysala-yi Haft Mas'ala* (*A Resolution to the Seven Controversies*), henceforth *FHM*. In *FHM*, Imdādullah showcased a hermeneutic that channeled a deep commitment to the normative boundaries of the *sharī'a* while also striving to secure intra-Muslim harmony and solidarity.

FHM was written in 1894, five years before Imdādullah's death. It is a relatively short text (around ten pages) that contains Imdādullah's discussion on seven contested ritual practices and doctrinal questions. These are (1) the celebration of the Prophet's birthday (*mawlid*), (2) transmission of blessings to the deceased (*fātiḥa-yi murawwaja*), (3) celebrating saints' anniversaries and listening to music ('*urs wa samā*'), (4) calling out the name of someone other than God (*nidā'-yi ghayr Allāh*), (5) holding a second prayer congregation (*jamā'at-i thānīya*), (6) God's capacity to lie (*imkān-i kizb*), and (7) God's capacity to create a second Muḥammad (*imkān-i naẓīr*). Since the *mawlid* was the most contested and eagerly debated ritual in India, it was also the problem that received the longest discussion in *FHM*. Also, in his treatment of the *mawlid* issue Imdādullah put into action the broader hermeneutical principles and strategies that in his view one should apply to any such controversial issue.

FHM was one of the first works that attempted the complicated task of resolving the disputed questions that animated the Deobandī-Barelvī controversy. Imdādullah was personally invested in resolving this conflict, since he had disciples from both the Barelvī and the Deobandī schools, though he has come to be best known as the Sufi master of the founders of Deoband. Although Imdādullah was not comprehensively trained as a legal scholar (as his Deobandī disciples were), the text is a remarkable example of a Sufi scholar's interpretation of complicated legal questions about the limits of heretical innovation in Islam. Imdādullah strove to bring Deobandīs and Barelvīs closer by identifying common ground in their ideological positions. But ironically, following the publication of this text, his ecumenical exegesis had the opposite effect, with each group claiming that he had endorsed its reformist program.

The ambiguity of Imdādullah's discourse also generated a fair degree of consternation within Deoband circles, as his Deoband disciples were compelled to address questions regarding the limits of master-disciple disagreement and to justify aspects of his thought that seemed at odds with their reform project. Ultimately, any possibility of interpretive plurality in *FHM* was laid to rest through a prominent Deoband scholar's fascinating dream narrative concerning *FHM*, discussed later in this chapter, in which the Prophet Muhammad himself appeared on earth to decide in favor of the Deoband *'ulamā'*. The mobilization of this dream narrative revealed an important ambiguity in how the Deoband pioneers presented their relationship with Imdādullah. At the same time as they insisted on no disagreement with their Sufi master they also oneirically mobilized the Prophet to establish the superiority of their position. These are the kinds of ambiguities and tensions that this chapter brings into view. Let me begin, though, by briefly introducing Imdādullah and his scholarly career, especially in relation to his role and place in the Deoband hierarchy and in South Asian Muslim intellectual traditions more broadly.

Ḥājī Imdādullah: An Exilic Traditionalist Sufi

Born in 1814, Ḥājī Imdādullah was a curious personality who traversed multiple intellectual, ideological, linguistic, and physical spaces. As someone who lived almost the entirety of the nineteenth century (he died in 1899), he also embodied the transitional character of the moment in which he lived. As Seema Alavi has recently argued, Imdādullah was among a number of nineteenth-century South Asian Muslim scholars who created and benefited from a variety of transnational intellectual and social networks.[2]

Imdādullah's original name at birth was Imdād Ḥusayn, but he was later given the title of Imdādullah by one of his early mentors, Muḥammad Isḥāq. As the twentieth-century biographer Muḥammad Anwar al-Ḥasan Sherkotī commented, in a rather sectarian moment of speculation: "Ḥājī Ṣāhib must have dropped 'Ḥusayn' from his name because it carried associations of polytheism" (on account, of course, of the name's association with Shī'ism).[3] Imdādullah was only seven when his mother, Bībī Ḥusaynī (d. 1824), a native of Nānautah, passed away, and his father Ḥāfiẓ Muḥammad Amīn, had died before his birth. Right before her death, Bībī Ḥusaynī had willed that Imdādullah, the third of her children, not be subjected to any scolding or strict physical discipline in his educational training.[4] It was as if she were nurturing on her deathbed what was later to become her son's trademark temperate and conflict-averse outlook. Imdādullah began the process of memorizing the Qur'ān when he was seven but did not complete this task until much later, after he moved to Mecca.

A decisive moment of his intellectual career occurred when, at the age of sixteen, he traveled to Delhi with Mamlūk 'Alī (d. 1851), then president of the Department of Eastern Studies at Delhi College. It was at Delhi College that Imdādullah received his first round of education in Persian and Arabic. Imdādullah's Sufi master, who trained him in all the major Sufi orders, was the thunderously named Miyānjī Nūr Muḥammad Jhanjhānvī (d. 1843) from the village of Jhanjhāna in Muzaffargarh in Uttar Pradesh.[5] Before he became a major Sufi master, Jhanjhānvī used to teach the Qur'ān and Persian to children at a local mosque in the village of Lohārī (today in Haryāna), some fifty-three kilometers from Jhanjhāna. His food, accommodation, and a salary of two rupees a month were paid for by an affluent woman in the area known as Iqbāl Baygam; he would take every Friday off to visit his home in Jhanjhāna. Jhanjhānvī was later trained in the Chishtī Sufi path by the famed scholar Shāh 'Abdul Rahīm Fāṭimī Wilāyatī (d. 1831). It was in Jhanjhānvī's discipleship that Imdādullah became an expert in the Chishtī Ṣābirī Sufi path. Indeed, Jhanjhānvī's death in 1843 was said to have so devastated Imdādullah, who was then twenty-nine, that he apparently ventured off for days to the wilderness in Panjāb, abstaining from any food or drink. These conditions were ripe for his being visited in dreams and visions by Sufi luminaries of the past, including Mu'īnuddin Chishtī, who revealed to Imdādullah the secrets of the path.[6] Imdādullah maintained an active Sufi lodge, Khānqāh-yi Imdādīya, in his native village, Thāna Bhavan, while he was in India; it was burned down during the Indian Mutiny of 1857.[7]

Imdādullah was thus a noted Sufi master who was mentored and trained by the most influential *'ulamā'* of modern South Asia. His writings include several seminal essays on various aspects of Sufi meditation, thought, and practice, arguably the most famous of which is the meditation text *The Light of Hearts* (*Ziyā' al-Qulūb*), admirably analyzed by Scott Kugle.[8] He also composed plentiful poetry in both Persian and Urdu, including such well-known pieces as "The Greater *Jihād*" (*Jihād-i Akbar*) and "The Garden of Knowledge" (*Gulzār-i Ma'rifat*). Imdādullah holds a coveted place in the intellectual genealogies of Chishtī Sufism and the Deoband madrasa.[9] His legacy today is dominated by his role as the Sufi master of the pioneers of Deoband: Qāsim Nānautvī, Rashīd Aḥmad Gangohī, and then later Ashraf 'Alī Thānvī. As this chapter will show, a defining feature of Imdādullah's personality was his proclivity for compromise and mutual understanding and his dislike of antagonism, polemical warfare, and discord. However, his penchant for avoiding conflict and his generally mild temperament did not keep him from playing a prominent and at times actively militaristic role in anticolonial resistance.

Imdādullah was charged with sedition on account of his alleged organization of militias against the British in the 1857 Mutiny. The precise scope and nature of his involvement in the war are difficult to determine. However, the hagiographic sources confidently portray Imdādullah as a "hero of the war" who was at the forefront of organizing and participating in active combat.[10] Aided by his close associates, including Nānautvī, Gangohī, and his bosom Sufi colleague Muḥammad Zāmin (d. 1857), Imdādullah is said to have successfully orchestrated an attack on a British tank as it was passing from the town of Shāmlī in Sāharanpūr district. Unfortunately, Zāmin was shot during the battle and died, a tragedy intensely memorialized in Deoband hagiography. In the aftermath of the Shāmlī battle, the British were determined to arrest Imdādullah. But he miraculously escaped all such attempts.

The most iconic and frequently retold story involves the moment when Imdādullah, while on the run, took refuge in a horse stable in Anbālā district in Uttar Pradesh. It was owned by one of his loyalists, a local notable called Rāo 'Abdullah. When the British collector of the district (charged with supervising the district's general administration) got word of this hiding place, he came out to 'Abdullah's stable to find and arrest Imdādullah under the pretext of inspecting some new horses. 'Abdullah and his confederates could do nothing but wait helplessly for Imdādullah's capture. But when the collector pushed open the door of the stable, there was no one inside. Imdādullah had miraculously disappeared. His bed, prayer mat, and water container for ablutions were all in place. Even the earth was still moist from the water used for ablution. But he could not be seen anywhere. And as soon as the British collector left, Imdādullah became visible again, seated on his prayer mat. His elevated spiritual status had allowed him to become invisible to others.[11] Soon thereafter, he traveled to Panjāb, paid a visit to the shrine of Sufi master Farīd al-Dīn Ganj Shakar (d. 1265) in Pākpattan, and made his way to the Karachi port. From there, in 1859, he boarded a ship that took him to Mecca and never returned again to India.[12] His last four decades in exile earned him the title "Muhājir Makkī," or "the Meccan Exile."

Though physically removed from India, Imdādullah remained intimately connected to Muslim intellectual circles. While in exile, he trained and cultivated a number of disciples who went on to become some of the most prominent Muslim scholars in South Asia. His disciples included not only the Deoband pioneers but also many of their opponents. In fact, Maulvī 'Abdul Samī', the arch-anti-Deoband polemicist and author of the scathing *Glistening Lights* whom we met in earlier chapters, was also one of Imdādullah's close disciples. After taking him as a disciple in India, Imdādullah maintained active correspondence with Samī' during his later Meccan years, including during the height of the latter's debate with the Deoband pioneers. Imdādullah's diverse and at times fractious followers are a crucial backdrop to *FHM* and its ensuing controversy. Imdādullah was keenly aware of the diversity in his pool of disciples and of their competing claims over his intellectual legacy. Indeed, the contention over who represented Imdādullah's true intellectual heirs, a contention I will explore through much of the latter half of this chapter, was an important facet of his self-imagination as a scholar. As he once put it, in a vivid celebration of ambiguity: "Every one interprets me through the color of his own lens, whereas I don't match any of those colors. I am like water. When you pour water in a bottle, it begins to look like the color of the bottle."[13]

Imdādullah found his accommodationist temperament increasingly at odds with the climate of intensifying polemical encounters that gripped the North Indian Muslim intellectual elite by the late nineteenth century. He acutely realized that he was a misfit in this new climate and frequently expressed his dejection and regret about it. For instance, following the publication of *Glistening Lights*, in a July 1887 letter (in Persian) to 'Abdul Samī', Imdādullah registered his displeasure at the "discursive acerbity" (*tayz qalamī*) and the "self-gratifying petulance" (*ghayẓ-i nafsānī*) that characterized the work, telling Samī', "This is not the style of scholars and the intellectual elite." Imdādullah also urged Samī' to refrain from responding to any rebuttals to the text: "Your objective was to express the truth. That was done. Now stop!" (*Qaṣd-i shumā iẓhār-i ḥaqq būd. Ẓāhir shud. Bas!*)[14]

A couple of months later, in another letter to Samī', Imdādullah lamented the polemical fires blazing in Muslim India with more explicit emotion: "Hearing about the conflict between Sufi brothers [in India] makes me sorrowful. It would be good to remain agreeable, keep away ill feelings, and maintain cordial relations. This is a responsibility of the scholarly class [*mawjib-i az diyār-i ma'ārif ast*]."[15] As I will have occasion to reiterate, Imdādullah's efforts to maintain intra-*'ulamā'* harmony were driven by a deep concern to protect the power, integrity, and gravitas of the scholarly elite in the eyes of the masses. His was a thoroughly hierarchical project invested in preserving the differential of intellectual and social capital that accorded the scholarly class its aura and prestige. Polemical entanglements and skirmishes weakened the integrity of this hierarchy; that was the main threat that he sought to contain and confront.

Imdādullah never acquired comprehensive training in Islamic law, though he had studied preliminary texts on jurisprudence and on the Ḥadīth. His Deoband disciples often explained their master's lack of expertise in the legal tradition by casting him as the possessor of knowledge bestowed by God (*'ilm-i laddunī*) that was said to have endowed him with mastery over both scriptural and mystical affairs. According to this logic, Imdādullah received knowledge directly from God, hence rendering the acquisition of formal training in particular knowledge traditions unnecessary. Take, for instance, Qāsim Nānautvī's response when he was once asked, "Is Ḥājī Imdādullah a genuine scholar?" Nānautvī retorted, "The usual meaning of 'a scholar' is irrelevant here because it is from the pure essence of God that he has been made a scholar."[16] At another point when someone shed doubt on Imdādullah's being a scholar, Nānautvī grew tearful and shot back, "What is so important about being a scholar? He is a maker of scholars [*'ālim gar*]."[17]

Ashraf 'Alī Thānvī advanced a similar argument by pointing to Imdādullah's possession of mystic knowledge: "Although Imdādullah was not among the most famous scholars of the *sharī'a*," Thānvī admitted, "he was adorned from head to foot by the jewels of the light of mystic knowledge [*nūr-i 'irfān*]."[18] Once someone asked Thānvī: "Why do so many people leave the *'ulamā'* and flock to Ḥajī Ṣāḥib's service?" Thānvī replied succinctly, "We own words; he owns the meaning" (*Hamāray pās alfāẓ hayn awr wahān ma'ānī*).[19] On another occasion, Thānvī made a curious rhetorical move by boasting of his own scholarly prowess while simultaneously affirming his master's intellectual superiority: "Ḥājī Ṣāhib had only read till the *Kāfiya* [an important early text in the Niẓāmī madrasa curriculum], and I have read so much that I could write another *Kāfiya*. But Hazrat's knowledge was such that in comparison to him the specialists in law and jurisprudence grasped no reality."[20]

These statements show the concerted interest Deoband pioneers took in framing their master's apparent lack of training in the *sharī'a* in a manner that kept the latter's religious authority intact. But for all his lack of expertise in matters of law and jurisprudence, Imdādullah was quite comfortable assembling normative legal arguments in *FHM*. In fact, as I hope to show in what follows, Imdādullah's discursive strategies in *FHM* escaped any obvious categorization. By creatively drawing on multiple logics and sources of knowledge including law, mystical knowledge, and everyday experience, Imdādullah devised a hermeneutic of reconciliation that was thoroughly heterological, eluding facile binaries like law/mysticism, inclusive/exclusive, and moderate/extreme. I now turn to a more detailed exploration of this hermeneutic.

A Hermeneutics of Reconciliation: The Structure of *Faysala-i Haft Mas'ala*

What drove Imdādullah to compose *FHM*? And why did he feel compelled to urgently take up the task of achieving rapprochement between the rival groups of South Asian *'ulamā'*? He addressed these questions at the outset:

> I believe that it is among the absolutely established principles that mutual harmony is a source of worldly and religious blessings and disunity is a cause of worldly and religious harm. These days certain secondary issues [*masā'il-i far'īya*] have produced such disagreement that they have resulted in all kinds of malignant and contentious disputes. And the time of the scholarly elite and the religion of the masses are going to waste. For in truth these disputes are driven by differences of mere semantics, and the goals of the competing parties are the same. I feel greatly perturbed by the general condition of Indian Muslims and especially of those with whom I am personally connected. Therefore, I felt compelled to write and publish a brief treatise on the aforementioned problems. I sincerely hope that it will resolve these conflicts and controversies.[21]

He went on to share his rationale for selecting the issues that the text focused on. By selecting controversies that occupied his disciples, he explained, he could keep his task manageable and also increase the chances of finding a resolution. He further explained that he had given priority of order and coverage to the most contentious issues followed by the ones that were less so. Hence the celebration of the Prophet's birthday was the first problem tackled. Imdādullah concluded his introduction to the treatise with a stern message for his readers: "If you benefit from this treatise, remember me in your prayers. But please don't bother with a rebuttal. I have no intention of engaging in [further] debates" (3).

There was much in Imdādullah's exposition that the Deoband pioneers would have endorsed with no hesitation. For instance, much like his Deoband disciples, Imdādullah insisted that it was a heretical innovation—a concept he defined as the introduction of the nonsalvational into the domain of salvation (*ghayr dīn ko dīn mayn dākhil kar līya jāway*)—to view as obligatory the particularities attached to the *mawlid*, like standing up in reverence to the Prophet (*qiyām*) (4). Imdādullah also argued that the line between permissibility and heresy was crossed when an actor began to confuse the particularities of the *mawlid* with obligatory practices such as praying and fasting. His explanation of this principle went like this:

> If one believes that if the *mawlid* is not held on its designated date, or if the standing up at the end of the ceremony [*qiyām*] does not take place, or if the provision of sweets is not arranged for, then the blessings [of the ceremony] will not be received, then certainly this belief is prohibited. Such a belief represents a transgression of legal limits. *Just as understanding a permissible action as prohibited and blameworthy is unjustified, so too is turning a permissible practice into an obligation* [emphasis mine]. In short, in both of these cases there is a transgression of limits [*ta'adī-yi ḥudūd*]. (4)

This was a remarkable example of a Sufi master proffering legal arguments based on subtle distinctions and boundaries. But while the legal dimension of Imdādullah's argument corresponded seamlessly with that of his Deoband disciples, the emphasis of his thought, unlike theirs, was on determining the intention with which an act was undertaken. Imdādullah made the curious argument that if one understood or intended the particularities of the *mawlid* (like standing up, distributing sweets, or specifying a date) as necessary, in the sense not of meeting a normative legal requirement but of receiving certain blessings, then that was not censurable. His elaboration of this point is worth considering in his own words:

> While performing certain rituals, one must attend to certain specifications, without which the profound effect [*asr-i khāṣ*] of those rituals is not realized. For instance, some rituals must be performed while standing. If performed while sitting, they will not produce their profound effect. With this consideration, if one understands standing up during the performance of the *mawlid* as necessary and the proof for arriving at this conclusion is the experience, mystical illuminations, or inspiration of the inventors of these practices [*mūjidān-i 'amal kā tajrabah, kashf yā ilhām*], then that is not heretical innovation. (4–5)

Having established his fidelity to the normative boundaries of the law, Imdādullah went on to offer possibilities of knowledge that went beyond the law and its limits, namely knowledge through experience and nondiscursive illuminations. Notice that this heterological approach did not posit or depend on a law/mysticism binary. To the contrary, for Imdādullah, the profound effect of religious experience was available only if and when the normative boundaries of the law were not transgressed or violated. Honoring legal boundaries was a prerequisite for the achievement of experiential and mystical knowledge necessary to engage the specificities of a ritual such as the *mawlid* in a spiritually effective and normatively legitimate fashion.

Central to Imdādullah's hermeneutic was his mobilization of the category of *maṣlaḥa*, commonly translated as "public welfare" or "public" interest. In Imdādullah's hands, however, *maṣlaḥa* was employed less in its legal sense of public welfare than in the sense of expedience or convenience. If the specific forms and particularities of a ritual such as the *mawlid* had been designated as such because of an attached expedience, then those forms and particularities could not be called heretical innovations, he argued. So for instance, if one designated a specific date for the *mawlid* to take place, such as the twelfth *rabīʿ al-awwal*, because of the expected convenience afforded by the ease of continuity from one year to the next, then that specification would not constitute a heretical innovation. Similarly, with respect to the *qiyām*, Imdādullah reasoned that "if one does not believe standing during the performance of the *mawlid* to be worship in its essence but instead regards hallowing the remembrance of the Prophet as the ultimate object of worship and has designated this form because of an associated expediency, then that is not heretical innovation" (5). He further asserted that "the detailed arguments on these problems are extensive, and for every instance there exists a separate reasoning. Certain forms of expediency [*maṣāliḥ*] are also mentioned in treatises on the celebration of the Prophet's birthday" (5).

Imdādullah's invocation of expediency as a normative legitimizer of particularities and specifications attached to a ritual reveals his confidence in the unspoken collective consensus of a community. If a community agreed to and formalized a specific form of a ritual on account of certain conveniences that it provided them, then there was no need to outlaw that form, he argued. Even if the particularities of a ritual were not sanctioned by the normative sources of the religion, so long as they were woven into the social fabric of a community, they could not be deemed illegitimate. For Imdādullah, the ritual life of a community could not be divorced from its specific conditions and from considerations of its own ease and convenience. In a clever move, Imdādullah made normative space for the *mawlid* and the specific forms in which it was practiced in India through recourse to the expedience and convenience of the public on the one hand, and to the experiential demands of the ritual on the other.

Time, Reason, and Community

Imdādullah's understanding of *maṣlaḥa* was also informed by the way he approached the relationship between a community's ritual life and time. He explained this relationship most elaborately in his discussion of the ritual of distributing and praying over food for the transmission of blessings to the deceased, an issue he considered the second most controversial after the *mawlid*. Imdādullah narrated the history of this ritual to show the reasoning and process through which its specific forms and elements became current among South Asian Muslims. Below I present some highlights from this historical sketch. It offers a particularly good example of how Imdādullah appealed to the interrelatedness of time, ritual, and communal norms as a way to legitimize new forms and specificities that over time became attached to a ritual practice. As he told the story:

> It seems that the practice of preparing food and offering it to the destitute as a way of transmitting blessings to the deceased existed among the early Muslim community, though it seems that in that era people used to make the intention of transmitting blessings silently in their hearts without enunciation. Then among later Muslims it occurred to some people that during the five daily prayers, although the intention to pray could be made silently, the masses were encouraged to enunciate their intentions so as to harmonize the heart and tongue. Similarly, in this case, they rea-

soned, it would be preferable to enunciate a prayer after the preparation of food: for example, saying, "O God, may the rewards from this food reach [the soul of] such and such a person." Later, someone further reasoned that this food for charity would satisfy the heart even more if the person offering it placed it in front of him or her while saying the prayer. So that was what began to happen. Then someone thought that the prospects of a supplication's acceptance would rise if some parts of the Qur'an were also recited at this moment, so, short verses from the Qur'an began to be recited. And then it was thought that raising one's hands while saying a prayer was among the Prophet's practices. So people began to raise their hands over the food as they said a prayer. (7–8)

These new additions to the ritual were not objectionable, Imdādullah argued. This was so because these incremental additions and innovations were inspired by what one might call the community's common sense accumulated over layers of time and collective experience. It was this notion of public reason informed by a combination of expedience and a community's unsaid affective consensus that formed Imdādullah's understanding of the idea of *maṣlaḥa* or the Urdu *maṣlaḥat*. When a ritual traveled over time, he gently reminded his readers, it acquired new forms and specificities in accordance with the temperament and collective taste, sensibilities, and aesthetics of a community. Such new forms and specificities, so long as they did not oppose the normative order of the religion, could not be called heretical innovations.

Note in passing the significant contrast between Imdādullah's reading of this ritual and its history and the approach of Shāh Muḥammad Ismā'īl and Ashraf 'Alī Thānvī to this very ritual, as discussed earlier in chapter 7. Ismā'īl and Thānvī had lamented the manner in which people were no longer mindful of the original purpose for which this ritual had been undertaken (the transmission of blessings to the deceased through an act of charity). Instead, Ismā'īl and Thānvī protested, people were attached only to the external forms of this ritual at the expense of recognizing its meaning and objective. And this blind unarticulated attachment to specific forms and procedures had generated a widespread culture of affectation and insincerity in the manner and attitude with which this ritual was undertaken. So Ismā'īl and Thānvī concluded.

While Imdādullah would also have found affectation and hollow intentions reprehensible, he articulated a strikingly different conception of the interaction of time, ritual, and community. In contrast to Ismā'īl and Thānvī, Imdādullah seemed unperturbed by the absence of the articulation of the ritual's reason or purpose during its performance. For Imdādullah, the performative and the cognitive went hand in hand. The reason for a ritual was embedded in its practice, which in turn was informed by a series of collective experiences, experiments, and deliberations. At the heart of the difference between Imdādullah's attitude and that of Ismā'īl's and Thānvī's was their differing approaches to the impact of time and history on the development of a community's ritual life. For the latter, time and history had the corrupting influence of burying the original purpose and reason of a ritual that in their view became calcified in the ever-hardening shell of new forms and specificities. But Imdādullah did not imagine the evolution of history and time in such ominous terms. For him, reason and form evolved together with the passage of time. Reason was not divorced from form. In fact, it was precisely in the disciplined practice of a ritual, as fashioned by a community's experiences and preferences over time, that its reason was located. Reason, experience, and time worked in tandem. So rather than reminding the masses of their responsibility to an original time by exhorting them to shed accreted forms and specificities, Imdādullah carved normative space for such forms and specificities under the category of *maṣlaḥa* or public reason/expedience.

Imdādullah applied a similar hermeneutic while addressing the contention surrounding the ritual of commemorating the death anniversaries of Sufi masters (*'urs*). *'Urs*, literally meaning "wedding," is a widespread and long-standing ritual that marks a Sufi master's death anniversary, or wedding/union with the ultimate beloved, God. The textual foundations of this ritual are often traced to an evocative saying of the Prophet, "Sleep the sleep of brides" (*nim ka nawmat al-'urūs*), which connects death and divine love in arresting erotic imagery. Just as the wedding night marks the consummation of a worldly marriage, the moment of death consummates marriage with the divine. Often lasting a few days, *'urs* combines text, space, and ritual as the memory of a Sufi master is honored through panegyric recitations of the master's discourses, meditation exercises, and the offering of food for the transmission of blessings, among other such reverential practices. These activities usually take place at the shrine or burial place of Sufi masters, thus connecting the physical space marking their union with the divine to their discursive and bodily charisma.[22] Among the controversies attached to this ritual is the practice of listening to devotional music as a form of meditation (*samā‘*), a practice that has been intensely contested through much of Muslim history. And as with the dispute surrounding the celebration of the Prophet's birthday, the festival-like ambience found frequently at *‘urs* gatherings has been a subject of much contention, originating in the Prophet's statement "Do not turn my grave into a site of festivity" (*Lā tattakhidū qabrī ‘īdan*).

Imdādullah exonerated the *‘urs* from the charge of heresy by highlighting the different ways in which it served the community's interests and devotional needs. First, he argued, the *‘urs* fulfilled the pious objective of transmitting blessings to the souls of esteemed Sufi sages. Second, it provided a venue for people from a Sufi order to meet each other every year, thus nourishing mutual love. Moreover, Imdādullah pointed out, since several Sufi masters gathered at the *‘urs*, it allowed aspiring disciples to look for and find a master (9). But what about the Prophet's reprimand against festivities at his gravesite? Imdādullah claimed that it applied only to situations where people engaged in excessive celebration, pomp, and decorative display while gathering at graves. This was so because such conviviality contravened the foundational purpose of visiting graves: reflecting on death and the afterlife. However, Imdādullah stressed, this prophetic saying could not be taken to prohibit gathering at gravesites altogether. If that were the case, then the crowds of people who visited the Prophet's grave in Medina would all count as heretics (9). Again, much as in his approach toward the *mawlid* and *īṣāl-i sawāb*, the community's experience and expedience were key factors in Imdādullah's hermeneutical strategy of legitimizing the specifications attached to *‘urs*.

Critically, however, this recourse to expediency and experience was qualified by the categorical affirmation of the legal principle that an actor must not view nonobligatory acts as obligatory. Imdādullah at once established his fidelity to the law and its limits while also pointing to avenues of knowledge and experience that went beyond the law. But the emphasis of his exposition, it would be fair to say, was less on preventing the simulation of obligatory acts by nonobligatory ones (as was the case with Deoband scholars) and more on securing normative allowance for rituals like the *mawlid* in a manner that did not transgress the boundaries of the *sharī'a*. The middle ground Imdādullah strove to reach is perhaps best captured by a statement of his that I also quoted earlier: "Just as understanding a permissible action as prohibited and blameworthy is unjustified, so too is turning a permissible practice into an obligation" (4).

The Etiquette of Pastoral Regulation

Let me return to the *mawlid*. Imdādullah was at pains to underscore that scholars who prohibited the excesses of the masses during such rituals had to do so in a cautious and discerning way. He insisted that they must not rush to condemn a practice universally before carefully ascertaining the specific conditions in which it took place and investigating the intentions of its practitioners. For Imdādullah, the specter of heretical innovation should be raised only selectively, in situations where major doctrinal corruptions such as believing a nonobligatory practice like the *qiyām* to be obligatory were incontrovertibly established. Otherwise, attaching the label of heretical innovation to a particular ritual like the Prophet's birthday celebration in a generalized and blanket manner was unjustified. As he wrote, "Some scholars, merely after witnessing certain excesses of the ignorant masses, such as singing, reciting, and so on, as they take place in the assemblies of the ignorant, impose a single and uniform injunction on all the celebrations of the Prophet's birthday. This is also contrary to justice" (5).

If one followed such a harsh policy of doctrinal policing, Imdādullah hypothetically reasoned, then one would have to prohibit even sermons and preaching assemblies, since one might argue that the mingling of men and women at such venues could generate unwanted sexual temptations. One could not preemptively strike down devotional rituals and pious practices to prevent the sporadic intrusion of moral harm and corruption. Or, as he teasingly put it, quoting a Persian saying, "Because of one flea you don't burn the entire carpet" (*Bahr-i kīkay tū galīmeh rā ma sūz*) (6). Imdādullah also advanced the principle that "when a person is found practicing a ritual in an objectionable manner, the focus of a scholar should be on educating that person and correcting his practice rather than on prohibiting the ritual altogether" (10). Prohibition would only create more problems, Imdādullah stressed. In all likelihood, such a person would not abandon the ritual in any case, so pressuring him or her to do so would only make things worse.

It was not only scholars whom Imdādullah urged to keep a cautious and positive attitude. In an intriguing move, he further argued that the people in a community must not rush to firm conclusions about the reason behind a scholar's censure of someone in their community. In other words, if they saw someone being censured by a scholar, they must not presume that such censuring necessarily implied the corruption or moral failing of the person censured. Although such censuring might well have taken place because of a corrupt attitude or practice, such as understanding the *qiyām* as a legal obligation, there could be a number of other possibilities (5).

Imdādullah offered the following situations as examples of moments when a scholar's objection to a given practice might not be inspired by normative legal considerations. For instance, suppose a saintly or elderly figure entered an assembly and everyone stood up in respect but one person kept his seat. In this situation, the person who did not stand up might be censured, not because of abandoning a normative legal obligation, but because of opposing the rules of the assembly. Similarly, it was a widespread practice in India that after the completion of the Qur'ān during the month of Ramaḍān (as part of the nightly *tarāwīḥ* prayers), sweets were distributed. Now someone who did not distribute sweets might be censured. But, and this was Imdādullah's point, the person would be censured, not for the violation of any law, but for opposition to a beneficial tradition (5).

It seems as though Imdādullah was keen to rescue the pastoral concerns of the scholarly elite from the sledgehammer of positive law. The pastoral efforts of scholars to reform and protect the everyday lives of the masses could not be reduced to normative legal considerations. By highlighting nonlegal factors that could cause someone to be censured, he tried to lighten a censure's communal and doctrinal weight. Rather than rushing to the conclusion that a person who was rebuked by a scholar must have committed the egregious crime of opposing God's law and its limits, members of a community should adopt a more generous and less incriminating attitude in such moments, Imdādullah suggested. An expansive and flexible hermeneutic open to entertaining multiple possibilities, rather than one that was rigidly accusatory, provided the best opportunity to lower the heat of debate among Indian Muslims. Imdādullah's most difficult task, however, was to resolve the thorny issue of the Prophet's knowledge of the unknown. I turn now to that discussion.

Celebrating Ambiguity

While engaging the question of the Prophet's knowledge of the unknown, Imdādullah advanced a characteristically nuanced position that people on both sides of the debate would have found at once a vindication and a reprimand. Imdādullah explicitly affirmed the Prophet's capacity to appear at multiple locations during the *mawlid*. As he put it:

> As far as the belief that the Prophet himself appears on the occasion of his birthday celebration is concerned, to declare this belief as unbelief and polytheism is excessive. This is so because the Prophet's appearance at this gathering is possible, according to both rational [*'aqlan*] and revelatory [*naqlan*] proofs. Those who are at a certain level [of spiritual accomplishment] can indeed detect the light of the Prophet's presence. And as far as the doubt regarding how the Prophet knows that he has to be present at multiple locations simultaneously, this is a weak doubt. When one considers the breadth of the Prophet's spiritual knowledge that is established from both traditional proofs and mystical revelations, this is a trivial matter. (6)

Imdādullah was quick to qualify this capacious statement by adding "But from this it does not become necessary to believe that the Prophet possesses 'knowledge of the unknown' [*'ilm-i ghayb*]. Knowledge of the unknown is among the specificities of God's essence" (6). He nevertheless pointed out that "*it is not essential to God's being that his creation possess knowledge of the unknown* [emphasis mine]; that knowledge is gifted to creation through the signs of divine lordship. Not only is such knowledge possible; it can also be actualized. So how could a belief in something possible be polytheism and unbelief?" (6).

This was not the end to Imdādullah's hermeneutical gymnastics. He introduced a further caveat: the potential knowledge of the unknown possessed by the Prophet need not be actualized. In his words, "Now of course, for every possible thing, actuality is not necessary." To hold such a belief, he went on, "is contingent on finding a proof. If someone finds a proof—for example, if he experiences an unveiling [of divine secrets] or is informed by someone else who has gone through an unveiling—in that case the belief is valid. Otherwise, without any proof, it would be a fanciful mistake. In such a situation, it would be necessary for him to retreat from his error" (6). Imdādullah concluded his examination of this problem with the declaration "But it [belief in the Prophet's knowledge of the unknown] cannot be polytheism and unbelief in any way" (6).

In characteristic style, Imdādullah strove to highlight the varied dimensions of the issue in an effort to find common ground and to show the legitimacy of the concerns and assumptions undergirding each competing position. The gist of his position was familiar, namely that the Prophet's knowledge of the unknown was possible though not necessary and that while such knowledge was essential to God's being, he could grant it to his creation, including to the Prophet. Therefore, one could not regard belief in the Prophet's capacity to possess such knowledge as heresy or unbelief.

But crucial to note here is not just the content of Imdādullah's position. Equally instructive is the way he presented and articulated that position. In particular, note the contrast between his argumentative temperament and that of the Deobandī and Barelvī pioneers described in the previous chapters. Imdādullah's focus was less on conclusively establishing his position over that of his rivals than on elucidating the multiple interpretive possibilities and ambiguities attached to a particular doctrinal problem. He strove to exhibit the multiplicity of ways in which a question could be addressed in order to relax the finality or absoluteness of any singular stance. Instead of seeking to prove and firmly establish a doctrinal claim, he fashioned a hermeneutic that explored, invited, and celebrated ambiguity.

Such ambiguity, however, was neither vacuous nor unrestricted and open to any interpretive move. To the contrary, while strictly grounding himself in the normative boundaries of the tradition, Imdādullah also sought to display the nuance and ambiguity available within the parameters of those normative boundaries. By celebrating ambiguity, he labored to craft a hermeneutic that was above all invested in securing and preserving the integrity of human relations. In fact, Imdādullah explicitly went beyond interpretive matters and presented a somewhat detailed blueprint for how scholars and the laity should approach and resolve their differences. As part of this program, he also prescribed particular attitudes and sensibilities, the cultivation of which, in his view, could prevent the germination of discord and antagonism. Imdādullah's prescriptions, to which I now turn, offer an illuminating example of a code of conduct designed by a Sufi master to encourage mutual harmony and understanding among his rival disciples.

The Etiquette of Disagreement

Imdādullah exhorted the scholarly elite to treat their differences in a manner that did not injure the credibility of their opponents or destroy everyday social relations between factions. As he advised, "They [the scholarly elite] should not harbor any enmity and scorn for another faction. Also, they should not view their opponents with antipathy and ridicule, or judge them to be heretical or as people who have gone astray. . . . And they should keep the conventions of mutual amity and open communication, the expression of peace and love, and the exchange of greetings current" (6). Imdādullah further advised his disciples to abstain from writing refutations and repudiations, and as he put it, from "writing *fatwās* and from signing and sealing *fatwās*, for that is foolishness!" (6). The most remarkable illustration of his proposed method for encouraging amity and goodwill among his warring disciples was seen in his recipe for how they must engage the most contentious issue of standing up in reverence to the Prophet during his birthday celebration (the *qiyām*).

At the crux of Imdādullah's proposal was the plea to extend to the other with whom one disagreed the benefit of doubt and to voice one's own opinions on contentious issues in a restrained and gentle fashion. Moreover, he suggested that one remain mindful of not attacking others' doctrinal commitments and sensibilities regarding how they performed their everyday religious life. So, for instance, he proposed that if an opponent of the *qiyām* participated in a gathering hosted by its proponents, then it was best if the *qiyām* did not take place there so as to prevent any disruption. But, he continued, if the *qiyām* were in fact to take place, then its opponents should also reciprocate the gesture of reconciliation by addressing the excesses and the transgressions of the masses only in a gentle fashion. A gentle approach, he gently pleaded, would be more beneficial to their overall project of religious reform (6).

Crucially, Imdādullah's point was not that the opposing parties should retreat from or abandon their positions altogether. Rather, they should articulate and air their opinions in a manner that cast the intentions of their opponents in the best possible light. By such means, he hoped, the eruption of unrest and controversy could be prevented.

So, what did such a nonincendiary attitude look like? Imdādullah offered concrete suggestions addressing this question. With regard to the scholarly elite, he advised the proponents of controversial practices like the *mawlid* to adopt the following view regarding the opponents of this practice: even though they occasionally prohibit and abstain from the *mawlid*, there is much common ground in our overall views and positions. On the other hand, Imdādullah contended, "The opponents of the *mawlid* must also give a favorable interpretation of the position of the proponents: that they [the proponents] too must support the *mawlid* because of this very reason of minimizing dissent or because they have been overpowered by their love for the Prophet" (7).

Imdādullah's advice to the common people is best put in his own words: "As for the laity, they should follow the research provided by a devout and serious scholar. They should not oppose people who hold other points of view, and they should especially refrain from insulting the dignity of the *'ulamā'* of other religious groups, for doing so is tantamount to 'small mouth and big talk.' From backbiting and envy, even good deeds go to waste" (7). Further, he lectured, "The masses should not read complicated books and articles that contain intellectual expositions on contentious questions. That is the job of the *'ulamā'* [the scholars]" (7). In a brief yet revealing moment, Imdādullah declared his own practice regarding the *mawlid* and admitted that he did indeed participate in it. In fact, he went a step further by announcing: "I am indeed attached to that assembly and find it a source of pleasure and satisfaction" (7). But it is perhaps Imdādullah's description of his practice concerning the *fātiḥa*, the transmission of blessings to the deceased, that best captures the spirit of his thought and attitude: "I am not bound to any specific form of this ritual, but I don't denounce those who are" (9).

Imdādullah concluded his exposition with a "will" (*waṣīyat*) in which he made the curious move of affirming his loyalty to the Deoband project by extolling his disciple Rashīd Aḥmad Gangohī, who was one of the founders of the Deobandī school. In what reads like a postscript, this will was addressed to the opponents and proponents of Deoband and Gangohī. Imdādullah advised the opponents of Deoband to consider Gangohī's presence in India a source of utmost good fortune and a supreme blessing. He urged them to seek from him spiritual guidance and tutelage. Imdādullah described Gangohī as someone who combined apparent and inner perfections and whose thought bore no trace of egoism. And as if protecting his disciple from polemical cross-fires, he implored the followers and supporters of Deoband to avoid bringing up disputatious issues in Gangohī's presence (13–14). "Don't involve him in your fights!" (14). The final sentence was as simple and pithy as it was penetrating and meaningful: "Everyone should avoid expending his precious life on [unrewarding] conflicts and polemics, for that veils the true beloved [God]" (14).

Beyond the Law/Sufism Binary

Ḥājī Imdādullah's discourse in *FHM* creatively drew from multiple sources of knowledge, including legal reasoning, mystical knowledge, and personal experience. This was not a Sufi defense of popular customs and rituals articulated against the ire of legal reformists, as a hasty recourse to the law/Sufism binary would push us to assume. Certainly, even a cursory reading of this text makes abundantly clear that Imdādullah disapproved of the intensity with which his *'ulamā'* disciples, especially his Deoband disciples, were critiquing rituals such as the *mawlid* in India. However, even while registering his disapproval, he was careful to secure the legitimacy and credibility of his argument according to the protocols of normative legal reasoning. Imdādullah did not abandon the law or the normative precepts attached to it. Rather, he went beyond the law as he took a hermeneutical approach that joined the mystical to the legal and delicately balanced the sovereignty of divine law with the integrity of human relations.

Indeed, as I said earlier, the cornerstone of Imdādullah's project was his desire to preserve the integrity of human relations. Even amid the most hostile disagreements, the etiquette of keeping current conventions of everyday social relations needed to remain uninjured. Imdādullah was also very sensitive to preserving the integrity of the pastoral relationship between religious scholars and the common folk. One of the things he found most disturbing about a culture of polemics and incessant antagonism was its capacity to weaken the bond of trust and respect between the scholarly elite and the masses. Ultimately, untempered animosity between rival factions of religious scholars, regardless of which side of the debate they took, could only harm their overall stature and aura in the long run. This was so because as group polemics and name-calling between factions escalated, the masses would feel freer to impugn the authority of scholars from the opposing ideological camp. Imdādullah warned his *'ulamā'* disciples that even if they succeeded in scoring a doctrinal point or two, if the fire from their polemical warfare raged out of control, it would only burn down the entire edifice of the religious authority they held over the masses. Reducing the heat of this polemical fire was imperative to maintaining the traditional hierarchy that distinguished the knowledgeable scholarly class from the cattle-like masses they had been entrusted to guide and command.

The scholar-commoner hierarchy also informed Imdādullah's views on controversial theological questions. For instance, in his discussion on God's capacity to lie (*imkān-i kizb*) and his capacity to create a second Muḥammad (*imkān-i naẓīr*), Imdādullah advised scholars to minimize conversations and debates on these sensitive issues. If they had to exercise their intellectual prowess, he further counseled, they should do so either in private or through the exchange of brief letters rather than by the publication of elaborate books and treatises. Curiously, he went on to suggest that if scholars could not contain the desire to write a book or article on such delicate subjects, they should do so only in Arabic. Otherwise, they might harm the masses by embroiling the latter in issues beyond their capacity and understanding. And the masses, Imdādullah forcefully underscored, should be formally prohibited from speaking about and discussing such matters (13). Note that this prohibition stood in some contrast to his earlier principle that the masses should not be prohibited from engaging in a ritual even if the manner in which they did so required reform and correction. Imdādullah was not willing to show flexibility or take any risks when it came to theological matters. Theological land mines were best altogether avoided, lest they do irreparable damage to the integrity of established intellectual and social norms.

Hermeneutically, the balancing act Imdādullah strove to strike throughout *FHM* was that of protecting the primacy of religious obligations while also making normative space for widely practiced customs and devotional rituals. While negotiating this balancing act, Imdādullah presented himself as a cautious realist. He was careful to categorically declare that understanding a nonobligatory practice as obligatory constituted a heretical innovation. Moreover, he emphasized that one must not pressure others to take part in nonobligatory rituals, a sentiment best summed up in his statement that "from repeated and undue insistence, even a commendable practice can turn into a sin" (5). However, the realist in him was quick to add that if that was not the case, a practice could not be categorized as a heretical innovation.

The key to his argument was the intentionality of the actor. As long as the intention of the actor was not to turn a normatively optional ritual into an obligation upon oneself or anyone else, then that ritual remained permissible. However, if one insisted to the point of making an optional ritual obligatory, then that insistence became impermissible. Furthermore, by warning his followers against the tendency to stick labels on other people on the basis of their apparent actions, Imdādullah registered his displeasure with drawing hasty conclusions about the intentions of the actor. His message to his disciples was clear and simple: you must not make any assumptions about the intentions of the actor; you must not second-guess the intentions of the actor. In contrast to his Deoband disciples who tried to reform or abolish long-established habits and customs, Imdādullah was more of a realist in acknowledging the difficulty of such a transformative project. The regulation and enforcement of divine law must not fracture the integrity of human relations, he argued.

This subtle disagreement and *FHM*'s susceptibility to varied interpretations and readings provided the conditions for a fair bit of contestation over the precise verdict that Imdādullah had delivered in this text. *FHM* generated a great deal of controversy. The opponents of Deoband pounced on it as a clear repudiation of the school by its own master. Meanwhile the pioneers of Deoband scrambled to dispel any such impression of internal rifts and insisted that the text fully endorsed their reform project. Even so, the tensions made visible by *FHM* were apparent. The ways in which the Deoband pioneers negotiated these tensions present an intriguing study of how a master-disciple disagreement is framed, packaged, and circumscribed. It is to some highlights of this negotiation seen in the aftermath of *FHM*'s publication that I now turn. The moments of intra-Deobandī tensions and disagreement that I explore in what follows showcase how disagreement with and devotion to a master can go together—though ultimately, as I will show, the Deoband pioneers deliberately dyed Imdādullah's message in colors that best matched their reformist fabric.

Who Is the Author?

Ironically, one of the main issues of contention that arose in the initial years following *FHM*'s publication related not to its content but to the question of authorship. Even during Imdādullah's life, a widespread rumor began circulating around North India that *FHM* was in fact written not by him but by his then enterprising disciple Ashraf 'Alī Thānvī. In fact, for a significant period of time, this treatise was included in the list of Thānvī's books. A measure of the controversy surrounding the issue of authorship can be gleaned from a story narrated by a devotee of Imdādullah's in India, a certain Ḥājī Sayyid Nūr al- Ḥasan, in which he described the circumstances of a meeting between the two in Mecca:

> In India, in the village *khurja* [in the district Bulandshahr], I was once casually conversing with a certain Khān Ṣāḥib. When the topic of *Fayṣala-yi Haft Mas'ala* came up, he suggested that Ḥājī Imdādullah had not written this essay but that someone else had and then had later attributed it to

> Ḥājī Ṣāḥib. This provocation left my heart in doubt and apprehension. Therefore, when I left for Mecca to perform the Hajj, I took a copy of *Fayṣala-yi Haft-Mas'ala* with me. I decided that when I saw Ḥājī Ṣāḥib, I would read out to him the entire essay word by word to check whether he wrote all of it. Prior to my departure, I met Maulvī Muḥammad Sābiq, who was also heading to Mecca for Ḥajj. I shared this plan of mine with him. He agreed and we decided to visit Ḥājī Imdādullah together. When we reached Mecca, we went to Ḥājī Ṣāḥib's house, and I brought the essay with me. At the time when we were about to kiss his feet [*jis waqt ham qadam bos huway*], he immediately fixed his gaze on Maulvī Sābiq Ṣāḥib and said to him, "Mr. Muḥammad Sābiq [Miān Muḥammad Sābiq], people in India are embroiled in all kinds of strange conflicts. I have also heard that several people have been raising doubts over *Fayṣala-yi Haft Mas'ala*, claiming that it is not written by me [*faqīr*]. But alas! They don't realize that rather than speculating on who wrote the essay, they should focus on the truth that it contains."[23]

He went on to confirm that he was indeed the author of this treatise. He then proceeded to recount and explain the content of *FHM* in detail, starting with the first problem and proceeding all the way to problem number 7.

As Nūr al-Ḥasan put it, "[He explained *FHM*] in such a convincing and thorough fashion that there remained no need for me to read the article word by word to him to verify its authenticity. After hearing Ḥājī Ṣāḥib's explanation, I left his house in peace, and I said to Maulvī Muḥammad Sābiq, 'There you go, we have been satisfied in such a conclusive manner that we did not even need to ask the question. So praise belongs to God.'"[24]

This narrative underscores the controversial character of *FHM* at the time of its release. But more than authorship, it was the content of this text, especially the possibility that Imdādullah might have contravened his Deoband disciples' positions on important normative questions, that was the crux of the controversy. Both Thānvī and Gangohī, the younger and older stalwarts of the Deoband hierarchy, downplayed such a conflict between them and their Sufi master. To the contrary, they argued (an argument I will explore more fully in a moment) that *FHM* in fact reaffirmed their viewpoint. But for all their attempts to dispel any traces of disagreement, at other moments such tensions were obvious. For example, in his monumental biography of Gangohī *Remembering Rashid* (*Tazkirat ar-Rashīd*), 'Āshiq Ilāhī recounts that in the era when the frenzy over *FHM* was at its peak, Gangohī expressed his irritation over the text's reception: "In India everything is fine and there is nothing to worry about. But nowadays," he continued with veiled sarcasm, "we are receiving all kinds of strange news from Arabia."[25]

In what follows, I analyze in more depth the specific points of tension connected to Imdādullah's relationship with his chief Deoband disciples that came under discussion in the immediate aftermath of *FHM*. These points of tension and the discourses surrounding them not only display the subtle but significant internal diversity of positions on the limits of normativity in the early years of Deoband but also reveal a tradition marked by a remarkable capacity for dialogue, deliberation, and argument over thorny questions of managing disagreement in relationships of love, devotion, and discipleship.

The Limits of Disagreement in a Master-Disciple Relationship:

The tensions between Ḥājī Imdādullah and his Deoband disciples can be best analyzed by considering a series of letters between Ashraf 'Alī Thānvī and an anonymous Deobandī questioner who wrote to him in the days following *FHM*'s publication. The questioner sought from Thānvī a convincing rebuttal to the specific doubts and objections raised against the school by its opponents, especially in relation to the credibility of Imdādullah's relationship with his chief Deoband disciples (including Thānvī himself). A self-described sympathizer of Deoband, this questioner requested from Thānvī intellectual ammunition to counter the allegations leveled against the sincerity of Imdādullah's spiritual connection with his Deobandī disciples. In this correspondence, the questioner played the devil's advocate as he listed and explained the specific points of contention he desired Thānvī to address.

In his initial letter to Thānvī, this anonymous questioner raised three issues of contention.

> The first point of contention is whether some of Ḥājī Ṣāḥib's beliefs and practices, as articulated in *FHM*, are genuinely what he believes in or whether they are based on some form of political expedience, meant to assuage the political elite and notables in Mecca. If what he endorses is contrary to what he believes, then he is guilty of dissimulation. In effect he is cast under the sign of the *rawāfiḍ* [a derogatory term for the *Shī'ī*], which would stand in complete contradiction to his external and internal perfections [*ẓāhirī awr bāṭinī kamālāt*]. And if he actually believes in what he wrote, then what is one to make of his relationship with his [Deoband] disciples, who call those very beliefs and practices heretical and misguided? What is one to think of them if their own master opposes what they preach?[26]

The second question addressed a more general and broader issue: Did the institution of the master-disciple relationship require disciples to obey their Sufi master in all matters of religion? Or was it enough for them to demonstrate obedience only in the realm of mystical practices, such as meditation and devotional exercises, and to rely on their own knowledge and judgment when it came to problems of jurisprudence? The reason why this was important to clarify, the questioner explained, was that if the latter were true and the master opposed his disciple in the realm of law and ritual practices, then the master's greatness could not be sustained in the disciple's heart. And as a consequence, the master-disciple relationship could not blossom. On the other hand, if the disciple felt that the beliefs and practices of his master opposed the dicta of the divine norm (*shar'*) and the prophetic model (*sunna*) then he could not maintain a loving relationship with his master. In fact, let alone loving the master, under such circumstances, the master could not even be imagined as eligible for such a lofty status. The heart of the issue was that if the master did not agree with his disciple on the distinction between truth and falsehood, on what was permissible and what constituted misguidance, then how could he serve as the means of enabling the disciple to journey through the spiritual stages [*manāzil*] that lead to God? As the questioner elaborated: "Even if one were to concede that disagreement on matters of practice has occurred since ancient times with no impact on matters regarding the [Sufi] path [*mu'āmalat-i ṭarīqat*], one can reply, first, that this disagreement is no paltry matter. And second, to condone this disagreement would amount to trivializing the established requirement for seekers of truth to look for a master who is a scholar in complete harmony with the prophetic norm [*kāmil-i muttabi'-i sunna*]" (99–100).

The questioner then went on to apply these abstract issues that informed his queries to the specific case of Ḥājī Imdādullah's apparent disagreements with the Deoband pioneers. If one were to accept the premise, he wondered, that the master and disciple must enjoy complete compatibility and that they must be similar in their outlook, doctrinal orientation, and practice (*hum khayāl, hum 'aqīda awr hum 'amal*), then in light of the disagreements between Ḥājī Imdādullah and his disciples, it was apparent that these folk (*hazrāt*) did not meet the requisite test of master-disciple harmony.

The third point of contention raised by the questioner shifted attention from the sincerity or strength of Imdādullah's relationship with his disciples to the question of who the true inheritors of Imdādullah's legacy were, Deobandī scholars such as Rashīd Aḥmad Gangohī and Ashraf 'Ali Thānvī, or the opponents of Deoband like 'Abdul Samī'. As the questioner framed the issue:

> Ḥājī Ṣāḥib's disciples can be divided into two distinct camps, both made up of *'ulamā'*. In one camp, we find people like Maulvī Aḥmad Ḥasan Ṣāḥib Kānpūrī and Shāh 'Abdul Ḥaqq Muhājir Makkī, whose beliefs and practices are like those of Ḥājī Ṣāḥib and other Chishtī Sufis of the Ṣābirīya and Qudūsīya varieties. The other camp consists of Deoband scholars like Maulvī Rashīd Aḥmad Gangohī, Maulvī Ashraf 'Alī Thānvī, and the late Maulvī Muḥammad Qāsim Nānautvī, who call the beliefs and practices of the first group heretical and misguided, to the extent of sometimes even anathematizing them with unbelief and polytheism. So, which of these two camps is the rightful custodian of Ḥājī Ṣāḥib's legacy? And what should one make of Ḥājī Ṣāḥib's practice of bestowing his discipleship upon people from two groups so starkly opposite in their beliefs and practices? (101)

Now let us turn to Thānvī's answers to these incisive questions. Thānvī premised his entire response to these three queries on a distinction he drew between absolute epistemic disagreement and relative differences of opinion. The first category consisted of absolute and irreconcilable differences, while the second represented disagreements generated by contingent factors such as disparity of knowledge about the issue or problem at hand. Thānvī explained that to comprehend the nature of the disagreement in this context, one had to be attentive to the nature of the disputed problems at hand. The debate, he lectured, concerned rituals that were permissible in essence but that became ugly and undesirable because of being accompanied by certain contingent corrupting influences. For example, controversial practices such as the *mawlid* and the recitation of the Qur'ān on the eleventh day of a Sufi master's death belonged to this category. According to Thānvī, one could hold two kinds of opinions about such practices. One could outright deny that the corruptions attached to a practice were in fact undesirable. A person who harbored such an opinion would indeed be sinful and misguided. Moreover, if this were Imdādullah's opinion, then certainly his disagreement with the pioneers of Deoband would be absolute and irreconcilable, Thānvī readily admitted (102).

The other response, Thānvī continued, was to understand these corruptions as undesirable and to prohibit others from engaging in practices infected by them, but to give the masses the benefit of doubt as to whether their practices were indeed corrupted, and thus to permit them to take part in such practices. Now on the surface this permission might be seen as evidence of an obvious disagreement with those who did not permit such practices. However, Thānvī cautioned, a disagreement of this second variety was not substantive or real. Rather, it was the product of a single instance of error caused by a lack of knowledge and investigation of the lives of the masses in question. Such an error could be committed by scholars, saints, and even by the Prophet, Thānvī pointed out. And this kind of an error did not diminish someone's greatness (*'aẓmat*), majesty (*shān*), perfection (*kamāl*), or proximity to God (*qurb-i ilāhī*). Thānvī contended that the disagreement between Imdādullah and his Deoband disciples was of this second variety. It was not real or substantive. It was only a result of Imdādullah's lack of knowledge about the conditions of the masses in India that had given him an unduly optimistic view of their devotional lives (103–4).

Thānvī's argument was based on Imdādullah's physical absence from India. Since Imdādullah lived in Mecca and had been away from India for a while, he did not possess the necessary data to assess the religious lives of the Indian Muslim masses. But since this error in judgment was only a product of deficiency in empirical knowledge, it did not tarnish his saintly authority or the capacity to help his disciples achieve proximity to God. Even the Prophet, he further reasoned, could have committed an error because of lacking empirical knowledge about something. For instance, "Say someone added poison to the Prophet's food and he inadvertently ate it. This mistake would not undermine his greatness in the hearts of his Companions. They would not fault the Prophet for consuming poison. Rather, they would reason that the food he ate was permissible and that he would never have eaten it if he had known about its poisoned condition" (105).

Thānvī analogized that if an instance of inadvertently transgressing the law did not reduce the Prophet's greatness in the hearts of his Companions, then neither should a mistake like Imdādullah's faulty assessment of the Indian masses hold any consequence for the greatness of a master in the hearts of his disciple. But what about the fact that Imdādullah himself took part in rituals like the *mawlid* that his Deoband disciples opposed? Here Thānvī's defense rested on similar grounds. Imdādullah, Thānvī claimed, used to take part only in those rituals that were free of any corruption. Moreover, Thānvī suggested that the unblemished rectitude of Imdādullah's own conduct had much to do with his generous confidence in the conduct of others. While warranted on occasion, such confidence was mostly misplaced. But why was Imdādullah's permissive outlook not affected or influenced by the prohibitive stance of his Deoband disciples, if indeed he was so close to them? And even more seriously, if the Deoband pioneers prohibited practices that Imdādullah engaged in, did that in effect equate to their censuring their own master?

In responding to these questions (which the questioner had also raised), Thānvī again mobilized his trademark distinction between the essentially permissible nature of an act and the contingent conditions of corruption that turned that act into a heretical innovation. He issued a reminder that when Deoband *'ulamā'* called the *mawlid* a heretical innovation, their censure was directed not toward the act itself but toward the corruptions attached to it. These corruptions, Thānvī insisted, were neither a part of Imdādullah's practice nor something he condoned or permitted. Therefore, there was no true opposition between the positions of Imdādullah and those of his Deoband disciples.

Thānvī summed up his argument with a useful comparative statement: "The gist of Hājī Imdādullah's speech and actions is that these practices are permissible if they are free of any corruption, and the upshot of the legal opinion of the [Deoband] *'ulamā'* is that these practices are impermissible if they are contaminated by any corruption. So there is no point of debate here" (104). Thānvī did concede that "with regard to the question of whether in most instances these corruptions do actually exist or not, yes there is disagreement" (104). But this disagreement, Thānvī emphatically underscored, *was only an empirical difference* that did not justify casting aspersions on Imdādullah, compromising the position of the Deoband pioneers, or raising any doubts about the purity or strength of their master-disciple relationship.

A striking feature of Thānvī's defense strategy was the deterministic character of his argument; had Imdādullah known what the Deoband scholars knew about the conditions on the ground, he would have arrived at the same conclusion as they had. Moreover, of particular significance is the way Thānvī framed the entire conversation concerning Imdādullah's positions in *FHM*. Rather than focus on the specificities of Imdādullah's arguments in *FHM*, Thānvī shifted the focus to the empirical foundation of those arguments. In this way, he reformulated the terms of the conversation so that they were most favorable to the position of the Deoband scholars. Why? Because if empirical knowledge of conditions on the ground was considered a vital yardstick for measuring an argument, then of course the position of the Deoband pioneers actually based in India would easily trounce that of their master sitting far away in Mecca.

The Marks of a "True" Disciple

On the question of who should be regarded as the "true" disciples of Imdādullah, the Deobandis or those among his disciples who were their opponents, Thānvī began on a sarcastic note, commenting: "I cannot vouch for the moral rectitude of all of Hājī Imdādullah's disciples" (106). In a curious and ambiguous move, he went on to excoriate "certain people of knowledge" (*ahl-i 'ilm*) for misunderstanding and misrepresenting Imdādullah's ideological orientation by taking literally the words uttered by him in a state of mystical ecstasy (*ḥāl*). According to Thānvī, opinions expressed on complex problems (*gahray masā'il*), especially when uttered in a state of ecstasy, could not be taken in their literal sense. Rather, in such moments, the interpreter was obligated to adopt a more sophisticated hermeneutic that probed the inner modalities of seemingly apparent statements (107). Thānvī did not specify which exactly of Imdādullah's opinions were delivered in a state of ecstasy. But in bringing up his master's ecstatic state, Thānvī in one move hit two targets: attributing any unfavorable opinions in *FHM* to a state of ecstasy and undermining the hermeneutical skills and aptitude of his opponents.

Finally, while responding to the question of why Imdādullah had awarded his tutelage to scholars of two groups so opposed and conflicting in their normative disposition, Thānvī reassumed the stance of empiricism. He argued that Imdādullah had cultivated relations with scholars opposed to Deoband who harbored dubious beliefs and habits because he had lacked the requisite empirical knowledge about them and their practice. Intellectual confusion or deficiency was not the reason for this error (107). Why this same lack of empirical knowledge did not prevent him from making the Deoband pioneers his disciples was a question Thānvī did not entertain.

But such ambiguities aside, this exchange between Thānvī and the Deobandī questioner highlights the keenness of the Deoband pioneers to package Imdādullah's intellectual legacy in a manner most favorable to their reform agenda. Thānvī's painstaking efforts to extinguish any suspicion of a fracture in their relationship show his enormous concern to mold Imdādullah's memory in accordance with the narrative interests of the Deoband project.

Oneiric Operations

Perhaps the most fascinating way in which Deoband *'ulamā'* sought to rescue their reform program from the potential threat posed by their own master is found in the narration of a dream concerning *FHM* by one of

Rashīd Aḥmad Gangohī's close associates, Mawlānā Ḥāfiẓ Aḥmad, the principal of Deoband seminary at the time this text was published. In this dream, none other than Prophet Muḥammad himself intervened in this matter and decided in favor of Gangohī and the Deoband *'ulamā'*. In contrast to Thānvī's interpretive gymnastics just discussed, this dream narrative did not seek to align Imdādullah's opinions with those of his Deoband disciples but rather to present the latter as overriding the former. Let me present a brief extract from Ḥāfiẓ Aḥmad's remarkable dream to show how this goal was achieved. Aḥmad narrated:

> In the dream, there was a big hall. Ḥājī Imdādullah was present and so was I, and we were debating the *Fayṣala-yi Haft Mas'ala*. Ḥājī Ṣāḥib said, "Why are the [Deoband] *'ulamā'* being so extreme in this matter? There is room for flexibility." To which I then said, "Sir [*hazrat*], there can be no flexibility; if there is, the limits of doctrines will be violated." He replied, "This is clearly intolerance." I responded with a great deal of reverence, "Sir, whatever you say is right, but sir, the jurists can only oppose this [the corrupt practices of the masses]." At the end of this tense exchange, Ḥājī Ṣāḥib said, "Well then, let's cut this debate short. What if the author of the *sharī'a* himself decides on this matter?" I said, "Well, after that who can dare contradict whatever is decided?" Ḥājī Ṣāḥib said, "Then in this place the author of the *sharī'a* himself will decide between you and me." "After hearing this I was extremely happy that today I would have the pleasure of being visited by the Prophet. After some time Ḥājī Ṣāḥib said, "Be prepared, get ready, the Prophet is coming." Within minutes I saw a huge crowd gathering in front of the hall. As it approached I saw the Prophet in front, and behind him all the Companions. And the Prophet's splendor was shown in that his garb was exactly like that of Mawlānā Rashīd Aḥmad Gangohī. He was wearing a long shirt, very thin, without a vest. And he was wearing a cap made of five corners, just like the *'ulamā'* of Deoband. When the Prophet entered the hall, Ḥājī Ṣāḥib stood reverentially in one corner of the hall, and I went and stood in the opposite corner with the same amount of reverence, with my hands folded. (91–93)
>
> The Prophet crossed over and came toward me, came very close to me, put his hands on my shoulder, and then loudly proclaimed, "This

> boy is right in all that he is saying." When I heard this, there was no end to my joy. And with it too the status of Ḥājī Ṣāḥib further rose in my mind. I thought to myself, "What exalted status has God bestowed on our spiritual masters that the Prophet can so casually appear to them and address them." After I observed the Prophet's kindness and generosity I gained the courage to ask, "Sir, in the Prophetic tradition, the blessed appearance about which we have learned is different from what you are wearing now. This is Hazrat Gangohī's garb." The Prophet replied, "My original garb is what you have read about, but in this moment I have adopted Mawlānā Gangohī's appearance because I know how much you adore him." With this reply, my commitment and devotion to Hazrat Gangohī only multiplied. The elevated status of proximity to God enjoyed by our masters became self-evident. With that the Prophet with his entourage returned on the same path that they had come. And then I woke up. (94)

There are a number of noteworthy moments and moves in Aḥmad's dream. First note the invocation of the Prophet as the "author of the *sharī'a*." While the *sharī'a* represents the divine normative order, the Prophet is presented in this formulation as a synecdoche for divine law. Note also the way this dream kills two birds with one stone: at the same time as it honors Imdādullah for his intimate proximity to the Prophet, it mobilizes the Prophet to discredit Imdādullah's project of hermeneutical hospitality in the *FHM*. And remarkably it is precisely through Imdādullah's religious authority that this authority is weakened. The Prophet's journey to the earthly realm has been made possible by Imdādullah, or more precisely, by his elevated spiritual status, which affords him the privilege to extend the most premium of all invitations. But on accepting this invitation and arriving at the scene, the Prophet decides against Imdādullah and in favor of the Deoband *'ulamā'*. In effect, Imdādullah dug his own grave.

It is also significant that the Prophet does not appear alone. He comes with an entourage of all his Companions, confirming an endorsement from the complete spectrum of prophetic normative authority in the Sunnī worldview. As I mentioned in chapter 7, the Companions are a critical feature of the Sunnī traditionalist understanding of the Prophet's normative model, the *sunna*, signifying the noblest touchstone of imitation.

Note also the rather instrumentalist Indianization of the Prophet in this dream. In establishing his affinity for the *'ulamā'* of Deoband, the Prophet not only endorses their position but also dons their clothing. This gesture of kinship underscores the embodied nature of the Prophet's affirmation of the Deoband project. He shows his approval of the Deobandī position in substance and in appearance. However, curiously, this dream subverts the normal order of imitation. Rather than the Deoband pioneers imitating the Prophet, it is the Prophet who imitates the Deoband pioneers—Gangohī, to be even more specific.

Cold, Bleak, Disenchanted?

There are several other instances in the Deoband archive where we find dreams that strategically Indianize the Prophet and establish his affection for Deoband scholars. For example, in his well-known polemical text *The Conclusive Proofs* (discussed at several points in this book), the prominent Deoband scholar Khalīl Aḥmad Sāharanpūrī narrates a story in which the Prophet appears in a Deobandī scholar's dream (the name of the scholar is unspecified) and begins speaking to him in Urdu. Obviously bewildered, this scholar asks the Prophet, "Sir, I thought you were an Arab, how is it that you are speaking in Urdu?"[27] The Prophet responds, "I have learned this language because of my profound relationship with the *'ulamā'* of Deoband."[28]

The mobilization of such dream narratives shows that although it might seem uncharacteristic of the staunch rationalist puritans that Deoband scholars are often made out to be, the oneiric imagination occupied an important place in Deobandī thought and discourse. Throughout Muslim history, dreams have been important vehicles for constructing and advancing moral arguments. They also serve as critical receptacles of spiritual insight, indicating the health enjoyed by or the disease afflicting the human soul.[29] Participating in this long-standing tradition, in this instance, the Deoband *'ulamā'* drew on the oneiric imagination for the competitive purpose of establishing the supremacy of their doctrinal positions over those of their rivals. This competitive function and its intimacy with modern conditions notwithstanding, they had no modern, rationalist qualms about the significance of dreams as an avenue for encountering the Prophet and, through doing so, advancing moral arguments.

The Deobandī embrace of the oneiric imagination does not sit comfortably with historian Francis Robinson's claim that modern Indian madrasas like Deoband "produced a dwindling stream, relatively at least, of *turbaned graduates* able to see the world only through the *prism of revelation* [emphases mine]."[30] In a burst of Weberian determinism, Robinson says of modern Indian Muslim reformers like the Deoband scholars: "These puritan Muslims began to dispense with the great network of saints and ancestors through whom they once came close to God. . . . These Muslims increasingly seemed to find the world a cold, bleak, disenchanted place."[31] I admire and consider myself a beneficiary of Robinson's erudite scholarship on South Asian Islam. However, I must respectfully but forcefully disagree with him here. These statements are incredibly problematic. Let us leave aside for a moment the unfortunate selection of the descriptor "turbaned graduates" for the Deoband *'ulamā'* (turbaned graduates as opposed to unturbaned graduates of secular universities?). More importantly, describing Deoband scholars' worldview as "cold, bleak, and disenchanted" ignores the fact that even the strictest of them did not reject the existence of miracles, jinns, and other supernatural elements not entirely in sync with a disenchanted view of the world. But most importantly, the enchanted/disenchanted binary is singularly unhelpful in attending to the internal logics and complexities of Deobandī or for that matter Barelvī conceptions of religious reform.[32]

As I have striven to show throughout this book, approaching the question of Muslim reform in modern South Asia through a narrative of inherent competition between puritan disenchantment and mystical enchantment is at once inaccurate and conceptually impoverished. Deoband pioneers were capable of viewing the world beyond the prism of revelation and of engaging multiple intellectual disciplines and traditions. More crucially, the very suggestion that revelation must somehow stand in opposition to networks of saints rests on the unsound assumption that mysticism and revelation constitute an oppositional binary. It was not revelation/law versus mysticism but competing understandings of the relationship between divine sovereignty, prophetic authority, and ritual practice that were at the heart of intra-Muslim contestations like the

Barelvī-Deobandī controversy. The enchantment/disenchantment binary, much like the law/mysticism binary, is attractive in the way it simplifies a complicated narrative. But it is a fundamentally misleading way of approaching Muslim intellectual traditions and debates.

Questioning Liberal Secular Moderation

In concluding this chapter, it might be useful to briefly consider the effect or outcome of *FHM*. Was Imdādullah successful in achieving the task he had set himself in this text: easing tensions between *'ulamā'* groups in India and defusing the intensity with which the Deoband pioneers prohibited particular practices? While the question is difficult to answer conclusively, the evidence at hand indicates that the answer is no. The Barelvī-Deobandī dispute only intensified in the decades following the publication of *FHM* in 1894. And the pioneers of Deoband, like Thānvī and Gangohī, continued to forbid practices like the *mawlid* with no less resolve and severity. In a certain sense, then, one might describe *FHM* as a tragic text that could not realize the future it had hoped and aspired for. But despite its tragic nature, perhaps its most remarkable aspect, as I have labored to show throughout this chapter, was the way it fashioned a hermeneutic of reconciliation that operated across multiple logics simultaneously: those of the law, mysticism, and everyday expedience. *FHM* was a heterological text through and through.

Moreover, and this is a point I wish to insist upon, *FHM* did not participate in a liberal secular operation of "moderating" religion so as to render it more peaceful, inclusive, or tolerant. The demand to moderate religion, a demand most often made of Islam and Muslims today, is often inextricable from the desire to manage and regulate religion in a manner most conducive to liberal secular governance. As Ananda Abeysekara has usefully reminded us, the word *moderate* is derived from the Latin *moderare*, meaning to "tame," "control," "reduce," and "restrain."[33] Religion that is moderated is religion that is sufficiently tamed and domesticated so as to pose no threat to the sovereignty of the modern state (be it avowedly religious or secular). The necessity for moderation arises from an irresolvable contradiction that afflicts the logic of modern state sovereignty: the very diversity and pluralism that form the identity of the liberal state also threaten that identity. The promise of freedom and autonomy for all citizens is a central tenet that sustains the liberal secular state. However, pluralism and difference threaten the survival of that freedom.[34]

Given the constantly hovering crisis posed by this irresolvable contradiction, moderating religion and religious life emerges as a way of resolving the crisis. But such a crisis cannot be resolved because of the inherently contradictory character of the modern liberal state that must redress religious difference and inequality (which constantly threaten its promise of freedom and equality for all citizens) while also remaining neutral to religion and religious difference. As Saba Mahmood has asked, "How could a state that sought to eliminate religious inequality do so without making religious difference part of its political vocabulary?"[35] This question brings into sharp focus the aporetic condition of political secularism and of modern state sovereignty: an irresolvable condition that cannot be resolved by making appeals to religious moderation, tolerance, and inclusion. In fact, far from a solution to any problem, the trope of moderation is symptomatic of the problem itself. The sovereign secular demand for religion to be moderated signifies the limits and irresolvable contradictions of secularism and modern sovereignty. Elsewhere I have more fully developed this argument regarding the entwinement of the aporias of secularism and the discourse of moderate Islam.[36] Here I rehearse its gist to draw an important contrast between liberal secular discourses of religious moderation and tolerance and the logic of intrareligious reconciliation at work in Ḥājī Imdādullah's *FHM*.

What we find in Imdādullah's discourse is something quite different. His efforts to harmonize human relations were not tethered to the sovereign concerns and anxieties of the state. Rather, Imdādullah was most concerned with protecting the authority and integrity of the scholarly elite from what he saw as the corrosive threat of rampant controversy and intra-*'ulamā'* antagonism. Allowing such debate to get out of hand, he argued, not only produced unseemly factionalism among religious scholars but, perhaps more importantly, also undermined their stature in the eyes of the masses.

Notice that Imdādullah was not advancing a liberal secular argument for moderating religion to neutralize difference as a way to achieve religious equality. To the contrary, an illiberal logic of preserving a hierarchical difference between the scholarly elite and their followers, the masses, was at the center of Imdādullah's mission. In presenting such a hierarchical vision of religious authority, Imdādullah displayed his fidelity to the traditionalist formulation "The masses are like a herd of cattle" (*Al-'awāmm ka-l-an'ām*). Moreover, the affirmation of this hierarchical vision of religious authority was not intended to cultivate a liberal subject subservient to the interests and sovereignty of the modern state.[37]

Rather, the imperative of safeguarding the aura of the religious elite was bound up with their status as the inheritors of the Prophet's mantle and the interpreters of divine norms. In Imdādullah's religious imaginary, safeguarding the sanctity of the *'ulamā'* translated into honoring the Prophet's spiritual pedigree and upholding God's sovereign power. It was not fashioning equal citizens before a supposedly neutral state that channeled Imdādullah's discourse. Rather, he strove to fashion a pious community with carefully calibrated boundaries and expectations of normative authority. To put it differently, his was not a liberal quest to moderate religion in the service of the state. Instead, he aimed to ameliorate intrareligious conflict to ensure the integrity of a theologically grounded narrative of how knowledge, power, and community must interact and cohere.

The broader point is this: Imdādullah's hermeneutic of reconciliation does not lend itself neatly for categorization as a mystical inclusivist push for tolerance and religious moderation, the way a good Muslim/bad Muslim binary that equates mysticism with peace, tolerance, and moderate Islam might hasten us to do. To the contrary, it was precisely such a binary that his discourse disrupted and brought into question. This was so not only because of his illiberal logic of the normative relationship between the religious elite and the masses but also on account of the multiple logics and knowledge sources that drove his arguments. *FHM* was not the work of a liberal inclusivist mystic admonishing his exclusivist *sharī'a*-minded disciples. We will go fundamentally wrong by reducing Imdādullah's tensions with his Deoband disciples or his strivings for intrareligious harmony in *FHM* to a law/Sufism divide. Such a perspective would miss and erase the nuances, the ambiguities, the hermeneutical layers, and indeed the tragedy enshrined in this text. And these are some of the elements that I have sought to present and detail in what has preceded in this chapter.

A Final Word on Imdādullah and his Relationship with His Deoband Disciples

In closing, a quick word on the intra-Deoband relations that were discussed here. As highlighted in this chapter, the relationship between Ḥājī Imdādullah and the pioneers of the Deoband madrasa such as Rashīd Aḥmad Gangohī was at times tense and ambiguous. However, for all their differences and disagreements, the foundations of this relationship were never challenged, and Imdādullah remained indispensable to the narrative of the early Deoband movement. Further, the founders of Deoband and then Ashraf ʻAlī Thānvī continued to regard Imdādullah as their primary spiritual master and as the fountainhead of their religious lives. Indeed, Imdādullah's relationship with his Deoband disciples presents an excellent example of a master-disciple context in which hermeneutical disagreement did not fracture the integrity of that relationship. Moreover, Imdādullah and Deoband pioneers like Gangohī did not look for 100 percent compatibility with each other. A tolerable amount of incompatibility was a feature that had always characterized their relationship and one that both had come to terms with. Ultimately, the Deoband pioneers saw their difference with Imdādullah as one of style, not substance.

Once, after Imdādullah had passed on, someone said to Thānvī, as if lodging a complaint: "Ḥājī Ṣāhib used to be very flexible and patient, but you are very strict." Thānvī's reply was memorable. He said that both he and Imdādullah had the same objective: reform (of the public). But Imdādullah possessed a charisma (*bā barkat*) that he did not. Playing on the rhyming words *barkat* (charisma) and *ḥarkat* (action), Thānvī argued that people like him who lacked the charisma of an Imdādullah could do the work of reform only through strict action. As he summed up, "We do reform through *ḥarkat*, and he does reform though *barkat*" (*Hum ḥarkat se iṣlāḥ kartay hain awr ḥazrat barkat se iṣlāḥ kartay hain*).[38] In a quintessentially Thānvī-esque move, in one stroke he honored his master's charismatic authority, established his subservience to that authority, and authorized his own distinct temperament and method of reform.

Epilogue

The central argument pursued in this book has been that intra-Muslim rivalries, like the Barelvī-Deobandī polemic, should be approached as moments of contestation between competing rationalities of tradition and reform. These rationalities become centrally visible during specific moments when the limits of the normative and the heretical, identity and difference, are authoritatively debated. Each chapter in this book has shown ways in which authoritative religious actors sought to strategically control the boundaries of tradition. By focusing on a specific context of antagonism in nineteenth-century Muslim India, I have described two opposing narratives of the relationship between divine sovereignty, prophetic charisma, and the boundaries of ritual practice. The protagonists of these narratives constructed their religious authority by identifying an object of dissatisfaction and then proposing a program of reform to overcome that dissatisfaction.

Shāh Muḥammad Ismā'īl and the Deoband pioneers crafted as their object of critique prevalent attitudes and practices dominant in the public sphere that in their view posed an imminent threat to divine sovereignty. As an antidote, they advanced a reform project that called for the abandonment of such practices as a way to restore the radical alterity of divine sovereignty. They also argued for an imaginary of the Prophet that emphasized his humanity as the marker of his perfection. On the other hand, it was precisely such a notion of reform that Fazl-i Ḥaqq Khayrābādī and later Aḥmad Razā Khān sought to overcome. They vigorously defended long-standing rituals and devotional practices that in their view were indispensable to tradition. Moreover, they claimed that the Prophet's exceptionality, as affirmed through such qualities as his unrivaled capacity for intercession or his access to knowledge of the unknown, was non-negotiable. In fact, the exceptionality of divine sovereignty was established precisely through the affirmation of the Prophet's ontological exceptionality. Divine sovereignty and prophetic charisma were inseparable. To sum up, this book has argued that these rival narratives of tradition and reform in nineteenth-century Muslim India were animated by competing political theologies that corresponded with competing understandings of law and normative practice in everyday life. In advancing this argument, I have tried to question commonplace understandings of the Barelvī-Deobandī controversy as one reflective of an inherent clash between Islamic law and Sufism, legal and mystical Islam, or "hard" and "soft" Islam. These popular binaries break down once the relevant sources and archives are read in some detail.

By shifting the analytical focus to political theology, I have also sought to show that what may seem like arcane intra-*'ulamā'* debates were in fact embedded in crucial questions of power, morality, and social order. Could one raise both hands while praying over food distributed on the occasion of someone's death? Was standing up during the celebration of the Prophet's birthday permissible? To our modern sensibilities, these questions might seem reflective of obscure if not petty and inconsequential squabbles of an eccentric scholarly elite. A few years ago, in the Q&A session following a talk I had delivered to a diaspora South Asian Muslim audience in northern Virginia, an audience member wondered, "How did these scholars [Barelvī and Deobandī] have so much time on their hands to be debating such petty issues?" I am not sure this book will satisfy such expressions of dismissive skepticism, but it has nonetheless striven to make understandable the sorts of logics, stakes, and concerns that drove the controversy and made it so intense.

What I have tried to show throughout this book is that the debates over theology, law, and ritual that occupied nineteenth-century South Asian *'ulamā'* were entangled in profound anxieties and aspirations over large questions of sovereignty, knowledge, law, temporality, and embodiment. This has involved asking of authoritative religious actors from the past questions they would not have asked of themselves, connecting their thought to larger themes not always centrally visible in the problem space where they operated. My goal has been to detail the specificities of competing moral arguments while also capturing the deeper conceptual and philosophical problems that gave those arguments their normative weight and urgency.

Questioning the Secular by Navigating Tradition

A conceptually attuned examination of intra-Muslim traditions of moral argument also offers the promise of undermining and bringing into question the secular promise of canonizing religion into disciplinary binaries. In the last few decades, disturbing the religion-secular binary has dominated the problem space of the study of religion. Even though this book has not directly engaged the question of the secular, here I want to briefly suggest ways in which it might speak to some of the concerns raised in what one might term critical secularism studies. Several important works have sought to question the universality of liberal secular modernity and the often-assumed opposition between religion and the secular. In different ways, these works have shown that the secular, rather than being the inverse of religion, is better understood as a regime of discursive and institutional power that constantly regulates and manages what does and does not count as religion. Put more simply: it is precisely by defining religion as its "other" that the secular defines itself.[1] Moreover, the secular reorganization of religion as reducible to propositional beliefs and as belonging to the private sphere of individual piety packages religion in a manner most conducive to liberal political rule.

These genealogical investigations of secular power have been especially inspired by the work of anthropologist Talal Asad. Asad's thought was the pioneering force behind the now familiar argument that rather than representing opposite domains of life, the modern categories of "religion" and "secularism" are mutually dependent. One of his clearest articulations of this argument is found in his insightful critique of Wilfred Cantwell Smith's views on religion: "I would urge that 'religion' is a modern concept not because it is reified but because it has been linked to its Siamese twin 'secularism.' Religion has been part of the restructuration of practical times and spaces, a rearticulation of practical knowledges and powers, of subjective behaviors, sensibilities, needs, and expectations in modernity. But that applies equally to secularism, whose function has been to try to guide that rearticulation and to define 'religions' in the plural as a species of (non-rational) belief."[2]

In Asad's view, secularism, much like any religion, normalizes itself by valorizing certain virtues, sensibilities, and forms of embodiment that seek to cultivate particular kinds of subjects and affective registers. Most importantly, for Asad, secular assumptions about the normative role of religion in society, as belonging to the "private" spheres of inner belief and the family, and the political rationality that authorizes those assumptions, that of political secularism, are anything but universal. Rather, like any ideological construct, the secular is also contingently authorized in arbitrary conjunctures of specific historical, institutional, and discursive forces.[3] In his work, Asad has particularly explored with much depth and nuance the connections between political secularism (the doctrine mandating the separation of religion and state), the secular (a conceptual force yielding formidable yet often ineffable power), and secularity (the kinds of life, affects, and attitudes fostered by secularism and the secular). The power and diffusion of secularism as a normative ideal owe precisely to the operation and cooperation of these ideas as family concepts at multiple strata of society, Asad's scholarly oeuvre suggests.

Asad's genealogical critiques have done much to interrupt the self-congratulatory narrative of secular modernity's alleged eclipse of tradition and religion. They have also disrupted the often-assumed universality of such liberal virtues as individual sovereignty, freedom, and the separation of religion and politics. More recently, building on Asad's work, scholars like Hussein Agrama and Saba Mahmood have shown that political secularism remains arrested in an irresolvable paradox: the modern secular state must redress religious inequality while also remaining neutral and indifferent to religion and religious difference. And for all its claims of neutrality, bias toward the majority population remains integral to the very structure and organizing logic of the modern secular state.[4]

This book has built on Asad's and his interlocutors' work through a route different from that of offering another genealogical critique of the secular. Instead it has tried to shift inquiry from secular colonial regimes of "religion making" to critical conjunctures of authoritative native discourses and debates on the boundaries of religion.[5] In addition to genealogical critique, bringing into view alternative logics of life and critique can also advance the labor of provincializing and unsettling the conceptual hegemony of the secular. That is precisely what this book has tried to do by providing a thick description of some of the moral antagonisms that animated a specific discursive tradition in colonial South Asia. By so doing, I have tried to describe in some detail a tradition of moral argument that did not always operate according to the codes, expectations, and normative desires of liberal secular politics. While operating under the shadow of colonial power, the *'ulamā'* discourses and debates addressed in this book were not subsumed by that power. A cautionary word is in order here. This conceptual positioning is not meant to undermine the significance or power of the secular colonial discursive economy. Indeed, colonialism in India served as the very condition of possibility for the efflorescence of religious reform movements like the ones discussed in this book. Also, as Deoband scholar Manẓūr Nu'mānī's views on knowledge explored in chapter 11 showed, *'ulamā'* discourses and modern secular conceptions of religion often converged.

Moreover, I have not attempted the conceptually questionable task of putting on display an example of an "alternative modernity." Nor have I sought to unearth "native agency" from the rubbles of colonial power. Several scholars have convincingly shown the conceptual poverty of the so-called alternative modernities argument and of the gesture to impute agency to natives, as I had occasion to detail in the conclusion to Part I of this book.[6] What I have sought to do instead is to show the internal workings of a discursive tradition that often did not operate according to the colonizing grammar of secular conceptuality. The competing imaginaries of tradition described in this book were not available for the secular division of life into disciplinary binaries like law/Sufism, moderate/extremist, reformist/traditionalist, religious/secular, belief/practice, and public/private. Even as they were enveloped by the social and institutional conditions of colonial secular modernity, the participants of this tradition did not organize their lives through the prism of such binaries. Instead, their lives and thought point to these binaries' limits. Their rival narratives of tradition and reform depended on moral questions, expectations, and anxieties that did not fit neatly with the calculus of liberal secular thought or governance. Moreover, the actors who participated in these debates, despite their intense disagreements, shared certain underlying expectations about the practices, events, and convictions that were worthy of dispute and that therefore demanded resolution.

These actors may have fought relentlessly over how to understand a particular practice or event. But what was never in question was the significance of that practice or event to the achievement of moral excellence. The stakes of their contentions and conflicts were secured through an underlying covenant about the goods, virtues, and excellences that ought to be valued, preserved, and inculcated.

As the anthropologist David Scott so eloquently put it:

> Tradition is not merely an inheritance, something that you get. Tradition is not a passive, absorptive relation between the past and the present. Rather tradition presupposes an active relation in which the present calls upon the past. In this sense then, tradition always implies an ensemble of practices and institutions that actively produce and reproduce the virtues understood to be *internal to that tradition* [emphasis mine]. In this sense too, tradition is not principally about what happened in the past: it is less nostalgia than memory, and memory more as a source of sustenance and vision.[7]

This book has described specific moments in the career of a discursive tradition, that of Islam in late eighteenth- and nineteenth-century South Asia, when it was invested with competing moral goods and understandings of normativity. Through a reading of the texts and contexts that animated an ongoing intra-Muslim disagreement, it has sought to capture some of the complexity and dynamism of South Asian Muslim intellectual traditions. In doing so, I have tried to bring into central view the aspirations, anxieties, and ambiguities that marked the religious thought of seminal modern South Asian *'ulamā'*. While one may not share their points and modes of contention, the palimpsest of logics and conflicts that informed their religious imaginaries displays ample depth, nuance, tension, and ambiguity. This book has striven to detail some of those logics and conflicts in the hope of elucidating a nineteenth-century intra-Muslim debate that continues to influence the religious lives of South Asian Muslims, both within and beyond South Asia, in profound ways.

postscript

Listening to the Internal "Other"

In January 2016, on a balmy Saturday morning in Lāhore, I ventured to a famous Islamic bookstore in the historic and densely populated Anārkalī Bāzār area. I was looking to acquire personal copies of some books I had tired of repeatedly requesting on interlibrary loan back in the United States. I asked the store attendant, a tall and slightly rotund man in his late thirties or early forties, sporting a thick beard, and clad in a spotless white *shalwār kamīz*, whether he had a copy of Ashraf ʻAlī Thānvī's short Urdu epistle *Guarding Faith* (*Ḥifẓ al-Īmān*). Readers might remember this text from my discussion of it in chapter 11. My seemingly innocuous question turned this store attendant, who until this point, I must admit, had been more distracted then attentive, visibly anxious. Without uttering a word, he gently unearthed a copy of the text from a large intimidating pile of books, and slid it toward me. Once confident that I had safely secured it in my hands, he softly but audibly murmured, as if schooling a newly enrolled student during orientation: "This is one of the books they have banned. If they find me selling it, I can be immediately locked up and charged by the antiterrorism court for spreading sectarianism." This store attendant was referring to a recent drive, on the part of the Pakistani military establishment, in collaboration with the then provincial government, to ban Islamic books deemed to contain any sectarian or hateful content. Thānvī's *Ḥifẓ al-Īmān*, due to its entanglement in the Barelvī-Deobandī controversy, was thus judged as one such book.

The process of putting texts and authors on this list of forbidden books was often quite random and haphazard, however. There was a gaping disconnect between the law enforcement agencies charged with implementing this program and the intellectual field constituted by "Islamic books." Humorous stories of the provincial Panjāb police knocking on doors looking for long-dead authors, with queries (in Panjābī) such as "*Ay Shiblī Nu'mānī kithe hunda hay?*" (Where can I find Shiblī Nu'mānī? [d. 1914]) circulated among the urban intelligentsia more attuned to the landscape of South Asian Islam, providing welcome laughter and entertainment. But such state-engineered attempts at moderating religion, hideously apparent in their design to assuage and placate Western imperial desires and visions of "good religion," are ultimately more tragic and violent than they are humorous. The impulse to divest the public sphere of religious controversy also evinces a particularly anxious and suspicious attitude toward the discursive site of the polemic. That a polemic can easily slip into violence is the working assumption that animates the desire to ban all combustible materials (such as polemical texts) that, if brought together, might ignite a polemical fire. However, this quest and strategy is always destined to fail. For as the anthropologist Michael Taussig famously argued, the attempt to erase and deface an object only makes it more visible and prominent.[1]

The polemical encounter described in this book offers a valuable corrective to the widely held notion that polemics must always result in violence, or that they are by nature unfortunate occurrences. It is tempting to read the nineteenth-century intra-Muslim conflict that occupied this book as the opening act of the tragic saga of intra-Muslim violence and sectarian warfare that engulfed postcolonial South Asia. While these moments are not completely disconnected, such a teleological reading would be unduly simplistic and indeed problematic. Note that for all the intensity of disagreement, bitterness, and acerbic sarcasm that pervaded the beginnings of the Barelvī-Deobandī controversy and its early nineteenth-century antecedents, no shots were fired. This was a remarkable instance of a vigorously fought intellectual conflict that despite its high stakes and high polemical temperatures did not result in physical violence. The Barelvī-Deobandī controversy is a telling example of a vehement and impassioned, yet layered and complex tradition of intra-Muslim critique and disagreement. One does not have to celebrate or sympathize with its competing political theologies to find it worthy of some reflection and instruction.

Moreover, as Saba Mahmood has argued, making religious intransigence and excess causal explanations for the exacerbation of intrareligious tensions and sectarian violence in postcolonial Muslim societies is an insidious liberal fallacy. Such a diagnosis, invariably carrying the prescription of a higher dose of secularism as the solution to religious discord, masks the intimacy of religious inequality and the structural paradoxes haunting political secularism. Though Mahmood formulated her argument while examining the context of modern Egypt, her point is equally applicable to South Asia: that for all its claims to religious neutrality, the political and legal structuring of the modern state necessitates its involvement in and production of religious difference. As she so pointedly summed up the underlying contradiction at the heart of political secularism: "Secularism as a statist project aims to make religious difference inconsequential to politics while at the same time embedding majoritarian religious norms in state institutions, laws, and practices."[2]

What I have striven to do throughout this book is to offer a competing logic of life and tradition not so easily amenable or reducible to the oppressive grid of intelligibility informing the modern state's management of religious difference and conflict. In so doing, I have tried to listen eagerly and sympathetically to what one might call an internal "other." As I made clear in the Introduction, though I am marked as a South Asian Muslim, I am not trained in or a part of the madrasa tradition. Indeed, it was at a very late stage of my undergraduate education in the United States that I first even heard of madrasa institutions like Deoband. Names such as Ashraf ʿAlī Thānvī, Aḥmad Razā Khān, and Ḥājī Imdādullah entered my vocabulary even later, when I began my graduate work. I distinctly remember that during my first introductory course on Islam at Macalester College, the instructor brought up Abū Aʿlā Mawdūdī at some point in class and asked for my reflections on his place in Pakistan. "Never heard of him," was my honest answer, much to his visible (and legitimate) surprise.

A childhood colonized by cricket and dominated by Bollywood, Lollywood, Panjābī, and Pashto cinema only partially explains this ignorance. A more useful and more widely applicable explanation lies in the curse of the colonial legacy of the tripartite education system that brutally divides a country into private elite schools (with instruction in English), public middle-class schools (with instruction in Urdu), and lower-middle-class madrasa schools (with instruction in Urdu and Arabic).[3] This division, a persisting colonial legacy, has had catastrophic sociological and psychological consequences. It is both a symptom and a generator of a broader polarity between pathological political theologies of religious fundamentalism that "mummify" a dynamic tradition and suffocating varieties of liberal secular fundamentalism that cannot approach religious actors or thought with any nuance and sympathy.[4] Such polarization does not usefully contribute to the project of exploring the complexities and tensions in Muslim intellectual texts and contexts.

In settings like Pakistan, one often encounters the casual bandying of terms like *mullah*, with the explicit connotation of signifying the assumed backwardness of the male religious scholar. Other instances of such smug liberal secular fundamentalism are found in abundance in popular print and online media, especially in English. Read almost any major Pakistani English daily for a few months and you are bound to find appallingly shallow stories, editorial essays, and cartoons that uncritically reproduce sensationalized stereotypes of religious scholars and madrasa graduates. Often, these caricatured depictions take the form of seizing on an extreme case of an embarrassing *fatwā* or fringe opinion to target an entire tradition and its inhabitants for the perverse gratification of liberal mockery.[5] The phenomenon of madrasaphobia is of course by no means restricted to Pakistan or to media in English. Rather, as I noted in the Introduction, it is global. It is common across the border in India, elsewhere in South Asia and the global South, and in imperial centers and satellites dotting the global North. But glibly caricaturing an entire tradition because of the actions of a select few within it is not only intellectually wanting and unproductive; it is grossly unjust. As Muhammad Qasim Zaman, in his shining recent book *Islam in Pakistan: A History*, so aptly puts it: "Contemporary 'ulama have done better at acquiring Western learning, and at benefiting from so doing, than the [Western educated] modernists have in developing a credible grounding in the Islamic tradition and in enhancing the religious credentials that go with any such accomplishment."[6] It is precisely this power imbalance and lopsided pressure on the *'ulamā'* to modernize and embrace the disciplining protocols of liberal secular citizenship with no expectation of any reciprocal engagement with their discursive universe on the part of the modernist elite that nourishes not only madrasaphobia, but that also empowers violently pathological readings of the Muslim tradition. After all, the refusal to engage a tradition on its own terms or to complicate stereotypical depictions of its custodians can only amplify and dramatize its most extreme expressions. As Zaman trenchantly sums up, "Among the blind spots most damaging to the modernists' own cause has been their unwillingness to see much nuance or internal differentiation among their conservative rivals. The need to recognize such nuance and to build on it is not a matter of intellectual generosity; it is pragmatic politics."[7]

Of course, as I made clear in the Introduction, responding to madrasaphobia with the hagiographic romanticization of madrasa actors and traditions of knowledge is also inadequate and unhelpful. A far more intellectually robust and responsible strategy would involve listening eagerly, carefully, and critically to the layered logics of life that compose *'ulamā'* traditions of knowledge and that inform their internal debates. One does not have to agree with or embody a logic of life to be able to listen to it and learn from it sympathetically and with humility. The academic study of religion presents and promises an excellent avenue and set of tools to execute readings of a tradition that are attentive to its internal voices and logics. It is precisely this exercise in listening to the internal "other" that inspired the pages of this book, an exercise through which I labored to honor and remember a complicated, contentious, and formidable fragment of the heritage of South Asian Islam and modern Muslim thought more broadly.

appendix

Suggestions for Teaching This Book

Recommended Chapters for Various Courses

Different parts of this book will suit different kinds of undergraduate/graduate courses and pedagogical purposes. Here are some recommendations. I am assuming a class session of an hour and twenty minutes that meets twice a week; instructors can adapt these suggestions based on their specific teaching context:

—To instructors wishing to give students a sense of modern Muslim reformist thought and activism for a single class session in an introductory course on Islam, I would recommend assigning chapter 2.

—To add South Asian perspectives and debates in seminars on Islamic law, assigning chapters 6, 7, and 9 over two class sessions would work best; for a single class session, chapter 6 and then either chapter 7 or 8 would be best.

—Instructors teaching upper-level courses on South Asian religions, religion and colonialism in South Asia, or South Asian Islam can employ a couple of different configurations: (a) Introduction and chapters 2 and 5; or (b) Introduction and chapters 6, 7, and 9 spread over two or three class sessions. For a single class session, either chapter 2 or chapters 6 and 7 will work best.

—Courses on Muslim political thought or political theology (with focus on Islam or otherwise) will most benefit from chapters 3, 4, and 5.

—For seminars on Sufism, the Introduction and chapter 12 will work well together.
—Courses on religion, gender, and sexuality interested in gendered discourses on religious reform in modernity will find useful select discussions in chapter 2 (especially the subsection on widow remarriage) and in chapters 8 and 10.
—Seminars with a focus on *'ulamā'* discourses and problems of religious authority in modern Islam will be best served by the Introduction and chapters 7, 9, 10, and 11 over two class sessions.
—Students in advanced undergraduate seminars or graduate seminars on the specific theme of modern South Asian Islam will benefit from reading the entire book spaced into three class sessions: Introduction and Part I, chapters 6, 7, 8, and 9 from Part II, and then the remainder of the book.

In undergraduate courses, staging hypothetical in-class debates in which students prepare and argue competing Muslim scholarly positions on contested legal, theological, and ethical issues can work as a profitable exercise.

Possible Discussion Questions for Each Chapter

Below are some discussion questions connected with each chapter of the book that will work well for varied purposes including in-class discussions, take-home exam questions, and reflection/response papers.

Introduction

—What is the law/Sufism binary, why is it problematic, and how is it entangled with the broader Good Muslim/Bad Muslim discourse?
—What alternate conceptual framing and argument does the author propose and advance as a way to overcome binary understandings of Muslim reformist thought and intra-Muslim intellectual debates?

Chapter 1

—What does *political theology* mean, and how is that concept mobilized in this chapter and book?
—What were some of the major shifts in the sociology of sovereignty during South Asia's transition from late Mughal imperialism to British colonialism?

Chapter 2

—What were some of the major objects and arenas of moral reform that occupied Shāh Muḥammad Ismā'īl during his career as a scholar and activist? Identify and explain at least two.
—In authorizing his reform project, how did he describe the theological and moral problems/dissatisfactions that he found in early nineteenth-century North India?

Chapter 3

—How did Shāh Muḥammad Ismā'īl's approach to religious reform differ from and overlap with that of his illustrious grandfather Shāh Walī Ullah?
—In Ismā'īl's view, in what ways was divine sovereignty threatened in the world he inhabited, and through what sorts of arguments and discursive strategies did he try to counter that threat?

Chapter 4

—In chapter 4, the author argues, "Ismā'īl equated the loss of Muslim sovereignty more with the extinction of such public markers of identity (primarily concerning distinctly Muslim practices) than with the loss of a Muslim state or political power per se" (p. 105). What does this mean, and how does this argument reflect key aspects of Ismā'īl's political thought and theory of prophetic politics?
—Despite their contrasting tone and discursive styles, how did Ismā'īl's broader arguments in *Manṣab-i Imāmat* and *Taqvīyat al-Īmān* come together as part of a coherent reform agenda?

Chapter 5

—Describe and explain Shāh Muḥammad Ismā'īl's understanding and critique of prophetic intercession (*shafā'at*). What political assumptions and imaginaries informed his critique?

—What were the central aspects of Fazl-i Ḥaqq Khayrābādī's counterargument in defense of prophetic intercession? What sort of political attachments and worldview animated his theology?

—Identify and explain two major points that sustained Ismā'īl's and Khayrābādī's respective arguments on the twin controversies about God's capacity to create another Prophet Muḥammad (*imkān-i naẓīr*) and God's capacity to lie (*imkān-i kizb*).

Chapter 6

—What sorts of political, institutional, and technological conditions facilitated the emergence of competing Muslim reformist groups and movements in late nineteenth-century South Asia?

—What does the concept of *maslak* mean? What are some of the ambiguities associated with this concept?

Chapter 7

—Describe and explain the concept of heretical innovation (*bid'a*). In addition to its being a legal concept, how according to the author does *bid'a* operate as a narrative category? Address the latter question with reference to the author's analysis of the thought of the late medieval jurist Ibrāhim al-Shāṭibī.

—Describe and explain the concept of *rasm* or custom. How did Muslim intellectual discourses on this concept transform from the eighteenth to the nineteenth centuries, and why is that transformation significant? Hint: See the author's analysis of Shāh Walī Ullah's discourse on *rasm* and its contrast with that of his later followers.

—How did Shāh Muḥammad Ismā'īl and the Deoband pioneer Ashraf 'Alī Thānvī define and understand the category of *bid'a*?

Identify and explain at least three major aspects of their interpretive strategies. How was their definition and understanding of *bid'a* connected to and anchored by particular notions of law, history, and time?

Chapter 8

—What is the ritual of the *mawlid*, and why did it generate such controversy among Muslim scholars in colonial South Asia?

—What were the major interpretive moves through which Ashraf 'Alī Thānvī made his case for categorizing the *mawlid* as practiced in his time a heretical innovation? Do you find his argument convincing? Why or why not?

Chapter 9

—Identify and discuss any three major aspects of Aḥmad Razā Khān's rebuttal to Deobandī discourses on *bid'a*. What were the key legal arguments through which he launched his rebuttal?

—How did Aḥmad Razā Khān understand and present the relationship between tradition and time? Why was this relationship so central to his thought and argument?

—Make a list of all the scholars from the Muslim tradition that Khān cited and mobilized as part of his attack on the Deoband school. What do you notice about his citational practice? What work do these citations do for his religious authority?

Chapter 10

—In chapter 10 the author argues that for all their disagreement there were also important points of convergence between the views of Aḥmad Razā Khān and his Deobandī opponents on *bid'a* and the everyday ritual life of the masses. What were these points of convergence?

—How does the author connect the Barelvī-Deobandī dispute over the definition and application of heretical innovation to the broader theme of "competing political theologies?" How did this polemical encounter reflect deeper concerns and anxieties regarding the interaction of power, politics, and social order?

Chapter 11

—Imagine you meet someone completely unfamiliar with the Barelvī-Deobandī polemic. How would you describe to such a person the controversy surrounding Prophet Muḥammad's "knowledge of the unknown" (*'ilm al-ghayb*)? What are the central features of Deobandī and Barelvī positions on this controversy?

—How was the debate around the nature and scope of the Prophet's "knowledge of the unknown" connected to defining religion in modernity? Address this question with reference to the author's analysis of the Deoband scholar Manẓūr Nu'mānī's contribution to this debate.

Chapter 12

—Who was Ḥajī Imdādullah, and what were the key features and ingredients of what the author describes as Imdādullah's "Hermeneutics of Reconciliation?" Address this question with reference to Imdādullah's discussion on the *mawlid* and on any one other matter of controversy as presented in his text *Resolution to the Seven Controversies* (*Fayṣala-yi Haft Mas'ala*).

—What doubts regarding the authenticity of Ḥajī Imdādullah's relationship as the Sufi master of the Deoband pioneers were generated by *Resolution to the Seven Controversies*? How did Ashraf 'Alī Thānvī strive to address and overcome those doubts? Do you find his defense convincing? Why or why not?

Glossary

Al-'awāmm ka-l-an'ām: "The masses are like a herd of cattle." A Muslim traditionalist trope that signifies the hierarchy of the relationship between the masses and the Muslim scholarly elite while reinforcing the pastoral authority of the latter.

bid'a (pl. *bida'*): Heretical innovation; doctrines, devotional practices, and rituals that oppose the normative model of the Prophet.

fasād al-zamān: Corruption over time.

fatāwa (sing. *fatwā*): Legal opinion.

'ilm al-ghayb: Knowledge of the unknown. The scope and character of the Prophet's knowledge of the unknown were issues of massive contestation among *'ulamā'* of modern South Asia.

iltizām mā lā yalzim: Making obligatory that which is not obligated. A trope frequently employed by Deoband scholars to critique the tendency of the masses to partake in simply permissible acts with a commitment and intensity exclusively reserved for obligatory acts.

imām: Prayer leader or Muslim spiritual or political leader.

imkān-i kizb: God's capacity to lie.

imkān-i naẓīr: God's capacity to create another Prophet Muḥammad.

jihād: Literally "to strive"; warfare.

kufr: Unbelief.

maslak (pl. *masālik*): Derived from the Arabic term *sulūk* or proper conduct, *maslak* is a normative orientation required for the cultivation of a subject's virtues and ethical formation. In the modern South Asian context, *maslak* also signals a normative orientation that defines a particular reform movement, such as Deobandī, Barelvī, or Ahl-i Ḥadīth.

mawlid: Annual celebration of Prophet Muḥammad's birthday, usually takes place on the twelfth day of *rabī' al-awwal* (third month in the Islamic calendar).

mubāḥ (pl. *mubāḥāt*): Simply permissible practices; practices that are neither obligatory nor forbidden.

mujāhidīn: those who take part in jihād.

qiyām: Standing up as a show reverence to the Prophet during his birthday celebration.

raf' al-yadayn: Raising both hands during prayers; a practice that generates intense debate and controversy between Ḥanafī scholars and the nonconformist Ahl-i Ḥadīth in South Asia.

rasm (pl. *rusūm*): Customs and conventions regularly practiced in a community.

shafā'at: Intercession, especially prophetic intercession.

sharī'a: Divine normative order; Islamic law.

sunna (pl. *sunan*): Normative model of the Prophet.

takfīr: To declare someone else an unbeliever; to anathematize.

'ulamā'(sing. *'ālim*): Traditionally educated Muslim scholars; the Muslim scholarly elite.

Notes

Foreword

1. Marc Gaborieau, *Le Mahdi incompris: Sayyid Ahmad Barelvi (1786–1831) et le millénarisme en Inde* (Paris: CNRS Editions, 2010).

Introduction

1. "200 Weddings Redone in UP after a Fatwa," *Times of India*, September 5, 2006.

2. Ibid.

3. "Court Convicts Imam and Son for Blasphemy," *Dawn*, January 11, 2011.

4. Qādrī was executed by the Pakistani government in February 2016. He has since emerged as a polarizing figure in debates surrounding blasphemy and extremism in the country. While many decry Qādrī as an emblem of intolerance and extremist violence, he has also caught the imagination of several people, especially in urban populations, as a defender of prophetic honor. In fact, the fallout from Qādrī's execution served as a key catalyst for the emergence and rise to fame of the political party Teḥrīk-i Labbayk Yā Rasūl Allāh (Here I am at your service, O Messenger of God), currently led by the firebrand cleric Khādim Rizvī, which emerged as the fifth-largest party in the 2018 general elections, bagging over two million votes on a platform largely centered on defending the blasphemy law.

5. "Court Convicts Imam."

6. On the movement and afterlives of these South Asian Muslim polemics in diaspora contexts such as South Africa, see the excellent study of Brannon Ingram, *Revival from Below: The Deoband Movement and Global Islam* (Berkeley: University of California Press, 2018).

7. The idea of reform, as imagined by the actors who occupy this book, did not always equate to the notion of a radical reformation. Rather, reform for them corresponded to the category of *iṣlāḥ*, or the process of repairing, mending, and correcting faulty attitudes of faith and habits of life. The work of reform

involved both the preservation and the reenergizing of tradition. For more on this conception of reform in Muslim intellectual thought and history, see Ebrahim Moosa and SherAli Tareen, "Revival and Reform in Islam," in *Islamic Political Thought*, ed. Gerhard Bowering (Princeton, NJ: Princeton University Press, 2015), 202–19.

8. Throughout this book, I use the term *divine sovereignty* in the sense that the actors whose thought occupies this book invoke it: as God's absolute sovereign power and capacity that establishes God's exceptional oneness (*tawhīd*) and distinction. Other than *tawhīd*, in the context of this project, categories frequently invoked to convey this modality of divine sovereignty include *qudra* (*qudrat* in Persian or Urdu) or *qudrat-i ilāhī*, and *ikhtiyār*. The varied and often shifting modalities in which the concept of divine sovereignty operates in premodern and modern Muslim intellectual thought are ably interrogated, though with different thematic foci, in Muhammad Qasim Zaman, "The Sovereignty of God in Modern Islamic Thought," *Journal of the Royal Asiatic Society* 25, no. 3 (July 2015): 389–418; Andrew March, "Genealogies of Sovereignty in Islamic Political Theology," *Social Research* 80, no. 1 (Spring 2013): 293–320; Ahmed Abdel Meguid, "Reversing Schmitt: The Sovereign as a Guardian of Rational Pluralism and the Peculiarity of the Islamic State of Exception in al-Juwaynī's Dialectical Theology," *European Journal of Political Theory*, published online September 12, 2017, https://doi.org/10.1177%2F1474885117730672.

The scholars whose thought animates this book primarily belonged to Delhi, the northern part of the Gangetic Plain. While the term *Indian Muslims* is less specific and at times anachronistic, I use it in this book for purposes of style, as *Hindustani-speaking Muslims* and *North Indian Muslims* sound either bulky or too specific in terms of what these scholars imagined as their audience. I also use *Indian Muslims* and *South Muslims* interchangeably for phraseological variety.

9. For a useful survey and analysis of the Barelvī-Deobandī controversy in Pakistan, see Mohammad Waqas Sajjad, "For the Love of the Prophet: Deobandi-Barelvi Polemics and the Ulama in Pakistan" (PhD diss., Graduate Theological Union, 2018).

10. For more on the history and knowledge traditions of madrasas in South Asia, see Ebrahim Moosa, *What Is a Madrasa?* (Chapel Hill: University of North Carolina Press, 2015). See also Robert Hefner and Muhammad Qasim Zaman, eds., *Schooling Islam: The Culture and Politics of Modern Muslim Education* (Princeton, NJ: Princeton University Press, 2007).

11. For a brilliant analysis of some of these moments of internal criticism, in South Asia and beyond, see Muhammad Qasim Zaman, *Modern Islamic Thought in a Radical Age: Religious Authority and Internal Criticism* (New York: Cambridge University Press, 2012).

12. Kecia Ali, *The Lives of Muhammad* (Cambridge, MA: Harvard University Press, 2014), 43.

13. Arshad Alam, *Inside a Madrasa: Knowledge, Power, and Islamic Identity in India* (New Delhi: Routledge, 2011); Naveeda Khan, *Muslim Becoming: Aspiration and Skepticism in Pakistan* (Durham, NC: Duke University Press, 2012).

14. See, for instance, Sunniport (www.Sunniport.com), Falaah Research Foundation (www.falaah.co.uk), and the Ahlus Sunnah Forum (http://ahlussunnah.boards.net).

15. Talal Asad, "Anthropology and the Analysis of Ideology," *Man*, n.s., 14 (1979): 607–27.

16. Talal Asad, "Responses," in *Powers of the Secular Modern: Talal Asad and His Interlocutors*, ed. David Scott and Charles Hirschkind (Stanford, CA: Stanford University Press, 2016), 212.

17. Talal Asad, *The Idea of an Anthropology of Islam* (Washington, DC: Center for Contemporary Arab Studies, Georgetown University, 1986).

18. Talal Asad, "Thinking about Tradition, Religion, and Politics in Egypt Today," *Critical Inquiry* 42, no. 1 (Autumn 2015): 169.

19. Ananda Abeysekara, "Theravāda Buddhist Encounters with Modernity: A Review Essay," *Journal of Buddhist Ethics* 25 (2018): 333–71.

20. Ananda Abeysekara, *Colors of the Robe: Religion, Identity, and Difference* (Columbia: University of South Carolina Press, 2003).

21. Ashraf ʻAlī Thānvī, *Malfūẓāt-i Ashrafīya* (Multān: Idārah-yi Ta'līfāt-i Ashrafīya, 1981), 132.

22. Aḥmad Razā Khān, *Maqāl-i ʻUrafā' fī I'zāz-i Shar'-i ʻUlamā' Sharī'at o' Ṭarīqat* (Karāchī: Idārah-yi Taṣnīfāt-i Imām Aḥmad Razā Khān, n.d.).

23. Mahmood Mamdani, *Good Muslim, Bad Muslim: America, the Cold War, and the Roots of Terror* (New York: Penguin Random House, 2005).

24. Elizabeth Hurd, *Beyond Religious Freedom: The New Global Politics of Religion* (Princeton, NJ: Princeton University Press, 2015).

25. Cheryl Benard, Andrew Riddile, and Peter Wilson, *Civil Democratic Islam: Partners, Resources, and Strategies* (Santa Monica, CA: RAND, 2003), 25.

26. Ibid., 47.

27. Ibid., 37.

28. Ibid., 25.

29. Ibid., 46.

30. Hedieh Mirahmadi, Mehreen Farooq, and Waleed Ziad, *Traditional Muslim Networks: Pakistan's Untapped Resource in the Fight against Terrorism* (Washington, DC: WORDE, 2010).

31. Ibid., 2.

32. The term *Wahhābī* refers to the late eighteenth-century Muslim reform movement in Arabia founded by the scholar Muḥammad Ibn al-Wahhāb (d. 1792). Despite some doctrinal convergence, the equation of Deobandīs with Wahhābīs represents a polemical accusation from the colonial era with little substance. In reality, these two brands of reform were radically different; while the Wahhābīs underplayed if they did not reject the canonical authority of the four Sunnī schools of law, conformity to the legal tradition was the touchstone of the Deobandīs. The British Orientalist W. W. Hunter (d. 1900) popularized the notion of the "Indian Wahhabis." The opponents of the Deoband school, such as the Barelvīs, also frequently called the Deobandīs "Wahhābīs" as a way to undermine their authority and to present them as extremist radicals. In adopting the term *Deobandī-Wahhābī* with no hesitation or reflection, the authors of the WORDE seem insouciantly unaware of this polemically charged colonial legacy.

33. Mirahmadi, Farooq, and Ziad, *Traditional Muslim Networks*, 13.

34. See Lisa Curtis and Haider Mullick, *Reviving Pakistan's Pluralist Traditions to Fight Extremism* (Washington, DC: Heritage Foundation, 2009).

35. Fait Muedini, *Sponsoring Sufism: How Governments Promote "Mystical Islam" in Their Domestic and Foreign Policies* (New York: Palgrave Macmillan, 2015), 2.

36. Ibid.

37. See Azfar Moin, *The Millennial Sovereign: Sacred Kingship and Sainthood in Islam* (New York: Columbia University Press, 2010).

38. See Nile Green, *Sufism: A Global History* (Chichester: Wiley Blackwell, 2012).

39. Carl Ernst, *The Shambhala Guide to Sufism* (Boston: Shambhala Publications, 1997), 18–32.

40. Katherine Ewing, introduction to *Sufi Politics: Rethinking Islam, Scholarship, and the State in South Asia and Beyond*, ed. Katherine Ewing and Rosemary Corbett (New York: Columbia University Press, forthcoming). A fuller elaboration of this argument and some of its implications for Sufism in Pakistan is found in Ewing's earlier pioneering monograph *Arguing Sainthood: Modernity, Psychoanalysis, and Islam* (Durham, NC: Duke University Press, 1997).

41. Pnina Werbner, "The Making of Muslim Dissent: Hybridized Discourses, Lay Preachers, and Radical Rhetoric among British Pakistanis," *American Ethnologist* 23, no. 1 (February 1996): 102–29.

42. Ibid., 106–11.

43. Marc Gaborieau, *Un autre Islam*: *Inde, Pakistan, Bangladesh* (Paris: Albin Michel, 2007), 142.

44. David Pinault, *Notes from the Fortune-Telling Parrot: Islam and the Struggle for Religious Pluralism in Pakistan* (London: Equinox, 2008).

45. Ibid., 9.

46. Ibid., 42.

47. For more on the conceptual problems attached to this argument and the insidious political agendas that motivate it, see Gregory A. Lipton, "Secular Sufism: Neoliberalism, Ethnoracism, and the Reformation of the Muslim Other," *Muslim World* 101, no. 3 (2011): 427–40; and SherAli Tareen, "Park 51," in *Frequencies: A Genealogy of Spirituality*, Web-based project curated by John Modern and Kathryn Lofton, Social Science Research Council, December 2011, http://frequencies.ssrc.org/2011/12/13/park-51.

48. Aamir Mufti, *Enlightenment in the Colony: The Jewish Question and the Crisis of Postcolonial Culture* (Princeton, NJ: Princeton University Press, 2007), 19.

49. The category "hyper-rationalist and hyper-literalist techno-Islamism," one should mention in passing, is as clunky as it is unhelpful. For more on the conceptual and political problems attached to such hypersecularist approaches to the study of Islamism, see Irfan Ahmad's excellent study *Religion as Critique: Islamic Critical Thinking from Mecca to the Marketplace* (Chapel Hill: University of North Carolina Press, 2017).

50. Saba Mahmood, "Secularism, Hermeneutics, Empire: The Politics of Islamic Reformation," *Public Culture* 19, no. 2 (2006): 323–47.

51. Some of the studies on Indian Muslim reform movements include Barbara Metcalf, *Islamic Revival in British India: Deoband, 1860–1900* (Princeton, NJ: Princeton University Press, 1982); Francis Robinson, *The 'Ulama of Farangi Mahall and Islamic Culture in South Asia* (New Delhi: Orient Longman, 2001); Muhammad Qasim Zaman, *Custodians of Change: The Ulama in Contemporary Islam* (Princeton, NJ: Princeton University Press, 2002); Dietrich Reetz, *Islam in the Public Sphere: Religious Groups in India, 1900–1947* (New Delhi: Oxford University Press, 2006); Usha Sanyal, *Devotional Islam and Politics in British India: Ahmad Riza Khan Barelwi and His Movement, 1870–1920* (Delhi: Oxford University Press, 1996); and Harlan Otto Pearson, *Islamic Reform and Revival in Nineteenth-Century India: The Tarīqah-i-Muhammadīyah* (Delhi: Yoda Press, 2008).

52. Zaman's pioneering work *Custodians of Change* represents an important exception to this trend. With coverage of both Arabic and Urdu sources, this book is much more attuned to the complexity of Muslim scholarly discourses in South Asia. It mostly focuses, however, on the postcolonial context of traditionally educated Muslim scholars in Pakistan. Zaman's more recent book on the prominent late nineteenth- and twentieth-century Deoband thinker Ashraf 'Alī Thānvī, *Ashraf 'Ali Thanawi: Islam in Modern South Asia* (Oxford: Oneworld Publications, 2008), deals with Islam in colonial India more directly. In this

book, I build on this work by examining in some depth hitherto unexplored aspects of Thānvī's thought (see chapters 7 and 8).

53. Saba Mahmood, *Politics of Piety: The Islamic Revival and the Feminist Subject* (Princeton, NJ: Princeton University Press, 2005), 35.

54. Pearson left the academy to work in the private sector soon after completing his dissertation at Duke University's Department of History.

55. Ebrahim Moosa, introduction to "The Deoband Madrasa," ed. Ebrahim Moosa, special issue, *Muslim World* 99, no. 3 (July 2009): 427.

56. I am thankful to Margrit Pernau for pushing me to clarify this point.

chapter one. Thinking the Question of Sovereignty in Early Colonial India

1. Ashraf ʿAlī Thānvī, *Arwāḥ-yi Salāsa* (Karāchī: Dār al-Ishāʿat, 2001), 49.

2. Ibid., 49–50.

3. In her instructive study *Building Histories: The Archival and Affective Lives of Five Monuments in Modern Delhi* (Chicago: University of Chicago Press, 2016), Mrinalani Rajagopalan has shown that the Jāmiʿ mosque, the biggest mosque in Delhi, established in the seventeenth century by the Mughal emperor Shāhjahān (d. 1666), was a site of potent anticolonial and secular nationalist mobilization in the twentieth century, revealing the limits of colonial power and of archival definitions of the mosque as a purely religious space (88–89). One might add to Rajagopalan's analysis the observation that a century earlier, as seen in the narrative above, the Jāmiʿ mosque was also a site where fierce intra-Muslim contestations over and competing visions of the community's normative life during its transition to colonial rule became centrally visible. The critical importance of the Jāmiʿ mosque as a symbolic and material theater of intra-Muslim contest and a clear indication of the creeping shadow of colonial power most dramatically manifested in Ismāʿīl's eventually getting banned from delivering sermons or teaching lessons there by the British resident officer, an episode I will get to later in this section.

4. A. Thānvī, *Arwāḥ-yi Salāsa*, 49–50.

5. Robert Orsi, *History and Presence* (Cambridge, MA: Harvard University Press, 2016), 10.

6. Christopher Bayly, *Indian Society and the Making of the British Empire* (Cambridge: Cambridge University Press, 1988).

7. Marcia Hermansen, "Eschatology," in *The Cambridge Companion to Classical Islamic Theology*, ed. Tim Winter (Cambridge: Cambridge University Press, 2010), 308–24.

8. Shaun Marmon, "The Quality of Mercy: Intercession in Mamluk Society," *Studia Islamica* 87 (1998): 125–39.

9. Carl Schmitt was a major theorist of political theology who lived from 1888 to 1985. He is most well known for his proposition that the sovereign is the one who decides on the state of exception. Carl Schmitt, *Political Theology: Four Chapters on the Concept of Sovereignty* (Cambridge, MA: MIT Press, 1986), 36.

10. Paul Kahn, *Political Theology: Four New Chapters on the Concept of Political Theology* (New York: Columbia University Press, 2012), 18.

11. Graham Hammill and Julia Lupton, introduction to *Political Theology and Early Modernity*, ed. Graham Hammill and Julia Lupton (Chicago: University of Chicago Press, 2012), 1.

12. Ibid.

13. In probing the political projects and aspirations that inform and underlie theological discourses and debates, I find myself in profound agreement with Ovamir Anjum's thoughtful observation that "the political domain of thinking in any thought-world is grounded in its fundamental commitments and often silent presuppositions. Modern scholars have often understood Islamic political thought through the study of classical treatises on the caliphate, but have largely ignored the theoretical underpinnings of political life in epistemology, theology, and legal theory." Ovamir Anjum, *Politics, Law, and Community in Islamic Thought: The Taymiyyan Moment* (Cambridge: Cambridge University Press, 2012), 9.

14. Schmitt, *Political Theology*, 46.

15. Ibid., 1–55.

16. Ibid., 43.

17. David Gilmartin, "Rethinking the Public through the Lens of Sovereignty," *South Asia: Journal of South Asian Studies* 38, no. 3 (September 2015): 371–86.

18. Mithi Mukherjee, *India in the Shadows of Empire: A Legal and Political History, 1774–1950* (New Delhi: Oxford University Press, 2010), xv.

19. Ibid., xvi.

20. Christopher Bayly, *Empire and Information: Intelligence Gathering and Social Communication in India, 1780–1870* (Cambridge: Cambridge University Press, 1999) and *Indian Society*.

21. Sudipta Kaviraj, *The Trajectories of the Indian State* (Ranikhet: Permanent Black, 2010), 51.

22. Ibid.

23. Ibid., 40.

24. Bernard Cohn, "Representing Authority in Victorian India," in *The Invention of Tradition*, ed. Eric Hobsbawm and Terence Ranger (Cambridge: Cambridge University Press, 1992), 173.

25. Ibid.

26. Ibid., 169–70.

27. Ibid., 172.

28. Ibid., 178.

29. My reading here is inspired by conversations with David Gilmartin.

30. Margrit Pernau, *Ashraf into Middle Classes: Muslims in Nineteenth-Century Delhi* (New Delhi: Oxford University Press, 2013).

31. Ibid., 1–57 and 179–297.

32. Ibid., 423.

33. Azfar Moin, *The Millennial Sovereign: Sacred Kingship and Sainthood in Islam* (New York: Columbia University Press, 2010), 5.

34. Ibid., 2–22.

35. To reiterate, the polemical encounter considered in this section occurred sometime in 1826, a moment in Indian history when British colonial rule had already taken hold but had not yet completely overridden the Mughal Empire that it replaced; that development takes place later in 1857. Thus, in many ways, this time period can be characterized as one of gradual but definite transition from Mughal to British colonial rule.

chapter two. The Promise and Perils of Moral Reform

1. Mirzā Ḥayrat Dihlavī, *Ḥayāt-i Ṭayyiba* (Lāhore: Islāmī Academy Nāshirān-i Kutub, 1984), 41–51.

2. Ibid., 47.

3. Ibid., 44.

4. Ibid., 43.

5. To avoid confusion, I use Sayyid Aḥmad instead of the last name Barelvī.

6. For an excellent analysis and overview of Sayyid Aḥmad's intellectual and political career, see Sana Haroon, "Reformism and Orthodox Practice in Early Nineteenth-Century Muslim North India: Sayyid Ahmed Shaheed Reconsidered," *Journal of the Royal Asiatic Society* 21, no. 2 (April 2011): 177–98. As Haroon informs us in this article, while undergoing military training at Tonk, Sayyid Aḥmad had developed a reputation as a mystic sage who could perform miracles to spiritually and materially benefit other people and at times even animals, and who could foretell the future. To quote one example: "He ran his hands over sick people and read prayers over water which he then gave them to drink, causing them to become well again. His prayers caused a blind man to see again, sick oxen to be able to pull carts again, and a dried up cow to produce milk again" (182).

7. Ghulām Rasūl Mehr, introduction to *Taqwīyat al-Īmān* (Karāchī: Siddīqī Trust, n.d.), 15.

8. Charles Hambrick-Stowe, *Charles Finney and the Spirit of American Evangelicalism* (Grand Rapids, MI: William B. Eerdmans, 1996), 37.

9. Ashraf 'Alī Thānvī, *Arwāḥ-yi Salāsa* (Karāchī: Dār al-Ishā'at, 2001), 56–58. Chāndnī Chowk is one of the oldest and busiest markets in Old Delhi and exists today in North Central Delhi. It was originally built in the seventeenth century by the Mughal emperor Shāhjahān and was designed by his daughter Jahānārā (d. 1681).

10. Tanika Sarkar, *Rebels, Wives, Saints: Designing Selves and Nations in Colonial Times* (London: Seagull Books, 2009), 122.

11. Ibid., 121.

12. Ibid., 68.

13. For instance, Sarkar, *Rebels, Wives, Saints*; Tanika Sarkar, *Hindu Wife, Hindu Nation: Community, Religion, and Cultural Nationalism* (Bloomington: Indiana University Press, 2001); Lata Mani, *Contentious Traditions: The Debate on Sati in Colonial India* (Berkeley: University of California Press, 1998); Ashis Nandy, *The Savage Freud and Other Essays on Possible and Retrievable Selves* (Princeton, NJ: Princeton University Press, 1995).

14. A. Thānvī, *Arwāḥ-yi Salāsa*, 71.

15. Ismā'īl's sister (we are not told her name) was first married to their first cousin (son of Shāh Rafī' al-Dīn) Maulvī 'Abdul Raḥmān, who passed away only a few days after marriage.

16. A. Thānvī, *Arwāḥ-yi Salāsa*, 68–71.

17. Curiously, exactly the same chain of events transpired with Deoband founder Qāsim Nānautvī a few dacades later, according to Nānautvī's biographer and major Deoband scholar Manāẓar Aḥsan Gīlānī. This was clearly Gīlānī's attempt to narratively conjoin Ismā'īl's and Nānautvī (and by extension Deoband's) reform programs. Manāẓar Aḥsan Gīlānī, *Savāniḥ-i Qāsimī*, vol. 2 (Lāhore: Maktabah-yi Raḥmānīya, 1976), 10.

18. A. Thānvī, *Arwāḥ-yi Salāsa*, 71.

19. As Sarkar argued, "Reformers tried to respond to orthodox charges that remarriage was gross immorality by a counter-charge that precisely its absence stimulated immorality and sinfulness" (*Rebels, Wives, Saints*, 144).

20. Mirzā Dihlavī, *Ḥayāt-i Ṭayyiba*, 135–48.

21. Ibid.

22. Ibid., 140.

23. Ibid., 141.

24. Ibid., 141–42.

25. Ibid., 144–45.

26. Ibid., 146.

27. Ibid., 147.

28. Apart from his most well-known and fiercely controversial text, *Taqwīyat al-Īmān*, on divine sovereignty, some of Ismā'īl's other prominent texts include *'Abaqāt*, which is a commentary on Walī Allah's mystical work *Lama'āt* (on the doctrine of ontological monism, *waḥdat al-wujūd*); *Manṣab-i Imāmat*, a tract on political theory (discussed in detail in chapter 4); and *Izāḥ al-Ḥaqq*, an exposition of the legal rules and hermeneutical principles relevant to the concept of heretical innovation (*bid'a*) in Islam.

29. In addition to the founders of Deoband, some of Ismā'īl's most ardent supporters included the founder of the Alīgarh Muslim University, Sayyid Aḥmad Khān, and the prominent twentieth-century scholar Abu'l Ḥasan 'Alī Nadvī (d. 1999). Nadvī translated *Taqwīyat al-Īmān* into Arabic and played an important role in popularizing this text in the Arab Middle East.

30. Quoted in Sayyid Muḥammad Na'īmuddīn, *Aṭyab al-Bayān fī Radd Taqwīyat al-Īmān* (Bombay: Razā Academy, 1998), 206.

31. Ismā'īl has also been accused of plagiarizing his work in *Taqwīyat al-Īmān* from the well-known *Kitāb al-Tawḥīd* (Book on divine unity), by the eighteenth-century Arab reformer Muḥammad ibn 'Abd al-Wahhāb (d. 1792). However, that claim has not been substantiated. I am not aware of any evidence that explicitly connects Ismā'īl to Ibn 'Abd al-Wahhāb's followers or thought.

32. Na'īmuddīn, *Aṭyab al-Bayān fī Radd Taqwīyat al-Īmān*, 38.

33. A. Thānvī, *Arwāḥ-yi Salāsa*, 74.

34. Ibid., 75.

35. Ibid.

36. Ibid.

37. Shaykh Muḥammad Ikrām, *Mawj-i Kawsar* (Lāhore: Idārah-yi Saqāfat-i Islāmīya, 2014), 21.

38. Ibid., 37.

39. This letter belongs to a collection of Sayyid Aḥmad's (and a few of Ismā'īl's) letters, speeches, and sermons that were hand copied by a certain Mawlānā 'Ubaydullah Ghulām Ḥusayn in 1883, some fifty years after Sayyid Aḥmad's death. From Siālkot in Panjāb, Ghulām Ḥusayn came from a family of scholars closely connected to Sayyid Aḥmad's intellectual lineage; an accomplished scholar, poet, and oral historian, he is said to have copied a number of such rare texts. His library, not well kept by his descendants, was eventually bought by a book merchant in Lāhore, 'Abdul Rashīd, through whose publishing house, Maktabah-yi Rashīdīya, the original manuscript form of Ghulām Ḥusayn's copied text was published in November 1975. This is the text, printed though preserved in its manuscript form, that I have relied on in this discussion.

40. By "corrupt rebels," Sayyid Aḥmad meant the "rebellious" tribes and groups of Afghanistan and Khurāsān, an invocation through which he tried to indigenize the *jihād* campaign.

41. Sayyid Aḥmad Barelvī, *Makātīb-i Sayyid Aḥmad Shahīd* (Lāhore: Maktabah-yi Rashīdīya, 1975), 18.

42. Ibid.

43. Ibid.

44. See, for instance, ibid., 18; Shāh Muḥammad Ismā'īl, "Maktūbat-i Shāh Ismā'īl Dihlavī," unpublished manuscript, MS 102, p. 26, Punjab University Library manuscript collections, Lāhore.

45. Barelvī, *Makātīb*, 13.

46. Ibid.

47. On the legacy of Sayyid Aḥmad and his movement in the Pashtūn northwest region, see Sana Haroon's excellent study *Frontier of Faith: Islam in the Indo-Afghan Borderland* (New York: Columbia University Press, 2007). For a fascinating if at times documentarian study of the *jihād* movement from the perspective of the Pashtūn tribes, see Altaf Qadir, *Sayyid Ahmad Barailvi: His Movement and Legacy from the Pakhtun Perspective* (New Delhi: Sage Publications, 2015).

48. Khushtar Nūrānī, *Taḥrīk-i Jihād awr British Government: Aik Taḥqīqī Muṭāla'a* [The *jihād* movement and the British government: A scholarly investigation] (Delhi: Idārah-yi Fikr-i Islāmī, 2014), 152–55.

49. Ibid., 155–56.

50. For the analysis conducted here, I have considered different sections of two versions of this text: first, a Persian manuscript of around two hundred folios that mostly includes Maḥbūb 'Alī's discussion on grave visitation, and second, the contemporary scholar Khushtar Nūrānī's reproduction of the section of the text in Arabic dealing with Maḥbūb 'Alī 's eyewitness account in Nūrānī's book *Taḥrīk-i Jihād awr British Government*. While informative, Nūrānī's work is clearly invested in establishing Sayyid Aḥmad's *jihād* movement as an enabler of British colonialism, and this explains his interest in replicating an eyewitness account by a seeming renegade from this movement. Maḥbūb 'Alī 's account is not, however, always conducive to Nūrānī's project. In any case, I have primarily drawn on Nūrānī's book as a site to access a selection of Maḥbūb 'Alī's text that was unfortunately not included in the manuscript I worked with. I was not able to obtain the full original manuscript at the time this book was going to press. I thank and acknowledge Professor Javaid Mujaddidi for alerting me to the existence and significance of *Ta'rīkh al-Ā'ima*.

51. Sayyid Maḥbūb 'Alī Dihlavī, "Ta'rīkh al-Ā'ima fī Dhikr Khulafā' al-Umma," in Nūrānī, *Taḥrīk-i Jihād*, 157.

52. Sayyid Maḥbūb ʻAlī Dihlavī, "Ta'rīkh al-Ā'ima fī Dhikr Khulafā' al-Umma," unpublished manuscript, Rotograph 319, Punjab University Library manuscript collections, Lāhore.

53. Abū ʻUmar was one of Shāh Muḥammad Ismāʻīl's nicknames, as one of his sons was named ʻUmar.

54. S. Dihlavī, "Ta'rīkh al-Ā'ima," in Nūrānī, *Taḥrīk-i Jihād*, 183–96.

55. Ibid., 194.

56. Ibid.

57. Ibid., 195.

58. "Īn chunīn mardum bandah rā mī goyand keh īn-kas munkir-i wilāyat-i awliyā' shudah ast wa mazhab-i wahhābīyān ikhtiyār kardeh ẓāhiran az qawl-i īshān chūnān maʻlūm mī shawad keh khud rā az awliyā' Allāh shumardeh and. . . . Dar khānah nishisteh har cheh mī khwāhand bak bak mī kunand. . . . Na-mī dānand keh ightirā' wa buhtān bad-i balā'ī ast keh dīn wa dunyā bisabab-i ān kharāb mī shawad. . . . Īn mardum mānind-i aḥwāl-i rawāfiz shudeh ast keh har kas-rā mukhālif-i ʻandiyyeh' khwīsh mī dānand az ū tabarā' mī namāyand wa mī goyand keh īn munkir-i imāmān-i dīn ast." S. Dihlavī, "Ta'rīkh al-Ā'ima," fols. 2–3.

59. Ayesha Jalal, *Partisans of Allah: Jihad in South Asia* (Cambridge, MA: Harvard University Press, 2008), 16.

60. For more on premodern and modern Muslim intellectual discourses on *jihād*, see the chapters on *jihād* in Jonathan Brockopp, ed., *Islamic Ethics of Life: Abortion, War, and Euthanasia* (Columbia: University of South Carolina Press, 2003). See also Paul Heck, "'Jihad' Revisited," *Journal of Religious Ethics* 32, no. 1 (Spring 2004): 95–128.

61. Jalal, *Partisans of Allah*, 8–9.

62. Ibid., 36.

63. For an incisive and brilliant analysis of the problems attached to such ethno-racial readings of Muslim thought and history, see Gregory Lipton, *Rethinking Ibn ʻArabi* (New York: Oxford University Press, 2018). On some of the conceptual and historiographic shortcomings of the Arab exclusivism/Persian inclusivism binary, especially in the South Asian context, see SherAli Tareen, review of *Muslim Cosmopolitanism in the Age of Empire*, by Seema Alavi, *International Journal of Asian Studies* 15, no. 1 (January 2018): 126–31.

64. Ibid., 105. Notice the liberal secular imaginary at work in these series of binaries: belief/faith, inner/outer, spiritual/ritual, ethical/pragmatic, moral/material, private/public, inclusive/exclusive, universal/particular, and of course, most pertinent in the context of *jihād*, violence/politics; these binary framings do often come in a neat package.

65. Ibid., 106.

66. Ibid.

67. Talal Asad, *On Suicide Bombing* (New York: Columbia University Press, 2009), 7–64.

68. Roxanne L. Euben, "Jihād and Political Violence," *Current History* 101 (November 2002): 365.

69. For an excellent demonstration of such a depiction, see S. M. Ikrām's *Mawj-i Kawsar*.

70. Sayyid Abu'l A'lā al-Mawdūdī, preface to *Shāh Ismā'īl Shahīd*, by 'Abdullah Butt (Lāhore: Ta'mīr Printing Press, 1974), 19.

71. An excellent illustration of such a narrative is found in Ghulām Rājā, *Imtiyāz-i Ḥaqq: Fazl-i Ḥaqq Khayrābādī aur Shāhīd Dihlavī ke Siyāsī Kirdār ka Taqābulī Jā'iza* (Lāhore: Maktabah-yi Qādirīya, 1979).

72. Sayyid Aḥmad, *Makātīb*, 28.

chapter three. Reenergizing Sovereignty

1. Shāh Muḥammad Ismā'īl, *Taqwīyat al-Īmān* (Karāchī: Ṣiddīqī Trust, n.d.), 48.

2. *Taqwīyat al-Īmān* was originally composed in Arabic as a text called *Repelling Transgression* (*Radd al-Ishrāk*), the first part of which Ismā'īl had himself translated into Urdu; that is what we know today as *Taqwīyat al-Īmān*. The remainder of *Radd al-Ishrāk* was later translated into Urdu and published by a certain Maulvī Sulṭān Muḥammad as a text called *Remembrance of Brothers* (*Tazkīr al-Ikhwān*). Ghulām Rasūl Mehr (d. 1971), among Ismā'īl's foremost biographers, informs us that four major early manuscript and print editions of this text ranging from 1837 to 1854 have formed the basis for later printed editions. Of these four, the two printed editions were published by Dār al-'Ulūm Publishing in Delhi in 1847 and Muḥsinī Publishing in Calcutta in 1854. Mehr admitted, without offering details, that "certain passages of the text in these editions were altered" (Ghulām Rasūl Mehr, "Muqaddima," in Ismā'īl, *Taqwīyat al-Īmān* (Karāchī), 37–38). For my analysis in this book, I have primarily relied on two printed editions of *Taqwīyat al-Īmān*, the one published by Ṣiddīqī Trust in Karāchī (n.d.) and the one published by Maṭba' Aḥmadī in Lāhore (n.d.). The specific editions are noted in individual citations.

3. John Modern, *Secularism in Antebellum America* (Chicago: University of Chicago Press, 2011), 62.

4. For more on the role of the newly emerging printing presses in northern India in the production and dissemination of *Taqwīyat al-Īmān* and other such reformist texts, see Harlan Otto Pearson, *Islamic Reform and Revival in Nineteenth-Century India: The Tarīqah-i-Muhammadīyah* (Delhi: Yoda Press, 2008).

5. Ismā'īl, *Taqwīyat al-Īmān* (Karāchī), 44; Qur'ān 2:99.

6. Shāh ʻAbdul Qādir, *Mūziḥ al-Qur'ān* (Calcutta: n.p., 1829).

7. Khurram ʻAlī, "Naṣīḥat al-Muslimīn," MS Urdu 13 b, British Library Manuscript Collections, London.

8. Ismāʻīl, *Taqwīyat al-Īmān* (Karāchī), 48–49.

9. Shaykh Muḥammad Ikrām, *Rūd-i Kawsar* (Lāhore: Idārah-yi Saqāfat-i Islāmīya, 2005), 572.

10. For more on Pānīpatī's thought and career, especially the context of his views on law, see Sajida Alvi, "Qāzī Sanā'Allāh Pānīpatī, an Eighteenth-Century Indian Ṣūfī-ʻĀlim: A Study of His Writings in Their Sociopolitical Context," in *Islamic Studies Presented to Charles J. Adams*, ed. Wael Hallaq and Donald Little (Leiden: E. J. Brill, 1991), 11–26.

11. Qāzī Sanā'ullah Pānīpatī, *Mā Lā Budda Min-Hu* (Karāchī: Qadīmī Kutub Khāna, 1956), 98–99.

12. Ibid., 118.

13. For more on shifting notions of the public in modern South Asia, see Brannon Ingram, Barton Scott, and SherAli Tareen, eds., *Imagining the Public in Modern South Asia* (London: Routledge, 2016).

14. Fākhir Allāhabādī was among the earliest and most prominent exponents of the nonconformist school of thought in South Asia, which took the shape of a more defined group, the Ahl-i Ḥadīth, in the nineteenth century. Allāhabādī had also authored an important Persian text, *Qur'at al-ʻAynayn fī Isbāt Sunnat-i Rafʻ al-Yadayn*, in which he tried to establish the normative legitimacy of raising both hands during prayers. Curiously, Shāh Muḥammad Ismāʻīl, in his own book on this subject, which had similar aims and a remarkably similar title (*Tanwīr al-ʻAynayn fī Isbāt-i Rafʻ al-Yadayn*), had drawn heavily on Allāhabādī's work. Moreover, Allāhabādī's friendship with Walī Ullah is notable as an indication not only of the latter's rather flexible attitude regarding socializing with nonconformist scholars but also of the fluidity of movement across varied ideologies that characterized the eighteenth century. While Walī Ullah's attachment to the Ḥanafī canon was at times ambiguous, and while he did play with the idea of forging a composite Sunnī legal school that drew from all four existing Sunnī schools, he remained nonetheless committed to his hermeneutical identity as a Ḥanafī scholar. But that identity did not prevent him from harboring close friendships and social relations with scholars who did not share it.

15. A nonconformist scholar is one who does not assent to the canonical authority of the four legal schools in Sunnī Islam, including the Ḥanafī school that dominates South Asia; see chapter 6 for a fuller discussion on these doctrinal variations in the South Asian context.

16. ʻUbaydullah Sindhī, *Shāh Walī Ullah awr un kī Siyāsī Taḥrīk* (Lāhore: Sindh Sāgar Academy, 2008), 82. This story has shorter and longer versions, which appear in different editions. I have recounted here the fuller version.

17. Shāh Muḥammad Ismā'īl, *Īzāḥ al-Ḥaqq al-Ṣarīḥ fī Aḥkām al-Mayyit wa al-Zarīḥ* (Karāchī: Qadīmī Kutub Khāna, 1976), 73.

18. Ismā'īl, *Taqwīyat al-Īmān* (Karāchī), 48–173.

19. Interestingly, Ismā'īl also argued that the association of such privileged forms of knowledge with nondivine entities was heresy regardless of whether those knowledges were considered essential (*dhātī*) to that entity or as gifted to them by God (*'aṭā'ī*). The question of knowledge and its relationship to sovereignty is discussed more extensively in chapter 11.

20. Ismā'īl, *Taqwīyat al-Īmān* (Karāchī), 61.

21. Ibid., 49–50.

22. Qur'ān 9:31. Quoted in Ismā'īl, *Taqwīyat al-Īmān* (Karāchī), 55.

23. Quoted in ibid., 165.

24. Quoted in ibid., 173.

25. I have borrowed this insight from the brilliant work of Arvind Mandair on colonialism and Sikh reform; see Arvind Mandair, *Religion and the Specter of the West: Sikhism, India, Postcoloniality, and the Politics of Translation* (New York: Columbia University Press, 2009). Indeed, much of my analysis here is indebted to Mandair's thought.

26. Ismā'īl, *Taqwīyat al-Īmān* (Lāhore), 38.

27. Ismā'īl, *Taqwīyat al-Īmān* (Karāchī), 101.

28. Ibid., 100.

29. Shāh Muḥammad Ismā'īl, *Yak Roza* (Multān: Farūqī Kutub Khāna, n.d.). In addition to *imkān-i kizb* or God's capacity to lie, the notion of God's capacity to renege on a promise and the dispute surrounding it are less commonly referred to as *imkān-i khalf-i wa'īd*.

30. Ibid., 14.

31. Giorgio Agamben, *Homo Sacer: Sovereign Power and Bare Life* (Stanford, CA: Stanford University Press, 1998), 44–45.

32. Ibid., 45.

33. Qur'an 36:81–82 (translation mine).

34. Ismā'īl, *Yak Roza*, 2.

35. Ibid., 3.

36. Ibid.

37. Ibid.

38. Qur'ān 3:59 (translation mine).

39. Ismā'īl, *Yak Roza*, 4.

40. Ibid.

41. Ibid.

42. Ibid.

43. Jean Elshtain, *Sovereignty, God, State, and Self* (New York: Basic Books, 2008), 21.

44. Ibid.

45. Francis Oakley, *Politics and Eternity: Studies in the History of Medieval and Early-Modern Political Thought* (Leiden: E. J. Brill, 1999), 43–44.

46. Ibid., 44.

chapter four. Salvational Politics

1. For a useful survey of medieval and early modern Indo-Muslim political thought, especially as reflected in key Persian texts, see Muzaffar Alam, *The Languages of Political Islam: India, 1200–1800* (Chicago: University of Chicago Press, 2004), esp. 35–80.

2. For an engaging analysis of Sunnī political thought in early and medieval Islam, see Ovamir Anjum, *Politics, Law, and Community in Islamic Thought: The Taymiyyan Moment* (New York: Cambridge University Press, 2012), 1–136.

3. See Alam, *Languages of Political Islam*, 35–80.

4. The word *kamāl* (pl. *kamālāt*) is often translated as "perfection." I find that translation somewhat inadequate, as it does not communicate the attributive sense or processual nature of the term. I instead render it as "talent," a translation that also works better with the modality of Ismā'īl's usage in this context.

5. Shāh Muḥammad Ismā'īl, *Manṣab-i Imāmat* (Delhi: Maṭba'-i Fārūqī, 1899), 29–30. Subsequent page citations from this work are to this edition and are given parenthetically in the text.

6. Quoted in ibid., 55.

7. Ismā'īl's statement here also reminds us that the common translation of *'amr bi'l ma'rūf* as "commanding the good" is not always adequate or accurate. In this case, for example, enjoining goodness does not entail so much a hierarchical sovereign command issued from a position of power but rather an attempt to guide, advise, and engage the politically powerful in moral instruction and pedagogy. The cultivation of virtue through pedagogy is far more central to the modality of *'amr bi'l ma'rūf* here (and in many other contexts) than the "command to do good." *'Amr bi'l ma'rūf* thus signifies more a process of moral embodiment than an instant sovereign decision or command to become good or convert into goodness.

chapter five. Intercessory Wars

1. Shāh Muḥammad Ismā'īl, *Taqwīyat al-Īmān* (Lāhore: Maṭba' Aḥmadī, n.d.), 18.

2. Quoted in ibid., 24. The context of this Ḥadīth is the famous revelation of the "warning verse" in the Qur'ān (26:214) in which God instructs the Prophet to "warn his most intimate kin" (*'ashīrat al-aqribīn*).

3. Qur'ān 72:21–22. Quoted in Shāh Muḥammad Ismā'īl, *Taqwīyat al-Īmān* (Karāchī: Ṣiddīqī Trust, n.d.), 95.

4. Ibid.

5. Ibid., 96.

6. Qur'ān 10:18. Quoted in Ismā'īl, *Taqwīyat al-Īmān* (Lāhore), 4.

7. Qur'ān 23:88. Quoted in ibid., 5.

8. Qur'ān 20:109.

9. Qur'ān 34:23.

10. Ismā'īl, *Taqwīyat al-Īmān* (Karāchī), 100.

11. Ibid., 101–2.

12. Ibid., 102–3.

13. Ibid., 103.

14. Ismā'īl, *Taqwīyat al-Īmān* (Lāhore), 22.

15. Ibid., 23.

16. Ibid.

17. Ismā'īl, *Taqwīyat al-Īmān* (Karāchī), 68.

18. Ibid.

19. It is useful to note that the invocation of the *Chamār* as an object of denigration in the context of intra-Muslim debates is a feature seen throughout the nineteenth century, with far fewer if any such references in the late eighteenth century. The interaction between British colonial reconfigurations of caste categories like *Chamār* and the formation of taboos surrounding such categories among the North Indian Muslim scholarly elite is a subject deserving of more intensive research and reflection. For more on the colonial and contemporary politics of caste, especially in relation to the former "untouchables"/Dalits, see Ramnarayan Rawat and K. Satyanarayana, eds., *Dalit Studies* (Durham, NC: Duke University Press, 2016); Anupama Rao, *The Caste Question: Dalits and the Politics of Modern India* (Berkeley: University of California Press, 2009); Rupa Viswanath, *The Pariah Problem: Caste, Religion, and the Social in Modern India* (New York: Columbia University Press, 2014); and Nathaniel Roberts, *To Be Cared For: The Power of Conversion and the Foreignness of Belonging in an Indian Slum* (Berkeley: University of California Press, 2016).

20. Arvind Mandair, *Religion and the Specter of the West: Sikhism, India, Postcoloniality, and the Politics of Translation* (New York: Columbia University Press, 2009), 234; Martin Heidegger, *Metaphysical Foundations of Logic* (Bloomington: Indiana University Press, 1984), 160.

21. Heidegger, *Metaphysical Foundations of Logic*, 160.

22. Ibid., 161.

23. Ibid., 162.

24. Ibid.

25. To clarify, this is my reading of Ismā'īl's political theology; he did not frame his argument through the categories of individual and collective obligations in Islamic law.

26. Chapters in the next section examine the relationship between political theology, law, and conceptions of ideal publics in greater depth.

27. Fazl-i Rasūl Badāyūnī, *'Aqīda-yi Shafā'at Kitāb wa Sunnat kī Rawshnī Mayn* (Badāyūn: Tāj al-Fuḥūl Academy, 2009), 84. Muḥammad Mūsā Dihlavī was the son of Shāh Rafī'al-Dīn (Ismā'īl's uncle).

28. Margrit Pernau has usefully informed us concerning the paper trail of this text. After its composition in prison, it was "smuggled out on various scraps of paper and cloth and secretly sent to his son in India. The latter subsequently reconstructed the fragments of text and forwarded them to those Indian scholars who had chosen to migrate to Mecca after 1857. From there they arrived back in India on the eve of the First World War. They were mentioned publicly for the first time in 1914." Pernau concluded from this book history, a conclusion with which I concur, that "alterations to the substance and structure of the text cannot be ruled out, but neither is there any evidence of such alteration." Margrit Pernau, *Ashraf into Middle Classes: Muslims in Nineteenth-Century Delhi* (New Delhi: Oxford University Press, 2013), 229–30.

29. Fazl-i Ḥaqq Khayrābādī, *Al-Thawra al-Hindīya (Bāghī-yi Hindustān)* (Lāhore: Maktabah-yi Qādirīya, 1997), 252.

30. For a useful account of the contributions of the Khayrābādī school to Islamic theology and philosophy in South Asia, see Asad Ahmad and Reza Pourjavady, "Theology in the Indian Subcontinent," in *The Oxford Handbook of Islamic Theology*, ed. Sabine Schmidtke (Oxford: Oxford University Press, 2016), 606–24.

31. Asīd al-Ḥaqq Badāyūnī, *Khayrābādīyāt* (Lāhore: Maktaba A'lā Hazrat, 2011), 24–25.

32. 'Abd al-Ḥayy al-Ḥasanī, *Nuzhat al-Khawāṭir wa Bahjat al-Masāmi' wa-l-Nawāẓir*, vol. 7 (Dār Arafāt: Ṭayyab Academy, 1993), 384.

33. A. Badāyūnī, *Khayrābādīyāt*, 89–102.

34. This title is also often attributed to 'Alī ibn Abī Ṭālib.

35. Fazl-i Rasūl Badāyūnī, *Al-Bawāriq al-Muḥammadīya li-Rajm al-Shayāṭīn al-Najdīya* (Lāhore: Dār al-Islām, 2014); Fazl-i Rasūl Badāyūnī, *Al-Fawz al-Mubīn bi Shafā'at al-Shāfi'īn*, in *Majmū'a Rasā'il-i Fazl-i Rasūl* (Karāchī: Maktabah Barakāt al-Madīna; Dār al-Un'mān, 2010); Fazl-i Rasūl Badāyūnī, *Sayf al-Jabbār al-Maslūl 'alā a'dā' al-Abrār* (Lāhore: Maktabah-yi Rizvīya, 1973); Fazl-i Rasūl Badāyūnī, *Iḥqāq al-Ḥaqq wa Ibṭāl al-Bāṭil* (Badāyūn: Tāj al-Fuḥūl Academy, 2007); Fazl-i Rasūl Badāyūnī, *Al-Mu'taqad al-Muntaqad* (Istānbul: Ḥakīkat Kitābevi, 1985).

36. F. Badāyūnī, *Majmū'a Rasā'il*, 7–95.

37. Fazl-i Rasūl Badāyūnī, *Majmū'a Rasā'il*; *Al-Bawāriq al-Muḥammadīya*; *Sayf al-Jabbār*; *Fawz al-Mubīn*; *Iḥqāq al-Ḥaqq*; *Al-Mu'taqad al-Muntaqad*.

38. Badāyūnī had written this text at the request of a Meccan scholar.

39. Ibid., 131.

40. For a more detailed examination of Khayrābādī's relations with the British and of his role in the Mutiny of 1857, see Jamal Malik, "Letters, Prison Sketches, and Autobiographical Literature: The Case of Fadl-e Haqq Khairabadi in the Andaman Penal Colony," *Indian Economic and Social History Review* 43, no. 1 (March 2006): 77–100.

41. al-Ḥasanī, *Nuzhat al-Khawāṭir*, 384.

42. A. Badāyūnī, *Khayrābādīyāt*, 107.

43. For more on the Aḥmadī doctrine of prophecy and its place in Muslim thought, see Yohanan Friedmann's classic *Prophecy Continuous: Aspects of Ahmadi Religious Thought and Its Medieval Background* (Berkeley: University of California Press, 1989). See also Adil Khan's excellent book *From Sufism to Ahmadiyya: A Muslim Minority Movement in South Asia* (Bloomington: Indiana University Press, 2015).

44. Khayrābādī also wrote another major and well-known text on the subject of *imkān-i naẓir* called *Imtinā'-i Naẓīr*, or the *Impossibility of Another Muhammad*, sometime between 1848 and 1853. This text was composed in response to Sayyid Aḥmad's disciple Ḥaydar 'Ālī Tonkī's (d. 1865) refutation of Khayrābādī's refutation of Ismā'īl's thought (A. Badayūnī, *Khayrābādīyāt*, 135, 162–71).

45. Fazl-i Ḥaqq Khayrābādī, *Taḥqīq al-Fatwā fī Ibṭāl al-Ṭughwā* (Lāhore: Maktabah-yi Qādirī, 1979), 261; subsequent page citations are to this edition and will be given parenthetically in the text. Ahmad Dallal had argued that among major eighteenth- and nineteenth-century Muslim revivalist scholars, Muḥammad ibn 'Abd al-Wahhāb stood in a league of his own when it came to charging other Muslims of unbelief (*takfīr*) for acts that in his view committed the credal violation of compromising divine sovereignty (Ahmad Dallal, "The Origins and Objectives of Islamic Revivalist Thought: 1750–1850," *Journal of the American Oriental Society* 113, no. 3 [1993]: 341–59). In light of this observation, it is informative that in the nineteenth-century Indian context of the polemic under consideration it was Khayrābādī and later Aḥmad Razā Khān, scholars at the opposite end of the ideological spectrum from ibn 'Abd Wahhāb, who passed the judgment of unbelief on their rivals. This is not simply to point out that anathematizing was not the business solely of Wahhābīs but also to highlight that such judgments were prompted by varied logics of doctrinal transgression, including the charge of causing affront to the status of the Prophet. The exclusionary logics and ideologies that impelled the arrows of anathema varied considerably and were shot in unpredictable directions.

46. Quoted in Khayrābādī, *Taḥqīq al-Fatwā*, 265.

47. Khayrābādī, *Taḥqīq al-Fatwā*, 267. A Ḥadīth Qudsī is a prophetic saying in which the Prophet transmitted God's words. Unlike a regular prophetic saying, the chain of transmission (*isnād*) for a Ḥadīth Qudsī originates not with the Prophet but with God.

48. Qur'ān 2:253.

49. For an illuminating overview of such traditions of prophetology in Islam, see Carl Ernst, "Muhammad as the Pole of Existence," in *Cambridge Companion to Muhammad*, ed. Jonathan Brockopp (Cambridge: Cambridge University Press, 2009). Also see Anne Marie Schimmel, *And Muhammad Is His Messenger: The Veneration of the Prophet in Islamic Piety* (Chapel Hill: University of North Carolina Press, 1985).

50. Qur'ān 48:10.

51. Qur'ān 33:40. For a fascinating discussion of the intriguing interpretations and transformations of the category "seal" or *khatm/khātim*, see Friedmann's monumental work *Prophecy Continuous*.

52. Qur'ān 36:81–82 (translation mine).

53. Qur'ān 36:78 (translation mine).

54. Qur'ān 3:59 (translation mine).

55. With this sentence Khayrābādī closed his brief initial rejoinder in response to *Taqwīyat al-Īmān*, *Objection against Taqwīyat al-Īmān's Controversial Passage* (*Taqrīr-i I'tirāz bar 'Ībārat-i Taqwīyat al-Īmān*). This text appears at the end of the printed edition of *Taḥqīq al-Fatwā*.

56. Shāh Muḥammad Ismā'īl, *Yak Roza* (Multān: Farūqī Kutub Khāna, n.d.), 25.

57. Carl Schmitt, *Political Theology: Four Chapters on the Concept of Sovereignty* (Cambridge, MA: MIT Press, 1986), 44.

58. See John Modern, *Secularism in Antebellum America* (Chicago: University of Chicago Press, 2011), and Michael Warner, "The Evangelical Public Sphere," A. S. W. Rosenbach Lectures, University of Pennsylvania, March 2009, https://repository.upenn.edu/rosenbach/2/.

59. Though concerned with a slightly later period, on the history of the book and especially the impact of the commercialization of print on the formation of reading practices and publics in nineteenth-century North India, see the fascinating study by Ulrike Stark, *An Empire of Books: The Naval Kishore Press and the Diffusion of the Printed Word in Colonial India* (New Delhi: Permanent Black, 2007).

60. Mandair, *Religion and the Specter*, 175–239.

61. Ibid.

62. Ibid., 61.

63. Gananath Obeyesekere, "Religious Symbolism and Political Change in Ceylon," *Modern Ceylon Studies* 1, no. 1 (1970): 43–63. As Ananda Abeysekara has usefully pointed out, Obeyesekere's argument was not that Protestant Buddhism is equivalent to Protestantism but rather that it was amplified with echoes of a Protestant ethos (Ananda Abeysekara, "Protestant Buddhism and 'Influence': The Temporality of a Concept," *Qui Parle* 28, no. 1 [2019]: 1–75). Also, Obeyesekere's point was not that Protestant Buddhists were any less or more Buddhist than other Buddhists. Rather, *Protestant Buddhist* is an appellation that captures the diffusion of colonial capillary power in the life of a discursive tradition in nineteenth-century Ceylon. Obviously, Protestantism is itself not an unchanging monolith or a singular substance, in any moment in history, including the modern colonial moment. As Barton Scott has brilliantly argued, in the context of modern South Asia "The very iterability of the 'Protestant' ensured that each citation of the original would diverge from it, thereby calling the unity of that original into question." J. Barton Scott, *Spiritual Despots: Modern Hinduism and the Genealogies of Self-Rule* (Chicago: University of Chicago Press, 2015), 132.

64. Ibid., 78–85; David Scott, *Conscripts of Modernity: The Tragedy of Colonial Enlightenment* (Durham, NC: Duke University Press, 2004), 98–132; Ananda Abeysekara, "Religious Studies' Mishandling of Origin and Change: Time, Tradition, and Form-of-Life in Buddhism," *Cultural Critique* 98 (Winter 2018): 8.

65. Abeysekara, "Religious Studies' Mishandling," 8–9.

66. Abeysekara, "Protestant Buddhism."

67. Mandair, *Religion and the Specter*, 78.

68. David Scott, *Refashioning Futures: Criticism after Postcoloniality* (Princeton, NJ: Princeton University Press, 1999), 8–9.

chapter six. Reforming Religion in the Shadow of Colonial Power

1. Ashraf 'Alī Thānvī, *Arwāḥ-yi Salāsa* (Karāchī: Dār al-Ishā'at, 2001), 209–10.

2. On the perpetuation of the category of "Wahhābī" as a symbol of Muslim extremism in colonial South Asia, see Ilyse Morgenstein Fuerst, *Indian Muslim Minorities and the 1857 Rebellion: Religion, Rebels and Jihad* (London: I. B. Tauris, 2017). While Fuerst focuses on the British Orientalist contributions to the ominous signification of this term, it is interesting to note its attachment to a "black foreign Muslim scholar" in this particular narrative, signaling a narrative gesture toward the transnational purchase of the category "Wahhābī" as a marker of intra-Muslim "otherness" by the late nineteenth century.

3. A. Thānvī, *Arwāḥ-yi Salāsa*, 209–10. We are not told in what language the black foreigner communicated with the local congregants, though one can guess that it was classical Arabic, since that was and remains the lingua franca of the Muslim scholarly elite.

4. Ibid.

5. For more on the emergence of the mosque as a site of intra-Muslim contest in colonial South Asia, see Sana Haroon's forthcoming essay "The Fragmentation of South Asian Mosque Practice under the Colonial State," unpublished paper in author's possession.

6. For arguably the best and most incisive analysis of the dizzying array of Muslim scholarly responses to British colonialism, and of the variety of Muslim reformist, revivalist, and modernist movements that catapulted during this moment, see chapter 1 of the monumental recent book by Muhammad Qasim Zaman, *Islam in Pakistan: A History* (Princeton, NJ: Princeton University Press, 2018), 14–53.

7. Quoted in Bernard Cohn, "Representing Authority in Victorian India," in *The Invention of Tradition*, ed. Eric Hobsbawm and Terence Ranger (Cambridge: Cambridge University Press, 1992), 165.

8. David Gilmartin, "Democracy, Nationalism, and the Public: A Speculation on Colonial Muslim Politics," *South Asia* 14, no. 1 (1991): 123–40.

9. Ibid.

10. Julia Stephens, "The Politics of Muslim Rage: Secular Law and Religious Sentiment in Late Colonial India," *History Workshop Journal* 77 (2014): 45–64.

11. For an arresting study on the colonial reconfiguration of religion as an increasingly defined and competitive category in South Asia, see Teena Purohit's splendid book *The Aga Khan Case: Religion and Identity in Colonial India* (Cambridge, MA: Harvard University Press, 2012).

12. Arvind Mandair, *Religion and the Specter of the West: Sikhism, India, Postcoloniality, and the Politics of Translation* (New York: Columbia University Press, 2009).

13. For more focused analyses of varied and intersecting threads of intrareligious and interreligious polemics in colonial South Asia, see the collection of essays in Kenneth Jones, ed., *Religious Controversy in British India: Dialogues in South Asian Languages* (Albany: State University of New York Press, 1992). On Muslim-Christian polemics, see Avril Powell, *Muslims and Missionary in Pre-Mutiny India* (Richmond, Surrey: Curzon Press, 1993).

14. In his insightful dissertation, S. Akbar Zaidi has offered the useful reminder that these debates and polemics were not restricted to the eminent pioneers and leaders of major Muslim reformist groups but also enveloped "hun-

dreds, if not thousands" (17) of other lesser-known Urdu writers and publicists in late nineteenth-century North India. The intensity as well as the amount of such polemical activity, Zaidi rightly points out, militates against the presence in this period of the conception of a unified Indian Muslim "nation" (*qawm*). S. Akbar Zaidi, "Contested Identities and the Muslim Qaum in Northern India: c. 1860–1900" (PhD diss., Cambridge University, 2009).

15. On Deobandī support of the Pakistan movement, see Venkat Dhulipala, *Creating a New Medina: State Power, Islam, and the Quest for Pakistan in Late Colonial North India* (New Delhi: Cambridge University Press, 2015). On Madanī's opposition, see Barbara Metcalf, *Husain Ahmad Madani: The Jihad for Islam and India's Freedom* (London: OneWorld Press, 2008). For later twentieth-century developments in Deobandī political thought, see Muhammad Qasim Zaman, *The Ulama in Contemporary Islam: Custodians of Change* (Princeton, NJ: Princeton University Press, 2002), 87–111, and Barbara Metcalf, "'Traditionalist' Islamic Activism: Deoband, Tablighis, and the Talibs," in "After September 11: 2001 Essays Archive," Social Science Research Council, 2001, http://essays.ssrc.org/sept11/essays/metcalf.htm.

16. See Muhammad Qasim Zaman, *Modern Islamic Thought in a Radical Age: Religious Authority and Internal Criticism* (New York: Cambridge University Press, 2012), and SherAli Tareen, "Revolutionary Hermeneutics: Translating the Qur'ān as a Manifesto for Revolution," *Journal of Religious and Political Practice* 3, nos. 1–2 (2017): 1–24.

17. To be precise, Nānautvī and Khān did not spar with each other directly. However, a major part of Khān's later attack on the Deobandī ideology was centered on Nānautvī's views, especially the controversy surrounding his position on God's capacity to produce a second Muḥammad (*imkān-i naẓīr*) as presented in Nānautvī's book *Cautioning the Public* (*Taḥzīr al-Nās*).

18. Louis Dumont, *Religion, Politics, and History in India: Collected Papers in Indian Sociology* (The Hague: Mouton, 1971), 118, quoted in Gyanendra Pandey, *The Construction of Communalism in Colonial North India* (Delhi: Oxford University Press, 1990), 4.

19. Quoted in Muḥammad Iqbāl Qurayshī, *Bid'at kī Ḥaqīqat awr us ke Aḥkām* (Lāhore: Idārah-yi Islāmīyāt, 2000), 27.

20. Ashraf 'Alī Thānvī, *Al-Ifādāt al-Yawmīya*, vol. 3 (Multān: Idārah-yi Ta'līfāt-i Ashrafīya, n.d.), 235–37.

21. Aḥmad Razā Khān, *Al-Dawlat al-Makkīya bi-l-Mādat al-Ghaybīya* (Lāhore: Nazir Sons, 2000), 289. I have used both the Lāhore and Karāchī editions of this text in this book and have specified which for each citation.

22. Rashīd Aḥmad Gangohī, *Fatāwā-yi Rashīdīya* (Karāchī: Muḥammad Karkhānah-yi Islāmī Kutub, 1987), 423.

chapter seven. Law, Sovereignty, and the Boundaries of Normative Practice

1. Michel Foucault, "A Preface to Transgression," in *Religion and Culture: Michel Foucault*, ed. Jeremy Carrette (New York: Routledge, 1999), 60.

2. Mary Douglas, *Purity and Danger* (London: Routledge, 2002), 50.

3. Muḥyīuddīn al-Nawawī, *Al-Arba'īn* (Cairo: Maktabat al-Khānjī, 2005), 5–7.

4. Maribel Fierro, "The Treatises against Innovations '(kutub al-bida'),'" *Der Islam* 68, no. 1 (1992): 204–46. These examples appear on 211–16 and 220.

5. Umar F. Abd-Allah, "Creativity, Innovation and Heresy in Islam," in *Voices of Islam*, vol. 5, ed. Omid Safi (Westport, CT: Praeger, 2007), 15.

6. I should note here my profound disagreement with Mehran Kamrava's approach toward engaging the topic of innovation in Islam in his volume *Innovation in Islam* as a problem of "overarching conservative inertia" that needs fixing. Rather than trying to diagnose "obstacles to innovation" in a bid to overcome them, far more analytically profitable is the task of closely navigating the competing logics of innovation, normativity, and heresy that are invested in and divested from the category of *bid'a* in particular conjunctures of authoritative discourse and debate. Such an approach might help one avoid the formulation of such noxious questions as "Why has the West developed and modernized, while the Muslim world has lagged behind?" or the advancement of such unfortunate sweeping civilizational declarations as "Gone are the days when Islamic intellectual achievements—in mathematics and astronomy, artillery and industry, medicine, philosophy, and physics—paved the way and helped inform Europe's scientific revolution. Islam's own internal scientific revolution was aborted, its spirit of discovery dampened, its contribution to world civilization now much smaller than that of Europe." These comments are yawningly ridiculous. Mehran Kamrava, ed., *Innovation in Islam: Traditions and Contributions* (Berkeley: University of California Press, 2011), cover page and 3.

7. Muhammad Qasim Zaman's *Ashraf 'Ali Thanawi: Islam in Modern South Asia* (Oxford: Oneworld Publications, 2008), 17.

8. Ibid., 30.

9. Different aspects of Thānvī's scholarly oeuvre have been brilliantly explored in three dissertations: in chronological order, Darakhshan Khan, "Fashioning the Pious Self: Middle Class Religiosity in Colonial India" (PhD diss., University of Pennsylvania, 2016); Ali Mian, "Surviving Modernity: Ashraf 'Ali Thanvi and the Making of Muslim Orthodoxy in Colonial India" (PhD diss., Duke University, 2015), and Fareeha Khan, "Traditionalist Approaches to Shari'ah Reform: Mawlana Ashraf 'Ali Thanawi's Fatwa on Women's Right to Divorce" (PhD diss., University of Michigan–Ann Arbor, 2008).

10. Christine Korsgaard, *The Sources of Normativity* (Cambridge: Cambridge University Press, 1996), 8, 9.

11. See Brett Wilson, "Failure of Nomenclature: The Concept of Orthodoxy in the Study of Islam," *Comparative Islamic Studies* 3, no. 2 (2007): 169–94.

12. Roberto Esposito, *Two: The Machine of Political Theology and the Place of Thought* (New York: Fordham University Press, 2016).

13. I thank Arvind Mandair for bringing Esposito's book to my attention.

14. Esposito, *Two*, 23.

15. Arvind Mandair, "Decolonizing Secularism's 'Conceptual Matrix,'" *Comparative Studies of South Asia, Africa, and the Middle East* 38, no. 2 (2018): 443–51.

16. See Arvind Mandair, *Religion and the Specter of the West: Sikhism, India, Postcoloniality, and the Politics of Translation* (New York: Columbia University Press, 2009).

17. For instance, see Robert Langer and Udo Simon, "The Dynamics of Orthodoxy and Heterodoxy: Dealing with Divergence in Muslim Discourses and Islamic Studies," *Die Welt des Islams: International Journal for the Study of Modern Islam* 48, nos. 3/4 (2008): 273–88.

18. Gil Anidjar, *Blood: A Critique of Christianity* (New York: Columbia University Press, 2016). In his magisterial work *What Is Islam? The Importance of Being Islamic*, Shahab Ahmed took issue with an earlier formulation of my conceptualization of normativity by noting, correctly I would add, that the enforcement of normativity is not the exclusive domain of the *'ulamā'* in Muslim thought and history (though perhaps he somewhat downplays the role and significance of the *'ulamā'* in this regard). I have found Ahmed's observation helpful in refining and reformulating my phraseology. However, I should clarify that the source of normativity (expert knowledge/authority or otherwise) was hardly the central thrust of my critique of the category of orthodoxy. Far more central to my argument was and is the attempt to wrest the examination of intra-Muslim contestation from the juggernaut of conceptual matrices that replicate and advance the machine of secular political theology, as I just explained. However, I should mention in passing that Ahmed's attachment to the category of orthodoxy seems at first view somewhat surprising and puzzling. After all, is not the valuable project of disrupting dominant legal prescriptive understandings of orthodoxy in Islam at the core of his text? But on closer inspection, his hesitance to abandon the promise and category of orthodoxy is actually not all that surprising. For another central motif of his book is the replacement of one vision of orthodoxy (based on prescriptive law) with another (grounded in love, philosophy, poetry, etc.). This desire for a competing orthodoxy comes through in especially pronounced terms in his frequent historicist empiricist declarations of the number

of times a text was copied, or the volume of readership it achieved, to demonstrate the "centrality" and "dominance" of particular texts and authors to Muslim life (primarily in what he terms the "Bengal to Balkans Complex"; Ahmed, *What Is Islam?*, 7–106). This paradoxical desire to undo dominant understandings of the orthodox while concurrently building new monuments of orthodoxy is a central conceptual tension running through his book.

19. Pierre Bourdieu, *The Logic of Practice* (Stanford, CA: Stanford University Press, 1990), 54. Note that *doxa* is by no means the same as orthodoxy.

20. Ibid., 55.

21. Ibid.

22. Pierre Bourdieu, *Outline of a Theory of Practice* (Stanford, CA: Stanford University Press, 1990), 166.

23. Bourdieu, *Logic of Practice*, 60–61.

24. Hayden White, "The Value of Narrativity," in *On Narrative*, ed. W. J. T. Mitchell (Chicago: University of Chicago Press, 1980), 22–23.

25. For more on al-Shāṭibī and his legal thought, see Khalid Masud, *Shatibi's Philosophy of Islamic Law* (Kuala Lumpur: Islamic Book Trust, 2002).

26. Ebrahim Moosa, *Ghazālī and the Poetics of Imagination* (Chapel Hill: University of North Carolina Press, 2005), 43.

27. Paul Ricoeur, "Narrative Time," in Mitchell, *On Narrative*, 179.

28. Ibrāhīm al-Shāṭibī, *Al-I'tiṣām* (Beirut: Dār al-Kitāb al-'Arabī, 2005), 13. Subsequent citations to this work are to this edition and are given parenthetically in the text.

29. Qur'ān 3:103, my translation.

30. I have chosen here not to give *munkar* the usual translations of "wrong," "evil," "rejected," etc. I have tried to capture instead the idiomatic sense that al-Shāṭibī intends here, which is "the opposite of the normative and the commonly found and accepted."

31. See Ashraf 'Alī Thānvī, *Iṣlaḥ al-Rusūm* (Lāhore: Idārah-yi Ashrafīya, 1958), and Shāh Muḥammad Ismā'īl, *Īzāḥ al-Ḥaqq* (Karāchī: Qadīmī Kutub Khāna, 1976).

32. I have preferred to translate *irtifāqāt* more idiomatically as "instruments of moral cultivation" and not as "supports of civilization," in order to wrest Walī Ullah's thought from the Western colonial histories and their category of civilization. See Talal Asad, "Conscripts of Western Civilization?," in *Dialectical Anthropology: Essays in Honor of Stanley Diamond*, ed. C. Gailey, vol. 1 (Gainesville: University Press of Florida, 1992), 333–51. Moreover, I find cosmological, ritual, and sociopolitical processes of moral cultivation central to his purposes in this text, especially in his mobilization of the category of *irtifāqāt*. Though I have used my own translations in the course of this discussion, and though I ever so mildly disagree with Marcia Hermansen on this par-

ticular translation choice, I nonetheless remain indebted to her seminal English translation of this text. See Marcia Hermansen, *The Conclusive Argument from God: Shah Wali Allah of Delhi's Hujjat Allah al-Baligha* (Leiden: E. J. Brill, 1996).

33. Norbert Elias, *The Civilizing Process: Sociogenetic and Psychogenetic Investigations* (Cambridge: Wiley Blackwell, 2000).

34. Shāh Walī Ullah, *Ḥujjat Allāh al-Bāligha*, vol. 1 (Beirut: Dār al-Jīl, 2005), 100. Subsequent citations of this work are to this edition and are given parenthetically in the text.

35. Talal Asad, *Genealogies of Religion: Discipline and Reasons of Power in Christianity and Islam* (Baltimore: Johns Hopkins University Press, 1993), 290. As Asad memorably wrote, "My concern is to argue against the idea that social life can be likened to a work of art, because social life as a whole is not constructed out of preexisting matter as works of art are. Life is essentially itself. Only the part of it that can be narrativized may be said to be 'made up' like a story by an artist."

36. The "Highest Council" (*al-malā' al a'lā*), or assembly of angels most proximate to God, and the "Supernum Plenum" (*ḥaẓīrat al-quds*), or holy enclave where the best among the assembly of angels gather and individual souls meet the highest spirit, are metaphysical concepts recurrently employed by Walī Ullah in this text. They signify the cosmological workings of the divine normative order and plan governing human salvation. For more on these concepts, see Hermansen, *Conclusive Argument from God*, 46–47.

37. Sa'īd Aḥmad Pālanpūrī, *Raḥmat Allāh al-Wāsi'a, Sharḥ Ḥujjat Allāh al-Bāligha*, vol. 1 (Deoband: Maktabah-yi Hijāz, 2000).

38. Ibid., 509.

39. Sigmund Freud, *Totem and Taboo: Resemblances between the Psychic Lives of Savages and Neurotics* (New York: Barnes and Noble, 2005), 32.

40. Ashraf 'Alī Thānvī, *Al-Ifādāt al-Yawmīya*, vol. 9 (Multān: Idārah-yi Ta'līfāt-i Ashrafīya, 1984), 149.

41. Ismā'īl, *Īzāḥ al-Ḥaqq*, 94.

42. This text was originally composed in Persian—likely toward the end of Ismā'īl's life, as it was left unfinished—and was later translated into Urdu. I have not been able to unearth the original Persian manuscript and thus have relied on the Urdu translation of Mi'rāj Muḥammad Bāriq.

43. Ismā'īl, *Īzāḥ al-Ḥaqq*, 93–95.

44. Ibid.

45. Ibid.

46. Jean-Luc Nancy, "Finite History," in *The States of "Theory": History, Art, and Critical Discourse*, ed. David Carroll (New York: Columbia University Press, 1990), 149.

47. My analysis here is indebted to and inspired by the work of Ananda Abeysekara. See Ananda Abeysekara, *The Politics of Postsecular Religion: Mourning Secular Futures* (New York: Columbia University Press, 2008), 33–83.

48. Ashraf ʻAlī Thānvī, *Wa'ẓ al-Dīn al-Khāliṣ* (Lāhore: Idārah-yi Islāmīya, 2001), 25.

49. Ibid.

50. Ibid.

51. Ismāʻīl, *Īzāḥ al-Ḥaqq*, 5–35.

52. Khalīl Aḥmad Sāharanpūrī, *Al-Barāhīn al-Qāṭiʻa ʻalā Ẓalām al-Anwār al-Sāṭiʻa* (Karāchī: Dār al-Ishāʻat, 1987), 30–170.

53. Ismāʻīl, *Īzāḥ al-Ḥaqq*, 5–35.

54. In Muḥammad Zayd Nadvī, *Fiqh-i Ḥanafī Ke Uṣūl wa Ẓawābiṭ* (Karāchī: Zam Zam, 2003), 125–26.

55. Ibid.

56. Thānvī here was referring to the Muʻtazilītes.

57. In M. Nadvī, *Fiqh-i Ḥanafī Ke Uṣūl*, 125–26.

58. Ibid.

59. Ashraf ʻAlī Thānvī, *Bidʻat kī Ḥaqīqat awr us ke Aḥkām awr Masā'il* (Lāhore: Idārah-yi Islāmīyāt, 2001), 62–63.

60. Ibid., 43.

61. al-Nawawī, *Al-Arbaʻīn*, 5–7.

62. A. Thānvī, *Bidʻat kī Ḥaqīqat*, 43.

63. Ashraf ʻAlī Thānvī, *Maqālāt-i Ḥikmat* (Lāhore: Idārah-yi Ta'līfāt-i Ashrafīya, 1977), 136.

64. In M. Nadvī, *Fiqh-i Ḥanafī Ke Uṣūl*, 135.

65. A. Thanvī, *Al-Ifādāt al-Yawmīya*, 9:98.

66. Muḥammad ibn ʻĀbidīn, *Radd al-Muhtār ʻalā Durr al-Mukhtār*, vol. 2, *Bāb al-Witr wa-l-Nawāfil* (Beirut: Dār al-Kutub al-ʻIlmīya, 1994), 6.

67. Aḥmad Ibn ʻAlī Ibn Ḥajar al-Asqalānī, *Fatḥ al-Bāri Sharḥ Ṣaḥiḥ al-Bukhārī* (Beirut: Dār al-Kutub al-ʻIlmīya, 2003), 2:437.

68. Ibid.

69. Ashraf ʻAlī Thānvī, *Al-Tablīgh* (Deoband: Idārah-yi Ta'līfāt-i Awlīya, 1901), 23.

70. Ibid.

71. A. Thānvī, *Bidʻat ki Ḥaqīqat*, 62.

72. A. Thānvī, *Al-Tablīgh*, 11–15.

73. A. Thānvī, *Al-Ifādāt al-Yawmīya*, 9:48.

74. Ibid.

75. For an intriguing account of shifting Muslim traditional representations of Zayd's life and of his relationship to the Prophet, see David Powers,

Zayd: The Little-Known Story of Muḥammad's Adopted Son (Philadelphia: University of Pennsylvania Press, 2014).

76. Ibid., 95–123.

77. This was a reference to verse 33:37 in the Qur'ān (in the chapter "The Parties/Groups" [*Aḥzāb*]), the pertinent part of which reads: "When Zayd had finished with her, We gave her to you in marriage, so that there should be no difficulty for the believers concerning the wives of their adopted sons, when they have finished with them" (translation from Powers, *Zayd*, 2). This verse, in which God gives the Prophet the green light to marry Zaynab, is one of the rare occasions in the Qur'ān where a member of the early Muslim community, in this case Zayd, is mentioned by name.

78. A. Thānvī, *Al-Ifādāt al-Yawmīya*, 48.

79. Ibid.

80. Ibid.

81. Ibid.

82. Ibrahim Essa, *The Televangelist*, trans. Jonathan Wright (Cairo: Hoopoe Press, 2016). This novel was written in Arabic and then translated into English.

83. Ibid., 17.

84. Quoted in ibid., 21.

85. Quoted in ibid.

86. Ibid., 17–23.

87. Quoted in ibid., 22–23.

88. Ibid.

89. Quoted in Powers, *Zayd*, 34.

90. Ibid., 35. Zaynab, and indeed her family, had at first resisted this marriage proposal, citing Zayd's status as a former slave (of the Prophet, though during Muḥammad's preprophetic years). Eventually, she had to yield in light of verse 36 of chapter 33: "When God and His messenger have decided a matter, it is not for any believing man or woman to have any choice in the affair" (33). The racial dynamics involved here are also interesting. Zayd was not only a slave but also much darker skinned than the "fair-skinned" Zaynab. Add to the mix the intriguing fact that Zayd's first wife (with whom he remained married) was the Prophet's surrogate mother and black Ethiopian slave Baraka, also known as Umm Ayman. Much as Zaynab had resisted marrying Zayd, Zayd had been lukewarm about the Prophet's earnest proposal that he marry Umm Ayman, perhaps, as David Powers has speculated, because she was "a dark-skinned woman" (31).

91. Ibid., 37.

92. Translation from ibid.

93. For more on the possible implications of this verse and of Zayd's disinheritance as the Prophet's adopted son for the concept and institution of prophecy in Islam, see ibid., 97–123.

94. Ibid., 49–57.

95. Essa, *Televangelist*, 25.

96. Quoted in ibid., 21.

chapter eight. Forbidding Piety to Restore Sovereignty

1. See Marion Katz, *The Birth of the Prophet Muhammad: Devotional Piety in Sunni Islam* (London: Routledge, 2007).

2. Jalāl al-Dīn al-Suyūṭī, "Ḥusn al-Maqṣid fī 'Amal al-Mawlid," in *Al-Ḥawī lil-Fatāwī* (Beirut: Dār al-Kutub al-'Ilmīya, 1975), 1:192.

3. Taqī al-Dīn Ibn Taymīya, *Iqtiḍā al-Ṣirāṭ al-Mustaqīm li Mukhālafat Aṣḥāb al-Jahīm* (Cairo: Al-Maktabah al-Tawfīqīya, 2000), 2:123.

4. Ibid.

5. For more on premodern Muslim legal debates on the legitimacy of the *mawlid*, see Raquel Ukeles, "Innovation or Deviation: Exploring the Boundaries of Islamic Devotional Law" (PhD diss., Harvard University, 2006), 200–239.

6. Ashraf 'Alī Thānvī, *Ṭarīqah-yi Mawlid Sharīf* (Lāhore: Idārah-yi Islāmīyāt, 1976). Subsequent citations are to this edition and are given parenthetically in the text. This treatise was originally published in 1899 as part of Thānvī's much larger work on *bid'a* entitled *Mending Conventions* (*Iṣlāḥ al-Rusūm*). The section on *mawlid* from this text was later separately published as *Ṭarīqah-yi Mawlid Sharīf.* I have compared the original text with its later reprint and found no discrepancies or omissions.

7. By "erotic modes of being" I am referring to Thānvī's concern that practices such as putting up lights, using excessive decorations, allowing the intermingling of men and women, and allowing good-looking boys to sing imbued the community with an *eros* that inherently opposed the cultivation of a sober subject and by extension the nurturing of a community committed to the ideal of sobriety in its everyday practice.

8. Costas Douzinas and Ronnie Warrington, *Justice Miscarried: Ethics, Aesthetics and the Law* (New York: Harvester Wheatsheaf, 1999), 83.

9. Michel De Certeau, *The Practice of Everyday Life* (Berkeley: University of California Press, 1984), 50.

10. Barbara Metcalf, *Islamic Revival in British India: Deoband, 1860–1900* (Princeton, NJ: Princeton University Press, 1982), 351.

11. Muhammad Qasim Zaman, *The 'Ulama in Contemporary Islam: Custodians of Change* (Princeton, NJ: Princeton University Press, 2002), 13.

12. Ashraf ʿAlī Thānvī, *Iṣlāḥ al-Rusūm* (Lāhore: Idārah-yi Ta'līfāt-i Ashrafīya, 1958), 10–40.

13. Ibid., 48.

14. Ibid.

15. In thinking through the co-emergence of the passional and the utilitarian in Thānvī's thought, I have benefited greatly from conversations with Ali Mian and Margrit Pernau, as I have benefited from their own work on different aspects of Thānvī's thought and career.

chapter nine. Retaining Goodness

1. On the multiple ways in which the trope of *takfīr* has been deployed, imagined, and contested in Muslim intellectual thought and history, see Camilla Adang, Hassan Ansari, and Maribel Fierro, eds., *Accusations of Unbelief in Islam: A Diachronic Perspective on Takfīr* (Leiden: E. J. Brill, 2016).

2. Aḥmad Razā Khān, *Ḥusām al-Ḥaramayn ʿalā Manḥar al-Kufr wa-l-Mayn* (Lāhore: Maktabah-yi Nabawīya, 1975), 11.

3. The "Holy Sanctuaries" here are Mecca and Medina, the two most sacred cities in the Islamic tradition.

4. ʿAbdul Samīʿ, "*Anwār-i Sāṭiʿa dar Bayān-i Mawlūd wa-l-Fātiḥa*," Aʿlā Ḥazrat Network, n.d., accessed February 16, 2018, www.alahazratnetwork.org; Khalīl Aḥmad Sāharanpūrī, *Al-Barāhīn al-Qāṭiʿa ʿalā Ẓalām al-Anwār al-Sāṭiʿa* (Karāchī: Dār al-Ishāʿat, 1987).

5. Best known for his polemical encounters and his six-volume Arabic polemical text against Christian missionaries *Revealing Truth* (*Iẓhār al-Ḥaqq*), following the 1857 uprising, Kayrānwī fled to Mecca where he spent the latter half of his life. For more on his life, thought, and activities, see Avril Powell, *Muslims and Missionaries in Pre-Mutiny India* (Richmond, Surrey: Curzon Press, 1993), and Seema Alavi, *Muslim Cosmopolitanism in the Age of Empire* (Cambridge, MA: Harvard University Press, 2015).

6. Muḥammad Charyākotī, "*Ṣāḥib-i Anwār-i Sāṭiʿa*," in *Anwār-i Sāṭiʿa dar Bayān-i Mawlūd wa-l-Fātiḥa*, by ʿAbdul Samīʿ (Charyākot: Idārah-yi Furogh-i Islām, 2010), 11–13.

7. This does not mean that Samīʿ was a bad or rebellious student. Rather, his opposition to Deobandī positions reflects (a) the porosity of South Asian Muslim intellectual networks across ideological divisions, and (b) the internal variations and temperamental diversity within the Deoband school (which I discuss more thoroughly in chapter 12). Samīʿ found himself temperamentally closer to the likes of Qāsim Nānautvī and Imdādullah than to the more hardline Deoband pioneers like Gangohī and Sāharanpūrī.

8. This was the same press that later printed Ashraf ʻAlī Thānvī's famous *Heavenly Ornaments* (*Bihishtī Zaywar*) in 1905.

9. Aḥmad Razā Khān, *Al-Fatāwā al-Rizvīya* (Gujarāt: Markaz-i Ahl-i Sunnat, 2006), vol. 15.

10. Ashraf ʻAlī Thānvī, *Al-Ifādāt al-Yawmīya* (Multān: Idārah-yi Ta'līfāt-i Ashrafīya, n.d), 4:58–59.

11. Ibid., 6:83. For more on the debates between the Āryā Samāj founder Dayānanda Saraswatī (d. 1883) and the Deoband pioneers, see my "Polemic of Shahjahanpur: Religion, Miracles, History," *Islamic Studies* 51, no. 1 (2012): 49–67. See also Fuad Naeem, "Interreligious Debates, Rational Theology, and the ʻUlamā' in the Public Sphere: Muḥammad Qāsim Nanautvī and the Making of Modern Islam in South Asia" (PhD diss., Georgetown University, 2015). For Āryā intra- and inter-religious polemical encounters in colonial India, see Kenneth Jones, *Arya Dharm: Hindu Consciousness in 19th-Century Punjab* (Berkeley: University of California Press, 1976).

12. See Natana DeLong-Bas, *Wahhabi Islam: From Revival and Reform to Global Jihad* (New York: Oxford University Press, 2004); David Commins, *The Wahhabi Mission and Saudi Arabia* (London: I. B. Tauris, 2006); and Samira Haj, *Reconfiguring Islamic Tradition: Reform, Rationality and Modernity* (Stanford, CA: Stanford University Press, 2009).

13. Usha Sanyal, *Devotional Islam and Politics in British India: Ahmad Riza Khan Barelwi and His Movement, 1870–1920* (Delhi: Oxford University Press, 1996), 49–68.

14. Ibid., 51.

15. Muḥammad Masʻūd Aḥmad, *Ḥayāt-i Mawlānā Aḥmad Razā Khān Barelvī* (Siālkot: Islāmī Kutub Khānā, 1981), 83–97.

16. This seminary was originally named Miṣbāḥ al-Tahzīb (The lamp of moral cultivation).

17. M. Aḥmad, *Ḥayāt-i Mawlānā*, 122.

18. See Aḥmad Zaynī Daḥlān, *Al-Durar al-Sanīya fī-Radd ʻalā al-Wahhābīya* (Istanbul: Dār al-Shafqa, n.d.).

19. Aḥmad Razā Khān, *Al-Dawlat al-Makkīya bi-l-Mādat al-Ghaybīya* (Lāhore: Nazir Sons, 2000).

20. Nasīm Bastāvī and Muḥammad Ṣābir, *Aʻlā Ḥazrat Barelvī: Ḥālāt-i Mujaddid* (Lāhore: Maktabah-yi Nabavīya, 1976), 47–51.

21. Ebrahim Moosa, introduction to "The Deoband Madrasa," ed. Ebrahim Moosa, special issue, *Muslim World Journal* 99, no. 3 (July 2009): 427.

22. On the emergence and flourishing of hierarchical normative imaginaries in Muslim thought and social history, see Louise Marlow, *Hierarchy and Egalitarianism in Islamic Thought* (Cambridge: Cambridge University Press, 2002).

23. In the context of South Asia, the term *sharīf* (pl. *shurafā'*) can have an explicitly Islamic connotation meaning descendants of the Prophet (usually *sayyids*) or may simply refer to clans that have historically served as the landed elite in the region. For more on their role in the politics of colonial and postcolonial South Asia, see David Gilmartin, *Empire and Islam: Punjab and the Making of Pakistan* (Berkeley: University of California Press, 1988).

24. Aḥmad Razā Khān, *Irā'at al-Adab li Fāḍil al-Nasab*, in *Al-Fatāwā al-Rizvīya*, 9:201–77.

25. Ibid., 206.

26. Ibid., 202.

27. Ibid., 204.

28. Ibid., 255.

29. Ibid., 253.

30. Aḥmad Razā Khān, *Iqāmat al-Qiyāma 'alā Ṭā'in al-Qiyām li Nabī Tihāma*, in *Al-Fatāwā al-Rizvīya*, vol. 26.

31. Muḥammad al-Qasṭalānī, *Al-Mawāhib al-Ladunīya bi'l-Minaḥ al-Muḥammadīya* (Beirut: Al-Maktab al-Islāmī, 1991), quoted in A. Khān, *Iqāmat al-Qiyāma*, 543.

32. Abū 'Īsā al-Tirmidhī, *Jāmi' al-Tirmidhī*, vol. 1 (Delhi: Amīn, n.d.), 206.

33. A. Khān, *Iqāmat al-Qiyāma*, 525–31.

34. Ibid., 546–50.

35. Ibid., 532.

36. Ibid., 537.

37. Sāharanpūrī, *Al-Barāhīn al-Qāṭi'a*, 39.

38. *Pākhāna* usually refers to the latrine or the lavatory but can also at times be used to refer to excrement. It seems that Sāharanpūrī meant it here in this latter sense. A possible alternate reading of this sentence as "animal manure that is kept in latrines" is less plausible, as Sāharanpūrī seems most interested here in the benefit or goodness inherent in *pākhāna* rather than in its secondary uses, such as the capacity to serve as storage space.

39. Sāharanpūrī, *Al-Barāhīn al-Qāṭi'a*, 39.

40. Ibid.

41. A. Khān, *Iqāmat al-Qiyāma*, 539–43.

42. Ibid., 540–42.

43. Ibid., 544–45.

44. Ibn Ḥajar al-Haytamī, *Al-Jawhar al-Munaẓẓam Muqaddima fī Ādāb al-Safar* (Lāhore: Al-Maktabah al-Qādirīya fi'l Jāmi'a al-Niẓāmīya), 12, quoted in ibid., 531.

45. A. Khān, *Iqāmat al-Qiyāma*, 504–34.

46. Ibid., 547.

47. Aḥmad Razā Khān, *Al-Ḥujja al-Fā'iḥa li Ṭīb al-Tā'īn wa-l-Fātiḥa*, in *Al-Fatāwā al-Rizvīya*, 9:580.

48. Ibid., 582.

49. A. Khān, *Iqāmat al-Qiyāma*, 547.

50. Aḥmad Ibn Ḥanbal, *Musnad Aḥmad Ibn Ḥanbal*, vol. 6 (Beirut: Dār al-Fikr, n.d.), 368.

51. al-Ḥākim al-Nīsāpūrī, *Al-Mustadrak 'alā Ṣaḥīḥayn fi-l-Ḥadīth* (Beirut: Dār al-Fikr, n.d), 6:572, quoted in A. Khān, *Iqāmat al-Qiyāma*, 513.

52. Abū Ḥāmid al-Ghazālī, *'Ihyā' 'Ulūm al-Dīn Kitāb al-Samā ' wa al-Wajd* (Cairo: Al-Mashhad al-Husaynī, n.d.), 305.

53. Samī', *Anwār-i Sāṭi'a*, 52.

54. Both Nasafī and Taftazānī were from Samarqand, in what is today the country of Uzbekistan in Central Asia.

55. Quoted in Samī', *Anwār-i Sāṭi'a*, 52.

56. Muḥammad al-Hirawī, *Sharḥ Kitāb al-Fiqh al-Akbar* (Beirut: Dār al-Kutub al-'Ilmīya, 2006), Quoted in Samī', *Anwār-i Sāṭi'a*, 52.

57. Quoted in ibid.

58. Ibid., 53.

59. Ibid.

60. Sāharanpūrī, *Al-Barāhīn al-Qāṭi'a*, 75.

61. Ibid., 76.

62. Ibid., 78.

63. Ibid.

64. Ibid., 79.

65. Ibid.

66. Sayyid Ja'far Barzanjī, *'Iqd al-Jawhar fī Mawlid al-Nabī al-Azhar* (Lāhore: Jāmi'a Islamīya, n.d.), 25.

67. Daḥlān, *Al-Durar al-Sanīya*, 18.

68. al-Nīsāpūrī, *Al-Mustadrak*, 1:116.

69. A. Khān, *Iqāmat al-Qiyāma*, 521.

70. Ibid.

71. Ibn Māja, *Sunan Ibn Māja* (Cairo: Dār al-Ḥadīth, 1998), Ḥadīth 3950, quoted in ibid., 522.

72. Shāh Walī Ullah, *Al-Durr al-Thamīn fi Mubasharāt al-Nabī al-Amīn* (Faisalābād: Kutub Khānā-i 'Alawīya Rizvīya, n.d.), 40.

73. Quoted in A. Khān, *Al-Ḥujja al-Fā'iḥa*, 575.

74. Shāh Walī Ullah, *Al-Intibāh fī Salāsil Awlīyā' Allāh* (Delhi: Barqī Press, n.d.), 100.

75. Shāh 'Abdul 'Azīz, *Tuḥfat Ithnā 'Asharīya* (Lāhore: Sohail Academy, n.d), 214. "*Umūr-i Takvīnīya*" (sing. *amr-i takvīnī*) refers to divine orders or

commands by virtue of which things are the way they are. One may think of this concept as the divine commands that order the ontology of the world. *Umūr-i Takvīnīya* is contrasted with the idea of "*Umūr-i Taklīfīya*" (sing. *amr-i taklīfī*). *Umūr-i Taklīfīya* means divine normative orders that institute legal prescriptions to be followed by subjects. See Michel Chodkiewicz, *The Spiritual Writings of Amir 'Abdul Kader* (Albany: State University of New York Press, 1995), 220, and Michael Sells, *Mystical Languages of Unsaying* (Chicago: University of Chicago Press, 1994), 250.

76. Shāh 'Abdul 'Azīz, *Tafsīr-i 'Azīzī* (Delhi: Lāl Kūwān, n.d.), 206.

77. Shāh Rafī' al-Dīn, *Fatāwā Shāh Rafī' al-Dīn* (Delhi: Maṭba'-i Mujtabā'ī, n.d.), quoted in A. Khān, *Al-Ḥujja al-Fā'iḥa*, 591–92.

78. Ibid., quoted in A. Khān, *Al-Ḥujja al-Fā'iḥa*, 592.

79. A. Khān, *Iqāmat al-Qiyāma*, 584.

80. Ibid.

81. Ibid.

chapter ten. Convergences

1. Yasīn Akhtar Miṣbāḥī, *Imām Aḥmad Razā: Radd-i Bid'āt wa Munkarāt* (Karāchī: Idārah-yi taṣnīfāt-i Imām Aḥmad Razā, 1985), 529.

2. Ibid.

3. Ibn al-Humām, *Sharḥ Fatḥ al-Qadīr* (Beirut: Dār al-Fikr, 1900), quoted in Aḥmad Razā Khān, *Iqāmat al-Qiyāma 'alā Ṭā'in al-Qiyām li Nabī Tihāma*, in *Al-Fatāwā al-Rizvīya* (Gujarāt: Markaz-i Ahl-i Sunnat, 2006), 26:530.

4. A. Khān, *Iqāmat al-Qiyāma*, 531.

5. Faisal Devji, "Gender and the Politics of Space: The Movement for Women's Reform in Muslim India, 1857–1900," *South Asia: Journal of South Asian Studies* 14, no. 1 (1991): 150.

6. A. Khān, *Iqāmat al-Qiyāma*, 536.

7. Ibid., 534.

8. Ibid., 536.

9. Ibid., 467–68.

10. Ibid., 468.

11. Ibid., 534–35.

12. Ibid., 535.

13. Ibid., 459.

14. Ibid., 459–60.

15. Ibid., 460.

16. Ibid.

17. SherAli Tareen, "Contesting Friendship in Colonial Muslim India," *South Asia: Journal of South Asian Studies* 38, no. 3 (August 2015): 419–34.

18. See ibid.

19. Ibid., 426–32.

20. Miṣbāḥī, *Imām Aḥmad Razā*, 540.

21. Ibid.

22. Ibid.

23. Ibid., 543–49.

24. Ibid., 544.

25. Ibid.

26. Ibid., 545.

27. Ibid.

28. Ibid., 546.

29. Ibid.; it is interesting to note here that the term *randī*, meaning "dancing girl" in the late nineteenth century, today primarily has come to mean "prostitute."

30. Ibid.

31. Ibid.

32. Ibid.

33. al-Ḥākim al-Nīsāpūrī, *Al-Mustadrak 'alā Ṣaḥīḥayn fi-l-Ḥadīth* (Beirut: Dār al-Fikr, n.d), 3:78, quoted in A. Khān, *Iqāmat al-Qiyāma*, 513.

34. I thank David Gilmartin for suggesting to me the possibility of such a theorization.

chapter eleven. Knowing the Unknown

1. Khān also anathematized the other founder of Deoband, Qāsim Nānautvī, on the charge of denying the finality of the Prophet. That is a separate debate that will not be dealt with in this chapter.

2. Khalīl Aḥmad Sāharanpūrī, *Al-Barāhīn al-Qāṭi'a 'alā Ẓalām al-Anwār al-Sāṭi'a* (Karāchī: Dār al-Ishā'at, 1987), 50–55.

3. 'Abdul Samī', *Anwār-i Sāṭi'a dar Bayān-i Mawlūd wa-l-Fātiḥa*, in Sāharanpūrī, *Al-Barāhīn al-Qāṭi'a*, 53.

4. Ibid.

5. Ibid., 54–57.

6. Ibid.

7. Sāharanpūrī, *Al-Barāhīn al-Qāṭi'a*, 53.

8. Qur'ān 6:59.

9. Sāharanpūrī, *Al-Barāhīn al-Qāṭi'a*, 55.

10. 'Abd Allāh ibn Aḥmad Nasafī, *Al-Baḥr al-Rā'iq fī Sharḥ Kanz al-Daqā'iq fī Furū' al-Ḥanafīya* (Beirut: Dār al-Kutub al-'Ilmīya, 1997); Muḥammad ibn 'Alī Haskafī, *Al-Durr al-Mukhtār fī Sharḥ Tanwīr al-Abṣār* (Calcutta: Maṭba' Ishtiyāq Lithographic Company, 1827).

11. Sāharanpūrī, *Al-Barāhīn al-Qāṭi'a*, 55.

12. Ibid., 53–56.

13. Ibid., 53.

14. Ashraf 'Alī Thānvī, *Ḥifẓ al-Īmān* (Deoband: Dār al-Kitāb Deobandī, n.d.), 2.

15. Ibid., 14.

16. Ibid., 15. For a revelatory proof that demonstrated the Prophet's lack of access to absolute hidden knowledge, Thānvī presented the Prophet's declaration in the Qur'ān "Had I possessed knowledge of the unknown, I would have multiplied all good" (Qur'ān 7:188).

17. Khān included Gangohī in this list because Sāharanpūrī wrote *Conclusive Proofs* at Gangohī's behest. Gangohī had also endorsed the contents of the text. Therefore, in Khān's opinion, although Sāharanpūrī was the apparent author, he merely served as a ventriloquist for the views of his master and founder of the Deoband school, Gangohī.

18. Aḥmad Razā Khān, *Ḥusām al-Ḥaramayn 'alā Manḥar al-Kufr wa-l-Mayn* (Lāhore: Maktabah-yi Nabawīya, 1975), 24.

19. Ibid.

20. Ibid., 23–28.

21. Ibid., 27.

22. Ibid., 29.

23. Ibid.

24. Aḥmad Razā Khān, *Al-Dawlat al-Makkīya bi-l-Mādat al-Ghaybīya* (Lāhore: Nazir Sons, 2000), 272.

25. A. Khān, *Ḥusām al-Ḥaramayn*, 29.

26. Khān replicated this argument in much of *The Meccan Gift* (*Al-Dawlat al-Makkīya*).

27. A. Khān, *Ḥusām al-Haramayn*, 29.

28. Ibid.

29. Ibid., 32.

30. Rashīd Aḥmad Gangohī, *Fatāwā-yi Rashīdīya* (Karāchī: Muḥammad Karkhāna-i Islāmī Kutub, 1987), 234–38.

31. Ibid., 454.

32. Ibid.

33. Ibid., 453.

34. Usha Sanyal, *Devotional Islam and Politics in British India: Ahmad Riza Khan Barelwi and His Movement, 1870–1920* (Delhi: Oxford University Press, 1996), 233.

35. *Muhannad* is an Arabic word meaning "sword made of Indian steel" and thus is not a coincidental choice for the title of a book written by and in defense of Indian scholars.

36. Khalīl Aḥmad Sāharanpūrī, *Al-Muhannad 'alā al-Mufannad* (Lāhore: Al-Mīzān, 2005), 22–73.

37. Manẓūr Nu'mānī, *Fayṣala Kun Munāẓara* (Karāchī: Dār al-Ishā'at, n.d.), 61–95. Subsequent citations to this work are to this edition and are given parenthetically in the text.

38. Nu'mānī borrowed this statement from Khān's prominent text on hidden knowledge *The Meccan Gift*, discussed earlier. Quoted in Nu'mānī, *Faysala Kun Munāẓara*, 194.

39. Remember, the original question from which this debate had erupted concerned the Prophet's capacity to visit multiple venues during the *mawlid* ceremony.

40. Nu'mānī cited the verse in the Qur'ān "Certain of the desert Arabs round about you are hypocrites, as well as [desert Arabs] among the Medina folk: they are obstinate in hypocrisy: thou knowest them not" (Qur'ān 9:101).

41. Qur'ān 36:69.

42. Margrit Pernau, *Ashraf into Middle Classes: Muslims in Nineteenth-Century Delhi* (New Delhi: Oxford University Press, 2013), 271.

43. Ibid.

44. Nu'mānī's hermeneutic here amplifies and adds another important illustration of Abdulkader Tayob's claim in his erudite study *Religion in Modern Islamic Discourse* (New York: Columbia University Press, 2009) that from the nineteenth century onwards, "time after time, religion and the religious emerge as the key terms around which new meanings of Islam were found and articulated" (16). While Tayob largely focused his analysis on the thought of Muslim modernist, Islamist, and feminist scholars, the examples of Nu'mānī and also of Thānvī as discussed earlier in chapter 7 (in the context of his analysis of the Prophet's decision to marry Zaynab bint Jaḥsh) display the creative ways in which Muslim traditionalist scholars also contributed to the modern conceptual formations of religion as a distinct category of life.

45. Rashīd Aḥmad Gangohī, *Fatāwā Rashīdīya* (Lāhore: Maktabah-yi Raḥmānīya, n.d.), 225.

46. A. Khān, *Al-Dawlat al-Makkīya*, 277.

47. My theoretical stance here is indebted to Ananda Abeysekara, "Identity for and against Itself: Religion, Criticism, and Pluralization," *Journal of the American Academy of Religion* 72, no. 4 (2004): 973–1001.

chapter twelve. Internal Disagreements

1. Muḥammad Iqbāl Qurayshī, *Ma'ārif-i Gangohī* (Lāhore: Idārah-yi Islāmīyāt, 1976), 67.

2. Seema Alavi, *Muslim Cosmopolitanism in the Age of Empire* (Cambridge, MA: Harvard University Press, 2015). I do disagree, however, with many aspects of her reading of Imdādullah's thought, as the contrast in my own and her analysis of his textual corpus will make abundantly clear.

3. Muḥammad Sherkotī, *Ḥayāt-i Imdād* (Karāchī: Madrasa Arabīya Islāmīya, 1965), 53.

4. Nisār Aḥmad Fārūqī, *Navādir-i Imdādīya* (Gulbargah, Karnātaka: Sayyid Gīsūdarāz Taḥqīqātī Academy, 1996), 26.

5. Sherkotī, *Ḥayāt-i Imdād*, 58.

6. Fārūqī, *Navādir-i Imdādīya*, 28–30.

7. Sherkotī, *Ḥayāt-i Imdād*, 83.

8. Scott Kugle, *Sufis and Saints' Bodies: Mysticism, Corporeality, and Sacred Power in Islam* (Chapel Hill: University of North Carolina Press, 2007).

9. For more on Imdādullah's place in and contributions to the Chishtī order, see Carl W. Ernst and Bruce B. Lawrence, *Sufi Martyrs of Love: The Chishti Order in South Asia and Beyond* (New York: Palgrave Macmillan, 2002), 105–26.

10. Sayyid Naẓar Zaydī, *Ḥājī Imdādullah Muhājir Makkī Sīrat o Savāniḥ* (Gujarāt: Maktabah-yi Ẓafar, 1978), 43.

11. Sherkotī, *Ḥayāt-i Imdād*, 59.

12. Fārūqī, *Navādir-i Imdādīya*, 36.

13. Ashraf 'Alī Thānvī, *Qiṣṣaṣ al-Akābir li-Ḥiṣṣaṣ al-Aṣāghir* (Multān: Idārah-yi Ta'līfāt-i Ashrafīya, 2006), 84.

14. Fārūqī, *Navādir-i Imdādīya*, 72.

15. Ibid., 74. Imdādullah used to send letters to India either via the postal system or through different acquaintances traveling back and forth from India to Mecca. He began almost all of his letters with the chain of transmission through which that particular letter was to reach its intended recipient. The content of his letters ranged from everyday matters such as complaints over the unavailability of money order facilities in Mecca and expressions of protest over the exorbitant price at which Aḥmad al-Taḥṭāwī's (d. 1816) marginalia on Haskafī's *Durr-al Mukhtār* was being sold in Mecca (fifteen *riyāl*), accompanied with a request for some copies to be sent from India, to more complex matters of normative practice and doctrine.

16. Ashraf 'Alī Thānvī, *Imdād al-Mushtāq ilā Ashraf al-Akhlāq* (Karāchī: Dār al-Ishā'at, 1976), 14.

17. Fārūqī, *Navādir-i Imdādīya*, 27.

18. Ibid., 15.

19. Fārūqī, *Navādir-i Imdādīya*, 27.

20. A. Thānvī, *Arwāḥ-yi Salāsa* (Karāchī: Dār al-Ishā'at, 2001), 138.

21. Ḥājī Imdādullah, *Fayṣala-yi Haft Mas'ala* (Karāchī: M. H. Sa'īd, n.d.), 3. Subsequent page citations are to this edition and are given parenthetically in the text.

22. Nile Green, *Making Space: Sufis and Settlers in Early Modern India* (New Delhi: Oxford University Press, 2012), 33–64.

23. Sherkotī, *Ḥayāt-i Imdād*, 131–32.

24. Ibid.

25. Quoted in ibid., 133.

26. Jamīl Thānvī, ed., *Sharḥ-i Fayṣala-yi Haft Mas'ala* (Lahore: Jāmi'a-yi Ziyā' al-'Ulūm, 1971), 98. Subsequent page citations are to this edition and are given parenthetically in the text.

27. Khalīl Aḥmad Sāharanpūrī, *Al-Barāhīn al-Qāṭi'a 'alā Ẓalām al-Anwār al-Sāṭi'a* (Karāchī: Dār al-Ishā'at, 1987), 30.

28. Ibid.

29. See Amira Mittermaier, *Dreams That Matter: Egyptian Landscapes of the Imagination* (Berkeley: University of California Press, 2010).

30. Francis Robinson, *Islam and Muslim History in South Asia* (New Delhi: Oxford University Press, 2000), 125.

31. Ibid., 127.

32. For a compelling critique of the very category of "disenchantment," especially when heralded as a signature achievement of the modern West, see Jason Josephson-Storm, *The Myth of Disenchantment: Magic, Modernity, and the Birth of the Human Sciences* (Chicago: University of Chicago Press, 2017).

33. Ananda Abeysekara, "The Im-possibility of Critique: The Future of Religion's Memory," *Religion and Culture* 11, no. 3 (2010): 213–46.

34. Ananda Abeysekara, *The Politics of Postsecular Religion: Mourning Secular Futures* (New York: Columbia University Press, 2007).

35. Saba Mahmood, *Religious Difference in a Secular Age: A Minority Report* (Princeton, NJ: Princeton University Press, 2016), 74.

36. SherAli Tareen, "Islam, Democracy, and the Limits of Secular Conceptuality," *Journal of Law and Religion* 29, no. 1 (2014): 1–17.

37. I should briefly note here my disagreement with the conclusion Seema Alavi draws from her reading of *FHM* that Imdādullah embodied and articulated an "individual centered Muslim cosmopolitanism" or that he "hoped to unite the *umma* across continents . . . and meet the European civilizational challenge" (Alavi, *Muslim Cosmopolitanism*, 248, 251). As I have elaborated in greater detail elsewhere, "At the heart of *Faysala-yi Haft Mas'ala* was an argu-

ment not for the centrality of the individual or for social leveling but exactly to the contrary. Imdādullah's foremost concern was in fact to maintain the integrity of the hierarchy between the *'ulama'* elite and the masses. He wrote this text in response to and as a way to mitigate the explosion of intra-*'ulama'* polemics in North India that perturbed him precisely because in his view such polemics threatened the erosion of the stature and authority of the scholarly elite in the eyes of the masses. . . . His project was at once thoroughly entwined to the local North Indian context of Barelvī-Deobandī polemics, and deeply invested in upholding a hierarchical elitist vision of maintaining the pastoral authority and supremacy of the *'ulama'* over the masses." SherAli Tareen, review of *Muslim Cosmopolitanism in an Age of Empire*, by Seema Alavi, *International Journal of Asian Studies* 15, no. 1 (January 2018): 131.

38. A. Thānvī, *Arwāḥ-yi Salāsa*, 132.

Epilogue

1. See, for instance, Charles Taylor, *A Secular Age* (Cambridge, MA: Harvard University Press, 2007), Arvind Mandair, *Religion and the Specter of the West: Sikhism, India, Postcoloniality and the Politics of Religion* (New York: Columbia University Press, 2009), Russell McCutcheon, "'They Licked the Platter Clean': On the Co-dependency of the Religious and the Secular," *Method and Theory in the Study of Religion* 19 (2007): 173–99, and John Modern, *Secularism in Antebellum America* (Chicago, University of Chicago Press, 2011).

2. Talal Asad, "Reading a Modern Classic: W. C. Smith's *The Meaning and End of Religion*," *History of Religions* 40, no. 3 (February 2001): 205–21.

3. Talal Asad, *Formations of the Secular: Christianity, Islam, Modernity* (Stanford, CA: Stanford University Press, 2003).

4. Hussein Agrama, *Questioning Secularism: Islam, Sovereignty, and the Rule of Law in Modern Egypt* (Chicago: University of Chicago Press, 2012); Saba Mahmood, *Religious Difference in a Secular Age: A Minority Report* (Princeton, NJ: Princeton University Press, 2016).

5. On religion making, see Markus Dressler and Arvind Mandair, *Secularism and Religion-Making* (New York: Oxford University Press, 2011).

6. For a most convincing example of this argument, see David Scott, *Conscripts of Modernity: The Tragedy of Colonial Enlightenment* (Durham, NC: Duke University Press, 2004), 98–132.

7. David Scott, *Refashioning Futures: Criticism after Postcoloniality* (Princeton, NJ: Princeton University Press, 1999), 115.

postscript. Listening to the Internal "Other"

1. Michael Taussig, *Defacement: Public Secrecy and the Labor of the Negative* (Stanford, CA: Stanford University Press, 1999).

2. Saba Mahmood, *Religious Difference in a Secular Age: A Minority Report* (Princeton, NJ: Princeton University Press, 2016), 206. For a fuller analysis of this argument, see my "Disrupting Secular Power and the Study of Religion: Saba Mahmood," in *Cultural Approaches to Studying Religion: An Introduction to Theories and Methods*, ed. Sarah Bloesch and Meredith Minister (London: Bloomsbury Press, 2018), 155–72. For those unfamiliar with Mahmood's work who might object that self-avowedly "Islamic" states like Pakistan cannot be approached through the category of political secularism, remember that at the heart of her project is the attempt to disrupt the binary of Western and non-Western secularism. Her argument is that while the precise trajectory of religious inequality is historically specific to each context, the inextricability of secularism from liberal political rule is derived from analogous conundrums and paradoxes involved in the modern state's management of religious difference.

3. I realize that these class categories and corresponding patterns of education are fluid and dynamic; I use them here primarily for heuristic purposes to present broad outlines of a division.

4. On the "mummifying" of religious tradition, see Ebrahim Moosa, *Ghazālī and the Poetics of Imagination* (Chapel Hill: University of North Carolina Press, 2005), 61.

5. For a couple among countless such examples, see "India's Darul Uloom Deoband Issues Fatwa against Nail Polish for Women," *Express Tribune*, November 5, 2018; Fatima Raza, "According to This 'Scholar,' 'Sins Such as Murder and Rape Will Be Ignored as Long as You Pray,'" *Express Tribune*, October 26, 2018.

6. Zaman, *Islam in Pakistan*, 266.

7. Ibid., 277.

Select Bibliography

Sources in Islamicate Languages

Sources in Arabic

al-Asqalānī, Aḥmad Ibn 'Alī Ibn Ḥajar. *Fatḥ al-Bārī fī Sharḥ Ṣaḥīḥ al-Bukhārī*. Beirut: Dār al-Kutub al-'Ilmīya, 2003.

Badāyūnī, Fazl-i Rasūl. *Al-Mu'taqad al-Muntaqad*. Istānbul: Ḥakīkat Kitābevi, 1985.

Barzanjī, Sayyid Ja'far. *'Iqd al-Jawhar fī Mawlid al-Nabī al-Azhar*. Lāhore: Jāmi'a Islāmīya, n.d.

Daḥlān, Aḥmad Zaynī. *Al-Durar al-Sanīya fī-Radd 'alā al-Wahhābīya*. Istānbul: Dār al-Shafqa, n.d.

al-Ghazālī, Abū Ḥamīd. *'Ihyā' 'Ulūm al-Dīn Kitāb al-Samā' wa al-Wajd*. Cairo: Al-Mashhad al-Husaynī, n.d.

Ḥanbal, Aḥmad Ibn. *Musnad Aḥmad Ibn Ḥanbal*. Vol. 6. Beirut: Dār al-Fikr, n.d.

al-Ḥasanī, 'Abd al-Ḥayy. *Nuzhat al-Khawāṭir wa Bahjat al-Masāmi' wa-l-Nawāẓir*. Vol. 7. Dār Arafāt: Ṭayyab Academy, 1993.

Haskafī, Muḥammad ibn. 'Alī. *Al-Durr al-Mukhtār fī Sharḥ Tanwīr al-Abṣār*. Calcutta: Maṭba' Ishtiyāq Lithographic Company, 1827.

al-Haytamī, Ibn Ḥajar. *Al-Jawhar al-Munaẓẓam Muqaddima fī Ādāb al-Safar*. Lāhore: Al-Maktabah al-Qādirīya fi'l Jāmi'a al-Niẓāmīya.

al-Hirawī, Muḥammad. *Sharḥ Kitāb al-Fiqh al-Akbar*. Beirut: Dār al-Kutub al-'Ilmīya, 2006.

Ibn 'Ābidīn, Muḥammad. *Radd al-Muhtār 'alā Durr al-Mukhtār*. Beirut: Dār al-Kutub al-'Ilmīya, 1994.

Ibn Humām, al-Kamāl. *Sharḥ Fatḥ al-Qadīr*. Beirut: Dār al-Fikr, 1900.

Ibn Māja [Abū 'Abdillāh Muḥammad ibn Yazīd Ibn Mājah al-Rab'ī al-Qazwīnī]. *Sunan Ibn Māja*. Cairo: Dār al-Ḥadīth, 1998.

Ibn Taymīya, Taqī al-Dīn. *Iqtiḍā al-Ṣirāṭ al-Mustaqīm li Mukhālafat Aṣḥāb al-Jahīm*. Cairo: Al-Maktabah al-Tawfīqīya, 2000.

Khān, Aḥmad Razā. *Al-Dawlat al-Makkīya bi-l-Mādat al-Ghaybīya*. Karāchī: Maktabah-yi Rizvīya, n.d.

———. *Al-Dawlat al-Makkīya bi-l-Mādat al-Ghaybīya*. Lāhore: Nazir Sons, 2000.

———. *Ḥusām al-Ḥaramayn 'alā Manḥar al-Kufr wa-l-Mayn*. Lāhore: Maktabah-yi Nabawīya, 1975.

Khayrābādī, Fazl-i Ḥaqq. *Al-Thawra al-Hindīya (Bāghī-yi Hindustān)*. Lāhore: Maktabah-yi Qādirīya, 1997.

Nasafī, 'Abd Allāh ibn Aḥmad. *Al-Baḥr al-Rā'iq fī Sharḥ Kanz al-Daqā'iq fī Furū' al-Ḥanafīya*. Beirut: Dār al-Kutub al-'Ilmīya, 1997.

al-Nawawī, Muḥyīuddīn. *Al-Arba'īn*. Cairo: Maktabat al-Khānjī, 2005.

al-Nīsāpūrī, al-Ḥākim. *Al-Mustadrak 'alā Ṣaḥīḥayn fi-l-Ḥadīth*. Beirut: Dār al-Fikr, n.d.

al-Qasṭalānī, Muḥammad. *Al-Mawāhib al-Ladunīya bi'l-Minaḥ al-Muḥammadīya*. Beirut: Al-Maktab al-Islāmī, 1991.

Raysūnī, Aḥmad. *Naẓarīyat al-Maqāṣid 'inda al-Imām al-Shāṭibī*. Herndon, VA: Al-Ma'had al-'Ālamī li-l-fikr al-Islāmī [International Institute of Islamic Thought Press], 1991.

Sāharanpūrī, Khalīl Aḥmad. *Al-Muhannad 'alā al-Mufannad*. Lāhore: Al-Mīzān, 2005.

Sarakhsī, Muḥammad ibn Aḥmad. *Al-Nukat*. Hyderābād: Lajnat Iḥyā' al-Ma'ārif al-Nu'mānīya, 1958.

al-Shāṭibī, Ibrāhīm. *Al-I'tiṣām*. Beirut: Dār al-Kitāb al-'Arabī, 2005.

al-Suyūṭī, Jalāl al-Dīn. "Ḥusn al-Maqṣid fī 'Amal al-Mawlid." In *al-Ḥawī lil-Fatāwī*. Beirut: Dār al-Kutub al-'Ilmīya, 1975.

al-Tirmidhī, Abū 'Īsā. *Jāmi' al-Tirmidhī*. Vol. 1. Delhi: Amīn, n.d.

Walī Ullah, Shāh. *Ḥujjat Allāh al-Bāligha*. Vols. 1 and 2. Beirut: Dār al-Jīl, 2005.

———. *Al-Inṣāf fī Bayān Sabab al-Ikhtilāf*. Cairo: Al-Maṭba' al-Salafīya wa Maktabatuhā, 1965.

Sources in Persian

'Azīz, Shāh 'Abdul. *Tafsīr-i 'Azīzī*. Delhi: Lāl Kūwān, n.d.

———. *Tuḥfat Ithnā 'Asharīya*. Lāhore: Sohail Academy, n.d.

Badāyūni, Fazl-i Rasūl. *Al-Bawāriq al-Muḥammadīya li-Rajm al-Shayāṭīn al-Najdīya*. Lāhore: Dār al-Islām, 2014.

———. *Al-Fawz al-Mubīn bi Shafā'at al-Shāfi'īn*. In *Majmū'a Rasā'il-i Fazl-i Rasūl*. Karāchī: Maktabah Barakāt al-Madīna; Dār al-Nu'mān, 2010.

———. *Iḥqāq al-Ḥaqq wa Ibṭāl al-Bāṭil*. Badāyūn: Tāj al-Fuḥūl Academy, 2007.

———. *Majmū'a Rasā'il-i Fazl-i Rasūl*. Karāchī: Maktabah Barakāt al-Madīna; Dār al-Un'mān, 2010.

———. *Sayf al-Jabbār al-Maslūl 'alā a'dā' al-Abrār*. Lāhore: Maktabah-yi Rizvīya, 1973.

Barelvī, Sayyid Aḥmad. *Makātīb-i Sayyid Aḥmad Shāhīd*. Lāhore: Maktabah-yi Rashīdīya, 1975.

Dihlavī, Maḥbūb 'Alī. "Ta'rīkh al-Ā'ima fī Dhikr Khulafā' al-Umma." Unpublished manuscript, Rotograph 319, Punjab University Library manuscript collections, Lāhore.

Fuyūḍ al-Ḥaramayn. Delhi: Maṭba'-i Aḥmadī, n.d.

Ismā'īl, Shāh Muḥammad. "Maktūbāt-i Shāh Ismā'īl Dihlavī." Unpublished manuscript, MS 102, Punjab University Library manuscript collections, Lāhore.

———. *Manṣab-i Imāmat*. Delhi: Maṭba'-i Faruqi, 1899.

———. *Ṣirāṭ-i Mustaqīm*. Delhi: Maṭba'-i Mujtabā'ī, 1905.

———. *Yak Roza*. Multān: Farūqī Kutub Khāna, n.d.

Khayrābādī, Fazl-i Ḥaqq. *Taḥqīq al-Fatwā fī Ibṭāl al-Tughwā*. Lāhore: Maktabah-yi Qādirī, 1979.

Pānīpatī, Sanā'ullah. *Mā Lā Budda Min-Hu*. Karāchī: Qadīmī Kutub Khāna, 1956.

Rafī' al-Dīn, Shāh. *Fatāwā Shāh Rafī' al-Dīn*. Delhi: Maṭba'-i Majtabai, n.d.

Walī Ullah, Shāh. *Al-Durr al-Thamīn fī Mubasharāt al-Nabī al-Amīn*. Faisalabād: Kutub Khānā-i 'Alawīya Rizvīya, n.d.

———. *Al-Intibāh fī Salāsil Awlīyā' Allāh*. Delhi: Barqī Press, n.d.

Sources in Urdu

Aḥmad, Muḥammad Mas'ūd. *Ḥayāt-i Mawlānā Aḥmad Razā Khān Barelvī*. Siālkot: Islāmī Kutub Khānā, 1981.

Aḥmad, Qiyām al-Dīn. *Hindustān Mein Wahhābī Taḥrīk*. Karāchī: Nafīs Academy, 1976.

'Alī, Khurram. "Naṣīḥat al-Muslimīn." MS Urdu 13 b, British Library Manuscript Collections, London.

A'ẓamī, Abu'l Ḥasan. *Hazrat Thānvī ke Pasandīda Wāqi'āt*. Karāchī: Dār al-Ishā'at, 2004.

Badāyūnī, Asīd al-Ḥaqq. *Khayrābādīyāt*. Lāhore: Maktabah A'lā Hazrat, 2011.

Badāyūnī, Fazl-i Rasūl. *'Aqīda-yi Shafā'at Kitāb wa Sunnat kī Rawshnī Mayn*. Badāyūn: Taj al-Fuḥūl Academy, 2009.

Bastāvī, Nasīm, and Muḥammad Ṣābir. *Ā'lā Ḥazrat Barelvī: Ḥālāt-i Mujaddid*. Lāhore: Maktaba-yi Nabavīya, 1976.

Butt, 'Abdullah. *Shāh Ismā'īl Shahīd*. Lāhore: Qawmī Kutub Khāna, 1974.

Charyākotī, Muḥammad. "*Ṣāḥib-i Anwār-i Sāṭi'a*." In *Anwār-i Sāṭi'a dar Bayān-i Mawlūd wa-l-Fātiḥa*, by 'Abdul Samī', 11–13. Charyākot: Idārah-yi Furogh-i Islām, 2010.

Dihlavī, Abū Muḥammad Raḥīm Bakhsh. *Ḥayāt-i Walī*. Delhi: Shāh Walī Ullah Public Library.

Dihlavī, Mirzā Ḥayrat. *Ḥayāt-i Ṭayyiba*. Lāhore: Islāmī Academy Nāshirān-i Kutub, 1984.

Fārūqī, Nisār Aḥmad. *Navādir-i Imdādīya*. Gulbargah, Karnātaka: Sayyid Gīsū-darāz Taḥqīqātī Academy, 1996.

Gangohī, Rashīd Aḥmad. *Fatāwā Rashīdīya*. Lāhore: Maktabah Raḥmanīya, n.d.

———. *Fatawā-yi Rashīdīya*. Karāchī: Muḥammad Karkhānah-yi Islāmī Kutub, 1987.

———. *Makātīb-i Rashīdīya*. Lāhore: Idārah-yi Islāmiyyāt, 1996.

Gīlānī, Manāẓar Aḥsan. *Musalmānon kī Firqa Bandīyon kā Afsāna*. Delhi: Nadwat al-Muṣannifīn, 1953.

———. *Savāniḥ-yi Qāsimī*. 3 vols. Lāhore: Maktabah-yi Raḥmānīya, 1976.

al-Ḥasan, Muḥammad Anwar. *Ḥayāt-i Imdād*. Deoband: Kutubkhānah-yi Qāsimī, 1976.

Ikrām, Shaykh Muḥammad. *Mawj-i Kawsar*. Lāhore: Idārah-yi Saqāfat-i Islāmīya, 2014.

———. *Rūd-i Kawsar*. Lāhore: Idārah-yi Saqāfat-i Islāmīya, 2005.

Illāhī, Muḥammad ʻĀshiq. *Tazkirat al-Khalīl*. Karāchī: Maktabat al-Shaykh, 1977.

———. *Tazkirat al-Rashīd*. Karāchī: Maktabah-yi Baḥr al-ʻUlūm, 1978.

Imdādullah, Ḥājī. *Fayṣala-yi Haft Mas'ala*. Karāchī: M. H. Saʻīd, n.d.

Ismāʻīl, Shāh Muḥammad. *ʻAbaqāt*. Hyderābād: al-Lajna al-Islamīya, 1962.

———. *Īzāḥ al-Ḥaqq al-Ṣarīḥ fī Aḥkām al-Mayyit wa al-Zarīḥ*. Karāchī: Qadīmī Kutub Khāna, 1976.

———. *Khuṭbāt al-Tawḥīd*. Multān: ʻAbdul Tawwāb Academy, 1989.

———. *Taqwīyat al-Īmān*. Lāhore: Maṭbaʻ Aḥmadī, n.d.

———. *Taqwīyat al-Īmān*. Karāchī: Ṣiddīqī Trust, n.d.

Khān, Aḥmad Razā. *Dāmān-i Bāgh-i Subḥān al-Subūḥ*. In *Al-Fatāwā al-Rizvīya*, vol. 15.

———. *Al-Fatāwā al-Rizvīya*. Gujarāt: Markaz-i Ahl al-Sunnat Barakāt-i Razā, 2006.

———. *Al-Ḥujja al-Fā'iḥa li Ṭīb al-Tāʻīn wa-l-Fātiḥa*. In *Al-Fatāwā al-Rizvīya*, vol. 9.

———. *Ihlāk al-Wahhābīyīn ʻalā Tawhīn Qubūr al-Muslimīn*. In *Al-Fatāwā al-Rizvīya*, vol. 15.

———. *Iqāmat al-Qiyāma ʻalā Ṭāʻin al-Qiyām li Nabī Tihāma*. In *Al-Fatāwā al-Rizvīya*, vol. 26.

———. *Irā'at al-Adab li Fāḍil al-Nasab*. In *Al-Fatāwā al-Rizvīya*, vol. 9.

———. *Al-Kawkaba al-Shahābīya fī Kufrīyāt ʻabī Wahhābīya*. In *Al-Fatāwā al-Rizvīya*, vol. 15.

———. *Kullīyāt-i Makātīb-i Razā*. Haridvār: Dār al-ʻUlūm Qādirīya Ṣābirīya Barakāt-i Razā, 2005.

———. *Al-Maḥajja al-Muʼtamana li āya Mumtaḥana*. In *Al-Fatāwā al-Rizvīya*, vol. 14.

———. *Malfūẓāt*. Lāhore: Kamyāb Dār al-Tablīgh, 1977.

———. *Maqāl-i ʻUrafāʼ fī Iʻzāz-i Sharʻ-i ʻUlamāʼ Sharīʻat o Ṭarīqat*. Karāchī: Idārah-yi Taṣnīfāt-i Imām Aḥmad Razā Khān, n.d.

———. *Rasāʼil-i Rizvīya*. Lāhore: Maktabah-yi Ḥamīdīya, 1974.

———. *Rimāḥ al-Qahhār ʻalā Kufr al-Kuffār*. In *Al-Fatāwā al-Rizvīya*, vol. 15.

———. *Risāla-yi Taʻzīyadārī*. Faisalābād: al-Jamāl, 1970.

———. *Sall al-Suyūf al-Hindīya ʻalā Kufrīyāt Bābā ʻan al-Najdīya*. In *Al-Fatāwā al-Rizvīya*, vol. 15.

———. *Subḥān al-Subūḥ ʻan ʻAyb-i Kidhb-i Maqbūḥ*. In *Al-Fatāwā al-Rizvīya*, vol. 15.

Khān, Muḥammad Abdul Ghanī. *Ahl-i Sunnat awr Ahl-i Bidʻat; Aik Ḥaqīqat, Aik Jāʼiza Yaʻnī al-Junnat li Ahl-i Sunnat*. Karāchī: Al-Maktabah al-Bunūrīya, 1978.

Makkī, Ḥājī Imdādullah. *Kullīyāt-i Imdādīya*. Karāchī: Dār al-Ishāʻat, 1976.

———. *Maktūbāt-i Imdādīya*. Karāchī: Dar al-Ishāʻat, 1976.

———. *Shamāʼim-i Imdādīya*. Shāhkot: Kutub Khāna-yi Sharaf al-Rashīd, 1966.

Masʻūd, Khālid. *Athārwīn Sadī ʻĪswī Mayn Bar-i Ṣaghīr Mayn Islāmī Fikr ke Rahnumā*. Islāmābād: Idārah-yi Taḥqīqāt-i Islāmī, 2008.

al-Mawdūdī, Sayyid Abu'l Aʻlā. Preface to *Shāh Ismāʻīl Shahīd*, by ʻAbdullah Butt. Lāhore: Taʻmīr Printing Press, 1974.

Mehr, Ghulām Rasūl. Introduction to *Taqwīyat al-Īmān*. Karāchī: Ṣiddīqī Trust, n.d.

Miṣbāḥī, Yasīn Akhtar. *Chand Mumtāz ʻUlamāʼ-yi Inqilāb 1857*. New Delhi: Dār al-Kalām, 2008.

———. *Imām Aḥmad Razā: Radd-i Bidʻāt wa Munkarāt*. Karāchī: Idārah-yi Taṣnīfāt Imām Aḥmad Razā, 1985.

Nadvī, Muḥammad Zayd. *Fiqh-i Ḥanafī Ke Uṣūl wa Zawābiṭ*. Karāchī: Zam Zam, 2003.

Nadvī, Sayyid Abu'l Ḥasan ʻAlī. *Karvān-i Īmān wa ʻAzīmat*. Lāhore: Sayyid Aḥmad Shahīd Academy, 1980.

Naʻīmuddīn, Sayyid Muḥammad. *Aṭyab al-Bayān fī Radd Taqwīyat al-Īmān*. Bombay: Razā Academy, 1998.

Nānautvī, Muḥammad Qāsim. *Farāʼiz-i Qāsimīya*. Delhi: Idārah-yi Adabīyāt-i Dillī,1980.

———. *Taṣfīyat al-ʻAqāʼid*. Karāchī: Dār al-Ishāʻat, 1976.

Nu‘mānī, Manẓūr. *Fayṣala Kun Munāẓara*. Karāchī: Dār al-Ishā‘at, n.d.

———. *Shāh Muḥammad Ismā‘īl awr Mu‘ānidīn-i ahl-i Bid‘at ke Ilzāmāt*. Gujrānwāla: Maktabah-yi Madīna, 1976.

———. *Taḥqīq-i Mas'ala-i Īṣāl-i Sawāb*. Baraylī: al-Furqān, 1943.

Nūrānī, Khushtar. *Taḥrīk-i Jihād awr British Government: Aik Taḥqīqī Muṭāla‘a*. Delhi: Idārah-yi Fikr-i Islāmī, 2014.

Pālanpūrī, Sa‘īd Aḥmad. *Raḥmat Allāh al-Wāsi‘a, Sharḥ Ḥujjat Allāh al-Bāligha*. Vol. 1. Deoband: Maktabah-yi Hijāz, 2000.

Pānīpatī, Sanā'ullah. *Mā Lā Budda Min-Hu*. Karāchī: Qadīmī Kutub Khāna, 1956.

Qādir, Shāh ‘Abdul. *Mūziḥ al-Qur'ān*. Calcutta: n.p., 1829.

Qādrī, Muḥammad Ayūb. *Jang-i Āzādi 1857: Wāqi‘āt wa Shakhṣīyāt*. Karāchī: Pak Academy, 1976.

Qādrī, Sayyid Muḥammad. *Fāzil Barelvī awr Umūr-i Bid‘at*. Lāhore: Razā Publications, 1981.

Qāsimī, Akhlāq Ḥusayn. *Shāh Ismā‘īl Shahīd aur un ke Nāqid*. Sarghoda: Zunūrayn Academy, 1985.

al-Qāsimī, Muḥammad ‘Ubaydullah. *Dār al-‘Ulūm Deoband*. Deoband: Shaykh al-Hind Academy Dār al-‘Ulūm Deoband, 2000.

Quraysḥī, Muḥammad Iqbāl. *Bid‘at kī Ḥaqīqat awr us ke Aḥkām*. Lāhore: Idārah-yi Islāmīyāt, 2000.

———. *Ma‘ārif-i Gangohī*. Lāhore: Idārah-yi Islamīyat, 1976.

Rafī‘ al-Dīn, Shāh. *Fatāwā-yi Shāh Rafī‘ al-Dīn*. Delhi: Maṭba‘-i Majtabai, n.d.

al-Raḥmān, Ḥāfiẓ Fuyūz. *Ḥājī Imdādullah Muhājir Makkī awr Unn ke Khulafā'*. Karāchī: Majlis-i Nashrīyāt-i Islām, 1997.

Rājā, Ghulām. *Imtiyāz-i Ḥaqq: Fazl-i Ḥaqq Khayrābādī aur Shahīd Dihlavī ke Siyāsī Kirdār kā Taqābulī Jā'iza*. Lāhore: Maktabah-yi Qādirīya, 1979.

Rizvī, Muḥammad Ḥasan ‘Alī. *Muhāsaba-i Deobandīyat bā Jawāb-i Muṭāla‘a-i Barelvīyat: Deobandīyat par aik Tarīkhī nā-Qābil-i Tardīd Dastāvayz*. Mubārakpūr: Jāmi‘a-yi Ashrafīya, 1998.

Rūmī, Abu'l Auṣāf. *Deoband se Baraylī Tak*. Allāhabād: Makatabah-yi ‘Irfān, n.d.

Ṣafdar, Muḥammad Sarfarāz. *Mas'ala-i ‘Ilm-i Ghayb wa Ḥāzir o Nāẓir*. Gujrānwālā: Maktabah-yi Ṣafdarīya, 1997.

Sāharanpūrī, Khalīl Aḥmad. *‘Aqā'id-i ‘Ulamā'-yi Deoband aur Ḥusām al-Ḥaramayn*. Karāchī: Dār al-Ishā‘at, 1976.

———. *Al-Barāhīn al-Qāṭi‘a ‘alā Ẓalām al-Anwār al-Sāṭi‘a*. Karāchī: Dār al-Ishā‘at, 1987.

———. *Fatāwā -yi Khalīlīya*. Karāchī: Maktabat al-Shaykh, 1977.

Samī‘, ‘Abdul. *Anwār-i Sāṭi‘a dar Bayān-i Mawlūd wa-l-Fātiḥa*. A‘lā Ḥazrat Network, n.d., accessed February 16, 2018, www.alahazratnetwork.org.

Sarvar, Muḥammad. *Armaghān-i Shāh Walī Ullah: Shāh Walī Ullah ke Ta'līmāt wa Afkār awr Savāniḥ-i Ḥayāt, 'Arabī wa Fārsī Taṣnīfāt se Intikhāb*. Lāhore: Idārah-yi Saqāfat-i Islāmīya, 1971.

———. *Ifādāt wa Malfūẓāt-i Hazrat 'Ubaydullah Sindhī*. Lāhore: Sindh Sāgar Academy, 1972.

Shahābī, Intiẓamūllah. *Ḥayāt-i 'Allāma Fazl-i Ḥaqq Khayrābādī*. Lucknow: Apnā Prakāshan, 1966.

Sherkotī, Muḥammad. *Ḥayāt-i Imdād*. Karāchī: Madrasa Arabīya Islāmīya, 1965.

Shervānī, Muḥammad. *Bāghī-yi Hindustān: Shahīd-i Tāḥrīk-i Āzādī-yi 'Ulamā' Fazl-i Ḥaqq Khayrābādī ke Faqīd al-Masal 'Ilmī Adabī awr Mujāhadāna Kārnāmay*. Hyderābād: Anwār al-Muṣṭafā, 1985.

Sindhī, 'Ubaydullah. *Shāh Walī Ullah awr un kā Falsafa*. Lāhore: Sindh Sāgar Academy, 1998.

———. *Shāh Walī Ullah awr un kā Naẓarīya-i Inqilāb*. New Delhi: Farīd Book Depot, 2004.

———. *Shāh Walī Ullah awr un kī Siyāsi Taḥrīk*. Lāhore: Sindh Sāgar Academy, 2008.

Ṭayyib, Muḥammad Qārī. *Khuṭbāt-i Ḥakīm al-Islām*. Deoband: Fayṣal Publishing House, 1984.

———. *Maslak-i 'Ulamā'-yi Deoband*. Karāchī: Dar al-Ishā'at, 1976.

Thānvī, Ashraf 'Alī. *Arwāḥ-yi Salāsa*. Karāchī: Dār al-Ishā'at, 2001.

———. *Bid'at kī Ḥaqīqat awr us ke Aḥkām awr Masā'il*. Lāhore: Idārah-yi Islāmīyāt, 2001.

———. *Ḥifẓ al-Īmān*. Deoband: Dār al-Kitāb Deobandī, n.d.

———. *Al-Ifādāt al-Yawmīya*. Multān: Idārah-yi Ta'līfāt-i Ashrafīya, 1984.

———. *Imdād al-Fatāwā*. Deoband: Zakarīya Book Depot, 1994.

———. *Imdād al-Mushtāq ilā Ashraf al-Akhlāq*. Karāchī: Dār al-Ishā'at, 1976.

———. *Iṣlāḥ al-Rusūm*. Lāhore: Idārah-yi Ta'līfāt-i Ashrafīya, 1958.

———. *Islām awr 'Aqlīyāt*. Lāhore: Idārah-yi Islāmīyāt, 1994.

———. *Malfūẓāt-i Ashrafīya*. Multān: Idārah-yi Ta'līfāt-i Ashrafīya, 1981.

———. *Maqālāt-i Ḥikmat*. Lāhore: Idārah-yi Ta'līfāt-i Ashrafīya, 1977.

———. *Marqūmāt-i Imdādīya*. Delhi: Maktabah-yi Burhān, 1979.

———. *Qiṣṣaṣ al-Akābir li-Ḥiṣṣaṣ al-Aṣāghir*. Multān: Idārah-yi Ta'līfāt-i Ashrafīya, 2006.

———. *Al-Tablīgh*. Deoband: Idārah-yi Ta'līfāt-i Awlīyā, 1901.

———. *Ṭarīqah-yi Mawlid Sharīf*. Lāhore: Idārah-yi Islāmīyāt, 1976.

———. *Wa'ẓ al-Dīn al-Khāliṣ*. Lāhore: Idārah-yi Islāmīya, 2001.

Thānvī, Jamīl, ed. *Sharḥ-i Fayṣala-yi Haft Mas'ala*. Lāhore: Jāmi'a-yi Ziyā' al-'Ulūm, 1975.

Zaydī, Sayyid Naẓar. *Ḥājī Imdādullah Muhājir Makkī Sīrat o Savāniḥ*. Gujarāt: Maktabah-yi Ẓafar, 1978.

Sources in Western Languages

Abd-Allah, 'Umar F. "Creativity, Innovation and Heresy in Islam." In *Voices of Islam*, vol. 5, edited by Omid Safi, 1–22. Westport, CT: Praeger, 2007.

Abeysekara, Ananda. *Colors of the Robe: Religion, Identity, and Difference*. Columbia: University of South Carolina Press, 2003.

———. "Identity for and against Itself: Religion, Criticism, and Pluralization." *Journal of the American Academy of Religion* 72, no. 4 (2004): 973–1001.

———. "The Im-possibility of Critique: The Future of Religion's Memory." *Religion and Culture* 11, no. 3 (2010): 213–46.

———. *The Politics of Postsecular Religion: Mourning Secular Futures*. New York: Columbia University Press, 2008.

———. "Protestant Buddhism and 'Influence': The Temporality of a Concept." *Qui Parle* 28, no. 1 (2019): 1–75.

———. "Religious Studies' Mishandling of Origin and Change: Time, Tradition, and Form-of-Life in Buddhism." *Cultural Critique* 98 (Winter 2018): 22–71.

———. "Theravāda Buddhist Encounters with Modernity: A Review Essay." *Journal of Buddhist Ethics* 25 (2018): 333–71.

———. "The Un-translatability of Religion; The Un-translatability of Life: Thinking Talal Asad's Thought Unthought in Religious Studies." *Method and Theory in the Study of Religion* 23, no. 3 (2011): 257–82.

Adang, Camilla, Hassan Ansari, and Maribel Fierro, eds. *Accusations of Unbelief in Islam: A Diachronic Perspective on Takfīr*. Leiden: E. J. Brill, 2016.

Agamben, Giorgio. *Homo Sacer: Sovereign Power and Bare Life*. Stanford, CA: Stanford University Press, 1998.

Agrama, Hussein. *Questioning Secularism: Islam, Sovereignty, and the Rule of Law in Modern Egypt*. Chicago: University of Chicago Press, 2012.

Ahmad, Asad, and Reza Pourjavady. "Theology in the Indian Subcontinent." In *The Oxford Handbook of Islamic Theology*, edited by Sabine Schmidtke, 606–24. Oxford: Oxford University Press, 2016.

Ahmad, Irfan. *Islamism and Democracy in India: The Transformation of Jamaat-e-Islami*. Princeton, NJ: Princeton University Press, 2009.

———. *Religion as Critique: Islamic Critical Thinking from Mecca to the Marketplace*. Chapel Hill: University of North Carolina Press, 2017.

Ahmed, Shahab. *What Is Islam? The Importance of Being Islamic*. Princeton, NJ: Princeton University Press, 2015.

Alam, Arshad. *Inside a Madrasa: Knowledge, Power, and Islamic Identity in India*. New Delhi: Routledge, 2011.

Alam, Muzzafar. *The Crisis of Empire in Mughal North India: Awadh and the Punjab, 1707–48*. Delhi: Oxford University Press, 1986.

———. *The Languages of Political Islam: India, 1200–1800*. Chicago: University of Chicago Press, 2004.
Alavi, Seema. *Muslim Cosmopolitanism in the Age of Empire*. Cambridge, MA: Harvard University Press, 2015.
Ali, Ahmed. *Al-Qur'ān: A Contemporary Translation*. Princeton, NJ: Princeton University Press, 1993.
Ali, Kecia. *The Lives of Muhammad*. Cambridge, MA: Harvard University Press, 2014.
Alvi, Sajida. "Qāzī Sanā'Allāh Pānīpatī, an Eighteenth-Century Indian Ṣūfī-'Ālim: A Study of His Writings in Their Sociopolitical Context." In *Islamic Studies Presented to Charles J. Adams*, edited by Wael Hallaq and Donald Little, 11–26. Leiden: E. J. Brill, 1991.
Anidjar, Gil. *Blood: A Critique of Christianity*. New York: Columbia University Press, 2016.
Anjum, Ovamir. *Politics, Law, and Community in Islamic Thought: The Taymiyyan Moment*. Cambridge: Cambridge University Press, 2012.
Arendt, Hannah. *On Revolution*. New York: Penguin Books, 2006.
Asad, Muhammad. *The Message of the Qur'ān: The Full Account of the Revealed Arabic Text Accompanied by Parallel Transliteration*. Bristol, UK: Book Foundation, 2003.
Asad, Talal. "Anthropology and the Analysis of Ideology." *Man*, n.s., 14 (1979): 607–27.
———. "Conscripts of Western Civilization?" In *Dialectical Anthropology: Essays in Honor of Stanley Diamond*, vol. 1, edited by C. Gailey, 333–51. Gainesville: University Press of Florida, 1992.
———. *Formations of the Secular: Christianity, Islam, Modernity*. Stanford, CA: Stanford University Press, 2003.
———. *Genealogies of Religion: Discipline and Reasons of Power in Christianity and Islam*. Baltimore: Johns Hopkins University Press, 1993.
———. *The Idea of an Anthropology of Islam*. Washington, DC: Center for Contemporary Arab Studies, Georgetown University, 1986.
———. *On Suicide Bombing*. New York: Columbia University Press, 2009.
———. "Reading a Modern Classic: W. C. Smith's *The Meaning and End of Religion*." *History of Religions* 40, no. 3 (February 2001): 205–21.
———. "Responses." In *Powers of the Secular Modern: Talal Asad and His Interlocutors*, edited by David Scott and Charles Hirschkind, 206–42. Stanford, CA: Stanford University Press, 2016.
———. "Thinking about Tradition, Religion, and Politics in Egypt Today." *Critical Inquiry* 42, no. 1 (Autumn 2015): 166–214.
Assmann, Jan. *Politische Theologie zwischen Ägypten und Israel*. Munich: Carl Friedrich von Siemens, 1992.

Bakhtin, Mikhail. *The Bakhtin Reader: Selected Writings of Bakhtin, Medvedev and Voloshinov*. London: E. Arnold, 1994.

Balibar, Etienne. *Spinoza and Politics*. London: Verso, 1998.

Baljon, J. M. S. *Religion and Thought of Shah Wali Allah Dihlawi, 1702–1763*. Leiden: E. J. Brill, 1986.

Bayly, Christopher. *Empire and Information: Intelligence Gathering and Social Communication in India, 1780–1870*. Cambridge: Cambridge University Press, 1999.

———. *Indian Society and the Making of the British Empire*. Cambridge: Cambridge University Press, 1988.

———. *Rulers, Townsmen and Bazaars: North Indian Society in the Age of British Expansion, 1770–1870*. Cambridge: Cambridge University Press, 1983.

Bayly, Susan. "Hindu Kingship and the Origin of Community: Religion, State, and Society in Kerala, 1750–1850." *Modern Asian Studies* 18, no. 2 (1984): 177–213.

Benard, Cheryl, Andrew Riddile, and Peter Wilson. *Civil Democratic Islam: Partners, Resources, and Strategies*. Santa Monica, CA: RAND, 2003.

Benjamin, Walter. *Gesammelte Schriften*. Edited by Rolf Teidemann and Hermann Schweppenhauser. Frankfurt: Suhrkamp, 1972–89.

Bourdieu, Pierre. *The Logic of Practice*. Stanford, CA: Stanford University Press, 1990.

———. *Outline of a Theory of Practice*. Cambridge: Cambridge University Press, 1977.

Brockopp, Jonathan, ed. *Islamic Ethics of Life: Abortion, War, and Euthanasia*. Columbia: University of South Carolina Press, 2003.

Brown, Wendy. *Regulating Aversion: Tolerance in the Age of Empire*. Princeton, NJ: Princeton University Press, 2006.

Canguilhem, Georges. *The Normal and the Pathological*. New York: Zone Books, 1989.

Chagatai, M. Ikram. *Shah Wali Ullah (1702–63): His Religious and Political Thought*. Lāhore: Sang-e-Meel Publications, 2005.

Chakrabarty, Dipesh. *Habitations of Modernity: Essays in the Wake of Subaltern Studies*. Chicago: University of Chicago Press, 2002.

Chodkiewicz, Michel. *The Spiritual Writings of Amir 'Abdul Kader*. Albany: State University of New York Press, 1995.

Cohn, Bernard. *An Anthropologist among Historians and Other Essays*. Oxford: Oxford University Press, 1987.

———. *Colonialism and Its Forms of Knowledge: The British in India*. Princeton, NJ: Princeton University Press, 1996.

———. "Representing Authority in Victorian India." In *The Invention of Tradition*, edited by Eric Hobsbawm and Terence Ranger, 165–210. Cambridge: Cambridge University Press, 1992.

Commins, David. *The Wahhabi Mission and Saudi Arabia*. London: I. B. Tauris, 2006.

cooke, miriam, and Bruce B. Lawrence, eds. *Muslim Networks from Hajj to Hip Hop*. Chapel Hill: University of North Carolina Press, 2005.

Curtis, Lisa, and Haider Mullick. *Reviving Pakistan's Pluralist Traditions to Fight Extremism*. Washington, DC: Heritage Foundation, 2009.

Dallal, Ahmad. "The Origins and Objectives of Islamic Revivalist Thought: 1750–1850." *Journal of the American Oriental Society* 113, no. 3 (1993): 341–59.

Dalmia, Vasudha. *The Nationalization of Hindu Traditions: Bharatendu Harishchandra and Nineteenth Century Banaras*. New Delhi: Oxford University Press, 1996.

De Certeau, Michel. *Heterologies: Discourses on the Other*. Minneapolis: University of Minnesota Press, 1985.

———. *The Practice of Everyday Life*. Berkeley: University of California Press, 1984.

———. *The Writing of History*. New York: Columbia University Press, 1988.

DeLong-Bas, Natana. *Wahhabi Islam: From Revival and Reform to Global Jihad*. New York: Oxford University Press, 2004.

Derrida, Jacques. *Aporias: Dying-Awaiting (One Another) at the "Limits of Truth."* Stanford, CA: Stanford University Press, 1993.

———. "Theology of Translation." In *Eyes of the University: Right to Philosophy 2*, translated by Jan Plug et al., 64–82. Stanford, CA: Stanford University Press, 2003.

Devji, Faisal. "Gender and the Politics of Space: The Movement for Women's Reform in Muslim India, 1857–1900." *South Asia: Journal of South Asian Studies* 14, no. 1 (1991): 141–53.

Dhulipala, Venkat. *Creating a New Medina: State Power, Islam, and the Quest for Pakistan in Late Colonial North India*. New Delhi: Cambridge University Press, 2015.

Douglas, Mary. *Purity and Danger*. London: Routledge, 2002.

Douzinas, Costas, and Ronnie Warrington. *Justice Miscarried: Ethics, Aesthetics and the Law*. New York: Harvester Wheatsheaf, 1999.

Dressler, Markus, and Arvind Mandair. *Secularism and Religion-Making*. New York: Oxford University Press, 2011.

Dumont, Louis. *Homo Hierarchicus: The Caste System and Its Implications*. Chicago: University of Chicago Press, 1980.

———. *Religion, Politics, and History in India: Collected Papers in Indian Sociology*. The Hague: Mouton, 1971.

Eaton, Richard. *Essays on Islam and Indian History*. New Delhi: Oxford University Press, 2000.

———. *The Rise of Islam and the Bengal Frontier*. Berkeley: University of California Press, 1993.

Elias, Norbert. *The Civilizing Process: Sociogenetic and Psychogenetic Investigations*. Cambridge: Wiley Blackwell, 2000.

Elshtain, Jean. *Sovereignty, God, State, and Self.* New York: Basic Books, 2008.

Ernst, Carl. *Eternal Garden: Mysticism, History, and Politics at a South Asian Sufi Center*. Albany: State University of New York Press, 1992.

———. "Muhammad as the Pole of Existence." In *Cambridge Companion to Muḥammad*, edited by Jonathan Brockopp, 123–38. Cambridge: Cambridge University Press, 2009.

———. "Muslim Studies of Hinduism? A Reconsideration of Persian and Arabic Translations from Sanskrit." *Iranian Studies* 36 (2003): 173–95.

———. "Reconfiguring South Asian Islam: The 18th and 19th Centuries." *Journal of Comparative Islamic Studies*, forthcoming.

———. *The Shambhala Guide to Sufism*. Boston: Shambhala Publications, 1997.

Ernst, Carl W., and Bruce B. Lawrence. *Sufi Martyrs of Love: The Chishti Order in South Asia and Beyond*. New York: Palgrave Macmillan, 2002.

Ernst, Carl W., and Richard C. Martin, eds. *Rethinking Islamic Studies: From Orientalism to Cosmopolitanism*. Columbia: University of South Carolina Press, 2010.

Esposito, Roberto. *Two: The Machine of Political Theology and the Place of Thought*. New York: Fordham University Press, 2016.

Essa, Ibrahim. *The Televangelist*. Translated by Jonathan Wright. Cairo: Hoopoe Press, 2016.

Euben, Roxanne L. "Jihād and Political Violence." *Current History* 101 (November 2002): 365–76.

Ewing, Katherine. *Arguing Sainthood: Modernity, Psychoanalysis, and Islam*. Durham, NC: Duke University Press, 1997.

———. Introduction to *Sufi Politics: Rethinking Islam, Scholarship, and the State in South Asia and Beyond*, edited by Katherine Ewing and Rosemary Corbett. New York: Columbia University Press, forthcoming.

Fierro, Maribel. "The Treatises against Innovations '(kutub al-bida').'" *Der Islam* 68, no. 1 (1992): 204–46.

Foucault, Michel. "A Preface to Transgression." In *Religion and Culture: Michel Foucault*, edited by Jeremy Carrette, 57–72. New York: Routledge, 1999.

Freitag, Sandria. *Collective Action and Community: Public Arenas and the Emergence of Communalism in North India.* Berkeley: University of California Press, 1989.

———. "Contesting in Public: Colonial Legacies and Contemporary Communalism." In *Contesting the Nation: Religion, Community, and the Politics of Democracy in India*, edited by David Ludden, 211–34. Philadelphia: University of Pennsylvania Press, 1996.

Freud, Sigmund. *Totem and Taboo: Resemblances between the Psychic Lives of Savages and Neurotics.* New York: Barnes and Noble, 2005.

Friedmann, Yohanan. *Prophecy Continuous: Aspects of Ahmadi Religious Thought and Its Medieval Background.* Berkeley: University of California Press, 1989.

———. *Shaykh Ahmad Sirhindi, An Outline of His Thought and a Study of His Image in the Eyes of Posterity.* Montreal: McGill University, Institute of Islamic Studies, 1971.

Fuerst, Ilyse Morgenstein. *Indian Muslim Minorities and the 1857 Rebellion: Religion, Rebels and Jihad.* London: I. B. Tauris, 2017.

Gaborieau, Marc. *Un autre Islam: Inde, Pakistan, Bangladesh.* Paris: Albin Michel, 2007.

———. *Le Mahdi incompris: Sayyid Ahmad Barelvi (1786–1831) et le millénarisme en Inde.* Paris: CNRS Editions, 2010.

Gilmartin, David. "Customary Law and Shariat in British Punjab." In *Shariat and Ambiguity in South Asian Islam*, edited by Katherine Ewing, 43–62. Berkeley: University of California Press, 1988.

———. "Democracy, Nationalism, and the Public: A Speculation on Colonial Muslim Politics." *South Asia* 14, no. 1 (1991): 123–40.

———. *Empire and Islam: Punjab and the Making of Pakistan.* Berkeley: University of California Press, 1988.

———. "Rethinking the Public through the Lens of Sovereignty." *South Asia: Journal of South Asian Studies* 38, no. 3 (September 2015): 371–86.

Gilmartin, David, and Bruce B. Lawrence, eds. *Beyond Turk and Hindu: Rethinking Religious Identities in Islamicate South Asia.* Gainesville: University Press of Florida, 2000.

Green, Nile. *Making Space: Sufis and Settlers in Early Modern India.* New Delhi: Oxford University Press, 2012.

———. *Sufism: A Global History.* Chichester: Wiley Blackwell, 2012.

Habermas, Jürgen. *The Structural Transformation of the Public Sphere.* Translated by T. Burger and F. Lawrence. Cambridge, MA: MIT Press, 1989.

Haj, Samira. *Reconfiguring Islamic Tradition: Reform, Rationality and Modernity.* Stanford, CA: Stanford University Press, 2009.

Hallaq, Wael. *Authority, Continuity and Change in Islamic Law*. Cambridge: Cambridge University Press, 2005.

———. *The Origins and Evolution of Islamic Law*. Cambridge: Cambridge University Press, 2005.

———. *Shari'a: Theory, Practice, Transformations*. Cambridge: Cambridge University Press, 2009.

Hambrick-Stowe, Charles. *Charles Finney and the Spirit of American Evangelicalism*. Grand Rapids, MI: William B. Eerdmans, 1996.

Hammill, Graham, and Julia Lupton, eds. Introduction to *Political Theology and Early Modernity*, edited by Graham Hammill and Julia Lupton, 1–22. Chicago: University of Chicago Press, 2012.

Hardy, Peter. *The Muslims of British India*. Cambridge: Cambridge University Press, 1972.

Haroon, Sana. "The Fragmentation of South Asian Mosque Practice under the Colonial State." Unpublished paper in author's possession.

———. *Frontier of Faith: Islam in the Indo-Afghan Borderland*. New York: Columbia University Press, 2007.

———. "Reformism and Orthodox Practice in Early Nineteenth-Century Muslim North India: Sayyid Ahmed Shaheed Reconsidered." *Journal of the Royal Asiatic Society* 21, no. 2 (April 2011): 177–98.

Harrison, Peter. *"Religion" and the Religions in the English Enlightenment*. New York: Cambridge University Press, 1993.

Heck, Paul. "'Jihad' Revisited." *Journal of Religious Ethics* 32, no. 1 (Spring 2004): 95–128.

Hefner, Robert, and Muhammad Qasim Zaman, eds. *Schooling Islam: The Culture and Politics of Modern Muslim Education*. Princeton, NJ: Princeton University Press, 2007.

Heidegger, Martin. *Metaphysical Foundations of Logic*. Bloomington: Indiana University Press, 1984.

Hermansen, Marcia. *The Conclusive Argument from God: Shah Wali Allah of Delhi's Hujjat Allah al-Baligha*. Leiden: E. J. Brill, 1996.

———. "Eschatology." In *The Cambridge Companion to Classical Islamic Theology*, edited by Tim Winter, 308–24. Cambridge: Cambridge University Press, 2010.

———. *Shah Wali Allah's Treatise on Juristic Disagreement*. Louisville, KY: Fons Vitae, 2011.

Hurd, Elizabeth. *Beyond Religious Freedom: The New Global Politics of Religion*. Princeton, NJ: Princeton University Press, 2015.

Ingram, Brannon. *Revival from Below: The Deoband Movement and Global Islam*. Berkeley: University of California Press, 2018.

Ingram, Brannon, J. Barton Scott, and SherAli Tareen, eds. *Imagining the Public in Modern South Asia*. London: Routledge, 2016.

Iqbal, Muhammad. *The Reconstruction of Religious Thought in Islam*. Dubai: Kitab al-Islamīya, n.d.

Jackson, Sherman. *On the Boundaries of Theological Tolerance in Islam: Abu Hamid al-Ghazali's "Faysal al-Tafriqa Bayn al-Islam wa al-Zandaqa."* Karāchī: Oxford University Press, 2002.

Jalal, Ayesha. *Partisans of Allah: Jihad in South Asia*. Cambridge, MA: Harvard University Press, 2008.

Jalbani, G. N. *Teachings of Shah Waliyullah of Delhi*. Lāhore: S. H. Muḥammad Ashraf, 1996.

Jameson, Fredric. *A Singular Modernity: Essay on the Ontology of the Present*. London: Verso, 2002.

Jonas, Hans. *The Gnostic Religion: The Message of the Alien God and the Beginnings of Christianity*. Boston: Beacon Press, 1963.

Jones, Kenneth. *Arya Dharm: Hindu Consciousness in 19th-Century Punjab*. Berkeley: University of California Press, 1976.

———, ed. *Religious Controversy in British India: Dialogues in South Asian Languages*. Albany: State University of New York Press, 1992.

Josephson-Storm, Jason. *The Myth of Disenchantment: Magic, Modernity, and the Birth of the Human Sciences*. Chicago: University of Chicago Press, 2017.

Kahn, Paul. *Political Theology: Four New Chapters on the Concept of Political Theology*. New York: Columbia University Press, 2012.

Kamrava, Mehran, ed. *Innovation in Islam: Traditions and Contributions*. Berkeley: University of California Press, 2011.

Kantorowicz, Ernst. *The King's Two Bodies*. Princeton, NJ: Princeton University Press, 1957.

Katz, Marion. *The Birth of the Prophet Muḥammad: Devotional Piety in Sunni Islam*. London: Routledge, 2007.

Kaviraj, Sudipta. "The Imaginary Institution of India." In *Subaltern Studies 7*, edited by Partha Chatterjee and Gyanendra Pandey, 1–39. Oxford: Oxford University Press, 1993.

———. *The Trajectories of the Indian State*. Ranikhet: Permanent Black, 2010.

Khalid, Adeeb. *Islam after Communism: Religion and Politics in Central Asia*. Berkeley: University of California Press, 2007.

———. *The Politics of Muslim Cultural Reform: Jadidism in Central Asia*. Berkeley: University of California Press, 1998.

Khan, Adil. *From Sufism to Ahmadiyya: A Muslim Minority Movement in South Asia*. Bloomington: Indiana University Press, 2015.

Khan, Darakhshan. "Fashioning the Pious Self: Middle Class Religiosity in Colonial India." PhD diss., University of Pennsylvania, 2016.

Khan, Fareeha. "Traditionalist Approaches to Shari'ah Reform: Mawlana Ashraf 'Ali Thanawi's Fatwa on Women's Right to Divorce." PhD diss., University of Michigan–Ann Arbor, 2008.

Khan, Naveeda. *Muslim Becoming: Aspiration and Skepticism in Pakistan*. Durham, NC: Duke University Press, 2012.

Kim, David. *Melancholic Freedom: Agency and the Spirit of Politics*. New York: Oxford University Press, 2007.

Korsgaard, Christine. *The Sources of Normativity*. Cambridge: Cambridge University Press, 1996.

Koselleck, Reinhart. *Futures Past: On the Semantics of Historical Time*. New York: Columbia University Press, 2004.

Kugle, Scott. *Sufis and Saints' Bodies: Mysticism, Corporeality and Sacred Power in Islam*. Chapel Hill: University of North Carolina Press, 2007.

Laine, James. "Mind and Mood in the Study of Religion." *Religion* 40, no. 4 (October 2010): 239–49.

———. *Shivaji: Hindu King in Islamic India*. Oxford: Oxford University Press, 2004.

Langer, Robert, and Udo Simon. "The Dynamics of Orthodoxy and Heterodoxy: Dealing with Divergence in Muslim Discourses and Islamic Studies." *Die Welt des Islams: International Journal for the Study of Modern Islam* 48, nos. 3/4 (2008): 273–88.

Lawrence, Bruce, ed. *The Rose and the Rock: Mystical and Rational Elements in the Intellectual History of South Asian Islam*. Durham, NC: Duke University Programs in Comparative Studies in Southern Asia and Islamic and Arabian Development Studies, 1979.

Lelyveld, David. *Aligarh's First Generation: Muslim Solidarity in British India*. Princeton, NJ: Princeton University Press, 1978.

Lipton, Gregory A. *Rethinking Ibn 'Arabi*. New York: Oxford University Press, 2018.

———. "Secular Sufism: Neoliberalism, Ethnoracism, and the Reformation of the Muslim Other." *Muslim World* 101, no. 3 (2011): 427–40.

Lorenzen, David. "Who Invented Hinduism." *Comparative Studies in Society and History* 41, no. 4 (October 1999): 630–59.

MacIntyre, Alasdair. *Three Rival Versions of Moral Enquiry: Encyclopedia, Tradition, Genealogy*. Notre Dame, IN: University of Notre Dame Press, 1991.

Mahdi, Muhsen. *Al-Farabi and the Foundations of Islamic Political Philosophy*. Chicago: University of Chicago Press, 2001.

Mahmood, Saba. *Politics of Piety: The Islamic Revival and the Feminist Subject*. Princeton, NJ: Princeton University Press, 2005.

———. *Religious Difference in a Secular Age: A Minority Report*. Princeton, NJ: Princeton University Press, 2016.

———. "Secularism, Hermeneutics, Empire: The Politics of Islamic Reformation." *Public Culture* 19, no. 2 (2006): 323–47.

Malik, Jamal. "Letters, Prison Sketches, and Autobiographical Literature: The Case of Fadl-e Haqq Khairabadi in the Andaman Penal Colony." *Indian Economic and Social History Review* 43, no. 1 (March 2006): 77–100.

Mamdani, Mahmood. *Good Muslim, Bad Muslim: America, the Cold War, and the Roots of Terror*. New York: Penguin Random House, 2005.

Mandair, Arvind. "Decolonizing Secularism's 'Conceptual Matrix.'" *Comparative Studies of South Asia, Africa, and the Middle East* 38, no. 2 (2018): 443–51.

———. *Religion and the Specter of the West: Sikhism, India, Postcoloniality, and the Politics of Translation*. New York: Columbia University Press, 2009.

Mani, Lata. *Contentious Traditions: The Debate on Sati in Colonial India*. Berkeley: University of California Press, 1998.

March, Andrew. "Genealogies of Sovereignty in Islamic Political Theology." *Social Research* 80, no. 1 (Spring 2013): 293–320.

Marlow, Louise. *Hierarchy and Egalitarianism in Islamic Thought*. Cambridge: Cambridge University Press, 2002.

Marmon, Shaun. "The Quality of Mercy: Intercession in Mamluk Society." *Studia Islamica* 87 (1998): 125–39.

Masud, Khalid. "The Definition of Bid'a in the South Asian Fatawa Literature." *Annales Islamologiques* 27 (1993): 55–75.

———. *Shatibi's Philosophy of Islamic Law*. Kuala Lumpur: Islamic Book Trust, 2002.

McCutcheon, Russell. "'They Licked the Platter Clean': On the Co-dependency of the Religious and the Secular." *Method and Theory in the Study of Religion* 19 (2007): 173–99.

Meguid, Ahmed Abdel. "Reversing Schmitt: The Sovereign as a Guardian of Rational Pluralism and the Peculiarity of the Islamic State of Exception in al-Juwaynī's Dialectical Theology." *European Journal of Political Theory*, published online September 2017. http://dx.doi.org/10.1177/1474885117730672.

Metcalf, Barbara. *Husain Ahmad Madani: The Jihad for Islam and India's Freedom*. London: OneWorld Press, 2008.

———. *Islamic Revival in British India: Deoband, 1860–1900*. Princeton, NJ: Princeton University Press, 1982.

———, ed. *Islam in South Asia in Practice*. Princeton, NJ: Princeton University Press, 2009.

———. "'Traditionalist' Islamic Activism: Deoband, Tablighis, and the Talibs." In "After September 11: 2001 Essays Archive." Social Science Research Council, 2001. http://essays.ssrc.org/sept11/essays/metcalf.htm.

Metcalf, Thomas. *Ideologies of the Raj*. Cambridge: Cambridge University Press, 1995.

Mian, Ali. "Surviving Modernity: Ashraf 'Ali Thanvi and the Making of Muslim Orthodoxy in Colonial India." PhD diss., Duke University, 2015.

Mirahmadi, Hedieh, Mehreen Farooq, and Waleed Ziad. *Traditional Muslim Networks: Pakistan's Untapped Resource in the Fight against Terrorism*. Washington, DC: WORDE, 2010.

Mitchell, W. J. T., ed. *On Narrative*. Chicago: University of Chicago Press, 1980.

Mittermaier, Amira. *Dreams That Matter: Egyptian Landscapes of the Imagination*. Berkeley: University of California Press, 2010.

Modern, John. *Secularism in Antebellum America*. Chicago: University of Chicago Press, 2011.

Moin, Azfar. *The Millennial Sovereign: Sacred Kingship and Sainthood in Islam*. New York: Columbia University Press, 2010.

Moosa, Ebrahim. "Allegory of the Rule (Ḥukm): Law as Simulacrum in Islam?" *History of Religions* 38, no. 1 (August 1998): 1–24.

———. "The Dilemma of Islamic Rights Schemes." *Journal of Law and Religion* 15, no. 2 (2000–2001): 185–215.

———. *Ghazālī and the Poetics of Imagination*. Chapel Hill: University of North Carolina Press, 2005.

———. Introduction to "The Deoband Madrasa," edited by Ebrahim Moosa, special issue, *Muslim World* 99, no. 3 (July 2009): 427–35.

———. "The Poetics and Politics of Law after Empire: Reading Women's Rights in the Contestations of Law." *Journal for Islamic and Near Eastern Law* 15, nos. 1/2 (2000–2001): 185–215.

———. *What Is a Madrasa?* Chapel Hill: University of North Carolina Press, 2015.

Moosa, Ebrahim, and SherAli Tareen. "Revival and Reform in Islam." In *Islamic Political Thought*, edited by Gerhard Bowering, 202–19. Princeton, NJ: Princeton University Press, 2015.

Muedini, Fait. *Sponsoring Sufism: How Governments Promote "Mystical Islam" in Their Domestic and Foreign Policies*. New York: Palgrave Macmillan, 2015.

Mufti, Aamir. "The Aura of Authenticity." *Social Text* 10, no. 64 (2000): 87–103.

———. *Enlightenment in the Colony: The Jewish Question and the Crisis of Postcolonial Culture*. Princeton, NJ: Princeton University Press, 2007.

Mukherjee, Mithi. *India in the Shadows of Empire: A Legal and Political History, 1774–1950*. New Delhi: Oxford University Press, 2010.

Naeem, Fuad. "Interreligious Debates, Rational Theology, and the 'Ulamā' in the Public Sphere: Muḥammad Qāsim Nanautvī and the Making of Modern Islam in South Asia." PhD diss., Georgetown University, 2015.

Nancy, Jean-Luc. "Finite History." In *The States of "Theory": History, Art, and Critical Discourse*, edited by David Carroll, 149–72. New York: Columbia University Press, 1990.

Nandy, Ashis. *The Savage Freud and Other Essays on Possible and Retrievable Selves*. Princeton, NJ: Princeton University Press, 1995.

Nicholson, Andrew. *Unifying Hinduism: Philosophy and Identity in Indian Intellectual History*. New York: Columbia University Press, 2010.

Oakley, Francis. *Politics and Eternity: Studies in the History of Medieval and Early-Modern Political Thought*. Leiden: E. J. Brill, 1999.

Oberoi, Harjot. *The Construction of Religious Boundaries: Culture, Identity, and Diversity in the Sikh Tradition*. Chicago: University of Chicago Press, 1994.

Obeyesekere, Gananath. "Religious Symbolism and Political Change in Ceylon." *Modern Ceylon Studies* 1, no. 1 (1970): 43–63.

Orsi, Robert. *Between Heaven and Earth: The Religious World People Make and the Scholars Who Study Them*. Princeton, NJ: Princeton University Press, 2005.

———. *History and Presence*. Cambridge, MA: Harvard University Press, 2016.

Pandey, Gyanendra. *The Construction of Communalism in Colonial North India*. Delhi: Oxford University Press, 1990.

Pannikar, K. N. *Culture, Ideology, Hegemony: Intellectuals and Social Consciousness in Colonial India*. New Delhi: Tulika, 1998.

Pearson, Harlan Otto. *Islamic Reform and Revival in Nineteenth-Century India: The Tarīqah-i-Muhammadīyah*. Delhi: Yoda Press, 2008.

Pennington, Brian. *Was Hinduism Invented? Britons, Indians, and the Colonial Construction of Religion*. New York: Oxford University Press, 2005.

Pernau, Margrit. *Ashraf into Middle Classes: Muslims in Nineteenth-Century Delhi*. New Delhi: Oxford University Press, 2013.

Pinault, David. *Notes from the Fortune-Telling Parrot: Islam and the Struggle for Religious Pluralism in Pakistan*. London: Equinox, 2008.

Platts, John. *A Dictionary of Urdū, Classical Hindī, and English*. London: Oxford University Press, 1964.

Powell, Avril. *Muslims and Missionaries in Pre-Mutiny India*. Richmond, Surrey: Curzon Press, 1993.

Powers, David. *Zayd: The Little-Known Story of Muḥammad's Adopted Son*. Philadelphia: University of Pennsylvania Press, 2014.

Purohit, Teena. *The Aga Khan Case: Religion and Identity in Colonial India*. Cambridge, MA: Harvard University Press, 2012.

Qadir, Altaf. *Sayyid Ahmad Barailvi: His Movement and Legacy from the Pakhtun Perspective*. New Delhi: Sage Publications, 2015.

Rahman, Fazlur. *Islam and Modernity: Transformation of an Intellectual Tradition*. Chicago: University of Chicago Press, 1982.

———. *Prophecy in Islam: Philosophy and Orthodoxy*. London: Allen and Unwin, 1958.

———. *Revival and Reform in Islam: A Study in Islamic Fundamentalism*. Oxford: Oneworld Publications, 2000.

Rajagopalan, Mrinilani. *Building Histories: The Archival and Affective Lives of Five Monuments in Modern Delhi*. Chicago: University of Chicago Press, 2016.

Rao, Anupama. *The Caste Question: Dalits and the Politics of Modern India*. Berkeley: University of California Press, 2009.

Rawat, Ramnarayan. "Colonial Archive versus Colonial Sociology: Writing Dalit History." In *Dalit Studies*, edited by Ramnarayan Rawat and K. Satyanarayana, 53–73. Durham, NC: Duke University Press, 2016.

Rawat, Ramnarayan, and K. Satyanarayana, eds. *Dalit Studies*. Durham, NC: Duke University Press, 2016.

Reetz, Dietrich. *Islam in the Public Sphere: Religious Groups in India, 1900–1947*. New Delhi: Oxford University Press, 2006.

Ricoeur, Paul. *Memory, History, Forgetting*. Chicago: University of Chicago Press, 2004.

———. "Narrative Time." In Mitchell, *On Narrative*, 169–90.

Roberts, Nathaniel. *To Be Cared For: The Power of Conversion and the Foreignness of Belonging in an Indian Slum*. Berkeley: University of California Press, 2016.

Robinson, Francis. *Islam and Muslim History in South Asia*. New Delhi: Oxford University Press, 2000.

———. *The 'Ulama of Farangi Mahall and Islamic Culture in South Asia*. New Delhi: Orient Longman, 2001.

Roy, Rammohan. *Raja Ram Mohun Roy, His Life, Writings and Speeches*. Madras: G. A. Natesan, 1925.

Sajjad, Mohammad Waqas. "For the Love of the Prophet: Deobandi-Barelvi Polemics and the Ulama in Pakistan." PhD diss., Graduate Theological Union, 2018.

Sanyal, Usha. *Devotional Islam and Politics in British India: Ahmad Riza Khan Barelwi and His Movement, 1870–1920*. Delhi: Oxford University Press, 1996.

Sarkar, Tanika. *Hindu Wife, Hindu Nation: Community, Religion, and Cultural Nationalism*. Bloomington: Indiana University Press, 2001.

———. *Rebels, Wives, Saints: Designing Selves and Nations in Colonial Times*. London: Seagull Books, 2009.

Schimmel, Anne Marie. *And Muhammad Is His Messenger: The Veneration of the Prophet in Islamic Piety*. Chapel Hill: University of North Carolina Press, 1985.

———. *Islam in the Indian Subcontinent*. Leiden: E. J. Brill, 1990.

Schmitt, Carl. *Political Theology: Four Chapters on the Concept of Sovereignty*. Cambridge, MA: MIT Press, 1986.

Scott, David. *Conscripts of Modernity: The Tragedy of Colonial Enlightenment*. Durham, NC: Duke University Press, 2004.

———. *Formations of Ritual: Colonial and Anthropological Discourses on the Sinhala Yaktovil*. Minneapolis: University of Minnesota Press, 1994.

———. *Refashioning Futures: Criticism after Postcoloniality*. Princeton, NJ: Princeton University Press, 1999.

Scott, David, and Charles Hirschkind. *Powers of the Secular Modern: Talal Asad and His Interlocutors*. Stanford, CA: Stanford University Press, 2006.

Scott, J. Barton. *Spiritual Despots: Modern Hinduism and the Genealogies of Self-Rule*. Chicago: University of Chicago Press, 2015.

Sells, Michael. *Mystical Languages of Unsaying*. Chicago: University of Chicago Press, 1994.

Smith, Wilfred Cantwell. *The Meaning and End of Religion*. Minneapolis, MN: Fortress Press, 1991.

Steingass, Francis. *A Comprehensive Persian-English Dictionary*. London: Trubner, 1957.

Sommerville, C. John. *The Secularization of Early Modern England: From Religious Culture to Religious Faith*. New York: Oxford University Press, 1992.

Stark, Ulrike. *An Empire of Books: The Naval Kishore Press and the Diffusion of the Printed Word in Colonial India*. New Delhi: Permanent Black, 2007.

Stephens, Julia. "The Politics of Muslim Rage: Secular Law and Religious Sentiment in Late Colonial India." *History Workshop Journal* 77 (2014): 45–64.

Subramanyam, Sanjay. *Society and Circulation: Mobile People and Itinerant Cultures in South Asia, 1750–1950*. Delhi: Permanent Black, 2003.

Sugirtharajah, R. S. *The Bible and Empire: Postcolonial Explorations*. Cambridge: Cambridge University Press, 2005.

Tareen, SherAli. "Competing Political Theologies in Islam: Intra-Muslim Polemics on the Limits of Prophetic Intercession (*Shafa'at*)." *Political Theology* 12, no. 3 (June 2011): 418–33.

———. "Contesting Friendship in Colonial Muslim India." *South Asia: Journal of South Asian Studies* 38, no. 3 (2015): 419–34.

———. "Deoband Madrasa." In *Oxford Bibliographies Online: Islamic Studies*, edited by Tamara Sonn. Oxford University Press, March 2011. www.oxfordbibliographies.com/view/document/obo-9780195390155/obo-9780195390155-0019.xml.

———. "Disrupting Secular Power and the Study of Religion: Saba Mahmood." In *Cultural Approaches to Studying Religion: An Introduction to Theories and Methods*, edited by Sarah Bloesch and Meredith Minister, 155–72. London: Bloomsbury Press, 2018.

———. "Islam, Democracy, and the Limits of Secular Conceptuality." *Journal of Law and Religion* 29, no. 1 (2014): 1–17.

———. "Mawdudi." In *Oxford Bibliographies Online: Islamic Studies*, edited by Tamara Sonn. Oxford University Press, May 2011. www.oxfordbibliographies.com/view/document/obo-9780195390155/obo-9780195390155-0129.xml.

———. "Normativity, Heresy and the Politics of Authenticity in South Asian Islam." In "The Deoband Madrasa," edited by Ebrahim Moosa, special issue, *Muslim World* 99, no. 3 (July 2009): 521–52.

———. "Park 51." In *Frequencies: A Genealogy of Spirituality*, Web-based project curated by John Modern and Kathryn Lofton. Social Science Research Council, December 2011. http://frequencies.ssrc.org /2011/12/13/park-51.

———. "Polemic of Shahjahanpur: Religion, Miracles, History." *Islamic Studies* 51, no. 1 (2012): 49–67.

———. Review of *Muslim Cosmopolitanism in the Age of Empire*, by Seema Alavi. *International Journal of Asian Studies* 15, no. 1 (January 2018): 126–31.

———. "Revolutionary Hermeneutics: Translating the Qur'ān as a Manifesto for Revolution." *Journal of Religious and Political Practice* 3, nos. 1–2 (March 2017): 1–24.

Taussig, Michael. *Defacement: Public Secrecy and the Labor of the Negative*. Stanford, CA: Stanford University Press, 1999.

Taylor, Charles. *Modern Social Imaginaries*. Durham, NC: Duke University Press, 2006.

———. *A Secular Age*. Cambridge, MA: Harvard University Press, 2007.

———. *Sources of the Self: The Making of the Modern Identity*. Cambridge, MA: Harvard University Press, 1989.

Taylor, Mark, ed. *Critical Terms for Religious Studies*. Chicago: University of Chicago Press, 1998.

Tayob, Abdulkader. *Religion in Modern Islamic Discourse*. New York: Columbia University Press, 2009.

Thapar, Romilla. *Cultural Pasts: Essays in Early Indian History*. Oxford: Oxford University Press, 1987.

Tripp, Charles. *Islam and the Moral Economy: The Challenge of Capitalism*. Cambridge: Cambridge University Press, 2006.

Ukeles, Raquel. "Innovation or Deviation: Exploring the Boundaries of Islamic Devotional Law." PhD diss., Harvard University, 2006.

Van der Veer, Peter. *Religious Nationalism: Hindus and Muslims in India*. Berkeley: University of California Press, 1994.

Viswanath, Rupa. *The Pariah Problem: Caste, Religion, and the Social in Modern India*. New York: Columbia University Press, 2014.

Viswanathan, Gauri. *Outside the Fold: Conversion, Modernity, and Belief*. Princeton, NJ: Princeton University Press, 1998.

Voll, John. *Islam: Continuity and Change in the Modern World*. 2nd ed. Syracuse, NY: Syracuse University Press, 1994.

Warner, Michael. "The Evangelical Public Sphere." A. S. W. Rosenbach Lectures, University of Pennsylvania, March 2009. https://repository.upenn.edu/rosenbach/2/.

———. *Publics and Counterpublics*. New York: Zone Books, 2002.

Wehr, Hans. *A Dictionary of Modern Written Arabic*. Urbana, IL: Spoken Language Services, 1994.

Werbner, Pnina. "The Making of Muslim Dissent: Hybridized Discourses, Lay Preachers, and Radical Rhetoric among British Pakistanis." *American Ethnologist* 23, no. 1 (February 1996): 102–29.

White, Hayden. *The Content of the Form: Narrative Discourse and Historical Representation*. Baltimore: Johns Hopkins University Press, 1987.

———. "The Value of Narrativity." In Mitchell, *On Narrative*, 1–23.

Wilson, Brett. "Failure of Nomenclature: The Concept of Orthodoxy in the Study of Islam." *Comparative Islamic Studies* 3, no. 2 (2007): 169–94.

Zaidi, S. Akbar. "Contested Identities and the Muslim Qaum in Northern India: c. 1860–1900." PhD diss., Cambridge University, 2009.

Zaman, Muhammad Qasim. "Arabic, the Arab Middle East, and the Definition of Muslim Identity in Twentieth-Century India." *Journal of the Royal Asiatic Society* 8, no. 1 (April 1998): 59–81.

———. *Ashraf 'Ali Thanawi: Islam in Modern South Asia*. Oxford: Oneworld Publications, 2008.

———. "Commentaries, Print and Patronage: *Ḥadīth* and the Madrasas in Modern South Asia." *Bulletin of the School of Oriental and African Studies*, 62, no. 1 (January 1999): 60–81.

———. "Consensus and Religious Authority in Modern Islam: The Discourses of the 'Ulamā'." In *Speaking for Islam: Religious Authorities in Muslim*

Societies, edited by Gudrun Kramer and Sabine Schmidtke, 153–80. Leiden: E. J. Brill, 2006.

———. *Islam in Pakistan: A History*. Princeton, NJ: Princeton University Press, 2018.

———. *Modern Islamic Thought in a Radical Age: Religious Authority and Internal Criticism*. New York: Cambridge University Press, 2012.

———. "Modernity and Religious Change in South Asian Islam." *Journal of the Royal Asiatic Society* 14, no. 3 (November 2004): 253–63.

———. Review of *Rethinking Tradition in Modern Islamic Thought*, by Daniel Brown. *Journal of Islamic Law and Society* 5, no. 2 (1998): 266.

———. "The Sovereignty of God in Modern Islamic Thought." *Journal of the Royal Asiatic Society* 25, no. 3 (July 2015): 389–418.

———. *The Ulama in Contemporary Islam: Custodians of Change*. Princeton, NJ: Princeton University Press, 2002.

Index

Page numbers in italics refer to figures.

SherAli Tareen

is associate professor of religious studies at Franklin and Marshall College. He is co-editor of *Imagining the Public in Modern South Asia*.

CPSIA information can be obtained
at www.ICGtesting.com
Printed in the USA
LVHW081327100120
643239LV00015B/626/P

9 780268 106706